OCP:
Oracle 10*g* Administration II
Study Guide

OCP: Oracle 10g™ Administration II Study Guide

Doug Stuns

Tim Buterbaugh

Bob Bryla

Wiley Publishing, Inc.

Publisher: Neil Edde
Acquisitions and Developmental Editor: Jeff Kellum
Production Editor: Mae Lum
Technical Editors: Ashok Hanumanth, Robert Wahl
Copyeditor: Sarah Lemaire
Compositor: Laurie Stewart, Happenstance Type-O-Rama
Graphic Illustrator: Jeffrey Wilson, Happenstance Type-O-Rama
CD Coordinator: Dan Mummert
CD Technician: Kevin Ly
Proofreaders: James Brook, Nancy Riddiough
Indexer: Jack Lewis
Book Designer: Bill Gibson, Judy Fung
Cover Designer: Archer Design
Cover Photographer: Photodisc and Victor Arre

Library of Congress Card Number: 2004094993

ISBN-13: 978-0-7821-4368-3
ISBN-10: 0-7821-4368-7

Manufactured in the United States of America

10 9 8 7 6 5 4

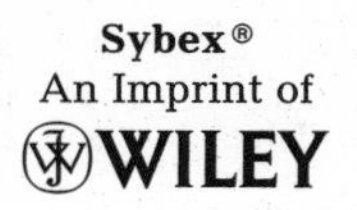

To Our Valued Readers:

Thank you for looking to Sybex for your Oracle 10*g* exam prep needs. The OCP certification is designed to validate knowledge of advanced database administration tasks and an understanding of the Oracle database architecture and how its components work and interact with one another. With Oracle continuing to lead the database market, pursuit of the OCP designation is a worthy and wise endeavor.

We at Sybex are proud of the reputation we've established for providing Oracle certification candidates with the practical knowledge and skills needed to succeed in the highly competitive IT marketplace. It has always been Sybex's mission to teach individuals how to utilize technologies in the real world, not to simply feed them answers to test questions. Just as Oracle is committed to establishing measurable standards for certifying database professionals, Sybex is committed to providing those professionals with the means of acquiring the skills and knowledge they need to meet those standards.

As always, your feedback is important to us. If you believe you've identified an error in the book, please visit the Customer Support section of the Wiley web site. And if you have general comments or suggestions, feel free to drop me a line directly at nedde@wiley.com. At Sybex we're continually striving to meet the needs of individuals preparing for certification exams.

Good luck in pursuit of your Oracle certification!

Neil Edde
Publisher—Certification
Sybex, an imprint of Wiley

Wiley Publishing, Inc.
End-User License Agreement

To Cathy, Brant, and Brea.
—Doug Stuns

To Jeaneanne and Gillian, the ladies that I love—and to Arren, Brandon, and Nicholas, who help me watch over them.
—Tim Buterbaugh

To MC, CM, CR, ES—y'all rock.
—Bob Bryla

Acknowledgments

First, I want say what a blessing it was to be able to write this book. I am very thankful for the time and privilege. I am truly thankful to the Lord, my savior, for making this all possible.

Thanks to Mae and Jeff for direction and guidance throughout the writing of this book. Sarah, your edits and suggestions greatly improved this book and made my job much easier. Thanks to Ashok Hanumanth and Robert Wahl for the technical edits and reviews, which enhanced the quality of this writing—greatly.

Finally, I want to thank my wife Cathy, my son Brant, and my daughter Brea for allowing me the time to work on this book. It has been greatly appreciated.

—Doug Stuns

I would like to thank the following people, without whom I would not have been able to accomplish this:

To Jeff Kellum and Mae Lum at Sybex, for giving me a chance (and being patient with me) as a new author. To Matt Weishan for recommending me to Sybex. To Matt Hall, Gary Brite, Barry Trout, Jerry Dennington, and Mark Moehling for helping me in my DBA career, and in my life. To Barry Heck and Steve Kell, two of the smartest DBAs I know, for answering all of my stupid questions. But above all, to my wife and kids, for remembering who I was when I came out from behind the laptop.

—Tim Buterbaugh

This book wouldn't be possible without the love and support from my family throughout the long nights and weekends when I still managed to find time to help the kids with their homework before bedtime. I loved every minute of it.

Thanks also to my professional colleagues, both past and present, who provided me with inspiration, support, and guidance and who pushed me a little further to take a risk now and then, starting with that math teacher in high school, whose name eludes me at the moment, who introduced me to computers on a DEC PDP-8 with a teletype and a paper tape reader.

—Bob Bryla

Contents at a Glance

Contents

Introduction

There is high demand for professionals in the information technology (IT) industry, and Oracle certifications are the hottest credential in the database world. You have made the right decision to pursue your Oracle certification, because achieving your Oracle certification will give you a distinct advantage in this highly competitive market.

Most readers should already be familiar with Oracle and do not need an introduction to the Oracle database world. For those who aren't familiar with the company, Oracle, founded in 1977, sold the first commercial relational database and is now the world's leading database company and second-largest independent software company, with revenues of more than $10 billion, serving more than 145 countries.

Oracle databases are the de facto standard for large Internet sites, and Oracle advertisers are boastful but honest when they proclaim, "The Internet Runs on Oracle." Almost all big Internet sites run Oracle databases. Oracle's penetration of the database market runs deep and is not limited to dot-com implementations. Enterprise resource planning (ERP) application suites, data warehouses, and custom applications at many companies rely on Oracle. The demand for DBA resources remains higher than others during weak economic times.

This book is intended to help you pass the Oracle Database 10g: Administration II Exam, which will establish your credentials as an Oracle Certified Professional (OCP). The OCP certification is a prerequisite for obtaining an Oracle Certified Master (OCM) certification. Using this book and a practice database, you can learn the necessary skills to pass the 1Z0-043 Oracle Database 10g: Administration II exam.

Why Become Oracle Certified?

The number one reason to become an OCP is to gain more visibility and greater access to the industry's most challenging opportunities. Oracle certification is the best way to demonstrate your knowledge and skills in Oracle database systems.

Certification is proof of your knowledge and shows that you have the skills required to support Oracle core products. The Oracle certification program can help a company to identify proven performers who have demonstrated their skills and who can support the company's investment in Oracle technology. It demonstrates that you have a solid understanding of your job role and the Oracle products used in that role.

OCPs are among the best paid in the IT industry. Salary surveys consistently show the OCP certification to yield higher salaries than other certifications, including Microsoft, Novell, and Cisco.

So whether you are beginning your career, changing your career, or looking to secure your position as a DBA, this book is for you!

Oracle Certifications

Oracle certifications follow a track that is oriented toward a job role. These are database administration, application developer, and web application server administrator tracks. Within each track, Oracle has a multi-tiered certification program.

Within the administration track there are three tiers:

- The first tier is the Oracle 10*g* Certified Associate (OCA). To obtain OCA certification, you must pass the 1Z0-042 Oracle Database 10*g*: Administration I exam in a proctored setting.
- The second tier is the Oracle 10*g* Certified Professional (OCP), which builds on and requires OCA certification. To obtain OCP certification, you must attend an approved Oracle University hands-on class and pass the 1Z0-043 Oracle Database 10*g*: Administration II exam in a proctored setting.
- The third and highest tier is the Oracle 10*g* Certified Master (OCM), which builds on and requires OCP certification. To obtain OCM certification, you must attend advanced-level classes and take a two-day, hands-on practical exam.

The material in this book addresses only the Administration II exam. Other Sybex books—which can be found at `http://www.sybex.com`—can help students new to the DBA world prepare for the OCA exam 1Z0-042 Oracle Database 10*g*: Administration I. You can also get information on the Oracle upgrade exam, Oracle Database 10*g*: New Features for Administrators (exam 1Z0-040).

See the Oracle website at `http://www.oracle.com/education/certification` for the latest information on all of Oracle's certification paths, along with Oracle's training resources.

Oracle DBA Certification

The role of the DBA has become a key to success in today's highly complex database systems. The best DBAs work behind the scenes, but are in the spotlight when critical issues arise. They plan, create, maintain, and ensure that the database is available for the business. They are always watching the database for performance issues and to prevent unscheduled downtime. The DBA's job requires broad understanding of the architecture of Oracle database and expertise in solving problems.

Because this book focuses on the DBA track, we will take a closer look at the different tiers of the DBA track.

Oracle Database 10*g* Administrator Certified Associate

The Oracle 10*g* Administrator Certified Associate (OCA) certification is a streamlined, entry-level certification for the database administration track and is required to advance toward the more senior certification tiers. This certification requires you to pass one exam that demonstrates your knowledge of Oracle basics:

- 1Z0-042 Oracle Database 10*g*: Administration I

Oracle Database 10*g* Administrator Certified Professional

The OCP tier of the database administration track challenges you to demonstrate your enhanced experience and knowledge of Oracle technologies. The Oracle 10*g* Administrator Certified Professional (OCP) certification requires achievement of the OCA certification, attendance at one or more approved Oracle University classes, and successful completion of the following exam:

- 1Z0-043 Oracle Database 10*g*: Administration II

The approved courses for OCP candidates include the following:

- Oracle Database 10*g*: Administration I
- Oracle Database 10*g*: Administration II
- Oracle Database 10*g*: Introduction to SQL
- Oracle Database 10*g*: New Features for Administrators
- Oracle Database 10*g*: Program with PL/SQL

If you already have your OCP in 9*i* or earlier and have elected to take the upgrade path, you are not required to take the Oracle University class to obtain your OCP for Oracle 10*g*.

You should verify this list against the Oracle education website (`www.oracle.com/education`), as it can change without any notice.

Oracle Database 10*g* Certified Master

The Oracle Database 10*g* Administration Certified Master (OCM) is the highest level of certification that Oracle offers. To become a certified master, you must first obtain OCP certification, then complete advanced-level classes at an Oracle Education facility, and finally pass a hands-on, two-day exam at an Oracle Education facility. The classes and practicum exam are offered only at an Oracle Education facility and may require travel.

Details on the required coursework for the OCM exam were not available when this book was written.

Oracle 10*g* Upgrade Paths

Existing Oracle Professionals can upgrade their certification in several ways:

- An Oracle9*i* OCP can upgrade to 10*g* certification by passing the 1Z0-040 Oracle Database 10*g*: New Features for Administrators exam.
- An Oracle8*i* OCP can upgrade directly to 10*g* by passing the 1Z0-045 Oracle Database 10*g*: New Features for Oracle8*i* OCPs exam.
- Oracle 7.3 and Oracle 8 DBAs must first upgrade to an Oracle9*i* certification with the 1Z0-035 Oracle9*i* DBA: New Features for Oracle 7.3 and Oracle 8 OCPs exam and then

upgrade the 9*i* certification to 10*g* with the 1Z0-040 Oracle Database 10*g*: New Features for Administrators exam.

Oracle Database 10*g* Administrator Special Accreditations

New to the Oracle certification program are the Oracle Database 10*g* Administrator Special Accreditation programs. These accreditations formally recognize the specialized knowledge of OCPs, in particular database administration areas such as high availability, security, and 10*g* Grid Control. OCPs who pass one of these special accreditation exams receive a certificate that formally recognizes their specialized competency.

Oracle Database 10*g* DBA Assessment

Oracle also provides an optional (and free) prerequisite to all of the proctored exams—the Oracle Database 10*g* DBA Assessment online exam:

- 1Z0-041 Oracle Database 10*g*: DBA Assessment

This exam evaluates your proficiency with basic administration and management of an Oracle 10*g* database and upon passing this online exam, you receive a certificate of completion from Oracle University. While anybody can take this exam, it is designed for those new to Oracle 10*g*, and it is an excellent measurement of how familiar you are with the new Oracle 10*g* database.

Oracle Exam Requirements

The Oracle Database 10*g*: Administration II exam covers several core subject areas. As with many typical multiple-choice exams, there are several tips that you can follow to maximize your score on the exam.

Skills Required for the Oracle Database 10*g*: Administration II Exam

To pass the Oracle 10*g* Administration II exam, you need to master the following subject areas in Oracle 10*g*:

Using Globalization Support

Customize language-dependent behavior for the database and individual sessions.

Specify different linguistic sorts for queries.

Use datetime datatypes.

Query data using case-insensitive and accent-insensitive searches.

Obtain Globalization support configuration information.

Securing the Oracle Listener

Secure the listener.

Remove default EXTPROC entry and add a separate listener to handle external procedure calls.

Configuring Recovery Manager (RMAN)

Configure database parameters that affect RMAN operations.

Change RMAN default settings with `CONFIGURE`.

Manage RMAN's persistent settings.

Start RMAN utility and allocate channels.

Using Recovery Manager

Use the RMAN `BACKUP` command to create backup sets and image copies.

Enable block change tracking.

Manage the backups and image copies taken with RMAN with the `LIST` and `REPORT` commands.

Diagnostic Sources

Use the alert log and database trace files for diagnostic purposes.

View alerts using Enterprise Manager (EM).

Adjust thresholds for tracked metrics.

Control the size and location of trace files.

Recovering from Non-Critical Losses

Recover temporary tablespaces.

Recover a redo log group member.

Recover index tablespaces.

Recover read-only tablespaces.

Recreate the password file.

Database Recovery

Recover the control file.

Explain reasons for incomplete recovery.

Perform incomplete recovery using EM.

Perform incomplete recovery using RMAN.

Perform incomplete recovery using SQL.

Perform database recovery following a `RESETLOGS` operation.

Flashback Database

Determine which flashback technology to use for each recovery situation.

Configure and use Flashback Database.

Monitor the Flashback Database.

Use the Enterprise Manager Recovery Wizard to flashback database.

Manage (or maintain) the Flash Recovery Area.

Recovering from User Errors

Recover a dropped table using Flashback technology.

Perform a Flashback table operation.

Manage the Recycle Bin.

Recover from user errors using Flashback Versions Query.

Perform transaction-level recovery using Flashback Transaction Query.

Dealing with Database Corruption

Define block corruption and list its causes and symptoms.

Detect database corruptions using the following utilities: ANALYZE, DBVERIFY.

Detect database corruptions using the `DBMS_REPAIR` package.

Implement the `DB_BLOCK_CHECKING` parameter to detect corruptions.

Repair corruptions using RMAN.

Automatic Database Management

Use the Database Advisors to gather information about your database.

Use the SQL Tuning Advisor to improve database performance.

Use automatic undo retention tuning.

Monitoring and Managing Storage

Tune redo writing and archiving operations.

Issue statements that can be suspended upon encountering space condition errors.

Reduce space-related error conditions by proactively managing tablespace usage.

Reclaim wasted space from tables and indexes using the segment shrink functionality.

Estimate the size of new tables and indexes.

Use different storage options to improve the performance of queries.

Rebuild indexes online.

Automatic Storage Management

Set up initialization parameter files for ASM and database instances.

Execute SQL commands with ASM filenames.

Start up and shut down ASM instances.

Administer ASM disk groups.

Use RMAN to migrate your database to ASM.

Monitoring and Managing Memory

Implement Automatic Shared Memory Management (ASMM).

Manually configure SGA parameters for various memory components in the SGA.

Use Automatic PGA Memory Management (APMM).

Managing Resources

Configure the Resource Manager.

Assign users to Resource Manager groups.

Create resource plans within groups.

Specify directives for allocating resources to consumer groups.

Automating Tasks with the Scheduler

Simplify management tasks by using the Scheduler.

Create a job, program, schedule, and window.

Reuse Scheduler components for similar tasks.

View information about job executions and job instances.

Tips for Taking the Administration II Exam

Use the following tips to help you prepare for and pass the exam:

- The exam contains about 55–80 questions to be completed in 90 minutes. Answer the questions you know first, so that you do not run out of time.
- Many questions on the exam have answer choices that at first glance look identical. Read the questions carefully. Do not just jump to conclusions. Make sure that you clearly understand exactly what each question asks.
- Some of the questions are scenario-based. Some of the scenarios contain nonessential information and exhibits. You need to be able to identify what's important and what's not important.

- Do not leave any questions unanswered. There is no negative scoring. After selecting an answer, you can mark a difficult question or one that you're unsure of and come back to it later.
- When answering questions that you're not sure about, use a process of elimination to get rid of the obviously incorrect answers first. Doing this greatly improves your odds if you need to make an educated guess.
- If you're not sure of your answer, mark it for review and then look for other questions that may help you eliminate any incorrect answers. At the end of the test, you can go back and review the questions that you marked for review.

You should be familiar with the exam objectives, which are included in the front of this book as a perforated tear-out card. You can also find them at www.oracle.com/education/certification/objectives/43.html. In addition, if you would like information on recommended classes and passing scores, visit www.oracle.com/education/certification/news/beta_043.html.

Where Do You Take the Certification Exam?

The Oracle Database 10*g* certification exams are available at any of the more than 900 Thomson Prometric Authorized Testing Centers around the world. For the location of a testing center near you, call 1-800-891-3926. Outside the United States and Canada, contact your local Thomson Prometric Registration Center.

To register for a proctored Oracle Certified Professional exam:

- Determine the number of the exam you want to take. For the OCP exam, it is 1Z0-043.
- Register with Thomson Prometric online at www.prometric.com or in North America by calling 1-800-891-EXAM (800-891-3926). At this point, you will be asked to pay in advance for the exam. At the time of this writing, the exams are $125 each and must be taken within one year of payment.
- When you schedule the exam, you'll get instructions regarding all appointment and cancellation procedures, the ID requirements, and information about the testing-center location.

You can schedule exams up to six weeks in advance or as soon as one working day before the day you wish to take it. If something comes up and you need to cancel or reschedule your exam appointment, contact Thomson Prometric at least 24 hours or one business day in advance.

What Does This Book Cover?

This book covers everything you need to pass the Oracle Database10*g*: Administration II exam. Each chapter begins with a list of exam objectives.

Chapter 1 This chapter discusses how to configure Recovery Manager, including configuring database parameters, RMAN default and persistent settings, and RMAN utility fundamentals.

Chapter 2 This chapter explains how to use Recovery Manager to perform backups, enable block change tracking, and retrieve RMAN with the `LIST` and `REPORT` commands.

Chapter 3 This chapter discusses the various non-critical losses to an Oracle database and how to recover from these losses.

Chapter 4 In this chapter, you will learn to perform database recovery. Specific cases of database recovery are covered such as control file recovery, incomplete recovery with RMAN and SQL, and recovery through `RESETLOGS`.

Chapter 5 This chapter explains how to configure, use, and monitor the Flashback Database. You will learn how to manage the Flashback Database using both Recovery Manager (RMAN) and Enterprise Manager (EM).

Chapter 6 This chapter discusses how to recover from user errors. This includes using and configuring Flashback Drop, Flashback Versions Query, Flashback Transaction Query, and Flashback Table.

Chapter 7 This chapter explains how to deal with database corruption. You'll learn what block corruption is, and how to detect database corruption with the ANALYZE and DBVERIFY utilities, the `DBMS_REPAIR` package, and the `DB_BLOCK_CHECKING` parameter. This chapter also explains how to repair database corruption using Recovery Manager (RMAN).

Chapter 8 In this chapter, we discuss Oracle's automatic database management features. You will learn about the Common Manageability Infrastructure (CMI), including the automatic workload repository, server-generated alerts, automated routine maintenance, and the advisory framework.

Chapter 9 In this chapter, you'll learn about Automatic Storage Management (ASM). It introduces the ASM architecture and how to create a special type of Oracle instance: an ASM instance. In addition, this chapter describes in detail how to create and manage disk volumes in an ASM environment.

Chapter 10 This chapter describes Oracle's globalization support features. You will learn about linguistic sorting and searching, datetime datatypes, and how to configure the database to support different language and territorial conventions.

Chapter 11 This chapter discusses the management of Oracle resources. You will learn about the Database Resource Manager (DRM) and how it can be used to manage resources. You will learn to create resource plans, resource consumer groups, and resource plan directives.

Chapter 12 In this chapter, we discuss the new Oracle Scheduler. You will learn how the Scheduler can be used to automate repetitive DBA tasks. You will also learn to create the objects necessary to schedule jobs, including job, schedule, program, window, job group, and window group objects.

Chapter 13 This chapter explains the various methods for monitoring and managing disk storage. It not only shows you how to optimize the disk space for redo log files using the Redo Logfile Size Advisor, it also introduces a number of table types that can optimize disk space, performance, or both, such as index-organized tables and two types of clustered tables. In addition, this chapter shows you how to suspend and resume a long-running operation that runs out of disk space without restarting the operation.

Chapter 14 This chapter discusses methods of securing the Oracle listener. You will also learn about Oracle's diagnostic resources and how to access and manage them. You will learn about automatic memory management features, including the Automatic Shared Memory Management (ASMM) and Automatic PGA Memory Management (APMM) features.

Throughout each chapter, we include Real World Scenario sidebars, which are designed to give a real-life perspective on how certain topics affect our everyday duties as DBAs. Each chapter ends with a list of Exam Essentials, which give you a highlight of the chapter, with an emphasis on the topics that you need to be extra familiar with for the exam. The chapter concludes with 20 review questions, specifically designed to help you retain the knowledge presented. To really nail down your skills, read and answer each question carefully.

How to Use This Book

This book can provide a solid foundation for the serious effort of preparing for the Oracle 10*g* Administration II exam. To best benefit from this book, use the following study method:

1. Take the Assessment Test immediately following this introduction. (The answers are at the end of the test.) Carefully read over the explanations for any questions you get wrong, and note which chapters the material comes from. This information should help you plan your study strategy.
2. Study each chapter carefully, making sure that you fully understand the information and the test objectives listed at the beginning of each chapter. Pay extra close attention to any chapter related to questions you missed in the Assessment Test.
3. Complete all hands-on exercises in the chapter, referring back to the chapter text so that you understand the reason for each step you take. If you do not have an Oracle database available, be sure to study the examples carefully.
4. Answer the Review Questions related to that chapter. (The answers appear at the end of each chapter, after the "Review Questions" section.) Note the questions that confuse or trick you, and study those sections of the book again.
5. Take the two Bonus Exams that are included on the accompanying CD. This will give you a complete overview of what you can expect to see on the real test.
6. Remember to use the products on the CD included with this book. The electronic flashcards and the Sybex Test Engine exam preparation software have been specifically designed to help you study for and pass your exam.

To learn all the material covered in this book, you'll need to apply yourself regularly and with discipline. Try to set aside the same time period every day to study, and select a comfortable and quiet place to do so. If you work hard, you will be surprised at how quickly you learn this material. All the best!

What's on the CD?

We have worked hard to provide some really great tools to help you with your certification process. All of the following tools should be loaded on your workstation when you're studying for the test.

The Sybex Test Engine Preparation Software

This test preparation software prepares you to pass the 1Z0-043 Oracle Database 10*g* Administration II exam. In this test, you will find all of the questions from the book, plus two additional bonus exams that appear exclusively on the CD. You can take the Assessment Test, test yourself by chapter, or take the practice exams. The test engine will run on either a Microsoft Windows or Linux platform.

Here is a sample screen from the Sybex Test Engine:

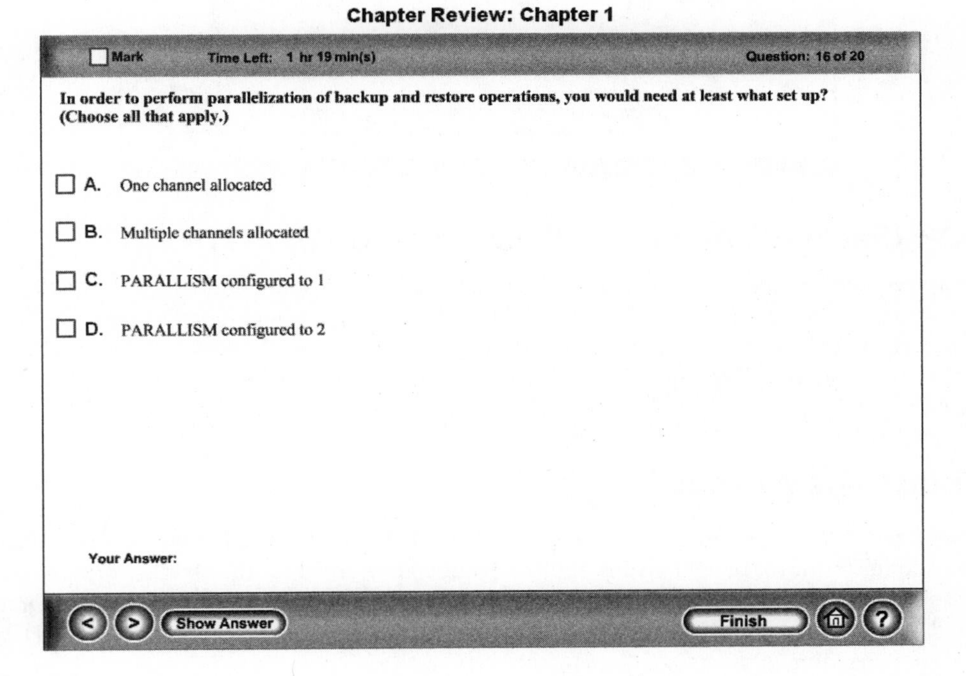

Electronic Flashcards for PC and Palm Devices

After you read the *OCP: Oracle 10g Administration II Study Guide*, read the Review Questions at the end of each chapter and study the practice exams included in the book and on the CD. You can also test yourself with the flashcards included on the CD.

The flashcards are designed to test your understanding of the fundamental concepts covered in the exam. Here is what the Sybex Flashcards interface looks like:

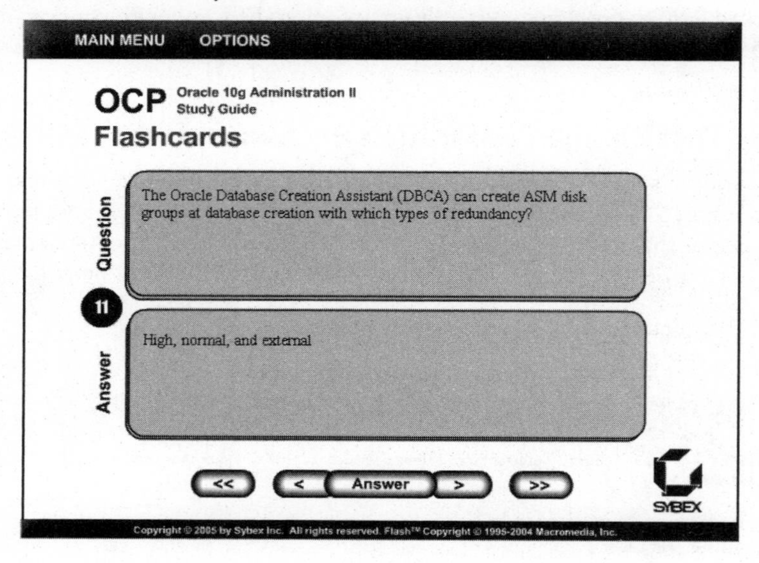

*OCP: Oracle 10*g *Administration II Study Guide* in PDF

Many people like the convenience of being able to carry their Study Guide on a CD, which is why we included the book in PDF format. This will be extremely helpful to readers who fly or commute on a bus or train and prefer an e-book, as well as to readers who find it more comfortable reading from their computer. We've also included a copy of Adobe Acrobat Reader on the CD.

About The Authors

Doug Stuns, OCP, has been an Oracle DBA for more than 15 years and has worked as lead database administrator for many Fortune 500 companies. He worked for the Oracle Corporation in consulting and education roles for five years and is the founder and owner of SCS, Inc., an Oracle-based consulting company that has been in business for more than five years. To contact Doug, you can e-mail him at `stuns@scs-corp.net`.

Tim Buterbaugh is an OCP with over six years of experience with Oracle databases. He currently works as a DBA for EDS in Madison, Wisconsin. He is also the co-founder of 3rdsystems, Inc. with his wife, Jeaneanne. To contact Tim, you can e-mail him at `tim@3rdsystems.com`.

Bob Bryla is an Oracle 8, 8*i*, 9*i* and 10*g* Certified Professional with more than 15 years of experience in database design, database application development, training, and database administration. He is an Internet database analyst and Oracle DBA at Lands' End in Dodgeville, Wisconsin. To contact Bob, you can e-mail him at `rjbryla@centurytel.net`.

Assessment Test

1. The process of configuring a database to back up the control file with each backup is called?
   A. Control file backup
   B. Control file autobackup
   C. Automatic control file backup
   D. Control file automatic backup

2. What is the new Oracle Database 10*g* feature that makes the channels more resilient?
   A. Automated channel redundancy
   B. Channel redundancy
   C. Automated channel fail over
   D. Channel fail over

3. What command would you use to set a persistent setting in RMAN so that backups are all written to a tape device?
   A. `CONFIGURE DEFAULT DEVICE TYPE TO TAPE MEDIA`
   B. `CONFIGURE DEFAULT DEVICE TYPE TO TAPE`
   C. `CONFIGURE DEFAULT DEVICE TYPE TO SBT`
   D. `CONFIGURE DEFAULT DEVICE TYPE TO SBT_TAPE`

4. The `CONTROL_FILE_RECORD_KEEP_TIME` initialization parameter should be set to what value? (Choose all that apply.)
   A. The initialization parameter should be set to 0 when the RMAN repository is being used.
   B. The initialization parameter should be set to greater than 0 with the RMAN repository utilizing the recovery catalog only.
   C. The initialization parameter should be set to greater than 0 with the RMAN repository utilizing the control file or the recovery catalog.
   D. The initialization parameter should be set to 0 with the RMAN repository utilizing the control file or the recovery catalog.
   E. The initialization parameter should never be set to 0 if you are using RMAN.

5. The `BACKUP` command has the ability to do what? (Choose all that apply.)
   A. The `BACKUP` command can make bit-for-bit copies of a file.
   B. The `BACKUP` command can improve performance by multiplexing backup files.
   C. The `BACKUP` can take advantage of the block change tracking capability.
   D. The `BACKUP` command cannot store data in incremental backups.
   E. The `BACKUP` command can store data in cumulative incremental backups only.

6. Which commands are required to perform a compressed RMAN backup? (Choose all that apply.)
   - A. BACKUP AS COMPRESSED BACKUPSET DATABASE
   - B. BACKUP AS COMPRESSED COPY OF DATABASE
   - C. CONFIGURE DEVICE TYPE DISK BACKUP TYPE TO COMPRESSED BACKUPSET
   - D. CONFIGURE DEVICE TYPE DISK BACKUP TYPE COMPRESS
   - E. BACKUP DATABASE COMPRESS

7. The RATE option performs what function during RMAN backups?
   - A. The RATE option increases RMAN throughput to the desired RATE value.
   - B. The RATE option increases system throughput to the desired RATE value.
   - C. The RATE option limits RMAN to only back up at a designated RATE value.
   - D. The RATE option increases RMAN to back up at a designated RATE value.

8. What two values are required to identify a database incarnation within the recovery catalog?
   - A. DBID
   - B. DATABASE NAME
   - C. DB_KEY
   - D. DATABASE_VALUE

9. What is the most efficient order in which to create a new default temporary tablespace named TEMP2 and have that tablespace available as the default tablespace for users?
   - A. Perform the CREATE TEMPORARY TABLESPACE temp2 command and then the ALTER USER *username* TEMPORARY TABLESPACE temp2 command.
   - B. Perform the CREATE TEMPORARY TABLESPACE temp2 command and then the ALTER DATABASE DEFAULT TEMPORARY TABLESPACE temp2 command.
   - C. Perform the DROP TABLESPACE temp2, CREATE TEMPORARY TABLESPACE temp2 command and then the ALTER DATABASE TEMPORARY TABLESPACE temp2 command.
   - D. Perform the CREATE TEMPORARY TABLESPACE temp2 command.

10. What is the correct command sequence for recovering a missing tempfile named temp?
    - A. STARTUP MOUNT, CREATE TEMPORARY TABLESPACE temp TEMPFILE
    - B. STARTUP NOMOUNT, DROP TABLESPACE temp, CREATE TEMPORARY TABLESPACE temp TEMPFILE
    - C. STARTUP MOUNT, DROP TABLESPACE temp, CREATE TEMPORARY TABLESPACE temp TEMPFILE
    - D. STARTUP, DROP TABLESPACE temp, CREATE TEMPORARY TABLESPACE temp TEMPFILE

11. You are faced with a media failure for a tablespace that is currently read-only. The only backup of the read-only tablespace was made one week ago when the tablespace was read-write. What do you have to do to recover this tablespace? (Choose all that apply.)

    A. You only need to restore the datafile for this tablespace because the tablespace is read-only.

    B. You only need to restore and recover the datafile for this tablespace because the tablespace you have restored is read-write.

    C. You only need to restore and recover the datafile for this tablespace because the tablespace has a different SCN in the header.

    D. You only need to recover the datafile for this tablespace because the tablespace is read-only.

12. User-managed recovery requires which major difference from using RMAN?

    A. User-managed recovery uses the `UNTIL SCN` clause.

    B. User-managed recovery uses the `UNTIL SEQUENCE` clause.

    C. User-managed recovery uses the `UNTIL TIME` clause.

    D. User-managed recovery requires the DBA to directly manage the recovery.

13. Why does control file recovery require special steps when using RMAN without the recovery catalog? (Choose all that apply.)

    A. Special steps are required when recovering control files because they are not part of the physical database.

    B. Special steps are required when recovering control files because they contain RMAN metadata information.

    C. Special steps are required when recovering a database when the RMAN repository is not available for that database.

    D. Special steps are required when recovering control files because they cannot be easily rebuilt.

14. Logical corruption has been introduced into the database. You need to recover the database to the point-in-time prior to the introduction of the corruption. The logical corruption was introduced at 6:30 P.M. on September 6, 2004.

    A.
    ```
    run
    {
    set until time '06-SEP-2004 6:25:00';
    restore database;
    recover database;
    }
    ```

    B.
    ```
    run
    {
    set until time '06-SEP-2004 18:25:00';
    recover database;
    }
    ```

C.
```
run
{
set until time '06-SEP-2004 18:25:00';
restore database;
}
```

D.
```
run
{
set until time '06-SEP-2004 18:25:00';
restore database;
recover database;
}
```

15. You have a backup from two days ago. It is discovered that corruption was introduced today at 6:30 P.M. You perform an incomplete recovery of the database to 6:25 P.M. before the corruption. One day later you have a media failure, and you need to recover but you only have the same backup that was used to perform an incomplete recovery prior to the corruption. What will happen to the recovery attempt for the media failure?

A. The media recovery will fail because you have performed a RESETLOGS to recover from the corruption and you have not taken another backup after the RESETLOGS operation.

B. The media recovery will be successful because you can perform a RESETLOGS to recover from an incomplete recovery to a new point-in-time greater than the RESETLOGS operation.

C. The media recovery will fail because you always must take a backup following an incomplete recovery with RESETLOGS to open the database.

D. The media recovery will only be successful if you recover the database back to the original time of 6:25 P.M. before the corruption.

16. Where are the flashback database logs stored? (Choose all that apply.)

A. Flashback database logs are stored in the flash recovery area.

B. Flashback database logs are stored at the location specified by the FLASH_DATABASE_LOG_DEST parameter.

C. Flashback database logs are stored at the location specified by the DB_RECOVERY_FILE_DEST parameter.

D. Flashback database logs are stored at the location specified by the FLASH_DATABASE_RETENTION_TARGET parameter.

17. Which of the following statements are correct regarding warnings at flash recovery thresholds? (Choose all that apply.)

A. At 90 percent, there is a full warning and obsolete files are removed.

B. At 85 percent, there is a full warning.

C. At 95 percent, there is a full warning and obsolete files are removed.

D. At 95 percent, there is a full warning.

18. What files are considered transient in the flash recovery area? (Choose all that apply.)

A. Flashback logs

B. Multiplexed redo logs

C. Control files

D. Datafiles

E. RMAN working files

19. Which initialization parameter will not create files in the flash recovery area? (Choose all that apply.)

A. `LOG_ARCHIVE_DEST`

B. `LOG_ARCHIVE_DEST_DUPLEX`

C. `LOG_ARCHIVE_DEST_`*`n`*

D. `LOG_ARCHIVE_DUPLEX_DEST`

20. What command is equivalent to the `DROP TABLE` command of Oracle 9*i* or earlier versions?

A. `DROP TABLE` *`table_name`*

B. `DROP TABLE PURGE` *`table_name`*

C. `PURGE TABLE` *`table_name`*

D. `PURGE TABLE` *`recycle_bin_object`*

21. How would you assure that the triggers you need enabled are enabled and the triggers you need disabled are disabled after a Flashback Table recovery? (Choose all that apply.)

A. Make sure that all triggers are enabled before a table is Flashback Table recovered.

B. Make sure that all triggers that need to be disabled are disabled before the Flashback Table command is executed with the `ENABLE TRIGGERS` option.

C. Manually enable and disable all triggers after the Flashback Table recovery.

D. Make sure that all triggers are disabled before a table is Flashback Table recovered.

22. How can you identify multiple objects dropped with the same name in the Recycle Bin?

A. In the `RECYCLEBIN` view, the column `ORIGINAL_NAME` will be unique.

B. In the `RECYCLEBIN` view, the column `OBJECT_NAME` will be unique.

C. In the `RECYCLEBIN` view, the columns `ORIGINAL_NAME` and `ORGINAL_NAME` will be different.

D. None of the above.

23. A user accidentally deleted a customer identified by 46435 from the `customers` table on September 6, 2004 at 3:30 P.M. Which of the following recovery approaches will successfully recover `CUSTOMER_ID 46435` with the least impact on database operations?

A. Perform the following RMAN incomplete recovery after restarting the database in `MOUNT` mode:

```
run
{
```

```
set until time '06-SEP-2004 15:25:00';
restore database;
recover database;
}
```

B. Perform the following DML transaction utilizing Flashback Query:

```
insert into customers
select * from customers where customer_id = 46435
as of timestamp to_timestamp ('06-SEP-2004 15:25:00')
where customer_id = 46435;
```

C. Perform a user-managed recovery after restoring database files after starting the database in MOUNT mode:

```
recover database until time '06-SEP-2004 15:25:00'
alter database open resetlogs
```

D. None of the above.

24. DB_BLOCK_CHECKING performs checksums on modified blocks only on what database objects?

A. All database objects by default

B. All database objects if DB_BLOCK_CHECKING is TRUE

C. All non-system tablespace objects if DB_BLOCK_CHECKING is FALSE

D. All system tablespace objects only if DB_BLOCK_CHECKING is TRUE

25. What is the correct syntax for performing a block media recovery for corrupt blocks in datafile 4 and 5 with blocks 5 and 6, respectively?

A. `RMAN> blockrecover datafile 4-5 block 5-6;`

B. `SQL> blockrecover datafile 4 and 5 block 5 and 6;`

C. `RMAN> blockrecover datafile 4 block 5;`
`RMAN> blockrecover datafile 5 block 6;`

D. `RMAN> blockrecover datafile 4 and 5 block 5 and 6;`

26. What is the name of the DBMS_REPAIR procedure used to identify index entries that point to corrupt data blocks?

A. DUMP_ORPHAN_KEYS

B. DUMP_ORPHAN_KEY

C. DUMP_CHILD_KEYS

D. DUMP_ORPHANS_KEYS

27. What type of backup should not be used to support RMAN block media recovery (BMR)?

A. Any incremental backup should not be used to support BMR.

B. Only a differential incremental backup should not be used to support BMR.

C. Full backups should not be used to support BMR.

D. Only a cumulative incremental backup should not be used to support BMR.

28. You create a new table, populate it, and build several indexes on the table. When you issue a query against the table, the optimizer does not choose to use the indexes. Why might this be?

A. The indexed columns are not used in the `where` clause of the query.

B. There are no statistics available for the table.

C. There is a small number of rows in the table.

D. The query contains a hint instructing the optimizer not to use the indexes.

E. All of the above.

29. You are concerned about keeping statistics up-to-date for the `NOODLE` table, a table that is the target of frequent DML operations. In response, another DBA issues the command `ALTER TABLE NOODLE MONITORING`. What is the result of this action? (Choose the best answer.)

A. The action resolves the issue.

B. The action has no effect.

C. The action only partially resolves the issue.

D. The action has a detrimental effect regarding the issue.

E. None of the above.

30. You have created a new table. How long do you have to wait to be sure that Oracle has automatically gathered optimizer statistics for the table and loaded them into the AWR?

A. Not more than 30 minutes.

B. Up to seven days.

C. Until the next scheduled automated statistics collection job is run.

D. Optimizer statistics are not stored in the AWR.

E. You must gather the statistics manually when a new table is created. Oracle will collect them automatically after that.

31. You are concerned about the operating system performance as well as SQL execution plan statistics. Which `STATISTICS_LEVEL` parameter would be the minimum required to ensure that Oracle will collect these types of statistics?

A. `BASIC`

B. `TYPICAL`

C. `ADVANCED`

D. `ALL`

E. None of these settings will achieve the desired result.

32. An ASM disk group can manage database files from how many different databases?

A. 1

B. 2

C. Limited only by disk space.

D. ASM disk groups manage tablespaces, not database files.

33. High redundancy disk groups must have how many failure groups? (Choose the best answer.)

   A. 1, because high redundancy disk groups rely on external RAID hardware or software

   B. 2

   C. Exactly 3

   D. 3 or more

34. Automatic Storage Management (ASM) disk group mirroring is done at which level?

   A. Tablespace level

   B. Extent level

   C. Segment level

   D. Datafile level

35. Identify two valid types of Oracle instances.

   A. RMAN

   B. DSKMGR

   C. ASM

   D. DBMS

   E. RDBMS

36. A new workstation has been added at your location in Spain. This machine will be used to run an application that connects to your database in the United States. A technician installs the Oracle client and the application. The user on the new machine notices that performance seems to be sluggish compared to the existing workstations. The technician swears that the application is configured identically on all machines, and has ruled out network issues. What is the most likely cause? (Choose the best answer.)

   A. Defective hardware

   B. Client character set

   C. Client `NLS_LANGUAGE` setting

   D. Server `NLS_LANGUAGE` setting

   E. Routing tables

37. You are setting up a new database instance that needs to support several languages. Conserving storage is a high priority. Point-in-time recovery is absolutely required. How would you go about choosing a character set to use?

   A. Choose a Unicode character set.

   B. Choose the smallest Unicode character set.

   C. Investigate multi-byte character sets to find one that supports the languages that you need.

   D. Use a single-byte Unicode character set.

   E. Investigate single-byte character sets to find one that supports the languages you need.

38. Your database uses a single-byte character set and has the following parameters set:

```
NLS_LENGTH_SEMANTICS = CHAR
```

You create a table as shown here:

```
SQL> create table XYZ (
      NAME  varchar2(30) );
Table created.
```

How many characters will you be able to store in the NAME column?

A. 15

B. 30

C. It depends on the size of a byte on the server platform.

D. It depends on the character set.

E. Somewhere between 7 and 15.

39. Your client NLS_LANG parameter is set to AMERICAN. You create a session to a server that has an NLS_LANGUAGE setting of FRENCH. You issue the following SQL statement:

```
ALTER SESSION SET NLS_LANGUAGE=ITALIAN;
```

Which language setting will govern client-side NLS operations?

A. AMERICAN

B. FRENCH

C. ITALIAN

D. It depends on the operation.

E. None of the above.

40. You want to set up DRM to allocate CPU resources between seven resource consumer groups. The groups should be allocated only CPU unused by the SYS_GROUP group. Six of the groups will get 15 percent and the remaining group will receive 10 percent. Which of the following would achieve all of these objectives with the least amount of effort?

A. Create a simple plan.

B. Create a complex plan with one sub-plan.

C. Create a complex plan with more than one sub-plan.

D. Create a simple plan with one sub-plan.

E. Create a simple plan with more than one sub-plan.

41. You are creating a complex plan. You need to limit the degree of parallelism for an existing consumer group. Which DRM element do you need to create?

A. Sub-plan

B. Group allocation

C. Resource

D. Resource plan directive

E. Parallel directive

42. You have finished building all of your DRM objects in the pending area. Your PC is currently down, so you ask another DBA to validate it from her PC. She sends you back the following screen capture:

```
SQL> begin
  2      dbms_resource_manager.validate_pending_area;
  3  end;
SQL> /

PL/SQL procedure completed successfully.
```

What do you know about the status of the pending area? (Select the best answer.)

A. The pending area was successfully validated.

B. The pending area has been scheduled for validation.

C. You are unsure if the other DBA submitted the correct pending area.

D. The pending area was successfully validated and is now active.

E. Nothing.

43. You want to create the elements for a resource plan that allocates twice as much CPU to one group than to another. Which of the following do you use?

A. Create a plan with `CPU_MTH` set to `EMPHASIS`.

B. Create plan directives with `CPU_MTH` set to `EMPHASIS`.

C. Create a plan with `CPU_MTH` set to `RATIO`.

D. Create a plan with `CPU_MTH` set to `WEIGHT`.

E. Create plan directives with `CPU_MTH` set to `RATIO`.

44. You want to create a scheduler job that is very similar to an existing job. Neither of these jobs requires any arguments. What is the best way to create the new job?

A. `DBMS_SCHEDULER.COPY_JOB`

B. `DBMS_SCHEDULER.CREATE_JOB_AS`

C. `DBMS_SCHEDULER.COPY_SCHEDULER_OBJECT`

D. Reuse the same job.

E. There is no way to copy a job.

45. You execute the following PL/SQL block:

```
SQL> begin
  2    DBMS_SCHEDULER.SET_SCHEDULER_ATTRIBUTE(
  3    'LOG_HISTORY', '60');
  4  end;
SQL> /

PL/SQL procedure successfully completed.
```

What is the result of this action?

A. Job and window logs will be updated every 60 minutes.

B. Job logs will be automatically purged after 60 days.

C. Window logs will be automatically purged after 60 days.

D. Job and window logs will be limited to the most recent 60 days.

E. Job and window logs will be automatically purged after 60 days.

46. You have created a new job by copying an existing job. When you attempt to execute the new job, it doesn't work. Why might this be?

A. The job must be modified in some way to differentiate it from the original job.

B. The job can only be executed within a certain window.

C. The job is disabled.

D. When a job is copied, the objects referenced by the job must be validated.

E. The new job must be registered in the `JOB_TABLE` table.

47. Consider the index `HR.IDX_PK_EMP` on the table `HR.EMPLOYEES` and the following `ALTER INDEX` command:

```
ALTER INDEX HR.IDX_PK_EMP COALESCE;
```

Which of the following commands accomplishes the same task as this command? (Choose the best answer.)

A. `ALTER TABLE HR.EMPLOYEES SHRINK SPACE CASCADE;`

B. `ALTER TABLE HR.EMPLOYEES SHRINK SPACE;`

C. `ALTER TABLE HR.EMPLOYEES SHRINK SPACE COMPACT;`

D. `ALTER INDEX HR.IDX_PK_EMP REBUILD;`

48. Which type of queue is supported by sorted hash clusters?

A. DEQUE

B. LIFO

C. FIFO

D. A queue represented by a two-way linked list

49. If you have two redo log groups with four members each, how many disks does Oracle recommend to keep the redo log files?

A. 8

B. 2

C. 1

D. 4

50. Which of the following statements is *not* true about segment shrink operations?

A. The compaction phase of segment shrink is done online.

B. During the compaction phase, the entire segment is locked but only for a very short period of time.

C. When the second phase of segment shrink occurs, the high watermark (HWM) is adjusted.

D. User DML can block the progress of the compaction phase until the DML is committed or rolled back.

E. Using the `COMPACT` keyword, the movement of the HWM can occur later during non-peak hours by running the command without the `COMPACT` keyword.

51. What is the purpose of the overflow area for an index-organized table (IOT)?

A. The overflow area helps to reduce row chaining in the IOT.

B. The overflow area allows you to store some or all of the non-primary key data in an IOT row in another tablespace, improving performance.

C. The overflow area is used when there is a duplicate value for the primary key in the IOT.

D. The overflow area stores the index information for indexed columns that are not part of the primary key.

52. You are concerned about ORA-00600 messages that have been appearing in the alert log, and you want to know if any new ones appear. Which Oracle feature might be of use? (Choose the best answer.)

A. AWR

B. Advisory framework

C. Server-generated alerts

D. Alert monitor

E. ADDM

53. You wish to restrict remote access to your database by using Valid Node Checking. Which file do you need to configure?

A. `listener.ora`

B. `lsnrctl.ora`

C. `tnsnav.ora`

D. `sqlnet.ora`

E. `init.ora`

54. Several users call to report that their sessions appear to be hung. They mention that the problem started within the last few minutes. You attempt to connect, but your session hangs as well. What would be the best place to look for the cause of the problem?

 A. `listener.log`

 B. Alert log

 C. EM Database Control

 D. Trace files

 E. `sqlnet.log`

55. A user sends you a SQL script that they say is running very slowly. The explain plan reveals no problems. How might you go about determining the problem?

 A. Execute an extended explain plan.

 B. Run the script with SQL tracing enabled.

 C. Check for locks on objects referenced in the script.

 D. Run the script with background tracing enabled.

 E. Run the script with `TIMED_STATISTICS` enabled.

Answers to Assessment Test

1. B. The control file autobackup is the name of the process that automates the backup of the control file with every backup. See Chapter 1 for more information.

2. C. Automated channel fail over requires that multiple channels be allocated. If one channel fails, the backup or recovery operation will use the other channel to complete the operation. See Chapter 1 for more information.

3. C. The command that sets the persistent setting that directs RMAN to back up to tape is `CONFIGURE DEFAULT DEVICE TYPE TO SBT`. See Chapter 1 for more information.

4. C, E. The `CONTROL_FILE_RECORD_KEEP_TIME` initialization parameter should never be set to 0 if you are using RMAN. If this value is set to 0, there is a potential to lose backup records. See Chapter 1 for more information.

5. B, C. The `BACKUP` command can take advantage of multiplexing datafiles to the same backup set. The `BACKUP` command can also use the block change tracking capability. See Chapter 2 for more information.

6. A, C. The correct methods of compressing a backup are to use the command `BACKUP AS COMPRESSED BACKUPSET DATABASE` and to set persistent settings by using `CONFIGURE DEVICE TYPE DISK BACKUP TYPE TO COMPRESSED BACKUPSET`. See Chapter 2 for more information.

7. C. The `RATE` option limits the system resource usage that RMAN will consume performing backup operations. See Chapter 2 for more information.

8. A, C. The `DBID` and `DB_KEY` are required to identify the database incarnation when using SQL*Plus to query the recovery catalog tables. See Chapter 2 for more information.

9. B. The most efficient way to create a new default temporary tablespace named `TEMP2` is to create the temporary tablespace `TEMP2`. Next, perform the `ALTER DATABASE DEFAULT TEMPORARY TABLESPACE temp2` command. This will make `TEMP2` the default temporary tablespace for all users. You can perform the `ALTER USER` *`username`* `TEMPORARY TABLESPACE temp2` command, but this could be more time-consuming than identifying all the users. See Chapter 3 for more information.

10. C. The correct command sequence for recovering a missing tempfile named `temp` is as follows:

    1. `STARTUP MOUNT`
    2. `DROP TABLESPACE temp`
    3. `CREATE TEMPORARY TABLESPACE temp TEMPFILE`

    The database must be mounted, and then the tablespace information needs to be dropped from the data dictionary. Then the tablespace can be created. See Chapter 3 for more information.

11. B, C. You need to restore and recover the tablespace of the read-only tablespace because the tablespace was read-write when the backup was taken. If the tablespace was backed up read-write, the datafile has changed or has a different SCN in the datafile header. This will require recovery. See Chapter 3 for more information.

12. D. User-managed recovery requires the DBA to directly manage the recovery process. The DBA must determine which database files to restore and from what backup, as well as which archive logs to apply. See Chapter 4 for more information.

13. B, C. Control files contain the RMAN repository when not using the recovery catalog that contains metadata about the backups that are used to perform the recovery. This information is not available when recovering a control file. See Chapter 4 for more information.

14. D. The correct RMAN commands would be as follows:

```
run
{
set until time '06-SEP-2004 18:25:00';
restore database;
recover database;
}
```

The closest time to 6:30 P.M. would be 18:25. You need to use both the `RESTORE DATABASE` and `RECOVER DATABASE` commands. See Chapter 4 for more information.

15. B. You can now recover through an incomplete recovery, which uses `RESETLOGS` to open the database. In previous Oracle versions, you had to take a backup immediately following an incomplete recovery, because the redo log sequences got reset, making the backup unusable. See Chapter 4 for more information.

16. A, C. The flashback database logs must be stored in the flash recovery area. The actual location in the flash recovery area is determined by the `DB_RECOVERY_FILE_DEST` parameter. See Chapter 5 for more information.

17. A, D. At 90 percent full, a warning is sent to the alert log, and obsolete files are removed. At 95 percent full, warnings are set to the alert log. See Chapter 5 for more information.

18. A, D, E. Flashback logs, datafiles, and RMAN working files are all considered transient by Oracle. These files will be overwritten during certain events. Multiplexed redo logs and control files are considered permanent and will not be overwritten, even when the flash recovery area is backed up to tape. See Chapter 5 for more information.

19. A, B, D. `LOG_ARCHIVE_DEST_DUPLEX` is not a valid initialization parameter. `LOG_ARCHIVE_DEST_`*n* is the only archive log initialization parameter that writes archive logs to the flash recovery area. See Chapter 5 for more information.

20. C. The command equivalent to the DROP TABLE command of Oracle 9*i* or earlier is PURGE TABLE *table_name*. The PURGE TABLE *recycle_bin_object* command only purges from the Recycle Bin. See Chapter 6 for more information.

21. B, C. The Flashback Table command by default disables all triggers unless the ENABLE TRIGGERS option is used. If the ENABLE TRIGGERS option is used, all enabled triggers at the time of the Flashback Table recovery are enabled. All disabled triggers at the time of the Flashback Table recovery are disabled. The last option is to manually enable and disable all triggers after the Flashback Table recovery has been performed. See Chapter 6 for more information.

22. B. The RECYCLEBIN view OBJECT_NAME column will provide a unique name of a database object, even if the OBJECT_NAME is the same. See Chapter 6 for more information.

23. B. The Flashback Query will query the deleted customer 46453 from the undo data, and the insert command will add the customer back to the customers table. There will be minimal impact on the database. See Chapter 6 for more information.

24. B. DB_BLOCK_CHECKING reports on all database objects if DB_BLOCK_CHECKING is TRUE. See Chapter 7 for more information.

25. C. The correct syntax to perform a block media recovery for corrupt blocks in two datafiles is to execute multiple BLOCKRECOVER commands, one for each datafile and block. See Chapter 7 for more information.

26. A. The DUMP_ORPHAN_KEYS is designed to identify index entries that point to corrupt data blocks. See Chapter 7 for more information.

27. A. All incremental backups will not support BMR because they contain only changed blocks. See Chapter 7 for more information.

28. E. Because you aren't given enough information to determine the availability of statistics, nor are you privy to the query itself, you can't rule out any valid possibilities. All of the choices listed are valid reasons why the optimizer might choose to not use an available index. See Chapter 8 for more information.

29. B. The MONITORING option of the ALTER TABLE command is deprecated in Oracle Database 10*g*. While it will not produce an error, it is treated as no operation by Oracle. Automatic DML monitoring is used instead. See Chapter 8 for more information.

30. D. The AWR does not store optimizer statistics. It stores dynamic performance statistics. Optimizer statistics are stored in the data dictionary. See Chapter 8 for more information.

31. D. The STATISTICS_LEVEL parameter must be set to ALL in order to instruct Oracle to automatically collect operating system and SQL execution plan statistics. See Chapter 8 for more information.

32. C. An ASM disk group can manage database files for essentially an unlimited number of different databases. Creating ASM disk groups is discussed in Chapter 9.

33. D. High redundancy disk groups require disks in at least three failure groups, but they can contain more if a higher level of redundancy or performance is desired. Controlling disk group redundancy is detailed in Chapter 9.

34. B. Disk group mirroring for ASM is done at the extent level. To learn about Automatic Storage Management mirroring, see Chapter 9.

35. C, E. ASM instances manage ASM disk groups, and RDBMS instances are the traditional and only type of instance available before Oracle Database 10*g*. Configuring ASM and RDBMS instances for Automatic Storage Management is covered in Chapter 9.

36. B. The most likely cause is that the Oracle client environment is using a character set that does not match the server and is not a strict subset of the server character set. In this situation, Oracle will perform automatic data conversion, which can impact performance. See Chapter 10 for more information.

37. E. If a single-byte character set can be found that fulfills all of your language requirements, you will save storage space over using a multi-byte character set. See Chapter 10 for more information.

38. B. A single-byte character set always uses only one byte to store a character, so using byte semantics isn't any different from using character semantics. See Chapter 10 for more information.

39. A. Client-side NLS operations are governed by the `NLS_LANG` environment variable settings. The server session was affected by the `ALTER SESSION` command, but it has no effect on client-side NLS operations because they don't involve the server session. See Chapter 10 for more information.

40. A. A simple plan can allocate CPU resources for up to eight consumer groups at the same level. By default, `SYS_GROUP` will be allocated 100 percent of level 1 CPU, and all other CPU allocation is done at level 2. Therefore, a simple plan will meet all of these requirements. See Chapter 11 for more information.

41. D. A resource plan directive needs to be created, which will define the plan, the consumer group, and resource allocation. See Chapter 11 for more information.

42. E. There can only be one pending area, so there is no question of whether it was the right one. The problem is that you don't know whether she issued the `set serveroutput on` statement before executing the procedure. Therefore, you don't know if errors were found, but were not displayed. See Chapter 11 for more information.

43. C. The resource allocation method is defined at the plan level, not at the plan directive level. The resource allocation method of `RATIO` indicates that the amounts allocated in subsequent plan directives will represent a weighted amount, rather than a percentage. See Chapter 11 for more information.

44. A. Scheduler jobs can be copied by using the `DBMS_SCHEDULER.COPY_JOB` procedure. See Chapter 12 for more information.

45. E. The SET_SCHEDULER_ATTRIBUTE procedure sets the purge rule for both job and window logs by default. If the WHICH_LOG parameter is specified, the procedure sets the purge rule for one specific log type. See Chapter 12 for more information.

46. C. By default, copied jobs are created in a disabled state. See Chapter 12 for more information.

47. A. Using the CASCADE keyword in any segment shrink operation will shrink the free space in any dependent objects such as indexes. Chapter 13 discusses segment shrink functionality.

48. C. Sorted hash clusters are similar to standard hash clusters, except that they store data sorted by non-primary key columns and make access by applications that use the rows in a first in, first out (FIFO) manner very efficiently; no sorting is required. Chapter 13 describes how sorted hash clusters are created and used.

49. D. Oracle recommends that you keep each member of a redo log group on a different disk. You must have a minimum of two redo log groups, and it is recommended that you have two members in each group. The maximum number of redo log groups is determined by the MAXLOGFILES database parameter. The MAXLOGMEMBERS database parameter specifies the maximum number of members per group. See Chapter 13 for more information.

50. B. During the compaction phase, locks are held only on individual rows, causing some minor serialization with concurrent DML operations. For more information about segment shrink, see Chapter 13.

51. B. If an IOT row's data exceeds the threshold of available space in a block, the row's data will be dynamically and automatically moved to the overflow area. For more information about index-organized tables, see Chapter 13.

52. C. Server-generated alerts would be the best answer. Oracle has a predefined alert that detects ORA-00600 messages in the alert log and will raise an alert when they are found. See Chapter 14 for more information.

53. D. The sqlnet.ora file must be manually edited to configure Valid Node Checking. See Chapter 14 for more information.

54. B. The alert log would be the best place to look for information. EM Database Control does allow alerts to be viewed; however, the metrics are unlikely to have been updated because the problem occurred within the last few minutes. See Chapter 14 for more information.

55. B. Running the script with SQL tracing enabled will produce a trace file detailing the execution of the SQL. This file can be used to troubleshoot the performance problem. See Chapter 14 for more information.

Configuring Recovery Manager

ORACLE DATABASE 10*G*: ADMINISTRATION II EXAM OBJECTIVES COVERED IN THIS CHAPTER:

✓ **Configuring Recovery Manager**
- Configure database parameters that affect RMAN operations.
- Change RMAN default settings with CONFIGURE.
- Manage RMAN's persistent settings.
- Start the RMAN utility and allocate channels.

Exam objectives are subject to change at any time without prior notice and at Oracle's sole discretion. Please visit Oracle's Training and Certification website (`http://www.oracle.com/education/certification/`) for the most current exam objectives listing.

The Oracle *Recovery Manager (RMAN)* is the recommended backup and recovery tool provided with the Oracle Database Server 10*g* software. RMAN was first introduced in Oracle 8, and Oracle has steadily made enhancements and improvements with each new release of Oracle to meet the heavy demands required for database backup and recovery.

RMAN has grown to meet the demands of exponentially larger database sizes and more stringent availability requirements. Database servers have grown in size with technology gains of CPU, bus architectures, and more efficient disk subsystems. Disk costs have steadily decreased to more affordable and acceptable levels and have now become an economic alternative to tape storage.

RMAN has been redesigned in Oracle 10*g* to support these contemporary database environments. RMAN now places more focus on backing up and recovering the changes to the database instead of the complete database. This allows RMAN to support backups of larger databases and recover in faster timeframes.

This chapter discusses configuring and setting up RMAN. Configuring RMAN is the first step in the RMAN process. RMAN must be set up and configured to each environment's requirements. We will walk through this process in detail through examples and demonstrations.

This chapter walks through the parameters for RMAN that are demonstrated in the configuration settings. You will perform the basics of starting RMAN and configuring or setting up RMAN. The remainder of this chapter focuses on more complex topics such as autobackups using the control file.

This chapter takes you through a review of the common RMAN features. The review will demonstrate these features with examples. Where applicable, you will walk through the new 10*g* features and capabilities of RMAN.

The next few chapters discuss topics such as "Using RMAN," "Recovering from Non-critical Losses," "Flashback Database," "Recovering from User Errors," and "Database Corruption."

Exploring the Features and Components of RMAN

RMAN has many capabilities to facilitate the backup and recovery process. RMAN comes in both web-based GUI and command-line versions. In general, RMAN performs and standardizes the backup and recovery process, which can reduce mistakes made during this process. Below is a list of some of the existing RMAN features:

- Backup databases, tablespaces, datafiles, control files, and archive logs
- Compressing backups by determining which blocks have changed, and backing up only those blocks
- Performing change-aware incremental backups
- Providing scripting capabilities to combine tasks
- Logging backup operations
- Integrating with third-party tape media software
- Providing reports and lists of catalog information
- Storing information about backups in a catalog in an Oracle database
- Offering performance benefits, such as parallel processing of backups and restores
- Creating duplicate databases for testing and development purposes
- Testing whether backups can be restored successfully
- Determining whether backups are still available in media libraries

RMAN has many improvements to support new functionality and different database failures that were not supported before Oracle 10*g*. In addition, RMAN can handle larger database backups and recoveries in quicker timeframes. This means less availability impact during the backup and recovery process. Here is a list of new 10*g* RMAN features:

- Migrating datafiles across operating system platforms
- User error recovery with flashback
- Automated tablespace point-in-time recovery (TSPITR)
- Dropping a database
- Using backup copies and flash recovery
- Creating and using RMAN backup copies
- Configuring default disk backup types
- Recovering datafiles not backed up
- Blocking change tracking
- Unregistering a database from the catalog
- Actual compression of RMAN backups
- Error-reporting improvements

RMAN has a rich feature set that is improving dramatically with each release of Oracle. These features allow you to back up and recover a database in almost any situation. Many of these new features address problems or difficulties that you will encounter in your daily tasks.

Other features such as flash recovery, block change tracking, and actual backup compression are innovations within RMAN that allow a DBA to support evolving database requirements.

The main components of RMAN are GUI or command-line access, the optional recovery catalog, the RMAN commands and scripting, and tape media connectivity. These components enable you to automate and standardize the backup and recovery process. Each component is described as follows:

GUI or command-line interface method The web-enabled GUI or *command-line interface (CLI)* provides access to Recovery Manager. This process spawns off-server sessions that connect to the *target database*, which is the database that will be backed up. The GUI access is provided through the Oracle Enterprise Manager's web-based console. The Oracle *Enterprise Manager (EM)* tool performs backups, exports/imports, data loads, performance monitoring/tuning, job and event scheduling, and standard DBA management, to mention a few. The EM tool is a web-based application and must be run through a browser.

Recovery catalog The *recovery catalog* is recovery information that is stored inside an Oracle database. This is similar to the RMAN repository stored in the control file, but information stored in the recovery catalog is more extensive. It is a special data dictionary of backup information that is stored in a set of tables, much like the data dictionary stores information about databases. The recovery catalog provides a method for storing information about backups, restores, and recoveries. This information can provide status on the success or failure of backups, operating system backups, datafile copies, tablespace copies, control file copies, archive log copies, full database backups, and the physical structures of a database.

RMAN commands RMAN commands enable different actions to be performed to facilitate the backup and restore of the database. These commands can be organized logically into scripts, which can then be stored in the recovery catalog database. The scripts can be reused for other backups, thus keeping consistency among different target database backups.

Tape media connectivity Tape media connectivity provides a method for interfacing with various third-party tape hardware vendors to store and track backups in *automated tape libraries (ATLs)*. Oracle supports many tape hardware devices. ATLs are tape units that use robotics arms and bar-coded tapes to automate the usage of multiple tapes for backup purposes.

RMAN Usage Considerations

RMAN backup is a physical backup method that was first developed with Oracle 8 and has steadily improved with each Oracle release. If you are going to use RMAN, you can use disk or tape. If you are using tape, a third-party media management library is needed to interface with your tape hardware.

There are two other methods of backup and recovery in the Oracle database: user-managed and the Oracle EXPORT utility. *User-managed backups* are essentially customized scripts that interact with the operating system capabilities such as `copy` and `compress` commands. These types of backups have been the mainstay of Oracle backups prior to and during the initial release of RMAN.

The *EXPORT utility* executed with the exp executable is essentially a logical backup utility that performs backups only on the logical components of the database. A logical backup consists of backing up the database at the tablespace level or backing up other logical database components such as a table. A physical backup consists of backing up the database files such as the datafiles, control files, and redo logs. This is one of the reasons EXPORT is typically not considered a stand-alone backup method but provides additional backup protection for RMAN or a user-managed backup.

what is a physical backup?

In Oracle 10*g*, there is a new EXPORT utility, which is different from the standard EXPORT utility that is executed with the exp command. The new Oracle 10*g* EXPORT utility that supports data pump technology is called expdp. The new expdp EXPORT utility does not have the same functionality as the standard exp EXPORT utility.

RMAN performs many recovery options that are not supported by other available backup and recovery methods. Table 1.1 compares the capabilities of each backup method.

Starting the RMAN utility is a very straightforward process. To start RMAN, you need to be at the command line at the operating system level. In the case of a Windows environment, you would be at the DOS prompt.

TABLE 1.1 Different Backup Methods Capabilities

Capability	RMAN	User-Managed	EXPORT Utility
Server parameter file backups	Supported	Supported	Not supported
Password file backups	Not supported	Supported	Not supported
Closed database backups	Supported	Supported	Not supported
Open database backups	Supported	Not supported	Not supported
Incremental backups	Supported	Not supported	Not supported
Corrupt block detection	Supported	Not supported	Supported
Automatic backup file	Supported	Not supported	Supported
Backup catalogs	Supported	Not supported	Supported
Media manager	Supported	Supported	Supported
Platform independent	Supported	Not supported	Supported

RMAN Repository and Control Files

The RMAN utility uses two methods of storing information about the target databases that are backed up. Oracle calls the collection of metadata about the target databases the *RMAN repository*. There are two methods of storing data in the RMAN repository. The first method is by accessing an RMAN catalog of information about backups. The second method is by accessing the necessary information about backups in the target database's control files.

Oracle recommends that you store RMAN backup data in the catalog database as opposed to the RMAN repository for most medium-sized to enterprise environments. This allows full functionality of the RMAN utility. This catalog is another Oracle database with special RMAN catalog tables that store metadata about backups, much the same way that the data dictionary stores data about objects in the database. When using the recovery catalog, backup scripts can be created and stored in the catalog database for later use, and multiple target database can be backed up from a central source. This catalog database can also be backed up so that the information is made safe.

The RMAN utility enables you to use a target database without utilizing the recovery catalog database. The target database is the database targeted by RMAN for backup or recovery actions. Because most of the recovery catalog information is stored in the target database's control file, RMAN supports the ability to use just the control file to perform backup and recovery operations. This method would be used if the overhead of creating and maintaining a recovery catalog were too great for an organization.

The recovery catalog database will be covered in more detail in the next section "RMAN Using the Recovery Catalog."

If you use RMAN without the recovery catalog, you are storing most of the necessary information about each target database in the target database's control file. In this case, the target database's control file is the repository. Thus, you must manage the target database's control file to support this. The `init.ora` or `spfile.ora` parameter `CONTROL_FILE_RECORD_KEEP_TIME` determines how long information that can be used by RMAN is kept in the control file. The default value for this parameter is 7 days and can be as many as 365 days. The greater the number, the larger the control file becomes to store more information.

The control file can only be as large as the operating system allows.

The information that is stored within the control file is stored in the reusable sections called *circular reuse records* and *non-circular reuse records*. These sections can grow if the value of the parameter `CONTROL_FILE_RECORD_KEEP_TIME` is 1 or more. The circular reuse records have non-critical information that can be overwritten if needed. Some of the non-circular reusable sections consist of datafiles and redo log information.

In the next section, we will discuss the recovery catalog in detail. The recovery catalog is not the default method of storing data in the RMAN repository. You must set up and configure the recovery catalog and database before you can utilize this capability.

RMAN Using the Recovery Catalog

Before demonstrating how to use the recovery catalog, let's discuss briefly its capabilities and components. The recovery catalog is designed to be a central storage place for multiple databases' RMAN information. Unlike using the control file as a repository, the recovery catalog can support multiple Oracle databases or an enterprise environment. This centralizes the location of the RMAN information instead of having this information dispersed in each target database's control file.

The main components of the RMAN recovery catalog support the logging of the backup and recovery information in the catalog. This information is stored in tables, views, and other databases' objects within an Oracle database. Here is a list of the components contained in a recovery catalog:

- Backup and recovery information that is logged for long-term use from the target databases
- RMAN scripts that can be stored and reused
- Backup information about datafiles and archive logs
- Information about the physical makeup, or schema, of the target database

The recovery catalog is similar to the standard database catalog in that the recovery catalog stores information about the recovery process as the database catalog stores information about the database. The recovery catalog must be stored in its own database, preferably on a server other than the server where the target database resides. To enable the catalog, an account with `CONNECT`, `RESOURCE`, and `RECOVERY_CATALOG_OWNER` privileges must be created to hold the catalog tables. Next, the catalog creation script command must be executed as the user `RMAN_USER` connected to the RMAN utility.

Let's walk through the creation of the recovery catalog step by step:

This example assumes that you have already built a database called `ora101rc` to store the recovery catalog. Oracle recommends that the default size of the recovery catalog database be about 115mb including datafiles and redo logs.

1. First, you must point to the database where the recovery catalog will reside. This is not the target database. The RMAN database will be called `ora101rc`. The `oraenv` shell script is provided by Oracle to switch to other databases on the same server. Use the following command:

```
Microsoft Windows XP [Version 5.1.2600]
(C) Copyright 1985-2001 Microsoft Corp.

C:\Documents and Settings\dstuns>set ORACLE_SID=ora101rc
```

2. Create the user that will store the catalog. Use the name RMAN with the password RMAN. Make DATA the default tablespace and TEMP the temporary tablespace:

```
C:\Documents and Settings\>sqlplus /nolog
SQL*Plus: Release 10.1.0.2.0 - Production on Sun Jun 13 06:17:34 2004
Copyright (c) 1982, 2004, Oracle.  All rights reserved.

SQL>
SQL> connect /as sysdba
SQL> create user rman_user identified by rman_user
2  default tablespace data
3  temporary tablespace temp;
User created.
```

3. Grant the appropriate permissions to the RMAN user:

```
SQL> grant connect, resource, recovery_catalog_owner to rman_user;

Grant succeeded.
SQL>
```

4. Launch the RMAN tool:

```
C:\Documents and Settings\>rman
Recovery Manager: Release 10.1.0.2.0 - Production
Copyright (c) 1995, 2004, Oracle.  All rights reserved.
```

5. Connect to the catalog with the user called RMAN that you created in step 2:

```
RMAN> connect catalog rman_user/rman_user

connected to recovery catalog database
recovery catalog is not installed
```

6. Finally, create the recovery catalog by executing the following command and specifying the tablespace that you want to store the catalog in:

```
RMAN> create catalog tablespace data;

recovery catalog created

RMAN>
```

Once the recovery catalog is created, there are a few steps that must be performed for each target database so that backup and recovery can be stored. The first step is registering the database. Once an incarnation of the database is registered, data may be stored in the recovery catalog for that particular target database. An incarnation of the database is a reference for a database in the recovery catalog.

Let's walk through registering a database and then using the recovery catalog by running a full backup:

```
C:\Documents and Settings>rman target /
Recovery Manager: Release 10.1.0.2.0 - Production
Copyright (c) 1995, 2004, Oracle.  All rights reserved.

connected to target database: ORA101T (DBID=2615281366)

RMAN> connect catalog "rman_user/rman_user@ora101rc";

connected to recovery catalog database

RMAN> register database;

database registered in recovery catalog
starting full resync of recovery catalog
full resync complete

RMAN>
```

Once the target database has been registered, you can back up the target database. This will store the backup data in the recovery catalog. From this point on, all of RMAN can be utilized in the backup and recovery process for the backed-up target database.

To perform this you must connect to the target database, which in this example is `ora101t` in the Windows XP environment. Then you can connect to the recovery catalog in the `ora101rc` database.

Once connected to the proper target and catalog, you can execute the appropriate RMAN backup script. This script will back up the entire database. Next, the database can be restored with the appropriate RMAN script. Finally, the database can be opened for use.

Let's walk through this example step by step:

1. Set the `ORACLE_SID to ora101t`, which is your target database, so that the database can be started in `MOUNT` mode with SQL*Plus:

   ```
   C:\Documents and Settings>set ORACLE_SID=ora101t

   C:\Documents and Settings>sqlplus /nolog
   SQL*Plus: Release 10.1.0.2.0 - Production on Sun Jun 13 07:06:16 2004
   Copyright (c) 1982, 2004, Oracle.  All rights reserved.

   SQL>
   SQL> connect /as sysdba
   Connected to an idle instance.
   SQL> startup mount
   ORACLE instance started.
   ```

```
Total System Global Area   88080384 bytes
Fixed Size                   787588 bytes
Variable Size              78642044 bytes
Database Buffers            8388608 bytes
Redo Buffers                 262144 bytes
Database mounted.
```

2. Start the RMAN utility at the command prompt and connect to the target and the recovery catalog database ora101rc:

```
C:\Documents and Settings>rman
Recovery Manager: Release 10.1.0.2.0 - Production
Copyright (c) 1995, 2004, Oracle.  All rights reserved.

RMAN> connect target

connected to target database: ORA101T (DBID=2615281366)

RMAN> connect catalog rman_user/rman_user@ora101rc;

connected to recovery catalog database

RMAN>
```

3. Once connected to the target and recovery catalog, you can back up the target database, including archive logs, to disk or tape. In this example, choose disk. Give the database name a format of db_%u_%d_%s, which means that a db_ will be concatenated to the backup set unique identifier and then concatenated to database name with the backup set number:

```
RMAN> run
2> {
3> allocate channel c1 type disk;
4> backup database format 'db_%u_%d_%s';
5> backup format 'log_t%t_s%s_p%p'
6> (archivelog all);
7> }

allocated channel: c1
channel c1: sid=49 devtype=DISK

Starting backup at 15-JUN-04
channel c1: starting full datafile backupset
channel c1: specifying datafile(s) in backupset
```

```
input datafile fno=00001
  name=C:\ORACLE\ORADATA\ORA101T\SYSTEM01.DBF
input datafile fno=00003
  name=C:\ORACLE\ORADATA\ORA101T\SYSAUX01.DBF
input datafile fno=00005
  name=C:\ORACLE\ORADATA\ORA101T\EXAMPLE01.DBF
input datafile fno=00002
  name=C:\ORACLE\ORADATA\ORA101T\UNDOTBS01.DBF
input datafile fno=00004
  name=C:\ORACLE\ORADATA\ORA101T\USERS01.DBF
channel c1: starting piece 1 at 15-JUN-04
channel c1: finished piece 1 at 15-JUN-04
piece handle=C:\WINDOWS\SYSTEM32\DB_04FODN6N_ORA101T_4
  comment=NONE
channel c1: backup set complete, elapsed time: 00:01:57
channel c1: starting full datafile backupset
channel c1: specifying datafile(s) in backupset
including current controlfile in backupset
channel c1: starting piece 1 at 15-JUN-04
channel c1: finished piece 1 at 15-JUN-04
piece handle=C:\WINDOWS\SYSTEM32\DB_05FODNAC_ORA101T_5
  comment=NONE
channel c1: backup set complete, elapsed time: 00:00:05
Finished backup at 15-JUN-04

Starting backup at 15-JUN-04
channel c1: starting archive log backupset
channel c1: specifying archive log(s) in backup set
input archive log thread=1 sequence=7 recid=1 stamp=527413772
input archive log thread=1 sequence=8 recid=2 stamp=527414322
input archive log thread=1 sequence=9 recid=3 stamp=528706062
channel c1: starting piece 1 at 15-JUN-04
channel c1: finished piece 1 at 15-JUN-04
piece handle=C:\WINDOWS\SYSTEM32\LOG_T528932180_S6_P1
  comment=NONE
channel c1: backup set complete, elapsed time: 00:00:09
Finished backup at 15-JUN-04
released channel: c1

RMAN>
```

4. Once the backup is complete, the database may be restored and recovered. The database must be mounted but not opened. In the restore and recovery script, choose three disk channels to utilize parallelization of the restore process. This is not necessary but improves the restore and recovery time. The RESTORE DATABASE command is responsible for the restore process within RMAN. RECOVER DATABASE is required because the database was in ARCHIVELOG mode and these files need to be applied to the datafiles to perform a complete recovery. Lastly, the database is opened:

```
RMAN> run
2> {
3> allocate channel c1 type disk;
4> allocate channel c2 type disk;
5> allocate channel c3 type disk;
6> restore database;
7> recover database;
8> alter database open;
9> }

allocated channel: c1
channel c1: sid=49 devtype=DISK

allocated channel: c2
channel c2: sid=48 devtype=DISK

allocated channel: c3
channel c3: sid=47 devtype=DISK

Starting restore at 15-JUN-04

channel c1: starting datafile backupset restore
channel c1: specifying datafile(s) to restore from backup set
restoring datafile 00001 to
  C:\ORACLE\ORADATA\ORA101T\SYSTEM01.DBF
restoring datafile 00002 to
  C:\ORACLE\ORADATA\ORA101T\UNDOTBS01.DBF
restoring datafile 00003 to
  C:\ORACLE\ORADATA\ORA101T\SYSAUX01.DBF
restoring datafile 00004 to C:\ORACLE\ORADATA\ORA101T\USERS01.DBF
restoring datafile 00005 to
  C:\ORACLE\ORADATA\ORA101T\EXAMPLE01.DBF
channel c1: restored backup piece 1
piece handle=C:\WINDOWS\SYSTEM32\DB_04FODN6N_ORA101T_4
```

```
  tag=TAG20040615T213412
channel c1: restore complete
Finished restore at 15-JUN-04

Starting recover at 15-JUN-04

starting media recovery
media recovery complete

Finished recover at 15-JUN-04

database opened
released channel: c1
released channel: c2
released channel: c3

RMAN>
```

A typical target database uses only about 120mb of space per year in the recovery catalog database for metadata storage.

Starting and Connecting to RMAN

There are a few other important notes regarding starting RMAN such as a target database designation and specifying a recovery catalog. We will explore activating these designations when starting RMAN.

RMAN can be started by launching the RMAN executable. RMAN can be stopped by exiting or quitting from the RMAN prompt.

Let's walk through this in more detail:

```
Microsoft Windows XP [Version 5.1.2600]
(C) Copyright 1985-2001 Microsoft Corp.

C:\Documents and Settings>rman

Recovery Manager: Release 10.1.0.2.0 - Production

Copyright (c) 1995, 2004, Oracle.  All rights reserved.
```

```
RMAN>

RMAN> exit

Recovery Manager complete.

C:\Documents and Settings>
```

Once in the RMAN utility, backup configuration changes and restores can be performed. In order to perform these RMAN activities, it is important to know the three database connection types using the RMAN utility. Table 1.2 describes the three database connections available with RMAN. The subsequent examples will walk through the most common database connections: target database and recovery catalog database connections.

TABLE 1.2 RMAN Database Connection Methods

Database Connection	Definition
Target database	The target database is the database that is targeted for backup and recovery. SYSDBA privilege is required to perform these tasks.
Recovery catalog database	The recovery catalog database is the optional database that stores information about the backup, recovery, and restore data.
Auxiliary database	The auxiliary database is the standby database, duplicate database, or auxiliary instance (standby or TSPITR).

There are two methods of connecting to the target database: from the command line and using the RMAN utility.

Let's walk through designating a target database with each method. First, connect from the command line:

1. Set the Oracle system identifier (SID):

```
Microsoft Windows XP [Version 5.1.2600]
(C) Copyright 1985-2001 Microsoft Corp.

C:\Documents and Settings>set ORACLE_SID=ora101c
```

2. Launch the RMAN executable, specifying the target and default connection on the command line. NOCATALOG is optional, but if left blank, this is the default.

```
C:\Documents and Settings>rman target / nocatalog

Recovery Manager: Release 10.1.0.2.0 - Production
```

```
Copyright (c) 1995, 2004, Oracle.  All rights reserved.

connected to target database: ORA101C (DBID=1736563848)

RMAN>
```

Next, we will show you how to connect to the target database within the RMAN utility. This is quite similar to the previous example, except that you are at the RMAN command prompt when you specify the target database. Let's walk through this example:

1. Set the Oracle system identifier (SID):

```
Microsoft Windows XP [Version 5.1.2600]
(C) Copyright 1985-2001 Microsoft Corp.

C:\Documents and Settings>set ORACLE_SID=ora101c
```

2. Launch the RMAN executable:

```
C:\Documents and Settings>rman

Recovery Manager: Release 10.1.0.2.0 - Production

Copyright (c) 1995, 2004, Oracle.  All rights reserved.

RMAN>
```

3. Connect to the target database by executing the `connect target` command:

```
RMAN> connect target

connected to target database: ORA101C (DBID=1736563848)

RMAN>
```

Connecting to a recovery catalog is a fairly straightforward process. Just as when connecting to the target database, there are two methods of performing this activity: on the command line and within the RMAN utility.

First, let's walk through an example of connecting to the recovery catalog at the command line:

1. Set the Oracle SID:

```
Microsoft Windows XP [Version 5.1.2600]
(C) Copyright 1985-2001 Microsoft Corp.

C:\Documents and Settings>set ORACLE_SID=ora101c
```

2. Launch the RMAN executable specifying the target, the catalog and catalog owner, and the database containing the catalog.

```
C:\Documents and Settings>rman target / catalog rman_user/rman_user@ora101rc

Recovery Manager: Release 10.1.0.2.0 - Production

Copyright (c) 1995, 2004, Oracle.  All rights reserved.

connected to target database: ORA101C (DBID=1736563848)
connected to recovery catalog database

RMAN>
```

Next, you will connect to both the target database and the recovery catalog database within the RMAN utility. This is quite similar to the previous example, except that you are at the RMAN command prompt when you specify the target database and recovery catalog database. Let's walk through this example:

1. Set the Oracle SID:

```
C:\Documents and Settings>set ORACLE_SID=ora101t
```

2. Start the RMAN utility and connect to the target database:

```
C:\Documents and Settings>rman

Recovery Manager: Release 10.1.0.2.0 - Production

Copyright (c) 1995, 2004, Oracle.  All rights reserved.

RMAN> connect target

connected to target database: ORA101T (DBID=2615281366)
```

3. Connect to the recovery catalog specifying the username and password of the RMAN catalog owner:

```
RMAN> connect catalog rman_user/rman_user@ora101rc;

connected to recovery catalog database

RMAN>
```

Describing Media Management Layer

The *media management layer (MML)* interface is an Application Programming Interface (API) that interfaces RMAN and different hardware vendors' tape devices. These tape devices, as mentioned earlier in this chapter, are automated tape libraries (ATLs).

All tape hardware vendors that wish to work with Oracle RMAN make their own MML. This is necessary because most tape hardware devices are proprietary and require different program calls. The MML is then linked in with Oracle database kernel, so that the RMAN server process and MML can read and write the Oracle data to the tape device. Figure 1.1 illustrates this concept.

FIGURE 1.1 The media management layer (MML)

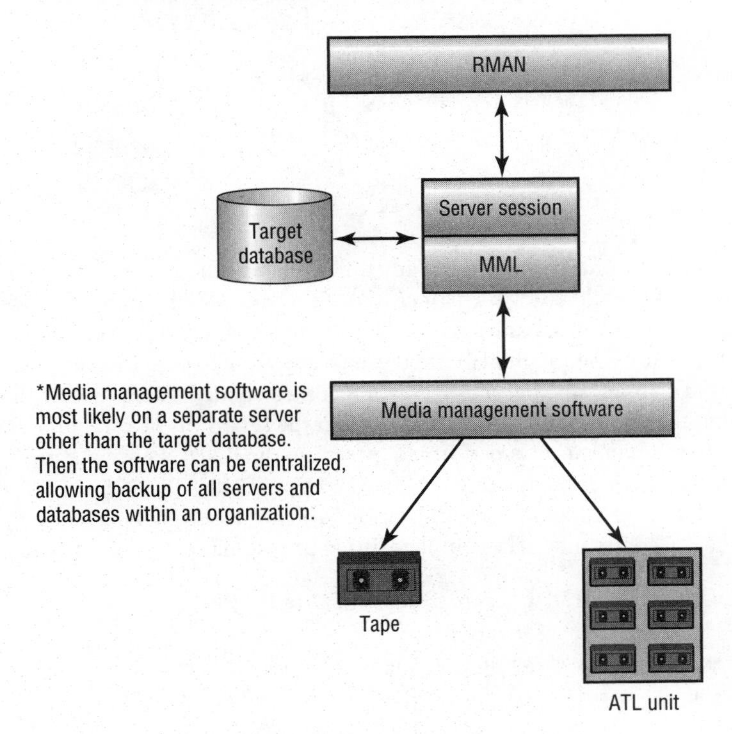

Describing Channel Allocation

Channel allocation is a method of connecting RMAN and the target database while also determining the type of I/O device that the server process will use to perform the backup or restore operation. Figure 1.2 illustrates this situation. The I/O device can be either tape or disk. Channels can be allocated manually or automatically.

FIGURE 1.2 Channel allocation

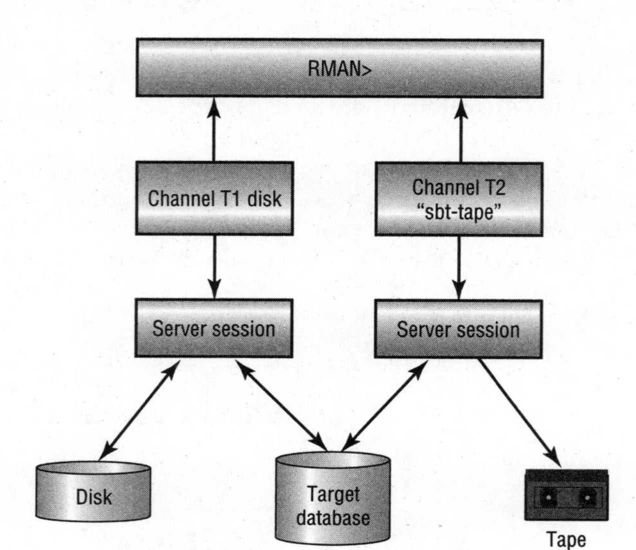

Manual channel allocation is performed any time you issue the command `ALLOCATE CHANNEL`. A manual command for allocating a channel is `ALLOCATE CHANNEL` *`channel name`* `TYPE DISK`. This is used for writing to a disk file system. The command `ALLOCATE CHANNEL` *`channel name`* `TYPE 'SBT_TAPE'` is another manual method used for writing to a tape backup system. These are the most common channel allocation usages. Allocating a channel is initiated with the `ALLOCATE CHANNEL` command, which starts a server process on the server of the target database.

Automatic channel allocation is performed by setting the RMAN configuration at the RMAN command prompt. This is done by using the `CONFIGURE DEFAULT DEVICE` or `CONFIGURE DEVICE` command. Automatic channel allocation is automatically used when executing the `BACKUP`, `RESTORE`, or `DELETE` commands. The complete listing of automatic channel allocation is as follows:

```
CONFIGURE DEVICE TYPE DISK backup|clear|parallelism n
CONFIGURE DEFAULT DEVICE TYPE to|clear
CONFIGURE CHANNEL DEVICE TYPE disk|equal
CONFIGURE CHANNEL n DEVICE TYPE disk|equal
```

There are some default naming conventions for the devices `ORA_MAINT_DISK_`*`n`* and `ORA_SBT_TAPE_`*`n`*. The following example shows that the default device type is set to disk and parallelism is set to 1. This means that if you don't allocate a channel manually, the parameters will be listed as follows:

```
RMAN> show all;

RMAN configuration parameters are:
CONFIGURE RETENTION POLICY TO REDUNDANCY 1; # default
```

```
CONFIGURE BACKUP OPTIMIZATION OFF; # default
CONFIGURE DEFAULT DEVICE TYPE TO DISK; # default
CONFIGURE CONTROLFILE AUTOBACKUP OFF; # default
CONFIGURE CONTROLFILE AUTOBACKUP FORMAT FOR DEVICE TYPE DISK TO '%F'; # default
CONFIGURE DEVICE TYPE DISK PARALLELISM 1 BACKUP TYPE TO BACKUPSET; # default
CONFIGURE DATAFILE BACKUP COPIES FOR DEVICE TYPE DISK TO 1; # default
CONFIGURE ARCHIVELOG BACKUP COPIES FOR DEVICE TYPE DISK TO 1; # default
CONFIGURE MAXSETSIZE TO UNLIMITED; # default
CONFIGURE ARCHIVELOG DELETION POLICY TO NONE; # default
CONFIGURE SNAPSHOT CONTROLFILE NAME TO 'C:\ORACLE\PRODUCT\10.1.0\DB_1\DATABASE\S
NCFORA101T.ORA'; # default

RMAN>
```

Multiple Backup Types on Your Tapes?

Your tape backup device could be supporting multiple backups that may be RMAN-based as well as normal file system backups. Most ATLs and the software support file system backups and RMAN backups are backed up with the same tape media. That means you could have each type of backup on a tape, especially since digital linear tapes (DLTs) support large storage volumes of 200GB or more per tape, meaning file system backups and RMAN backups could be interspersed on a single tape.

You should be aware that there are potentially two types of backups on the same tape. If you are heavily dependent on tapes for recovery operations, make sure that the tape cycle that your organization uses supports the requirements of the file system backup or the RMAN backup that is needed for the longest period of time.

For example, file system backups are needed for only one week until the next complete backup file system backup is taken on the weekend. RMAN backups may be needed up to a month to support business requirements. Therefore, you should store all the tapes for up to a month and if possible, procure additional tapes so you can keep backups separated.

There are also channel control options or commands that are used whether channels are allocated manually or automatically. *Channel control options* or *channel control commands* basically control the operating system resources that RMAN uses when performing RMAN operations. Channel control options or commands perform the functions described in Table 1.3.

TABLE 1.3 Channel Commands and Options

Channel Control Option or Command	Functions
ALLOCATE CHANNEL RATE or CONFIGURE CHANNEL RATE	Limits the I/O bandwidth in kilobytes, megabytes, or gigabytes
ALLOCATE CHANNEL or CONFIGURE CHANNEL MAXPIECESIZE	Limits the size of the backup pieces
ALLOCATE CHANNEL or CONFIGURE CHANNEL MAXSETSIZE	Limits the size of the backup sets
SEND	Sends vendor-specific commands to the Media Manager
ALLOCATE CHANNEL CONNECT or CONFIGURE CHANNEL CONNECT	Instructs a specific instance to perform an operation
ALLOCATE CHANNEL PARMS or CONFIGURE CHANNE PARMS	Sends vendor-specific parameters to the Media Manager

New with Oracle 10*g* is an *automated channel failover* for backup and restore operations. In order for this feature to function, multiple channels must be allocated. If there is a failure in the backup or restore operations, RMAN will complete the operation with the available channels. This can commonly happen when multiple backups attempt to use a one tape device or when there is an MML problem of some sort.

Error messages are reported in the V$RMAN_OUTPUT dynamic view. Error information is also logged to the screen or the RMAN log file when MML comes across any problems.

Parameters and Persistent Settings for RMAN

Configuring *persistent settings* or parameters for RMAN is handled through the configuration settings for each target database. There are many RMAN settings that help automate or simplify using RMAN. Be familiar with where these settings are located and how to modify them for a particular database environment. These settings are stored in the target databases control file or the recovery catalog.

This section explains how to display and set configuration parameters for RMAN and demonstrates these features with examples. You will then walk through the new RMAN parameters in Oracle 10*g*.

Let's show how you can display the configuration for a particular RMAN session. This is a fairly straightforward process that requires logging into RMAN and performing the SHOW ALL command:

1. Set the Oracle SID for the target database:

```
C:\Documents and Settings\dstuns>set ORACLE_SID=ora101c
```

2. Launch the RMAN utility from the command line:

```
C:\Documents and Settings\dstuns>rman

Recovery Manager: Release 10.1.0.2.0 - Production

Copyright (c) 1995, 2004, Oracle.  All rights reserved.

RMAN>
```

3. Connect to the target database:

```
RMAN> connect target

connected to target database: ORA101C (DBID=1736563848)

RMAN>
```

4. Perform the show all command to display all the configuration parameters:

```
RMAN> show all;

RMAN configuration parameters are:
CONFIGURE RETENTION POLICY TO REDUNDANCY 1; # default
CONFIGURE BACKUP OPTIMIZATION OFF; # default
CONFIGURE DEFAULT DEVICE TYPE TO DISK; # default
CONFIGURE CONTROLFILE AUTOBACKUP OFF; # default
CONFIGURE CONTROLFILE AUTOBACKUP FORMAT FOR DEVICE TYPE DISK TO '%F'; #
  ➥default
CONFIGURE DEVICE TYPE DISK PARALLELISM 1 BACKUP TYPE TO BACKUPSET; # default
CONFIGURE DATAFILE BACKUP COPIES FOR DEVICE TYPE DISK TO 1; # default
CONFIGURE ARCHIVELOG BACKUP COPIES FOR DEVICE TYPE DISK TO 1; # default
CONFIGURE CHANNEL DEVICE TYPE DISK FORMAT   '/oracle/flash_recovery_area/
  ➥ora101c
/%rec_area_%s_%p.bak';
CONFIGURE MAXSETSIZE TO UNLIMITED; # default
CONFIGURE ARCHIVELOG DELETION POLICY TO NONE; # default
CONFIGURE SNAPSHOT CONTROLFILE NAME TO 'C:\ORACLE\PRODUCT\10.1.0\DB_
  ➥1\DATABASE\S
```

```
NCFORA101C.ORA'; # default

RMAN>
```

There are some commonly used configuration settings that help you use RMAN. These settings are useful in daily operations:

- DEVICE TYPE
- BACKUP TYPE
- COMPRESSED BACKUPSET
- CHANNEL DISK DEVICE
- CHANNEL TAPE DEVICE

Let's learn how to modify or set each of these configuration settings in more detail.

To configure the default device to tape and then to disk, use the following command. This command sets the default media for RMAN to store the backup information:

```
RMAN>configure default device type to sbt;

RMAN>configure default device type to disk;
```

To configure the default backup type for an image copy and then for a backup set, use the following command. This parameter or setting configures the type of backup to be an image copy or a backup set:

```
RMAN>configure device type disk backup type to copy;

RMAN>configure device type disk backup type to backupset;
```

To configure a default device for either tape or disk to a compressed backup set, here are two specific examples:

```
RMAN>configure device type disk backup type to compressed backupset;

RMAN>configure device type sbt backup type to compressed backupset;
```

To configure disk devices and channels for specific formats, the next example shows that a channel is storing the output on disk and storing the name with the specific naming format. The `'ora_dev_'` string is concatenated to a special naming format. Formatting is an excellent method of naming your backups uniquely for easy identification.

See the following sidebar, "Format Specifications for the 10*g* RMAN FORMAT Option," for a more detailed listing of the FORMAT option's formatspec values. The complete information can be found in the Oracle Database 10*g* Recovery Manager Reference Guide, part number B10770-02.

Format Specifications for the 10*g* *RMAN FORMAT* Option

The following list includes some of the format specifications for the FORMAT option. For a complete listing, see the Oracle Database 10*g* Recovery Manager Reference Guide, part number B10770-02.

%a Specifies the activation ID of the database.

%c Specifies the copy number of the backup piece within a set of duplexed backup pieces.

%d Specifies the name of the database.

%D Specifies the current day of the month from the Gregorian calendar.

%e Specifies the archived log sequence number.

%f Specifies the absolute file number.

%F Combines the database identifier (DBID), day, month, year, and sequence number into a unique and repeatable generated name.

%h Specifies the archived redo log thread number.

%I Specifies the DBID.

%M Specifies the month in the Gregorian calendar in format *MM*.

%N Specifies the tablespace name.

%n Specifies the name of the database, padded on the right with *n* characters to a total length of eight characters.

%p Specifies the piece number within the backup set.

%s Specifies the backup set number.

%t Specifies the backup set timestamp.

%T Specifies the year, month, and day in the Gregorian calendar.

%u Specifies an eight-character name constituted by compressed representations of the backup set or image copy number.

%U Specifies a system-generated unique filename. (This is the default.)

Let's look at an example of configuring a disk device and channel for a specific format:

```
RMAN>configure channel device type disk format 'C:\backup\ora101c\
➥ora_dev_f%t_s%s_s%p';
```

The next example demonstrates how to configure tape devices and channels to utilize specific media management capabilities that control the tape hardware. In this case, some media managers allow you to pass in configuration settings with a PARMS string in the CONFIGURE command. Let's look at this example:

```
RMAN>configure channel device type sbt PARMS='ENV=mml_env_settings';

RMAN>configure device type sbt parallelism 3;
```

Configuring RMAN Settings with Enterprise Manager

RMAN settings can be configured using Enterprise Manager (EM). In Oracle 10*g*, EM is a web-based console, which allows most DBA activities to be performed from a GUI screen instead of from the typical command-line interface. The main home page can be accessed at `http://hostname.domain:EM portnumber/em`. The hostname is the server or machine and can be identified by typing **hostname** at the Unix or Windows command prompt. The domain name is the name of network you are on. The domain name varies for whatever network you are on, for instance, `sybex.com`. Also, the port number for the first database with EM agent running is 5500, which is the default. Each additional database increments this port number by 1. So, an additional database on this server will be listening on port 5501. In the examples in this chapter, you have installed the EM Database Control as opposed to Grid Control, which is an additional software component to support 10*g* Grid Control options.

We will demonstrate how to access EM. Once in the web application, you will navigate to the screens that are capable of modifying the configuration settings.

Let's look at the EM screens that allow the configuration of some of the RMAN settings:

1. First, enter **http://hostname.domain:5500/em** in the web browser to get to the EM main home page, which take you to the following login screen. The hostname is the name of the computer or server that is running EM, which is **dstuns-xp** and the network domain. At this point, enter the user id **SYS** and its password and connect as SYSDBA.

2. After logging in and clicking the Login button, the main EM Database Control main page appears, as you can see in the following graphic. (Notice that we saved this as two screens because of the size.) The Maintenance table will be selected to navigate to the maintenance screens that contain the screens that allow configuration modifications:

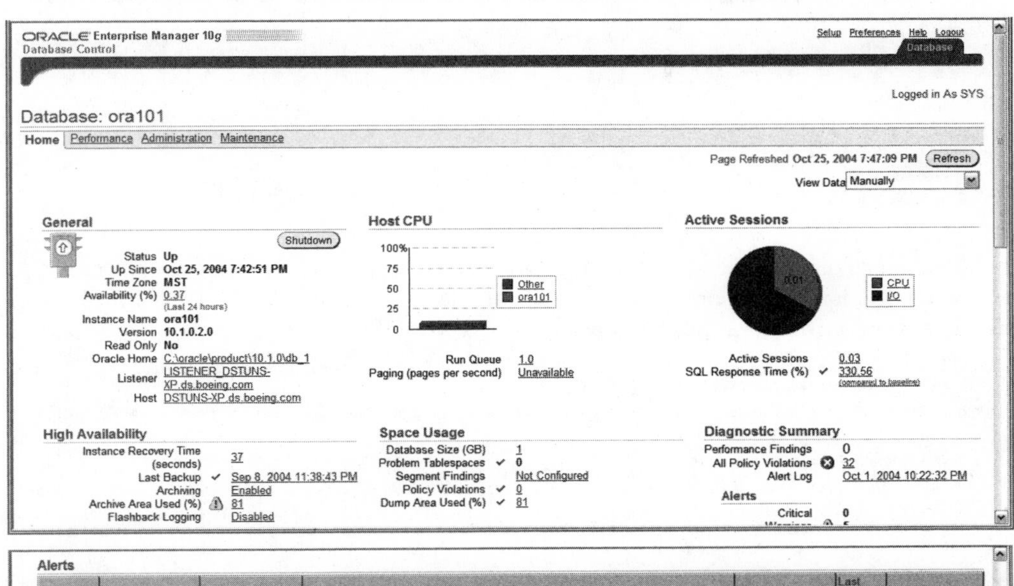

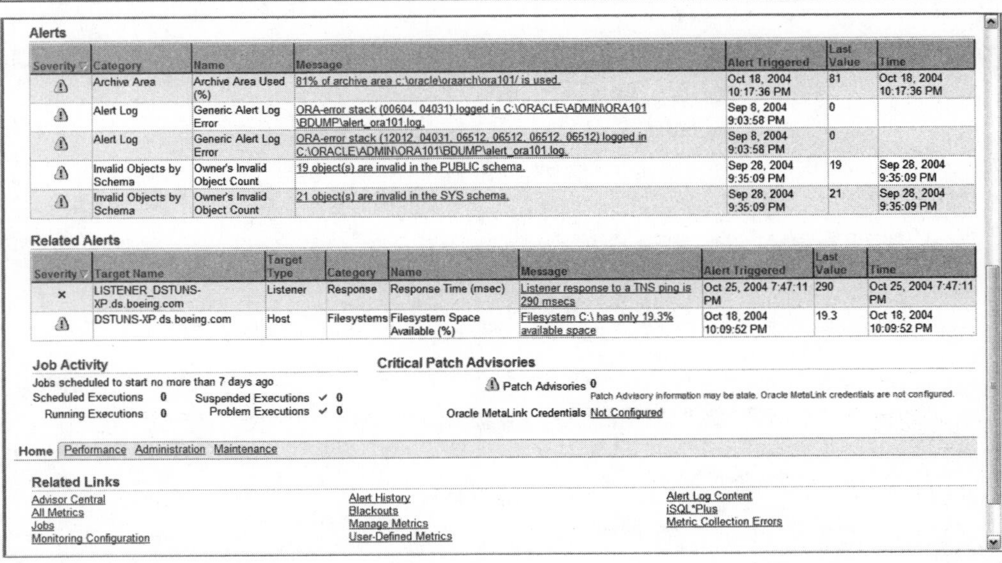

3. Next, select the Backup/Recovery section and click Configure Backup Settings, which will navigate to one of the configuration settings screens available in EM Database Control:

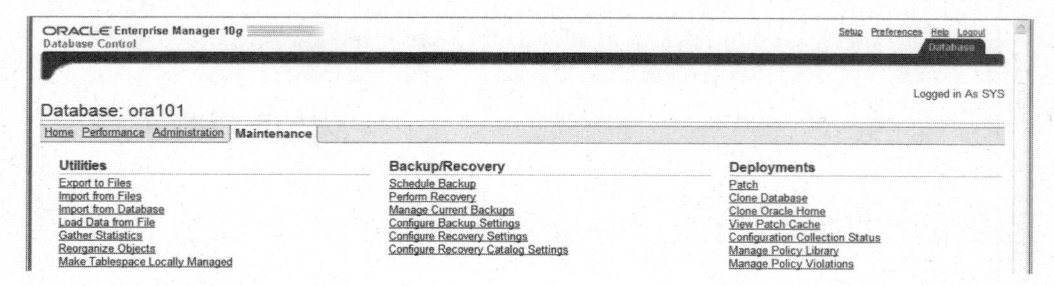

4. This screen displays the configuration settings for backups. These values can be modified, which will have the same effect as the RMAN command `CONFIGURE`. There are also configurations settings for recovery and the recovery catalog.

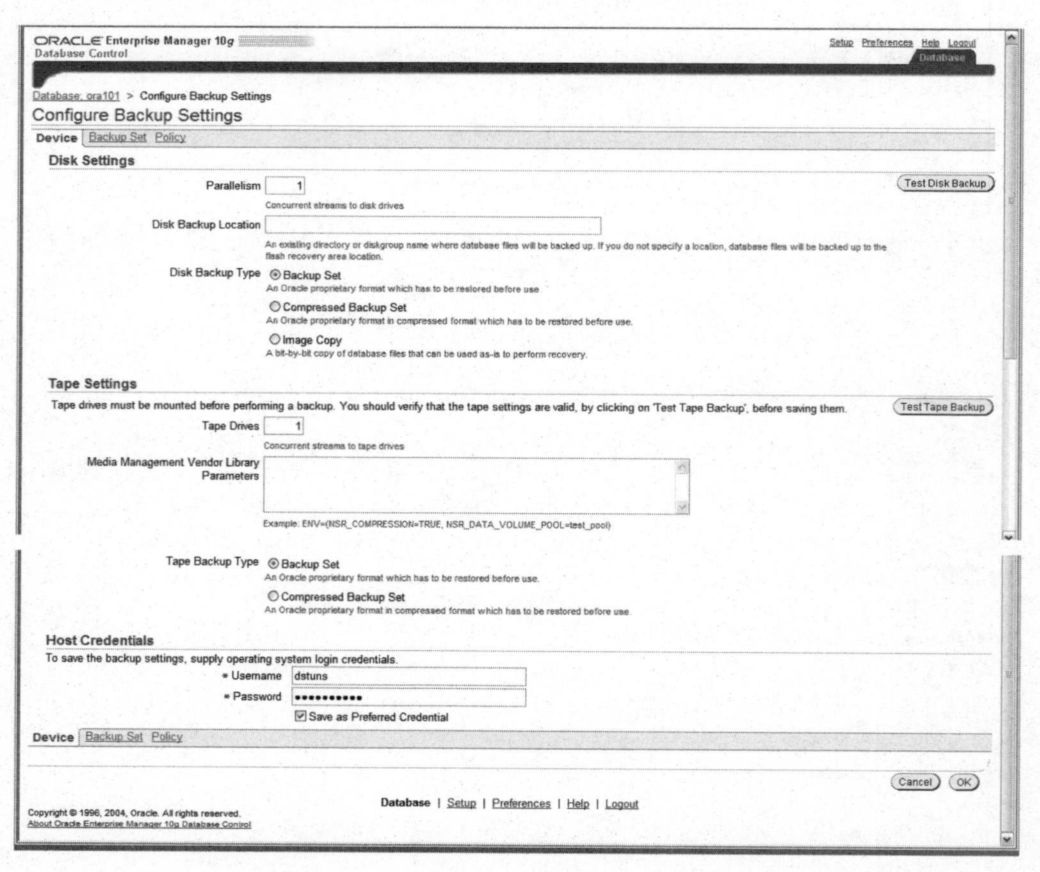

It is important to know that an account equal to the Windows Administrator account or that account itself should be used in the Host Credentials sections for the Windows environment. In the Unix environment, the Oracle account or similar privileged account should be used. This is because the EM 10*g* web applications essentially host out to the operating system to execute these commands with RMAN CLI.

Describing Retention Policies

The *retention policy* is the determined length of time that a backup is retained for use in a potential restore. The retention policy is determined by the configuration parameter RETENTION POLICY. This can be displayed with the SHOW ALL command.

Backups can be modified to block or obsolete their status from the retention policy. The commands CHANGE and KEEP modify the backup to be blocked from the retention policy. Two other commands—CHANGE and NOKEEP—obsoletes the backup from the existing retention policy.

Let's walk through an example of modifying a database retention policy:

```
RMAN> show all;

RMAN configuration parameters are:
CONFIGURE RETENTION POLICY TO REDUNDANCY 1; # default
CONFIGURE BACKUP OPTIMIZATION OFF; # default
CONFIGURE DEFAULT DEVICE TYPE TO DISK; # default
CONFIGURE CONTROLFILE AUTOBACKUP ON;
CONFIGURE CONTROLFILE AUTOBACKUP FORMAT FOR DEVICE TYPE DISK TO
  'c:\oracle\stagi
ng\ora101c\cf_%F';
CONFIGURE DEVICE TYPE DISK PARALLELISM 1 BACKUP TYPE TO BACKUPSET; # default
CONFIGURE DATAFILE BACKUP COPIES FOR DEVICE TYPE DISK TO 1; # default
CONFIGURE ARCHIVELOG BACKUP COPIES FOR DEVICE TYPE DISK TO 1; # default
CONFIGURE CHANNEL DEVICE TYPE DISK FORMAT
   '/oracle/flash_recovery_area/ora101c
/%rec_area_%s_%p.bak';
CONFIGURE MAXSETSIZE TO UNLIMITED; # default
CONFIGURE ARCHIVELOG DELETION POLICY TO NONE; # default
CONFIGURE SNAPSHOT CONTROLFILE NAME TO
  'C:\ORACLE\PRODUCT\10.1.0\DB_1\DATABASE\S
NCFORA101C.ORA'; # default

RMAN>
```

Next, you should have a retention policy set to a number of days. You will arbitrarily set 30 days retention as a monthly backup retention period. (In real life, this value would be agreed upon by the IT management.) What this means is that backups are kept for only 30 days within the recovery catalog. You will do this with the `CONFIGURE RETENTION POLICY TO RECOVERY WINDOW OF n DAYS` configuration setting, as seen here:

```
RMAN> configure retention policy to recovery window of 30 days;

new RMAN configuration parameters:
CONFIGURE RETENTION POLICY TO RECOVERY WINDOW OF 30 DAYS;
new RMAN configuration parameters are successfully stored

RMAN>
```

Next, let's create a backup and use the `TAG` clause to mark this backup with a unique name called `MONTHLY_BACKUP`. `TAG` is a clause that identifies a specific name to a backup so that it can be more easily identified. So this backup is governed by the retention policy you created of 30 days:

```
RMAN> run
2> {
3> allocate channel c1 type disk;
4> backup database format 'db_%u_%d_%s' tag monthly_backup;
5> backup format 'log_t%t_s%s_p%p'
6> (archivelog all);
7> }
```

Next, you can modify or change this backup so that the backup will not be kept until the end of retention policy. Let's learn how to cause a backup to expire so that it is not protected by the retention policy:

```
RMAN> change backupset tag monthly_backup nokeep;

allocated channel: ORA_DISK_1
channel ORA_DISK_1: sid=162 devtype=DISK
keep attributes for the backup are deleted
backup set key=6 recid=6 stamp=531831641

RMAN>
```

Next, you can modify or change the backup to block the 30-day retention policy you just had expire. Let's look at the command that blocks or excludes this backup from expiring in 30 days, which is the existing retention policy. You will set this backup to be kept until 01-DEC-04 by using the KEEP UNTIL TIME clause:

```
RMAN> change backupset tag monthly_backup keep until time '01-DEC-04' logs;

using channel ORA_DISK_1
keep attributes for the backup are changed
backup will be obsolete on date 01-DEC-04
archived logs required to recover from this backup will expire when
  ➥this backup expires
backup set key=6 recid=6 stamp=531831641

RMAN>
```

Configuring the Control File Autobackup

RMAN can be configured to automatically back up the control file and other server parameter files whenever information impacting the control file is changed or modified. This is a valuable asset to a backup because this allows RMAN to recover the database even if the control file or server parameter file is lost. This process is called *control file autobackup*.

The common naming of the server parameter file and control file allow RMAN to search and restore these files without accessing the RMAN repository. Once the control file is restored and mounted, the RMAN repository becomes available. RMAN can then use the repository information to restore datafiles and archive logs.

Configuring the autobackup of the control file is a straightforward process that is handled by the CONFIGURE command. Let's walk through an example:

```
RMAN> configure controlfile autobackup on;

using target database controlfile instead of recovery catalog
new RMAN configuration parameters:
CONFIGURE CONTROLFILE AUTOBACKUP ON;
new RMAN configuration parameters are successfully stored

RMAN>
```

You can also configure the format of the autobackup of the control file. This is performed by specifying a format setting in the CONFIGURE command. Let's look at an example:

```
RMAN> configure controlfile autobackup format
2> for device type disk to 'c:\oracle\staging\ora101c\cf_%F';
```

```
new RMAN configuration parameters:
CONFIGURE CONTROLFILE AUTOBACKUP FORMAT FOR DEVICE TYPE DISK TO
  'c:\oracle\stagi
ng\ora101c\cf_%F';
new RMAN configuration parameters are successfully stored

RMAN>
```

Summary

This chapter presented an overview of RMAN capabilities and components. We walked through starting, setting up, and configuring RMAN. The chapter used specific examples, which showed how to build the recovery catalog and establish connectivity using the recovery catalog and control file.

There was a demonstration using Enterprise Manager to configure RMAN settings. We discussed channel allocation and media management in conceptual format to show their importance to RMAN.

Throughout this chapter, we described the many new 10*g* features and capabilities that have been added to the existing RMAN functionality.

Exam Essentials

Know how to configure database parameters that affect RMAN operations. You should know the database parameters that impact RMAN operations. These parameters include `CONTROL_FILE_KEEP_TIME` and others.

Know how to change RMAN default settings with *CONFIGURE*. Make sure you know the many capabilities of RMAN's existing 9*i* features and the new 10*g* features. Be aware that there are four main components of RMAN: GUI or CLI, optional recovery catalog, RMAN commands, and tape media connectivity. Understand the concepts surrounding RMAN repository, RMAN recovery catalog, channel allocation, and MML interface. This includes creating, configuring, and using these features.

Understand how to manage RMAN's persistent settings. Know how to modify and display RMAN settings and parameters. Be aware of the persistent settings that are used to automate daily RMAN activities.

Understand starting RMAN utility and channel allocation. Be aware of the review activities relating to starting and stopping RMAN and the connection types associated with the RMAN utility such as target database and recovery catalog. Understand what the media management layer and channel allocation are and how they work with RMAN.

Review Questions

1. What is the parameter that determines the capacity of the RMAN repository?
   - A. CONTROLFILE_RECORD_KEEP_TIME
   - B. CONTROL_FILE_KEEP_TIME
   - C. CONTROL_FILE_RECORD_KEEP_TIME
   - D. CONTORL_FILE_RECORD_TIME

2. What privileges must be granted to allow an account to create the recovery catalog? (Choose two.)
   - A. RECOVERY_CATALOG_OWNER
   - B. DBA
   - C. RESOURCE
   - D. SELECT ANY DICTIONARY TABLE

3. What are the types of devices that channel allocation can utilize? (Choose all that apply.)
   - A. TYPE DISK
   - B. DISK TYPE
   - C. TYPE SBT_TAPE
   - D. TYPE FLASH_AREA

4. Which command configures a device so that channel allocation is automatically available during backup, restore, or delete?
   - A. CONFIGURE DEVICE TYPE TO DISK
   - B. CONFIGURE CHANNEL DEVICE TYPE DISK
   - C. CHANNEL DEVICE TYPE DISK CONFIGURE
   - D. CONFIGURE DEVICE CHANNEL TYPE DISK

5. What is the name of the API that interfaces RMAN with different tape devices?
   - A. Media Library Interface
   - B. Media Manager Library Interface
   - C. Management Media Interface
   - D. Media Management Layer

6. What backup capability is not supported with RMAN?
   - A. Password file backups
   - B. Closed database backups
   - C. Control file backups
   - D. Open database backups

7. What are the database connection types available with RMAN? (Choose all that apply.)
   A. Target database
   B. Recovery catalog
   C. Third-party database
   D. Auxiliary database

8. What is the main purpose of channel control options or commands?
   A. To control channel access options
   B. To control the operating system resources RMAN uses when performing RMAN operations
   C. To control manual channel allocation
   D. To control automatic channel allocation

9. The `FORMAT` command within the RMAN utility performs what function?
   A. It provides the capability for unique identification.
   B. It provides the capability to recreate channel devices.
   C. It provides the capability to rebuild channel devices.
   D. It provides the capability to rebuild disk devices.

10. What command displays the settings for automatic channel setup?
    A. `SHOW CONFIGURATION`
    B. `SHOW CHANNEL`
    C. `SHOW ALL`
    D. `SHOW DEVICE`

11. Which new 10*g* feature allows Oracle RMAN to store larger databases?
    A. The `COMPRESSED BACKUPSET` command
    B. Block change tracking
    C. The flash recovery area
    D. Automated tablespace point-in-time recovery (TSPITR)

12. Which new 10*g* feature allows Oracle RMAN to back up larger databases more efficiently?
    A. The `COMPRESSED BACKUPSET` command
    B. The Oracle Flashback Database
    C. Block change tracking
    D. Automated tablespace point-in-time recovery (TSPITR)

13. The BACKUP command is different from image copies in what way?

A. A backup set is stored in proprietary format using the BACKUP command.

B. A backup set can be compressed using the BACKUP command.

C. The RESTORE command must be used during recovery.

D. All of the above

14. Which RMAN components are *not* required to utilize Recovery Manager? (Choose all that apply.)

A. Media management layer (MML)

B. Command line interface (CLI)

C. Recovery catalog

D. Enterprise Manager (EM)

15. What do you call the RMAN information stored in the control files that is written over when necessary?

A. Writeable information

B. Non-reusable information

C. Circular reuse records

D. Non-circular reuse

16. In order to perform parallelization of backup and restore operations, you would need at least what set up? (Choose all that apply.)

A. One channel allocated

B. Multiple channels allocated

C. PARALLISM configured to 1

D. PARALLISM configured to 2

17. After database login to Enterprise Manager, what is required in order to perform most backup and recovery tasks? (Choose all that apply.)

A. System database account

B. Sys database account

C. Oracle Unix operating system account

D. Administrator Windows operating system account

18. Which of the following statements is true about RMAN persistent settings?

A. Persistent settings can control device type.

B. Persistent settings can control backup type.

C. Persistent settings can control channel device.

D. All of the above

19. Where are RMAN persistent settings stored? (Choose all that apply.)

    A. Target database catalog

    B. Recovery catalog database

    C. Control file

    D. Parameter file

20. What feature is *not* a new feature of Oracle 10*g* RMAN?

    A. User error recovery with flashback

    B. Automated tablespace point-in-time recovery (TSPITR)

    C. Compressing backups by only backing up changed blocks

    D. Compressing the backup sets regardless of whether blocks in the datafiles are mainly used

Answers to Review Questions

1. C. The CONTROL_FILE_RECORD_KEEP_TIME parameter is the parameter that determines the size of the RMAN repository or target database's control file when not using the recovery catalog.

2. A, C. The RECOVERY_CATALOG_OWNER and RESOURCE privileges are required to create the recovery catalog. The DBA privilege includes RESOURCE and CONNECT and will work, but this role has many additional privileges that are unneeded. SELECT ANY DICTIONARY TABLE is not required.

3. A, C. The TYPE DISK parameter allocates a channel to disk. The TYPE SBT_TAPE parameter allocates a channel to tape. These are the two correct device types.

4. B. The correct configure command is CONFIGURE CHANNEL DEVICE TYPE DISK. When using the CONFIGURE command, the information is stored as a default so that it doesn't need to be specified in backup, restores, or deletes.

5. D. The Media Management Layer (MML) is the API that interfaces RMAN with different vendor tape devices.

6. A. Password file backups are not supported with the RMAN utility.

7. A, B, D. The database connection types supported with RMAN are target database, recovery catalog, and auxiliary database.

8. B. The channel options and commands are used to control the operating system resources that RMAN uses. Specifically, the RATE and DURATION options protect a RMAN backup from consuming all operating system resources.

9. A. The FORMAT command allows for unique identification of a backup or image copy.

10. C. The SHOW ALL command displays all configuration settings, including automated channel setup settings. These are also known as the persistent settings.

11. A. The COMPRESSED BACKUPSET command allows you to compress backup sets to a smaller size, allowing for storage of larger databases.

12. C. Block change tracking allows RMAN to back up only changed blocks from the last backup. The blocks are identified in a journaling system to expedite the process.

13. D. All of the answers describe capabilities of the BACKUP command that are not available when using the image copy method of backing up.

14. A, C, D. The command-line interface is always required to use RMAN. EM, the recovery catalog, and MML are not mandatory to use RMAN.

15. C. The circular reuse records contain information that will be written over when necessary.

16. B, D. Multiple channels are needed to allow backup or recovery functions to be processed over each. The PARALLISM parameter can be configured to a number greater than 1, and this allocates multiple channels for parallelization.

17. C, D. EM uses the operating system account with significant privileges to run RMAN to perform operations. The Oracle account is needed on Unix and the administrator account or its equivalent in the Windows environment.

18. D. RMAN persistent settings can control or define devices, backups, and channels. Persistent settings control all values available in the `SHOW ALL` command.

19. B, C. Persistent settings are stored in the control file of the target database when using the control file as the repository. Persistent settings are also stored in the recovery catalog when using the recovery catalog as the repository.

20. C. Compression backup by backing up only changed blocks was the primary method of compression prior to 10*g*. Now with 10*g*, backups can be compressed regardless of the used or unused blocks.

Using Recovery Manager

ORACLE DATABASE 10*G*: ADMINISTRATION II EXAM OBJECTIVES COVERED IN THIS CHAPTER:

✓ **Using Recovery Manager**

- Use the RMAN BACKUP command to create backup sets and image copies.
- Enable block change tracking.
- Manage the backups and image copies taken with RMAN with the LIST and REPORT commands.

Exam objectives are subject to change at any time without prior notice and at Oracle's sole discretion. Please visit Oracle's Training and Certification website (`http://www.oracle.com/education/certification/`) for the most current exam objectives listing.

This chapter provides a hands-on understanding of using Recovery Manager (RMAN), focusing on RMAN backups. Understanding RMAN backups is one of the most important activities for a DBA using the RMAN utility. Emphasis is placed on the two distinct methods: image copies and backup sets. With the introduction of Oracle Database 10*g* (Oracle 10*g*) the RMAN utility has been advanced to support improvements such as block change tracking and the compression of backups. Having a good understanding of RMAN is critical for every DBA. Since the advent of RMAN, Oracle has steadily shifted the backup emphasis toward the use of RMAN opposed to the traditional method of backing up databases. As databases get larger and have greater availability requirements, this emphasis will surely continue. A good understanding of RMAN is a cornerstone for performing Oracle database backups.

This chapter walks through the image copy and backup set backup methods. You will perform examples using the new Oracle 10*g* capabilities of compressing backups and implementing block change tracking. You will also see examples of incremental and whole database backups and walk through examples of showing backup status using the RMAN `LIST` and `REPORT` commands and dynamic views.

RMAN Commands

The RMAN utility has a rich command set that is used to support the backup and restore operations of an Oracle database. The Oracle Database Recovery Manager Reference, 10*g* Release 1 (10.1), part number B10770-02, contains the complete list of commands and diagrams of how to utilize each command. In addition, this document has a listing of key and reserved words. This document is a valuable asset to utilizing RMAN commands and working with RMAN in general.

Table 2.1 lists all commands and clauses from the Oracle Database Recovery Manager Reference, 10*g* Release 1 (10.1). These are all the available commands and clauses that can be used in RMAN. These commands can be used interactively or in RMAN scripts that run these commands and clauses as a small program.

TABLE 2.1 RMAN Commands and Clauses

Command	Description
`@`	Run a command file.
`@@`	Run a command file in the same directory as another command file that is currently running. The `@@` command differs from the `@` command only when run from within a command file.
`ALLOCATE CHANNEL`	Establish a channel, which is a connection between RMAN and a database instance.
`ALLOCATE CHANNEL FOR MAINTENANCE`	Allocate a channel in preparation for issuing maintenance commands such as `DELETE`.
`allocOperandList`	A subclause that specifies channel control options such as PARMS and FORMAT.
`ALTER DATABASE`	Mount or open a database.
`archivelogRecordSpecifier`	Specify a range of archived redo logs files.
`BACKUP`	Back up database files, copies of database files, archived logs, or backup sets.
`BLOCKRECOVER`	Recover an individual data block or set of data blocks within one or more datafiles.
`CATALOG`	Add information about a datafile copy, archived redo log, or control file copy to the repository.
`CHANGE`	Mark a backup piece, image copy, or archived redo log as having the status UNAVAILABLE or AVAILABLE; remove the repository record for a backup or copy; override the retention policy for a backup or copy.
`completedTimeSpec`	Specify a time range during which the backup or copy completed.
`CONFIGURE`	Configure persistent RMAN settings. These settings apply to all RMAN sessions until explicitly changed or disabled.
`CONNECT`	Establish a connection between RMAN and a target, auxiliary, or recovery catalog database.

TABLE 2.1 RMAN Commands and Clauses *(continued)*

Command	Description
connectStringSpec	Specify the username, password, and net service name for connecting to a target, recovery catalog, or auxiliary database. The connection is necessary to authenticate the user and identify the database.
CONVERT	Converts datafile formats for transporting tablespaces across platforms.
CREATE CATALOG	Create the schema for the recovery catalog.
CREATE SCRIPT	Create a stored script and store it in the recovery catalog.
CROSSCHECK	Determine whether files managed by RMAN, such as archived logs, datafile copies, and backup pieces, still exist on disk or tape.
datafileSpec	Specify a datafile by filename or absolute file number.
DELETE	Delete backups and copies, remove references to them from the recovery catalog, and update their control file records to status DELETED.
DELETE SCRIPT	Delete a stored script from the recovery catalog.
deviceSpecifier	Specify the type of storage device for a backup or copy.
DROP CATALOG	Remove the schema from the recovery catalog.
DROP DATABASE	Delete the target database from disk and unregister it.
DUPLICATE	Use backups of the target database to create a duplicate database that you can use for testing purposes or to create a standby database.
EXECUTE SCRIPT	Run an RMAN stored script.
EXIT	Quit the RMAN executable.
fileNameConversionSpec	Specify patterns to transform source to target filenames during BACKUP AS COPY, CONVERT, and DUPLICATE.

TABLE 2.1 RMAN Commands and Clauses *(continued)*

Command	Description
FLASHBACK	Return the database to its state at a previous time or system change number (SCN).
formatSpec	Specify a filename format for a backup or copy.
HOST	Invoke an operating system command-line subshell from within RMAN or run a specific operating system command.
keepOption	Specify that a backup or copy should or should not be exempt from the current retention policy.
LIST	Produce a detailed listing of backup sets or copies.
listObjList	A subclause used to specify which items will be displayed by the LIST command.
maintQualifier	A subclause used to specify additional options for maintenance commands such as DELETE and CHANGE.
maintSpec	A subclause used to specify the files operated on by maintenance commands such as CHANGE, CROSSCHECK, and DELETE.
obsOperandList	A subclause used to determine which backups and copies are obsolete.
PRINT SCRIPT	Display a stored script.
QUIT	Exit the RMAN executable.
recordSpec	A subclause used to specify which objects the maintenance commands should operate on.
RECOVER	Apply redo logs and incremental backups to datafiles restored from backup or datafile copies in order to update them to a specified time.
REGISTER	Register the target database in the recovery catalog.
RELEASE CHANNEL	Release a channel that was allocated with an ALLOCATE CHANNEL command.

TABLE 2.1 RMAN Commands and Clauses *(continued)*

Command	Description
`releaseForMaint`	Release a channel that was allocated with an `ALLOCATE CHANNEL FOR MAINTENANCE` command.
`REPLACE SCRIPT`	Replace an existing script stored in the recovery catalog. If the script does not exist, then REPLACE SCRIPT creates it.
`REPORT`	Perform detailed analyses of the content of the recovery catalog.
`RESET DATABASE`	Inform RMAN that the SQL statement ALTER DATABASE OPEN RESETLOGS has been executed and that a new incarnation of the target database has been created, or reset the target database to a prior incarnation.
`RESTORE`	Restore files from backup sets or from disk copies to the default or to a new location.
`RESYNC`	Perform a full resynchronization, which creates a snapshot control file and then copies any new or changed information from that snapshot control file to the recovery catalog.
`RUN`	Execute a sequence of one or more RMAN commands, which are one or more statements executed within the braces of RUN.
`SEND`	Send a vendor-specific quoted string to one or more specific channels.
`SET`	Set the value of various attributes that affect RMAN behavior for the duration of a `RUN` block or a session.
`SHOW`	Display the current CONFIGURE settings.
`SHUTDOWN`	Shut down the target database. This command is equivalent to the SQL*Plus SHUTDOWN command.
`SPOOL`	Write RMAN output to a log file.
`SQL`	Execute a SQL statement from within RMAN.

TABLE 2.1 RMAN Commands and Clauses *(continued)*

Command	Description
`STARTUP`	Start up the target database. This command is equivalent to the SQL*Plus STARTUP command.
`SWITCH`	Specify that a datafile copy is now the current datafile, that is, the datafile pointed to by the control file. This command is equivalent to the SQL statement ALTER DATABASE RENAME FILE as it applies to datafiles.
`UNREGISTER DATABASE`	Unregister a database from the recovery catalog.
`untilClause`	A subclause specifying an upper limit by time, SCN, or log sequence number. This clause is usually used to specify the desired point-in-time for an incomplete recovery.
`UPGRADE CATALOG`	Upgrade the recovery catalog schema from an older version to the version required by the RMAN executable.
`VALIDATE`	Examine a backup set and report whether its data is intact. RMAN scans all of the backup pieces in the specified backup sets and looks at the checksums to verify that the contents can be successfully restored.

The following is an example of performing a job command from multiple RMAN commands in a `RUN` block. These commands can be grouped together inside the `RUN` command and brackets `{}`. This allows you to group multiple commands together and run them as if they were one command.

There are benefits of grouping commands together in a `RUN` block, which allows you to perform different types of backups such as weekly or monthly backups. You may want to back up only part of the database or the whole database. These `RUN` blocks can be saved as RMAN scripts, which can be called for these repeated backup tasks. This keeps consistency in the backup process because you eliminate some of the user interaction that occurs when running RMAN commands interactively.

Let's look at grouping commands together into a `RUN` block. This example will perform a complete database backup stored in a special format and will use the `TAG` command to name the backup `monthly_backup`. The archive logs will be stored in a special format as well. Let's walk through running the `RUN` block.

Here is the script:

```
RMAN> run
2> {
3> allocate channel c1 type disk;
4> backup database format 'db_%u_%d_%s' tag monthly_backup;
5> backup format 'log_t%t_s%s_p%p'
6> (archivelog all);
7> }

allocated channel: c1
channel c1: sid=162 devtype=DISK

Starting backup at 18-JUL-04
channel c1: starting full datafile backupset
channel c1: specifying datafile(s) in backupset
input datafile fno=00001 name=C:\ORACLE\ORADATA\ORA101C\SYSTEM01.DBF
input datafile fno=00003 name=C:\ORACLE\ORADATA\ORA101C\SYSAUX01.DBF
input datafile fno=00005 name=C:\ORACLE\ORADATA\ORA101C\EXAMPLE01.DBF
input datafile fno=00002 name=C:\ORACLE\ORADATA\ORA101C\UNDOTBS01.DBF
input datafile fno=00004 name=C:\ORACLE\ORADATA\ORA101C\USERS01.DBF
channel c1: starting piece 1 at 18-JUL-04
channel c1: finished piece 1 at 18-JUL-04
piece handle=C:\WINDOWS\SYSTEM32\DB_0DFR66MU_ORA101C_13 comment=NONE
channel c1: backup set complete, elapsed time: 00:02:07
Finished backup at 18-JUL-04

Starting backup at 18-JUL-04
current log archived
channel c1: starting archive log backupset
channel c1: specifying archive log(s) in backup set
input archive log thread=1 sequence=59 recid=54 stamp=528701976
input archive log thread=1 sequence=60 recid=55 stamp=529542042
input archive log thread=1 sequence=61 recid=56 stamp=529542953
channel c1: starting piece 1 at 18-JUL-04
channel c1: finished piece 1 at 18-JUL-04
piece handle=C:\WINDOWS\SYSTEM32\LOG_T531831661_S14_P1 comment=NONE
channel c1: backup set complete, elapsed time: 00:01:11
Finished backup at 18-JUL-04
Starting Control File Autobackup at 18-JUL-04
```

```
piece handle=C:\ORACLE\STAGING\ORA101C\CF_C-1736563848-20040718-00 comment=NONE
Finished Control File Autobackup at 18-JUL-04
released channel: c1

RMAN>
```

Backup Sets and Image Copies

Let's go into more detail about backup sets and how to use them. Database files in backup sets are stored in a special RMAN format and must be processed with the RESTORE command before these files are usable. This can take more time and effort during the recovery process. In the following sections, you will look at an example of using the BACKUP command and the BACKUP AS COPY or the deprecated COPY command. While the COPY command is still supported in Oracle 10*g*, this command has been replaced with BACKUP AS COPY. The COPY command may not be supported in future releases of Oracle Database.

Creating Backup Sets

The RMAN BACKUP command is used to perform the backup set backup process. The backup set backup process consists of using the BACKUP command instead of the COPY or BACKUP AS COPY command. This section contains an example of the BACKUP command.

In this example, you are backing up the database ora101t and storing in two backup sets: FULL DATAFILE BACKUPSET and ARCHIVE LOG BACKUP SET. FULL DATAFILE BACKUPSET is made up of two backup pieces. ARCHIVE LOG BACKUPSET is comprised on one backup piece. The *backup piece* is the actual file within the backup set. The *backup set* is a logical grouping of backup pieces that is stored in a proprietary format.

The first backup piece has the majority of the datafiles. This is called DB_04FODN6N_ORA101T_4. The second backup piece has the control file. This backup set is called DB_05FODNAC_ORA101T_5. The last backup piece has all of the archive logs and is called LOG_T528932180_S6_P1. All of these are stored in the C:\WINDOWS\System32 directory by default.

```
C:\Documents and Settings>rman
Recovery Manager: Release 10.1.0.2.0 - Production
Copyright (c) 1995, 2004, Oracle.  All rights reserved.

RMAN> connect target

connected to target database: ORA101T (DBID=2615281366)

RMAN> run
```

```
{
allocate channel c1 type disk;
backup database format 'db_%u_%d_%s';
backup format 'log_t%t_s%s_p%p'
(archivelog all);
}

allocated channel: c1
channel c1: sid=49 devtype=DISK

Starting backup at 15-JUN-04
channel c1: starting full datafile backupset
channel c1: specifying datafile(s) in backupset
input datafile fno=00001 name=C:\ORACLE\ORADATA\ORA101T\SYSTEM01.DBF
input datafile fno=00003 name=C:\ORACLE\ORADATA\ORA101T\SYSAUX01.DBF
input datafile fno=00005 name=C:\ORACLE\ORADATA\ORA101T\EXAMPLE01.DBF
input datafile fno=00002 name=C:\ORACLE\ORADATA\ORA101T\UNDOTBS01.DBF
input datafile fno=00004 name=C:\ORACLE\ORADATA\ORA101T\USERS01.DBF
channel c1: starting piece 1 at 15-JUN-04
channel c1: finished piece 1 at 15-JUN-04
piece handle=C:\WINDOWS\SYSTEM32\DB_04FODN6N_ORA101T_4 comment=NONE
channel c1: backup set complete, elapsed time: 00:01:57
channel c1: starting full datafile backupset
channel c1: specifying datafile(s) in backupset
including current controlfile in backupset
channel c1: starting piece 1 at 15-JUN-04
channel c1: finished piece 1 at 15-JUN-04
piece handle=C:\WINDOWS\SYSTEM32\DB_05FODNAC_ORA101T_5 comment=NONE
channel c1: backup set complete, elapsed time: 00:00:05
Finished backup at 15-JUN-04

Starting backup at 15-JUN-04
channel c1: starting archive log backupset
channel c1: specifying archive log(s) in backup set
input archive log thread=1 sequence=7 recid=1 stamp=527413772
input archive log thread=1 sequence=8 recid=2 stamp=527414322
input archive log thread=1 sequence=9 recid=3 stamp=528706062
channel c1: starting piece 1 at 15-JUN-04
channel c1: finished piece 1 at 15-JUN-04
piece handle=C:\WINDOWS\SYSTEM32\LOG_T528932180_S6_P1 comment=NONE
```

```
channel c1: backup set complete, elapsed time: 00:00:09
Finished backup at 15-JUN-04
released channel: c1

RMAN>
```

Backup sets have an inherent performance capability called *multiplexing*. Multiplexing the files in a backup set is when multiple files get read and then each of the file blocks gets written to the same backup set. These blocks are interspersed together. Image copies cannot be multiplexed. Figure 2.1 displays the interspersing of three datafiles into one backup set.

FIGURE 2.1 Multiplexing backup sets

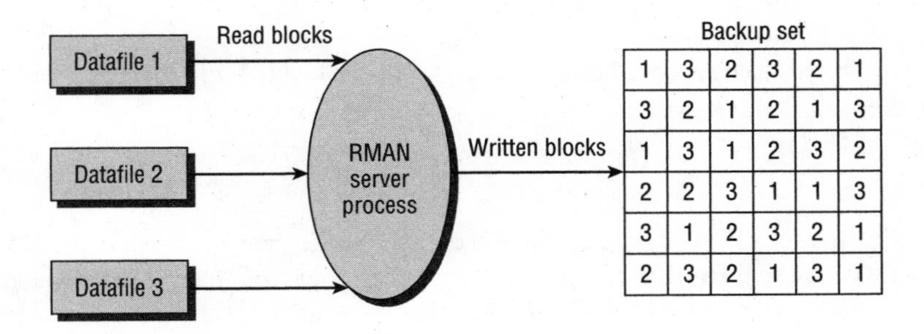

Creating Image Copies

Let's go into some detail about image copies and how they function. *Image copies* are actual copies of the database files, archive logs, or control files and are not stored in a special RMAN format. Image copies can be stored only on disk.

An image copy in RMAN is equivalent to an operating system copy command such as cp or dd in Unix, or COPY in Windows. Thus, no RMAN restore processing is necessary to make image copies usable in a recovery situation. This can improve the speed and efficiency of the restore and recovery process in most cases. However, there is also a price for this restore efficiency—the size of image copy backups. The image copy backup cannot be compressed and requires much more space than a backup set.

Let's look at an example of using the RMAN COPY command to create an image copy of various database files. This example shows the command necessary to perform an image copy.

In this example, you are backing up the system datafile and current control file as image copies to the C:\oracle\staging\ora101t directory:

```
RMAN> run { allocate channel ch1 type disk;
copy
datafile 1 to 'C:\oracle\staging\ora101t\SYSTEM01.DBF' ,
current controlfile to 'C:\oracle\staging\ora101t\CONTROL01.ctl';}
```

```
allocated channel: ch1
channel ch1: sid=52 devtype=DISK

Starting backup at 16-JUN-04
channel ch1: starting datafile copy
input datafile fno=00001 name=C:\ORACLE\ORADATA\ORA101T\SYSTEM01.DBF
output filename=C:\ORACLE\STAGING\ORA101T\SYSTEM01.DBF tag=TAG20040616T233305 re
cid=7 stamp=529025661
channel ch1: datafile copy complete, elapsed time: 00:01:17
channel ch1: starting datafile copy
copying current controlfile
output filename=C:\ORACLE\STAGING\ORA101T\CONTROL01.CTL tag=TAG20040616T233305 r
ecid=8 stamp=529025663
channel ch1: datafile copy complete, elapsed time: 00:00:03
Finished backup at 16-JUN-04
released channel: ch1
RMAN>
```

In Oracle 10*g*, there is a new backup command that simplifies image copies: BACKUP AS COPY. The benefit of this image copy is that you can perform image copies of an entire database, multiple tablespaces, datafiles, and archive logs without having to specify all of the individual files. In the previous image copy example, the location of the SYSTEM01.DBF file must be known before you do the copy. This requires a lot of extra work. Now you can just back up the whole database with one image copy command.

Let's take a look at how easily this new Oracle 10*g* command performs an image copy of an entire database. Let's use the TAG parameter to give this image copy a unique name:

```
C:\Documents and Settings\dstuns>rman

Recovery Manager: Release 10.1.0.2.0 - Production

Copyright (c) 1995, 2004, Oracle.  All rights reserved.

RMAN> connect target

connected to target database: ORA101T (DBID=2615281366)

RMAN> backup as copy tag "062504_backup" database;

Starting backup at 12-SEP-04
using target database controlfile instead of recovery catalog
```

```
allocated channel: ORA_DISK_1
channel ORA_DISK_1: sid=50 devtype=DISK
channel ORA_DISK_1: starting datafile copy
input datafile fno=00001 name=C:\ORACLE\ORADATA\ORA101T\SYSTEM01.DBF
output filename=C:\ORACLE\FLASH_RECOVERY_AREA\ORA101T\ORA101T\DATAFILE\O1_MF_SYS
TEM_0N8WXSTO_.DBF tag=062504_BACKUP recid=13 stamp=536663184
channel ORA_DISK_1: datafile copy complete, elapsed time: 00:01:15
channel ORA_DISK_1: starting datafile copy
input datafile fno=00003 name=C:\ORACLE\ORADATA\ORA101T\SYSAUX01.DBF
output filename=C:\ORACLE\FLASH_RECOVERY_AREA\ORA101T\ORA101T\DATAFILE\O1_MF_SYS
AUX_0N8X05CM_.DBF tag=062504_BACKUP recid=14 stamp=536663219
channel ORA_DISK_1: datafile copy complete, elapsed time: 00:00:35
channel ORA_DISK_1: starting datafile copy
input datafile fno=00005 name=C:\ORACLE\ORADATA\ORA101T\EXAMPLE01.DBF
output filename=C:\ORACLE\FLASH_RECOVERY_AREA\ORA101T\ORA101T\DATAFILE\O1_MF_EXA
MPLE_0N8X18D8_.DBF tag=062504_BACKUP recid=15 stamp=536663243
channel ORA_DISK_1: datafile copy complete, elapsed time: 00:00:26
channel ORA_DISK_1: starting datafile copy
input datafile fno=00002 name=C:\ORACLE\ORADATA\ORA101T\UNDOTBS01.DBF
output filename=C:\ORACLE\FLASH_RECOVERY_AREA\ORA101T\ORA101T\DATAFILE\O1_MF_UND
OTBS1_0N8X21TT_.DBF tag=062504_BACKUP recid=16 stamp=536663253
channel ORA_DISK_1: datafile copy complete, elapsed time: 00:00:07
channel ORA_DISK_1: starting datafile copy
input datafile fno=00006 name=C:\ORACLE\ORADATA\ORA101T\INDEX01.DBF
output filename=C:\ORACLE\FLASH_RECOVERY_AREA\ORA101T\ORA101T\DATAFILE\O1_MF_IND
EXES_0N8X29D5_.DBF tag=062504_BACKUP recid=17 stamp=536663260
channel ORA_DISK_1: datafile copy complete, elapsed time: 00:00:08
channel ORA_DISK_1: starting datafile copy
input datafile fno=00004 name=C:\ORACLE\ORADATA\ORA101T\USERS01.DBF
output filename=C:\ORACLE\FLASH_RECOVERY_AREA\ORA101T\ORA101T\DATAFILE\O1_MF_USE
RS_0N8X2JS0_.DBF tag=062504_BACKUP recid=18 stamp=536663265
channel ORA_DISK_1: datafile copy complete, elapsed time: 00:00:03
Finished backup at 12-SEP-04

Starting Control File Autobackup at 12-SEP-04
piece handle=C:\ORACLE\FLASH_RECOVERY_AREA\ORA101T\ORA101T\AUTOBACKUP\2004_09_12
  \O1_MF_N_536663267_0N8X2PJT_.BKP comment=NONE
Finished Control File Autobackup at 12-SEP-04

RMAN>
```

Compressed Backups

New with Oracle 10*g* RMAN is the capability to compress backups. In previous versions, reducing the size of backups was performed by backing up only used blocks and skipping unused blocks. This had limited effectiveness because this would reduce only the backup sizes of datafiles that were oversized or had significant free space.

With 10*g*, you can now compress backups regardless of the contents of the datafiles. This allows real compression of backups. *Compressed backups* work only with backup sets, not image copies. This includes database, tablespace, and datafile backup sets.

In the next section, you will create a compressed backup set. You will also configure a compressed backup to use a default device. You will walk through each of these capabilities in detail.

Image copies are exact copies of the Oracle database files. This means that the files do not compress as backup sets do. The files are stored in original format and not in the format of an RMAN backup set. Image copies cannot be compressed.

Creating Compressed Backup Sets for RMAN

Creating a compressed backup set is a fairly straightforward process. This is accomplished using the BACKUP AS COMPRESSED command. This functions as a normal backup set, but the backup set is compressed. Let's see how to create a compressed backup set:

```
RMAN> backup as compressed backupset database;

Starting backup at 17-JUN-04
allocated channel: ORA_DISK_1
channel ORA_DISK_1: sid=34 devtype=DISK
channel ORA_DISK_1: starting compressed full datafile backupset
channel ORA_DISK_1: specifying datafile(s) in backupset
input datafile fno=00001 name=C:\ORACLE\ORADATA\ORA101T\SYSTEM01.DBF
input datafile fno=00003 name=C:\ORACLE\ORADATA\ORA101T\SYSAUX01.DBF
input datafile fno=00005 name=C:\ORACLE\ORADATA\ORA101T\EXAMPLE01.DBF
input datafile fno=00002 name=C:\ORACLE\ORADATA\ORA101T\UNDOTBS01.DBF
input datafile fno=00004 name=C:\ORACLE\ORADATA\ORA101T\USERS01.DBF
channel ORA_DISK_1: starting piece 1 at 17-JUN-04
channel ORA_DISK_1: finished piece 1 at 17-JUN-04
piece handle=C:\ORACLE\FLASH_RECOVERY_AREA\ORA101T\ORA101T\BACKUPSET\
➥2004_06_17\O1_MF_NNNDF_TAG20040617T000017_0F2JD5H7_.BKP comment=NONE
channel ORA_DISK_1: backup set complete, elapsed time: 00:01:37
channel ORA_DISK_1: starting compressed full datafile backupset
channel ORA_DISK_1: specifying datafile(s) in backupset
```

```
including current controlfile in backupset
channel ORA_DISK_1: starting piece 1 at 17-JUN-04
channel ORA_DISK_1: finished piece 1 at 17-JUN-04
piece handle=C:\ORACLE\FLASH_RECOVERY_AREA\ORA101T\ORA101T\BACKUPSET\
  ➥2004_06_17\01_MF_NCNNF_TAG20040617T000017_0F2JH5WY_.BKP comment=NONE
channel ORA_DISK_1: backup set complete, elapsed time: 00:00:09
Finished backup at 17-JUN-04

RMAN>
```

A default device can be configured for compressed backups. This is activated by using the CONFIGURE command. When this command is executed, all backups using a designated device will be compressed until the configuration is modified. Let's look at this command for configuring a default device to use compressed backups:

```
RMAN> configure device type disk backup type to compressed backupset;

old RMAN configuration parameters:
CONFIGURE DEVICE TYPE DISK PARALLELISM 1 BACKUP TYPE TO BACKUPSET;
new RMAN configuration parameters:
CONFIGURE DEVICE TYPE DISK BACKUP TYPE TO COMPRESSED BACKUPSET
  PARALLELISM 1;
new RMAN configuration parameters are successfully stored
released channel: ORA_DISK_1
starting full resync of recovery catalog
full resync complete

RMAN>
```

Next, let's look at the resulting backup set sizes to verify that these backup sets are compressed. Look first at the standard backup set file for the database ora101t DB_01FODMV3_ORA101T_1.BKP. Next, compare it to the compressed backup set file NNNDF_TAG20040617T000017.BKP. Here is an example:

```
C:\WINDOWS\System32>dir *.BKP
06/15/2004  09:32 PM        548,052,992 DB_01FODMV3_ORA101T_1.BKP
06/17/2004  12:01 AM        109,101,056 NNNDF_TAG20040617T000017.BKP
```

As you can see, the compressed backup NNNDF_TAG20040617T000017.BKP is one-fifth the size of the non-compressed backup DB_01FODMV3_ORA101T_1.BKP.

Compressed database backup sets are compressed at approximately a 5-to-1 ratio, or 20 percent of the size of a standard backup set.

Full and Incremental Backups

The full and incremental backups are differentiated by how the data blocks are backed up in the target database. The *full backup* backs up all the data blocks in the datafiles, modified or not. An *incremental backup* backs up only the data blocks in the datafiles that were modified since the last incremental backup.

The full backup cannot be used as part of an incremental backup strategy. The baseline backup for an incremental backup is a level 0 backup. A level 0 backup is a full backup at that point in time. Thus, all blocks—modified or not—are backed up, allowing the level 0 backup to serve as a baseline for future incremental backups. The incremental backups can then be applied with the baseline—level 0—backup to form a full backup at some time in the future. The benefit of the incremental backup is that it is quicker, because not all data blocks need to be backed up.

Oracle incremental backups are designated as level 0 and level 1. A level 0 backup includes every block in the file except blocks that have never been used. A level 1 backup includes only those blocks that have been changed since the parent backup was taken. A level 0 backup is essentially a full backup, except a level 0 backup can be used as a parent to a level 1 backup.

There are two types of incremental backups: differential and cumulative. Both the differential and cumulative backups back up only modified blocks. The difference between these two types of incremental backups is in what the baseline database uses to identify the modified blocks that need to be backed up.

The *differential incremental backup* backs up only data blocks modified since the most recent backup at the same level or lower. A differential incremental backup determines which level 1 or level 2 backup has occurred most recently and backs up only blocks that have changed since that backup. The differential incremental backup is the default incremental backup.

The *cumulative incremental backup* backs up only the data blocks that have changed since the most recent backup of the next lowest level, or $n - 1$ or lower (with n being the existing level of backup). For example, if you are performing a level 2 cumulative incremental backup, the backup will copy data blocks only from the most recent level 1 backup. If no level 1 backup is available, then it will back up all data blocks that have changed since the most recent level 0 backup. This means that only one cumulative incremental backup needs to be restored instead of multiple differential incremental backups.

Full backups do not mean the complete database was backed up. In other words, a full backup can back up only part of the database and not all datafiles, control files, and logs.

Let's perform these two types of incremental backups: a differential incremental and a cumulative incremental backup.

Performing a Differential Incremental Backup

As stated in the preceding section, a differential incremental backup only backs up data blocks modified since the most recent backup at the same level or lower. The first incremental backup must be a level 0 backup that contains all used blocks. Next, you can perform a level 1 backup, which will pick up the changed blocks. Let's walk through the differential incremental backup:

```
RMAN> backup incremental level 0 database;

Starting backup at 25-JUL-04
allocated channel: ORA_DISK_1
channel ORA_DISK_1: sid=139 devtype=DISK
channel ORA_DISK_1: starting incremental level 0 datafile backupset
channel ORA_DISK_1: specifying datafile(s) in backupset
input datafile fno=00001 name=C:\ORACLE\ORADATA\ORA101C\SYSTEM01.DBF
input datafile fno=00003 name=C:\ORACLE\ORADATA\ORA101C\SYSAUX01.DBF
input datafile fno=00005 name=C:\ORACLE\ORADATA\ORA101C\EXAMPLE01.DBF
input datafile fno=00002 name=C:\ORACLE\ORADATA\ORA101C\UNDOTBS01.DBF
input datafile fno=00004 name=C:\ORACLE\ORADATA\ORA101C\USERS01.DBF
channel ORA_DISK_1: starting piece 1 at 25-JUL-04
channel ORA_DISK_1: finished piece 1 at 25-JUL-04
piece handle=C:\ORACLE\FLASH_RECOVERY_AREA\ORA101C\%REC_AREA_34_1.BAK
  ➥comment=NONE
channel ORA_DISK_1: backup set complete, elapsed time: 00:02:16
channel ORA_DISK_1: starting incremental level 0 datafile backupset
channel ORA_DISK_1: specifying datafile(s) in backupset
including current controlfile in backupset
channel ORA_DISK_1: starting piece 1 at 25-JUL-04
channel ORA_DISK_1: finished piece 1 at 25-JUL-04
piece handle=C:\ORACLE\FLASH_RECOVERY_AREA\ORA101C\%REC_AREA_35_1.BAK
  ➥comment=NONE
channel ORA_DISK_1: backup set complete, elapsed time: 00:00:09
Finished backup at 25-JUL-04

RMAN>
```

Next, let's see a level 1 incremental backup after some data has been changed in the database. The incremental level 1 backup will pick up the changes since the level 0 backup. Let's perform a level 1 incremental differential backup:

```
RMAN> backup incremental level 1 database;

Starting backup at 25-JUL-04
```

```
using channel ORA_DISK_1
channel ORA_DISK_1: starting incremental level 1 datafile backupset
channel ORA_DISK_1: specifying datafile(s) in backupset
input datafile fno=00001 name=C:\ORACLE\ORADATA\ORA101C\SYSTEM01.DBF
input datafile fno=00003 name=C:\ORACLE\ORADATA\ORA101C\SYSAUX01.DBF
input datafile fno=00005 name=C:\ORACLE\ORADATA\ORA101C\EXAMPLE01.DBF
input datafile fno=00002 name=C:\ORACLE\ORADATA\ORA101C\UNDOTBS01.DBF
input datafile fno=00004 name=C:\ORACLE\ORADATA\ORA101C\USERS01.DBF
channel ORA_DISK_1: starting piece 1 at 25-JUL-04
channel ORA_DISK_1: finished piece 1 at 25-JUL-04
piece handle=C:\ORACLE\FLASH_RECOVERY_AREA\ORA101C\%REC_AREA_36_1.BAK
  ➥comment=NONE
channel ORA_DISK_1: backup set complete, elapsed time: 00:00:57
channel ORA_DISK_1: starting incremental level 1 datafile backupset
channel ORA_DISK_1: specifying datafile(s) in backupset
including current controlfile in backupset
channel ORA_DISK_1: starting piece 1 at 25-JUL-04
channel ORA_DISK_1: finished piece 1 at 25-JUL-04
piece handle=C:\ORACLE\FLASH_RECOVERY_AREA\ORA101C\%REC_AREA_37_1.BAK
  ➥comment=NONE
channel ORA_DISK_1: backup set complete, elapsed time: 00:00:05
Finished backup at 25-JUL-04

RMAN>
```

Performing a Cumulative Incremental Backup

A cumulative incremental backup is different from the differential incremental backup in that it requires more space. The benefit of this is that cumulative incremental backups are usually faster and easier to restore because only one backup for a given level is needed to restore. A differential incremental backup compares between level 0 and level 1 and determines which one has most recently occurred to make the baseline comparison. Let's see a cumulative incremental backup:

```
RMAN> backup incremental level 1 cumulative database;

Starting backup at 25-JUL-04
using channel ORA_DISK_1
channel ORA_DISK_1: starting incremental level 1 datafile backupset
channel ORA_DISK_1: specifying datafile(s) in backupset
input datafile fno=00001 name=C:\ORACLE\ORADATA\ORA101C\SYSTEM01.DBF
input datafile fno=00003 name=C:\ORACLE\ORADATA\ORA101C\SYSAUX01.DBF
```

```
input datafile fno=00005 name=C:\ORACLE\ORADATA\ORA101C\EXAMPLE01.DBF
input datafile fno=00002 name=C:\ORACLE\ORADATA\ORA101C\UNDOTBS01.DBF
input datafile fno=00004 name=C:\ORACLE\ORADATA\ORA101C\USERS01.DBF
channel ORA_DISK_1: starting piece 1 at 25-JUL-04
channel ORA_DISK_1: finished piece 1 at 25-JUL-04
piece handle=C:\ORACLE\FLASH_RECOVERY_AREA\ORA101C\%REC_AREA_38_1.BAK
➥comment=NONE
channel ORA_DISK_1: backup set complete, elapsed time: 00:00:57
channel ORA_DISK_1: starting incremental level 1 datafile backupset
channel ORA_DISK_1: specifying datafile(s) in backupset
including current controlfile in backupset
channel ORA_DISK_1: starting piece 1 at 25-JUL-04
channel ORA_DISK_1: finished piece 1 at 25-JUL-04
piece handle=C:\ORACLE\FLASH_RECOVERY_AREA\ORA101C\%REC_AREA_39_1.BAK
➥comment=NONE
channel ORA_DISK_1: backup set complete, elapsed time: 00:00:03
Finished backup at 25-JUL-04

RMAN>
```

As you can see, performing a cumulative incremental backup is almost the same as running a differential incremental backup. The difference is all in how the backup is stored. As stated earlier, the cumulative incremental backup stores more complete information, which takes up more space. However, this negative aspect is compensated by the fact that recovery operations are more efficient.

Parallelization of Backup Sets

Parallelization of backup sets is performed by causing multiple backup sets to be concurrently backed up over multiple device channels. This is done by allocating multiple channels, one for each backup set that needs to be concurrently backed up before the backup process occurs. You can either modify the `CONFIGURE` settings for channel parallelism greater than 1 or use manual channel allocation.

Let's walk through an example of manually backing up in parallel:

1. Select the target database and start RMAN:

```
Microsoft Windows XP [Version 5.1.2600]
(C) Copyright 1985-2001 Microsoft Corp.

C:\Documents and Settings\dstuns>set ORACLE_SID=ora101c

C:\Documents and Settings\dstuns>rman
```

```
Recovery Manager: Release 10.1.0.2.0 - Production

Copyright (c) 1995, 2004, Oracle.  All rights reserved.

RMAN>
```

2. Start the BACKUP command in the backup script and allocate two channels: c1 and c2. Then specify datafile backups to c1 and archive logs to c2. This also backs up the control file:

```
RMAN> run
2> {
3> allocate channel c1 type disk;
4> allocate channel c2 type disk;
5> backup
6> (datafile 1,2,3 channel c1)
7> (archivelog all channel c2);
8> }

allocated channel: c1
channel c1: sid=137 devtype=DISK

allocated channel: c2
channel c2: sid=136 devtype=DISK

Starting backup at 25-JUL-04
channel c1: starting full datafile backupset
channel c1: specifying datafile(s) in backupset
input datafile fno=00001 name=C:\ORACLE\ORADATA\ORA101C\SYSTEM01.DBF
input datafile fno=00003 name=C:\ORACLE\ORADATA\ORA101C\SYSAUX01.DBF
input datafile fno=00002 name=C:\ORACLE\ORADATA\ORA101C\UNDOTBS01.DBF
channel c1: starting piece 1 at 25-JUL-04
channel c2: starting archive log backupset
channel c2: specifying archive log(s) in backup set
input archive log thread=1 sequence=63 recid=58 stamp=531002016
input archive log thread=1 sequence=64 recid=59 stamp=531162548
input archive log thread=1 sequence=65 recid=60 stamp=531162638
input archive log thread=1 sequence=66 recid=61 stamp=531306751
input archive log thread=1 sequence=67 recid=62 stamp=531321226
input archive log thread=1 sequence=68 recid=63 stamp=531342067
input archive log thread=1 sequence=69 recid=64 stamp=531356435
input archive log thread=1 sequence=70 recid=65 stamp=531363656
input archive log thread=1 sequence=71 recid=66 stamp=531381614
```

```
input archive log thread=1 sequence=72 recid=67 stamp=531399627
input archive log thread=1 sequence=73 recid=68 stamp=531417474
input archive log thread=1 sequence=74 recid=69 stamp=531474062
input archive log thread=1 sequence=75 recid=70 stamp=531475253
input archive log thread=1 sequence=76 recid=71 stamp=531496839
input archive log thread=1 sequence=77 recid=72 stamp=531514865
input archive log thread=1 sequence=78 recid=73 stamp=531533230
input archive log thread=1 sequence=79 recid=74 stamp=531551964
input archive log thread=1 sequence=80 recid=75 stamp=531572450
input archive log thread=1 sequence=81 recid=76 stamp=531590454
input archive log thread=1 sequence=82 recid=77 stamp=531761112
input archive log thread=1 sequence=83 recid=78 stamp=531761285
input archive log thread=1 sequence=84 recid=79 stamp=531766863
input archive log thread=1 sequence=85 recid=80 stamp=531784872
input archive log thread=1 sequence=86 recid=81 stamp=531831653
input archive log thread=1 sequence=87 recid=82 stamp=531849625
input archive log thread=1 sequence=88 recid=83 stamp=532443308
input archive log thread=1 sequence=89 recid=84 stamp=532445159
input archive log thread=1 sequence=90 recid=85 stamp=532445168
channel c2: starting piece 1 at 25-JUL-04
channel c1: finished piece 1 at 25-JUL-04
piece handle=C:\ORACLE\FLASH_RECOVERY_AREA\ORA101C\ORA101C\BACKUPSET\
  ➥2004_07_25
O1_MF_NNNDF_TAG20040725T141518_0J88QHW9_.BKP comment=NONE
channel c1: backup set complete, elapsed time: 00:02:53
channel c2: finished piece 1 at 25-JUL-04
piece handle=C:\ORACLE\FLASH_RECOVERY_AREA\ORA101C\ORA101C\BACKUPSET\
  ➥2004_ 07_25
O1_MF_ANNNN_TAG20040725T141518_0J88RXTM_.BKP comment=NONE
channel c2: backup set complete, elapsed time: 00:02:52
Finished backup at 25-JUL-04

Starting Control File Autobackup at 25-JUL-04
piece handle=C:\ORACLE\STAGING\ORA101C\CF_C-1736563848-20040725-00
  ➥comment=NONE
Finished Control File Autobackup at 25-JUL-04
released channel: c1
released channel: c2

RMAN>
```

The automated method of parallelizing your backup requires modifying the CONFIGURE setting of the parallelization parameter to the desired parallelization parameter. In the following example, you will use the parameter 3.

Let's walk through this example:

1. After connecting to the target database and starting RMAN, display the configuration settings:

```
RMAN> show all;

RMAN configuration parameters are:
CONFIGURE RETENTION POLICY TO RECOVERY WINDOW OF 30 DAYS;
CONFIGURE BACKUP OPTIMIZATION OFF; # default
CONFIGURE DEFAULT DEVICE TYPE TO DISK; # default
CONFIGURE CONTROLFILE AUTOBACKUP ON;
CONFIGURE CONTROLFILE AUTOBACKUP FORMAT FOR DEVICE TYPE DISK TO
  ➥'c:\oracle\staging\ora101c\cf_%F';
CONFIGURE DEVICE TYPE DISK PARALLELISM 1 BACKUP TYPE TO BACKUPSET; # default
CONFIGURE DATAFILE BACKUP COPIES FOR DEVICE TYPE DISK TO 1; # default
CONFIGURE ARCHIVELOG BACKUP COPIES FOR DEVICE TYPE DISK TO 1; # default
CONFIGURE CHANNEL DEVICE TYPE DISK FORMAT '/oracle/flash_recovery_area/ora101c
/%rec_area_%s_%p.bak';
CONFIGURE MAXSETSIZE TO UNLIMITED; # default
CONFIGURE ARCHIVELOG DELETION POLICY TO NONE; # default
CONFIGURE SNAPSHOT CONTROLFILE NAME TO 'C:\ORACLE\PRODUCT\10.1.0\DB_
1\DATABASE\S
NCFORA101C.ORA'; # default
```

2. Next, set the PARALLELISM setting to the desired value, in this case, 3.

```
RMAN>configure device type disk parallelism 3;

new RMAN configuration parameters:
CONFIGURE DEVICE TYPE DISK PARALLELISM 3 BACKUP TYPE TO BACKUPSET;
new RMAN configuration parameters are successfully stored

RMAN>
```

3. Then, execute a BACKUP command. The backup actions will be divided among the number of channels specified in the PARALLELISM configuration setting.

```
RMAN> backup
2> (datafile 1,2)
3> (datafile 3,4)
4> (archivelog all);
```

```
Starting backup at 25-JUL-04
allocated channel: ORA_DISK_1
channel ORA_DISK_1: sid=137 devtype=DISK
allocated channel: ORA_DISK_2
channel ORA_DISK_2: sid=136 devtype=DISK
allocated channel: ORA_DISK_3
channel ORA_DISK_3: sid=135 devtype=DISK
channel ORA_DISK_1: starting archive log backupset
channel ORA_DISK_1: specifying archive log(s) in backup set
input archive log thread=1 sequence=72 recid=67 stamp=531399627
input archive log thread=1 sequence=73 recid=68 stamp=531417474
input archive log thread=1 sequence=74 recid=69 stamp=531474062
input archive log thread=1 sequence=75 recid=70 stamp=531475253
input archive log thread=1 sequence=76 recid=71 stamp=531496839
input archive log thread=1 sequence=77 recid=72 stamp=531514865
input archive log thread=1 sequence=78 recid=73 stamp=531533230
input archive log thread=1 sequence=79 recid=74 stamp=531551964
input archive log thread=1 sequence=80 recid=75 stamp=531572450
input archive log thread=1 sequence=81 recid=76 stamp=531590454
channel ORA_DISK_1: starting piece 1 at 25-JUL-04
channel ORA_DISK_2: starting archive log backupset
channel ORA_DISK_2: specifying archive log(s) in backup set
input archive log thread=1 sequence=63 recid=58 stamp=531002016
input archive log thread=1 sequence=64 recid=59 stamp=531162548
input archive log thread=1 sequence=65 recid=60 stamp=531162638
input archive log thread=1 sequence=66 recid=61 stamp=531306751
input archive log thread=1 sequence=67 recid=62 stamp=531321226
input archive log thread=1 sequence=68 recid=63 stamp=531342067
input archive log thread=1 sequence=69 recid=64 stamp=531356435
input archive log thread=1 sequence=70 recid=65 stamp=531363656
input archive log thread=1 sequence=71 recid=66 stamp=531381614
channel ORA_DISK_2: starting piece 1 at 25-JUL-04
channel ORA_DISK_3: starting archive log backupset
channel ORA_DISK_3: specifying archive log(s) in backup set
input archive log thread=1 sequence=82 recid=77 stamp=531761112
input archive log thread=1 sequence=83 recid=78 stamp=531761285
input archive log thread=1 sequence=84 recid=79 stamp=531766863
input archive log thread=1 sequence=85 recid=80 stamp=531784872
input archive log thread=1 sequence=86 recid=81 stamp=531831653
```

```
input archive log thread=1 sequence=87 recid=82 stamp=531849625
input archive log thread=1 sequence=88 recid=83 stamp=532443308
input archive log thread=1 sequence=89 recid=84 stamp=532445159
input archive log thread=1 sequence=90 recid=85 stamp=532445168
channel ORA_DISK_3: starting piece 1 at 25-JUL-04
channel ORA_DISK_1: finished piece 1 at 25-JUL-04
piece handle=C:\ORACLE\FLASH_RECOVERY_AREA\ORA101C\%REC_AREA_19_1.BAK
  ➥comment=NONE
channel ORA_DISK_1: backup set complete, elapsed time: 00:01:03
channel ORA_DISK_1: starting full datafile backupset
channel ORA_DISK_1: specifying datafile(s) in backupset
input datafile fno=00001 name=C:\ORACLE\ORADATA\ORA101C\SYSTEM01.DBF
channel ORA_DISK_1: starting piece 1 at 25-JUL-04
channel ORA_DISK_2: finished piece 1 at 25-JUL-04
piece handle=C:\ORACLE\FLASH_RECOVERY_AREA\ORA101C\%REC_AREA_20_1.BAK
  ➥comment=NONE
channel ORA_DISK_2: backup set complete, elapsed time: 00:01:04
channel ORA_DISK_2: starting full datafile backupset
channel ORA_DISK_2: specifying datafile(s) in backupset
input datafile fno=00003 name=C:\ORACLE\ORADATA\ORA101C\SYSAUX01.DBF
channel ORA_DISK_2: starting piece 1 at 25-JUL-04
channel ORA_DISK_3: finished piece 1 at 25-JUL-04
piece handle=C:\ORACLE\FLASH_RECOVERY_AREA\ORA101C\%REC_AREA_21_1.BAK
  ➥comment=NONE
channel ORA_DISK_3: backup set complete, elapsed time: 00:01:05
channel ORA_DISK_3: starting full datafile backupset
channel ORA_DISK_3: specifying datafile(s) in backupset
input datafile fno=00002 name=C:\ORACLE\ORADATA\ORA101C\UNDOTBS01.DBF
channel ORA_DISK_3: starting piece 1 at 25-JUL-04
channel ORA_DISK_3: finished piece 1 at 25-JUL-04
piece handle=C:\ORACLE\FLASH_RECOVERY_AREA\ORA101C\%REC_AREA_24_1.BAK
  ➥comment=NONE
channel ORA_DISK_3: backup set complete, elapsed time: 00:01:00
channel ORA_DISK_3: starting full datafile backupset
channel ORA_DISK_3: specifying datafile(s) in backupset
input datafile fno=00004 name=C:\ORACLE\ORADATA\ORA101C\USERS01.DBF
channel ORA_DISK_3: starting piece 1 at 25-JUL-04
```

```
channel ORA_DISK_2: finished piece 1 at 25-JUL-04
piece handle=C:\ORACLE\FLASH_RECOVERY_AREA\ORA101C\%REC_AREA_23_1.BAK
  ➥comment=NONE
channel ORA_DISK_2: backup set complete, elapsed time: 00:01:18
channel ORA_DISK_3: finished piece 1 at 25-JUL-04
piece handle=C:\ORACLE\FLASH_RECOVERY_AREA\ORA101C\%REC_AREA_25_1.BAK
  ➥comment=NONE
channel ORA_DISK_3: backup set complete, elapsed time: 00:00:29
channel ORA_DISK_1: finished piece 1 at 25-JUL-04
piece handle=C:\ORACLE\FLASH_RECOVERY_AREA\ORA101C\%REC_AREA_22_1.BAK
  ➥comment=NONE
channel ORA_DISK_1: backup set complete, elapsed time: 00:01:50
Finished backup at 25-JUL-04

Starting Control File Autobackup at 25-JUL-04
piece handle=C:\ORACLE\STAGING\ORA101C\CF_C-1736563848-20040725-01
  ➥comment=NONE
Finished Control File Autobackup at 25-JUL-04

RMAN>
```

Backup Options

RMAN provides many options for the backup process. These options control filenames, backup performance, and the size of backups.

Options that control filenames are handled with FORMAT and TAG parameters with the BACKUP command. The RATE option limits backup I/O bandwidth usage on a computer. This limits RMAN from consuming all of a server's resources during backup operations. The DURATION option determines the maximum time a backup can process before being terminated. When backups exceed the DURATION option, the backups stop and are marked unusable.The last options impact the file sizes of backup sets and backup pieces. The options that control sizes are the MAXSETSIZE and MAXPIECESIZE. These options limit the size of backup sets and backup pieces.

Let's look at the options that control RMAN filenames, which are FORMAT and TAG options. The *FORMAT option* has many variables but the default format is %U. The default %U FORMAT variables are handled differently for the different types of files in an image copy. Table 2.2 lists some of the FORMAT options available.

TABLE 2.2 *FORMAT* options

Option	Description
%a	Specifies the activation ID of the database
%c	Specifies the copy number of the backup piece within a set of duplexed backup pieces
%d	Specifies the name of the database
%D	Specifies the current day of the month from the Gregorian calendar
%e	Specifies the archived log sequence number
%f	Specifies the absolute file number
%F	Combines the database ID (DBID), day, month, year, and sequence into a unique and repeatable generated name
%h	Specifies the archived redo log thread number
%I	Specifies the DBID
%M	Specifies the month in the Gregorian calendar in *MM* format
%N	Specifies the tablespace name
%n	Specifies the name of the database, padded on the right with *n* characters to a total length of eight characters
%p	Specifies the piece number within the backup set
%s	Specifies the backup set number
%t	Specifies the backup set timestamp
%T	Specifies the year, month, and day in the Gregorian calendar
%u	Specifies an eight-character name constituted by compressed representations of the backup set or image copy number
%U	Specifies a system-generated unique filename (this is the default setting)

The full set of FORMAT variables or specifications is described in Oracle Database Recovery Manager Reference 10*g*, Release 1 (10.1), part number B10770-02.

Let's look at examples of how to use the FORMAT option with backup sets and image copies:

```
RMAN> backup tablespace users format='user_bs_%d%p%s';


RMAN> backup as copy tablespace users format=
➥'C:\oracle\backups\ora101c\users_%d%p%s';
```

The *TAG option* is similar to the FORMAT option, but it is a user-specified string value. The TAG option can be used with image copies and backup sets. Let's look at an example of the TAG option:

```
RMAN> backup database tag weekly_backup;
```

The *RATE option* is designed to limit RMAN from using excessive system resources during backup and restore operations. The RATE option can be set with the CONFIGURE settings. Let's set the RATE option to read only 5MB per second:

```
RMAN> CONFIGURE CHANNEL DEVICE TYPE disk RATE 5M;
```

The MAXSETSIZE and MAXPIECESIZE parameters control the size of the backup sets and backup pieces. Setting the MAXSETSIZE parameter allows you to control the amount of files per backup set and can make RMAN create additional backup sets. This can have benefits in recovery options because you can recover multiple backup sets in parallel on different channels.

The MAXPIECESIZE parameter limits the size of a backup piece. By default, the RMAN utility will put the entire contents of a backup set into one backup piece, regardless of the size of the backup set. This parameter can be valuable for media managers that have size limitations.

For instance, if you have limitations of 2GB because of your media manager or operating system, the MAXPIECESIZE parameter can limit the size to 2GB, which will not violate the media management limitations. This will cause datafiles that are larger than 2GB to be split into backup pieces of 2GB.

Let's see how to set the MAXSETSIZE and MAXPIECESIZE parameters. The MAXSETSIZE can be used in both the CONFIGURE parameters and BACKUP command:

```
RMAN> configure channel device type disk maxsetsize=10G;
RMAN> backup database maxsetsize=10G;


RMAN> configure channel device type disk maxpiecesize = 2G;
```

Caution must be taken when using the `MAXSETSIZE` parameter. If the datafile being backed up is larger than the `MAXSETSIZE` parameter, the backup will fail.

Enabling and Disabling Block Change Tracking

Block change tracking is a new capability in Oracle 10*g*. The block change tracking process records the blocks modified since the last backup and stores them in a *block change tracking file*. RMAN uses this file to determine the blocks that were backed up in an incremental backup. This improves performance because RMAN doesn't have to scan the whole datafile during the backup.

In prior versions, RMAN had to scan the entire datafile. This wasn't significant on smaller databases, but larger databases took considerable time to back up, even if there were no significant block changes since the last backup. This change was a big improvement for large databases. The backup process is initiated with RMAN querying the block change tracking file to determine the changed blocks. Next, RMAN backs up only the changed blocks and skips the unchanged blocks. This reduces the amount of blocks required in backup to the amount of changes. See Figure 2.2 for more details.

FIGURE 2.2 Block change tracking

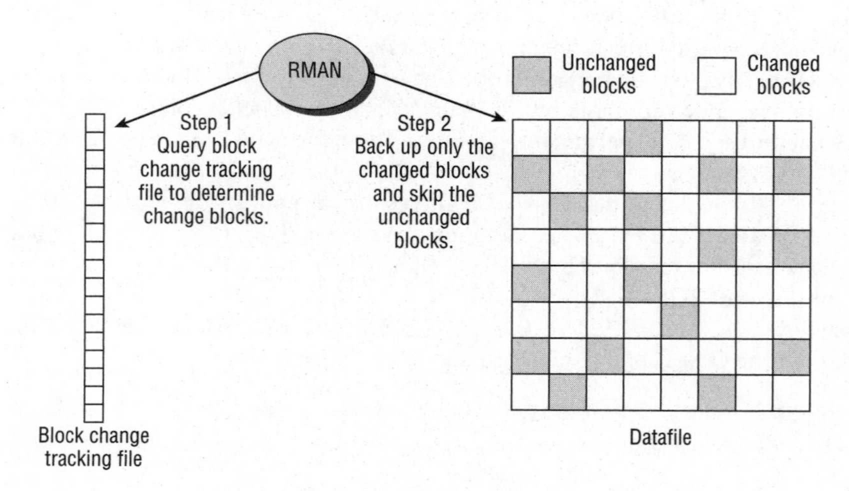

Block change tracking is enabled and disabled with a SQL command. By default, block change tracking is disabled. Block change tracking status can be verified by accessing a dynamic view V$BLOCK_CHANGE_TRACKING. Let's walk through these commands.

To enable block change tracking, take these steps:

```
C:\Documents and Settings>sqlplus /nolog
SQL*Plus: Release 10.1.0.2.0 - Production on Sun Jun 6 12:32:30 2004
Copyright (c) 1982, 2004, Oracle.  All rights reserved.
SQL> connect / as sysdba
Connected.

SQL> alter database enable block change tracking using
  2  file 'C:\oracle\block_track\ora101c_block_track.log';
Database altered.
SQL>
```

There is a new background process responsible for writing data to the block change tracking file, which is called the block change writer CTRW.

To verify the status of block change tracking, use this SELECT command:

```
SQL> select filename,status,bytes from v$block_change_tracking;
FILENAME
-----------------------------------------------------------------------

STATUS          BYTES
---------- ----------
C:\ORACLE\BLOCK_TRACK\ORA101C_BLOCK_TRACK.LOG
ENABLED      11599872
SQL>
```

To disable block change tracking, enter this command:

```
SQL> alter database disable block change tracking;
Database altered.
SQL>
```

Managing Backups with Enterprise Manager

Managing backup can be configured using Enterprise Manager (EM). As stated in Chapter 1, "Configuring Recovery Manager," EM is a web-based console that allows most DBA activities to be performed from a GUI screen instead of from the typical command-line interface (CLI).

In the examples in this book, you have installed Database Control opposed to Grid Control, which is an additional software component to support 10*g* Grid Control options.

The following steps demonstrate how to access EM Database Control. Once in the web application, you will see the screens that are capable of modifying managing backups. Let's look at the EM Database Control screens that allow the management of RMAN backups:

1. First, enter **`http://hostname.domain:5500/em`** in the web browser. The hostname is the name of the server or computer that you are running EM on. In this example, the hostname is `dstuns-xp`. The domain is the network domain that you have EM installed on. The domain value will vary depending on the network that you are running EM on. This will take you to the EM Database Control home page, where you can find the following login screen. At this point, enter the username SYS and SYS accounts passwords and connect as `SYSDBA`.

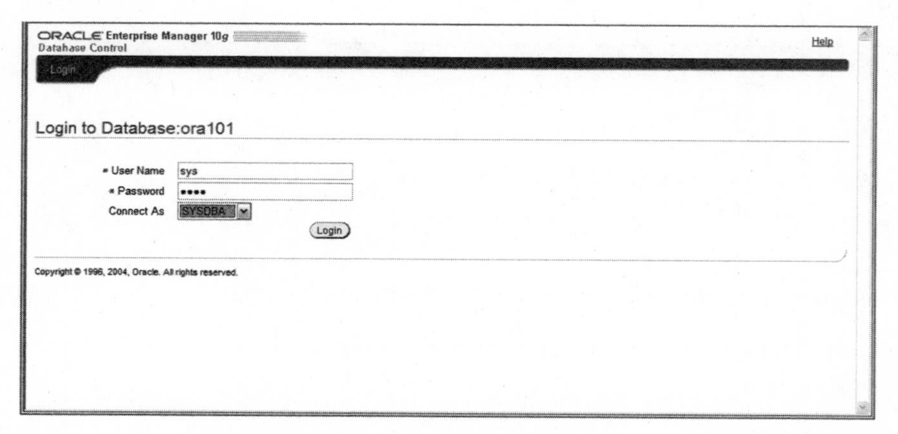

2. After you log in, the EM Database Control home page appears. (Notice that we saved this as two screens because of the size.) Choose the Maintenance tab to navigate to the maintenance screens that contain the screens that allow configuration modifications.

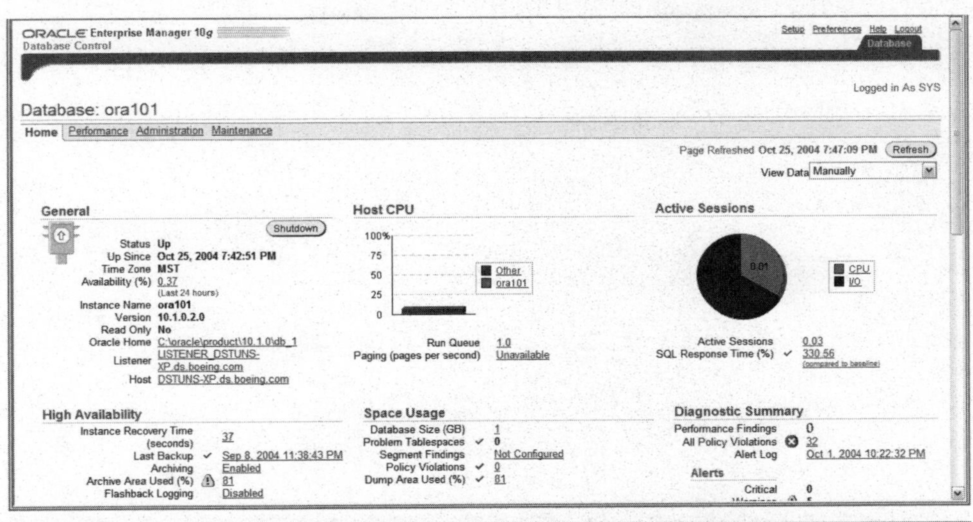

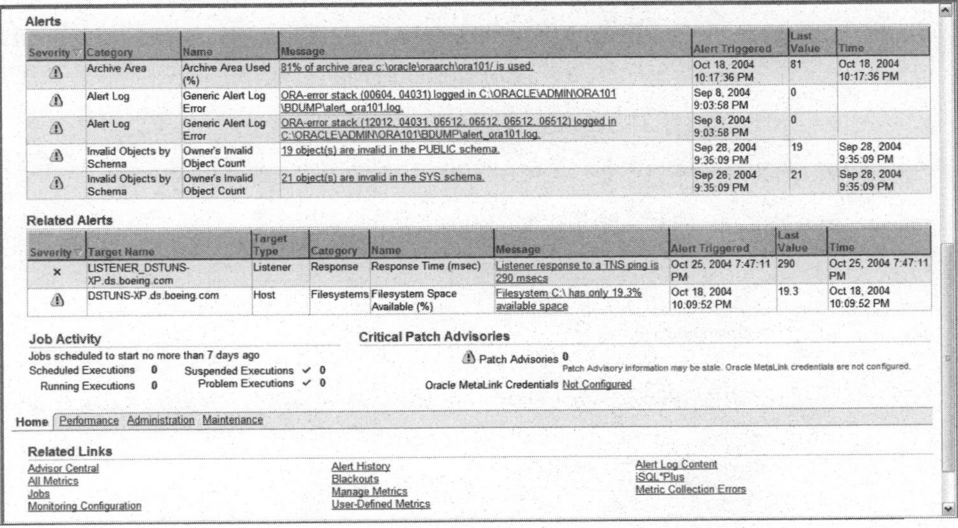

3. On the Maintenance screen, in the Backup/Recovery section, click the Manage Current Backups link, which will navigate to the Manage Current Backups screen available in EM Database Control.

4. On the Backup Set tab, notice four buttons: Catalog Additional Files, Crosscheck All, Delete All Obsolete, and Delete All Expired. These are the backup management options with EM.

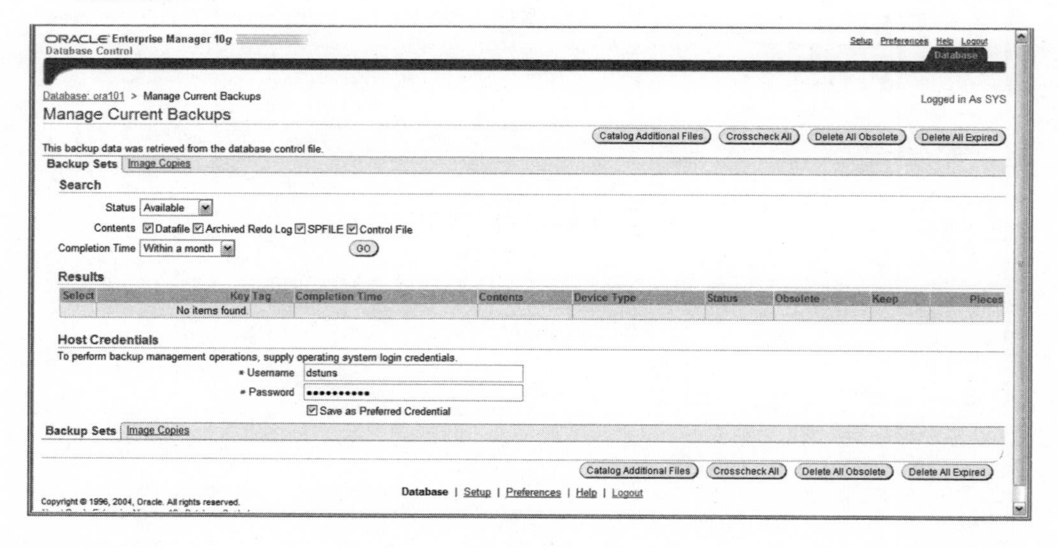

It is important to know that the Windows Administrator account or an account with the same privileges should be used in the Host Credentials section of the Manage Current Backups screen for the Windows environment. In a Unix environment, the Oracle user or similar privileged account should be used. This is because the EM Database Control web applications essentially host out to the operating system to execute these commands with the RMAN command-line interface.

Monitoring RMAN Backups

Monitoring actual sessions during RMAN backups or recoveries can be performed utilizing RMAN dynamic views. There are a few dynamic views that provide valuable information not provided in the general RMAN reporting features of the LIST, REPORT, and SHOW commands. These dynamic views are accessed through SQL*Plus as any database table or view would be. The RMAN dynamic views listed in Table 2.3 are stored in the target database.

TABLE 2.3 RMAN Dynamic Views

Dynamic View	Description
V$RMAN_OUTPUT	Displays messages reported by an RMAN job in progress.
V$RMAN_STATUS	Displays the success or failure of all completed RMAN jobs.
V$PROCESS	Shows currently active processes.
V$RECOVER_FILE	Shows the datafiles that require recovery.
V$SESSION	Shows active sessions.
V$SESSION_LONGOPS	Shows progress reports on RMAN backups and restores.
V$SESSION_WAIT	Shows the events causing sessions to wait.
V$BACKUP_SYNC_IO	Shows the rows when the I/O is synchronous to the backup process.
V$BACKUP_ASYNC_IO	Shows the rows when the I/O is asynchronous to the backup process.

It is important to know some information about the database that you will be using the RMAN or recovery catalog dynamic view on. Most of the recovery catalog views contain the columns DB_KEY and DBINC_KEY. It is important to get the target database value for these columns so that you can quickly specify the incarnation of the target database. This information is required to access the recovery catalog views.

Let's see how to get these values from querying some recovery catalog views:

1. First, query from the target database ora101c and get the database identifier (DBID) value:

```
SQL> connect system/manager@ora101c
Connected.
SQL>
SQL> select dbid from v$database;

      DBID
----------
1736563848

SQL>
```

2. Next, from the recovery catalog database, you may determine the DB_KEY and the current incarnation of the target database:

```
SQL> connect rman_user/rman_user@ora101rc
Connected.
SQL>
SQL> select db_key from rc_database where dbid = 1736563848;
```

If there are multiple incarnations of the target database, the most current incarnation can be identified by the following query:

```
SQL> select bs_key, backup_type, completion_time
  1 from rc_database_incarnation a, rc_backup_set b
  2 where a.db_key = b.db_key
  3 and a.db_key = b.db_key
  4 and a.current_incarnation = 'YES';
```

An incarnation is a unique backup of the target database that is identified by a unique DB_KEY value. A new incarnation is generated each time a database is opened with RESETLOGS or BACKUP CONTROLFILE, which essentially means an incomplete recovery. Recovery catalog views provide most the information about the target databases. All the recovery catalog views are stored in the recovery catalog database.

Using *LIST* Commands

The *LIST commands* are used to query the RMAN repository and get the data regarding the BACKUP command, COPY command and database incarnations. A *database incarnation* is a separate version of a physical database. The output of the LIST command displays the files that the CHANGE, CROSSCHECK, and DELETE commands have used.

The LIST command displays backup information by using the BY BACKUP and BY FILE options. There are also SUMMARY and VERBOSE options to condense or expand the output. Let's look at the LIST BACKUPSET with the BY BACKUP and SUMMARY options:

```
RMAN> LIST BACKUPSET BY BACKUP SUMMARY;

List of Backups
===============
Key     TY LV S Device Type Completion Time #Pieces #Copies Compressed Tag
------- -- -- - ----------- --------------- ------- ------- ---------- ---
1       B  F  A DISK        31-MAY-04       1       1       NO         TAG20031
➥T213343
2       B  F  A DISK        31-MAY-04       1       1       NO         TAG200
➥31T213343
3       B  F  A DISK        31-MAY-04       1       1       NO         TAG200
➥31T214614
4       B  F  A DISK        31-MAY-04       1       1       NO         TAG200
➥31T214614

RMAN>
```

As mentioned previously, this is a listing of backup sets by backup. In other words, for each backup, this shows the backup set that is associated with the backup. This can help identify which backup sets were completed with each backup or if you needed multiple backup sets with a backup.

You can also run the LIST command with BACKUP BY FILE. This will create a slightly different listing that shows backup sets by file. This use of the LIST command tends to be verbose. Let's take a look at this usage of the LIST command:

```
RMAN> list backupset by file;

List of Datafile Backups
========================
```

```
File Key     TY LV S Ckp SCN    Ckp Time  #Pieces #Copies Compressed Tag
---- ------- -  -- - ---------- --------- ------- ------- ---------- ---
1    2       B  F  A 609403     11-SEP-04 1       1       YES
➥TAG20040911T120548
2    2       B  F  A 609403     11-SEP-04 1       1       YES
➥TAG20040911T120548
3    2       B  F  A 609403     11-SEP-04 1       1       YES
➥TAG20040911T120548
4    2       B  F  A 609403     11-SEP-04 1       1       YES
➥TAG20040911T120548
5    2       B  F  A 609403     11-SEP-04 1       1       YES
➥TAG20040911T120548
6    2       B  F  A 609403     11-SEP-04 1       1       YES
➥TAG20040911T120548

List of Archived Log Backups
============================

Thrd Seq     Low SCN    Low Time  BS Key  S #Pieces #Copies Compressed Tag
---- ------- ---------- --------- ------- - ------- ------- ---------- ---
1    1       567536     06-SEP-04 3       A 1       1       YES
➥TAG20040911T120745
1    2       576049     06-SEP-04 3       A 1       1       YES
➥TAG20040911T120745
1    3       578090     06-SEP-04 3       A 1       1       YES
➥TAG20040911T120745
1    4       586421     07-SEP-04 3       A 1       1       YES
➥TAG20040911T120745
1    5       607356     07-SEP-04 3       A 1       1       YES
➥TAG20040911T120745

List of Controlfile Backups
===========================

CF Ckp SCN Ckp Time  BS Key  S #Pieces #Copies Compressed Tag
---------- --------- ------- - ------- ------- ---------- ---
647891     12-SEP-04 6       A 1       1       NO         TAG20040912T090747
609734     11-SEP-04 5       A 1       1       NO         TAG20040911T124220
```

```
609548     11-SEP-04 4     A 1     1     NO     TAG20040911T120813
567748     06-SEP-04 1     A 1     1     NO     TAG20040906T184954

RMAN>
```

As you can see, the LIST BACKUP BY FILE command separates the output into different physical database file categories. The LIST output is separated by datafiles, archive logs, and control files.

You can also list backups by querying V$BACKUP_FILES and RC_BACKUP_FILES. These dynamic views have the same information as supplied in the LIST and REPORT commands, which is discussed next.

Using *REPORT* Commands

The *REPORT commands* are used to query RMAN repository and get the data regarding which files need a backup, unneeded backups, database physical schema, and whether or not unrecoverable operations were performed on files. The output of the REPORT commands will generate more detailed information from the RMAN repository.

The RMAN repository must synchronize with the control file. In addition, the CHANGE, UNCATALOG, and CROSSCHECK commands should have been recently executed for the report to be completely accurate.

The REPORT command options include REPORT NEED BACKUP, REPORT OBSOLETE, and REPORT SCHEMA. Let's look at the REPORT OBSOLETE example. This report will display backups that are no longer needed based on the existing retention policy:

```
RMAN> REPORT OBSOLETE;

RMAN retention policy will be applied to the command
RMAN retention policy is set to recovery window of 30 days
Report of obsolete backups and copies
Type                 Key    Completion Time    Filename/Handle
-------------------- ------ ------------------ --------------------
Backup Set           1      31-MAY-04
  Backup Piece       1      31-MAY-04          C:\ORACLE\FLASH_RECOVERY_AREA\ORA
```

```
101C\%REC_AREA_2_1.BAK
Backup Set           2       31-MAY-04
  Backup Piece       2       31-MAY-04           C:\ORACLE\FLASH_RECOVERY_AREA\ORA
101C\%REC_AREA_3_1.BAK
Backup Set           3       31-MAY-04
  Backup Piece       3       31-MAY-04           C:\ORACLE\FLASH_RECOVERY_AREA\ORA
101C\%REC_AREA_4_1.BAK
Backup Set           4       31-MAY-04
  Backup Piece       4       31-MAY-04           C:\ORACLE\FLASH_RECOVERY_AREA\ORA
101C\%REC_AREA_5_1.BAK
Backup Set           5       31-MAY-04
  Backup Piece       5       31-MAY-04           C:\ORACLE\FLASH_RECOVERY_AREA\ORA
101C\%REC_AREA_6_1.BAK

RMAN>
```

Let's also look at displaying the database structure with the REPORT SCHEMA command. This will display the physical structure of the database (the physical schema is the actual location of the datafiles of the Oracle database):

```
RMAN> REPORT SCHEMA;

Report of database schema
File K-bytes    Tablespace           RB segs Datafile Name
---- ---------- -------------------- ------- -------------------
1        460800 SYSTEM               ***     C:\ORACLE\ORADATA\ORA101C\
  ➥SYSTEM01.DBF
2         25600 UNDOTBS1             ***     C:\ORACLE\ORADATA\ORA101C\
  ➥UNDOTBS01.DBF
3        245760 SYSAUX               ***     C:\ORACLE\ORADATA\ORA101C\
  ➥SYSAUX01.DBF
4          5120 USERS                ***     C:\ORACLE\ORADATA\ORA101C\
  ➥USERS01.DBF
5        153600 EXAMPLE              ***     C:\ORACLE\ORADATA\ORA101C\
  ➥EXAMPLE01.DBF

RMAN>
```

Working Examples Using RMAN

In the following sections, you will perform some common and practical examples that you may encounter in your daily routine. You will perform certain types of backups such as backing up the archived redo logs and using the image copy to back up an entire database.

You will also learn how to do certain tasks that are common in daily operations such as enabling ARCHIVELOG mode and scheduling a backup job in RMAN.

Enabling *ARCHIVELOG* Mode

Enabling ARCHIVELOG mode is a must-know process that is essential to managing an Oracle database. Enabling ARCHIVELOG mode is necessary for creating online backups and performing certain types of database recovery.

ARCHIVELOG mode allows backups to a point-in-time in the future and complete backups from media failure using online and offline backups. Without ARCHIVELOG mode enabled, the database cannot be rolled forward from the backup time of the database backup to the point of failure.

Let's see how to enable ARCHIVELOG mode:

1. Set LOG_ARCHIVE_START to TRUE in the `init.ora` file or in Oracle 9*i* or greater SPFILE by using the ALTER SYSTEM SET command in SQL*Plus:

```
LOG_ARCHIVE_START=TRUE

SQL> alter system set log_archive_start=true scope=spfile;
```

2. The `init.ora` or SPFILE parameters are used to specify the location and name of the ARCHIVELOG files. The LOG_ARCHIVE_DEST and LOG_ARCHIVE_FORMAT are just examples:

```
LOG_ARCHIVE_DEST=/d01/arch/ora101c
LOG_ARCHIVE_FORMAT= arch%s.arc
```

3. The database needs to be restarted in NOMOUNT mode, and then ARCHIVELOG mode needs to be enabled.

```
C:\Documents and Settings\dstuns>sqlplus  /nolog

SQL*Plus: Release 10.1.0.2.0 - Production on Mon Aug 2 22:33:01 2004

Copyright (c) 1982, 2004, Oracle.  All rights reserved.
```

```
SQL> connect / as sysdba
SQL> startup nomount
SQL> alter database archivelog;
```

4. Next the database must be opened:

```
SQL> alter database open;
```

At this point, the ARCHIVELOG mode is now enabled.

Using RMAN to Back Up Archived Redo Logs

Another important part of a complete database is including the archive logs. The archive logs are required to roll forward from online backups. The section describes an example of a complete database backup that includes the archive logs.

The first activity performed is backing up the database. Next, all redo logs that can be archived are flushed to archive logs in the file system. Next, the archive logs are backed up in the RMAN catalog by using the command BACKUP (ARCHIVELOG ALL), which backs up all available archive logs in the file system.

```
run {
    allocate channel c1 type disk;
    allocate channel c2 type disk;
    backup database;
    backup (archivelog all);
     }
```

Scheduling a Backup Job

An important function for routine jobs is to schedule backup jobs to be run on a regular basis. Many third-party media managers provide GUI tools that include scheduling tools which interact with the operating system's scheduling features. It is possible to use the basic scheduling capabilities of the operating system to execute an RMAN command file.

A typical backup command RUN block can be stored in a file such as DAILY_BACKUP.RCV. This file can then be put into a command-line sequence, which is called by CRON in Unix or AT in the Windows operating systems.

Let's look at what the command-line sequence would look like:

```
rman target sys/sys_password@target_db catalog
➥.rman_user/rman_password@rman_catalog_db@daily_backup.rcv
```

In this example, the RMAN utility is called with the target database SYS user and SYS password, followed by the target database SQL*Net service identifier, which in this case is called

TARGET_DB. Next, the CATALOG code word is specified with the RMAN catalog owner—which in this case is RMAN_USER—and the password of RMAN_PASSWORD. Then, the SQL*Net service identifier for the catalog database is specified, which in this case is called RMAN_CATALOG_DB. Lastly, the script file daily_backup.rcv is called out.

Real World Scenario

How to Clean Up From Manually Deleting Archive Logs

Let's look at an event that can occur in everyday database operations. A database is being rolled out to production soon, and most of the development staff is focused on meeting the delivery schedule. The database is in ARCHIVELOG mode, but the daily rigors of backup and recovery have not been enforced in development as stringently as in a production environment. The file system with the archive logs fills up before a backup is performed. The developers are unable to use the database because no log activity can be generated, so work comes to a halt. Finally, someone hastily deletes some of the archive logs to free up space.

The DBA now gets around to backing up the database with RMAN, but errors are generated because not all the archive logs are available. The problem is that the RMAN repository or the RMAN catalog knows the required archive logs that are needed since the last backup. RMAN will not allow you to back up the database without the complete set of archive logs.

What you need to do is reset the RMAN catalog or RMAN repository information to look at the existing archive logs only. This can be performed with RMAN command CHANGE ARCHIVELOG ALL CROSSCHECK. This command tells RMAN to use the available archive logs only and disregard the deleted ones. This information becomes the new baseline for this database. So, all future backups will not search for these deleted archive logs.

Summary

This chapter focused on how to use the RMAN product to perform backups. You learned the difference between the two backup methods available with RMAN: image copies and backup sets. You also learned how to create both image copies and backup sets with practical examples. This chapter also included detailed explanations of incremental and whole backups, along with examples.

In Oracle 10*g* RMAN, there have been significant improvements with each of these backup methods. Backup sets can be compressed, and they utilize block change tracking. You saw specific examples for each of these new features. This chapter provided a hands-on understanding of some of the fundamental RMAN concepts.

Exam Essentials

Know how to use Recovery Manager (RMAN). Understand how to use RMAN to perform the different types of commands and clauses. You should be able use the commands in `RUN` blocks and scripts.

Be able to use the RMAN *BACKUP* and *COPY* commands to create backup sets and image copies. Be aware of how to create both backup sets and image copies. Understand the differences of each of these backup methods. Know how to use compression for backup sets. Also make sure you understand how to use incremental and cumulative backups.

Know how to enable and disable block change tracking. Understand how to enable and disable block change tracking. Know how to use block change tracking after it has been enabled.

Know how to manage the backups and image copies taken with RMAN with the *LIST* and *REPORT* commands. Understand how to manage backups with the `LIST` command `BY BACKUP` and `BY FILE`. Understand how to manage backups with the `REPORT` command. Know how to identify obsolete backups.

Review Questions

1. How is block change tracking enabled?
   - **A.** With `ALTER DATABASE ENABLE BLOCK CHANGE TRACKING`
   - **B.** With `ALTER SYSTEM ENABLE BLOCK CHANGE TRACKING`
   - **C.** With a `INIT.ORA` parameter change
   - **D.** With a SPFILE parameter change
2. What type of backup is stored in a proprietary RMAN format?
   - **A.** Backup set
   - **B.** Image copy
   - **C.** Backup section
   - **D.** Backup group
3. What method is used to improve backup performance when creating backup sets?
   - **A.** Multicopy
   - **B.** Multiplecopy
   - **C.** Multiplex
   - **D.** Multiply
4. Which command creates an image copy?
   - **A.** `BACKUP AS COPY`
   - **B.** `BACKUP COPY`
   - **C.** `COPY AS BACKUP`
   - **D.** `COPY BACK`
5. Compressed backups work with which of the following commands?
   - **A.** `COPY AS BACKUP`
   - **B.** `BACKUP AS COPY`
   - **C.** `BACKUP`
   - **D.** `COPY`
6. What ratio are compressed backups sized to?
   - **A.** 30 percent
   - **B.** 40 percent
   - **C.** 70 percent
   - **D.** 20 percent

7. Which of the following best describes a full backup?
   - **A.** All datafiles of a database
   - **B.** All datafiles, archive logs, and control files
   - **C.** All datafiles and control files
   - **D.** All the used blocks in a datafile

8. Which type of backup backs up only data blocks modified since the most recent backup at the same level or lower?
   - **A.** Differential incremental backup
   - **B.** Different incremental backup
   - **C.** Cumulative backup
   - **D.** Cumulative incremental backup

9. Which type of backup must be performed first with an incremental backup?
   - **A.** Level 1
   - **B.** Level 0
   - **C.** Level 2
   - **D.** Level 3

10. Which backup option defines a user-defined name for a backup?
    - **A.** `FORMAT`
    - **B.** `NAME`
    - **C.** `TAG`
    - **D.** `FORMAT U%`

11. What action requires the `RESTORE` command?
    - **A.** Restoring a backup set
    - **B.** Restoring an image copy
    - **C.** Performing all RMAN recovery processes
    - **D.** All of the above

12. Which of the following most closely represents an image copy?
    - **A.** Unix `cp` command of a file
    - **B.** Bit-by-bit copy of a file
    - **C.** Windows `COPY` command of a file
    - **D.** All of the above

13. Which dynamic view displays the status of block change tracking?
    A. V$BLOCK_CHANGE
    B. V$BLOCK_CHANGE_TRACKING
    C. V$BLOCKCHANGE
    D. V$BLOCK_TRACKING
14. Which new Oracle 10*g* capability improves the backup efficency database of any size?
    A. Differential incremental backup
    B. Cumulative incremental backup
    C. Block change tracking
    D. Compressed backup
15. Where are RMAN dynamic views stored?
    A. Recovery catalog database
    B. Control file of the recovery catalog database
    C. Control file of the target database
    D. Target database
16. Which of the following can be used to monitor RMAN backups?
    A. LIST commands
    B. REPORT commands
    C. RMAN dynamic views
    D. All of the above
17. The LIST commands are best used to identify what about RMAN?
    A. How many times the database is restored
    B. Files impacted by the CHANGE, CROSSCHECK, and DELETE commands
    C. Only data in the recovery catalog
    D. All of the above
18. The REPORT command is best used to identify what about RMAN?
    A. Which files need a backup
    B. Unneeded backups
    C. Database physical schema
    D. If unrecoverable operations were performed on files
    E. All of the above

19. What should be done to generate accurate information from the REPORT command?
    A. Recently performed CHANGE command
    B. Recently performed UNCATALOG command
    C. Recently performed CROSSCHECK commands
    D. RMAN repository synchronized with the control file
    E. All of the above

20. Identify the methods used to schedule a backup job. (Choose all that apply.)
    A. A third-party GUI tool provided by the media management provider
    B. A file that is scheduled with the operating system scheduler
    C. Running the EM Maintenance utility
    D. Running RMAN from CLI

Answers to Review Questions

1. A. Block change tracking must be enabled with ALTER DATABASE ENABLE BLOCK CHANGE TRACKING. The physical location and name of the block change tracking file must be supplied.
2. A. The backup set is stored in a proprietary RMAN format, where only used blocks are backed up.
3. C. Multiplexing a backup is designed to improve the performance of the backup sets by copying multiple database files at the same time. Multiplexing can be used with image copies or backup sets.
4. A. The BACKUP AS COPY command is used to create an image copy backup.
5. C. Compressed backups work only with backup sets, not image copies. Thus compressed backups will work only with the BACKUP command.
6. D. Compressed backups compressed at a ratio of 5 to 1—20 percent—of the original size of a standard backup.
7. D. A full backup is best described by backing up all the used blocks in a datafile or any database file. A full backup can be taken on one database file.
8. A. A differential incremental backup only backs up blocks that have been modified since a backup at the same level or lower.
9. B. A level 0 backup is the first backup that is performed when implementing an incremental backup strategy. A level 0 backup copies all the used blocks as a baseline.
10. C. The TAG option is used to name a backup with a user-defined character string.
11. A. The RESTORE command is required only with a backup set recovery. This is because the backup set is stored in a RMAN proprietary format.
12. D. Image copies are similar to operating system copy commands. These equate to bit-by-bit copies of a file.
13. B. The V$BLOCK_CHANGE_TRACKING dynamic view shows the filename, status, and size of the block change tracking file.
14. C. Block change tracking improves the backup efficiency of large or small databases. With block change tracking, the backup time is proportional to the amount of changes that occurred in a database.
15. D. RMAN dynamic views are stored in the target database.
16. D. LIST, REPORT, and dynamic views all allow different types of monitoring of RMAN activities.
17. B. The LIST commands are used to determine files impacted by the CHANGE, CROSSCHECK, and DELETE commands.

18. E. The REPORT command is best used to identify which files need a backup, unneeded backups, database physical schema, and if unrecoverable operations were performed on files.

19. E. The REPORT command is accurate when the control and RMAN repository are synchronized, which can be performed by the CHANGE, UNCATALOG, and CROSSCHECK commands.

20. A, B. Third-party GUI tools provided from the media manager software and manually scripting a file incorporated with operating system scheduler are the two methods for scheduling a backup.

Recovering From Non-Critical Losses

ORACLE DATABASE 10*G*: ADMINISTRATION II EXAM OBJECTIVES COVERED IN THIS CHAPTER:

✓ **Recovering from Non-critical Losses**

- Recover temporary tablespaces.
- Recover a redo log group member.
- Recover index tablespaces.
- Recover read-only tablespaces.
- Recreate the password file.

Exam objectives are subject to change at any time without prior notice and at Oracle's sole discretion. Please visit Oracle's Training and Certification website (`http://www.oracle.com/education/certification/`) for the most current exam objectives listing.

This chapter provides a detailed explanation and examples of how to recover from non-critical losses. Non-critical losses are failure events that can be resolved without significantly impacting the operation of the database if performed properly. It is important to understand how to resolve these types of failures with minimal impact to the database operations. A DBA should be able to resolve non-critical losses quickly and leave the database in operational state throughout the recovery process.

In this chapter, you will walk through recovering a temporary tablespace, a redo log group member, an index tablespace, and a read-only tablespace. You will also re-create a password file to regain remote access to the database. You will see demonstrations and go through step-by-step examples performing each of these events and other related activities.

An Overview of Non-Critical Files

The recovery of non-critical files is an important matter that you should be familiar with so you can resolve them in an efficient manner. Non-critical files are essentially database files that do not have a critical impact on the operations of the database when they have been compromised. If recovery is performed properly, these files can be recovered or rebuilt in some cases with minimal impact to database operations.

Let's look at each of these non-critical database files specifically:

Temporary tablespaces *Temporary tablespaces* are non-critical database files that can be recovered without impacting the database operations. All database users need a temporary tablespace of some kind to perform database operations. Temporary tablespaces essentially provide the sorting operations. There are multiple types of temporary tablespaces that include local managed extents or tempfiles. You should know how to re-create a temporary tablespace if necessary. You should also know how to alter which tablespace is being used if necessary.

Redo log files Non-current *redo log files* members are also considered non-critical database files. However, the current redo log files can be critical during certain circumstances. The current and *non-current redo log file members* can be rebuilt with database commands so that database operations are not seriously impacted. A lost redo log group can be much more severe and doesn't fall into the category of a non-critical recovery.

Index tablespaces *Index tablespaces* fall in the non-critical database file category because often these tablespaces can be recovered without serious impact to database operations. Index tablespaces should only contain indexes, as the name implies. This means that the index tablespace can be re-created and the indexes can be rebuilt. Database performance will suffer during this period but the actual data is still available. If the tables are large, then performance slowdowns could prevent data access for normal operations and response times.

Indexes *Indexes* are also in the non-critical database file category because this database object can be rebuilt based on the tables. If the create index scripts are available and should be available, then these scripts can be run to rebuild a missing index.

Create index scripts should be kept current and readily available because they often need to be rebuilt to improve the performance of queries in routine database maintenance operations.

Read-only tablespaces *Read-only tablespaces* are by nature non-critical database files. These tablespaces are static or do not have data modifications like normal tablespaces. This allows recovery to be a fairly straightforward process under most circumstances. Typically, no redo log information needs to be applied to recover read-only tablespaces. All that is required is to restore the tablespace's associated datafile(s).

Password files Another type of non-critical database file is the *password file*. Password files contain the passwords for privileged administrative users such as SYSDBA and SYSOPER. This allows you to connect remotely to a database instance and perform database administrative functions. The password file can be deleted and re-created if necessary. It is important to know the contents of this file so that when the file is re-created, the accounts and passwords will be consistent.

These files, under certain situations, make up the non-critical database files of an Oracle database. They are important for the proper functioning of an Oracle database; if these files are not present, the database will not operate normally and may not start. However, with the proper understanding of how to recover or in some cases rebuild these files, you have the ability to make the impact of these losses non-critical.

The next sections walk you through the recovery or rebuild process of each of these objects.

Creating a New Temporary Tablespace

A temporary tablespace is responsible for various database sorting operations. A temporary tablespace is part of the physical database files, which the Oracle control file will expect to exist under normal operations. Because the temporary tablespace doesn't have any permanent objects stored within it, there is no change in the system change number (SCN) from the checkpoint process in the control file or file header. The database will continue to function normally, with the exception of creating temporary segments, which occurs when creating indexes or performing certain select statements. Because the temporary tablespace only has temporary data stored inside, this tablespace can be re-created and reassigned in the event of datafile loss.

For example, in a media failure such as a disk failure or controller failure, the temporary datafile could become unavailable. This would cause sorting operations such as creating indexes or select statements to fail. The remedy for this situation is to drop the tablespace—including its contents if they exist—which will remove the datafile and tablespace reference from the data dictionary. Then you simply create the temporary tablespace.

Real World Scenario

Before Shutdown, Always Check If the Backup Is Complete

RMAN backups called by media management vendors' software can be automated to the extent that your involvement as a DBA is minimal. This is sometimes executed and controlled by the backup coordinator, which may reside within the systems administrators group. When the backup terminates for some reason, it is often difficult for you to know the extent of a backup failure and why a backup has failed, unless good communication is set up, thus leaving the database partially in backup mode with some tablespaces and the associated datafiles active in backup. Furthermore, jobs could be incomplete and hanging in the recovery catalog.

What happens when the database goes down when a tablespace or all tablespaces are in is in backup mode? The datafile is not checkpointed so that it is consistent with the rest of the database. When the database is restarted, the datafile is marked as inconsistent and in need of recovery. This situation can come as an unwanted surprise when you are bouncing the database for some reason.

You can remedy this situation without recovery by issuing the `ALTER DATAFILE '`*`datafile name`*`' END BACKUP` command to fix this tablespace or by issuing the new Oracle 10*g* command `ALTER DATABASE END BACKUP` for all tablespaces at the same time. However, this situation can be avoided by checking the `V$BACKUP` table to validate that it is safe to shut down the database.

Let's see an example of creating a new temporary tablespace with the database up and running using a tempfile or locally managed extents:

```
SQL> create temporary tablespace temp2 tempfile
     ➥'C:\oracle\oradata\ora101t\temp2_01.dbf' size 100m
     ➥extent management local uniform size 128k;
```

You should use the `TEMPFILE` keyword and create the temporary tablespace as `TEMPORARY TABLESPACE` so that no permanent objects can be stored in the tablespace.

As you can see, being able to create a new temporary tablespace is an essential non-critical recovery task. Because there are no permanent objects in the temporary tablespace, you can easily re-create a new temporary tablespace. In the next sections, we will work with additional temporary tablespace issues. Specifically, you will learn how to deal with missing tempfiles and how to reassign the temporary tablespace.

Starting the Database with a Missing Tempfile

Starting a database with a missing tempfile is another non-critical recovery technique that you need to understand. A *tempfile* is a type of tablespace where management occurs locally or in the tablespace, as opposed to in the data dictionary. These types of tablespaces were first introduced in Oracle 8*i* and have significant improvements for sorting and space management. The tempfile can be used with all tablespaces as of Oracle9*i*. They are most commonly used with temporary tablespaces and are the default for the Database Configuration Assistant (DBCA) temporary tablespace creation.

The steps to start a database with a missing tempfile are fairly straightforward:

1. Start and mount the database if it is not already running:

```
C:\Documents and Settings\dstuns>sqlplus /nolog

SQL*Plus: Release 10.1.0.2.0 - Production on Sat Aug 21 19:08:48 2004

Copyright (c) 1982, 2004, Oracle.  All rights reserved.

SQL> connect / as sysdba
Connected.
SQL> startup mount
ORACLE instance started.

Total System Global Area   88080384 bytes
Fixed Size                   787588 bytes
Variable Size              78642044 bytes
Database Buffers            8388608 bytes
Redo Buffers                 262144 bytes
Database mounted.
SQL>
```

2. Next, drop the tablespace:

```
SQL> drop tablespace temp including contents;
```

3. Finally, re-create the temporary tablespace using the following command. In the Windows environment, use `C:\directory` to specify the file; in the Unix environment, use `/directory` to specify the file.

```
SQL> create temporary tablespace temp tempfile
     ➥'C:\oracle\oradata\ora101t\temp01.dbf' size 100m
     ➥extent management local uniform size 128k;

Tablespace created.
```

Altering the Default Temporary Tablespace for a Database

Another method for remedying the loss of a temporary tablespace is to modify the existing temporary tablespace to a new or different temporary tablespace. This can be accomplished by using the ALTER DATABASE DEFAULT TEMPORARY TABLESPACE command. This is a fairly straightforward process. First, there must be a temporary tablespace existing in the database. If not, you will need to create a temporary tablespace to switch as the default tablespace.

Let's walk through an example:

1. First, create a temporary tablespace if one doesn't exist:

```
SQL> create temporary tablespace temp2 tempfile
     ➥'C:\oracle\oradata\ora101t\temp2_01.dbf' size 100m
     ➥extent management local uniform size 128k;

Tablespace created.
```

2. Next, alter the default temporary tablespace to a different temporary tablespace using the following command:

```
SQL> alter database default temporary tablespace temp2;

Database altered.
```

You must have another temporary tablespace available. If you attempt to switch the default tablespace to a permanent tablespace, you will get an ORA-12904 default temporary tablespace cannot be altered to PERMENANT type error.

Re-creating Redo Log Files

Redo logs are important elements of the Oracle database physical structure. Redo logs contain all the transactions committed or uncommitted. An important standard for creating an Oracle database is to have *mirrored redo logs*, also referred to as *multiplexed* redo logs. Mirrored or multiplexed redo logs are multiple redo log members per redo log group.

If a redo log member is lost or deleted and the mirrored log member still exists, then the redo log member can be easily rebuilt. This is an example of a non-critical recovery. As long as one mirrored redo log is available, the Oracle database will continue to process archive logs until the switch to the next log file sequence.

Re-creating a redo log member is a fairly straightforward process. The command `ALTER DATABASE ADD LOGFILE MEMBER` will create a log file member if one has been lost or deleted.

Let's walk through an example of identifying and rebuilding a missing redo log file member:

1. First, identify that there is a missing redo log file member by looking at the trace files and alert log. The following is an excerpt from an alert log that shows that `REDO01.LOG` is missing:

```
ARC1: Evaluating archive   log 2 thread 1 sequence 24
Committing creation of archivelog
  'C:\ORACLE\ORAARCH\ORA101T\ARC00024_0527361115.001'
Sat Aug 21 22:37:31 2004
Errors in file
  c:\oracle\admin\ora101t\bdump\ora101t_lgwr_3464.trc:
ORA-00313: open failed for members of log group 1 of thread 1
ORA-00312: online log 1 thread 1:
  'C:\ORACLE\ORADATA\ORA101T\REDO01.LOG'
ORA-27041: unable to open file
OSD-04002: unable to open file
O/S-Error: (OS 2) The system cannot find the file specified.
ORA-27041: unable to open file
OSD-04002: unable to open file
O/S-Error: (OS 2) The system cannot find the file specified.

Sat Aug 21 22:37:31 2004
Errors in file
  c:\oracle\admin\ora101t\bdump\ora101t_lgwr_3464.trc:
ORA-00321: log 1 of thread 1, cannot update log file header
ORA-00312: online log 1 thread 1:
  'C:\ORACLE\ORADATA\ORA101T\REDO01.LOG'

Sat Aug 21 22:37:31 2004
Private_strands 7 at log switch
Sat Aug 21 22:37:31 2004
Errors in file
  c:\oracle\admin\ora101t\bdump\ora101t_lgwr_3464.trc:
ORA-00313: open failed for members of log group 1 of thread 1

Thread 1 advanced to log sequence 26
  Current log# 1 seq# 26 mem# 1:
    C:\ORACLE\ORADATA\ORA101T\REDO01_MIRROR.LOG
```

```
Sat Aug 21 22:37:31 2004
ARC1: Evaluating archive  log 3 thread 1 sequence 25
Committing creation of archivelog
  'C:\ORACLE\ORAARCH\ORA101T\ARC00025_0527361115.001'
```

2. Next, remove the REDO01.LOG redo log file from data dictionary. The REDO1.LOG cannot be the currently active redo log. It must be inactive.

```
SQL> alter database drop logfile member
     ➥'C:\ORACLE\ORADATA\ORA101T\REDO01.LOG';
```

3. Finally, re-create the missing REDO1.LOG redo log file by adding a new log called REDO1.LOG:

```
SQL> alter database add logfile member
     ➥'C:\ORACLE\ORADATA\ORA101T\REDO01.LOG' to group 1;
```

startup restrict

You should make sure that the database is in restrict mode if you do not have many redo logs, or the transaction volume could cause the redo log you are re-creating to cycle through to the current redo log. If the database is started in restrict mode, users will be restricted to administrative activities and the redo logs will not be heavily written to or advanced.

Recovering an Index Tablespace

Recovering the database with a missing index tablespace is another non-critical recovery technique that you need to understand. An index tablespace is a tablespace that should contain only indexes. Indexes are objects that can be created from the underlying database tables. Rebuild index scripts can be rerun to build the indexes in the index tablespace.

Let's walk through the process of recovering an index tablespace:

1. The first step is to start and mount the database if it is not already running:

```
C:\Documents and Settings\dstuns> sqlplus /nolog

SQL*Plus: Release 10.1.0.2.0 - Production on Sat Aug 21 19:08:48 2004

Copyright (c) 1982, 2004, Oracle.  All rights reserved.

SQL> connect / as sysdba
Connected.
SQL> startup mount
ORACLE instance started.
```

```
Total System Global Area   88080384 bytes
Fixed Size                   787588 bytes
Variable Size              78642044 bytes
Database Buffers            8388608 bytes
Redo Buffers                 262144 bytes
Database mounted.
SQL>
```

2. Next, drop the tablespace.

```
SQL> drop tablespace indexes including contents;
```

3. Finally, re-create the indexes tablespace.

```
SQL> create tablespace indexes
       ➥datafile 'C:\oracle\oradata\ora101t\index01.dbf' size 20m;

Tablespace created.
```

Re-creating Indexes

Re-creating indexes is required after rebuilding the index tablespace. The existing indexes will be gone because the tablespace was rebuilt from scratch. As long as you have the create index scripts, this is a non-critical recovery process.

It is very common to have copies of most of the indexes in your database to perform maintenance activities such as rebuilding a fragmented database for performance reasons. Rebuilding an index is a basic procedure.

Let's walk through rebuilding an index:

1. In this example, you have an index called `INDEX NAME OF_EXAMPLE_INDEX_PK.SQL`, which you are viewing through an operating system editor. This index is a primary key index, which is built with the `NOLOGGING` and `PARALLEL` options to improve the build time. The `NOLOGGING` option will not create redo information, so once the indexes are built, a backup should be performed shortly after the indexes are created:

```
CREATE  UNIQUE INDEX example_index_pk
 ON example_table
  ( column_one,
    column_two,
    column_three,
    column_four)
  PCTFREE    10
  INITRANS   2
  MAXTRANS   255
```

```
  TABLESPACE indexes
 STORAGE (
   INITIAL     1M
   NEXT        1M
   PCTINCREASE 0
   MINEXTENTS  1
   MAXEXTENTS  8192
   )
nologging
parallel (degree 4)
/
```

2. Now you can just run this create index script using the following command:

```
SQL> @create_example_index_pk
```

Rebuilding indexes can be a more difficult process if there is significant referential integrity in the database. You should discover the proper order or procedures to rebuild indexes in your database in the test or development database environment.

Recovering Read-Only Tablespaces

A read-only tablespace is a tablespace that contains static information. This means that in most cases, no media recovery is required. This type of read-only tablespace recovery is of a non-critical nature.

There are only a few times when media recovery is required with a read-only tablespace. The first is when the last backup of the read-only tablespace was taken when the tablespace was read-write and the tablespace was made read-only afterward. The second is when the tablespace was read-only when the last backup was taken, then was made read-write in between, and then was made read-only again. These two scenarios are really saying that the checkpoint process that updates the SCNs for the control file and file headers will need to be synchronized by the recovery process of applying log files. These two methods are the same as any other tablespace recovery. Read-only recovery is described in Table 3.1.

Because the most common method of read-only tablespace recovery is that no media recovery is needed, we will walk through an example of this approach. This is non-critical recovery method. Let's look at recovering a read-only tablespace in this manner.

TABLE 3.1 Read-Only Tablespace Recovery Scenarios

Read-Only Recovery Type	Description	Status
Read-only to read-only	Backup was taken read-only; no changes were made to the tablespace, and it was recovered to read-only.	Non-critical recovery.
Read-write to read-only	Backup was taken read-write, and the tablespace was recovered to read-only.	Critical recovery requires redo logs and the RECOVER command.
Read-only to read-write to read-only	Backup was taken read-only; the tablespace was modified read-write, and then recovered to read-only.	Critical recovery requires redo logs and the RECOVER command.

1. First, make the tablespace USERS read-only and force this statement to archive log by switching through the redo logs:

```
SQL> alter tablespace users read only;

Tablespace altered.

SQL> alter system switch logfile;

System altered.

SQL> alter system switch logfile;

System altered.

SQL> alter system switch logfile;

System altered.

SQL> alter system switch logfile;

System altered.
```

2. We are using a Windows environment for our example. If we were using Unix, the command is `cp` to copy the file. Next, shut down the database `ORA101T` and make a cold backup in the `C:\oracle\oradata\backup\ora101t` directory for restore purposes:

```
SQL> shutdown immediate
Database closed.
Database dismounted.
ORACLE instance shut down.

SQL> host
Microsoft Windows XP [Version 5.1.2600]
(C) Copyright 1985-2001 Microsoft Corp.

C:\Documents and Settings\dstuns> cd c:\oracle\oradata\backup\ora101t

c:\oracle\oradata\backup\ora101t> copy c:\oracle\oradata\ora101t\*
```

3. Again, we are using a Windows environment for our example. If we were using Unix, the command is `rm` to delete the file. Simulate a missing or lost `USERS` tablespace by deleting `users01.dbf`:

```
C:\oracle\oradata\backup\ora101t> cd ..\..\ora101t

C:\oracle\oradata\ora101t> delete users01.dbf
```

4. Start up the database to see the error:

```
SQL> startup
ORACLE instance started.

Total System Global Area   88080384 bytes
Fixed Size                   787588 bytes
Variable Size              78642044 bytes
Database Buffers            8388608 bytes
Redo Buffers                 262144 bytes
Database mounted.
ORA-01157: cannot identify/lock data file 4 - see DBWR trace file
ORA-01110: data file 4: 'C:\ORACLE\ORADATA\ORA101T\USERS01.DBF'
```

5. Shut down the database and do a restore of the `users01.dbf` read-only tablespaces datafile:

```
SQL> shutdown immediate
ORA-01109: database not open

Database dismounted.
```

```
ORACLE instance shut down.

SQL> host
Microsoft Windows XP [Version 5.1.2600]
(C) Copyright 1985-2001 Microsoft Corp.

C:\Documents and Settings\dstuns> cd c:\oracle\oradata\ora101t
C:\oracle\oradata\ora101t> copy c:\oracle\oradata\backup\ora101t\users01.dbf
➥users01.dbf

C:\oracle\oradata\ora101t> exit
```

6. Finally, start the database ORA101T without issue because the `user01.dbf` has been restored:

```
SQL> startup
ORACLE instance started.

Total System Global Area   88080384 bytes
Fixed Size                   787588 bytes
Variable Size              78642044 bytes
Database Buffers            8388608 bytes
Redo Buffers                 262144 bytes
Database mounted.
Database opened.
SQL>
```

As you can see, the USERS01.DBF datafile for the read-only tablespaces only needs to be restored. No recovery is required because there are no changes in the datafile. Essentially this means that the USERS01.DBF datafile's header does not change when database checkpointing updates SCN values in the normal read-write datafiles. So the USERS tablespace is static after it becomes read-only.

Re-creating the Password File

There are multiple methods for a database administrator to authenticate to an Oracle database. The standard method is to log in directly to the operating system of the server, connect directly to the database with *Inter-Process Control (IPC)*, and establish a local connection on the database, which does not need to use SQL*Net. This method requires the operating system's account to require the password for validation. Once in the secure operating system account, you can connect as SYSOPER or SYSDBA. *SYSOPER* has partial database administration privilege, which is good for operational support, and *SYSDBA* has full database administration privilege. In Unix, you would most likely be the Oracle user; and on Windows, you would be the administrator. The operating system account is local, which assures that the account is secure.

A second primary method is to connect remotely using SQL*Net and authenticate with a password file. This is how Enterprise Manager (EM) connects to the Oracle database. Remote connectivity requires a password file to be set up and configured to prevent unauthorized connections. In order to connect as SYSOPER or SYSDBA remotely, you need to know the defined password, which is created by the ORAPWD utility. Table 3.2 lists the ways that you can authenticate to the Oracle database.

TABLE 3.2 Administrative Authentication Methods

Connection Type	Connectivity Method	Authentication Method
Local	Local IPC connection	Operating system secure account
Remote	Remote SQL*Net connection	Oracle password file

The password file is required for all remote database administrative connections to an Oracle database using SYSOPER or SYSDBA. Re-creating a password file to allow connections of these types is another non-critical recovery scenario. Some key information must be known about the contents of the password files, information about the users who have remote password access through SYSDBA or SYSOPER. When this information is known, the password file can be quickly and easily re-created. Then remote access will be unaffected.

The ORAPWD executable is an Oracle utility that generates a password file for remote connections. ORAPWD should be run when the database is shut down. It is also best to run this utility in the directory this file needs to be located at. When using the ORAPWD, one should use the appropriate naming convention, which includes `orapw$ORACLE_SID`. The `$ORACLE_SID` reference is the name of the Oracle database. The file must be located in the `$ORACLE_HOME/dbs` directory in Unix and in `$ORACLE_HOME\database` in Windows. The `init.ora` file must also contain the `REMOTE_LOGIN_PASSWORDFILE` parameter, set to `SHARED` or `EXCLUSIVE`. This should already be set to either `SHARED` or `EXCLUSIVE`, so you likely won't need to do this step.

Let's walk through an example of rebuilding a password file:

1. First, shut down the database:

```
SQL> shutdown immediate
Database closed.
Database dismounted.
ORACLE instance shut down.
SQL> startup
```

2. Run the ORAPWD utility to build the password file in the `$ORACLE_HOME/dbs` directory in name convention `orapw$ORACLE_SID`. The `entries` option determines how many users can be stored in the password file:

```
orapwd file=orapwORA101T password=syspass entries=20
```

To see what users are utilizing the password file, keep a copy of the following query:

```
SQL> select * from v$pwfile_users;
USERNAME                       SYSDB SYSOP
------------------------------ ----- -----
SYS                            TRUE  TRUE
SQL>
```

Summary

In this chapter, you learned about non-critical recovery situations and methods. Non-critical losses are failures that do not impact database operations significantly or for a lengthy period of time. The key to resolving non-critical losses is to understand the correct methods of quickly recovering from the situation.

The non-critical database files that you need to recover are temporary tablespaces, redo log members, index tablespaces, indexes, read-only tablespaces, and password files. This chapter walked you through many examples using these types of database files.

In many cases, recovery is not needed—only rebuilding or altering an existing configuration. It is important to maintain the most current methods of recovering from these situations and save any required information such as scripts or query output. If this information is current and readily available, the non-critical loss can be resolved most efficiently.

Exam Essentials

Be aware of non-critical recovery situations. Make sure you are aware of the many situations that are considered a non-critical loss. Be aware of the six main areas of non-critical losses: temporary tablespaces, redo log members, index tablespaces, indexes, read-only tablespaces, and password files.

Understand non-critical recovery with temporary tablespaces. Know how to create a new temporary tablespace if needed. Know how to start the database with a missing tempfile. Understand how to alter the default temporary tablespace to a different tablespace.

Understand non-critical recovery with redo logs. Understand how to rebuild redo log members. Know how to identify that there is a missing redo log member from the alert log. Be aware of multiplexing or mirroring redo logs and why they are important.

Identify non-critical recovery with index tablespaces and contents. Know how to rebuild a missing index tablespace and the contents or indexes within the tablespace. Make sure to maintain scripts of the indexes so that these can be rebuilt quickly if necessary.

Understand non-critical recovery with read-only tablespaces. Be aware of how to recover a read-only tablespace. Understand the three different read-only tablespace scenarios that impact recovery.

Be aware of non-critical recovery with password files. Understand the two primary authentication methods for administrators. Know how to recover from the remote authentication method by rebuilding the password file.

Review Questions

1. Which of the following statements is true about non-critical losses?
   A. Non-critical losses require media recovery.
   B. Non-critical losses have a severe impact on database operations.
   C. Non-critical losses can be resolved quickly with little impact to database operations.
   D. Non-critical losses require the use of the `RECOVER` command.

2. Which of the following statements is true about temporary tablespaces?
   A. Temporary tablespaces most often contain some permanent objects.
   B. Temporary tablespaces are responsible for storing temporary or sort statements.
   C. Temporary tablespaces must be recovered with the `RECOVER` command.
   D. Temporary tablespaces cannot be managed locally.

3. Why is a missing tempfile considered a non-critical recovery situation?
   A. The tempfile is dictionary managed and can only contain some permanent objects.
   B. The tempfile is locally managed and can only contain some temporary objects.
   C. The tempfile is locally managed and can only contain temporary objects.
   D. The tempfile is dictionary managed and can only contain temporary objects.

4. How can you resolve a missing temporary tablespace quickly? (Choose all that apply.)
   A. Recover the tablespace immediately because restoring is not needed.
   B. Restore the tablespace from disk and not from tape.
   C. Run `CREATE TEMPORARY TABLESPACE` and then `ALTER DATABASE` to the new temporary tablespace.
   D. If a temporary tablespace exists, then run `ALTER DATABASE` to the existing temporary tablespace.

5. What must be done to recover a missing redo log file member?
   A. First perform a `ALTER DATABASE DROP LOGFILE MEMBER` *`filename`* and then `ALTER DATABASE ADD LOGFILE MEMBER` *`filename`* on the missing logfile member.
   B. Perform `ALTER DATABASE ADD LOGFILE MEMBER` *`filename`* on the missing logfile.
   C. Nothing is required if you have multiplexed redo logs.
   D. Nothing is required if you do not have multiplexed redo logs.

6. How would you know if you have lost a mirrored redo log member?
   A. The database would hang.
   B. The archive process would stop working.
   C. The alert log would display an error, and the database would hang.
   D. The alert log would display an error, and the database would process the archive logs.

7. What happens if the current or active online redo log group has a new member added?
   A. Nothing, the redo log member will be added.
   B. The redo log member will not be added because the log group is actively recording transactions.
   C. The redo log member will be added, but it will be out of sync until a log switch occurs.
   D. The redo log member will be added, but it will be empty.

8. What happens when you are recovering a temporary tablespace by switching to another available tablespace? (Choose all that apply.)
   A. The new temporary tablespace is made available if the tablespace is permanent.
   B. The new temporary tablespace is made available if the tablespace is temporary.
   C. You will receive an ORA-12904 error if the available tablespace is temporary.
   D. You will receive an ORA-12904 error if the available tablespace is permanent.

9. How can you rebuild the objects in the index tablespace most efficiently?
   A. Recover the index from tape.
   B. Rebuild the index with `LOGGING`.
   C. Rebuild the index with `NOLOGGING`.
   D. Rebuild the index in parallel with `NOLOGGING`.

10. What should be updated and readily accessible in case of a non-critical loss of a tablespace?
   A. Temporary segments
   B. `SELECT` statements using sorting
   C. Current index scripts
   D. Create table scripts

11. Which type of tablespace contains static data?
   A. Read-only tablespace
   B. Index tablespace
   C. Read-write tablespace
   D. Temporary tablespace

12. What is the result of starting an Oracle database with a missing read-only tablespace? (Choose two.)
   A. The database opens normally.
   B. The database only mounts.
   C. An `ORA-01157 cannot identify datafile halts the database from opening` error occurs.
   D. The database functions normally, and the read-only tablespace is static.

13. When connecting to an Oracle database locally to perform administrative functions, you are connecting with what access privilege?

    A. SQL*Net

    B. IPC

    C. SYSDBA

    D. SYSOPER

14. What is the proper way of creating a password supporting up to 10 users?

    A. `orapwd file=orapwORA101T password=syspass users=10`

    B. `orapwd file=orapwORA101T password=syspass entry=10`

    C. `orapwd file=orapwORA101T password=syspass entries=10`

    D. `orapass file=orapwORA101T password=syspass entries=10`

15. Which initialization parameter is required for remote access to the database?

    A. `REMOTE_LOGIN_PASSWORDFILE`

    B. `BREMOTE_LOGIN_PASSWORD_FILE`

    C. `REMOTE_PASSWORD_FILE`

    D. `REMOTE_LOGIN_FILE`

16. Which directory should the password file be stored in to function properly? (Choose all that apply.)

    A. `$ORACLE_HOME`

    B. `$ORACLE_HOME/dbs`

    C. `C:\$ORACLE_HOME\database`

    D. `$ORACLE_SID`

17. Before running the ORAPWD utility to generate a password file, what should be done?

    A. Start the database but make sure it isn't open.

    B. Start up the database.

    C. Start up the database in `MOUNT` mode.

    D. Shut down the database.

18. What do local connections to an Oracle database rely on for security and authentication of the user?

    A. Password file

    B. Database password

    C. Operating system password

    D. Listener password

19. The main reason that you need to restore and use the RECOVER command on a tablespace that was backed up read-write and converted to read-only is due to what? (Choose all that apply.)

A. The checkpointing process has changed the control file.

B. There have been changes to the tablespace.

C. The tablespace file header has been changed.

D. Read-only tablespaces require the RECOVER command.

20. Which situation is considered a non-critical loss to the database? (Choose all that apply.)

A. Loss of redo log group before archived

B. Loss of current or active redo member

C. Loss of archive log

D. Loss of current or active redo group

Answers to Review Questions

1. C. Non-critical losses have little impact on database operations if resolved properly.
2. B. Temporary tablespaces are responsible for storing temporary or sort segments. These are used in the sorting of select statements or in building indexes.
3. C. A missing tempfile can be re-created with the `create tablespace` command. Because the tempfile is locally managed and contains no permanent data, no restoring or recovering is needed. Therefore recovery can occur quickly with minimal impact to database operations.
4. C, D. A missing temporary tablespace can be quickly reassigned with the command `ALTER DATABASE` to an existing temporary tablespace if one is available. If one is not available, you will need to run `CREATE TEMPORARY TABLESPACE` and then perform the `ALTER DATABASE` command.
5. A. The missing redo log must first be dropped even though it doesn't exist physically in the file system. This removes the redo log metadata from the data dictionary. Next the log can be added back to database.
6. D. If your database has mirrored redo logs and a member is deleted, the database will function as normal. The error signaling that a log member has been deleted would be written to the alert log.
7. B. The redo log member will not be added to the current or active redo log group. Oracle will not allow this because transactions are actively being written to the redo log group.
8. B, C. You must use the `ALTER DATABASE DEFAULT TEMPORARY TABLESPACE` *`table name`* command on a temporary tablespace or you will receive an ORA-12904 error.
9. D. Rebuilding an index in parallel with `NOLOGGING` is the most efficient method of building an index to minimize the impact on database operations. You must be cautious not to use extensive server resources when you don't use the parallel rebuild option.
10. C. The index scripts must be current and stored locally so they can be accessed quickly and easily during an index tablespace rebuild.
11. A. The read-only tablespace contains only static or non-changing data.
12. B, C. The database will stop at the mount stage. This is due to the ORA-01157 error.
13. B. IPC is the method that the local administrative access uses to connect to the database.
14. C. The correct command to create a password file that supports 10 users is `orapwd file=orapwORA101T password=syspass entries=10`.
15. A. The initialization parameter required for remote access is `REMOTE_LOGIN_PASSWORDFILE`.
16. B, C. The `$ORACLE_HOME/dbs` is the Unix location for the password file, and `C:\$ORACLE_HOME\database` is the Windows location for the password file.
17. D. The database should be shut down before running the ORAPWD utility.

18. C. Local connections are secured by the operating system password logging on to an administrative account such as Oracle user in Unix and administrator in Windows.

19. A, B, C. The scenario of read-write to read-only tablespace requires the use of the RECOVER command, which will apply necessary redo changes to make the tablespace consistent with the control file. The checkpointing operation of Oracle will change the control file, and the header of the read-only tablespace will be modified, which equates to changes in the tablespace.

20. B, C. A non-critical loss should have limited impact on database operations. This means that incomplete recovery or media failure scenarios need to be performed. A loss of a redo group before archived will require incomplete recovery, which is the same as the loss of current or active redo log group. The current or active member or loss of archive will not significantly impact operations. A backup can be performed to eliminate the need for the archive log, and the database will function normally with the loss of a redo log member.

Database Recovery

ORACLE DATABASE 10*G*: ADMINISTRATION II EXAM OBJECTIVES COVERED IN THIS CHAPTER:

✓ **Database Recovery**

- Recover the control file.
- Explain reasons for incomplete recovery.
- Perform incomplete recovery using EM.
- Perform incomplete recovery using RMAN.
- Perform incomplete recovery using SQL.
- Perform database recovery following a RESETLOGS operation.

Exam objectives are subject to change at any time without prior notice and at Oracle's sole discretion. Please visit Oracle's Training and Certification website (`http://www.oracle.com/education/certification/`) for the most current exam objectives listing.

Recovering an Oracle Database 10*g* (Oracle 10*g*) can be performed in one of three ways: using traditional user-managed recovery procedures, Recovery Manager (RMAN), or Enterprise Manager (EM). As a DBA, you must have the ability to successfully recover your database to a normal state in many failure situations.

This chapter walks you through the steps for recovering the database in many situations. You will use the `RECOVER` command in different scenarios with user-managed recovery. The `RESTORE` and `RECOVER` commands will be utilized with RMAN to perform many different types of recovery. You will also look at new Oracle 10*g* features such as simplified `RESETLOGS` recovery, and you will use EM to perform an incomplete database recovery. We will include demonstrations and have step-by-step examples performing each of these events, as well as other related activities.

Understanding the Restore and Recovery Process

There are two main steps required to perform a database recovery: restoring and recovering. These are the same whether you perform a recovery using user-managed recovery procedures, Recovery Manager (RMAN), or Enterprise Manger (EM).

The restore process consists of copying the required physical files that are needed to begin the recovery of the database. If user-managed recovery is performed, the restore process will be a manual process that is based on operating systems commands or third-party tape management GUIs that help you retrieve the files from tape or disk and place the files in the appropriate locations. If using RMAN or EM to recover, this process will be performed by issuing the `RESTORE` command. The `RESTORE` command retrieves the required files from the backup media tape or disk and places the files in the appropriate location.

Once the files have been restored, the recovery process can begin. The recovery process is the process of taking a datafile and applying archived redo logs, which apply the changes that occurred in the database to the datafile.

Figure 4.1 shows the complete restore and recovery process. In this figure, a database backup was performed on August 1. Archive logs were generated from 101 through 322, at which point a database failure occurred on August 4. So the backup from August 1 was restored and archive logs 101 through 322 were applied to the backup to roll the backup forward to the point of the database failure.

FIGURE 4.1 The restore and recovery process

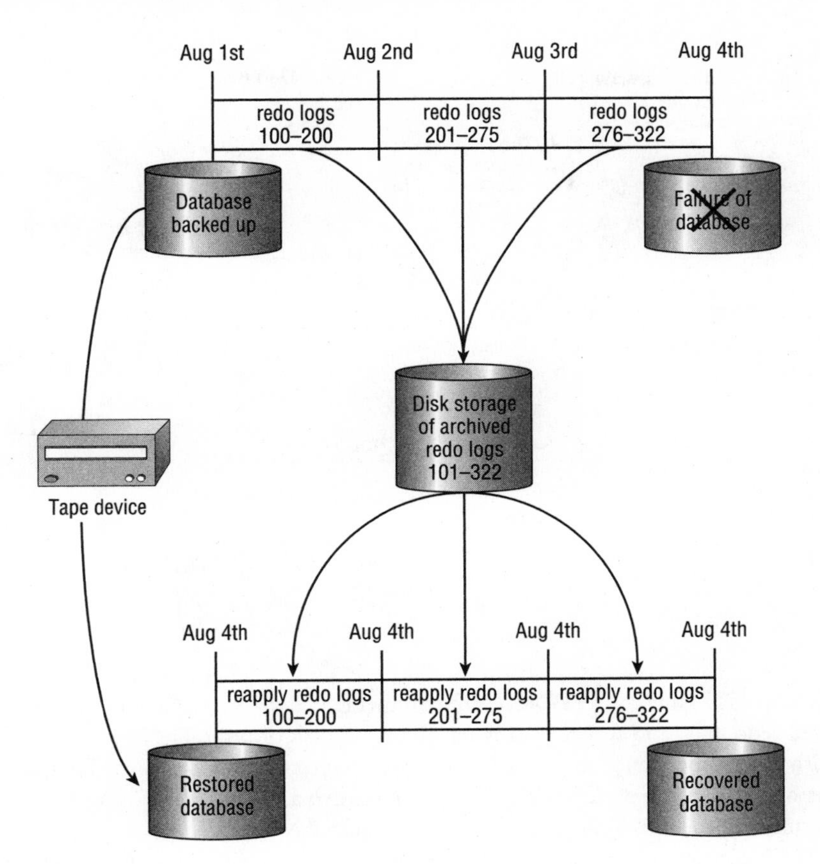

Server-Managed Recovery

Server-managed recovery consists of using the RMAN utility, which Oracle recommends for performing both backup and recovery processes. RMAN recovery is often termed server-manager recovery because the recovery is performed by a server process that initiates the recovery process. Figure 4.2 shows the server-managed recovery process.

FIGURE 4.2 Server-managed recovery

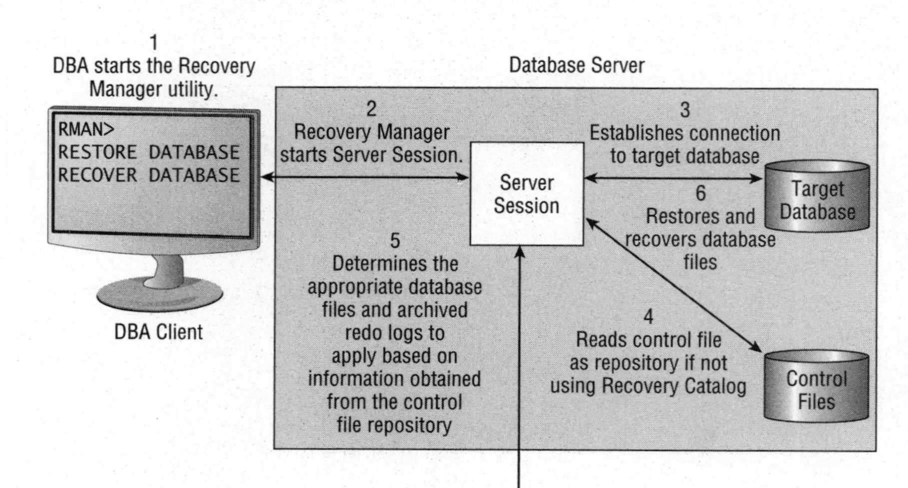

The first process is using the RESTORE command, which restores datafiles, tablespaces, control files, archived redo logs, and server parameter files from disk or tape. The RESTORE command is required with all backups made from the BACKUP command to create backups. The BACKUP command stores backups in a proprietary RMAN format called a BACKUPSET. If using the BACKUP AS COPY command, the RESTORE command is not required.

The RECOVER command is required with the BACKUP or BACKUP AS COPY command to roll the backup forward. The RECOVER command is responsible for applying the archived redo logs to the restored data files, if necessary, to apply the changes in the database that are not in the restored database files.

Let's walk through using the RESTORE and RECOVER command to restore a database from backup:

1. First, the target database must be in a mounted state to perform a full database recovery. The database can be open if you are performing online tablespace recovery or something less than full database recovery:

```
C:\Documents and Settings\dstuns> sqlplus /nolog

SQL*Plus: Release 10.1.0.2.0 - Production on Fri Sep 3 21:23:44 2004

Copyright (c) 1982, 2004, Oracle.  All rights reserved.
```

```
SQL> connect / as sysdba
Connected.
SQL> startup mount
ORACLE instance started.

Total System Global Area   88080384 bytes
Fixed Size                   787588 bytes
Variable Size              78642044 bytes
Database Buffers            8388608 bytes
Redo Buffers                 262144 bytes
Database mounted.
```

2. Next, run the RESTORE DATABASE and RECOVER DATABASE commands:

```
RMAN> run
2> {
3> allocate channel c1 type disk;
4> restore database;
5> recover database;
6> alter database open;
7> }

using target database controlfile instead of recovery catalog
allocated channel: c1
channel c1: sid=49 devtype=DISK

Starting restore at 03-SEP-04

channel c1: starting datafile backupset restore
channel c1: specifying datafile(s) to restore from backup set
restoring datafile 00001 to
  C:\ORACLE\ORADATA\ORA101T\SYSTEM01.DBF
restoring datafile 00002 to
  C:\ORACLE\ORADATA\ORA101T\UNDOTBS01.DBF
restoring datafile 00003 to
  C:\ORACLE\ORADATA\ORA101T\SYSAUX01.DBF
restoring datafile 00004 to C:\ORACLE\ORADATA\ORA101T\USERS01.DBF
restoring datafile 00005 to
  C:\ORACLE\ORADATA\ORA101T\EXAMPLE01.DBF
restoring datafile 00006 to C:\ORACLE\ORADATA\ORA101T\INDEX01.DBF
channel c1: restored backup piece 1
```

```
piece
  handle=C:\ORACLE\FLASH_RECOVERY_AREA\ORA101T\ORA101T\BACKUPSET
  \2004_09_03\01_MF_NNNDF_TAG20040903T213632_0MLKLMH2_.BKP
  tag=TAG20040903T213632
channel c1: restore complete
Finished restore at 03-SEP-04

Starting recover at 03-SEP-04

starting media recovery
media recovery complete

Finished recover at 03-SEP-04

database opened
released channel: c1

RMAN>
```

As you can see, the RESTORE command restored the datafiles from BACKUPSET. The RECOVER command then determines if any archived redo logs need to be applied. If so, these are applied to the database to make it consistent or to the point-in-time determined in the recovery process.

Archived redo logs are not usually restored with RMAN or server-managed recovery because RMAN automatically applies the backed-up logs for you. With user-managed recovery, you need to restore those to disk if there is no online copy of the archived redo logs available on disk.

User-Managed Recovery

User-managed recovery is the traditional recovery method where you directly manage the database files required to recover the database. You can use various operating system commands to restore the required files from tape or disk to perform the recovery process. In some cases, operating scripts are created to perform some of this functionality.

The basic procedure to perform user-managed recovery consists of first identifying the database files that need to be restored. Next, the database must be placed in the appropriate mode, either mounted or opened. Then the database files are restored from tape or disk to the appropriate location. Finally, the database can be recovered using the RECOVER command to apply archived redo logs to the database files if necessary.

Let's walk through an example of a user-managed recovery:

1. The first step is to identify the file that needs recovery. In this case, you will attempt to start the database with a missing datafile. The database cannot be started because of the missing datafile, so it should be shut down:

```
C:\Documents and Settings\dstuns> sqlplus /nolog

SQL*Plus: Release 10.1.0.2.0 - Production on Sat Sep 4 11:06:26 2004

Copyright (c) 1982, 2004, Oracle.  All rights reserved.

SQL> connect / as sysdba
Connected to an idle instance.
SQL> startup
ORACLE instance started.

Total System Global Area   88080384 bytes
Fixed Size                   787588 bytes
Variable Size              78642044 bytes
Database Buffers            8388608 bytes
Redo Buffers                 262144 bytes
Database mounted.
ORA-01157: cannot identify/lock data file 4 - see DBWR trace file
ORA-01110: data file 4: 'C:\ORACLE\ORADATA\ORA101T\USERS01.DBF'
```

2. Restore the USERS01.DBF file, which needs to be recovered. When the database is shut down, copy the datafile from the backup directory on the disk where the last database backup is stored:

```
C:\oracle\oradata\ora101t> copy ..\backup\ora101t\USERS01.DBF .
        1 file(s) copied.
C:\oracle\oradata\ora101t>
```

3. Then you can recover the database. The database must be mounted to perform a RECOVER DATABASE command. You are prompted to apply an archived redo log:

```
SQL> startup mount
ORACLE instance started.

Total System Global Area   88080384 bytes
Fixed Size                   787588 bytes
Variable Size              78642044 bytes
Database Buffers            8388608 bytes
Redo Buffers                 262144 bytes
```

```
Database mounted.
SQL>
SQL> recover database;
ORA-00279: change 489556 generated at 09/04/2004 10:39:15 needed for thread 1
ORA-00289: suggestion : C:\ORACLE\ORAARCH\ORA101T\ARC00050_0527361115.001
ORA-00280: change 489556 for thread 1 is in sequence #50


Specify log: {<RET>=suggested | filename | AUTO | CANCEL}
AUTO
ORA-00279: change 489835 generated at 09/04/2004 11:12:03 needed for thread 1
ORA-00289: suggestion :
  C:\ORACLE\ORAARCH\ORA101T\ARC00051_0527361115.001
ORA-00280: change 489835 for thread 1 is in sequence #51
ORA-00278: log file
  'C:\ORACLE\ORAARCH\ORA101T\ARC00050_0527361115.001' no
longer needed for this recovery


Log applied.
SQL>
```

4. Once the database has been recovered, it may be opened for normal use:

```
SQL> alter database open;

Database altered.

SQL>
```

As you can see, the restore process for user-managed recovery requires some user interaction. You must identify the missing file and determine the backup location. The file must be manually copied to the appropriate location. Then the RECOVER command can be executed. This method requires you to be directly involved with the activities in the recovery process. In contrast, RMAN does this work for you, which can simplify the effort.

Recovering Control Files

Control files are key database files required in the recovery process. Control files contain RMAN metadata information and the required repository information, if you're not using the Recovery Manager catalog. In Oracle 10*g*, RMAN has introduced control file autobackup, which allows you to configure RMAN to automatically back up the control file with other backups directly to the flash recovery area. This assures that you will have a control file for recovery purposes.

There are some methods of recovering the control file that you should be aware of. The first is using the control file autobackup to recover the control file. You should also be aware of how to create a new control file. The next sections walk you through each of these methods of recovering the control file.

Recovering a Control File Autobackup

Using the control file autobackup to recover the control file is a fairly straightforward process. You must first configure RMAN settings to perform a control file autobackup, which consists of enabling a configuration parameter. The *control file autobackup* configures all backups to automatically back up the control file. Once this has been configured, a RMAN backup should be performed. This backup will contain a control file that will be used for recovery operations. Then you can perform a recover control file operation. If you are not using the recovery catalog, you need to specify the database identifier (DBID) after connecting to the target database.

Let's walk through these steps without using the recovery catalog:

1. First, you must configure RMAN to perform a control file autobackup:

```
RMAN> connect target

connected to target database: ORA101T (DBID=2615281366)

RMAN> configure controlfile autobackup on;

using target database controlfile instead of recovery catalog
new RMAN configuration parameters:
CONFIGURE CONTROLFILE AUTOBACKUP ON;
new RMAN configuration parameters are successfully stored

RMAN>

RMAN> show all;

RMAN configuration parameters are:
CONFIGURE RETENTION POLICY TO REDUNDANCY 1; # default
CONFIGURE BACKUP OPTIMIZATION OFF; # default
CONFIGURE DEFAULT DEVICE TYPE TO DISK; # default
CONFIGURE CONTROLFILE AUTOBACKUP ON;
CONFIGURE CONTROLFILE AUTOBACKUP FORMAT FOR DEVICE TYPE DISK TO '%F'; #
  ➥default
```

```
CONFIGURE DEVICE TYPE DISK BACKUP TYPE TO COMPRESSED BACKUPSET PARALLELISM 1;
CONFIGURE DATAFILE BACKUP COPIES FOR DEVICE TYPE DISK TO 1; # default
CONFIGURE ARCHIVELOG BACKUP COPIES FOR DEVICE TYPE DISK TO 1; # default
CONFIGURE MAXSETSIZE TO UNLIMITED; # default
CONFIGURE ARCHIVELOG DELETION POLICY TO NONE; # default
CONFIGURE SNAPSHOT CONTROLFILE NAME TO 'C:\ORACLE\PRODUCT\10.1.0\
  ➥DB_1\DATABASE\S
NCFORA101T.ORA'; # default

RMAN>
```

2. Next, perform a backup with the control file autobackup enabled:

```
RMAN> run
2> {
3> backup database;
4> backup (archivelog all);
5> }

Starting backup at 04-SEP-04
allocated channel: ORA_DISK_1
channel ORA_DISK_1: sid=39 devtype=DISK
channel ORA_DISK_1: starting compressed full datafile backupset
channel ORA_DISK_1: specifying datafile(s) in backupset
input datafile fno=00001 name=C:\ORACLE\ORADATA\ORA101T\SYSTEM01.DBF
input datafile fno=00003 name=C:\ORACLE\ORADATA\ORA101T\SYSAUX01.DBF
input datafile fno=00005 name=C:\ORACLE\ORADATA\ORA101T\EXAMPLE01.DBF
input datafile fno=00002 name=C:\ORACLE\ORADATA\ORA101T\UNDOTBS01.DBF
input datafile fno=00006 name=C:\ORACLE\ORADATA\ORA101T\INDEX01.DBF
input datafile fno=00004 name=C:\ORACLE\ORADATA\ORA101T\USERS01.DBF
channel ORA_DISK_1: starting piece 1 at 04-SEP-04
channel ORA_DISK_1: finished piece 1 at 04-SEP-04
piece handle=
  ➥C:\ORACLE\FLASH_RECOVERY_AREA\ORA101T\ORA101T\BACKUPSET\
  ➥2004_09_04\01_MF_NNNDF_TAG20040904T124044_0MN6L0H4_.BKP comment=NONE
channel ORA_DISK_1: backup set complete, elapsed time: 00:01:27
Finished backup at 04-SEP-04

Starting backup at 04-SEP-04
current log archived
using channel ORA_DISK_1
channel ORA_DISK_1: starting compressed archive log backupset
```

```
channel ORA_DISK_1: specifying archive log(s) in backup set
input archive log thread=1 sequence=47 recid=41 stamp=535950026
input archive log thread=1 sequence=48 recid=42 stamp=535964440
input archive log thread=1 sequence=49 recid=43 stamp=535975236
input archive log thread=1 sequence=50 recid=44 stamp=535979525
input archive log thread=1 sequence=51 recid=45 stamp=535979527
input archive log thread=1 sequence=52 recid=46 stamp=535979533
input archive log thread=1 sequence=53 recid=47 stamp=535979589
input archive log thread=1 sequence=54 recid=48 stamp=535984936
channel ORA_DISK_1: starting piece 1 at 04-SEP-04
channel ORA_DISK_1: finished piece 1 at 04-SEP-04
piece handle=
  ➥C:\ORACLE\FLASH_RECOVERY_AREA\ORA101T\ORA101T\BACKUPSET\
  ➥2004_09_04\O1_MF_ANNNN_TAG20040904T124216_0MN6067V_.BKP comment=NONE
channel ORA_DISK_1: backup set complete, elapsed time: 00:00:43
Finished backup at 04-SEP-04

Starting Control File Autobackup at 04-SEP-04
piece handle=
  ➥C:\ORACLE\FLASH_RECOVERY_AREA\ORA101T\ORA101T\AUTOBACKUP\
  ➥2004_09_04\O1_MF_N_535984987_0MN6PG3P_.BKP comment=NONE
Finished Control File Autobackup at 04-SEP-04
```

3. Next, you simulate the missing control files by deleting all the control files. (The database will need to be shut down to perform this simulated failure.)

```
C:\oracle\oradata\ora101t\> delete *.ctl
```

4. Next, start the database in NOMOUNT mode, which is required because there is no control file to mount:

```
C:\Documents and Settings\dstuns> sqlplus /nolog

SQL*Plus: Release 10.1.0.2.0 - Production on Sat Sep 4 12:55:43 2004

Copyright (c) 1982, 2004, Oracle.  All rights reserved.

SQL> connect / as sysdba
Connected to an idle instance.
SQL> startup nomount
ORACLE instance started.

Total System Global Area   88080384 bytes
```

```
Fixed Size                    787588 bytes
Variable Size               78642044 bytes
Database Buffers             8388608 bytes
Redo Buffers                  262144 bytes
SQL>
```

5. Next, connect to RMAN and the target database. You will also need to specify the DBID to identify the database you are connecting to, because the control file contains this information and failure causes the control file to be unavailable. The DBID was obtained in step 1 from connecting to the target database before the failure was introduced:

```
RMAN> connect target /

connected to target database (not started)

RMAN> set dbid 2615281366;

executing command: SET DBID
```

6. Next, restore the control file from backup:

```
RMAN> restore controlfile from autobackup;

Starting restore at 04-SEP-04
using target database controlfile instead of recovery catalog
allocated channel: ORA_DISK_1
channel ORA_DISK_1: sid=49 devtype=DISK

recovery area destination: C:\oracle\flash_recovery_area\ora101t
database name (or lock name space) used for search: ORA101T
channel ORA_DISK_1: autobackup found in the recovery area
channel ORA_DISK_1: autobackup found:
  C:\ORACLE\FLASH_RECOVERY_AREA\ORA101T\ORA1
01T\AUTOBACKUP\2004_09_04\01_MF_N_535984987_0MN6PG3P_.BKP
channel ORA_DISK_1: controlfile restore from autobackup complete
output filename=C:\ORACLE\ORADATA\ORA101T\CONTROL01.CTL
output filename=C:\ORACLE\ORADATA\ORA101T\CONTROL02.CTL
output filename=C:\ORACLE\ORADATA\ORA101T\CONTROL03.CTL
Finished restore at 04-SEP-04

RMAN>
```

7. Next, mount the database and begin to recover the database:

```
RMAN> alter database mount;

database mounted
released channel: ORA_DISK_1

RMAN> recover database;

Starting recover at 04-SEP-04
Starting implicit crosscheck backup at 04-SEP-04
allocated channel: ORA_DISK_1
channel ORA_DISK_1: sid=49 devtype=DISK
Crosschecked 16 objects
Finished implicit crosscheck backup at 04-SEP-04

Starting implicit crosscheck copy at 04-SEP-04
using channel ORA_DISK_1
Crosschecked 8 objects
Finished implicit crosscheck copy at 04-SEP-04

searching for all files in the recovery area
cataloging files...
cataloging done

List of Cataloged Files
=======================
File Name:
  ➥C:\ORACLE\FLASH_RECOVERY_AREA\ORA101T\ORA101T\AUTOBACKUP\
  ➥2004_09_04\O1_MF_N_535984987_0MN6PG3P_.BKP

using channel ORA_DISK_1

starting media recovery

archive log thread 1 sequence 55 is already on disk as file
C:\ORACLE\ORADATA\OR
A101T\REDO03.LOG
archive log filename=C:\ORACLE\ORADATA\ORA101T\REDO03.LOG thread=1 sequence=55
media recovery complete
Finished recover at 04-SEP-04
```

8. Finally, open the database with RESETLOGS option for normal operations:

```
RMAN> alter database open resetlogs;

database opened

RMAN>
```

As you can see, recovering the control file requires some extra steps that are not part of your typical database recovery. This is because the control file has the information necessary to mount the database. If this is not available, the database cannot be mounted until the control file has been restored. Also, the control file contains RMAN information about the target database, which must be manually specified using the SET DBID command.

Re-creating a Control File

The procedure for creating a control file is a valuable recovery measure. The control file contains the physical map of an Oracle database. In other words, the control file has all the locations of the physical files, including datafiles, redo logs, and control files. The control file also has information about whether the database is in ARCHIVELOG mode, as well as RMAN metadata information.

The control file create script can be created with the command *ALTER DATABASE BACKUP CONTROL-FILE TO TRACE*. This command generates an ASCII representation of the binary control file as an Oracle trace file. The *ASCII backup control file* is in the form of data control language (DCL) statements or commands. The ASCII backup control file can be used to rebuild the binary control file. Either SPFILE or PFILE are required to start the database with appropriate initialization parameters when rebuilding the control file.

Let's walk through the steps for creating a control file:

1. First, create the ASCII control file:

```
C:\Documents and Settings\dstuns> sqlplus /nolog

SQL*Plus: Release 10.1.0.2.0 - Production on Sat Sep 4 15:09:25 2004

Copyright (c) 1982, 2004, Oracle.  All rights reserved.

SQL> connect / as sysdba
Connected.
SQL> alter database backup controlfile to trace;

Database altered.

SQL>
```

2. Next, display this trace file by locating the file in the UDUMP directory for the Oracle SID (ORACLE_SID) that you performed the command on. The backup control file has two

scenarios as the contents. The first is Set #1 NORESETLOGS case, and the second is Set #2 RESETLOGS case. The RESETLOGS case is used for incomplete recovery, and NORESETLOGS is used for complete recovery options:

```
C:\oracle\admin\ora101t\udump\> edit ora101t_ora_3428.trc

Dump file c:\oracle\admin\ora101t\udump\ora101t_ora_3428.trc
Sat Sep 04 15:09:41 2004
ORACLE V10.1.0.2.0 - Production vsnsta=0
vsnsql=13 vsnxtr=3
Oracle Database 10g Enterprise Edition Release 10.1.0.2.0 - Production
With the Partitioning, OLAP and Data Mining options
Windows XP Version V5.1 Service Pack 1
CPU             : 1 - type 586
Process Affinity: 0x00000000
Memory (A/P)    : PH:47M/510M, PG:745M/1249M, VA:1806M/2047M
Instance name: ora101t

Redo thread mounted by this instance: 1

Oracle process number: 12

Windows thread id: 3428, image: ORACLE.EXE (SHAD)


*** SERVICE NAME:(SYS$USERS) 2004-09-04 15:09:41.900
*** SESSION ID:(52.3) 2004-09-04 15:09:41.900
*** 2004-09-04 15:09:41.900
-- The following are current System-scope REDO Log Archival related
-- parameters and can be included in the database initialization file.
--
-- LOG_ARCHIVE_DEST=''
-- LOG_ARCHIVE_DUPLEX_DEST=''
--
-- LOG_ARCHIVE_FORMAT=ARC%S_%R.%T
--
-- DB_UNIQUE_NAME="ora101t"
--
-- LOG_ARCHIVE_CONFIG='SEND, RECEIVE, NODG_CONFIG'
-- LOG_ARCHIVE_MAX_PROCESSES=2
-- STANDBY_FILE_MANAGEMENT=MANUAL
-- STANDBY_ARCHIVE_DEST=%ORACLE_HOME%\RDBMS
```

```
-- FAL_CLIENT=''
-- FAL_SERVER=''
--
-- LOG_ARCHIVE_DEST_1='LOCATION=c:\oracle\oraarch\ora101t'
-- LOG_ARCHIVE_DEST_1='OPTIONAL REOPEN=300 NODELAY'
-- LOG_ARCHIVE_DEST_1='ARCH NOAFFIRM NOEXPEDITE NOVERIFY SYNC'
-- LOG_ARCHIVE_DEST_1='REGISTER NOALTERNATE NODEPENDENCY'
-- LOG_ARCHIVE_DEST_1='NOMAX_FAILURE NOQUOTA_SIZE NOQUOTA_USED NODB_UNIQUE_
  ➥NAME'
-- LOG_ARCHIVE_DEST_1='VALID_FOR=(PRIMARY_ROLE,ONLINE_LOGFILES)'
-- LOG_ARCHIVE_DEST_STATE_1=ENABLE
--
-- Below are two sets of SQL statements, each of which creates a new
-- control file and uses it to open the database. The first set opens
-- the database with the NORESETLOGS option and should be used only if
-- the current versions of all online logs are available. The second
-- set opens the database with the RESETLOGS option and should be used
-- if online logs are unavailable.
-- The appropriate set of statements can be copied from the trace into
-- a script file, edited as necessary, and executed when there is a
-- need to re-create the control file.
--
--     Set #1. NORESETLOGS case
--
-- The following commands will create a new control file and use it
-- to open the database.
-- Data used by Recovery Manager will be lost.
-- Additional logs may be required for media recovery of offline
-- Use this only if the current versions of all online logs are
-- available.
-- After mounting the created controlfile, the following SQL statement
-- will place the database in the appropriate protection mode:
--  ALTER DATABASE SET STANDBY DATABASE TO MAXIMIZE PERFORMANCE
STARTUP NOMOUNT
CREATE CONTROLFILE REUSE DATABASE "ORA101T" NORESETLOGS  ARCHIVELOG
    MAXLOGFILES 16
    MAXLOGMEMBERS 3
    MAXDATAFILES 100
    MAXINSTANCES 8
    MAXLOGHISTORY 454
```

```
LOGFILE
  GROUP 1 (
    'C:\ORACLE\ORADATA\ORA101T\REDO01_MIRROR.LOG',
    'C:\ORACLE\ORADATA\ORA101T\REDO01.LOG'
  ) SIZE 10M,
  GROUP 2 (
    'C:\ORACLE\ORADATA\ORA101T\REDO02.LOG',
    'C:\ORACLE\ORADATA\ORA101T\REDO02_MIRROR.LOG'
  ) SIZE 10M,
  GROUP 3 (
    'C:\ORACLE\ORADATA\ORA101T\REDO03.LOG',
    'C:\ORACLE\ORADATA\ORA101T\REDO03_MIRROR.LOG'
  ) SIZE 10M
-- STANDBY LOGFILE
DATAFILE
  'C:\ORACLE\ORADATA\ORA101T\SYSTEM01.DBF',
  'C:\ORACLE\ORADATA\ORA101T\UNDOTBS01.DBF',
  'C:\ORACLE\ORADATA\ORA101T\SYSAUX01.DBF',
  'C:\ORACLE\ORADATA\ORA101T\USERS01.DBF',
  'C:\ORACLE\ORADATA\ORA101T\EXAMPLE01.DBF',
  'C:\ORACLE\ORADATA\ORA101T\INDEX01.DBF'
CHARACTER SET WE8MSWIN1252
;
-- Configure RMAN configuration record 1
VARIABLE RECNO NUMBER;
EXECUTE :RECNO := SYS.DBMS_BACKUP_RESTORE.SETCONFIG('DEVICE
   TYPE','DISK BACKUP TYPE TO COMPRESSED BACKUPSET PARALLELISM 1');
-- Configure RMAN configuration record 2
VARIABLE RECNO NUMBER;
EXECUTE :RECNO := SYS.DBMS_BACKUP_RESTORE.SETCONFIG('CONTROLFILE
  ➥AUTOBACKUP','ON');
-- Commands to re-create incarnation table
-- Below log names MUST be changed to existing filenames on
-- disk. Any one log file from each branch can be used to
-- re-create incarnation records.
-- ALTER DATABASE REGISTER LOGFILE
  ➥'C:\ORACLE\ORAARCH\ORA101T\ARC00001_0520387048.001';
-- ALTER DATABASE REGISTER LOGFILE
  ➥'C:\ORACLE\ORAARCH\ORA101T\ARC00001_0527361115.001';
-- ALTER DATABASE REGISTER LOGFILE
```

```
    ➥'C:\ORACLE\ORAARCH\ORA101T\ARC00001_0535986437.001';
-- Recovery is required if any of the datafiles are restored backups,
-- or if the last shutdown was not normal or immediate.
RECOVER DATABASE
-- All logs need archiving and a log switch is needed.
ALTER SYSTEM ARCHIVE LOG ALL;
-- Database can now be opened normally.
ALTER DATABASE OPEN;
-- No tempfile entries found to add.
--
--     Set #2. RESETLOGS case
--
-- The following commands will create a new control file and use it
-- to open the database.
-- Data used by Recovery Manager will be lost.
-- The contents of online logs will be lost and all backups will be
  ➥invalidated.
-- Use this only if online logs are damaged. After mounting the created
-- controlfile, the following SQL statement will place the database in the
-- appropriate protection mode:
--  ALTER DATABASE SET STANDBY DATABASE TO MAXIMIZE PERFORMANCE
STARTUP NOMOUNT
CREATE CONTROLFILE REUSE DATABASE "ORA101T" RESETLOGS  ARCHIVELOG
    MAXLOGFILES 16
    MAXLOGMEMBERS 3
    MAXDATAFILES 100
    MAXINSTANCES 8
    MAXLOGHISTORY 454
LOGFILE
  GROUP 1 (
    'C:\ORACLE\ORADATA\ORA101T\REDO01_MIRROR.LOG',
    'C:\ORACLE\ORADATA\ORA101T\REDO01.LOG'
  ) SIZE 10M,
  GROUP 2 (
    'C:\ORACLE\ORADATA\ORA101T\REDO02.LOG',
    'C:\ORACLE\ORADATA\ORA101T\REDO02_MIRROR.LOG'
  ) SIZE 10M,
  GROUP 3 (
    'C:\ORACLE\ORADATA\ORA101T\REDO03.LOG',
    'C:\ORACLE\ORADATA\ORA101T\REDO03_MIRROR.LOG'
```

```
  ) SIZE 10M
-- STANDBY LOGFILE
DATAFILE
  'C:\ORACLE\ORADATA\ORA101T\SYSTEM01.DBF',
  'C:\ORACLE\ORADATA\ORA101T\UNDOTBS01.DBF',
  'C:\ORACLE\ORADATA\ORA101T\SYSAUX01.DBF',
  'C:\ORACLE\ORADATA\ORA101T\USERS01.DBF',
  'C:\ORACLE\ORADATA\ORA101T\EXAMPLE01.DBF',
  'C:\ORACLE\ORADATA\ORA101T\INDEX01.DBF'
CHARACTER SET WE8MSWIN1252
;
-- Configure RMAN configuration record 1
VARIABLE RECNO NUMBER;
EXECUTE :RECNO := SYS.DBMS_BACKUP_RESTORE.SETCONFIG('DEVICE
  ➥TYPE','DISK BACKUP TYPE TO COMPRESSED BACKUPSET PARALLELISM 1');
-- Configure RMAN configuration record 2
VARIABLE RECNO NUMBER;
EXECUTE :RECNO := SYS.DBMS_BACKUP_RESTORE.SETCONFIG('CONTROLFILE
  ➥AUTOBACKUP','ON');
-- Commands to re-create incarnation table below log names MUST be changed to
-- existing filenames on disk. Any one log file from each branch can be used to
-- re-create incarnation records.
-- ALTER DATABASE REGISTER LOGFILE
  ➥'C:\ORACLE\ORAARCH\ORA101T\ARC00001_0520387048.001';
-- ALTER DATABASE REGISTER LOGFILE
  ➥'C:\ORACLE\ORAARCH\ORA101T\ARC00001_0527361115.001';
-- ALTER DATABASE REGISTER LOGFILE
  ➥'C:\ORACLE\ORAARCH\ORA101T\ARC00001_0535986437.001';
-- Recovery is required if any of the datafiles are restored backups,
-- or if the last shutdown was not normal or immediate.
RECOVER DATABASE USING BACKUP CONTROLFILE
-- Database can now be opened zeroing the online logs.
ALTER DATABASE OPEN RESETLOGS;
-- No tempfile entries found to add.
--
```

3. Next, copy out the appropriate case needed to run. In this case, use the NORESETLOGS case, because you are recovering the database up to the point of failure. Let's look at the newly created copy of this trace file, which you will now call BACKUP_CONTROLFILE_NORESET.TXT:

```
STARTUP NOMOUNT
CREATE CONTROLFILE REUSE DATABASE "ORA101T" NORESETLOGS  ARCHIVELOG
```

```
    MAXLOGFILES 16
    MAXLOGMEMBERS 3
    MAXDATAFILES 100
    MAXINSTANCES 8
    MAXLOGHISTORY 454
LOGFILE
  GROUP 1 (
    'C:\ORACLE\ORADATA\ORA101T\REDO01_MIRROR.LOG',
    'C:\ORACLE\ORADATA\ORA101T\REDO01.LOG'
  ) SIZE 10M,
  GROUP 2 (
    'C:\ORACLE\ORADATA\ORA101T\REDO02.LOG',
    'C:\ORACLE\ORADATA\ORA101T\REDO02_MIRROR.LOG'
  ) SIZE 10M,
  GROUP 3 (
    'C:\ORACLE\ORADATA\ORA101T\REDO03.LOG',
    'C:\ORACLE\ORADATA\ORA101T\REDO03_MIRROR.LOG'
  ) SIZE 10M
-- STANDBY LOGFILE
DATAFILE
  'C:\ORACLE\ORADATA\ORA101T\SYSTEM01.DBF',
  'C:\ORACLE\ORADATA\ORA101T\UNDOTBS01.DBF',
  'C:\ORACLE\ORADATA\ORA101T\SYSAUX01.DBF',
  'C:\ORACLE\ORADATA\ORA101T\USERS01.DBF',
  'C:\ORACLE\ORADATA\ORA101T\EXAMPLE01.DBF',
  'C:\ORACLE\ORADATA\ORA101T\INDEX01.DBF'
CHARACTER SET WE8MSWIN1252
;
-- Configure RMAN configuration record 1
VARIABLE RECNO NUMBER;
EXECUTE :RECNO := SYS.DBMS_BACKUP_RESTORE.SETCONFIG('DEVICE
  TYPE','DISK BACKUP TYPE TO COMPRESSED BACKUPSET PARALLELISM 1');
-- Configure RMAN configuration record 2
VARIABLE RECNO NUMBER;
EXECUTE :RECNO := SYS.DBMS_BACKUP_RESTORE.SETCONFIG('CONTROLFILE
  ➥AUTOBACKUP','ON');
-- Commands to re-create incarnation table below log names MUST be changed to
-- existing filenames on disk. Any one log file from each branch can be used to
-- re-create incarnation records.
```

```
-- ALTER DATABASE REGISTER LOGFILE
   'C:\ORACLE\ORAARCH\ORA101T\ARC00001_0520387048.001';
-- ALTER DATABASE REGISTER LOGFILE
   'C:\ORACLE\ORAARCH\ORA101T\ARC00001_0527361115.001';
-- ALTER DATABASE REGISTER LOGFILE
   'C:\ORACLE\ORAARCH\ORA101T\ARC00001_0535986437.001';
-- Recovery is required if any of the datafiles are restored backups,
-- or if the last shutdown was not normal or immediate.
RECOVER DATABASE
-- All logs need archiving and a log switch is needed.
ALTER SYSTEM ARCHIVE LOG ALL;
-- Database can now be opened normally.
ALTER DATABASE OPEN;
```

4. Next, simulate the loss of all control files by deleting the control files for the database. This is performed with the database shut down:

```
C:\oracle\oradata\ora101t\> delete *.ctl
```

5. Now, use SQL*Plus and connect as SYSDBA. Then, run the BACKUP_CONTROLFILE_NORESET.TXT script:

```
C:\oracle\admin\ora101t\udump> sqlplus /nolog

SQL*Plus: Release 10.1.0.2.0 - Production on Sat Sep 4 15:44:37 2004

Copyright (c) 1982, 2004, Oracle.  All rights reserved.

C:\oracle\admin\ora101t\udump> sqlplus /nolog

SQL*Plus: Release 10.1.0.2.0 - Production on Sat Sep 4 15:44:37 2004

Copyright (c) 1982, 2004, Oracle.  All rights reserved.

SQL> connect / as sysdba
Connected to an idle instance.
SQL> @backup_controlfile_noreset.txt
ORACLE instance started.

Total System Global Area   88080384 bytes
Fixed Size                   787588 bytes
Variable Size              78642044 bytes
```

```
Database Buffers             8388608 bytes
Redo Buffers                  262144 bytes

Control file created.

PL/SQL procedure successfully completed.

PL/SQL procedure successfully completed.

ORA-00283: recovery session canceled due to errors
ORA-00264: no recovery required

ALTER SYSTEM ARCHIVE LOG ALL
*
ERROR at line 1:
ORA-00271: there are no logs that need archiving

Database altered.

SQL>
```

6. Verify that the control files have been rebuilt by going to the datafile directory listing the control files:

```
C:\oracle\oradata\ora101t> dir *.ctl
 Volume in drive C has no label.
 Volume Serial Number is 385B-CF22

 Directory of C:\oracle\oradata\ora101t

09/04/2004  03:48 PM         3,391,488 CONTROL01.CTL
09/04/2004  03:48 PM         3,391,488 CONTROL02.CTL
09/04/2004  03:48 PM         3,391,488 CONTROL03.CTL
               3 File(s)     10,174,464 bytes
               0 Dir(s)  18,775,740,416 bytes free

C:\oracle\oradata\ora101t>
```

As you can see, this process is fairly straightforward. The ASCII control file actually reproduces the binary control files. These can be verified by viewing the physical control files in the appropriate directory.

Performing an Incomplete Recovery

Incomplete recovery is a recovery that stops before the failure that forced the recovery. Another way of looking at incomplete recovery is that not all the transactions in the archived redo logs get applied to the database to make the database complete. With incomplete recovery, after the recovery process has ended, the database is still missing transactions that were in the database before the failure.

Incomplete recovery is sometimes called *database point-in-time recovery (DBPITR)* because this recovery is to a determined point-in-time.

RMAN incomplete recovery is performed by using the `SET UNTIL TIME` and `SET UNTIL SEQUENCE` clauses prior to the `RECOVER` command or the `UNTIL TIME` and `UNTIL SEQUENCE` clauses specified with the `RECOVER` commands. These clauses direct the recovery process to stop at a designated time, a redo log sequence, or a system change number (SCN) before full recovery is completed.

User-managed incomplete recovery is performed by using the `RECOVER DATABASE` command in conjunction with the `UNTIL TIME`, `UNTIL CHANGE`, or `UNTIL CANCEL` clauses. These have the same effect as the `SET UNTIL` clauses in RMAN, with the exception of the `UNTIL CANCEL` clause. The `UNTIL CANCEL` clause is designed to just stop the recovery process at a random point.

Table 4.1 describes the different types of incomplete recovery, and situations that might be best suited for their use for both RMAN and user-managed recovery operations.

TABLE 4.1 Incomplete Recovery Types and Uses

Recovery Type	Clause or Command	Usage
RMAN	`UNTIL TIME`	Stop recovery before a known time that introduces corruption in the database or some undesired event in the database that cannot be rolled back.
User-managed	`UNTIL TIME`	Stop recovery before a known time that introduces corruption in the database or some undesired event in the database that cannot be rolled back.
RMAN	`UNTIL SEQUENCE`	Stop before a known redo log sequence that introduces corruption or some undesired event in the database that cannot be rolled back.
RMAN	`UNTIL SCN`	Stop before a known SCN that introduces corruption or some undesired event in the database that cannot be rolled back. The SCN can be a more finite stopping point than a time or redo log sequence because it is by transaction.

TABLE 4.1 Incomplete Recovery Types and Uses *(continued)*

Recovery Type	Clause or Command	Usage
User-managed	UNTIL CHANGE	Stop before a SCN that introduces corruption or some undesired event in the database that cannot be rolled back. The SCN can be a more finite stopping point than a time or redo log sequence because it is by transaction.
User-managed	UNTIL CANCEL	Stop when administrator issues the CANCEL command. This is good for making a test database from backup, where the transactional stopping point is not important to the validity of the database.

Now that we have a high-level understanding of RMAN-based and user-managed incomplete recovery, we will take a look at RMAN-based incomplete recovery in more detail in the next section. RMAN-based incomplete recovery is very similar to user-managed incomplete recovery. RMAN-based incomplete recovery doesn't have a CANCEL-based option; however, RMAN-based incomplete recovery has SCN and SEQUENCE methods.

RMAN Incomplete Recovery

RMAN incomplete recovery can be performed by time, redo log sequence, or SCN. To perform an incomplete recovery, use the RECOVER DATABASE command with the *UNTIL TIME*, *SCN*, or *SEQUENCE* clause, or use the SET UNTIL clause prior to the RECOVER DATABASE command.

This section walks you through the steps for performing a time- and sequence-based incomplete recovery. Let's do a time-based recovery first:

1. Make sure the target database is started in MOUNT mode:

```
SQL> startup mount
ORACLE instance started.

Total System Global Area   88080384 bytes
Fixed Size                   787588 bytes
Variable Size              78642044 bytes
Database Buffers            8388608 bytes
Redo Buffers                 262144 bytes
Database mounted.
```

2. Make sure NLS_DATE_FORMAT is set to a value that you can reproduce in RMAN:

```
C:\> set NLS_DATE_FORMAT=DD-MON-YYYY HH24:MI:SS
```

3. Recover the database using the SET UNTIL TIME clause.

```
RMAN> run
2> {
3> set until time '06-SEP-2004 11:25:00';
4> restore database;
5> recover database;
6> }

executing command: SET until clause

Starting restore at 06-SEP-2004 11:50:05
using channel ORA_DISK_1

channel ORA_DISK_1: starting datafile backupset restore
channel ORA_DISK_1: specifying datafile(s) to restore from backup set
restoring datafile 00001 to C:\ORACLE\ORADATA\ORA101T\SYSTEM01.DBF
restoring datafile 00002 to C:\ORACLE\ORADATA\ORA101T\UNDOTBS01.DBF
restoring datafile 00003 to C:\ORACLE\ORADATA\ORA101T\SYSAUX01.DBF
restoring datafile 00004 to C:\ORACLE\ORADATA\ORA101T\USERS01.DBF
restoring datafile 00005 to C:\ORACLE\ORADATA\ORA101T\EXAMPLE01.DBF
restoring datafile 00006 to C:\ORACLE\ORADATA\ORA101T\INDEX01.DBF
channel ORA_DISK_1: restored backup piece 1
piece handle=
  ➥C:\ORACLE\FLASH_RECOVERY_AREA\ORA101T\ORA101T\BACKUPSET\
  ➥2004_09_06\O1_MF_NNNDF_TAG20040906T111843_0MSBJ797_.BKP
  ➥tag=TAG20040906T111843
channel ORA_DISK_1: restore complete
Finished restore at 06-SEP-2004 11:51:44

Starting recover at 06-SEP-2004 11:51:45
using channel ORA_DISK_1

starting media recovery

archive log thread 1 sequence 9 is already on disk as file
  ➥C:\ORACLE\ORAARCH\ORA101T\ARC00009_0535986437.001
archive log thread 1 sequence 10 is already on disk as file
  ➥C:\ORACLE\ORAARCH\ORA101T\ARC00010_0535986437.001
archive log filename=
  ➥C:\ORACLE\ORAARCH\ORA101T\ARC00009_0535986437.001 thread=1
```

```
sequence=9
archive log filename=
  ➥C:\ORACLE\ORAARCH\ORA101T\ARC00010_0535986437.001 thread=1
sequence=10
media recovery complete
Finished recover at 06-SEP-2004 11:52:00

RMAN>
```

4. Next, open the database with the RESETLOGS clause:

```
RMAN> alter database open resetlogs;

database opened

RMAN>
```

Next, let's walk through a specific example of using the sequence-based recovery, which uses a redo log sequence number to terminate the recovery process. There are some steps required to identify the redo log sequence number that require accessing the V$REDO_LOG_HISTORY dynamic view:

1. From the V$LOG_HISTORY table, get the sequence and thread information. In this case, you will recover up to sequence 3 and thread 1. These values are retrieved from the row with RECID 16:

```
SQL> select * from v$log_history;

RECID STAMP     THRD# SEQ# FIR_CHNG FIRST_TIM N_CHNG S_CHNG RESETLOG
----- --------- ----- ---- -------- --------- ------ ------ --------
14    536155296 1     1    562594   06-SEP-04 563149 562594 06-SEP-04
15    536155297 1     2    563149   06-SEP-04 563151 562594 06-SEP-04
16    536155302 1     3    563151   06-SEP-04 563154 562594 06-SEP-04
17    536155404 1     4    563154   06-SEP-04 563199 562594 06-SEP-04
```

2. Start the database in MOUNT mode:

```
SQL> startup mount
ORACLE instance started.

Total System Global Area   88080384 bytes
Fixed Size                   787588 bytes
Variable Size              78642044 bytes
Database Buffers            8388608 bytes
Redo Buffers                 262144 bytes
Database mounted.
```

3. Recover the database using the UNTIL SEQUENCE clause. Note that this will recover log sequences before 3, which is log sequence 1 and 2:

```
RMAN> run
2> {
3> set until sequence 3 thread 1;
4> restore database;
5> recover database;
6> }

executing command: SET until clause

Starting restore at 06-SEP-2004 13:22:07
using channel ORA_DISK_1

channel ORA_DISK_1: starting datafile backupset restore
channel ORA_DISK_1: specifying datafile(s) to restore from backup set
restoring datafile 00001 to C:\ORACLE\ORADATA\ORA101T\SYSTEM01.DBF
restoring datafile 00002 to C:\ORACLE\ORADATA\ORA101T\UNDOTBS01.DBF
restoring datafile 00003 to C:\ORACLE\ORADATA\ORA101T\SYSAUX01.DBF
restoring datafile 00004 to C:\ORACLE\ORADATA\ORA101T\USERS01.DBF
restoring datafile 00005 to C:\ORACLE\ORADATA\ORA101T\EXAMPLE01.DBF
restoring datafile 00006 to C:\ORACLE\ORADATA\ORA101T\INDEX01.DBF
channel ORA_DISK_1: restored backup piece 1
piece handle=
  ➥C:\ORACLE\FLASH_RECOVERY_AREA\ORA101T\ORA101T\BACKUPSET\
  ➥2004_09_06\01_MF_NNNDF_TAG20040906T111843_0MSBJ797_.BKP
tag=TAG20040906T111843
channel ORA_DISK_1: restore complete
Finished restore at 06-SEP-2004 13:23:46

Starting recover at 06-SEP-2004 13:23:46
using channel ORA_DISK_1

starting media recovery

archive log thread 1 sequence 1 is already on disk as file
  ➥C:\ORACLE\ORAARCH\ORA101T\ARC00001_0536154821.001
archive log thread 1 sequence 2 is already on disk as file
  ➥C:\ORACLE\ORAARCH\ORA101T\ARC00002_0536154821.001
archive log filename=
  ➥C:\ORACLE\ORAARCH\ORA101T\ARC00001_0536154821.001 thread=1
```

```
sequence=1
archive log filename=
  ➥C:\ORACLE\ORAARCH\ORA101T\ARC00002_0536154821.001 thread=1
sequence=2
media recovery complete
Finished recover at 06-SEP-2004 13:24:05

RMAN>
```

4. Open the database with the RESETLOGS clause:

```
RMAN> alter database open resetlogs;

database opened

RMAN>
```

Real World Scenario

Using Incomplete Recovery to Move a Database

Recovery operations can be used as tools to perform activities other the recovery from failure. For this reason, you (as the DBA) need to be familiar with the backup and recovery features and capabilities.

User-managed incomplete recovery options, such as utilizing the backup control file in conjunction with RECOVER DATABASE USING BACKUP CONTROLFILE UNTIL CANCEL, can be useful tools to move databases from one location to another. This approach can be used to move databases for any purpose such as testing or just moving to a new server. You must make sure that if you are moving to a new server that the Oracle database software and operating system are similar. The move database process can also be performed with the RMAN DUPLICATE TARGET DATABASE command.

This is a user-managed approach, which is performed by taking the hot or cold backup of the database you want to move and moving the datafiles and initialization files to the new location. Make the necessary changes in the ASCII control file to location references of all the physical database files such as redo logs and datafiles. Then validate that ORACLE_SID is sourced to the correct database and execute this control file at the SQL prompt as SYSDBA. This will generate a new database on a new server and in different locations. This can be used in many situations where hardware backup solutions integrated with storage area networks SAN and network area storage NAS devices are used with disk mirrored backups.

Performing User-Managed Incomplete Recovery

User-managed incomplete recovery can be performed by time, change, and cancelling. The method of performing incomplete recovery is using the *RECOVER DATABASE* command with the *UNTIL TIME*, *CHANGE*, or *CANCEL* clauses.

This section walks you through the steps for performing a time- and change-based incomplete recovery. Let's do a time-based recovery first:

1. Make sure NLS_DATE_FORMAT is set to a value that you can reproduce in SQL*Plus:

```
C:\> set NLS_DATE_FORMAT=DD-MON-YYYY HH24:MI:SS
```

2. Remove the datafile USERS01.DBF and restore USERS01.DBF from backup to simulate a recovery situation:

```
C:\oracle\oradata\ora101t\> delete USERS01.DBF
C:\oracle\oradata\ora101t\> copy
C:\oracle\backup\ora101t\USERS01.DBF .
```

Make sure you have tested the backup database before trying to simulate a failure by deleting a datafile.

3. Make sure the target database is started in MOUNT mode:

```
SQL> startup mount
ORACLE instance started.

Total System Global Area   88080384 bytes
Fixed Size                   787588 bytes
Variable Size              78642044 bytes
Database Buffers            8388608 bytes
Redo Buffers                 262144 bytes
Database mounted.
```

4. Recover the database using the SET UNTIL TIME clause:

```
SQL> recover database until time '06-SEP-2004 15:15:00';
ORA-00279: change 565007 generated at 09/06/2004 15:05:20 needed for thread 1
ORA-00289: suggestion : C:\ORACLE\ORAARCH\ORA101T\ARC00001_0536160481.001
ORA-00280: change 565007 for thread 1 is in sequence #1


Specify log: {<RET>=suggested | filename | AUTO | CANCEL}
auto
```

```
Log applied.
Media recovery complete.
SQL>
```

5. Open the database with the RESETLOGS clause:

```
SQL> alter database open resetlogs;

database opened

SQL>
```

Next, let's look at a specific example of using the cancel-based recovery, which is when you terminate the recovery process at random by issuing the CANCEL command. In this example, you will recover from an online backup using a backup control file that was created earlier when you used the ALTER DATABASE BACKUP CONTROLFILE TO TRACE command. Let's walk through a cancel-based recovery:

1. Copy the online backup of the all the datafiles that make up ora101t:

```
C:\oradata\oracle\ora101t\> copy C:\oracle\backup\ora101t\*.DBF .
```

2. View the backup control file to verify:

```
STARTUP NOMOUNT
CREATE CONTROLFILE REUSE DATABASE "ORA101T" RESETLOGS  ARCHIVELOG
    MAXLOGFILES 16
    MAXLOGMEMBERS 3
    MAXDATAFILES 100
    MAXINSTANCES 8
    MAXLOGHISTORY 454
LOGFILE
  GROUP 1 (
    'C:\ORACLE\ORADATA\ORA101T\REDO01_MIRROR.LOG',
    'C:\ORACLE\ORADATA\ORA101T\REDO01.LOG'
  ) SIZE 10M,
  GROUP 2 (
    'C:\ORACLE\ORADATA\ORA101T\REDO02.LOG',
    'C:\ORACLE\ORADATA\ORA101T\REDO02_MIRROR.LOG'
  ) SIZE 10M,
  GROUP 3 (
    'C:\ORACLE\ORADATA\ORA101T\REDO03.LOG',
    'C:\ORACLE\ORADATA\ORA101T\REDO03_MIRROR.LOG'
  ) SIZE 10M
```

```
-- STANDBY LOGFILE
DATAFILE
  'C:\ORACLE\ORADATA\ORA101T\SYSTEM01.DBF',
  'C:\ORACLE\ORADATA\ORA101T\UNDOTBS01.DBF',
  'C:\ORACLE\ORADATA\ORA101T\SYSAUX01.DBF',
  'C:\ORACLE\ORADATA\ORA101T\USERS01.DBF',
  'C:\ORACLE\ORADATA\ORA101T\EXAMPLE01.DBF',
  'C:\ORACLE\ORADATA\ORA101T\INDEX01.DBF'
CHARACTER SET WE8MSWIN1252
;
-- Configure RMAN configuration record 1
VARIABLE RECNO NUMBER;
EXECUTE :RECNO := SYS.DBMS_BACKUP_RESTORE.SETCONFIG('DEVICE TYPE',
  ➥'DISK BACKUP TYPE TO
  COMPRESSED BACKUPSET PARALLELISM 1');
-- Configure RMAN configuration record 2
VARIABLE RECNO NUMBER;
EXECUTE :RECNO := SYS.DBMS_BACKUP_RESTORE.SETCONFIG('CONTROLFILE
  AUTOBACKUP','ON');
```

3. Run the backup control file:

```
SQL> connect / as sysdba;
Connected to an idle instance.
SQL> @backup_control_reset.txt
ORACLE instance started.

Total System Global Area   88080384 bytes
Fixed Size                   787588 bytes
Variable Size              78642044 bytes
Database Buffers            8388608 bytes
Redo Buffers                 262144 bytes

Control file created.

PL/SQL procedure successfully completed.

PL/SQL procedure successfully completed.

SQL>
```

4. Issue the RECOVER DATABASE UNTIL CANCEL USING BACKUP CONTROLFILE command:

```
SQL> recover database until cancel using backup controlfile;
ORA-00279: change 566539 generated at 09/06/2004 17:41:21 needed for thr
ORA-00289: suggestion : C:\ORACLE\ORAARCH\ORA101T\ARC00004_0536167372.00
ORA-00280: change 566539 for thread 1 is in sequence #4


Specify log: {<RET>=suggested | filename | AUTO | CANCEL}

ORA-00279: change 567533 generated at 09/06/2004 18:03:37 needed   for thr
ORA-00289: suggestion : C:\ORACLE\ORAARCH\ORA101T\ARC00005_0536167372.00
ORA-00280: change 567533 for thread 1 is in sequence #5
ORA-00278: log file
  ➥'C:\ORACLE\ORAARCH\ORA101T\ARC00004_0536167372.001'
no longer needed for this recovery


Specify log: {<RET>=suggested | filename | AUTO | CANCEL}

ORA-00279: change 567535 generated at 09/06/2004 18:03:42 needed for thr
ORA-00289: suggestion : C:\ORACLE\ORAARCH\ORA101T\ARC00006_0536167372.00
ORA-00280: change 567535 for thread 1 is in sequence #6
ORA-00278: log file
  ➥'C:\ORACLE\ORAARCH\ORA101T\ARC00005_0536167372.001'
no longer needed for this recovery


Specify log: {<RET>=suggested | filename | AUTO | CANCEL}
CANCEL
Media recovery cancelled.
```

5. Open the database using the RESETLOGS clause:

```
SQL> alter database open resetlogs;

Database altered.

SQL>
```

Database Recovery Using Enterprise Manager

Recovering the database using Enterprise Manager (EM) performs the identical process of performing recovery with the RMAN command-line interface (CLI), except it is done through the EM web interface. EM uses the operating system commands to log on to the server and run the RMAN CLI.

In the following example, you will perform whole database recovery, which means that all the database files will be restored and recovered. This requires the database to be shut down and started in `MOUNT` mode. This section demonstrates how to perform a whole database recovery with EM. This is a fairly straightforward process.

Let's perform a recovery utilizing EM:

1. First, enter **`http://database: port/em`** in the web browser to get to the EM main home page. From the main page, you can get to the login screen. Enter the username **SYS** and the **SYS** accounts password, connect as **SYSDBA**, and click the Login button. The main EM home page opens. (This page is displayed as two screens here because of the size of the home page.)

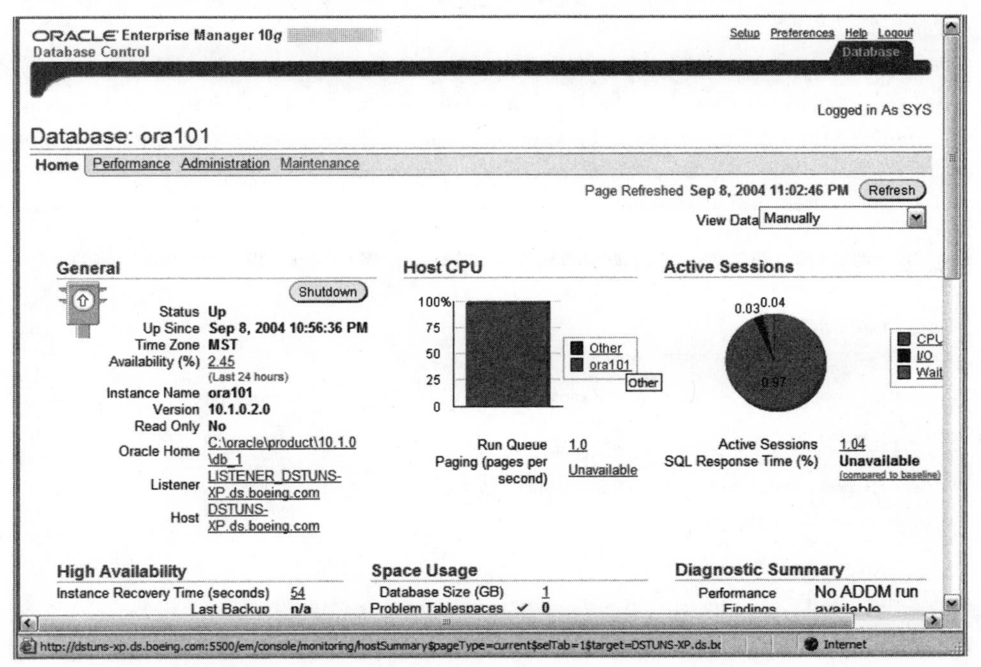

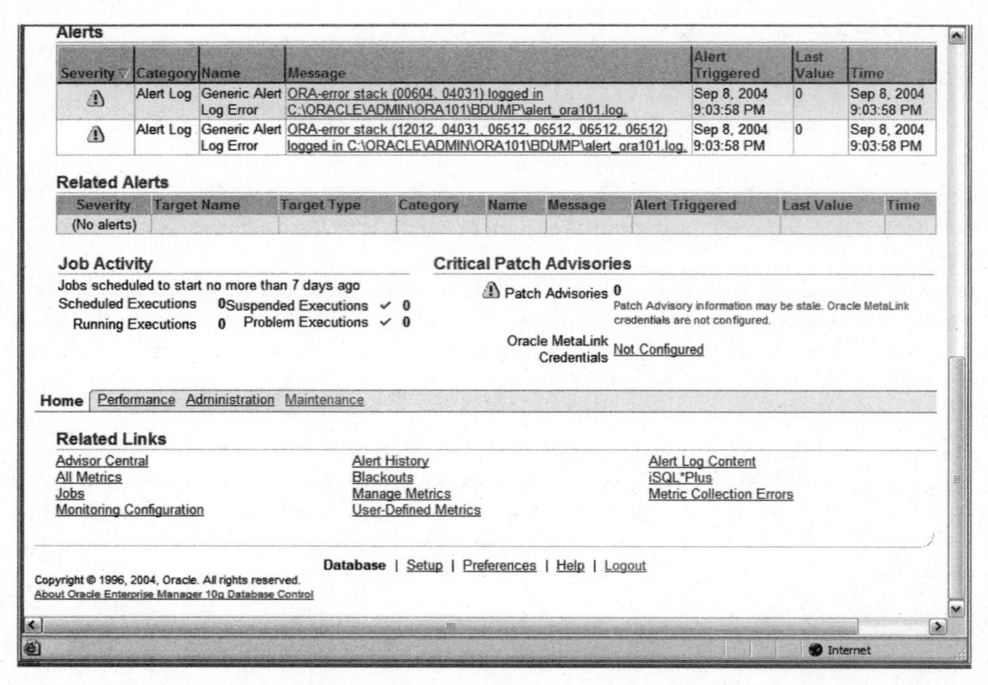

2. Select the Maintenance tab to navigate to the maintenance screens, which contain the screens that allow you to perform a recovery operation.

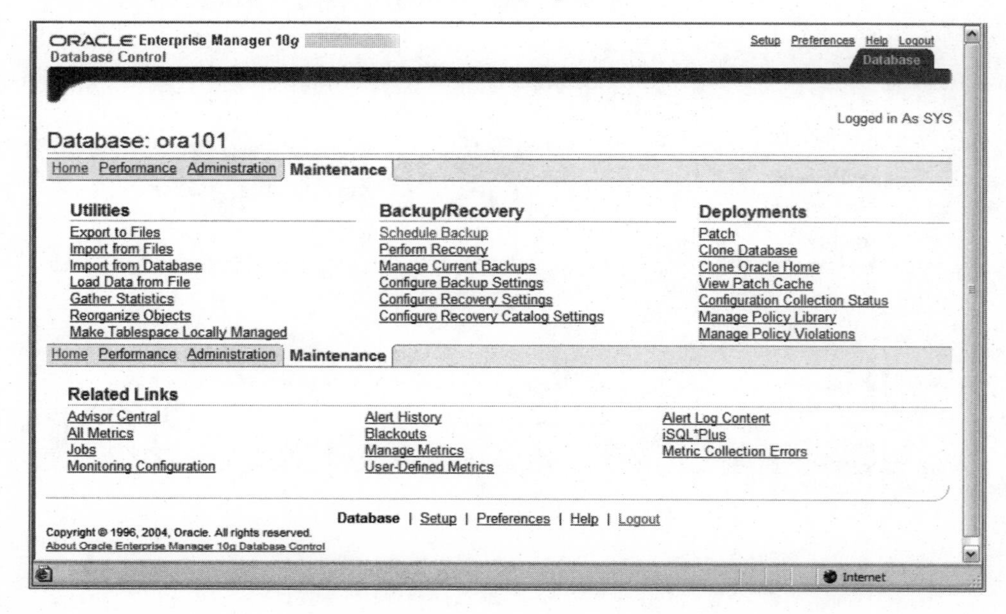

3. Select Perform Recovery under the Backup/Recovery section. The Perform Recovery: Type screen opens.

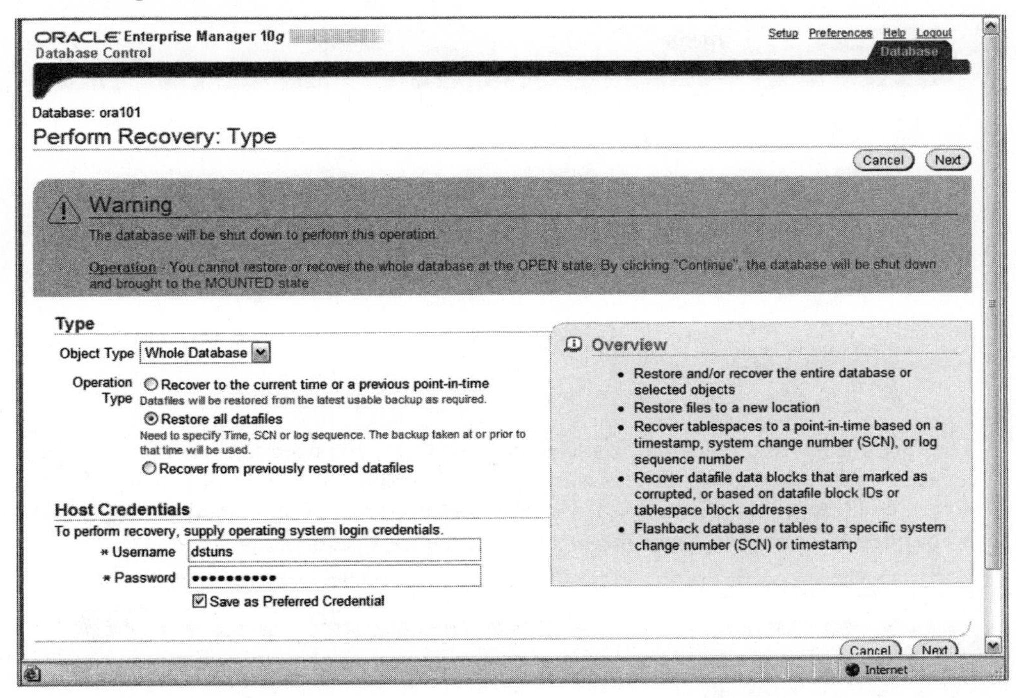

4. In the Perform Recovery: Type screen, select Whole Database from the Object Type list box. Enter the appropriate username and password with administrator privilege in Windows or Oracle user privilege in Unix. When this is completed, click Next. The Recovery Wizard screen opens. During this process, you are asked to wait until RMAN performs a shutdown on the database and startup mount.

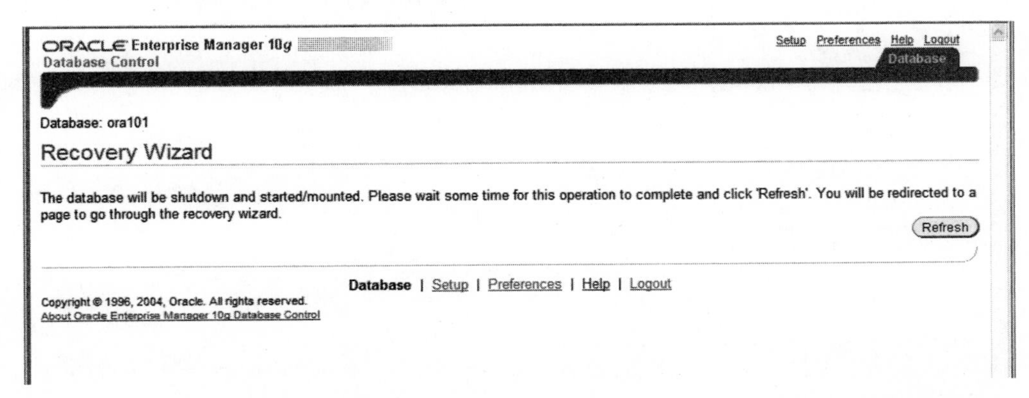

5. When the database is shut down, you will be directed to the Database: Ora101 screen to start the database in MOUNT mode by clicking the Startup button.

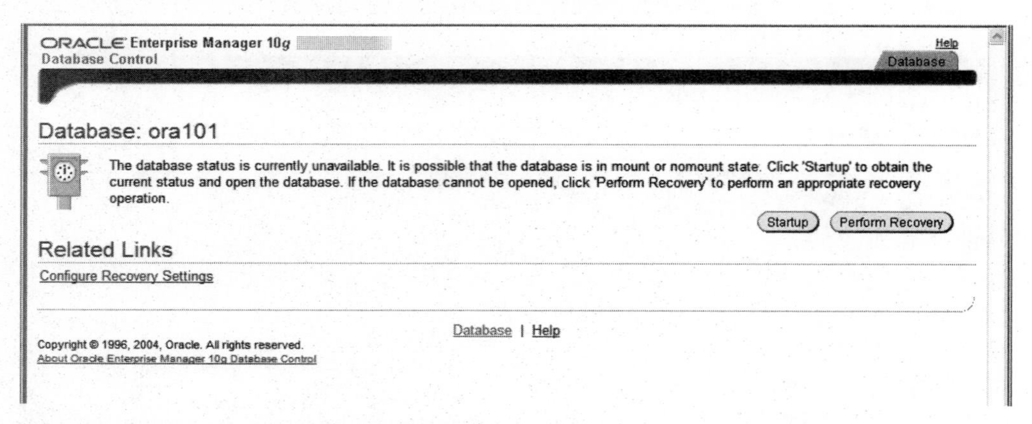

6. The Perform Recovery: Credentials screen opens. Here, you need to enter the host credentials username and password. This account needs to have administrator privilege for Windows and Oracle user privilege in Unix. You also need to enter the database credentials username and password. Once these are entered, click Continue.

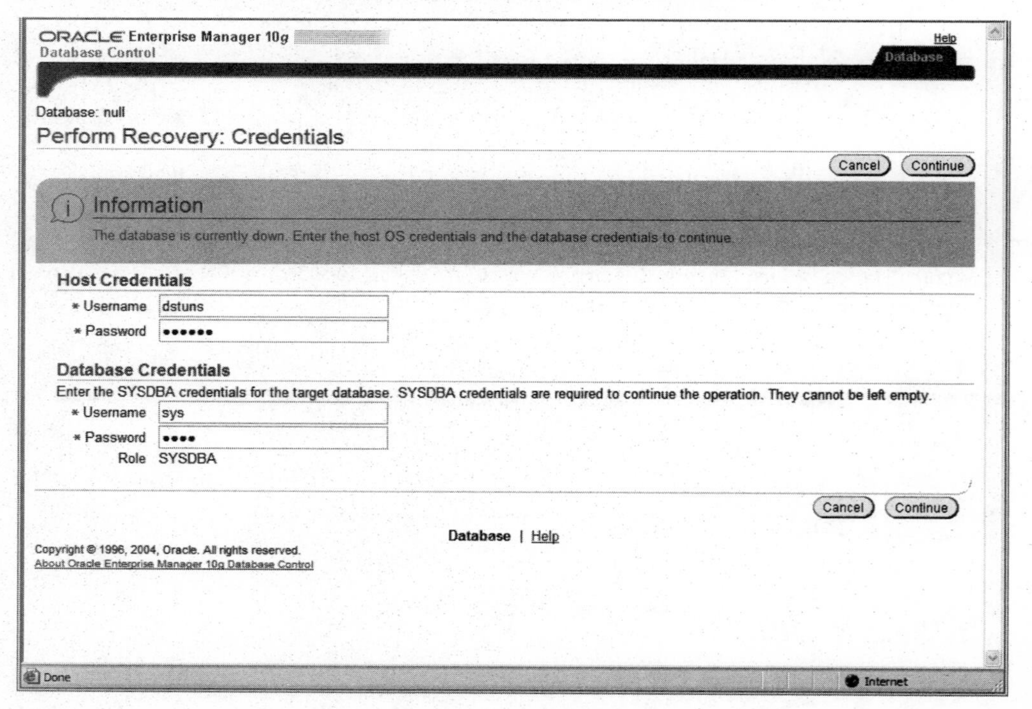

7. You are then directed back to the Perform Recovery: Type screen. Choose Whole Database from the Object Type list box. Enter the host credentials username and password of the equivalent Windows administrator account or Unix Oracle user account. Click Next.

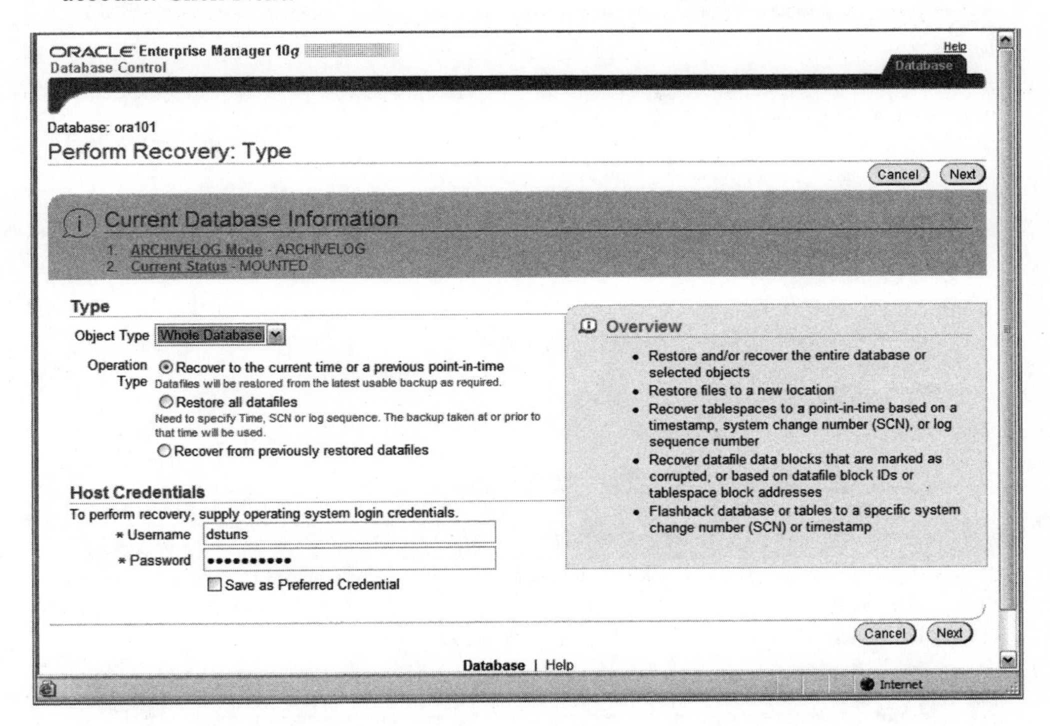

8. The Perform Recovery: Point-In-Time screen appears. Choose Recover To A Prior Point In Time radio button and then click Next.

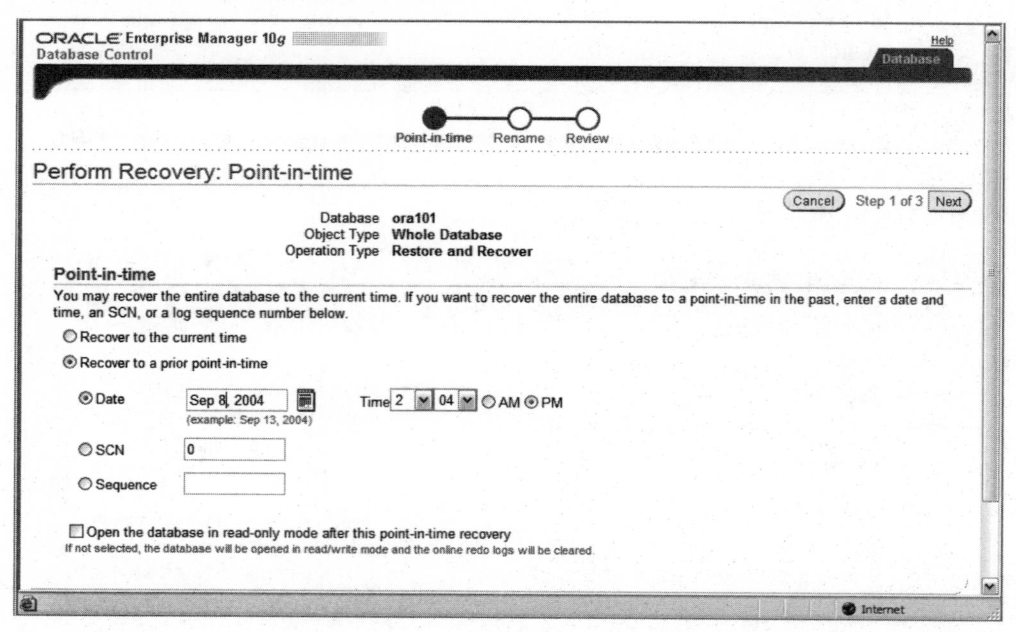

9. The Perform Recovery: Rename screen opens. Choose the No, Restore The Files To The Default Location radio button and then click Next.

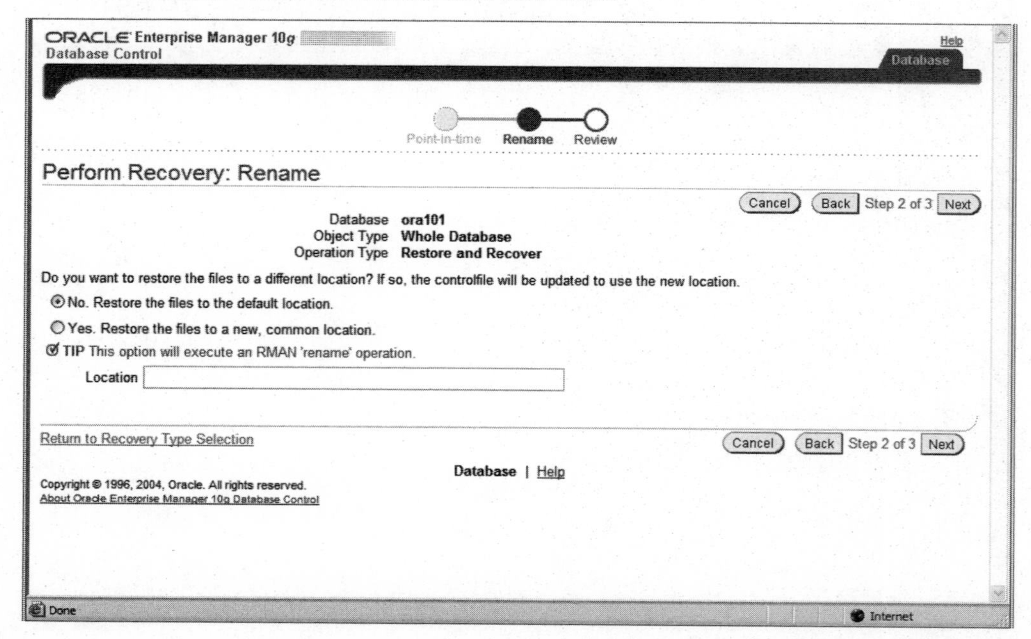

10. The Perform Recovery: Review screen opens. Here you can review the RMAN script that will be executed. Click the Submit button to submit the job.

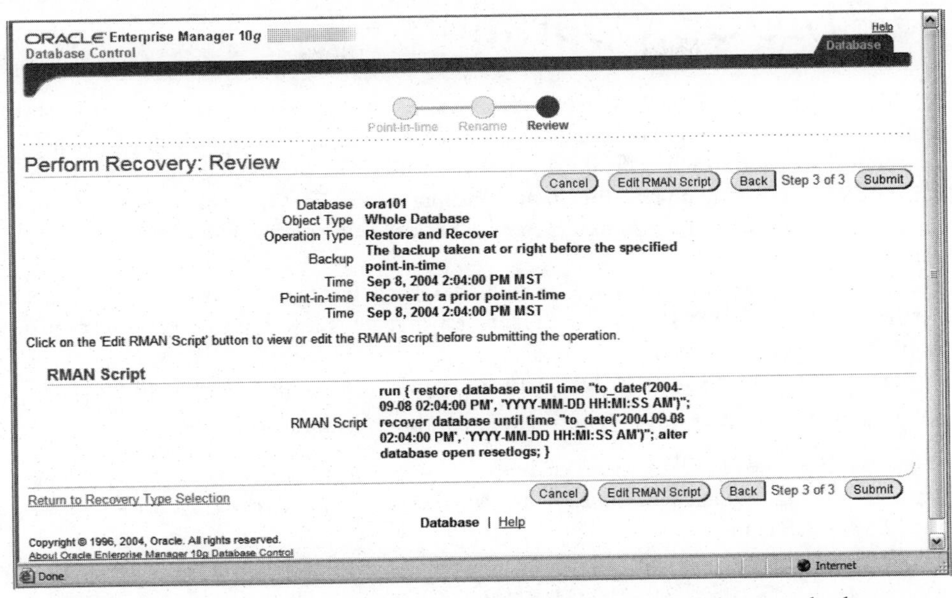

11. The final screen shows the output from the RMAN script and indicates whether or not the operation was successful.

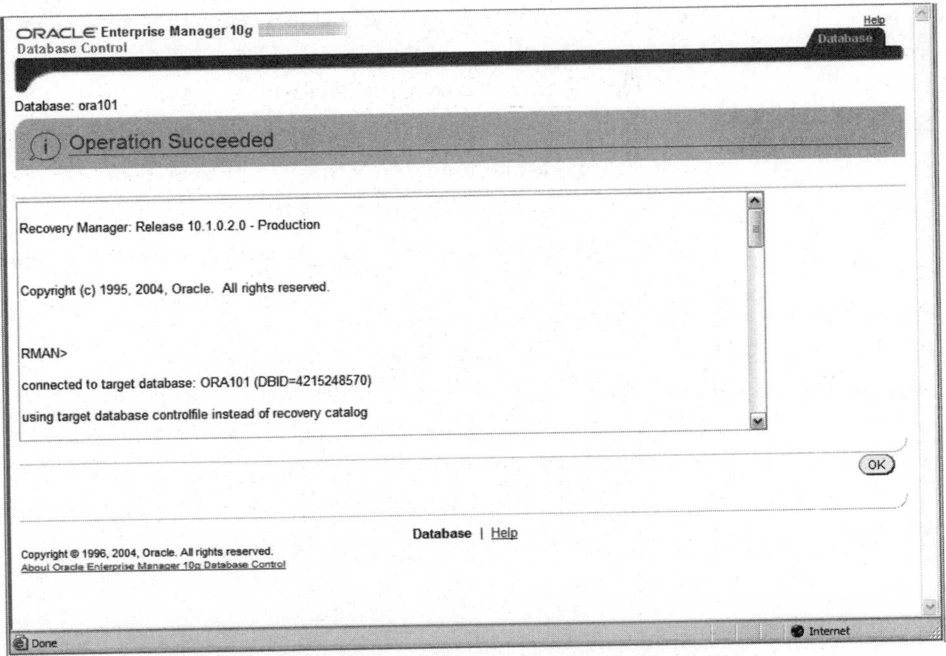

Performing a Recovery after a *RESETLOGS* Operation

The *RESETLOGS* clause is required in most incomplete recovery situations to open the database. This clause resets the redo log sequence for the Oracle database. In versions prior to Oracle 10*g*, this was a critical point because this invalidated your ability to use the backups prior to the use of RESETLOGS to recover again past the point of issuing the RESETLOGS. This is one of the reasons Oracle support always advised customers to take backup immediately following incomplete recovery.

In Oracle 10*g*, this problem has been remedied. Oracle has made revisions to the process of recovering through the RESETLOGS point. This new feature is internal to the recovery process; you don't need to do anything.

In order to test this new feature, here's an overview of the steps you need to take:

1. Make a new backup or have a good whole database backup available.
2. Force the redo log activity to archive logs.
3. Validate the log sequence number to perform your incomplete recovery, for which you use the RESETLOGS clause.
4. Shut down the database and delete the USERS01.DBF file to cause a recovery situation.
5. Start up the database in MOUNT mode and use RMAN to perform an incomplete recovery using the SET UNTIL SEQUENCE command.
6. When the incomplete recovery is complete, use the RESETLOGS clause to open the database.
7. To recover through the RESETLOGS, you need to simulate more database activity and force this activity to the archive logs. We will be using the USERS tablespace.
8. Shut down the database and delete the USERS01.DBF to cause another recovery situation.
9. Start up the database in MOUNT mode and use RMAN to perform a complete recovery.
10. When the recovery is complete, just use an ALTER DATABASE OPEN command.
11. Finally, view the V$LOG_HISTORY table and validate that the database activity is available in the database.

Let's go walk through this lengthy but straightforward procedure step by step:

1. Perform a backup if you do not have a good whole database backup:

```
RMAN> connect target

connected to target database: ORA101T (DBID=2615281366)

RMAN> run
2> {
```

```
3> allocate channel c1 type disk;
4> backup database;
5> backup (archivelog all);
6> }

using target database controlfile instead of recovery catalog
allocated channel: c1
channel c1: sid=36 devtype=DISK

Starting backup at 11-SEP-04
channel c1: starting compressed full datafile backupset
channel c1: specifying datafile(s) in backupset
input datafile fno=00001 name=C:\ORACLE\ORADATA\ORA101T\SYSTEM01.DBF
input datafile fno=00003 name=C:\ORACLE\ORADATA\ORA101T\SYSAUX01.DBF
input datafile fno=00005 name=C:\ORACLE\ORADATA\ORA101T\EXAMPLE01.DBF
input datafile fno=00002 name=C:\ORACLE\ORADATA\ORA101T\UNDOTBS01.DBF
input datafile fno=00006 name=C:\ORACLE\ORADATA\ORA101T\INDEX01.DBF
input datafile fno=00004 name=C:\ORACLE\ORADATA\ORA101T\USERS01.DBF
channel c1: starting piece 1 at 11-SEP-04
channel c1: finished piece 1 at 11-SEP-04
piece handle=
  ➥C:\ORACLE\FLASH_RECOVERY_AREA\ORA101T\ORA101T\BACKUPSET\
  ➥2004_09_11\O1_MF_NNNDF_TAG20040911T120548_0N6M4JBO_.BKP comment=NONE
channel c1: backup set complete, elapsed time: 00:01:36
Finished backup at 11-SEP-04

Starting backup at 11-SEP-04
current log archived
channel c1: starting compressed archive log backupset
channel c1: specifying archive log(s) in backup set
input archive log thread=1 sequence=1 recid=1 stamp=536194825
input archive log thread=1 sequence=2 recid=2 stamp=536194914
input archive log thread=1 sequence=3 recid=3 stamp=536209216
input archive log thread=1 sequence=4 recid=4 stamp=536227827
input archive log thread=1 sequence=5 recid=5 stamp=536587661
channel c1: starting piece 1 at 11-SEP-04
channel c1: finished piece 1 at 11-SEP-04
piece handle=
  ➥C:\ORACLE\FLASH_RECOVERY_AREA\ORA101T\ORA101T\BACKUPSET\
  ➥2004_09_11\O1_MF_ANNNN_TAG20040911T120745_0N6M8BSK_.BKP comment=NONE
```

```
channel c1: backup set complete, elapsed time: 00:00:18
Finished backup at 11-SEP-04

Starting Control File Autobackup at 11-SEP-04
piece handle=
  ➥C:\ORACLE\FLASH_RECOVERY_AREA\ORA101T\ORA101T\AUTOBACKUP\
  ➥2004_09_11\01_MF_N_536587693_0N6M936N_.BKP comment=NONE
Finished Control File Autobackup at 11-SEP-04
released channel: c1

RMAN>
```

2. Force all the redo log information to archive logs by executing `ALTER SYSTEM SWITCH LOGFILE`:

```
SQL> alter system switch logfile;

System altered.

SQL> alter system switch logfile;

System altered.

SQL> alter system switch logfile;

System altered.

SQL> alter system switch logfile;

System altered.
```

3. Verify the redo log sequence and thread number in the `V$LOG_HISTORY` table so that you can perform incomplete recovery to a redo log sequence:

```
SQL> select * from v$log_history;

RECID STAMP     THRD# SEQ# FIR_CHNG FIRST_TIM N_CHNG S_CHNG RESETLOG
----- --------- ----- ---- -------- --------- ------ ------ --------
8     536588583 1     6    609492   11-SEP-04 610333 567536 06-SEP-04
9     536588584 1     7    610333   11-SEP-04 610335 567536 06-SEP-04
10    536588589 1     8    610335   11-SEP-04 610338 567536 06-SEP-04

SQL>
```

4. Simulate a failure by shutting down the database and deleting the USERS01.DBF:

```
C:\Documents and Settings\dstuns> sqlplus /nolog

SQL*Plus: Release 10.1.0.2.0 - Production on Sat Sep 11 12:25:08 2004

Copyright (c) 1982, 2004, Oracle.  All rights reserved.

SQL> connect / as sysdba
Connected.
SQL> shutdown immediate
Database closed.
Database dismounted.
ORACLE instance shut down.
SQL> host

C:\oracle\oradata\ora101t\> del USERS01.DBF
```

5. Begin the recovery process by starting the database in MOUNT mode:

```
SQL> startup mount
ORACLE instance started.

Total System Global Area   88080384 bytes
Fixed Size                   787588 bytes
Variable Size              78642044 bytes
Database Buffers            8388608 bytes
Redo Buffers                 262144 bytes
Database mounted.
SQL>
```

6. Perform an incomplete recovery using the SET UNTIL SEQUENCE clause:

```
RMAN> connect target

connected to target database: ORA101T (DBID=2615281366)

RMAN> run
2> {
3> set until sequence 6 thread 1;
4> restore database;
5> recover database;
6> }
```

```
executing command: SET until clause
using target database controlfile instead of recovery catalog

Starting restore at 11-SEP-04
allocated channel: ORA_DISK_1
channel ORA_DISK_1: sid=49 devtype=DISK

channel ORA_DISK_1: starting datafile backupset restore
channel ORA_DISK_1: specifying datafile(s) to restore from backup set
restoring datafile 00001 to C:\ORACLE\ORADATA\ORA101T\SYSTEM01.DBF
restoring datafile 00002 to C:\ORACLE\ORADATA\ORA101T\UNDOTBS01.DBF
restoring datafile 00003 to C:\ORACLE\ORADATA\ORA101T\SYSAUX01.DBF
restoring datafile 00004 to C:\ORACLE\ORADATA\ORA101T\USERS01.DBF
restoring datafile 00005 to C:\ORACLE\ORADATA\ORA101T\EXAMPLE01.DBF
restoring datafile 00006 to C:\ORACLE\ORADATA\ORA101T\INDEX01.DBF
channel ORA_DISK_1: restored backup piece 1
piece handle=
  ➥C:\ORACLE\FLASH_RECOVERY_AREA\ORA101T\ORA101T\BACKUPSET\
  ➥2004_09_11\O1_MF_NNNDF_TAG20040911T120548_0N6M4JBO_.BKP
  ➥tag=TAG20040911T120548
channel ORA_DISK_1: restore complete
Finished restore at 11-SEP-04

Starting recover at 11-SEP-04
using channel ORA_DISK_1

starting media recovery

archive log thread 1 sequence 5 is already on disk as file
  ➥C:\ORACLE\ORAARCH\ORA101T\ARC00005_0536179727.001
archive log
  filename=C:\ORACLE\ORAARCH\ORA101T\ARC00005_0536179727.001
  thread=1
sequence=5
media recovery complete
Finished recover at 11-SEP-04

RMAN> alter database open resetlogs;
```

```
database opened

RMAN>
```

7. Simulate database activity by creating a table T1 and forcing this activity to the archived redo logs:

```
SQL> connect test/test
Connected.
SQL> create table t1(c1 char(20));

Table created.


SQL> connect / as sysdba
Connected.
SQL> alter system switch logfile;

System altered.

SQL> alter system switch logfile;

System altered.

SQL> alter system switch logfile;

System altered.

SQL> alter system switch logfile;

System altered.
```

8. Shut down the database and simulate a database failure by deleting the USERS01.DBF file:

```
SQL> shutdown immediate
Database closed.
Database dismounted.
ORACLE instance shut down.
SQL>

C:\oracle\oradata\ora101t\> del USERS01.DBF
```

9. Start the database in MOUNT mode and then perform a complete recovery in RMAN:

```
SQL> startup mount
ORACLE instance started.

Total System Global Area   88080384 bytes
Fixed Size                   787588 bytes
Variable Size              78642044 bytes
Database Buffers            8388608 bytes
Redo Buffers                 262144 bytes
Database mounted.
SQL>


C:\Documents and Settings\dstuns> rman

Recovery Manager: Release 10.1.0.2.0 - Production

Copyright (c) 1995, 2004, Oracle.  All rights reserved.

RMAN> connect target

connected to target database: ORA101T (DBID=2615281366)

RMAN> run
2> {
3> restore database;
4> recover database;
5> }

Starting restore at 11-SEP-04
using target database controlfile instead of recovery catalog
allocated channel: ORA_DISK_1
channel ORA_DISK_1: sid=49 devtype=DISK

channel ORA_DISK_1: starting datafile backupset restore
channel ORA_DISK_1: specifying datafile(s) to restore from backup set
restoring datafile 00001 to C:\ORACLE\ORADATA\ORA101T\SYSTEM01.DBF
restoring datafile 00002 to C:\ORACLE\ORADATA\ORA101T\UNDOTBS01.DBF
restoring datafile 00003 to C:\ORACLE\ORADATA\ORA101T\SYSAUX01.DBF
restoring datafile 00004 to C:\ORACLE\ORADATA\ORA101T\USERS01.DBF
restoring datafile 00005 to C:\ORACLE\ORADATA\ORA101T\EXAMPLE01.DBF
```

```
restoring datafile 00006 to C:\ORACLE\ORADATA\ORA101T\INDEX01.DBF
channel ORA_DISK_1: restored backup piece 1
piece handle=
  ➥C:\ORACLE\FLASH_RECOVERY_AREA\ORA101T\ORA101T\BACKUPSET\
  ➥2004_09_11\O1_MF_NNNDF_TAG20040911T120548_0N6M4JBO_.BKP
  ➥tag=TAG20040911T120548
channel ORA_DISK_1: restore complete
Finished restore at 11-SEP-04

Starting recover at 11-SEP-04
using channel ORA_DISK_1

starting media recovery

archive log thread 1 sequence 5 is already on disk as file
  ➥C:\ORACLE\ORAARCH\ORA101T\ARC00005_0536179727.001
archive log thread 1 sequence 1 is already on disk as file
  ➥C:\ORACLE\ORAARCH\ORA101T\ARC00001_0536589683.001
archive log thread 1 sequence 2 is already on disk as file
  ➥C:\ORACLE\ORAARCH\ORA101T\ARC00002_0536589683.001
archive log thread 1 sequence 3 is already on disk as file
  ➥C:\ORACLE\ORAARCH\ORA101T\ARC00003_0536589683.001
archive log thread 1 sequence 4 is already on disk as file
  ➥C:\ORACLE\ORAARCH\ORA101T\ARC00004_0536589683.001
archive log filename=
  ➥C:\ORACLE\ORAARCH\ORA101T\ARC00005_0536179727.001 thread=1
sequence=5
archive log filename=
  ➥C:\ORACLE\ORAARCH\ORA101T\ARC00001_0536589683.001 thread=1
sequence=1
archive log filename=
  ➥C:\ORACLE\ORAARCH\ORA101T\ARC00002_0536589683.001 thread=1
sequence=2
media recovery complete
Finished recover at 11-SEP-04

RMAN> alter database open;

database opened

RMAN>
```

10. Validate that you have recovered through the last RESETLOGS by verifying that the current V$LOG_HISTORY table shows the log sequence 6 and thread 1 followed by new redo logs files:

```
SQL> select * from v$log_history;

RECID STAMP     THRD# SEQ# FIR_CHNG FIRST_TIM N_CHNG S_CHNG RESETLOG
----- --------- ----- ---- -------- --------- ------ ------ --------
8     536588583 1     6    609492   11-SEP-04 610333 567536 06-SEP-04
9     536588584 1     7    610333   11-SEP-04 610335 567536 06-SEP-04
10    536588589 1     8    610335   11-SEP-04 610338 567536 06-SEP-04
11    536590054 1     1    609493   11-SEP-04 609880 609493 11-SEP-04
12    536590057 1     2    609880   11-SEP-04 609882 609493 11-SEP-04
13    536590062 1     3    609882   11-SEP-04 609885 609493 11-SEP-04
14    536590102 1     4    609885   11-SEP-04 609904 609493 11-SEP-04

SQL>
```

As you can see, this process requires a few steps to simulate. This is because you are simulating two failures and then performing two recoveries from the same backup. The first recovery is opening the databases with RESETLOGS option. The second recovery is using the same backup to recover past the first recovery with RESETLOGS to the complete recovery without opening the database with RESETLOGS.

Summary

In this chapter, you learned about database recovery in great detail. Database recovery can be performed with RMAN, user-managed, or EM methods. We discussed and demonstrated how to perform incomplete recovery using RMAN, user-managed, and EM methods. We also demonstrated recovery with control files. Incomplete recovery with RMAN is very similar to user-managed incomplete recovery. The main difference is there is CANCEL, a CHANGE-based option for only SCN with user-managed recovery. With RMAN-based recovery, there is no CHANGE-based option and there is the ability to use both SCN and redo log sequence.

You learned how to use the control file autobackup to perform a control file recovery, as well as how to rebuild or re-create a control file from an ASCII trace.

This chapter also discussed the new capabilities of Oracle 10*g* to recover through the RESETLOGS clause.

There are many options for performing database recovery. Some of these options are available for distinct recovery situations. It is important to be aware of all of these recovery methods so that you can be prepared for any failure situation.

Exam Essentials

Understand the different types of incomplete recovery. Make sure you are aware of the steps required for the three different types of incomplete recovery: user-managed, RMAN, and EM. Understand the different failure situations in which incomplete recovery should be used.

Know how to perform incomplete recovery using EM. Make sure you are familiar with the steps required to perform incomplete recovery using EM. Understand how to maneuver through the web screens to perform an incomplete recovery.

Know how to perform incomplete recovery using RMAN. Make sure you are familiar with the steps required to perform incomplete recovery using RMAN. Understand how to use the different RMAN commands for performing incomplete recovery.

Know how to perform incomplete recovery using SQL. Make sure you are familiar with the steps required to perform incomplete recovery using the traditional user-managed methods, which use SQL. Understand how to use the different commands for performing incomplete recovery using user-managed methods.

Understand database recovery using the *RESETLOGS* option. Be aware of how to recover a database using the `RESETLOGS` option. Know what the impacts of the improvements to the `RESETLOGS` option are for an incomplete database recovery.

Review Questions

1. What is another name for RMAN-based database recovery?

   A. User-managed recovery

   B. Server-managed recovery

   C. Traditional recovery

   D. Database recovery

2. What command is responsible for automating the backup of control files?

   A. `ALTER DATABASE CONTROLFILE AUTOBACKUP ON`

   B. `ALTER SYSTEM CONTROLFILE AUTOBACKUP ON`

   C. `CONFIGURE CONTROLFILE AUTOBACKUP ON`

   D. `ENABLE CONTROLFILE AUTOBACKUP`

3. What is the process to recover a control file?

   A. Start up database, restore control file, start up mount the database, recover the database, and open the database.

   B. Start up mount, restore control file, start up the database, recover the database, and open the database.

   C. Start up nomount, restore control file, start up mount the database, recover the database, and open the database.

   D. Start up force, restore control file, start up the database, recover the database, and open the database.

4. When recovering a control file without the recovery catalog, what special step must be performed to identify the target database? (Choose all that apply.)

   A. You must `CONNECT TARGET /` to the target database within RMAN.

   B. You must `STARTUP MOUNT` the database because the control file is missing.

   C. You must `SET DBID` to the target database so that the target database can be identified without the control file available.

   D. You must `CONNECT TARGET` *`database name`* to the target database within RMAN.

5. After you restore the control file, what must you do before you execute the RECOVER command to apply archive logs?

   A. The database must be restored with the RESTORE command.

   B. The database must be reconnected with the `CONNECT TARGET` *`database name`* command.

   C. The database must be started in `MOUNT` mode.

   D. The database must open for use with `ALTER DATABASE OPEN` command.

6. Which of the following methods should you use for creating a control file? (Choose all that apply.)
   - A. Dump the control file information to a trace file.
   - B. Use the `ALTER DATABASE BACKUP CONTROLFILE TO TRACE` command.
   - C. Use the `CREATE CONTROLFILE` command.
   - D. None of the above.

7. What are the two cases defined in the backup control file? (Choose two.)
   - A. `ALTER DATABASE OPEN`
   - B. `ALTER DATABASE OPEN RESETLOGS`
   - C. `ALTER DATABASE OPEN NORESETLOGS`
   - D. `ALTER DATABASE OPEN NORESET`

8. Which files need to be available and in the matching location of the ASCII control file in order to rebuild the control file? (Choose all that apply.)
   - A. Server file, PFILE or SPFILE
   - B. Datafiles
   - C. Control files
   - D. Redo logs

9. Which of the following descriptions best describes incomplete recovery? (Choose all that apply.)
   - A. Recovery that stops before the failure
   - B. Recovery that stops at the point of failure
   - C. Recovery that is missing transactions
   - D. Recovery that is not missing transactions

10. What are the required steps to perform a RMAN-based incomplete recovery with the `SET UNTIL TIME` clause?
    - A. Start up the database in `MOUNT` mode, verify or set the `NLS_DATE_FORMAT` environment variable, designate time with the `SET UNTIL TIME` *`time stamp`*, restore the necessary files with the `RESTORE DATABASE` command, recover the database with the `RECOVER DATABASE` command, and then open the database with the `ALTER DATABASE OPEN` command.
    - B. Start up the database in `NOMOUNT` mode, verify or set the `NLS_DATE_FORMAT` environment variable, designate the `SET UNTIL TIME` *`time stamp`*, restore the necessary files with the `RESTORE DATABASE` command, recover the database with the `RECOVER DATABASE` command, and then open the database with the `ALTER DATABASE OPEN RESETLOGS` command.
    - C. Start up the database in `MOUNT` mode, designate the `SET UNTIL TIME` *`time stamp`*, restore the necessary files with the `RESTORE DATABASE` command, recover the database with the `RECOVER DATABASE` command, and then open the database with `ALTER DATABASE OPEN NORESETLOGS` command.
    - D. Start up the database in `MOUNT` mode, verify or set the `NLS_DATE_FORMAT` environment variable, designate the `SET UNTIL TIME` *`time stamp`*, restore the necessary files with the `RESTORE DATABASE` command, recover the database with the `RECOVER DATABASE` command, and then open the database with `ALTER DATABASE OPEN RESETLOGS` command.

11. Which command is not a valid RMAN incomplete recovery run block?

A.
```
run
  {
   set until change 7563633;
   restore database;
   recover database;
  }
```

B.
```
run
  {
   set until time '06-SEP-2004 11:25:00';
   restore database;
   recover database;
  }
```

C.
```
run
  {
   set until SCN 7563633;
   restore database;
   recover database;
  }
```

D.
```
run
  {
   set until sequence 3 thread 1;
   restore database;
   recover database;
  }
```

12. Which of the following would be a reason for using incomplete recovery? (Choose all that apply.)

A. Stopping the recovery at a certain redo log sequence before a database corruption point

B. Stopping the recovery at a certain time when database corruption occurred

C. Stopping the recovery before a bad transaction is executed

D. Stopping the recovery only after applying all transactions

13. Which incomplete recovery capability is available to RMAN or user-managed methods?

A. `SET UNTIL TIME`

B. `UNTIL TIME`

C. `UNTIL SCN`

D. `UNTIL SEQUENCE`

14. When performing incomplete recovery, which command allows you to stop the recovery process at a random point?

A. `UNTIL SEQUENCE`, when performing a user-managed recovery

B. `UNTIL SCN`, when performing a RMAN-based recovery

C. `UNTIL CANCEL`, when performing a RMAN-based recovery

D. `UNTIL CANCEL`, when performing a user-managed recovery

15. Which command is required when performing an incomplete recovery?

    A. `ALTER DATABASE OPEN RESETLOGS`

    B. `ALTER DATABASE OPEN NORESETLOGS`

    C. `UNTIL CANCEL`

    D. `ALTER DATABASE OPEN`

16. When using EM to perform a whole database incomplete recovery, what sequence of events must occur? (Choose the best answer.)

    A. The database must be shut down and started in `NOMOUNT` mode.

    B. The database must be started in `MOUNT` mode.

    C. The database must be shut down and started in `MOUNT` mode.

    D. The database must be shut down and restarted.

17. Which credentials are needed to perform a recovery with EM? (Choose all that apply.)

    A. Database account with `SYSDBA` privilege

    B. Administrator account in Windows

    C. Oracle account in Unix

    D. Any Windows account

18. The `RESETLOGS` clause is required with which of the following types of incomplete recovery?

    A. Using the `UNTIL CANCEL` command and applying almost all the archived redo logs before cancelling recovery

    B. Using the `UNTIL TIME` command and stopping before the current time

    C. Using the `SET UNTIL SEQUENCE` command and stopping before the last redo log sequence

    D. All of the above

19. What is required to perform a `UNTIL SEQUENCE` recovery in RMAN?

    A. Identifying the sequence number with `V$LOGHISTORY`

    B. Identifying the sequence number with `V$LOG_HISTORY`

    C. Identifying the SCN number with `V$LOG_HISTORY`

    D. Identifying the SCN number with `V$LOGHISTORY`

20. What is required to recover your database through a `RESETLOGS` recovery from a backup created prior to the `RESETLOGS` recovery?

    A. `NORESETLOGS`

    B. `RESETLOGS`

    C. `UNTIL SEQUENCE`

    D. Nothing, this feature is automatic.

Answers to Review Questions

1. B. Server-managed recovery is another name for RMAN recovery because the server session performs the recovery process as it interacts with the target database.

2. C. The control file autobackup is enabled by setting parameters within RMAN by using `CONFIGURE CONTROLFILE AUTOBACKUP ON`.

3. C. The database needs to be started in `NOMOUNT` mode because there is not a control file available to `MOUNT` the database. Next, the control file can be restored. Once a restored control file is available, the database can be started in `MOUNT` mode so that standard database recovery can continue. When recovery is complete, the database can `OPEN` for normal use.

4. A, C. The target database is not identifiable by database name without the control file. So you must first use the `CONNECT TARGET /` command to connect. The target database needs to be identified by the database identifier (DBID) number with the command `SET DBID` *`database identifier`*. This database identifier number denotes the target database. When you are recovering the control file, the target database identification is not available because it is stored in the control file.

5. C. The database must be mounted before the `RECOVER` command can be executed. You first must restore control so you can `MOUNT` the database.

6. A, B. The `ALTER DATABASE BACKUP CONTROL FILE TO TRACE` command creates a user trace file, which stores an ASCII representation of the binary control file.

7. B, C. The two cases in the backup control file are opening the database with `RESETLOGS` or `NORESETLOGS`.

8. A, B. The server file, SPFILE or `PFILE` must be available to start the database with the right parameters, and the datafiles must be in the location matching the control file. The redo logs and control file will be rebuilt.

9. A, C. Incomplete recovery is a recovery that stops before the failure and a recovery that is missing transactions. Incomplete recovery is not complete or missing some data that was previously stored in the database prior to the failure.

10. D. The proper process of performing a RMAN based incomplete recovery utilizing a time stamp to determine the point-in-time to complete the recovery process is as follows: Start up the database in `MOUNT` mode, verify or set the `NLS_DATE_FORMAT` environment variable if not present, designate the `SET UNTIL TIME` *`time stamp`*, restore the necessary files with the `RESTORE DATABASE` command, recover the database with the `RECOVER DATABASE` command, and then open the database with `ALTER DATABASE OPEN RESETLOGS` command.

11. A. The `SET UNTIL CHANGE` command is not used with RMAN. This command is used during a user-managed incomplete recovery.

12. A, B, C. Incomplete recovery is designed to be able to stop at a desired point, before introducing undesired transactions to the database.

13. B. The UNTIL TIME clause is available in both user-managed and RMAN-based incomplete recovery methods.

14. D. The UNTIL CANCEL command is available only in user-managed recovery. This command allows you to stop the recovery process at a random point during redo log switches.

15. A. The ALTER DATABASE OPEN RESETLOGS command is required with every incomplete recovery. This is because the redo log sequence always needs to be reset.

16. C. When using EM, the database must be shut down and started in MOUNT mode so that a whole database backup can be performed when you are recovering the same database EM is connected to.

17. A, B, C. You need two credentials when running a recovery with EM: the correct operating system account and the correct database account. The correct operating system account is an account similar to the Oracle account in Unix or the administrator account in Windows. The database account is any account that has SYSDBA privilege.

18. D. The RESETLOGS clause is required with all incomplete recovery options. The RESETLOGS clause is required because you are opening the database to a point prior to the existing redo log entries. So the redo logs must be reset when the database is opened.

19. B. You need to know the redo log sequence number and thread to perform an UNTIL SEQUENCE recovery in RMAN. This can be obtained by querying the V$LOG_HISTORY dynamic view.

20. D. The new feature to recover your database through a prior RESETLOGS recovery is native with Oracle 10*g*. Oracle will recover the database through the RESETLOGS prior to recovery if necessary.

Understanding the Flashback Database

ORACLE DATABASE 10*G*: ADMINISTRATION II EXAM OBJECTIVES COVERED IN THIS CHAPTER:

✓ **Flashback Database**

- Determine which flashback technology to use for each recovery situation.
- Configure and use Flashback Database.
- Monitor the Flashback Database.
- Use the Enterprise Manager to manage the Flashback Database.
- Manage or (maintain) the Flash Recovery Area.

Exam objectives are subject to change at any time without prior notice and at Oracle's sole discretion. Please visit Oracle's Training and Certification website (`http://www.oracle.com/education/certification/`) for the most current exam objectives listing.

This chapter provides a detailed explanation and step-by-step instructions for using the new Oracle Database 10*g* (Oracle 10*g*) feature: the Flashback Database. We will discuss how to enable and disable the Flashback Database. We also discuss how to use the flash recovery area, which is required to use the Flashback Database. Additionally, you will use Enterprise Manager (EM) to configure and perform a Flashback Database recovery.

This chapter pays heavy attention on the workings of the Flashback Database. The overview of the Flashback Database explains its architecture in detail. This includes the flash recovery area, which is a prerequisite to setting up the Flashback Database. This chapter also describes the setup and configuration of the Flashback Database and explains in which situations you should use the Flashback Database. We will also discuss how to monitor the Flashback Database. You will see demonstrations and perform step-by-step examples performing each of these tasks, as well as other related activities.

An Overview of Flashback Technologies

Oracle Flashback Technologies were first developed in Oracle 9*i* with the advent of the Flashback Query. In Oracle 10*g*, there has been a significant extension of this technology. This chapter focuses on one specific Flashback Technology—the Oracle Flashback Database—but it is important to have a general understanding of all the Flashback Technologies and where these technologies are best used. This understanding will enable you to put the benefits of each of these technologies into context. The new Oracle 10*g* Flashback Technologies consist of the following:

- Flashback Database
- Flashback Drop
- Flashback Versions Query
- Flashback Transaction Query
- Flashback Table

Chapter 6, "Recovering from User Errors," will discuss Flashback Drop, Flashback Versions Query, Flashback Transaction Query, and Flashback Table in detail. It is important to note that all the flashback technologies, with the exception of the Flashback Database, are based on undo data. The Flashback Database is best used as a replacement for incomplete recovery of a complete database. The main benefit of the Oracle Flashback Database over incomplete database recovery is that the Flashback Database is much quicker and more efficient. The Flashback Database is not based on undo data but on flashback logs.

Flashback Drop, Flashback Versions Query, Flashback Transactions Query, and Flashback Table are best used to recover individual objects or rows within an object. The Flashback Drop provides a virtual Recycle Bin that allows a dropped object to be restored. The Flashback Versions Query and Flashback Transaction Query are designed to identify and allow you to fix rows of data that need to be reverted to a previous state. Flashback Table is designed to recover individual tables or groups of tables from errors such as when the table is updated with the wrong WHERE clause.

The Flashback Technologies, with the exception of the Flashback Database, are designed so that end users can repair their own errors. This reduces the need for the DBA to be involved in every recovery activity. The Flashback Database and sometimes the Flashback Table is a DBA activity because of their global impact to the database. The Flashback Database is best suited to recover from errors such as truncating a large table, an incomplete batch job, or a dropped user. The next sections will explain the Flashback Database in detail and show you how to use it.

An Overview of the Flashback Database

The *Flashback Database* is new to Oracle 10*g*. As mentioned previously, this feature builds upon the flash query capability that was first introduced in Oracle 9*i*. Now Flashback technology has been greatly extended, which includes flashback database, flashback query, flashback version query, flashback transaction query, flashback table, and flashback drop. There is one main difference with these flashback technologies and the new Oracle 10*g* Flashback Database: The Flashback Database relies on "before" images in the flashback logs, but traditional flashback technology relies on the undo data.

The Flashback Database allows you to flash the entire database back to a specific point-in-time. This is extremely useful to recover from errors such as truncating a large table, an incomplete batch job, or a dropped user. Flashback Database recovery is also the best choice for most logical corruptions such as a bad complex transaction that gets propagated throughout the database.

Real World Scenario

Limitations with the Flashback Database

Flashback Database recovery has some limitations that can impact the use of this valuable tool. *User errors* or logical corruptions are often the most difficult recovery processes because impact to the database is often not clearly known. These types of failures by themselves are where the Flashback Database is the most effective.

However, Flashback Database recovery cannot recover through some cases that are common occurrences in a lot of situations such as resizing a datafile to a smaller size or a deleted datafile. In these cases, Flashback Database recovery can be used with traditional incomplete recovery for an efficient recovery solution.

In the case of a deleted or resized datafile, the datafile would need to be restored with traditional methods to a point-in-time prior to the deletion or resizing of the datafile. Then you could use Flashback Database recovery to recover the rest of the database.

One major technological benefit of the Flashback Database is that it allows you to reverse user errors or logical corruption much quicker than performing a traditional incomplete recovery or using the Oracle Log Miner utility. The reason the Flashback Database recovery is much quicker than traditional recovery operations is due to the fact that recovery is no longer impacted by the size of the database. The mean time to recovery (MTTR) for traditional recovery is dependent on the size of the datafiles and archive logs that need to be restored and applied. Using Flashback Database recovery, recovery time is proportional to the number of changes that need to be backed out of the recovery process, not the size of datafiles and archive logs. This makes the Flashback Database recovery process the most efficient recovery process in most user error or logical corruption situations.

The Flashback Database architecture consists of the recovery writer *RVWR* background process and Flashback Database logs. When the Flashback Database is enabled, the RVWR process is started. *Flashback Database logs* are a new type of log file that contain a "before" image of physical database blocks. The RVWR writes the Flashback Database logs in the flash recovery area. Writing Flashback Database logs requires the flash recovery area to be enabled. The flash recovery area is a prerequisite to the Flashback Database because the Flashback Database logs are written to the flash recovery area. Figure 5.1 shows a diagram of the main components of the Flashback Database architecture.

FIGURE 5.1 Flashback Database architecture

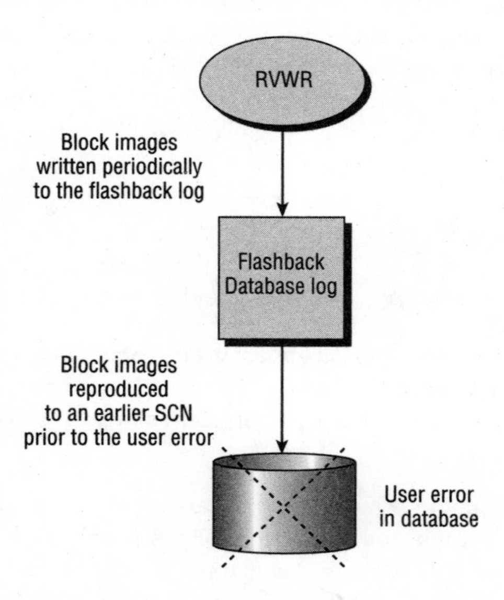

The Flashback Database is a nice substitute for incomplete recovery for logical corruption and user errors. However, there are some limitations to the Flashback Database that you should be aware of:

- Media failure cannot be resolved with the Flashback Database. You will still need to restore datafiles and recover archived redo logs to recover from media failure.

- Resizing datafiles to a smaller size, also called shrinking datafiles, cannot be undone with the Flashback Database.
- You cannot use the Flashback Database if the control file has been restored or recreated.
- Dropping a tablespace and recovery through RESETLOGS cannot be performed.
- You cannot flash back the database to an SCN prior to the earliest available SCN in the flashback logs.

Managing the Flash Recovery Area with Recovery Manager

Flash recovery is new with release Oracle 10*g*. The *flash recovery area* is designed to centralize the storage of all recovery files in a certain location on disk. The flash recovery area can use the local disk, a disk subsystem like a Storage Area Network (SAN) or Network Attached Storage (NAS), or Oracle *Automatic Storage Management (ASM)*. ASM is new with 10*g* and is part of the new Automation Features of 10*g*, which are designed to minimize the workload by simplifying the disk and file system configuration. ASM is targeted at the smaller end database market, which may not have a dedicated database administrator.

Flash recovery provides a couple of key benefits to the recovery process:

- All recovery files are stored in centralized location.
- It provides a much faster method of backing up and restoring because the information is written to disk as opposed to tape.

Flash recovery is created by initializing a database parameter. The size and location of the flash recovery area are also defined in a database parameter. This information is automatically recorded in the database alert log as files are added or deleted from the flash recovery area. There is also a database view that provides information about the status of the flash recovery area: `DBA_OUTSTANDING_ALERTS`.

The retention period of the files in the flash recovery area are determined by the Recovery Manager (RMAN) retention policy, which is defined by the RMAN `CONFIGURE RETENTION POLICY` command. This command specifies the number of days to retain backups. Only files with retention policies can be deleted from the flash recovery area. Files that exceed the retention policy or are obsolete are then deleted from the flash recovery area. Files that are not obsolete are not deleted and are available for restore.

The Oracle 10*g* database will send warnings to the alert log when the flash recovery area has reached 90 percent and 95 percent full. At 90 percent full, Oracle 10*g* will automatically remove files that are obsolete from the flash recovery area.

Now that we understand what is involved in managing the flash recovery area, we will walk through configuring the flash recovery area in the next sections. We will also write RMAN backups to the flash recovery area.

Configuring the Flash Recovery Area

Setting up a flash recovery area is fairly straightforward procedure. All that is required to create this feature is to add a couple of database parameters to your database.

Let's go through an example of setting up the flash recovery area:

1. Add the following database parameter for the size of the flash recovery area to the `init.ora` and/or SPFILE:

   ```
   SQL> alter system set db_recovery_file_dest_size=10M scope=both;
   ```

2. Add the following database parameter for the location of the flash recovery area:

   ```
   SQL> alter system set db_recovery_file_dest='
   ➥C:\oracle\flash_recovery_area\ora101t';
   ```

There are also commands to modify the size of and disable the recovery area. These commands are performed with a similar ALTER SYSTEM statement. Let's look at these commands:

To increase the size of the flash recovery area to 25MB, use this command:

```
SQL> alter system set db_recovery_file_dest_size=25mb;
```

To disable the flash recovery area, use this command:

```
SQL> alter system set db_recovery_file_dest='';
```

Using the Flash Recovery Area

As mentioned earlier, the flash recovery area is a centralized recovery area where recovery-related files can be managed. Before, Oracle 10*g* archive log files could get out of synch with backups and require manual cleanup. One characteristic of the flash recovery area is that these files are related with the datafiles and control files. This reduces the manual cleanup of unneeded archive logs. Once the flashback recovery area is set up, it is a straightforward process to perform a backup. You need to specify the flash recovery database to be the default for backups using the CONFIGURE command. Next, you can perform a BACKUP or BACKUP AS COPY command. The backup will be directed to the flash recovery area for centralized storage. You can also check the space consumed and other statistics about the flash recovery area by querying V$RECOVERY_FILE_DEST. This dynamic view displays all the information about the usage of the flash recovery area. You need to access RMAN and back up the recovery area.

Let's walk through performing an automated disk-based backup and recovery:

1. First, connect to the target database:

   ```
   C:\Documents and Settings\> set ORACLE_SID=ora101c

   C:\Documents and Settings\> rman
   Recovery Manager: Release 10.1.0.2.0 - Production
   Copyright (c) 1995, 2004, Oracle.  All rights reserved.
   ```

```
RMAN> connect target
connected to target database: ORA101C (DBID=1736563848)
RMAN>
```

2. Next, perform a backup of the target database:

```
RMAN> backup as copy database;

Starting backup at 22-JUN-04
allocated channel: ORA_DISK_1
channel ORA_DISK_1: sid=146 devtype=DISK
channel ORA_DISK_1: starting datafile copy
input datafile fno=00001 name=C:\ORACLE\ORADATA\ORA101C\SYSTEM01.DBF
output filename=C:\ORACLE\FLASH_RECOVERY_AREA\ORA101C\
  ➥%REC_AREA_7_1.BAK tag=TAG2
0040622T225613 recid=2 stamp=529541843
channel ORA_DISK_1: datafile copy complete, elapsed time: 00:01:15
channel ORA_DISK_1: starting datafile copy
input datafile fno=00003 name=C:\ORACLE\ORADATA\ORA101C\SYSAUX01.DBF
output filename=C:\ORACLE\FLASH_RECOVERY_AREA\ORA101C\
  ➥%REC_AREA_8_1.BAK tag=TAG2
0040622T225613 recid=3 stamp=529541892
channel ORA_DISK_1: datafile copy complete, elapsed time: 00:28:55
channel ORA_DISK_1: starting datafile copy
input datafile fno=00005 name=C:\ORACLE\ORADATA\ORA101C\EXAMPLE01.DBF
output filename=C:\ORACLE\FLASH_RECOVERY_AREA\ORA101C\
  ➥%REC_AREA_9_1.BAK tag=TAG2
0040622T225613 recid=4 stamp=529543607
channel ORA_DISK_1: datafile copy complete, elapsed time: 00:00:25
channel ORA_DISK_1: starting datafile copy
input datafile fno=00002 name=C:\ORACLE\ORADATA\ORA101C\UNDOTBS01.DBF
output filename=C:\ORACLE\FLASH_RECOVERY_AREA\ORA101C\
  ➥%REC_AREA_10_1.BAK tag=TAG
20040622T225613 recid=5 stamp=529543617
channel ORA_DISK_1: datafile copy complete, elapsed time: 00:00:08
channel ORA_DISK_1: starting datafile copy
input datafile fno=00004 name=C:\ORACLE\ORADATA\ORA101C\USERS01.DBF
output filename=C:\ORACLE\FLASH_RECOVERY_AREA\ORA101C\
  ➥%REC_AREA_11_1.BAK tag=TAG
20040622T225613 recid=6 stamp=529543621
channel ORA_DISK_1: datafile copy complete, elapsed time: 00:01:47
channel ORA_DISK_1: starting datafile copy
```

```
copying current controlfile
output filename=C:\ORACLE\FLASH_RECOVERY_AREA\ORA101C\
  ➥%REC_AREA_12_1.BAK tag=TAG
20040622T225613 recid=7 stamp=529543727
channel ORA_DISK_1: datafile copy complete, elapsed time: 00:00:03
Finished backup at 22-JUN-04

RMAN>
```

3. Finally, query the V$RECOVERY_FILE_DEST to determine if the SPACE_USED column value has increased.

```
SQL> select * from v$recovery_file_dest;

NAME                        SPACE_LI SPACE_US SPACE_REC NUM_FILES
-------------------------- -------- -------- --------- ---------
C:\flash_recovery_area\ora   214748   330852   2932735         5
```

The flash recovery area can also be used to create many types of Oracle database files. The flashback recovery area can contain datafiles, control files, online redo logs, miscellaneous RMAN files, and flashback logs. To fully take advantage of the flash recovery area, you can store files like redo logs, control files, and archived redo logs when these files are created.

There are few important facts you need to know about creating database files in the flash recovery area. We will discuss these unique behaviors for each initialization parameter that creates files in the flash recovery area. The following commands can be used to create online redo logs in the flash recovery area:

- CREATE DATABASE
- ALTER DATABASE ADD LOGFILE
- ALTER DATABASE ADD STANDBY LOGFILE
- ALTER DATABASE OPENRESET LOGS

Let's discuss some of the impacts of creating specific database files in the flash recovery area. There are some initialization parameters that decide the location of the online redo log files in general. These initialization parameters are

- DB_CREATE_ONLINE_LOG_DEST_*n*
- DB_RECOVERY_FILE_DEST
- DB_CREATE_FILE_DEST

These initialization parameters can be used to create the online redo log files and must be considered when creating the online redo logs in the flash recovery area.

The default size of the redo logs that are created in the flash recovery area is 100MB.

The following initialization parameters decide the location of the control files in general:

- CONTROL_FILES
- DB_CREATE_ONLINE_LOG_DEST_*n*
- DB_RECOVERY_FILE_DEST
- DB_CREATE_FILE_DEST

All these initialization parameters decide where the database control file is created and must be considered when creating the control file in the flash recovery area. There are some important behaviors to be aware of when using Oracle Managed Files. *Oracle Managed Files (OMF)* is a feature where Oracle creates the database files and manages these for you. This was the precursor to Automated Storage Management (ASM), which is new to 10*g*.

It is important to note that if you use both DB_RECOVERY_FILE_DEST and DB_CREATE_FILE_DEST initialization parameters with OMF, the control file will be created in the location of each parameter. When using DB_CREATE_ONLINE_LOG_DEST_*n* with OMF, the control files will be located in *n* number of locations with the first location as the primary control file. When using the DB_RECOVERY_FILE_DEST, the control file will be placed in the flash recovery area. The initialization parameters that impact the location of archived log files are

- LOG_ARCHIVE_DEST_*n*
- LOG_ARCHIVE_DEST
- LOG_ARCHIVE_DUPLEX_DEST

However, only the LOG_ARCHIVE_DEST_*n* parameter can be used to create archived log files in the flash recovery area.

As you can see, using the flash recovery area is relatively simple. Once the flash recovery area has been set up, you just need to use the CONFIGURE command to set the flash recovery area as the default for backups. Then you can perform backups normally. You can see from querying the V$RECOVERY_FILE_DEST dynamic view in the NUM_FILES column that five datafiles were added to the flash recovery area. You can also see the SPACE_LIMIT information and how much space you have used in the SPACE_USED column.

Database files can also be created from their conception in the flash recovery area. The method of creating files is the same as if you created these files otherwise. There are some limitations and defaults with some of the initialization parameters that we discussed. You should be aware of these limitations.

Backing Up the Flash Recovery Area

Backup of the flash recovery area is an important activity because this area contains important backup information that is critical to the recovery of the database. Oracle has developed special commands to back up the flash recovery area. This is performed to a tape device so that the backups to the flash recovery can be recovered if there is a disk failure that supports the flash recovery area.

There are two commands that are used in backing up the flash recovery area:

- BACKUP RECOVERY AREA backs up the whole recovery area.
- BACKUP RECOVERY FILES just backs up the files in the recovery area.

Here's the syntax for the two commands that back up the flash recovery area to a tape device:

```
RMAN> backup recovery area;

RMAN> backup recovery files;
```

As you can see, these commands are straightforward. The purpose of these commands is to protect the flash recovery area. These commands must be used with a tape device and a media manager configured to use with RMAN.

When backing up the flash recovery area, only datafiles and miscellaneous RMAN files will be backed up and removed. Current redo log files and control files are not backed up, made obsolete, and then removed because Oracle considers current redo log files and multiplexed control files to be *permanent*. While flashback logs are not backed up, they are still considered *transient*, the same as datafiles and RMAN working files.

Configuring the Flashback Database

In order to use the Flashback Database, the database must have multiple features configured prior to configuring the Flashback Database. The database must have ARCHIVE LOG enabled. As mentioned before, the flash recovery area must be configured to store the Flashback Database logs.

First, you can configure the Flashback Database, so the database must be shut down. Next, the database must be started in MOUNT mode. Then, the database parameter DB_FLASHBACK_RETENTION_TARGET can be set to the desired value, which is based on minutes. This value determines how far back in time you can flash back the database. This is like a baseline for the Flashback Database. Next, the Flashback Database can be enabled with the ALTER DATABASE FLASHBACK ON command. Finally, the database can be opened for normal use.

Let's walk through these steps in more detail:

1. Start the database in MOUNT mode:

```
SQL> connect / as sysdba
SQL> startup mount
ORACLE instance started.

Total System Global Area   88080384 bytes
Fixed Size                   787588 bytes
```

```
Variable Size             78642044 bytes
Database Buffers           8388608 bytes
Redo Buffers                262144 bytes
Database mounted.
```

2. Set the DB_FLASHBACK_RETENTION_TARGET parameter to the desired value. This value can be set as an initialization parameter if you're not using the SPFILE. This value is in minutes, which equates to three days:

```
SQL> alter set system db_flashback_retention_target=4320;
```

3. Enable the flashback capability:

```
SQL> alter database flashback on;
```

4. Now the database can be opened for normal use:

```
SQL> alter database open;
```

As you can see, enabling the Flashback Database is fairly simple. A key point for you is to know is how far back in time you need to be able to flash back from or know the DB_FLASHBACK_RETENTION_TARGET parameter value. The *DB_FLASHBACK_RETENTION_TARGET* value will determine how far back you can flash back the database to in minutes. In the preceding example, you specified the value of 4,320, which is for three days.

Using the Flashback Database with RMAN

The Flashback Database can be used with RMAN to perform recoveries. Using the RMAN interface to perform Flashback Database recovery is a straightforward process. Once the database is configured for the Flashback Database, you just need to start the database in MOUNT mode, and you are ready to perform a Flashback Database recovery. You also need to get either OLDEST_FLASHBACK_SCN or OLDEST_FLASHBACK_TIME from the V$FLASHBACK_DATABASE_LOG view. This will allow you to utilize the TO SCN or TO TIME clause in the FLASHBACK DATABASE clause. There is also the TO SEQUENCE clause, which uses the redo log sequence and thread to perform the recovery.

Let's walk through performing a Flashback Database recovery to a SCN:

1. First, query the V$FLASHBACK_DATABASE_LOG view to retrieve the OLDEST_FLASHBACK_SCN:

```
C:\Documents and Settings\dstuns> sqlplus /nolog

SQL*Plus: Release 10.1.0.2.0 - Production on Fri Oct 1 22:12:36 2004

Copyright (c) 1982, 2004, Oracle.  All rights reserved.

SQL> connect / as sysdba
Connected.
```

```
SQL> select oldest_flashback_scn, oldest_flashback_time
  2  from v$flashback_database_log;

OLDEST_FLASHBACK_SCN OLDEST_FLASHBACK_TIME
-------------------- ---------------------
              689316 29-SEP-04

SQL>
```

table to see scn numbers

2. Next, shut down and start the database in MOUNT mode:

```
SQL> shutdown
Database closed.
Database dismounted.
ORACLE instance shut down.
SQL>
SQL> startup mount
ORACLE instance started.

Total System Global Area   88080384 bytes
Fixed Size                   787588 bytes
Variable Size              78642044 bytes
Database Buffers            8388608 bytes
Redo Buffers                 262144 bytes
Database mounted.
SQL>
```

3. Next, issue the Flashback Database recovery from RMAN:

```
C:\Documents and Settings\dstuns> rman

Recovery Manager: Release 10.1.0.2.0 - Production

Copyright (c) 1995, 2004, Oracle.  All rights reserved.

RMAN> connect target

connected to target database: ORA101 (DBID=4215248570)

RMAN> flashback database to scn=689316;
```

```
Starting flashback at 01-OCT-04
using target database controlfile instead of recovery catalog
allocated channel: ORA_DISK_1
channel ORA_DISK_1: sid=158 devtype=DISK


starting media recovery

archive log thread 1 sequence 1 is already on disk as file
  ➥C:\ORACLE\ORAARCH\ORA101\ARC00001_0538108686.001
media recovery complete
Finished flashback at 01-OCT-04

RMAN>
```

4. Finally, open the database with the RESETLOGS option, because you recovered to a time prior to the current database:

```
SQL> alter database open resetlogs;

Database altered.
```

As you can see, the Flashback Database recovery is a fairly simple process. The V$FLASHBACK_DATABASE_LOG dynamic view is useful for both TO SCN and TO TIME recoveries. The Flashback Database recovery is a quick and efficient method for recovering from user errors or logical corruptions in the database. This is a great alternative to performing a traditional incomplete recovery.

The Flashback Database can also be performed in SQL*Plus with the FLASHBACK DATABASE command as well as RMAN.

Monitoring the Flashback Database

The Flashback Database can be monitored by using a few dynamic views: V$DATABASE, V$FLASHBACK_DATABASE_LOG, and V$FLASHBACK_DATABASE_STAT. These views provide some valuable information regarding the status of the Flashback Database and the supporting operations.

The V$DATABASE view displays if the Flashback Database is on or off. This tells you whether the Flashback Database is enabled or not.

Let's query the V$DATABASE view and see the results:

```
SQL> select flashback_on from v$database;

FLASHBACK_ON
------------
YES

SQL>
```

The V$FLASHBACK_DATABASE_LOG view is new to Oracle 10*g* and was created to support the Flashback Database. The main purpose of this view is to allow you determine the amount of space required in the recovery area to support the flashback activity generated by changes in the database. The values in the OLDEST_FLASHBACK_SCN and OLDEST_FLASHBACK_TIME columns give you information regarding how far back you can use the Flashback Database. This view also shows the size of the flashback data in the FLASHBACK_SIZE column. The column ESTIMATED_FLASHBACK_SIZE can be used to identify the estimated size of flashback data that you need for your current target retention. Shown next is an example of querying the V$FLASHBACK_DATABASE_LOG.

```
SQL> select
  1  oldest_flashback_scn,
  2  oldest_flashback_time,
  3  retention_target,
  4  estimated_flashback_size
  5  from v$flashback_database_log;

OLDEST_FLASH_SCN OLDEST_FLASH_TIME RET_TARGET EST_FLASHBACK_SIZE
---------------- ----------------- ---------- ------------------
689316           29-SEP-04         1440       298967040

SQL>
```

The V$FLASHBACK_DATABASE_STAT view is used to monitor the overhead of maintaining the data in the Flashback Database logs. This view allows you to make estimates regarding future Flashback Database operations. This is done by coming up with an estimate about potential required space.

Let's look at the V$FLASHBACK_DATABASE_STAT:

```
SQL> select * from v$flashback_database_stat;

BEGIN_TIM END_TIME FLAS_DATA DB_DATA REDO_DATA EST_FLASHBACK_SIZE
--------- -------- --------- ------- --------- ------------------
29-SEP-04 29-SEP-04  7774208  16531456 4586496                  0
```

```
29-SEP-04 29-SEP-04 12976128  26238976 7306240          294862848
29-SEP-04 29-SEP-04 11100160  23257088 7217152          293437440
29-SEP-04 29-SEP-04 10903552  23003136 7135232          296165376
29-SEP-04 29-SEP-04 11173888  22495232 6960128          300023808
29-SEP-04 29-SEP-04 12435456  23420928 7499264          304029696
29-SEP-04 29-SEP-04 13565952  27009024 8587264          304865280
29-SEP-04 29-SEP-04 12255232  23420928 7854080          301522944
29-SEP-04 29-SEP-04 11771904  22192128 7110144          303071232
29-SEP-04 29-SEP-04 10969088  21127168 7652352          308232192
29-SEP-04 29-SEP-04 11067392  20873216 8052736          322805760
29-SEP-04 29-SEP-04 11132928  21135360 7340544          350158848
29-SEP-04 29-SEP-04 19652608  49127424 10739200         425238528

13 rows selected.
SQL>
```

As you can see, the V$FLASHBACK_DATABASE_STAT dynamic view shows the utilization of the Flashback Database log. This is determined by the begin and end times.

Using the Flashback Database with Enterprise Manager

You can use the Flashback Database in Enterprise Manager (EM) just as you can in RMAN. You must have configured the flash recovery area and performed the same prerequisites you did with RMAN. This can be done manually in SQL, or you can simply go to the Maintenance and Configure Recovery Settings screens in EM to perform the same tasks.

Once the database is configured to support a Flashback Database, the recovery can be performed. The procedure for performing a Flashback Database recovery is done through the standard Maintenance and Perform Recovery options in the EM menu.

The following sections discuss and demonstrate how to configure, use, and monitor the Flashback Database using EM in more detail.

Configuring the Flashback Database with EM

To configure the Flashback Database with EM, you have to log in with a SYSDBA account. After logging into EM, you are directed to the Home page by default. Go to the Maintenance screen by clicking the Maintenance tab. Once in the Maintenance screen, choose Configure Recovery Settings under the Backup/Recovery section.

The Configure Recovery Settings screen allows you to set up all the parameters associated with the flash recovery area and the Flashback Database. The first parameter that can be configured is the FLASH_RECOVERY_AREA location and size. You can also enable FLASHBACK_LOGGING and FLASHBACK_RETENTION_TARGET. The following graphics show the Configure Recovery Settings screen in more detail. (This is broken into two graphics to display the entire screen.)

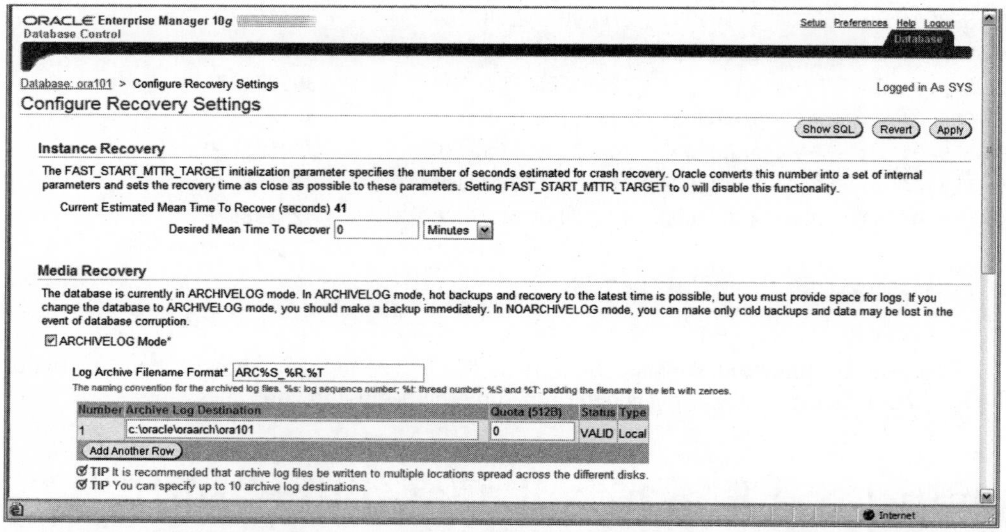

ORACLE Enterprise Manager 10g
Database Control

Setup Preferences Help Logout
Database

Database: ora101 > Configure Recovery Settings
Logged in As SYS

Configure Recovery Settings

Show SQL Revert Apply

Instance Recovery

The FAST_START_MTTR_TARGET initialization parameter specifies the number of seconds estimated for crash recovery. Oracle converts this number into a set of internal parameters and sets the recovery time as close as possible to these parameters. Setting FAST_START_MTTR_TARGET to 0 will disable this functionality.

Current Estimated Mean Time To Recover (seconds) **41**

Desired Mean Time To Recover 0 Minutes

Media Recovery

The database is currently in ARCHIVELOG mode. In ARCHIVELOG mode, hot backups and recovery to the latest time is possible, but you must provide space for logs. If you change the database to ARCHIVELOG mode, you should make a backup immediately. In NOARCHIVELOG mode, you can make only cold backups and data may be lost in the event of database corruption.

☑ ARCHIVELOG Mode*

Log Archive Filename Format* ARC%S_%R.%T

The naming convention for the archived log files. %s: log sequence number; %t: thread number; %S and %T: padding the filename to the left with zeroes.

Number	Archive Log Destination	Quota (512B)	Status	Type
1	c:\oracle\oraarch\ora101	0	VALID	Local

Add Another Row

TIP It is recommended that archive log files be written to multiple locations spread across the different disks.
TIP You can specify up to 10 archive log destinations.

Internet

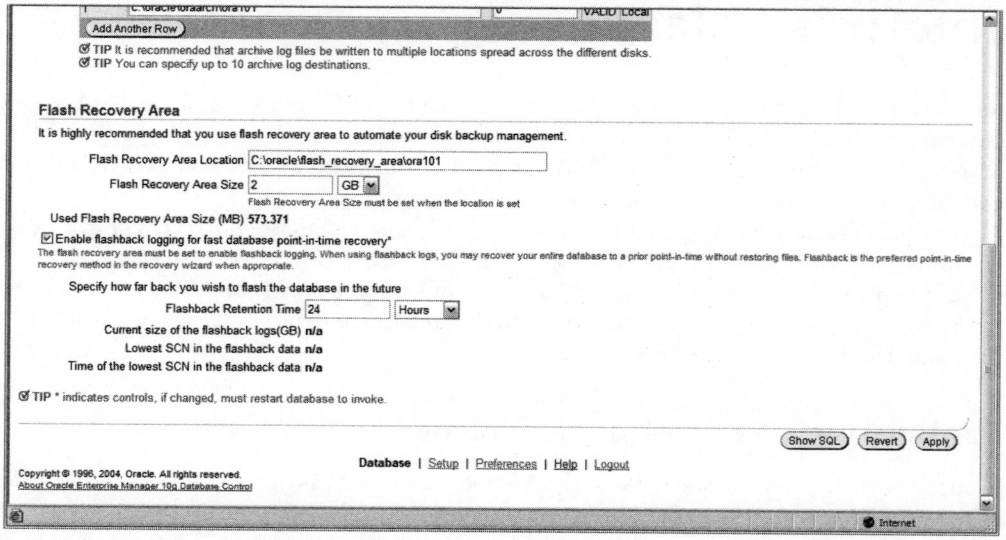

Add Another Row

TIP It is recommended that archive log files be written to multiple locations spread across the different disks.
TIP You can specify up to 10 archive log destinations.

Flash Recovery Area

It is highly recommended that you use flash recovery area to automate your disk backup management.

Flash Recovery Area Location C:\oracle\flash_recovery_area\ora101

Flash Recovery Area Size 2 GB

Flash Recovery Area Size must be set when the location is set

Used Flash Recovery Area Size (MB) 573.371

☑ Enable flashback logging for fast database point-in-time recovery*

The flash recovery area must be set to enable flashback logging. When using flashback logs, you may recover your entire database to a prior point-in-time without restoring files. Flashback is the preferred point-in-time recovery method in the recovery wizard when appropriate.

Specify how far back you wish to flash the database in the future

Flashback Retention Time 24 Hours

Current size of the flashback logs(GB) n/a

Lowest SCN in the flashback data n/a

Time of the lowest SCN in the flashback data n/a

TIP * indicates controls, if changed, must restart database to invoke.

Show SQL Revert Apply

Database | Setup | Preferences | Help | Logout

About Oracle Enterprise Manager 10g Database Control

Internet

As you can see, the flashback recovery area and Flashback Database can be easily configured in the Configure Recovery Settings screen. This allows you to quickly change values with pull-down menus and list boxes.

When enabling flashback logging within EM, you must restart the database for the changes to take effect. This is identified by the light blue asterisk and the note under the controls.

Using the Flashback Database with EM

After you have configured the Flashback Database with EM, you can use EM to perform a Flashback Database recovery. The Flashback Database recovery is performed like a normal recovery. When the Flashback Database is configured, EM determines by your selections in the screens whether you can recover with the Flashback Database. This option is then presented to you during the recovery process.

Let's walk through a Flashback Database recovery using an SCN number:

1. Log in to EM as a SYSDBA enabled user.

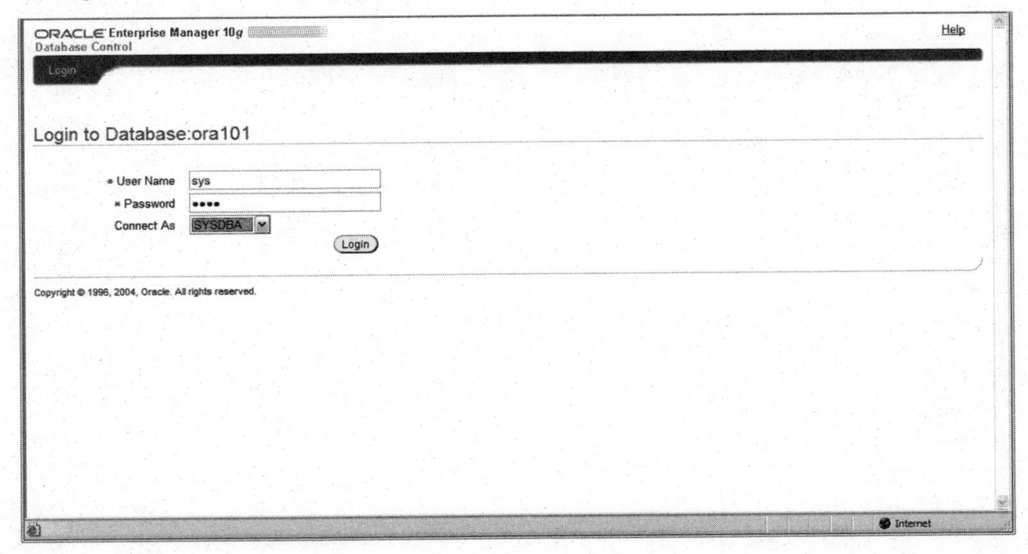

2. Once logged in, you are directed to the Home page. (This is broken into two graphics to display the entire screen.) Select the Maintenance screen.

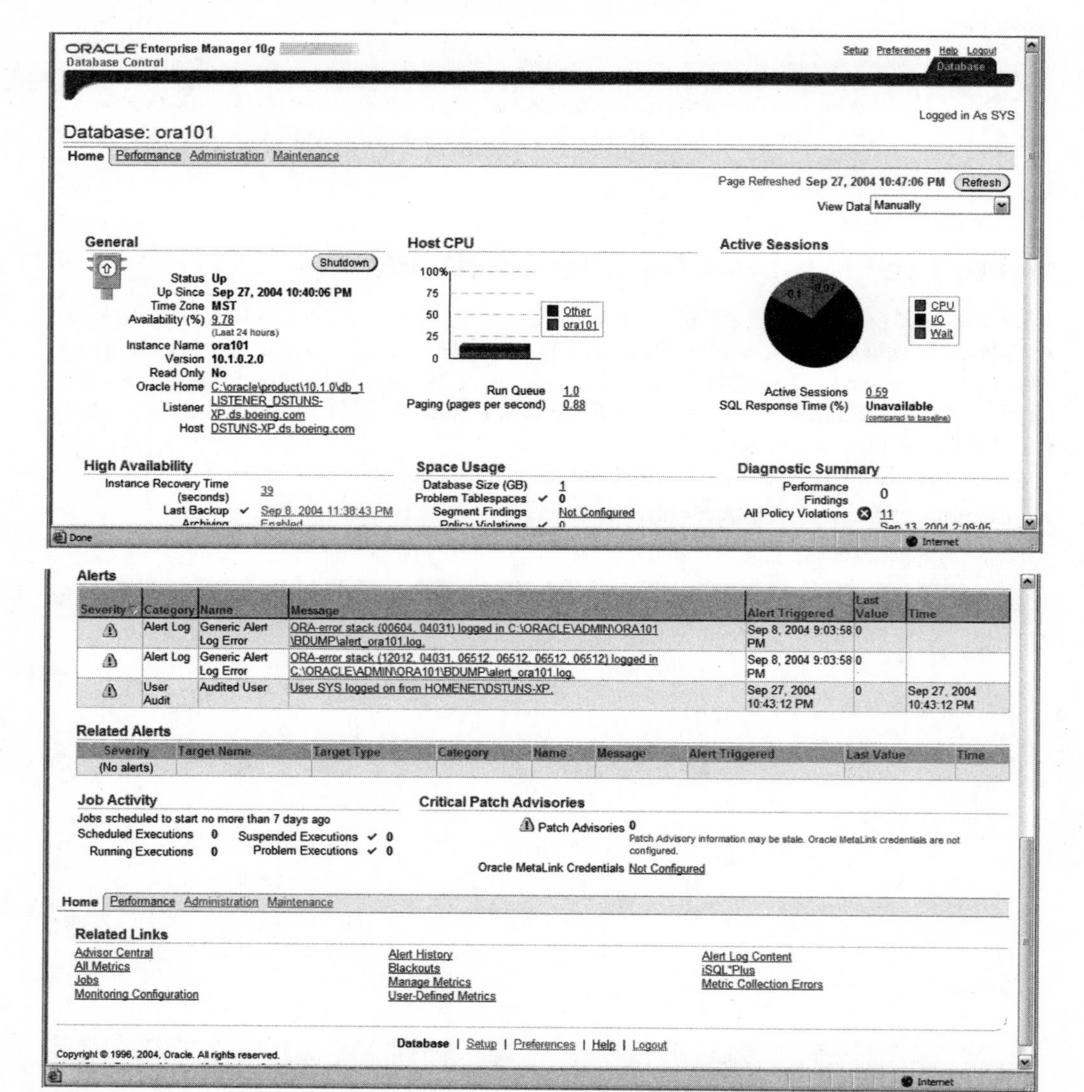

3. Choose the Perform Recovery option.

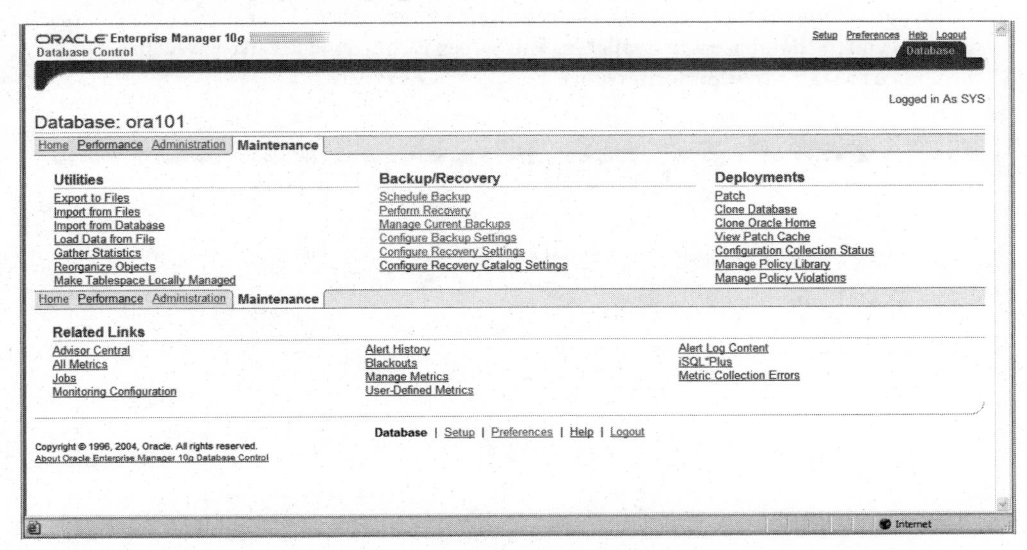

4. On the Perform Recovery: Type page, specify the type of recovery. Choose Datafiles in the Object Type drop-down list and choose Recover To Current Time Or A Previous Point-In-Time. Click the Next button.

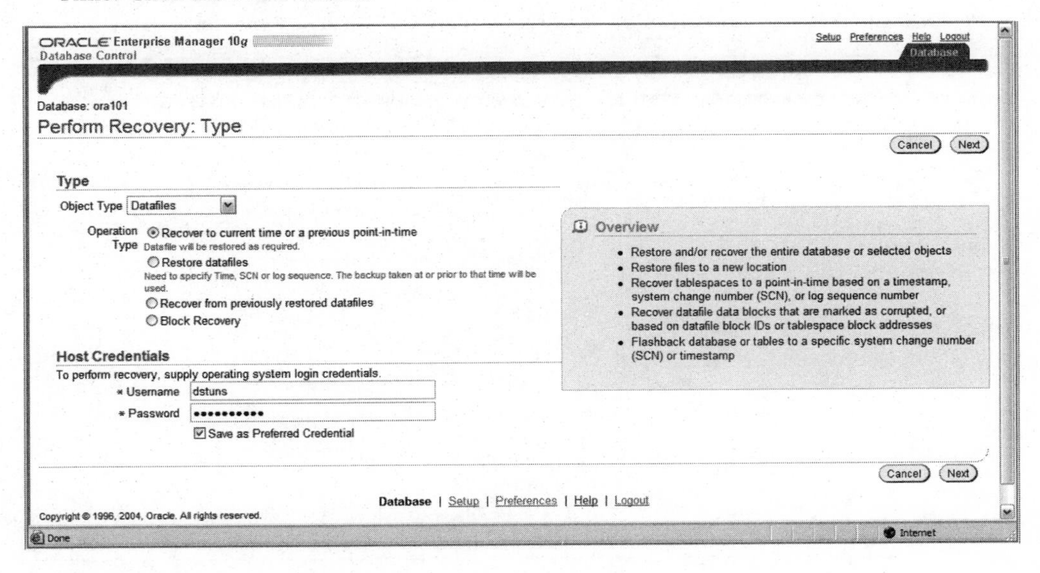

5. The database will need to be shut down and mounted to proceed with the recovery. After waiting about two or three minutes, click the Refresh button. An information screen appears that tells you the database is unavailable. This screen is called the Recovery Wizard. You have the choice to start up or perform recovery.

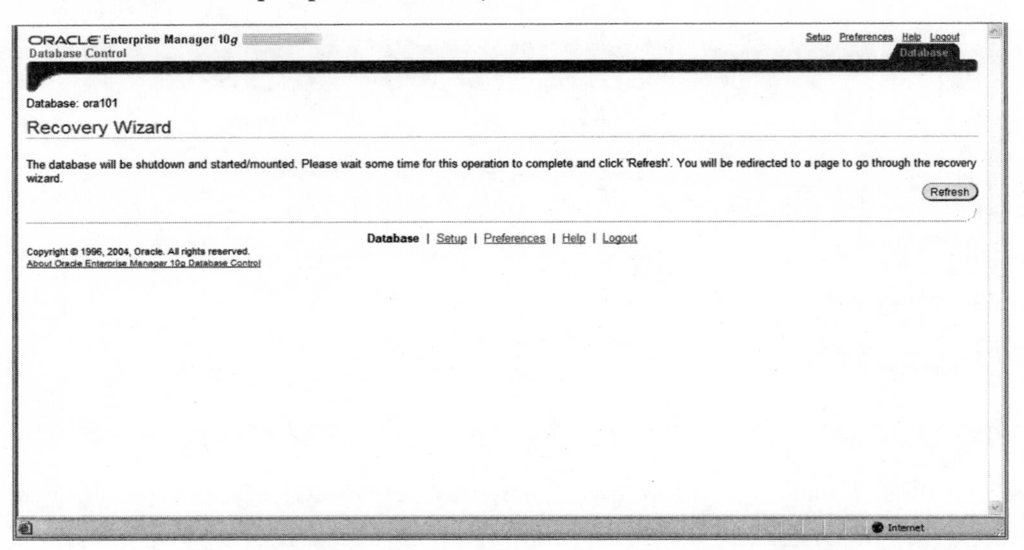

6. Perform the recovery operation by clicking the Perform Recovery button.

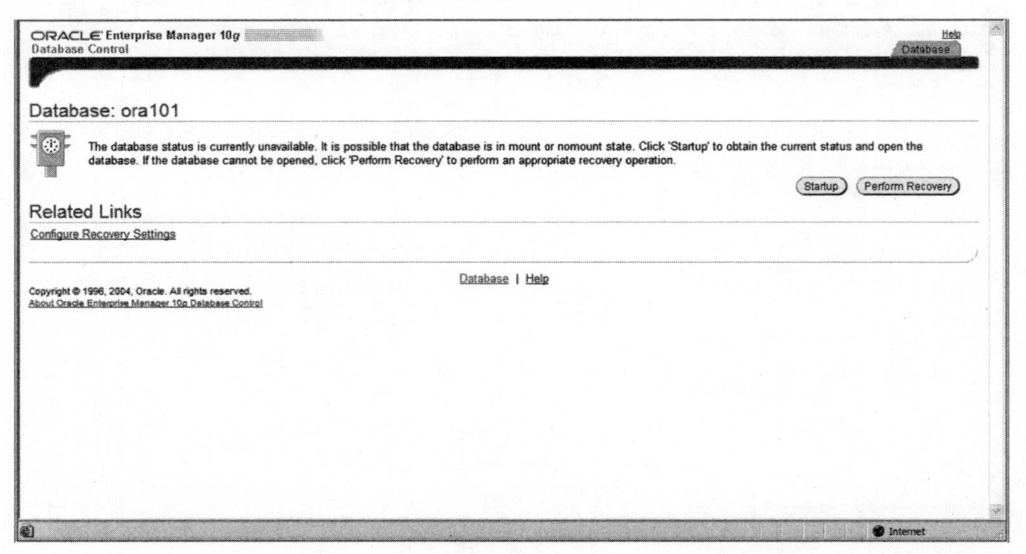

7. The Performance Recovery: Credentials screen appears, which has the required credentials for the host and database. If you have saved your preferred credentials, these fields will be filled with your accounts and passwords. Otherwise, enter the appropriate account information and click Continue.

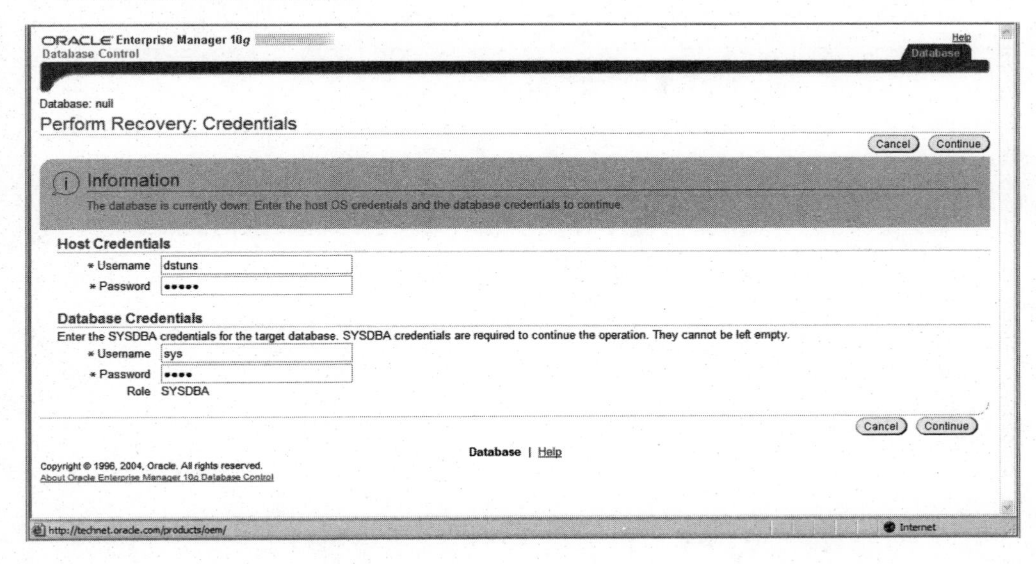

8. The Perform Recovery: Type screen appears. Choose the type of recovery you need to perform. In this example, choose Whole Database from the Object Type drop-down list and choose Recover To The Current Time Or A Previous Point-In-Time. Click Next.

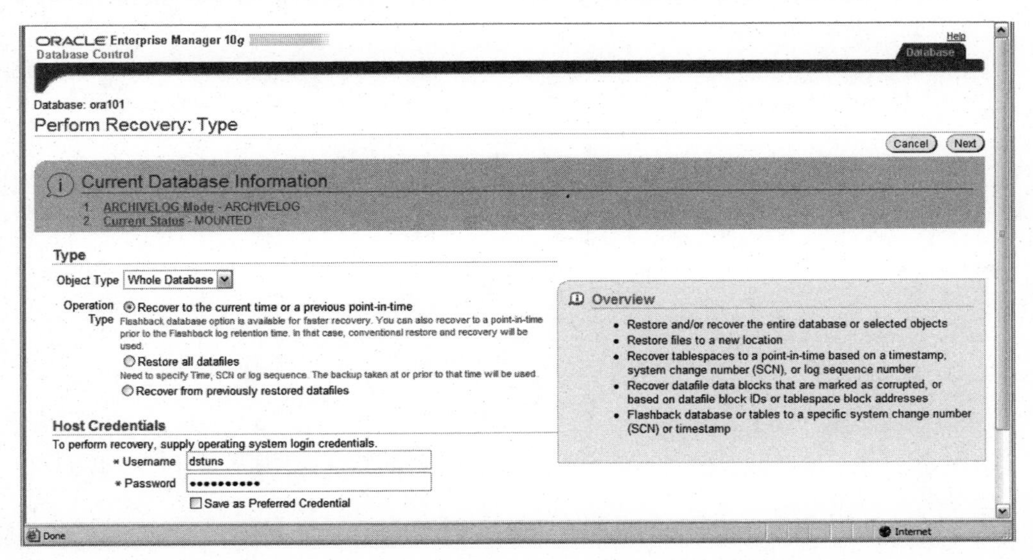

9. The Point-in-Time screen appears. The Point-In-Time screen determines if the Flashback Database capabilities are enabled and configured. If so, you can choose the time or the SCN to recover to. In this example, enter **689314** for the SCN, which is greater than the oldest flashback SCN. This helps determine that the Flashback Database recovery is the most efficient method of recovery and will utilize this. Click Next.

Database ora101
Object Type Whole Database
Operation Type Restore and Recover

Point-in-time

You may recover the entire database to the current time. If you want to recover the entire database to a point-in-time in the past, enter a date and time, an SCN, or a log sequence number below.

Recover to the current time

Recover to a prior point-in-time

TIP Flashback logging has been enabled in this database. You can consider using flashback by time or SCN to achieve faster database point-in-time recovery. If you choose to do a recovery by sequence, or if the time you want to recover back to falls out of the range of the flashback logs, Recovery Manager will be used to perform a conventional point-in-time recovery.

Oldest Flashback Time Sep 28, 2004 11:13:43 PM
Oldest Flashback SCN 689313

Date Sep 29, 2004 Time 2 30 AM PM
(example: Sep 29, 2004)

SCN 689314

Sequence 0

Open the database in read-only mode after this point-in-time recovery
If not selected, the database will be opened in read/write mode and the online redo logs will be cleared.

Return to Recovery Type Selection Cancel Step 1 of 4 Next

Database | Help

Copyright © 1996, 2004, Oracle. All rights reserved.
About Oracle Enterprise Manager 10g Database Control

Internet

10. The Perform Recovery: Flashback screen appears. The Perform Recovery: Flashback screen gives you the option of choosing Flashback Database recovery or standard point-in-time recovery. Select Yes, Use Flashback To Bring The Database Back To The Specified Point-In-Time. Click Next.

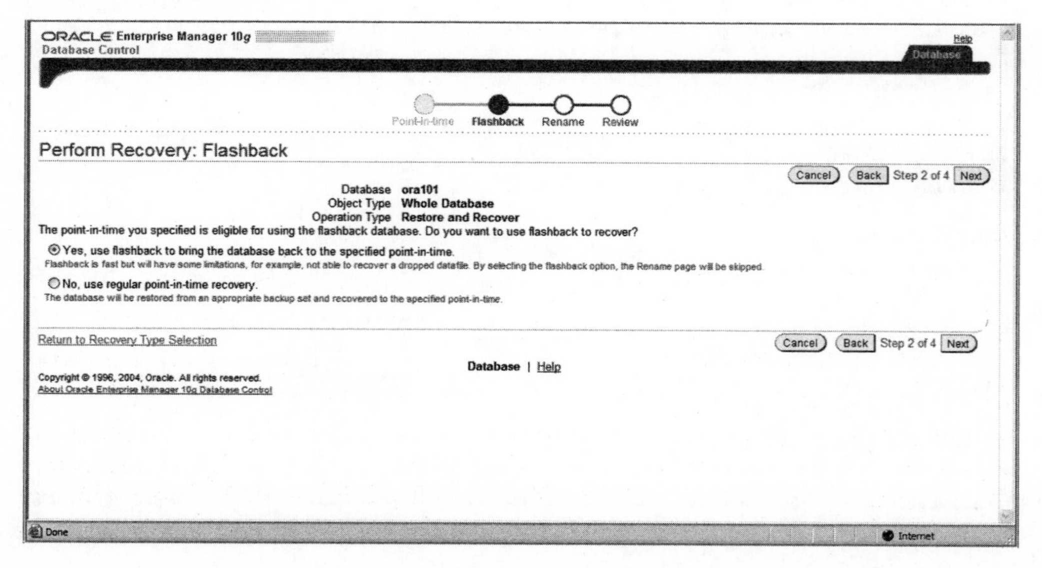

11. The Perform Recovery: Review screen appears, which displays the RMAN script that will perform the Flashback Database recovery.

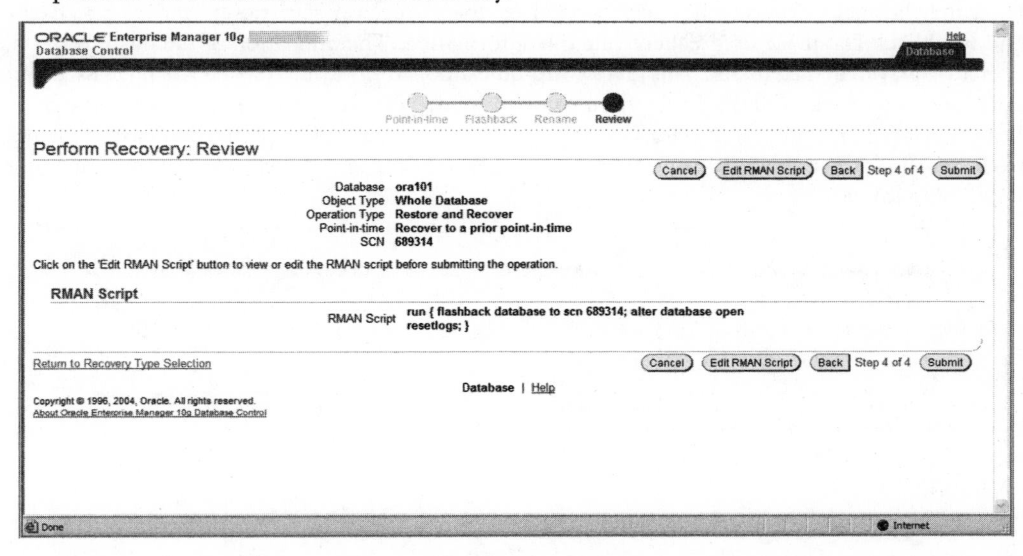

12. The final screen shows the output of the RMAN script and tells you if the recovery was successful.

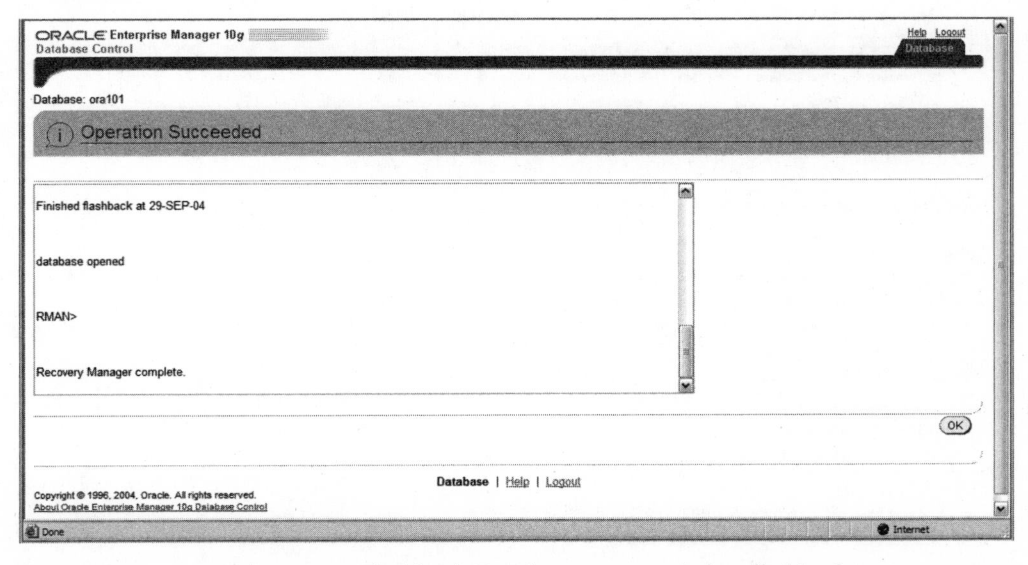

As you can see, performing a Flashback Database recovery is handled in the same way as a standard recovery. EM determines by your choices whether the Flashback Database recovery will be an option for your recovery situation. You are then presented with the choice of running the Flashback Database recovery.

Monitoring the Flashback Database with EM

Once the Flashback Database has been configured, there are many statistics for the flash recovery and Flashback Database that display valuable information. The utilization of the flash recovery area is displayed in megabytes. This gives you a quick look at how much space you have used and how much you have available in the flash recovery area. You also have the size of the Flashback Database logs in megabytes as well. This lets you know how much activity the database is writing to the Flashback Database logs during your defined retention period. Let's look at the Configure Recovery Settings screen.

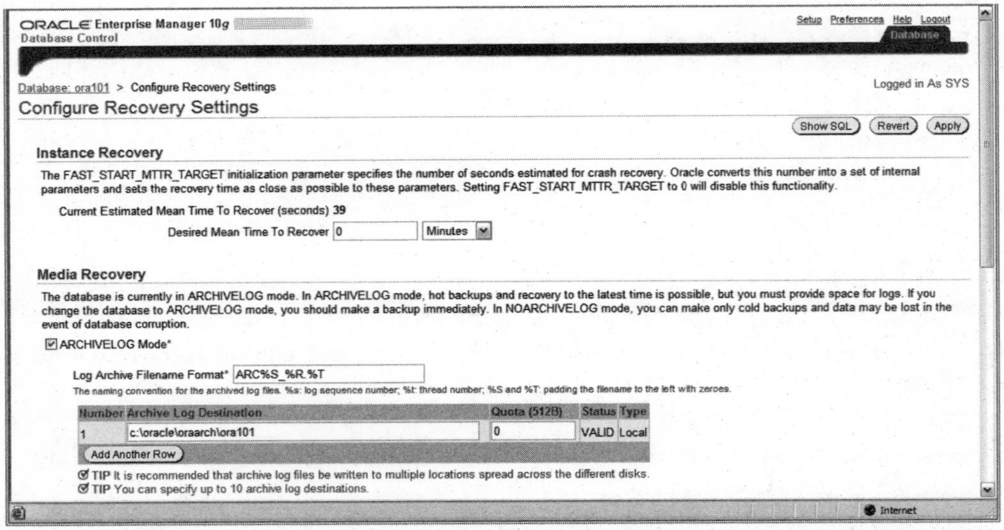

ORACLE Enterprise Manager 10g
Database Control

Setup Preferences Help Logout
Database

Database: ora101 > Configure Recovery Settings
Logged in As SYS

Configure Recovery Settings

Show SQL Revert Apply

Instance Recovery

The FAST_START_MTTR_TARGET initialization parameter specifies the number of seconds estimated for crash recovery. Oracle converts this number into a set of internal parameters and sets the recovery time as close as possible to these parameters. Setting FAST_START_MTTR_TARGET to 0 will disable this functionality.

Current Estimated Mean Time To Recover (seconds) **39**

Desired Mean Time To Recover 0 Minutes

Media Recovery

The database is currently in ARCHIVELOG mode. In ARCHIVELOG mode, hot backups and recovery to the latest time is possible, but you must provide space for logs. If you change the database to ARCHIVELOG mode, you should make a backup immediately. In NOARCHIVELOG mode, you can make only cold backups and data may be lost in the event of database corruption.

☑ ARCHIVELOG Mode*

Log Archive Filename Format* ARC%S_%R.%T

The naming convention for the archived log files. %s: log sequence number; %t: thread number; %S and %T: padding the filename to the left with zeroes.

Number	Archive Log Destination	Quota (512B)	Status	Type
1	c:\oracle\oraarch\ora101	0	VALID	Local

Add Another Row

TIP It is recommended that archive log files be written to multiple locations spread across the different disks.
TIP You can specify up to 10 archive log destinations.

Internet

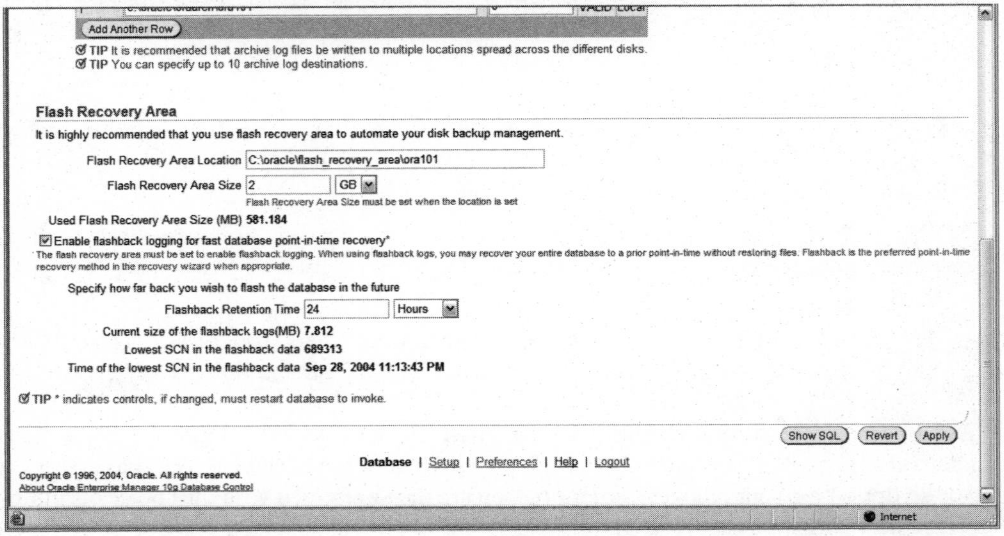

Add Another Row

TIP It is recommended that archive log files be written to multiple locations spread across the different disks.
TIP You can specify up to 10 archive log destinations.

Flash Recovery Area

It is highly recommended that you use flash recovery area to automate your disk backup management.

Flash Recovery Area Location C:\oracle\flash_recovery_area\ora101

Flash Recovery Area Size 2 GB

Flash Recovery Area Size must be set when the location is set

Used Flash Recovery Area Size (MB) **581.184**

☑ Enable flashback logging for fast database point-in-time recovery*

The flash recovery area must be set to enable flashback logging. When using flashback logs, you may recover your entire database to a prior point-in-time without restoring files. Flashback is the preferred point-in-time recovery method in the recovery wizard when appropriate.

Specify how far back you wish to flash the database in the future

Flashback Retention Time 24 Hours

Current size of the flashback logs(MB) **7.812**

Lowest SCN in the flashback data **689313**

Time of the lowest SCN in the flashback data **Sep 28, 2004 11:13:43 PM**

TIP * indicates controls, if changed, must restart database to invoke.

Show SQL Revert Apply

Database | Setup | Preferences | Help | Logout

About Oracle Enterprise Manager 10g Database Control

Internet

Some other useful information during Flashback Database recovery operations is stored in the Configure Recovery Settings screen as well. The lowest SCN available in the flashback data tells you how far back in the flashback logs you can recover by SCN. The lowest time tells you how far back in the flashback logs you can recover by a time reference.

You can also see the Flashback Database statistics are now displayed. These statistics show the utilization of the Flashback Database and activity that is being written to the logs. This is also a quick reference for the time and SCN limits if you need to perform a Flashback Database recovery.

Summary

In this chapter, you learned about the Flashback Database in detail. The Flashback Database is a new Oracle 10*g* solution that is best used to recover from logical corruption and user error. This is a new alternative to incomplete recovery or the Log Miner utility. The Flashback Database can be enabled and configured fairly easily. You must have the flash recovery area enabled to implement the Flashback Database.

You also learned how to use Enterprise Manager (EM) to enable and configure the Flashback Database and how to use the EM Perform Recovery capability by initiating the Recovery Wizard to perform a Flashback Database recovery. Monitoring of the Flashback Database can be performed through several dynamic views, which we covered in detail.

Exam Essentials

Understand the Flashback Database architecture. Make sure you are aware of the components that make up the Flashback Database architecture. Understand the Flashback Database logs and RVWR background process functionality.

Understand how to enable and disable the Flashback Database. Know how to configure the Flashback Database. Be aware of how to do this in EM and manually. Understand the flashback recovery area and how it is configured.

Know how to monitor the Flashback Database. Know the dynamic views that monitor the Flashback Database. Understand what each view contains. Be able to monitor the Flashback Database with EM.

Be aware of how to use the Enterprise Manager with the Flashback Database. Know how to use EM for recovery utilizing the Flashback Database. Understand the screens and methods to force Flashback Database recovery as an option.

Review Questions

1. What type of recovery is the Flashback Database best suited for? (Choose all that apply.)
   - **A.** User error
   - **B.** Physical corruption
   - **C.** Logical corruption
   - **D.** Media failure

2. Flashback Database recovery can recover from which of the following failure scenarios?
   - **A.** Loss of control file
   - **B.** Dropping a tablespace through `RESETLOGS`
   - **C.** A user error that resized datafiles to a smaller size
   - **D.** A large truncated table or group of tables

3. What new background process is responsible for writing before block images and recovering from the Flashback Database log?
   - **A.** RWVR
   - **B.** RVWR
   - **C.** RWRV
   - **D.** RVRW

4. What are the benefits of the flash recovery area in the recovery and backup process?
   - **A.** Recovery efficiency is improved because all files are stored on tape media for fast access.
   - **B.** Recovery efficiency is improved because the files are stored in multiple locations.
   - **C.** Recovery efficiency is improved because the files are stored in one location on tape.
   - **D.** Recovery efficiency is improved because the files are stored in one location on disk.

5. Where is information about the status of the flash recovery area displayed? (Choose all that apply.)
   - **A.** Alert log
   - **B.** Background trace files
   - **C.** `V$_OUSTANDING_ALERTS`
   - **D.** `DBA_OUTSTANDING_ALERTS`

6. How is the size of the flash recovery area determined? (Choose all that apply.)
   - **A.** The size is automatically allocated at 2 gigabytes.
   - **B.** Using the `ALTER SYSTEM` command to dynamically set the size.
   - **C.** With the initialization parameter `DB_RECOVERY_FILE_DEST_SIZE`.
   - **D.** Using the `ALTER TABLESPACE` command.

7. What type of backup commands can the flash recovery area be used for? (Choose all that apply.)

   A. BACKUP COPY

   B. BACKUP IMAGE

   C. BACKUP

   D. BACKUPSET

8. The flash recovery area space utilization and stored files can be identified by what method?

   A. DBA_OUTSTANDING_ALERTS

   B. V$OUTSTANDING_ALERTS

   C. V$RECOVERY_FILE_DEST

   D. DBA_RECOVERY_FILE_DEST

9. What parameter determines the length of time that the Flashback Database will store "before" images that can be used in the recovery process?

   A. DB_FLASHBACK_RETENTION_POLICY

   B. DB_FLASHBACK_RETENTION_TIME

   C. DB_FLASHBACK_RETENTION_STORE

   D. DB_FLASHBACK_RETENTION_TARGET

10. How is the DB_FLASHBACK_RETENTION_TARGET parameter measured?

    A. By SCN

    B. By redo log sequences

    C. By time in minutes

    D. By redo log sequence and threads

11. To enable the Flashback Database, what must be done to the database? (Choose all that apply.)

    A. It must be mounted.

    B. It must be opened with RESETLOGS.

    C. The flash recovery area must be created.

    D. The database must be in ARCHIVELOG mode.

12. When using the Flashback Database in a recovery situation, what information would be useful to know? (Choose all that apply.)

    A. Information about the smallest SCN number that is stored in the Flashback Database log

    B. Information about the earliest timestamp that is stored in the Flashback Database log

    C. Information about the greatest SCN number that is stored in the Flashback Database log

    D. Information about the latest timestamp that is stored in the Flashback Database log

13. How can you determine if the Flashback Database is turned on?
    - A. Query the DBA_FLASHBACK_DATABASE view.
    - B. Query the V$DATABASE dynamic view.
    - C. Check the initialization parameters.
    - D. Check the alert log.
14. Which of the following views can determine how much space you may need in the future in the Flashback Database logs?
    - A. V$DATABASE
    - B. V$FLASHBACK_DATABASE_STAT
    - C. V$FLASHBCK_DATABASE_LOG
    - D. DBA_FLASHBACK_LOG
15. What is the default size of a redo log file created in the flash recovery area?
    - A. 100MB
    - B. 150MB
    - C. 10MB
    - D. 50MB
16. Which initialization parameter will create archive logs to the flash recovery area?
    - A. ARCHIVE_LOG_DEST
    - B. ARCHIVE_DUPLEX_DEST
    - C. ARCHIVE_LOG_DEST_*n*
    - D. LOG_ARCHIVE_DEST_*n*
17. Which database files are permanently stored in the flash recovery area? (Choose all that apply.)
    - A. Datafiles
    - B. RMAN files
    - C. Control files
    - D. Current online redo logs
    - E. Archive logs
18. Which files will not be backed up in the flash recovery area when you're using the BACKUP RECOVERY AREA and BACKUP RECOVERY FILES commands? (Choose all that apply.)
    - A. Control files
    - B. Redo logs
    - C. Datafiles
    - D. Permanent files
    - E. Flashback logs

19. What is responsible for applying the "before" images to the database during a Flashback Database recovery?

A. LGWR

B. SMON

C. DBWR

D. RWVR

20. What administrative database activity cannot be undone with the Flashback Database recovery?

A. Dropped table

B. Dropped user

C. Resized datafiles to smaller size

D. Dropped tablespace

Answers to Review Questions

1. A, C. A Flashback Database recovery is best suited for a user error such as a truncated table or a logical corruption like an incomplete batch transaction affecting many tables. Media recovery situations cannot be performed with the Flashback Database recovery method.

2. D. A Flashback Database recovery can recover a large truncated table or group of tables.

3. B. The RVWR process is responsible for writing the "before" image information to the Flashback Database log. The Flashback Database log is read to perform the Flashback Database recovery.

4. D. The flash recovery area is a centralized storage area for backups on disk. This allows for a more efficient recovery process because the required files are in one location and are stored on disk instead of tape.

5. A, D. The Alert log reports space usage and other information about the flash recovery area. DBA_OUTSTANDING_ALERTS also show the information state of the flash recovery area.

6. B, C. The flash recovery area can be determined by either setting the initialization parameter DB_RECOVERY_FILE_DEST_SIZE or using the ALTER SYSTEM command.

7. A, C. The flash recovery area supports both the BACKUP and BACKUP COPY commands, which perform backup sets and image copies.

8. C. The dynamic view V$RECOVERY_FILE_DEST displays the space utilization and the amount of files that make up the flash recovery area.

9. D. The DB_FLASHBACK_RETENTION_TARGET parameter determines how much data is available to recover.

10. C. DB_FLASHBACK_RETENTION_TARGET is a parameter that is measured in minutes. This value determines how many minutes the Flashback Database should write data before this data gets overwritten.

11. A, C, D. To enable the Flashback Database, the flash recovery area must be created. The database must be mounted but not opened to turn on the Flashback Database. The database must also be in ARCHIVELOG mode.

12. A, B. The earliest timestamp and smallest SCN will tell you how far back you can recover the database. These values can be queried by the V$FLASHBACK_DATABASE_LOG dynamic view.

13. B. The V$DATABASE dynamic view has a new column called FLASHBACK_ON, which contains a value of YES or NO.

14. B. The V$FLASHBACK_DATABASE_STAT dynamic view shows the daily growth and utilization of the Flashback Database log. You can match daily activities to the daily utilization of the Flashback Database log.

15. A. The default size of a redo log file created in the flash recovery area is 100MB.

16. D. The LOG_ARCHIVE_DEST_*n* is the only initialization parameter that will create or write archive logs to the flash recovery area. ARCHIVE_LOG_DEST, ARCHIVE_DUPLEX_DEST, and ARCHIVE_LOG_DEST_*n* are not valid initialization parameters.

17. C, D. Control files and redo logs area considered permanent files in the flash recovery area. These files are not made obsolete and deleted, even when backed up to tape.

18. A, B, D, E. The flash recovery area will not back up redo log files, control files, or flashback logs with the BACKUP RECOVERY AREA and BACKUP RECOVERY FILES commands. Permanent files are considered to be current online redo logs and control files.

19. D. The RWVR process is responsible for writing the "before" images to the Flashback Database log. This process is also responsible for applying these to the database during a recovery.

20. C. Resizing of a tablespace or datafiles to a smaller size cannot be undone with Flashback Database recovery.

Recovering from User Errors

ORACLE DATABASE 10*G*: ADMINISTRATION II EXAM OBJECTIVES COVERED IN THIS CHAPTER:

✓ **Recovering from User Errors**

- Recover a dropped table using Flashback Technology.
- Perform Flashback Table operation.
- Manage the recycle bin.
- Recover from user errors using Flashback versions Query.
- Perform transaction level recovery using Flashback Transaction query.

Exam objectives are subject to change at any time without prior notice and at Oracle's sole discretion. Please visit Oracle's Training and Certification website (`http://www.oracle.com/education/certification/`) for the most current exam objectives listing.

This chapter provides a detailed explanation and walk-through of the new Oracle Database 10*g* (Oracle 10*g*) Flashback Technologies:

- Flashback Drop
- Flashback Versions Query
- Flashback Transaction Query
- Flashback Table

We will discuss and use the Recycle Bin to support these Flashback Technologies.

The Flashback Query was first introduced in Oracle 9*i* and is the foundation for the Oracle 10*g* Flashback Technologies. You will walk through examples of best practices of using each of these technologies. Additionally, you will use Enterprise Manager (EM) to perform Flashback Table recovery.

This chapter will focus on the workings of these Flashback Technologies. The overview of the Flashback Technologies will explain the architecture at a high level. This includes the Recycle Bin, which is a prerequisite to the Flashback Technologies. This will also include setup, configuration, and in which situations you should use each of the Flashback Technologies. You will see demonstrations and step-by-step examples performing each of these activities.

An Overview of Flashback Technologies

Flashback Technologies consist of the Flashback Drop, Flashback Versions Query, Flashback Transaction Query, Flashback Table, and the supporting Recycle Bin. The Flashback Query, first made available in Oracle 9*i*, and the rest of the Flashback Technologies that are new to Oracle 10*g* all rely on the undo data to rebuild dropped objects. *Undo data* are the records of the changes of each update to an Oracle database and the values that were overwritten by those updates. In addition, the Flashback Technologies are enabled by default.

All of the Flashback Technologies are designed to recover from user error or logical corruption:

- The Flashback Table is designed to recover a table in situations such as when you update a table with the incorrect `WHERE` clause. This makes significant changes to the table that would require you to recover the whole table.
- The Flashback Versions Query is designed to see individual changes in the rows from query so that you can recover an individual row or column within the row.

- The Flashback Drop is designed so that users can undrop a table that was dropped by mistake.
- The Flashback Transaction Query is designed to perform diagnostics on the changes that occur in a table or query.

All of these technologies can be used together to fix almost any user error or logical corruption that occurs in a database.

Using Flashback Drop

Flashback Drop is the process of saving a copy of the dropped database object and dependent objects in the Recycle Bin so that these objects can be recovered if necessary. The dropped database object is not removed from the database until the Recycle Bin is emptied. This provides a mechanism for a user to recover an accidental drop of a table. In previous releases of Oracle, you most likely needed to perform an incomplete recovery, import, or use Log Miner to recover dropped database objects. Flashback Drop is substantially faster than most other recovery mechanisms previously available. In addition, a Flashback Drop does not impact other users in the database to restore a dropped table, whereas incomplete recovery has database-wide impacts because there may be multiple database objects involved in a tablespace or datafile. Let's look at an example of the Flashback Drop capability that is performed by using the `FLASHBACK TABLE` *`table_name`* `TO BEFORE DROP` command.

```
SQL> flashback table t1
  2  to before drop;

Flashback complete.
SQL>
```

Many times, a user can drop a table by mistake or drop the wrong table. The Flashback Drop is designed to temporarily store the dropped object and dependent objects for a period of time, which can be seen in the Recycle Bin. Users can then recover these objects if necessary from the Recycle Bin. Figure 6.1 illustrates how this activity can occur.

FIGURE 6.1 An overview of Flashback Drop

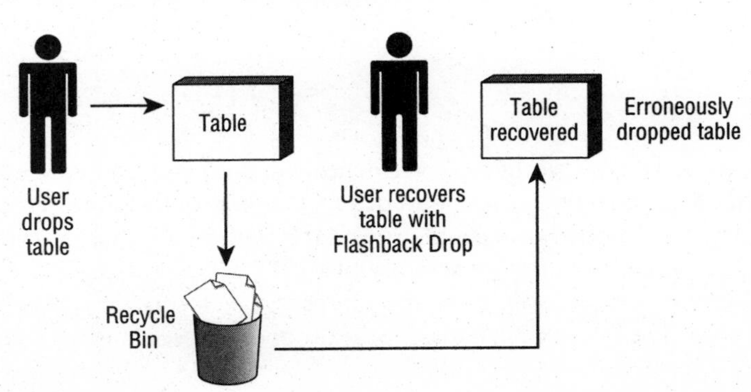

In order to fully comprehend Flashback Drop, you need to be aware of how the Recycle Bin works in detail. You should be aware of how the contents are stored in the Recycle Bin, including the naming conventions and versioning. You should understand space usage and limitations. In addition, you should be able to query and purge objects in the Recycle Bin. You will learn about all this in detail in the next section.

Understanding the Recycle Bin

The *Recycle Bin* is a logical storage container for all dropped tables and their dependent objects. As mentioned previously, when a table is dropped, the Recycle Bin stores the table and the table's dependent objects in the Recycle Bin so that these objects may be recovered later. The dependent objects that are stored in the Recycle Bin are indexes, constraints, triggers, nested tables, large binary object (LOB) segments, and LOB index segments. In the next few sections, we will focus on working with the Recycle Bin; the topics will include how objects are stored in the Recycle Bin, the naming conventions of objects, and querying objects. We will also discuss and demonstrate space pressure, purging objects in Recycle Bin, and space utilization. Let's look at these topics in more detail.

Working with the Recycle Bin

The Recycle Bin is enabled by default with Oracle 10*g*. The Recycle Bin receives database objects when the `DROP TABLE` command is executed. When this command is executed, tables and their dependent objects such as indexes are placed in the Recycle Bin. You need to use the Flashback Drop capability to recover these objects. The following example illustrates how this process works first with dropping the table `T1`:

```
SQL> select * from t1;

EMPLOYEE                 SALARY
-------------------- ----------
SCOTT                     10000
SMITH                     20000
JONES                     15000

SQL> drop table T1;

Table Dropped
```

After the table is dropped, you can see the table and dependent objects in the Recycle Bin. These objects have a unique naming convention to support dropped objects of the same name by different users. It is conceivable that another user could drop a table with same name, so Oracle takes this into account. The naming convention consists of a globalUID, which is a unique, 24-character long identifier, and a version number assigned by the database. The formatting is displayed like `BIN$`*`globalUID`*`$`*`version`*. The Recycle Bin name for the dropped object is always 30 characters in length.

There is a special command to view the Recycle Bin contents: *SHOW RECYCLEBIN*. The Recycle Bin can also be queried with the dynamic views USER_RECYCLEBIN and DBA_RECYCLEBIN. Let's view the Recycle Bin with the new SHOW RECYCLEBIN command and perform a standard database query on the RECYCLEBIN view within SQL*Plus:

```
SQL> show recyclebin;

ORIG NAME RECYCLEBIN NAME                OBJ TYPE DROP TIME
--------- ------------------------------ -------- -------------
T1        BIN$0ZVR8eDEQbK4s8G2Csf2kg==$0 TABLE    2004-10-25:20:51:34

SQL>
```

Next, let's look at the view RECYCLEBIN to query the contents of the Recycle Bin with a standard SQL statement:

```
SQL> select object_name as recycle_name, original_name, object_name
  2  from recyclebin;

RECYCLE_NAME                   ORIG_NAME OBJECT_NAME
------------------------------ --------- ------------------------------
BIN$0ZVR8eDEQbK4s8G2Csf2kg==$0 T1        BIN$0ZVR8eDEQbK4s8G2Csf2kg==$0
```

The data within the dropped tables, which are accessed through the Recycle Bin, can be queried just like any other database object. In order to query the object in the Recycle Bin, you must have the privileges that were needed to perform queries on the object before the object was dropped and placed in the Recycle Bin. You also need the FLASHBACK privilege. Let's query an object in the Recycle Bin by using the OBJECT_NAME in the Recycle Bin for table T1:

```
SQL> select * from "BIN$0ZVR8eDEQbK4s8G2Csf2kg==$0";

EMPLOYEE                 SALARY
-------------------- ----------
SCOTT                     10000
SMITH                     20000
JONES                     15000

SQL>
```

Using Flashback Drop to recover the table T1 is a fairly straightforward process. The Flashback Drop simply undoes the table drop command and removes the object from the Recycle Bin. This Flashback Drop is performed by specifying the Recycle Bin OBJECT_NAME in the RECYCLEBIN view of the dropped table with the FLASHBACK TABLE *table_name* TO BEFORE DROP command. We added the RENAME TO *table_name* option to change the original table name from T1 to T2. You can also see that the object is no longer in the Recycle Bin by performing a SHOW RECYCLEBIN command. When a Flashback Drop is performed, the object is removed from the Recycle Bin.

Let's walk through using a Flashback Drop to recover the dropped table T1 from the first example and rename the table to T2:

```
SQL> flashback table  "BIN$0ZVR8eDEQbK4s8G2Csf2kg==$0" to before drop
  2  rename to t2;

Flashback complete.

SQL> select * from t2;

EMPLOYEE                 SALARY
-------------------- ----------
SCOTT                     10000
SMITH                     20000
JONES                     15000

SQL> show recyclebin;
SQL>
```

As you can see, using the Recycle Bin and working with Flashback Drop is a fairly straightforward process. Tables and their dependent objects are stored in the Recycle Bin automatically in Oracle 10*g* once they are dropped. These objects can be recovered with the Flashback Drop operation.

The next section discusses and performs activities with the Recycle Bin in more detail. These Recycle Bin activities impact day-to-day operations such as space usage and maintenance operations.

Recycle Bin and Space Utilization

The Recycle Bin requires greater space utilization in the database, because dropped objects are still being stored after they have been dropped. This means that the original space allocation for the dropped tables and the dependent objects is maintained for extended periods of time in the original tablespace. The amount of space consumed by the dropped objects still counts against your tablespace quota.

There is a method to drop the objects from the Recycle Bin and to deallocate the space associated with the object all in one action. Of course, this means that you will not be able to rebuild this object if it has been removed from Recycle Bin. To permanently remove the object from the Recycle Bin and deallocate the space, you use the PURGE TABLE *original_table_name* command. This command provides the same functionality as the DROP TABLE command in Oracle releases prior to Oracle 10*g*.

You can also purge the object from the Recycle Bin with the PURGE TABLE *recycle_bin_object_name* command. The following command purges the table T1 after it has been placed in the Recycle Bin:

```
SQL> purge table "BIN$0ZVR8eDEQbK4s8G2Csf2kg==$0"

Table purged.
```

There is also a command that purges all the objects from a specified tablespace in the Recycle Bin. This command is the PURGE TABLESPACE command. The PURGE TABLESPACE command purges all dropped tables and dependent objects from the tablespace. Dependent objects such as LOBs, nested tables, and partitions will be purged from the specified tablespace, as well as the base table stored in a different tablespace because the dependent objects are dependent on the base table. The PURGE TABLESPACE *tablespace* USER *user* command removes only the tablespace contents of the specified username from the Recycle Bin. The following example purges the tablespace USERS with the user TEST from the Recycle Bin:

```
SQL> purge tablespace users user test;

Tablespace purged.
```

The command DROP USER *user* CASCADE drops the specified user and all of the objects owned by that user. The objects owned by the user are not placed in the Recycle Bin. Also, objects that are in the Recycle Bin and belong to the user are dropped. This DROP USER command bypasses the Recycle Bin and removes the objects immediately.

The contents of the Recycle Bin can be purged if desired. There are two commands that perform this capability:

- The PURGE RECYCLEBIN command is used to purge your own Recycle Bin. This command removes all objects from your Recycle Bin and deallocates all space associated with those objects.
- The PURGE DBA_RECYCLEBIN command removes all objects from all users' Recycle Bins. This effectively removes the Recycle Bin completely. You must have the SYSDBA system privilege to issue this command.

Let's see examples of these two commands and how they purge the Recycle Bin:

```
SQL> purge recyclebin;

Recyclebin purged.
```

```
SQL> connect / as sysdba;

Connected.

SQL> purge dba_recyclebin;

DBA Recyclebin purged.
```

Extents for the dropped database object are not deallocated until you purge the object or the tablespace runs out of free space.

The Recycle Bin is a logical storage container of the dropped objects based on existing allocated space in tablespaces. This means there is no preallocated space set aside for the Recycle Bin. This makes the Recycle Bin space dependent on the space available in the existing tablespaces. Therefore, the minimum time an object is stored in the Recycle Bin cannot be guaranteed.

The dropped objects in the Recycle Bin are kept in the Recycle Bin until new extents cannot be allocated in the tablespace to which the dropped objects belong. This situation is referred to as *space pressure*. User space quotas can also force the space pressure situation. Even though there is free space in the tablespace, the user's quota limits the space that can be utilized.

Real World Scenario

Reducing Space Pressure

Space management in most active databases can be a demanding job for any DBA. Large production databases can require significant effort to maintain adequate free extents for the most active tables, even with many monitoring tools. With the addition of the Flashback Drop capability and the Recycle Bin, this can place an additional burden on space management; the dropped objects can require increased available extents in a tablespace.

Flashback Drop adds a new level of safety for human errors and dropped tables for maintenance purposes. Dropped tables now have a copy available in the Recycle Bin by default. In order to keep copies of these tables for extended periods of time in the Recycle Bin and reduce the space pressure issue, you can remove many space-consuming database objects. Many times there are large indexes that can be purged with `PURGE INDEX` *`recycle_object_name`*. This can save large amounts of space and reduce the space pressure in a tablespace. Indexes can be easily and quickly rebuilt from a table in `PARALLEL` with `NOLOGGING` when required. Removing indexes reduces unneeded allocated extents from a tablespace where the table was dropped.

When space pressure arises, Oracle automatically reclaims space by overwriting objects in the Recycle Bin. Oracle selects certain objects for purging based on a first-in, first-out (FIFO) basis, so the first objects dropped are selected for purging. The purging of objects is done only as needed to meet space pressure, so the database purges as few as objects as possible to meet the space pressure needs. This minimalist approach of overwriting objects reduces performance impacts on transactions that encounter space pressure and maximizes the length of time a object can be available in the Recycle Bin.

Tablespaces that are configured with AUTO EXTEND storage requirements are purged from the Recycle Bin before the datafiles are extended for the tablespace.

As you can see, the Recycle Bin is a valuable new feature in Oracle 10*g*. The Recycle Bin reduces the need to perform incomplete recovery. It also reduces some of the workload on you because users can Flashback Drop their own objects. In previous versions, you needed to perform incomplete recovery or use the Import utility to rebuild a dropped table. This was a time-consuming process for you and other IT administration staff.

Limitations on Flashback Drop and the Recycle Bin

There are some limitations to the Flashback Drop that impact how you can use this technology, and there are certain objects that are excluded from the protection of the Recycle Bin. Be aware of the following limitations:

- Recycle Bin functionality is available only for non-system, locally managed tablespaces. If the table is a non-system, locally managed tablespace and some of the dependent objects are in a dictionary-managed tablespace, these dependent objects would be protected.
- There is no guaranteed timeframe for how long an object will be stored in the Recycle Bin. The time is determined by system activity that impacts space utilization.
- Data Manipulation Language (DML) or Data Definition Language (DDL) statements cannot be used on objects in the Recycle Bin.
- The Recycle Bin name of a table is required to query the table, not the original name.
- All dependent objects are retrieved when you perform a Flashback Drop, just as the objects are all added to the Recycle Bin when the base table is dropped. The only exception is when space pressure removes some dependent objects.
- Virtual Private Database (VPD) and fine-grained auditing (FGA) policies defined on tables are not protected for security reasons.
- Partitioned index-organized tables are not protected by the Recycle Bin.

Referential constraints are not protected by the Recycle Bin. Referential constraints must be replaced after the table has been rebuilt with the Flashback Drop.

As you can see, these limitations should be clearly understood. If you understand these limitations, you can more effectively utilize the Flashback Drop procedures and the Recycle Bin. As long as you also know the restrictions of the Flashback Drop technology, other alternatives can be made to support your database.

Using EM to Perform Flashback Dropped Tables

The Flashback Dropped Tables capability can be performed with Enterprise Manager (EM). The available Flashback Dropped Tables can be identified by schema in the Maintenance ➤ Recovery ➤ Dropped Objects screen. The targeted database objects can be identified to be Flashback Dropped.

The process to Flashback Drop leads you first through an object identification screen. Next, you are allowed to rename the object before you Flashback Drop the object. The last screen allows you to review your actions before the object is finally rebuilt.

Let's walk through this process in more detail:

1. Log in to EM as a SYSDBA-enabled user.

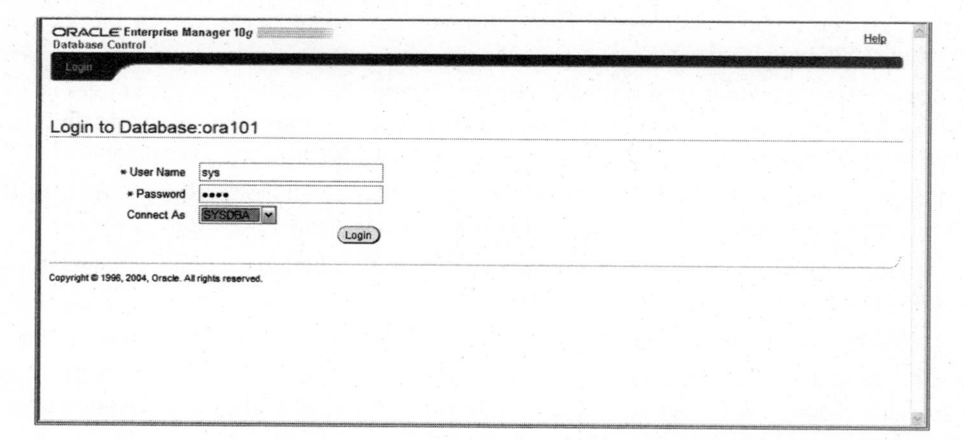

2. You will be redirected to the EM Home page, illustrated in the next two graphics.

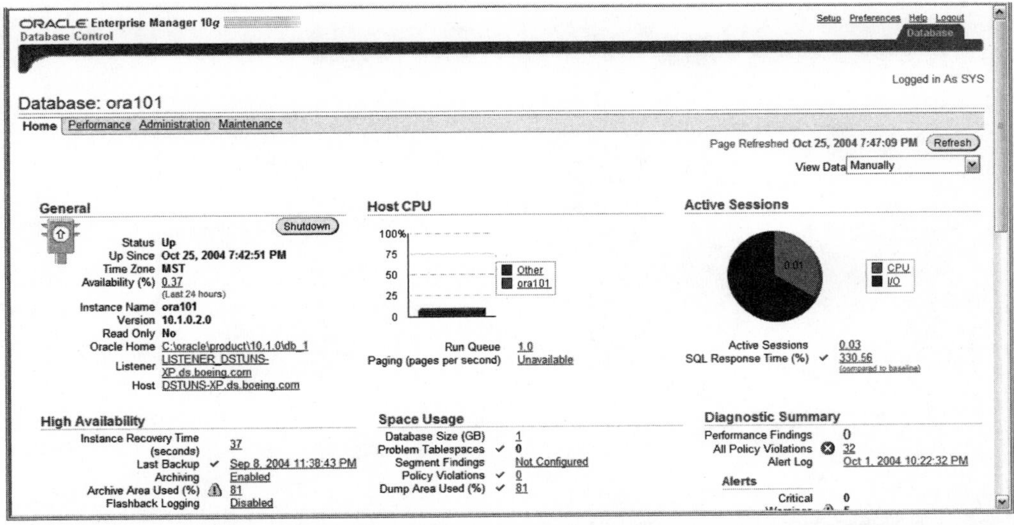

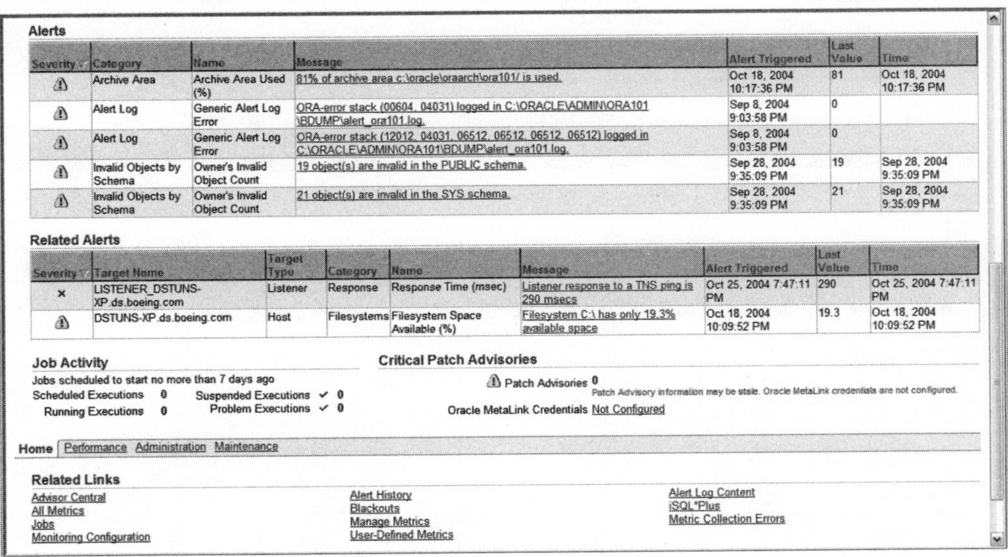

3. Select the Maintenance Tab.

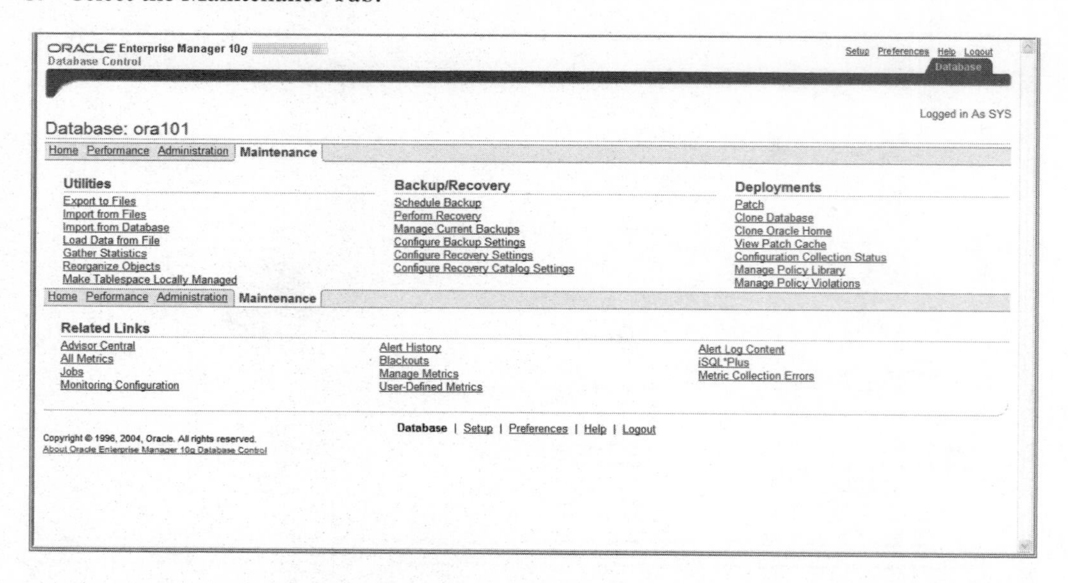

4. Once in the Maintenance menu, select the Perform Recovery option. You will be directed to the Perform Recovery: Type screen.

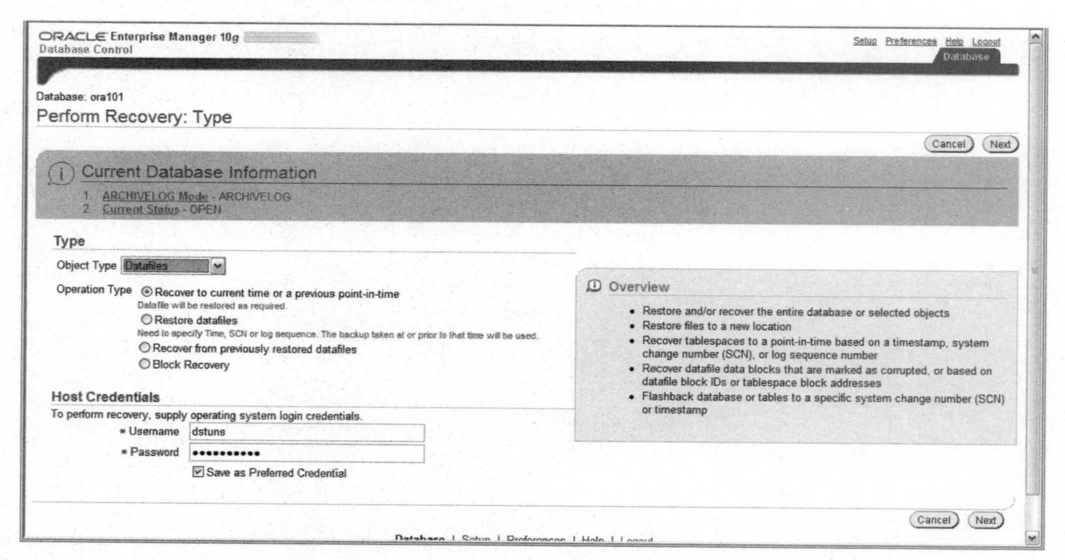

5. Select the Tables option from the Object Type drop-down list box.

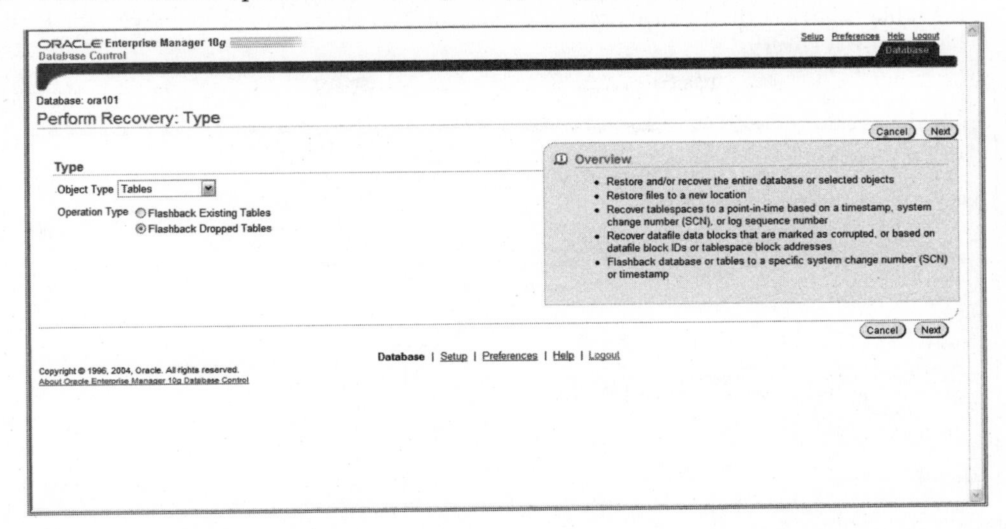

6. On the second Perform Recovery: Type screen, select the Flashback Dropped Tables radio button and click Next.

7. The Perform Recovery: Dropped Objects Selection screen appears. Click the Flashlight icon, select the schema owner Test, and click the Go button.

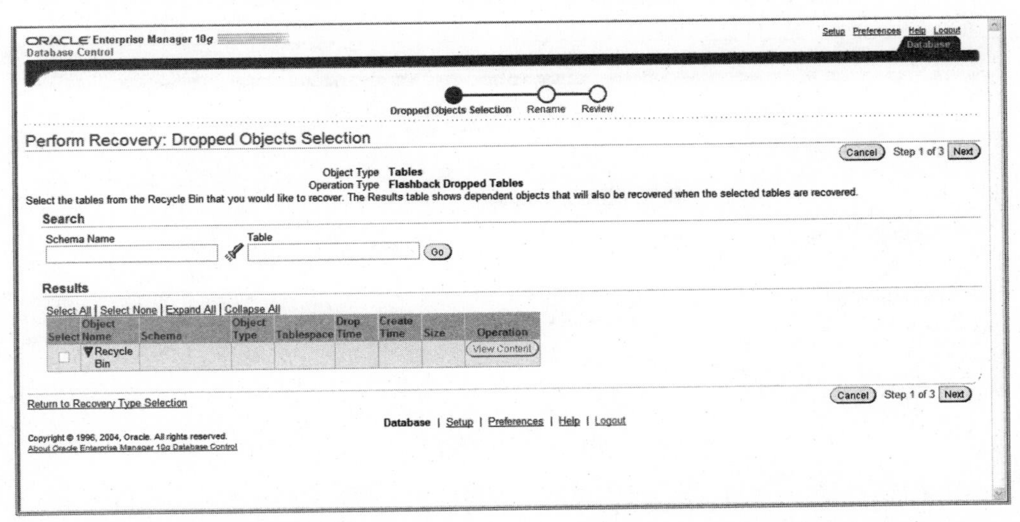

8. This will display all the tables that can be Flashback Drop recovered. In this example, it is the table T2. Select the T2 check box and click the Next button to proceed with the Flashback Drop recovery.

ORACLE Enterprise Manager 10g
Database Control
Setup Preferences Help Logout
Database
Dropped Objects Selection Rename Review

Perform Recovery: Dropped Objects Selection

Cancel Step 1 of 3 Next

Object Type Tables
Operation Type Flashback Dropped Tables

Select the tables from the Recycle Bin that you would like to recover. The Results table shows dependent objects that will also be recovered when the selected tables are recovered.

Search

Schema Name TEST Table Go

Results

Select All | Select None | Expand All | Collapse All

Select	Object Name	Schema	Object Type	Tablespace	Drop Time	Create Time	Size	Operation
☐	▼Recycle Bin							View Content
☑	T2	TEST	TABLE	USERS	2004-10-25:22:14:16	2004-10-25:22:13:56	8	View Content

Return to Recovery Type Selection

Cancel Step 1 of 3 Next

Database | Setup | Preferences | Help | Logout

About Oracle Enterprise Manager 10g Database Control

9. The Perform Recovery: Rename screen appears. At this point, you can choose to rename the table that you have selected to Flashback Drop recover. In this example, we will not rename the table. Click the Next button.

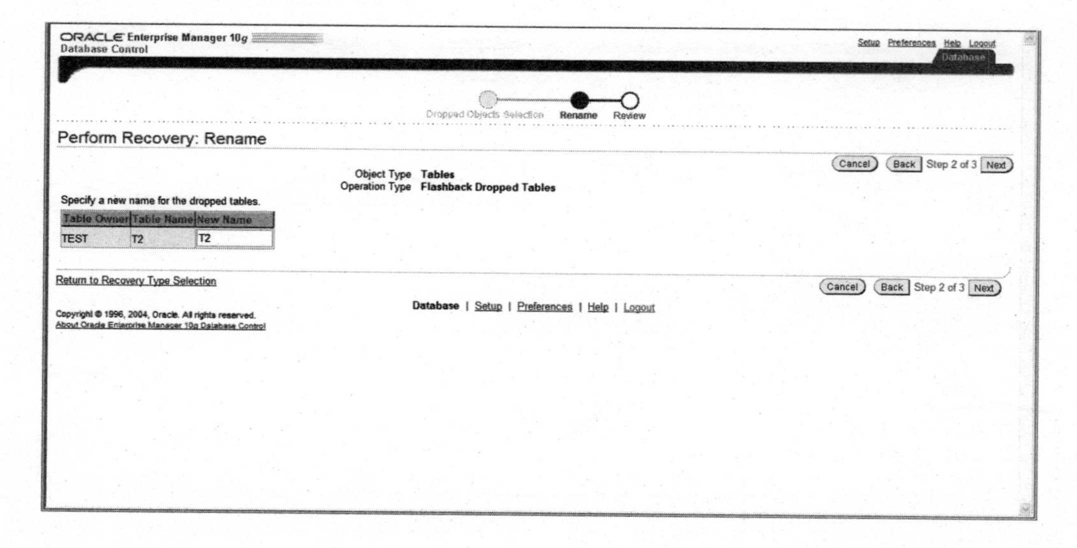

10. The Perform Recovery: Review screen appears, which shows the tables you have selected, and the names of the tables if you have changed their names. Click the Submit button to process the Flashback Drop recovery.

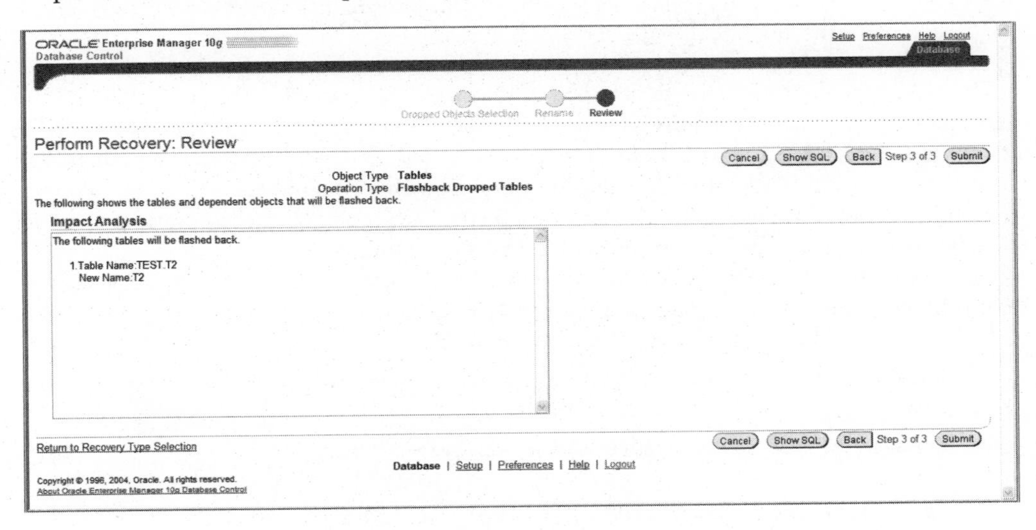

As you can see, EM performs the Flashback Drop in a straightforward manner. The standard recovery screen is selected initially. Choosing the Table option in the recovery screen determines that the Flashback Drop recovery will be initiated. By clicking the Show SQL button, you can see that the SQL command `FLASHBACK DROP` *`table_name`* `TO BEFORE DROP` is executed.

Using Flashback Versions Query

The *Flashback Versions Query* is an improvement to the Flashback Query technology first developed in Oracle 9*i*. Flashback Versions Query allows you to retrieve all of the versions of the rows that exist or existed between the times the query was executed to a determined point-in-time in the past. The Flashback Versions Query returns all the committed occurrences of the rows for a query of an object, while not displaying the uncommitted row versions.

Flashback Versions Query works by retrieving data from the `UNDO` tablespace. The `UNDO_RETENTION` initialization parameter, which is specified in seconds, determines how much committed undo data to keep in the database. If transactions need additional undo space and there is no more space in the `UNDO` tablespace, then Oracle will start reusing undo space. The `RETENTION GUARANTEE` tablespace and database option, which can be set on the `UNDO` tablespace, will protect unexpired undo data in this situation.

The default value for RETENTION in a tablespace is NO GUARANTEE. This value can be set during tablespace creation. This information can be viewed by querying the DBA_TABLESPACE view.

The privileges required to use the Flashback Versions Query are SELECT and FLASHBACK for each user. The Flashback Versions Query is performed with a new clause that can be added to a query statement: VERSIONS BETWEEN. The *VERSIONS BETWEEN* clause has two implementations. The first implementation is to specify the system change numbers (SCNs) to identify a start and stop point of the Flashback Versions Query. The second option uses a timestamp to identify a start and stop point of the Flashback Versions Query.

The VERSIONS BETWEEN clause can be used with SCN MINVALUE and MAXVALUE. Also, the VERSIONS BETWEEN clause can be used with TIMESTAMP TO_TIMESTAMP and TO_TIMESTAMP.

Let's look at a Flashback Versions Query in more detail:

1. First, execute some update statements to generate changes from the T1 table for employee JONES:

```
SQL> update t1 set salary=18000 where employee='JONES';
SQL>commit;
SQL> update t1 set salary=21000 where employee='JONES';
SQL>commit;
SQL> update t1 set salary=25000 where employee='JONES';
SQL>commit;
```

2. Next, query the table T1 with the VERSION BETWEEN option:

```
SQL> select salary from t1
  2  versions between
  3  scn minvalue and maxvalue
  4  where employee = 'JONES';

    SALARY
----------
     25000
     21000
     18000
SQL>
```

The following example uses the VERSIONS BETWEEN TIMESTAMP to identify the changes to the SALARY column in the T1 table for employee JONES:

```
SQL> select salary from t1
  2  versions between timestamp
```

```
  3  to_timestamp('2004-10-26 11:37:01','YYYY-MM-DD HH:MI:SS') and
  4  to_timestamp('2004-10-26 11:43:01','YYYY-MM-DD HH:MI:SS')
  5  where employee = 'JONES';

    SALARY
----------
     25000
     21000
     18000
SQL>
```

The VERSIONS BETWEEN clause cannot produce versions of the rows past when certain DDL commands modify the table specifications. This means that if you perform ALTER TABLE and add a new column or delete a column, this may not work through that change.

There are some new database functions that help you work with the Flashback Versions Query. The SCN_TO_TIMESTAMP function can be used to find the timestamp of an SCN. The inverse of this function is called TIMESTAMP_TO_SCN, which will find an SCN based on a timestamp.

Let's use one of these new functions in a SQL statement:

```
SQL> select current_scn,scn_to_timestamp(current_scn) from v$database;

CURRENT_SCN SCN_TO_TIMESTAMP(CURRENT_SCN)

----------- -------------------------------
     725638 26-OCT-04 11.37.03.000000000 AM
```

There are several new pseudocolumns that help you work with the Flashback Versions Query:

- VERSIONS_STARTTIME
- VERSIONS_STARTSCN
- VERSIONS_ENDTIME
- VERSIONS_ENDSCN
- VERSIONS_XID
- VERSIONS_OPERATION

These pseudocolumns are available for every Flashback Versions Query, and they can help identify when actual changes occur and how they were changed for specific queries.

Let's look at some of these pseudocolumns in an actual query:

```
SQL>
  1  select to_char(versions_starttime,'DD-MON HH:MI') "START DATE",
  2          to_char (versions_endtime, 'DD-MON HH:MI') "END DATE",
  3          versions_xid,
  4          versions_operation,
  5          employee,
  6          salary
  7          from test.tl
  8          versions between scn
  9          minvalue and maxvalue
 10*         where employee = 'JONES'

START DATE   END DATE     VERSIONS_XID     V EMPLOYEE SALARY
------------ ------------ ---------------- - -------- ----------
26-OCT 05:11              020018001F030000 U JONES    35000
26-OCT 05:06 26-OCT 05:11 0600270081000000 U JONES    31000
             26-OCT 05:06                    JONES    30000
```

As you can see, the pseudocolumns provide metadata about the versions of the row data in the T1 table. VERSIONS_XID is a unique identifier of the version metadata for that version of data. The V column is shortened for VERSIONS_OPERATION, which in this case displays a U for update, which shows how the data was changed. VERSIONS_STARTTIME and VERSIONS_ENDTIME is aliased to START DATE and END DATE, respectively. With the pseudocolumn information, you can identify when and how the data was changed. Table 6.1 describes each of these pseudocolumns.

TABLE 6.1 Flashback Pseudocolumns

Pseudocolumn	Description
VERSIONS_STARTSCN	Starting SCN when the row was first created. This identifies the SCN when the data first took on the values displayed in the row version. If NULL, the row version was created before the lower time bound of the query BETWEEN clause.
VERSIONS_STARTTIME	Starting TIMESTAMP when the row version was first created. This identifies the time when the data first took on the values displayed in the row version. If NULL, the row version was created before the lower time bound of the query BETWEEN clause.
VERSIONS_ENDSCN	Ending SCN when the row version expired. This identifies the row expiration SCN. If NULL, then either the row version is still current or the row corresponds to a DELETE operation.

TABLE 6.1 Flashback Pseudocolumns *(continued)*

Pseudocolumn	Description
VERSIONS_ENDTIME	Ending TIMESTAMP when the row version expired. This identifies the row expiration time. If NULL, then either the row version is still current or the row corresponds to a DELETE operation.
VERSIONS_XID	Identifier of the transaction that created the row version.
VERSIONS_OPERATION	This is the operation performed by the transaction that modified the data. The values are I for insertion, D for deletion, or U for update.

As you can see, the Oracle 10*g* Flashback Versions Query is a significant improvement over the Flashback Query in Oracle 9*i*. The Flashback Versions Query can specify query versions by timestamp or SCN. The operations that performed these changes are also identified. The Flashback Versions Query, in conjunction with other Flashback Technologies, has many valuable uses to help fix logical corruptions in the database and many other user errors.

The Flashback Versions Query VERSIONS BETWEEN clause can be used in DDL and DML subqueries.

Using Flashback Transaction Query

The *Flashback Transaction Query* is designed to be a diagnostic tool to help identify changes made to the database at the transaction level. This tool can be used to perform analysis on data for audits of transactions. With Flashback Transaction Query, you can identify all changes made within a specific time period, as well as perform transactional recovery of tables.

The Flashback Transaction Query is based on undo data and utilizes the UNDO_RETENTION initialization parameter to determine the amount of time to retain committed undo data in the database. The Flashback Transaction Query also uses the RETENTION GUARANTEE in the same manner as the previously discussed Flashback Versions Query.

The Flashback Transaction Query analysis and diagnostics are performed by querying the view *FLASHBACK_TRANSACTION_QUERY*. The data in this view allow analysis of a specific transaction or what changes were made at a specific time.

Using the FLASHBACK_TRANSACTION_QUERY view can help identify the table and operation that is performed against the table. This view can be large, so it is helpful to use a filter like the transaction identifier, which is in the column XID. The XID value was identified in the previous Flashback Versions Query example.

Let's query the FLASHBACK_TRANSACTION_QUERY to perform transactional analysis by specific transaction:

```
SQL> select table_name, operation, undo_sql
  2  from flashback_transaction_query
  3  where xid = '020018001F030000';

TABLE_NAME OPERATION UNDO_SQL
---------- --------- ------------------------------------------------
T1         UPDATE    update "TEST"."T1" set "SALARY" = '31000' where
  ➥ROWID = 'AAAMVBAAEAAAAFlAAC';
```

Another method is to use timestamps to narrow the transactional analysis to a certain point-in-time. Let's look at an example in more detail:

```
SQL> select table_name, operation, undo_sql
  2  from flashback_transaction_query
  3  where start_timestamp >= to_timestamp ('2004-10-26 06:45:00',
  ➥'YYYY-MM-DDHH:MI:SS')
  4  and table_owner = 'TEST';

TABLE_NAME OPERATION UNDO_SQL
---------- --------- ------------------------------------------------
T1         UPDATE update "TEST"."T1" set "SALARY" = '35000' where ROWID
  ➥ = 'AAAMVBAAEAAAAFlAAC';
T1         UPDATE update "TEST"."T1" set "SALARY" = '31000' where ROWID
  ➥ = 'AAAMVBAAEAAAAFlAAC';
T1         UPDATE update "TEST"."T1" set "SALARY" = '25000' where ROWID
  ➥ = 'AAAMVBAAEAAAAFlAAC';
T1         UPDATE update "TEST"."T1" set "SALARY" = '40000' where ROWID
  ➥ = 'AAAMVBAAEAAAAFlAAC';

SQL>
```

If you need to perform a transactional recovery of any values for the employee JONES, you can then update the row back to the prior SALARY value that is displayed in FLASHBACK_TRANSACTION_QUERY.

As you can see, the Flashback Transaction Query is a valuable addition to the Flashback Technologies. The Flashback Transactional Query is a diagnostic tool to help identify changes at the transactional level. There are many methods to query FLASHBACK_TRANSACTION_QUERY to see how and when data was changed.

The privilege required to use the Flashback Transaction Query is the system privilege FLASHBACK ANY TABLE.

Using Flashback Table

Flashback Table is a Flashback Technology that allows you to recover a table or set tables to a specific point-in-time without performing an incomplete recovery. All dependent objects are also recovered when using Flashback Table.

Flashback Table has some significant benefits over incomplete recovery:

- It is much faster and easier to use than incomplete recovery.
- Flashback Table does not impact the availability of the database.
- The DBA is not required to perform Flashback Table, so users can quickly recover from logical corruptions.

Like other Flashback Technologies, the Flashback Table is based on undo data and utilizes the UNDO_RETENTION initialization parameter to determine the amount of time to retain committed undo data in the database. The Flashback Table also uses RETENTION GUARANTEE in the same manner as the previously discussed Flashback Versions Query and Flashback Transaction Query.

The privilege required to use Flashback Table is the system privilege FLASHBACK ANY TABLE or FLASHBACK TABLE. You must also grant SELECT, INSERT, DELETE, and ALTER object privileges to the user performing the Flashback Table.

You can use the Flashback Table with either Enterprise Manager or with standard SQL commands. In the earlier section titled "Using EM to Perform Flashback Dropped Tables," we used EM to perform this. There are two main clauses that are used with the Flashback Table:

- The TO SCN clause can recover the Flashback Table to a certain SCN.
- The TO TIMESTAMP clause can recover the Flashback Table to a certain point-in-time.

The Flashback Table must have ROW MOVEMENT enabled with the following command: ALTER TABLE *tablename* ENABLE ROW MOVEMENT.

It is important to get the current SCN number from the database. The current SCN can be identified by querying the CURRENT_SCN column in the V$DATABASE view. To show that Flashback Table is recovered, you can create a change to the data. In the following example, you will update the SALARY for JONES to 50000 and then commit the transaction. Then you can Flashback Table to an SCN prior to the change for employee JONES. This change will be missing if the table is recovered to an SCN before the change is introduced.

Let's walk through performing a Flashback Table with SCN:

1. Enable ROW MOVEMENT on table T1:

```
SQL> alter table t1 enable row movement;

Table altered.

SQL>
```

2. Retrieve the current SCN before you modify the table:

```
SQL> select current_scn from v$database;

CURRENT_SCN
-----------
     771511

SQL>
```

3. Update a value in the table so you can verify the change was eliminated after you performed the Flashback Table operation to the SCN prior to the update:

```
SQL> update t1 set salary=50000 where employee = 'JONES';

1 row updated.

SQL> commit;

Commit complete.

SQL>
```

4. Perform the FLASHBACK TABLE command to recover the table to an SCN to a point-in-time before the update of JONES to a SALARY of 50000:

```
SQL> flashback table t1
  2   to scn 771511;
```

5. Query the table to verify the change was eliminated due to the Flashback Table to an SCN prior to the existence of the change:

```
SQL> select * from tl where employee='JONES';

EMPLOYEE                  SALARY
-------------------- ----------
JONES                      41000

SQL>
```

Triggers are disabled by default during the Flashback Table process. Triggers can be enabled with the ENABLE TRIGGERS option on the FLASHBACK TABLE command. This option enables all triggers that were enabled on the table before they were disabled by the Flashback Table operation. If you want certain triggers to be disabled, you can disable them with the ALTER TRIGGER command prior to performing a Flashback Table and then use the ENABLE TRIIGGERS clause.

Let's take a look at this Flashback Table option:

```
SQL> flashback table table_name
  2         to scn 771551
  3         enable triggers;
```

As you can see, the Flashback Table operation is a valuable recovery method. You might notice some similarity with Flashback Drop. Flashback Table is best used to recover a table that was updated with an incorrect WHERE clause. This can allow users to quickly and easily recover their own problems, without involving the DBA. In addition, the availability of the database is not compromised during the Flashback Table operation.

Summary

In this chapter, you learned about the Flashback Technologies in detail. The Flashback Technologies consist of the Flashback Drop, Flashback Versions Query, Flashback Transaction Query, and Flashback Table.

Flashback Query was first developed in Oracle 9*i* and is the basis for the rest of the Flashback Technologies developed in Oracle 10*g*. We discussed the Recycle Bin in detail, and you learned how to

- Drop tables to the Recycle Bin
- Query the Recycle Bin
- Recover tables from the Recycle Bin

- Purge the Recycle Bin
- Permanently remove objects from the Recycle Bin and deallocate the space allocated to them

You also learned how Flashback Drop works with the Recycle Bin and that when space pressure arises, Oracle automatically reclaims space by overwriting objects in the Recycle Bin.

The next section discussed and provided hand-on examples of using the Flashback Versions Query. This capability retrieves all versions of the rows that exist or existed between the times the query was executed to a determined point-in-time in the past. Flashback Versions Query works by retrieving data from the UNDO tablespace and uses either SCNs or timestamps to identify the start and stop points.

You then used the Flashback Transaction Query to diagnose and analyze transactional changes in data. You saw examples of how you can use this tool to perform transactional analysis using transaction identifiers or timestamps.

The last Flashback Technology discussed in this chapter was the Flashback Table. You use Flashback Table to recover a table or to set tables to a specific point-in-time without performing an incomplete recovery. All dependent objects are also recovered when using Flashback Table. Flashback Table has numerous benefits over incomplete recovery.

EM also can perform Flashback Technologies and you walked through performing a Flashback Table recovery within EM.

Exam Essentials

Know how to recover a dropped table using Flashback Drop. Make sure you are aware of how the Recycle Bin works for dropped objects. You should be able to identify objects in the Recycle Bin. You should be familiar with how to manage the Recycle Bin and be able to perform a Flashback Drop recovery of a dropped object.

Know how to recover from user errors with Flashback Versions Query. Know how to perform a Flashback Versions Query using timestamp or SCN information. Be aware of how undo data is used with Flashback Versions Query and how to protect this data. You should also know how to identify data with pseudocolumns.

Be aware of how to perform a transactional level recovery using Flashback Transaction Query. Know how to use the Flashback Transaction Query to diagnose and analyze changes in the database. Make sure you understand how to identify specific information with Flashback Transaction Query and how to use Data Manipulation Language (DML) to undo a transaction.

Understand how to perform a Flashback Table operation. Know how to perform a Flashback Table operation with a timestamp or an SCN. Be aware of how undo data is used in Flashback Table and how to protect this data.

Review Questions

1. Which underlying database technology is used by Flashback Drop, Flashback Table, and Flashback Versions Query to recover data?

   A. Redo logs

   B. Rollback segments

   C. Undo data

   D. Archive logs

2. Which of the following statements is true regarding the Recycle Bin? (Choose all that apply.)

   A. The Recycle Bin is a physical storage area of flashback dropped objects.

   B. The Recycle Bin is a logical container area of flashback dropped objects.

   C. The objects in the Recycle Bin are stored in the `UNDO` tablespace.

   D. The objects in the Recycle Bin are stored in the tablespace they were created in.

3. What actions does the Flashback Drop process perform?

   A. Back up table only

   B. Back up table and indexes only

   C. Back up table and referential constraints only

   D. Back up table and dependent objects

4. Which activity can occur with the Recycle Bin?

   A. All indexed-organized tables are protected by the Recycle Bin.

   B. System- and dictionary-managed tablespaces are stored in the Recycle Bin.

   C. Dependent objects of stored tables—including referential constraints—are stored in the Recycle Bin.

   D. Data Manipulation Language (DML) and Data Definition Language (DDL) can be run against objects in the Recycle Bin.

   E. None of the above.

5. One method of dropping objects and bypassing the Recycle Bin is to perform which command?

   A. `DROP USER` *`user`* `CASCADE`

   B. `DROP TABLE`

   C. `DROP TABLE INCLUDING CONTENTS`

   D. `DROP USER` *`user`*

6. Which command is responsible for removing the objects in multiple users from the Recycle Bin?

   A. PURGE RECYCLEBIN

   B. PURGE TABLESPACE *user*

   C. PURGE DBA_RECYCLEBIN

   D. PURGE TABLES *user*

7. What is the naming convention of a Recycle Bin object?

   A. BIN$*globalUID*$*version*

   B. BIN$*global*$*UIDversion*

   C. BIN$*globalUIDversion*

   D. BIN*globalUIDversion*

8. What two methods can be used to view the Recycle Bin?

   A. Run the SHOW RECYCLEBIN command.

   B. Query the view DBA_RECYCLEBIN.

   C. Query the view V$RECYCLEBIN.

   D. Query the view RECYCLEBIN.

9. What best describes the space pressure in the Recycle Bin?

   A. No free extents in the Recycle Bin, and objects being removed from the Recycle Bin to free up extents for non-Recycle Bin objects.

   B. No free extents in a tablespace, and objects being removed from the Recycle Bin to free up extents for non-Recycle Bin objects.

   C. No free extents in a tablespace, and objects being removed from the Recycle Bin to free up extents in a tablespace for non-Recycle Bin objects on a first in, first out (FIFO) basis.

   D. No free extents in the Recycle Bin tablespace and objects being removed from Recycle Bin tablespace to free up extents for non-Recycle Bin objects on a first in, first out (FIFO) basis.

10. If a tablespace is configured for AUTO EXTEND, what will occur when there are no free extents and there are objects in the AUTO EXTEND tablespace?

   A. The tablespace will autoextend to make more free space and Oracle will not remove Recycle Bin objects associated with the tablespace.

   B. The tablespace will not autoextend, and objects in the Recycle Bin will be removed to make space in the tablespace.

   C. The tablespace will autoextend to make more free space and Oracle will remove Recycle Bin objects associated with the tablespace.

   D. The tablespace will not autoextend, and objects in the Recycle Bin will be compressed to make space in the tablespace.

11. Which of the following statements best describes Flashback Versions Query?

    A. Flashback Versions Query is a query to perform diagnostics on version changes in row data on rows that existed between the times the query was executed to a determined point-in-time in the past.

    B. Flashback Versions Query is a method of querying all version changes on rows that existed between the times the query was executed to a determined point-in-time in the past.

    C. Flashback Versions Query is a query to perform diagnostics on table changes in row data on rows that existed between the times the query was executed to a determined point-in-time in the past.

    D. Flashback Versions Query is a method of querying all version changes on rows that existed between the times the query was executed to a determined point-in-time in the future.

12. What view can be used to query diagnostic information about transactional changes in the database?

    A. `FLASHBACK_TRANSACTION_QUERY`

    B. `DBA_TRANSACTION_QUERY`

    C. `V$TRANSACTION_QUERY`

    D. `V$FLASHBACK_TRANSACTION_QUERY`

13. What are the methods of performing a Flashback Versions Query? (Choose all that apply.)

    A. Flashback Versions Query can be performed by minimum and maximum SCN value.

    B. Flashback Versions Query can be performed by minimum and maximum sequence number.

    C. Flashback Versions Query can be performed by starting and ending timestamp.

    D. Flashback Versions Query can be performed by minimum and maximum undo value.

14. Which of the following statements is true regarding the `VERSIONS BETWEEN` clause?

    A. The `VERSIONS BETWEEN` clause only supports SCN.

    B. The `VERSIONS BETWEEN` clause only supports log sequences.

    C. The `VERSIONS BETWEEN` clause cannot produce versions past modifications to the table structure.

    D. The `VERSIONS BETWEEN` clause can produce versions past Data Definition Language (DDL) changes to an object.

15. Which pseudocolumn do you use to identify a unique row in a Flashback Versions Query?

    A. `VERSIONS_XID`

    B. `BVERSIONS_OPERATION`

    C. `VERSIONS_ENDTIME`

    D. `VERSION_STARTTIME`

16. Which of the following statements are true regarding the VERSIONS BETWEEN clause? (Choose all that apply.)
    - A. The VERSIONS BETWEEN clause may be used in DML statements.
    - B. The VERSIONS BETWEEN clause may be used in DDL statements.
    - C. The VERSIONS BETWEEN clause may be used to query past DDL changes to tables.
    - D. The VERSIONS BETWEEN clause may not be used to query past DML statements to tables.
17. Which of the following statements is true regarding implementing a Flashback Table recovery?
    - A. SCN is never needed to perform a Flashback Table recovery.
    - B. ROW MOVEMENT must be enabled to perform a Flashback Table recovery.
    - C. Only one table may be recovered to perform a Flashback Table recovery.
    - D. Flashback Table recovery does not use undo data to perform a Flashback Table recovery.
18. What happens to enabled triggers on a table after a FLASHBACK TABLE command is performed? (Choose all that apply.)
    - A. The triggers are disabled by default.
    - B. The triggers are enabled by default.
    - C. Disabled triggers remain disabled with the default FLASHBACK TABLE command.
    - D. All triggers are enabled if the ENABLE TRIGGER clause is used.
19. What method can you use to identify a DML operation and the SQL statement that has been performed against a row in a specific table for a schema owner? (Choose all that apply.)
    - A. Query DBA_TRANSACTION_QUERY for TABLE_NAME, OPERATION, and UNDO_SQL. Limit rows by START_SCN and TABLE_OWNER.
    - B. Query FLASHBACK_TRANSACTION_QUERY for TABLE_NAME, OPERATION, and UNDO_SQL. Limit rows by START_SCN and TABLE_OWNER.
    - C. Query FLASHBACK_TRANSACTION_QUERY for TABLE_NAME, OPERATION, and UNDO_SQL. Limit rows by START_TIMESTAMP and TABLE_OWNER.
    - D. Query DBA_TRANSACTION_QUERY for TABLE_NAME, OPERATION, and UNDO_SQL. Limit rows by START_SCN and TABLE_OWNER.
20. How can you protect the amount of time you can query information from the Flashback Transaction Query?
    - A. Add UNDO GUARANTEE to the UNDO tablespace.
    - B. Add RETENTION GUARANTEE to the UNDO tablespace.
    - C. Add RETENTION GUARANTEE to the Recycle Bin logical storage container.
    - D. Add UNDO GUARANTEE to the Recycle Bin logical storage container.

Answers to Review Questions

1. C. All the Flashback Technologies, with the exception of the Flashback Database, utilize the undo data to recover objects.

2. B, D. The Recycle Bin is a logical container of flashback dropped objects. The objects in the Recycle Bin are stored in the tablespace they were created in.

3. D. The Flashback Drop process is responsible for backing up tables and their dependent objects.

4. E. Only non-partitioned index-organized tables are protected by the Recycle Bin. Non-system and locally managed tablespaces are stored in the Recycle Bin. Referential constraints are not stored in the Recycle Bin. DML or DDL cannot be performed against objects in the Recycle Bin.

5. A. The command `DROP USER` *`user`* `CASCADE` drops the user and the database objects without recording a backup in the Recycle Bin. Objects in the Recycle Bin owned by the user will be removed from the Recycle Bin.

6. C. The `PURGE DBA_RECYCLEBIN` command purges the complete Recycle Bin for all users.

7. A. The naming convention of objects in the Recycle Bin consists of a globalUID and version number assigned by the database with `BIN$` prefixed, and a `$` between the globalUID and the version number. The formatting looks like `BIN$`*`globalUID`*`$`*`version`*.

8. A, D. The `SHOW RECYCLEBIN` command and querying the `RECYCLEBIN` view are two methods of viewing the contents of the Recycle Bin.

9. C. The Recycle Bin is not stored in a Recycle Bin tablespace. It is a logical container pointing to objects in the tablespace where the objects were originally created. Objects are removed from the Recycle Bin when there is a need for available extents in a non-system tablespace. The objects are removed on a first in, first out (FIFO) basis.

10. B. A tablespace with `AUTO EXTEND` enabled will not autoextend to make space for the Recycle Bin objects. The objects will be removed from the Recycle Bin in the standard first in, first out (FIFO) basis.

11. B. Flashback Versions Query is a method of querying all version changes on rows. The rows must exist from the time the query was executed to a point-in-time in the past. The query will not display committed data after the query has been executed.

12. A. The view `FLASHBACK_TRANSACTION_QUERY` is used as a diagnostic tool to identify version information about transactional changes to the database. This view can be used to view the DML statements that were executed against a row and in a specific table.

13. A, C. The Flashback Versions Query can be performed by either `MINVALUE` and `MAXVALUE SCN` or starting and ending `TO_TIMESTAMP` value.

14. C. The `VERSIONS BETWEEN` clause of the Flashback Versions Query cannot query past table modifications or DDL changes to a table.

15. A. VERSIONS_XID uniquely identifies a row in the Flashback Versions Query. The other pseudocolumns can narrow down the selection criteria and may identify multiple rows in a timeframe or SCN range.

16. A, B. The VERSIONS BETWEEN clause can be used in DML and DDL statements to identify data.

17. B. The command ALTER TABLE *table_name* ENABLE ROW MOVEMENT must be enabled to allow Flashback Table recovery.

18. A, C. The default action for the FLASHBACK TABLE command is that the triggers will be disabled. If you disable the triggers on a table, the triggers will stay disabled after the FLASHBACK TABLE command as well. Also, if you use the ENABLE TRIGGER clause, all enabled triggers on the table prior to the Flashback Table operation will be enabled and all disabled triggers will be disabled.

19. B, C. The proper method is to query the FLASHBACK_TRANSACTION_QUERY view. The TABLE_NAME, OPERATION, and UNDO_SQL columns should be queried to display the information about the transactional information. The transactional information from FLASHBACK_TRANSACTION_QUERY should then be narrowed down by START_TIMESTAMP or START_SCN. Then the information can be further narrowed down by TABLE_OWNER. Alternatively, the XID, if known, can be queried to identify the exact transaction, but that was not an option in this example.

20. B. Adding RETENTION GUARANTEE to the UNDO tablespace or during database creation to the UNDO tablespace will protect unexpired undo data in the UNDO tablespace. This is where the Flashback Transaction Query retrieves information about transaction changes to rows in the database.

Handling Block Corruption

ORACLE DATABASE 10*G*: ADMINISTRATION II EXAM OBJECTIVES COVERED IN THIS CHAPTER:

✓ **Dealing with Database Corruption**

- Define block corruption and list its causes and symptoms.
- Detect database corruptions using the following utilities: ANALYZE and DBVERIFY.
- Detect database corruptions using the DBMS_REPAIR package.
- Implement the DB_BLOCK_CHECKING parameter to detect corruptions.
- Repair corruptions using RMAN.

Exam objectives are subject to change at any time without prior notice and at Oracle's sole discretion. Please visit Oracle's Training and Certification website (`http://www.oracle.com/education/certification/`) for the most current exam objectives listing.

This chapter provides a detailed explanation and walk-through of techniques and utilities designed to deal with physical corruption. We will discuss and use the ANALYZE TABLE *table_name* command, the DBVERIFY utility, the DB_BLOCK_CHECKING initialization parameter, and the DBMS_REPAIR package. These utilities and methods are not new to Oracle 10*g*; most of them have been available since Oracle versions 7 and 8*i*. We will walk through some examples of using best practices for dealing with physical corruption. Additionally, you will use RMAN Block Media Recovery (BMR) to repair block corruption. This is a new Oracle 10*g* capability in RMAN.

This chapter concentrates on the workings of each of the preceding methods to identify and resolve physical corruption at the block level. The overview of the block corruption will explain how this occurs at a high level. We will also discuss how to identify block corruption and following that, we will demonstrate how to use each tool and utility to resolve block corruption.

An Overview of Block Corruption

Block corruption or *physical corruption* is when a block on a physical disk becomes unreadable or inconsistent to the state that the data is unusable. Block corruption can be caused by many different sources. It is often very difficult to diagnose the actual cause of the corruption.

Block corruption can be introduced by human error though the use of software, firmware, and hardware bugs. Block corruption can also be introduced by the environment that houses your Oracle database. This usually means hardware failure, but other factors can impact the way the memory and hardware function on a system that your Oracle database is installed on.

It is generally accepted that the cause of most block corruptions is human error. Often bugs, patches, or hardware can be introduced, causing block corruption. Most often, these causes of corruption can be remedied by having good operational procedures such as making changes to hardware and software in test environments before moving the changes to the production environments. Also, using redundant hardware such as mirrored disks can protect against hardware-caused block corruption.

Block Corruption Symptoms

The detection of block corruption involves using multiple diagnostic logs to identify that corruption has occurred. These methods include monitoring and reading the log files from the operating system, application, and database level. If audit functions are enabled at the operating system level, these audit logs can be reviewed as well.

System logs vary for each operating system:

- In a Windows environment, the Event Viewer shows the contents of the system log. The Event Viewer is evoked by choosing Control Panel ➤ Administrative Tools ➤ Computer Management.

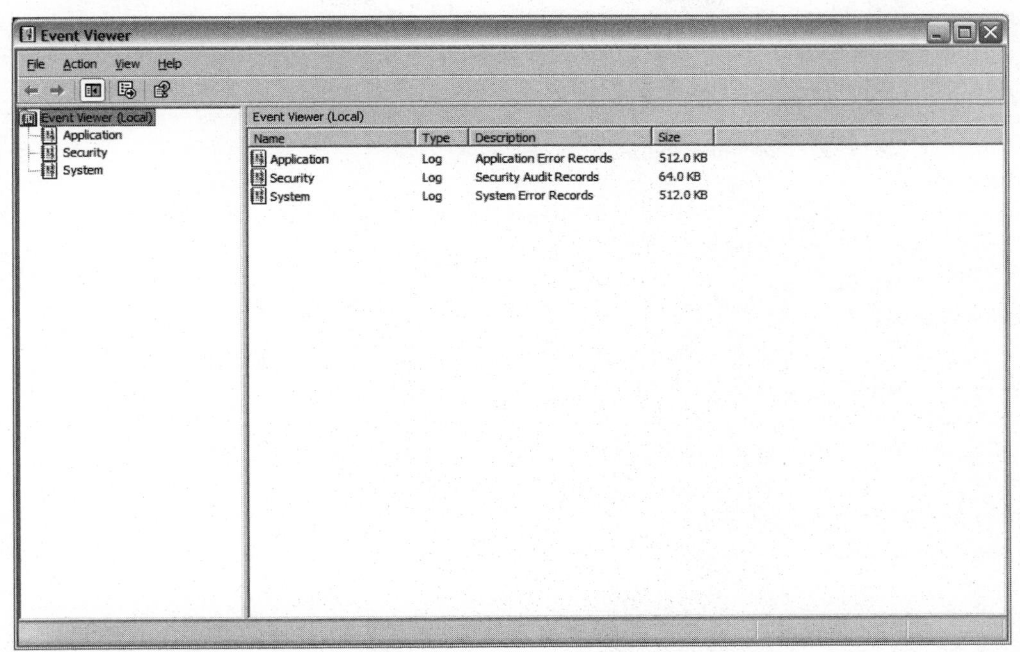

- In a Unix environment, the SYSLOG file contains the system log events. This is a file located in /var/adm/syslog in many Unix environments.

Application logs can vary for each application that is installed. You need to read your application administrator's guide to determine the location of these logs. In most cases, these logs indicate that there is a problem with a process or procedure in the application. The application logs don't often give detailed information about block corruption, but they are a good starting point.

Database logs and trace file references are located in the ALERT.LOG file and the associated trace files in the UDUMP or BDUMP directories. The ALERT.LOG often indicates that there is a problem at a high level. Then a trace file is spawned off in the UDUMP or BDUMP directory, which provides detail about the ALERT.LOG entry. The trace files provide the most detail about the corruption problems.

The following is an example of a trace file created in the UDUMP directory:

```
Dump file c:\oracle\admin\ora101\udump\ora101_ora_2236.trc
Fri Nov 16 16:21:35 2004
ORACLE V10.1.0.2.0 - Production vsnsta=0

*** 2004.11.16.15.53.02.000
```

```
*** SESSION ID:(11.9) 2004.05.08.11.51.09.000
kdbchk: row locked by non-existent transaction
        table=0   slot=0
        lockid=44   ktbbhitc=1
Block header dump:  0x01800005
 Object id on Block? Y
 seg/obj: 0xb6d  csc: 0x00.1cf5f  itc: 1  flg: -
  typ: 1 - USERS
     fsl: 0  fnx: 0x0 ver: 0x01

 Itl           Xid                  Uba         Flag  Lck        Scn/Fsc
0x01   xid:  0x0003.011.00000151    uba:
  0x008018fb.0645.0d  --U-    4  fsc
0x0000.0001cf60

data_block_dump
===============
tsiz: 0x6b8
hsiz: 0x18
pbl: 0x38088044
bdba: 0x01800008
flag=-----------
ntab=1
nrow=5
```

As you can see, detecting block corruption is a detailed process of monitoring system, application, and database output. This can be a time-consuming process. If possible, monitoring of the ALERT.LOG file should be performed on a daily basis. Many times, you can use operating system capabilities to perform a string search for Oracle errors and send these to you automatically. In the next few sections, you will use Oracle utilities to detect block corruption. You will look for block corruption in a specific table, and you will learn how to bypass these corrupt blocks.

Using Various Methods to Detect and Resolve Corruption

There are four methods for detecting corruption:

- The ANALYZE TABLE *table_name* VALIDATE STRUCTURE command
- The Oracle DBVERIFY utility used against the offline data files

- The init.ora parameter DB_BLOCK_CHECKING, which checks data and index blocks each time they are created or modified
- The DBMS_REPAIR package used against a table, index, or partition

Each method is described in the following sections.

Using the ANALYZE Utility

The ANALYZE TABLE *table_name* VALIDATE STRUCTURE command validates the integrity of the structure of the object being analyzed. This command is either successful or not successful at the object level. Therefore, if this command returns an error for the object being analyzed, you would need to completely rebuild it. If no error is returned, the object is free of corruption and does not need to be re-created. The following is an example of the ANALYZE command, when it detects an error and when it doesn't:

```
SQL> analyze table test.t3 validate structure;
*
ERROR at line 1:
ORA-01498: block check failure - see trace file

SQL> analyze table test.t3 validate structure;

Table analyzed.

SQL>
```

As you can see, using the ANALYZE command is a straightforward process. If the object has any corrupt blocks, the statement fails. This is a good starting point for identifying a database object that is corrupt.

Using the DBVERIFY Utility

DBVERIFY is an Oracle utility that is used to see whether corruption exists in a particular datafile. This utility is most often used on a backup of the database or when the database is not running. However, if necessary, the tool can be used on the database when it is online to minimize availability impacts on high-use databases. The output of a DBVERIFY command verifies index and data blocks that have processed with and without error, the total number of blocks processed, empty blocks, and blocks already marked as corrupt.

The DBVERIFY utility uses the term *pages* instead of *blocks*. This term refers to blocks within the Oracle datafile.

The Oracle DBVERIFY utility is executed by entering **dbv** at the command prompt. This utility has nine parameters that can be specified at execution:

- FILE
- START
- END
- BLOCKSIZE
- LOGFILE
- FEEDBACK
- PARAFILE
- USERID
- SEGMENT_ID

Table 7.1 describes these parameters.

TABLE 7.1 DBVERIFY Parameters

Parameter	Description	Default Value for Parameter
FILE	Datafile to be verified by the utility.	No default parameter
START	Starting block to begin verification.	First block in the datafile
END	Ending block to end verification.	Last block in the datafile
BLOCKSIZE	Block size of database. This should be the same as the init.ora parameter DB_BLOCK_SIZE.	8192
LOGFILE	Log file to store the results of running the utility.	No default parameter
FEEDBACK	Displays the progress of the utility by displaying a dot for each number of blocks processed.	0
PARAFILE	The parameter file to store options if you do not want to specify these on the command line.	No default parameter
USERID	Username and password.	No default parameter
SEGMENT_ID	The segment identifier.	No default parameter

This help information can also be seen by executing the DBV HELP=Y command, as in the following example:

```
C:\oracle\product\10.1.0\db_1\database>dbv help=y
DBVERIFY: Release 10.1.0.2.0 - Production on Fri Nov 5 20:08:57 2004
Copyright (c) 1982, 2004, Oracle.  All rights reserved.

Keyword     Description                    (Default)
----------------------------------------------------
FILE        File to Verify                 (NONE)
START       Start Block                    (First Block of File)
END         End Block                      (Last Block of File)
BLOCKSIZE   Logical Block Size             (8192)
LOGFILE     Output Log                     (NONE)
FEEDBACK    Display Progress               (0)
PARFILE     Parameter File                 (NONE)
USERID      Username/Password              (NONE)
SEGMENT_ID  Segment ID (tsn.relfile.block) (NONE)
C:\oracle\product\10.1.0\db_1\database>
```

To run the DBVERIFY utility, the BLOCKSIZE parameter must match your database block size, or the following error will result:

```
C:\oracle\oradata\ora101>dbv blocksize=2048 file=users01.dbf

DBVERIFY: Release 10.1.0.2.0 - Production on Fri Nov 5 20:12:14 2004

Copyright (c) 1982, 2004, Oracle.  All rights reserved.


DBV-00103: Specified BLOCKSIZE (2048) differs from actual (8192)

C:\oracle\oradata\ora101>
```

Once the BLOCKSIZE parameter is set to match the database block size, the DBVERIFY utility can proceed. There are two ways to run this utility: without the LOGFILE parameter specified, and with it specified.

Let's walk through both of these examples. First, without the LOGFILE parameter set:

```
C:\oracle\oradata\ora101>dbv blocksize=8192 file=users01.dbf
DBVERIFY: Release 10.1.0.2.0 - Production on Fri Nov 5 20:10:27 2004
Copyright (c) 1982, 2004, Oracle.  All rights reserved.
```

```
DBVERIFY - Verification starting : FILE = users01.dbf
DBVERIFY - Verification complete

Total Pages Examined         : 640
Total Pages Processed (Data) : 91
Total Pages Failing   (Data) : 0
Total Pages Processed (Index): 18
Total Pages Failing   (Index): 0
Total Pages Processed (Other): 128
Total Pages Processed (Seg)  : 0
Total Pages Failing   (Seg)  : 0
Total Pages Empty            : 403
Total Pages Marked Corrupt   : 0
Total Pages Influx           : 0
C:\oracle\oradata\ora101>
```

The following code demonstrates the DBVERIFY utility with the `LOGFILE` parameter set. The results of this command are written to the file `users01.log` and not to the screen. The results can be displayed by editing the log file.

```
C:\oracle\oradata\ora101>dbv blocksize=8192 file=users01.dbf
  ➥logfile=c:\temp\users01.log
DBVERIFY: Release 10.1.0.2.0 - Production on Fri Nov 5 20:14:00 2004
Copyright (c) 1982, 2004, Oracle.  All rights reserved.
C:\oracle\oradata\ora101>
```

In this second example, the output from the first example would appear in the file `c:\temp\users01.log`.

The DBVERIFY utility is a useful diagnostic tool to identify the physical structure of Oracle database files.

Using *DB_BLOCK_CHECKING*

The *DB_BLOCK_CHECKING* initialization parameter sets block checking at the database level. The default is set to `FALSE` for all non-system tablespaces. The `SYSTEM` tablespace is enabled by default. The `DB_BLOCK_CHECKING` parameter can be dynamically set with the `ALTER SYSTEM SET` statement. This parameter forces checks for corrupt blocks each time blocks are modified at the tablespace level. A checksum occurs every time a block is modified. The following is an excerpt from an `initora101.ora` file that gives information on the value of this parameter:

```
C:\oracle\product\10.1.0\db_1\database>edit initora101.ora

db_block_checking = TRUE
```

As you can see, setting the DB_BLOCK_CHECKING initialization parameter is fairly simple. Adding this parameter forces block checking at the database level. Like any verification procedure, this can place overhead on the database that can affect performance. The trade-off is that the database will be checked for block corruption each time a block is modified. This will catch corruption in near real time.

Using the *DBMS_REPAIR* Package

The *DBMS_REPAIR* package is a set of procedures that enables you to detect and fix corrupt blocks in tables and indexes. The DBMS_REPAIR package is made up of multiple stored procedures, as described earlier. Each of these procedures performs different actions. This section focuses on the CHECK_OBJECT procedure and the FIX_CORRUPT_BLOCKS procedure. Table 7.2 shows all of the procedures available in the DBMS_REPAIR package.

The general process for resolving physical corruption is to verify that you have corrupt data blocks and to determine their extent. Next, you need to put the list of corrupt data blocks in a holding table so the corrupt blocks can be identified. These blocks are then marked as corrupt so that they can be skipped over in a query or during normal usage of the table. We will also demonstrate how to fix an index and freelists that could be impacted by physical corruption in a table.

TABLE 7.2 *DBMS_REPAIR* Package

Procedure Name	Description
CHECK_OBJECT	Detects and reports corruptions in a table or index.
FIX_CORRUPT_BLOCKS	Marks blocks (that were previously identified by the CHECK_OBJECT procedure) as software corrupt.
DUMP_ORPHAN_KEYS	Reports index entries (into an orphan key table) that point to rows in corrupt data blocks.
REBUILD_FREELISTS	Rebuilds the freelists of the object.
SEGMENT_FIX_STATUS	Provides the capability to fix the corrupted state of a bitmap entry when segment space management is AUTO.
SKIP_CORRUPT_BLOCKS	When used, ignores blocks marked corrupt during table and index scans. If not used, you get an ORA-1578 error when encountering blocks marked corrupt.
ADMIN_TABLES	Provides administrative functions (create, drop, purge) for repair of orphan key tables. Note: These tables are always created in the SYS schema.

Let's walk through an example of how to detect and mark corrupt blocks:

1. Generate a trace file of the corrupt block, which is automatically created by the ANALYZE command.

```
SQL> connect / as sysdba
Connected.

SQL> analyze table test.t3 validate structure;
*
ERROR at line 1:
ORA-01498: block check failure - see trace file
```

2. View the trace file to determine bad block information. In this example, the bad block is 5. This is indicated by the output line nrow=5, highlighted at the end of this code listing.

```
Dump file c:\oracle\admin\ora101\udump\ora101_ora_2236.trc
Fri Nov 16 16:21:35 2004
ORACLE V10.1.0.2.0 - Production vsnsta=0

*** 2004.11.16.15.53.02.000
*** SESSION ID:(11.9) 2004.05.08.11.51.09.000
kdbchk: row locked by non-existent transaction
        table=0   slot=0
        lockid=44   ktbbhitc=1
Block header dump:  0x01800005
 Object id on Block? Y
 seg/obj: 0xb6d  csc: 0x00.1cf5f  itc: 1  flg: -
  typ: 1 - USERS
     fsl: 0  fnx: 0x0 ver: 0x01

 Itl           Xid                  Uba         Flag  Lck        Scn/Fsc
0x01   xid:  0x0003.011.00000151    uba:
  0x008018fb.0645.0d  --U-    4  fsc
0x0000.0001cf60

data_block_dump
===============
tsiz: 0x6b8
hsiz: 0x18
pbl: 0x38088044
bdba: 0x01800008
```

```
flag=-----------
ntab=1
nrow=5
```

3. Create the repair tables to store and retrieve information from running the DBMS_REPAIR package. The following is the example PL/SQL in a file called `repair_tab.sql`, which will be used to build the REPAIR_TABLE. This is a custom script that must be created by the DBA. After the script `repair_tab.sql` is run, query the DBA_OBJECTS table to verify that the REPAIR_TABLE has been created.

```
SQL> host repair_tab.sql
-- Create DBMS Repair Table
declare

begin

  dbms_repair.admin_tables
   (table_name => 'REPAIR_TABLE',
   table_type => dbms_repair.repair_table,
   action => dbms_repair.create_action,
   tablespace => 'USERS');

end;
/
SQL>
SQL> @repair_tab
PL/SQL procedure successfully completed.
SQL> select owner, object_name, object_type
     2> from dba_objects
     3> where object_name like '%REPAIR_TABLE';
OWNER          OBJECT_NAME      OBJECT_TYPE
-------------- ---------------- -------------------
SYS            DBA_REPAIR_TABLE VIEW
SYS            REPAIR_TABLE     TABLE
2 rows selected.
SQL>
```

4. Check the object, or table T3, to determine whether there is a corrupt block in the table. Even though you know this from the ANALYZE TABLE *table_name* VALIDATE STRUCTURE command, you need this information saved in REPAIR_TABLE. The following code calls the DBMS_REPAIR.CHECK_OBJECT procedure that has determined variables such as SCHEMA_NAME and

OBJECT_NAME. The corrupt blocks are then stored in REPAIR_TABLE and output is sent to the screen through the DBMS_OUTPUT.PUT_LINE procedure.

```
SQL> host edit check_obj.sql
--determine what block is corrupt in a table

set serveroutput on size 100000;
declare

   rpr_count int;

begin

   rpr_count := 0;

dbms_repair.check_object(
   schema_name => 'TEST',
   object_name => 'T3',
   repair_table_name => 'REPAIR_TABLE',
   corrupt_count => rpr_count);

dbms_output.put_line('repair block count: '
  ||to_char(rpr_count));

end;

SQL> @check_obj.sql
Server Output                     ON
PL/SQL procedure successfully completed.
repair block count: 1
SQL>
```

5. Verify that REPAIR_TABLE contains information about table T3 and the bad block. This query has been broken into three queries for display purposes:

```
SQL> select object_name, block_id, corrupt_type, marked_corrupt,
  2  corrupt_description, repair_description
  3  from repair_table;

OBJECT_NAME  BLOCK_ID  CORRUPT_TYPE MARKED_COR
-----------  --------  ------------ ----------
T3           3         1            FALSE
```

```
SQL> select object_name, corrupt_description
  2  from repair_table;

OBJECT_NAME CORRUPT_DESCRIPTION
----------- ------------------------------------------
T3          kdbchk: row locked by non-existent transaction
            table=0   slot=0
            lockid=44   ktbbhitc=1

SQL> select object_name, repair_description
  2  from repair_table;

OBJECT_NAME REPAIR_DESCRIPTION
----------- ---------------------------
T3          mark block software corrupt
```

6. A backup of the table should be created before any attempts are made to fix the block or mark the block as corrupt. Therefore, you should attempt to salvage any good data from the corrupted block before marking it as corrupt.

```
SQL> connect test/test
Connected.
SQL> create table t3_bak as
  2  select * from t3
  3  where dbms_rowid.rowid_block_number(rowid) = 5
  4  and dbms_rowid.rowid_to_absolute_fno (rowid, 'TEST','T3') = 4;

Table created.

SQL> select c1 from t3_bak;

      C1
--------
       1
       2
       3
       5
```

7. Mark block 5 as corrupt, but note that full table scans will still generate an ORA-1578 error.

```
SQL> host edit fix_blocks.sql

-- Create DBMS Fix Corrupt blocks
```

```
declare
     fix_block_count int;
  begin
     fix_block_count := 0;
  dbms_repair.fix_corrupt_blocks (
     schema_name => 'TEST',
     object_name => 'T3',
     object_type => dbms_repair.table_object,
     repair_table_name => 'REPAIR_TABLE',
     fix_count => fix_block_count);
     dbms_output.put_line('fix blocks count: ' ||
  to_char(fix_block_count));
  end;
  /


SQL>
SQL> @fix_blocks
fix blocks count: 1
PL/SQL procedure successfully completed.


SQL> select object_name, block_id, marked_corrupt
  2  from repair_table;

OBJECT_NAME                      BLOCK_ID MARKED_COR
------------------------------ ---------- ----------
T3                                      5 TRUE

SQL> select * from test.t3;
select * from test.t3
                     *
ERROR at line 1:
ORA-01578: ORACLE data block corrupted
  (file # 4, block # 5)
ORA-01110: data file 4: 'C:\oracle\oradata\ora101\users01.dbf'
```

8. Use the DUMP_ORPHAN_KEYS procedure to dump the index entries that point to the corrupt rows in the corrupt data blocks. This procedure displays the affected index entries. Therefore,

the index will need to be rebuilt. You must first create the ORPHAN_KEY_TABLE if it has not been created:

```
SQL> host more orphan_tab.sql

-- Create the orphan_table
declare

begin

  dbms_repair.admin_tables
   (table_name => 'ORPHAN_KEY_TABLE',
   table_type => dbms_repair.orphan_table,
   action => dbms_repair.create_action,
   tablespace => 'USERS');

end;
/
SQL>
SQL> @orphan_tab
PL/SQL procedure successfully completed.
```

9. Once the ORPHAN_KEY_TABLE is created, you can then dump the orphaned keys into this table. The following example dumps the data into the ORPHAN_KEY_TABLE:

```
SQL> host more orphan_dump.sql

-- Create DBMS Dump orphan/Index entries

declare
    orph_count int;
  begin
    orph_count:= 0;
  dbms_repair.dump_orphan_keys (
        schema_name => 'TEST',
        object_name => 'T3_PK',
        object_type => dbms_repair.index_object,
        repair_table_name => 'REPAIR_TABLE',
       orphan_table_name => 'ORPHAN_KEY_TABLE',
       key_count => orph_count);
```

```
        dbms_output.put_line('orphan-index entries: ' || to_char(orph_count));
    end;
    /



SQL>
SQL> @orphan_dump
orphan-index entries: 3
PL/SQL procedure successfully completed.

SQL> select index_name, count(*) from orphan_key_table
  2  group by index_name;

INDEX_NAME                       COUNT(*)
------------------------------ ----------
T3_PK                                   3
```

10. Mark the corrupt block as *skip enabled*. This allows for querying the table without retrieving the corrupt block, which would trigger an ORA-1578 error:

```
SQL> host more corrupt_block_skip.sql

-- Skips the corrupt blocks in the tables.

declare

  begin

    dbms_repair.skip_corrupt_blocks (
       schema_name => 'TEST',
       object_name => 'T3',
       object_type => dbms_repair.table_object,
       flags => dbms_repair.skip_flag);

    end;
    /

SQL> @corrupt_block_skip
PL/SQL procedure successfully completed.
```

```
SQL> select table_name, skip_corrupt from dba_tables
  2  where table_name = 'T3';

TABLE_NAME                     SKIP_COR
------------------------------ --------
T3                             ENABLED
```

11. Rebuild the freelists so that the corrupt block is never added to freelists of blocks. This will prevent this block from being used for future data entry. Rebuilding the freelists is performed with the procedure in the DBMS_REPAIR package called REBUILD_FREELISTS.

```
SQL> host more rebuild_freelists.sql

-- Removes the bad block from the freelist of blocks


declare
    begin
    dbms_repair.rebuild_freelists (
       schema_name => 'TEST',
       object_name => 'T3',
       object_type => dbms_repair.table_object);
    end;
    /

SQL> @rebuild_freelists
PL/SQL procedure successfully completed.
```

12. Finally, you can rebuild the index, and then the table T3 is ready for use.

```
SQL> drop index t3_pk;
Index dropped.
SQL> create index t3_pk on t3 (c1);
Index created.
```

As you can see, using the many procedures in the DBMS_REPAIR package to resolve physical corruption can be a lengthy process. These procedures are detailed, and you must enter the right variables. Make sure your SQL session has SET SERVEROUTPUT ON SIZE 100000, which allows the procedures to return output to the SQL session. This was defined in step 4 of the preceding instructions and remains active in the example until you log out of the SQL session.

Repairing corrupt blocks can result in the loss of data in those blocks. Furthermore, the repairs can result in logical inconsistencies between certain relationships in your database. Thus, you should perform careful analysis before using the DBMS_REPAIR package to determine the overall database effect. You should use this tool with the assistance of Oracle support, if possible.

There are some considerations that you should be aware of when using the DBMS_REPAIR package that could impact the usage of the utility. You should be aware of these situations so you can plan the best usage of the DBMS_REPAIR package. The following is a list of best practices for dealing with corruption. Physical corruption is a serious failure, and you may need to use a combination of recovery techniques to resolve the issue.

What is the extent of the corruption? Use the CHECK_OBJECT procedure and then verify REPAIR_TABLE.

What other options are available to resolve block corruption?

- Examine other methods of resolving corrupt objects if necessary, such as rebuilding an object if the data is available.
- Try to ignore the corruption by excluding the corrupt row from `select` statements.
- Perform incomplete recovery.

Real World Scenario

Keep Your Recovery Options Open

It is always a good idea to have more than one method to recover a database. You don't ever want to be in a situation where there is only one choice. This is readily apparent with block corruption. Block corruption can be a difficult recovery process, mainly because you are recovering at a block level. Referential integrity between row data and other database objects is common on complex database applications. Triggers can also make changes to row data that must be carefully handled. All of these complications make the chances of successfully performing block corruption recovery an uncertain option.

That is why you should have other methods at the database level, and for key tables, if possible. You need to make sure at a minimum that you have full RMAN backups or user-managed backups performed on a daily basis. Exporting individual key tables can be useful as well. The Flashback Tables and Flashback Versions Query can be useful for reconstructing row data.

Remember, it is better to lose some data and have an operational database by performing an incomplete recovery than to not have an operational database due to corruption in a key table.

What are the side effects of using DBMS_REPAIR on an object?

- Referential integrity constraints can be broken due to block corruption. You may need to repair these constraints, which can affect multiple tables.
- Triggers on tables can create logical corruption on tables because the physically corrupt rows in the database may impact the way triggers fire. Also, during the rebuild process, triggers need to be identified and thoroughly understood so that logical corruption does not get introduced.
- Freelist blocks can become inaccessible due to physical corruption. You need to utilize the REBUILD_FREELISTS procedure.
- Indexes can become out of sync from the table when data in the table is physically corrupt. You need to use the DUMP_ORPHAN_KEYS procedure to retrieve the necessary data.

As you can see, resolving physical corruption is a detailed and lengthy process. The DBMS_REPAIR package has many procedures designed for specific uses. It is a good idea to create small SQL scripts to run these individual procedures. You also need to make sure you are aware of all options available for resolving physical corruption. You may need to do more than just use the DBMS_REPAIR package. Follow the best practices for resolving physical corruption by determining the extent of the corruption, keeping all the recovery options open, and being aware of the impacts of using the DBMS_REPAIR package.

Block Media Recovery

Block Media Recovery (BMR) is a Recovery Manager (RMAN) feature that was new in Oracle 9i. BMR is used to recover an individual block or a group of corrupt blocks in a datafile. This allows you to recover individual data blocks instead of the whole datafile. BMR should be used as a supplement to datafile recovery, not as a replacement. BMR is best used where block corruption is minimal, not widespread. Block corruption cases that are not widespread where memory corruptions or sporadic I/O errors get written to disk are best suited for BMR.

Nevertheless, BMR has some major advantages over recovering the whole datafile. One big advantage of using BMR is that it reduces the mean time to recovery (MTTR), because only the affected blocks are restored and recovered instead of the whole datafile. Also, the operation of the database can be unaffected when using BMR, because the datafile does not have to be taken offline to restore and recover a block. Additionally, BMR can potentially recover when you have missing redo logs, if the redo records do not affect the blocks being recovered.

BMR has some limitations that you should be aware of:

- BMR must be used with RMAN.
- You must perform complete recovery of individual blocks. All redo logs must be applied to the block.
- You can never recover blocks marked corrupt from the media backup source. This is known as a media corrupt block.

- You must have a full RMAN backup, not an incremental backup. Remember, incremental backups back up only changed blocks.
- Media corrupt blocks are not accessible to users until the recovery is complete.

Let's look at how to perform a BMR. The first step you need to perform includes identifying the datafile and block that you need to recover.

As you learned in the section titled "Block Corruption Symptoms" earlier in this chapter, most detection of block corruption occurs in the ALERT.LOG and in associated trace files. The following is an example of output that is written in a trace file in the BDUMP directory:

```
ORA-01578: ORACLE data block corrupted (file # 5, block # 6)
ORA-01110: data file 7: 'c:\oracle\oradata\ora101\users01.dbf'
```

After viewing the trace file, you can now pinpoint the block corruption to file number 5 and block number 6. This is the sixth block in the USERS tablespace. With this information, you can run the RMAN command BLOCKRECOVER. Let's walk through an example:

```
C:\oracle\oradata\ora101> rman

Recovery Manager: Release 10.1.0.2.0 - Production

Copyright (c) 1995, 2004, Oracle.  All rights reserved.

RMAN> connect target

connected to target database: ORA101 (DBID=4215248570)

RMAN> blockrecover datafile 5 block 6;


Starting blockrecover at 06-NOV-04
using target database controlfile instead of recovery catalog
allocated channel: ORA_DISK_1
channel ORA_DISK_1: sid=145 devtype=DISK

starting media recovery
media recovery complete

Finished blockrecover at 06-NOV-04

RMAN>
```

As you can see, BMR is a nice supplement to datafile recovery options. The process is fairly quick and does not impact database operations, because you do not have to take the datafile offline to restore and recover. Remember, BMR is not designed to perform recovery of widespread block corruption. Widespread block corruption would be better resolved by datafile recovery or database recovery.

Summary

This chapter focused on how to identify and resolve physical corruption at the block level. We began with an overview of block corruption, how block corruption occurs, what the symptoms are, and how to identify block corruption using system logs, application logs, database logs, and trace files.

Next, we described in detail the methods for dealing with physical corruption. We discussed the `ANALYZE TABLE` *`table_name`* command, the DBVERIFY utility, the `DB_BLOCK_CHECKING` initialization parameter, and the `DBMS_REPAIR` package. You saw examples of how to use each of these methods to detect and repair block corruption.

Finally, we showed you how to use RMAN Block Media Recovery (BMR) to repair block corruption. This is a new Oracle 10*g* capability in RMAN and has many advantages over recovering the entire datafile.

Exam Essentials

Know how to detect database corruptions using *ANALYZE* and *DBVERIFY*. Make sure you understand how to detect database corruptions using the `ANALYZE` command against database objects like tables and indexes. You should be able to identify corruption using the DBVERIFY utility against datafiles.

Understand how to detect database corruptions using the *DBMS_REPAIR* package. Know how to detect database corruptions using the `CHECK_OBJECT` procedure in the `DBMS_REPAIR` package. Understand how to use many of the procedures in the `DBMS_REPAIR` package to resolve all aspects of database corruptions.

Know how to implement the *DB_BLOCK_CHECKING* initialization parameter to detect corruptions. Know how to set the `DB_BLOCK_CHECKING` initialization parameter. Understand how the `DB_BLOCK_CHECKING` parameter works to detect block corruptions.

Be able to repair corruptions with RMAN. Understand how to use RMAN to perform Block Media Recovery (BMR), when to use BMR, and its limitations.

Review Questions

1. What activity is responsible for causing most block corruption?
   A. Human errors that introduce bugs caused by hardware, software, or firmware
   B. Memory errors written to disk
   C. Random I/O errors written to disk
   D. A bad transaction that updates many tables

2. What is the most common way of detecting block corruption in the database?
   A. Monitoring the operating system log files
   B. Monitoring the application log files
   C. Monitoring the `ALERT.LOG` database log
   D. Monitoring the `ALERT.LOG` and associated trace files

3. What is the correct command to analyze the `EMPLOYEE` table in the schema owned by user `TEST`?
   A. `ANALYZE INDEX EMPLOYEE VALIDATE STRUCTURE`
   B. `ANALYZE TABLE` *`TEST.EMPLOYEE`* `VALIDATE STRUCTURE`
   C. `ANALYZE TABLE` *`EMPLOYEE`* `VALIDATE STRUCTURE`
   D. `ANALYZE INDEX` *`TEST.EMPLOYEE`* `VALIDATE STRUCTURE`

4. Which of the following is the most correct statement about what the `ANALYZE` command does?
   A. The `ANALYZE` command identifies the object and blocks where corruption exists.
   B. The `ANALYZE` command identifies the objects where corruption exists.
   C. The `ANALYZE` command identifies the table where corruption exists.
   D. The `ANALYZE` command identifies the index and the block where corruption exists.

5. The DBVERIFY utility reports output about corruption in which manner?
   A. The DBVERIFY utility identifies the amount of corrupt objects, not the amount of blocks in a table.
   B. The DBVERIFY utility identifies the amount of corrupt blocks, not the amount of objects in a datafile.
   C. The DBVERIFY utility identifies the amount of corrupt pages, not the amount of blocks in a datafile.
   D. The DBVERIFY utility identifies the amount of corrupt pages, not the amount of blocks in the database.

6. Which of the following is a correct statement about the DBVERIFY utility?
   A. The DBVERIFY utility can be executed only on online datafiles.
   B. The DBVERIFY utility can be executed on online datafiles and offline datafiles.
   C. The DBVERIFY utility can be executed only on offline datafiles.
   D. The DBVERIFY utility can be executed only on online datafiles and offline tablespaces.

7. What is the correct syntax for using the DBVERIFY utility to write to a file and to verify the DATA tablespace with a 4k database block size?

   A. `dbv blocksize=4096 file=data01.dbf logfile=c:\temp\data01.log`

   B. `dbv blocksize=4096 file=user01.dbf logfile=c:\temp\data01.log`

   C. `dbv file=data01.dbf blocksize=4k  logfile=c:\temp\data01.log`

   D. `dbverify blocksize=4096 file=data01.dbf logfile=c:\temp\data01.log`

8. The DB_BLOCK_CHECKING initialization parameter needs be enabled to verify what objects?

   A. Objects stored in the default tablespace of the SYS user

   B. Objects stored in the default tablespace of any application owner

   C. Objects stored in the default tablespace of the SCOTT user

   D. Objects stored in the default tablespace of the HR user

9. What statement best describes DB_BLOCK_CHECKING?

   A. DB_BLOCK_CHECKING is a utility that performs checksums on blocks every time the block is modified.

   B. DB_BLOCK_CHECKING is a database parameter that causes the Oracle to perform checksums on blocks every time the block is modified.

   C. DB_BLOCK_CHECKING is a command that performs checksums on blocks every time the checkpoint process occurs.

   D. DB_BLOCK_CHECKING is a database parameter that performs checksums on blocks every time the database checkpoint occurs.

10. How should you use the DBMS_REPAIR package to build a REPAIR_TABLE for the DATA tablespace that can help the diagnosis of corrupt rows in a table in that tablespace?

    A.
    ```
    declare
        begin
        dbms_repair.admin_table
        (table_name => 'REPAIR_TABLE',
        table_type => dbms_repair.repair_table,
        action => dbms_repair.create_action,
        tablespace => 'DATA01');
        end;
        /
    ```

    B.
    ```
    declare
        begin
        dbms_repair.admin_tables
        (table_name => 'REPAIR_TABLE',
        table_type => dbms_repair.repair_table,
        action => dbms_repair.create_action,
        tablespace => 'DATA');
        end;
        /
    ```

C.
```
declare
begin
dbms_repair.admin_table
(table_name => 'REPAIR_TABLE',
table_type => dbms_repair.repair_tables,
action => dbms_repair.create_action,
tablespace => 'DATA');
end;
/
```

D.
```
declare
begin
dbms_repair.admin_tables
(table_name => 'REPAIR_TABLE',
table_type => dbms_repair.repair_table,
action => dbms_repair.create_action,
tablespace => 'DATA');
end;
/
```

11. How should you use the DBMS_REPAIR package to verify REPAIR BLOCK COUNT and load REPAIR_TABLE for the EMPLOYEE table in the SCOTT schema with information of the object and block that is corrupt in the tablespace?

A.
```
set serveroutput on size 100000;
declare
rpr_count int;
begin
rpr_count := 0;
dbms_repair.check_objects(
schema_name => 'SCOTT',
object_name => 'EMPLOYEE',
repair_table_name => 'REPAIR_TABLE',
corrupt_count => rpr_count);
dbms_output.put_line('repair block count: '
||to_char(rpr_count));
end;
```

B.
```
set serverout on size 100000;
declare
rpr_count int;
begin
rpr_count := 0;
dbms_repair.check_objects(
schema_name => 'SCOTT',
object_name => 'EMPLOYEE',
repair_table_name => 'REPAIR_TABLESPACE',
corrupt_count => rpr_count);
dbms_output.put_line('repair block count: '
||to_char(rpr_count));
end;
```

C.
```
set serveroutput on size 100000;
    declare
    rpr_count int;
    begin
    rpr_count := 0;
    dbms_repair.check_object(
    schema_name => 'SCOTT',
    object_name => 'EMPLOYEE',
    repair_table_name => 'REPAIR_TABLE',
    corrupt_count => rpr_count);
    dbms_output.put_line('repair block count: '
    ||to_char(rpr_count));
    end;
```

D.
```
set serverout on size 100000;
    declare
    rpr_count int;
    begin
    rpr_count := 0;
    dbms_repair.check_object(
    schema_name => 'SCOTT',
    object_name => 'EMPLOYEE',
    repair_table_name => 'REPAIR_TABLE',
    corrupt_count => rpr_count);
    dbms_output.put_line('repair block count: '
    ||to_char(rpr_count));
    end;
```

12. What could be impacted by the DBMS_REPAIR package being used on a table?

A. A table related by a foreign key and primary key to the table repaired by the DBMS_REPAIR package could become unusable.

B. A trigger on the table repaired by the DBMS_REPAIR package could introduce logical corruption.

C. An index related to the table repaired by the DBMS_REPAIR package could become out of sync with the repaired table.

D. All of the above.

13. How should you use the DBMS_REPAIR package to identify problems with a primary key index on a corrupt table in the SCOTT schema with the EMPLOYEE_PK index? (Choose all that apply.)

A.
```
declare
  orph_count int;
begin
  orph_count:= 0;
dbms_repair.dump_child_keys (
     schema_name => 'SCOTT',
     object_name => 'EMPLOYEE_PK',
     object_type => dbms_repair.index_object,
     repair_table_name => 'REPAIR_TABLE',
    orphan_table_name => 'ORPHAN_KEY_TABLE',
```

```
     key_count => orph_count);
    dbms_output.put_line('orphan-index entries: ' || to_char(orph_count));
end;
/
```

B.
```
declare
  orph_count int;
begin
  orph_count:= 0;
dbms_repair.dump_orphan_key (
     schema_name => 'SCOTT',
     object_name => 'EMPLOYEE_PK',
     object_type => dbms_repair.index_object,
     repair_table_name => 'REPAIR_TABLE',
    orphan_table_name => 'ORPHAN_KEY_TABLE',
    key_count => orph_count);
   dbms_output.put_line('orphan-index entries: ' || to_char(orph_count));
end;
/
```

C.
```
declare
  orph_count int;
begin
  orph_count:= 0;
dbms_repair.dump_orphan_keys (
     schema_name => 'SCOTT',
     object_name => 'EMPLOYEE_PK',
     object_type => dbms_repair.index_object,
     repair_table_name => 'REPAIR_TABLE',
    orphan_table_name => 'ORPHAN_KEY_TABLE',
    key_count => orph_count);
   dbms_output.put_line('orphan-index entries: ' || to_char(orph_count));
end;
/
```

D.
```
declare
  orph_count int;
begin
  orph_count:= 0;
dbms_repair.dump_orphan_key (
     schema_name => 'SCOTT',
     object_name => 'EMPLOYEE_PK',
     object_type => dbms_repair.index_object,
     repair_table_name => 'REPAIR_TABLE',
    orphan_table_name => 'ORPHAN_KEY_VIEW',
    key_count => orph_count);
   dbms_output.put_line('orphan-index entries: ' || to_char(orph_count));
end;
/
```

14. What table can you query to identify the block that is corrupt?

A. DBA_CORRUPT_BLOCKS

B. REPAIR_TABLE

C. DBA_REPAIR_TABLE

D. CORRUPT_BLOCKS_TABLE

15. When determining how to resolve block corruption, what should you keep in mind?

A. The tables where the corruption is located

B. The block or blocks in the corrupt table

C. The extent of the corruption in the table or tables

D. The tables and indexes where the corruption is located

16. How should you use the DBMS_REPAIR package to rebuild freelists on a corrupt table?

A.
```
declare
    begin
    dbms_repair.rebuild_freelist (
       schema_name => 'SCOTT',
       object_name => 'EMPLOYEE',
       object_type => dbms_repair.table_object);
    end;
    /
```

B.
```
declare
    begin
    dbms_repair.rebuild_freelists (
       schema_name => 'SCOTT',
       object_name => 'EMPLOYEE',
       object_type => dbms_repair.object_table);
    end;
    /
```

C.
```
declare
    begin
    dbms_repair.repair_freelists (
       schema_name => 'SCOTT',
     object_name => 'EMPLOYEE',
     object_type => dbms_repair.table_object);
    end;
    /
```

D.
```
declare
    begin
    dbms_repair.rebuild_freelists (
       schema_name => 'SCOTT',
       object_name => 'EMPLOYEE',
       object_type => dbms_repair.table_object);
    end;
    /
```

17. Which of the following statements best describes using the DBMS_REPAIR package to resolve block corruption?
    - **A.** Resolving block corruption is a complex process, and you should be careful.
    - **B.** Resolving block corruption is a complex process, and you most often use the DBMS_REPAIR package even if the corruption is widespread.
    - **C.** Resolving block corruption is a complex process, and you should contact Oracle Support if possible.
    - **D.** Resolving block corruption is a complex process, and use of the DBMS_REPAIR package cannot introduce other problems in the database.

18. Before attempting to resolve block corruption with the DBMS_REPAIR package, what should you consider?
    - **A.** Examine other methods of resolving the corrupt objects by rebuilding the object if the data is available.
    - **B.** Attempt to exclude the corruption by excluding the row from `select` statements.
    - **C.** If possible, perform an incomplete recovery.
    - **D.** All of the above.

19. Which of the following is required to perform a block media recovery with RMAN? (Choose all that apply.)
    - **A.** The datafile number and block number of the corrupted block or blocks in the UDUMP trace file
    - **B.** The tablespace number and block number of the corrupted block or blocks
    - **C.** The datafile number and block number of the corrupted block or blocks
    - **D.** The ALERT.LOG information from the ORA-01578 error

20. Which of the following statements are true regarding BMR? (Choose all that apply.)
    - **A.** BMR must be performed with RMAN.
    - **B.** BMR may be performed with RMAN and SQL.
    - **C.** Incremental backups can be used to perform BMR.
    - **D.** Redo logs are not required to perform BMR if the redo log records don't affect the corrupt block.

Answers to Review Questions

1. A. Most block corruption is caused by human error introducing bugs with new hardware, software, or firmware changes.

2. D. Monitoring the ALERT.LOG and associated trace files is the best method for detecting block corruption in the database.

3. B. If the ANALYZE command is being run by a DBA account, you need to prefix the table name with the schema owner.

4. B. The ANALYZE command determines which object has corrupted indexes or tables, because the command returns an error if the statement does not process completely. The ANALYZE command does not identify which block is corrupt.

5. C. The DBVERIFY utility uses the term *pages* instead of blocks. The DBVERIFY utility determines the amount of corrupt pages in a datafile.

6. B. The DBVERIFY utility can be used on online and offline datafiles.

7. A . The correct syntax for the DBVERIFY utility to write the output to a log and specify a 4k block size is as follows: `dbv blocksize=4096 file=data01.dbf logfile=c:\temp\data01.log`.

8. A. DB_BLOCK_CHECKING is enabled for the SYSTEM tablespace by default. The SYS user default tablespace is SYSTEM.

9. B. DB_BLOCK_CHECKING is a database parameter that causes Oracle to perform checksums on blocks every time the block is modified.

10. B. The correct use of the DBMS_REPAIR package on the DATA tablespace is to use the ADMIN_TABLES procedure with the following parameters:

```
declare
   begin
   dbms_repair.admin_tables
   (table_name => 'REPAIR_TABLE',
   table_type => dbms_repair.repair_table,
   action => dbms_repair.create_action,
   tablespace => 'DATA');
   end;
   /
```

11. C. The DBMS_REPAIR package must be used with the CHECK_OBJECT procedure. If you want to verify REPAIR BLOCK COUNT, you must have SET SERVEROUTPUT ON SIZE. The following is the correct PL/SQL syntax for the DBMS_REPAIR package:

```
set serveroutput on size 100000;
   declare
```

```
rpr_count int;
begin
rpr_count := 0;
dbms_repair.check_object(
schema_name => 'SCOTT',
object_name => 'EMPLOYEE',
repair_table_name => 'REPAIR_TABLE',
corrupt_count => rpr_count);
dbms_output.put_line('repair block count: '
||to_char(rpr_count));
end;
```

12. D. Referential integrity constraints on related tables can be broken, indexes can become out of sync with the table data, and triggers on a table can cause logical corruption if they are not well understood when using the DBMS_REPAIR package on a table.

13. C. The DBMS_REPAIR package can be used to identify problems with a primary index by identifying orphaned keys in the index as they relate to the table being repaired for corruption. The correct usage of the DBMS_REPAIR.DUMP_ORPHANED_KEYS package procedure is as follows:

```
declare
    orph_count int;
  begin
    orph_count:= 0;
  dbms_repair.dump_orphan_keys (
       schema_name => 'SCOTT',
       object_name => 'EMPLOYEE_PK',
       object_type => dbms_repair.index_object,
       repair_table_name => 'REPAIR_TABLE',
      orphan_table_name => 'ORPHAN_KEY_TABLE',
      key_count => orph_count);
      dbms_output.put_line('orphan-index entries: ' || to_char(orph_count));
   end;
   /
```

14. B. REPAIR_TABLE will show OBJECT_NAME, BLOCK_ID, and if the block is MARKED_CORRUPT.

15. C. When determining how to resolve block corruption, you should determine the extent of the corruption first. Is the corruption limited to a few blocks or is it widespread?

16. D. The DBMS_REPAIR package can be used to rebuild freelists on a corrupt table with the following syntax:

```
declare
    begin
```

```
dbms_repair.rebuild_freelists (
   schema_name => 'SCOTT',
   object_name => 'EMPLOYEE',
   object_type => dbms_repair.table_object);
end;
/
```

17. C. Resolving block corruption can result in the loss of data in the blocks that are corrupt. You should contact Oracle Support, if possible.

18. D. Before using the DBMS_REPAIR package, consider other alternatives to resolve the block corruption. Make sure you understand how else to resolve block corruption, as a backup plan if necessary.

19. C, D. The ORA-01578 error in the ALERT.LOG specifies the datafile number and the block number.

20. A, D. BMR must be performed with RMAN only. Incremental backups cannot be used to perform BMR, because incremental backups consist of changed blocks only. All redo logs are not required to perform BMR if the damaged block does not require those redo logs.

Understanding Automatic Database Management

ORACLE DATABASE 10*G*: ADMINISTRATION II EXAM OBJECTIVES COVERED IN THIS CHAPTER:

✓ **Diagnostic Sources**

- Adjust thresholds for tracked metrics.

✓ **Automatic Database Management**

- Use the Database Advisors to gather information about your database.
- Use the SQL Tuning Advisor to improve database performance.
- Use automatic undo retention tuning.

Exam objectives are subject to change at any time without prior notice and at Oracle's sole discretion. Please visit Oracle's Training and Certification website (`http://www.oracle.com/education/certification/`) for the most current exam objectives listing.

With the release of Oracle Database 10*g* (Oracle 10*g*), Oracle has introduced the Common Manageability Infrastructure (CMI) and taken a big step forward in fulfilling their promise of a self-managing and self-tuning database. Composed of the Automatic Workload Repository (AWR), server-generated alerts, automated routine maintenance features, and the advisory framework, the components of the CMI simplify database administration through automation and intelligent design.

The AWR collects and processes performance statistics and metrics to be used for problem detection and self-tuning purposes. It also acts as the central storage repository for all elements of the CMI.

Server-generated alerts proactively monitor database events and metric levels. When metric threshold levels are exceeded, an alert is generated. Server-generated alerts can also send notification via e-mail or pager, execute operating system programs, execute PL/SQL scripts, or generate SNMP traps in response to alert situations.

The automated routine maintenance tasks handle many time-consuming tasks automatically. The automatic statistics collection and automatic DML monitoring features work together to collect and maintain up-to-date optimizer statistics. The Automatic Database Diagnostic Monitor (ADDM) analyzes performance statistics to identify and resolve system bottlenecks. Automatic SQL tuning optimizes SQL statement performance, and automatic undo retention management ensures adequate undo space is always available.

Lastly, the advisory framework provides analysis and recommendations on a number of key administrative areas. The *advisors* share a common interface to simplify usage and to allow ease of interaction between advisors. The SQL Tuning Advisor, for example, provides an interface to the automatic SQL tuning functionality. It offers analysis and recommendations for optimizing SQL statements to improve performance.

Together, these four components instantiate the CMI and simplify the tasks associated with Oracle database administration.

This chapter discusses each of these components of the CMI. You'll see how the AWR collects and manages performance statistics and metrics and provides a centralized repository for the CMI. You'll study server-generated alerts and learn to assign threshold levels to specific metrics.

This chapter also covers the automated routine maintenance functions, with an emphasis on automatic statistics collection and ADDM. Finally, you'll get an overview of the advisory framework, see how the common interface simplifies advisor usage, and walk through the SQL Tuning Advisor to demonstrate advisor usage. Through it all, we hope to show you how the CMI components interact, communicate, and leverage each other to support the self-managing and self-tuning concept.

Using the Automatic Workload Repository (AWR)

The *Automatic Workload Repository (AWR)* is the cornerstone of the CMI. AWR provides services to collect, process, maintain, and access database performance statistics and metrics for the database.

This section discusses the two elements that make up AWR:

- The statistics collection facility, which is charged with the collection of dynamic performance statistics
- The workload repository, where the statistics are stored for persistence

We'll also describe the Active Session History (ASH) buffer and how the *Manageability Monitor (MMON)* process captures statistics from ASH for inclusion in the workload repository.

Next, you'll learn how to use AWR to manage snapshots and baselines. Snapshots represent AWR's method of capturing statistics. Baselines define a range of snapshots that represent a particular workload. These baselines can be saved for comparison to monitor workload performance.

Finally, we'll show you the AWR views and even an HTML report you can run to see AWR data.

AWR Statistics Collection Facility

The statistics collection facility of AWR resides in memory and is responsible for the collection of dynamic performance statistics. All of the collected statistics are stored in fixed tables that are only accessible through fixed views. The statistics are also stored in the workload repository element of the AWR for persistent storage.

In the following sections, you'll learn what database performance statistics are and how they differ from optimizer statistics. You'll also look at how the MMON process calculates metrics from the statistics. Lastly, you'll see a few of the new performance statistics added in Oracle 10*g*.

Don't confuse AWR's statistics collection facility with Oracle's automatic statistics collection feature. AWR collects dynamic performance statistics. The automatic statistics collection feature collects optimizer statistics.

Database Performance Statistics

Unlike optimizer statistics, database performance statistics are not utilized by the query optimizer. Instead, they are used to measure the performance of the database over time. By analyzing these statistics, performance problems can be identified and resolved.

Database performance statistics are dynamic in nature, meaning that they are initialized at instance startup and are lost at instance shutdown. Unlike optimizer statistics, they are not stored in the data dictionary. Instead, they are stored in dynamic performance tables, more commonly known as *fixed tables*. Fixed tables are memory structures that emulate tables in that they can be queried and can be the object of views.

Database performance statistics fall into one of three categories:

- Cumulative values
- Metrics
- Sampled data

Cumulative value statistics, as the name implies, are statistics that accumulate over a period of time through continuous updating. These statistics are captured for the system as a whole, for individual sessions, for individual SQL statements, for segments, and for services (the 5 Ss, if you will). For example, the V$SYSSTAT view shows cumulative statistics for the system since startup. The V$SESSTAT view shows cumulative statistics for individual sessions.

Historically, cumulative statistics would exist only until instance shutdown, at which time they were lost. As you will see later in this chapter, the AWR allows many cumulative statistics to persist—even through database shutdowns—to provide cumulative statistics covering the database since its inception (or, at least, since migration to Oracle 10*g*).

Metrics are statistics that represent the rate of change in a cumulative statistics category. They are generally measured against a fixed unit type such as time, database calls, transactions, and so on. For example, the number of transactions per second would be one type of metric. Metrics are computed by the MMON process at varying intervals. Some are computed as often as once a second while others may be computed only once every 30 minutes. They represent delta values between snapshot periods.

Sampled data represents a sampling of the current state of all active sessions. These statistics are collected by the ASH sampler, which is covered later in this section.

New Statistics in Oracle 10*g*

Oracle has added many new statistics types in the new 10*g* release. The following list, though not exhaustive, contains many of the most important ones and their associated V$ view (these statistics are also maintained in the AWR):

- Time model statistics, which can be viewed with the V$SYS_TIME_MODEL view:
  - DB CPU
  - DB TIME
  - JAVA EXECUTION ELAPSED TIME
  - PL/SQL COMPILATION ELAPSED TIME
  - PL/SQL EXECUTION ELAPSED TIME
  - BACKGROUND CPU TIME
  - BACKGROUND ELAPSED TIME
  - CONNECTION MANAGEMENT CALL ELAPSED TIME
  - FAILED PARSE (OUT OF SHARED MEMORY) ELAPSED TIME
  - FAILED PARSE ELAPSED TIME

- HARD PARSE (BIND MISMATCH) ELAPSED TIME
- HARD PARSE (SHARING CRITERIA) ELAPSED TIME
- HARD PARSE ELAPSED TIME
- INBOUND PL/SQL RPC ELAPSED TIME
- PARSE TIME ELAPSED
- SEQUENCE LOAD ELAPSED TIME
- SQL EXECUTE ELAPSED TIME

- Operating system statistics, which can be viewed with the V$OSSTAT view:
  - AVG_BUSY_TICKS
  - AVG_IDLE_TICKS
  - AVG_IN_BYTES
  - AVG_OUT_BYTES
  - AVG_SYS_TICKS
  - AVG_USER_TICKS
  - BUSY_TICKS
  - IDLE_TICKS
  - IN_BYTES
  - NUM_CPUS
  - OUT_BYTES
  - RSRC_MGR_CPU_WAIT_TIME
  - SYS_TICKS
  - USER_TICKS
- Wait statistics, which can be viewed with the V$SERVICE_STATS view:
  - APPLICATION WAIT TIME
  - DB CPU
  - CONCURRENCY WAIT TIME
  - USER COMMITS
  - USER I/O WAIT TIME
  - CLUSTER WAIT TIME

While AWR collects the majority of base statistics (statistics collected in memory), not all legacy statistics have been converted to work with AWR. The following list shows the statistics that AWR collects and processes:

- Object statistics that determine both access and usage statistics of database segments
- Time model statistics based on time usage for activities, displayed in the V$SYS_TIME_MODEL and V$SESS_TIME_MODEL views

- Some of the system and session statistics collected in the V$SYSSTAT and V$SESSTAT views
- Some of the Oracle optimizer statistics, including those used by Oracle for self-learning and self-tuning
- Most expensive SQL statements (those that are producing the highest load on the system), based on criteria such as CPU time and elapsed time
- ASH statistics, capturing activity from recent sessions

Workload Repository

The workload repository element of AWR adds persistence to the statistics collection facility by providing a set of tables where performance data can be stored and accessed by other CMI components. It also acts as a repository for other CMI components to store persistent data.

The AWR consists of both the statistics collection facility and the workload repository. For simplicity, the general term *AWR* will be used when referring to the workload repository element.

In the following sections, you'll learn about the workload repository, how to enable it, and disk space considerations relating to it.

An Overview of the Workload Repository

The AWR adds persistence to the statistics collection facility. On a regular basis, the MMON process transfers cumulative statistics in memory to the workload repository tables on disk. This ensures that statistics can survive through instance crashes, or aren't lost when they are replaced by newer statistics.

The workload repository also ensures that historical data will be available for baseline comparisons, trend analysis, and to troubleshoot intermittently occurring problems. Before AWR, collecting this type of data required manual collection and management using Statspack or custom code.

Workload repository data is owned by the SYS user and is stored in the SYSAUX tablespace. In fact, the repository is one of the main clients of the SYSAUX tablespace. The data is stored in a collection of tables, all of which are named beginning with WR. By listing the table names, it is easy to get an idea of the types of data stored in the repository, as shown in this partial listing:

```
SQL> select table_name
from dba_tables
where tablespace_name = 'SYSAUX'
and substr(table_name, 1,2) = 'WR'
and rownum <= 20
order by 1;
```

```
TABLE_NAME
------------------------------
WRH$_ACTIVE_SESSION_HISTORY_BL
WRH$_BG_EVENT_SUMMARY
WRH$_BUFFER_POOL_STATISTICS
WRH$_CLASS_CACHE_TRANSFER_BL
WRH$_CR_BLOCK_SERVER
WRH$_CURRENT_BLOCK_SERVER
WRH$_DATAFILE
WRH$_DB_CACHE_ADVICE_BL
WRH$_DLM_MISC_BL
WRH$_ENQUEUE_STAT
WRI$_OPTSTAT_HISTGRM_HISTORY
WRI$_OPTSTAT_HISTHEAD_HISTORY
WRI$_OPTSTAT_IND_HISTORY
WRI$_OPTSTAT_OPR
WRI$_OPTSTAT_TAB_HISTORY
WRI$_SCH_CONTROL
WRI$_SCH_VOTES
WRI$_SQLSET_BINDS
WRI$_SQLSET_DEFINITIONS
WRM$_BASELINE
```

Once in the repository, the statistics can be accessed using data dictionary views. This makes them available to other Oracle manageability resources such as ADDM. They are also available to the users, and easily accessible should a third party wish to design their own monitoring tools.

Enabling AWR

To enable AWR, the STATISTICS_LEVEL initialization parameter must be set to TYPICAL or ALL. If it is set to BASIC, AWR statistics will not be gathered automatically, but they can be gathered manually by using procedures in the built-in DBMS_WORKLOAD_REPOSITORY package. Note that manually gathered statistics will not be as complete as statistics gathered automatically through AWR.

The workload repository is created automatically at database creation time. No manual action is required.

AWR Space Considerations

So how much disk space will be consumed by AWR using the default snapshot interval and retention period? A rough guideline is that an average system with an average of 10 concurrent active sessions will generate 200MB to 300MB of AWR data. This estimate assumes the default retention period of 7 days. The space used is determined by the number of active sessions, the snapshot interval, and the retention period.

Space consumption can be reduced by either increasing the snapshot interval (resulting in less frequent snapshots) or decreasing the retention period. Technically, you could also decrease your active sessions, but undoubtedly your users would not appreciate it. Any of these changes will reduce the disk space required, but they could also have a negative effect on other aspects of the system. By reducing the available statistics, the accuracy and validity of the following components may be reduced as well:

- ADDM
- SQL Tuning Advisor
- Undo Advisor
- Segment Advisor

It is the responsibility of the MMON process to purge data from the repository when it has reached the end of the retention period. This is accomplished on a nightly basis through an automated purge task defined in the Scheduler. The MMON process will use best efforts to complete the task in the designated management window.

Snapshots are removed in chronological order, for the most part. The exception is snapshots that belong to a baseline. These are retained (even past the retention period) until their associated baselines are removed.

Active Session History

In order to provide statistics on current session activity, Oracle 10*g* has introduced *Active Session History (ASH)*. In the following sections, you'll look at ASH and how it interacts with the AWR. You'll learn about the types of statistics that ASH captures and how to calculate ASH memory usage size. Lastly, you will be introduced to ASH views and look at how ASH data is stored in the AWR.

Sizing ASH

ASH is actually a first-in, first-out (FIFO) buffer in memory that collects statistics on current session activity. These statistics are gathered by extracting samples from `V$SESSION` every second. Because this kind of frequent gathering could quickly overwhelm the system, ASH continually ages out old statistics to make room for new ones.

ASH resides in the System Global Area (SGA) and its size is fixed for the lifetime of the instance. Its size is calculated using the following calculation:

The lesser of:

- Total number of CPUs × 2MB of memory
- 5 percent of the Shared Pool size

So, on a 16-processor system, with a Shared Pool size of 500MB, the size of the ASH buffer could be calculated as follows:

- ASH desired size: 16 × 2MB = 32MB
- 5 percent of Shared Pool size: 500MB × 5% = 25MB
- Final ASH size: 25MB

Because the desired ASH size exceeded 5 percent of the Shared Pool size, Oracle will choose the lesser size. There are, therefore, only two ways to increase the ASH buffer size:

- Increase the number of CPUs.
- Increase the Shared Pool size.

ASH Statistics

As stated previously, ASH samples statistics from all active sessions once every second. It can accomplish this effectively by directly accessing Oracle's internal memory structures (the `V_$SESSION` fixed table) so that no I/O is required. ASH, as the name implies, is only interested in active sessions. It does not sample inactive sessions.

The following types of data are sampled by ASH:

- `SQL_ID`
- SID
- Client ID, service ID
- Program, module, action
- Object, file, block
- Wait event number, actual wait time (if the session is waiting)

`SQL_ID` is a hash value that uniquely identifies a SQL statement in the database. `SQL_ID` is new in Oracle 10*g*.

ASH Views

The statistics in ASH can be viewed using the `V$ACTIVE_SESSION_HISTORY` fixed view. One row will be displayed for each active session per sample.

ASH and AWR

Because the data in the ASH represents a unique set of statistics, Oracle captures some of the ASH statistics to the workload repository for persistent storage. This process is handled in one of two ways.

Every 30 minutes, the MMON process flushes the ASH buffer of all data. In the process, it filters some of the data into the AWR. Due to the high volume of data, the MMON process doesn't filter all of the ASH data into the AWR. Instead, it filters out much of the data and retains only key elements.

If the ASH buffer fills in less than 30 minutes, the *Memory Monitor Light (MMNL)* process will flush out a portion of the buffer (to make room for the new statistics) and filter a portion of the flushed data to the AWR.

Using AWR

The primary interface for AWR is through Oracle Enterprise Manager (EM) Database Control. The link to access AWR can be found on the Administration page. Under Workload, click the Workload Repository link. From this page, you can manage AWR settings and snapshots.

Oracle also provides the DBMS_WORKLOAD_REPOSITORY package. This Application Program Interface (API) allows management of all AWR functionality, just as Database Control provides.

Examples shown in this chapter will focus primarily on the use of DBMS_WORKLOAD_REPOSITORY.

The DBMS_WORKLOAD_REPOSITORY package consists of the procedures listed in Table 8.1.

TABLE 8.1 *DBMS_WORKLOAD_REPOSITORY* Procedures

Name	Description
CREATE_SNAPSHOT	Creates manual snapshots
DROP_SNAPSHOT_RANGE	Drops a range of snapshots at once
CREATE_BASELINE	Creates a single baseline
DROP_BASELINE	Drops a single baseline
MODIFY_SNAPSHOT_SETTINGS	Changes the RETENTION and INTERVAL settings

AWR Snapshots

AWR collects performance statistics by taking snapshots of the system at specific intervals. In the following sections, we'll teach you how to determine the frequency of these snapshots. You'll also look at how you can create, modify, and drop snapshots, as well as the implications of each.

Using Snapshots

The snapshot pulls information from the fixed tables that hold performance statistics in memory, so, like ASH sampling, snapshot collection is not resource-intensive.

By default, AWR generates performance data snapshots once every hour. This is known as the *snapshot interval*. It also retains the snapshot statistics for seven days before automatically purging them. This is known as the *retention period*. The data from these snapshots is analyzed by the ADDM for problem detection and self-tuning.

To view the current AWR settings, you can use the DBA_HIST_WR_CONTROL view, as shown here:

```
SQL> Select snap_interval, retention
From dba_hist_wr_control;

SNAP_INTERVAL       RETENTION
-----------------   -----------------
+00000 01:00:00.0   +00007 00:00:00:0
```

As the query results show, the snapshot interval is set to one hour, and the retention period is set at seven days (the default values).

Each snapshot is assigned a unique snapshot ID, which is a sequence number guaranteed to be unique within the repository. The only exception to this is when using Real Application Clusters (RACs). In an RAC environment, AWR snapshots will query every node within the cluster. In this situation, the snapshots for all nodes will share a snapshot ID. Instead, they can be differentiated by the instance ID.

Creating Snapshots

There may be times when you want to collect snapshots that don't fall neatly into a schedule. For example, you may want to take snapshots during heavy loads, but the loads don't occur on a strict schedule. In that situation, you may want to create a snapshot manually. Here's an example of how to do that:

```
BEGIN
  DBMS_WORKLOAD_REPOSITORY.CREATE_SNAPSHOT();
END;
```

As you can see, the CREATE_SNAPSHOT function requires no parameters. It simply takes a snapshot of the system in its current state.

Modifying Snapshot Frequency

As mentioned earlier in this chapter, the snapshot interval and retention period can be modified from their default settings, though the risk of impacting Oracle's diagnostic tools needs to be weighed carefully.

If you are unsure of the current AWR settings, you can query the DBA_HIST_WR_CONTROL view, as shown earlier in the "Using Snapshots" section.

To make changes, use the procedure DBMS_WORKLOAD_REPOSITORY.MODIFY_SNAPHOT_SETTINGS. The parameters of this procedure are listed in Table 8.2.

TABLE 8.2 *MODIFY_SNAPSHOT_SETTINGS* Procedure Parameters

Parameter	Description
RETENTION	Length of time to retain snapshots (in minutes). Must be between 1,440 (one day) and 52,596,000 (100 years).
INTERVAL	Time interval between snapshots (in minutes). Must be between 10 and 525,600 (one year).
DBID	The database ID (defaults to the local DBID).

Both parameters RETENTION and INTERVAL are measured in minutes, so in the following example, you are setting the retention period to 10 days (14,400 minutes) and the snapshot interval to 45 minutes. The MODIFY_SNAPSHOT_SETTINGS procedure, as well as several others in this package, will also accept an optional database identifier. This parameter defaults to the local database identifier, so it won't be included in the examples:

```
BEGIN
  DBMS_WORKLOAD_REPOSITORY.MODIFY_SNAPSHOT_SETTINGS(
  RETENTION => 14400, INTERVAL => 45);
END;
```

Dropping Snapshots

To remove snapshots from the AWR, the DROP_SNAPSHOT_RANGE procedure is used. This procedure is designed to drop a range of snapshots, but it can also be used to drop individual snapshots by using the same snapshot ID for both the HIGH_SNAP_ID and LOW_SNAP_ID parameters. This is useful because no procedure exists to drop an individual snapshot. The parameters for this procedure are listed in Table 8.3.

TABLE 8.3 *DROP_SNAPSHOT_RANGE* Procedure Parameters

Parameter	Description
LOW_SNAP_ID	The lowest snapshot ID of range to drop
HIGH_SNAP_ID	The highest snapshot ID of range to drop
DBID	Optional database ID

In the following example, snapshots 316 through 320 would be dropped from the repository:

```
Exec DBMS_WORKLOAD_REPOSITORY.DROP_SNAPSHOT_RANGE(
➥LOW_SNAP_ID =>316, HIGH_SNAP_ID =>320);
```

AWR Baselines

A *baseline* is the definition of a pair of snapshots that denote a significant workload period. For example, snapshots could be taken at the start and end of a normal payroll processing job. These snapshots could then be used to define a baseline to compute performance deltas for a normal payroll processing job. This baseline can be retained for comparison to current system performance.

In this section, you'll learn how baselines are used and how to create and delete them.

Using Baselines

Baselines (and their associated snapshots) are not aged out of the workload repository using the RETENTION setting. Instead, they are kept for historical comparisons to current system behavior. The baseline must be dropped manually, at which time the related snapshots will also be removed.

Besides their analytical value, baselines can also be used to define threshold settings for Oracle's *server-generated alerts* facility. This functionality allows you to be notified whenever a threshold has been exceeded (for example, when a disk is 97 percent full).

AWR baselines also make an excellent tool for application performance and scalability testing. For example, a payroll application may be baselined with a small amount of test data to begin with. Then, as the test bed is increased, comparisons can be made to determine how well the application is scaling.

Creating Baselines

To create a baseline, the CREATE_BASELINE procedure is used. As you should remember, a baseline requires a beginning and ending snapshot ID, as well as a name. You can also specify an optional database identifier (DBID).

Table 8.4 lists the parameters for the CREATE_BASELINE procedure.

TABLE 8.4 *CREATE_BASELINE* Procedure Parameters

Parameter	Description
START_SNAP_ID	Lowest snapshot ID in the range
END_SNAP_ID	Highest snapshot ID in the range
BASELINE_NAME	Unique name for the baseline
DBID	Optional database ID

For example, if you want to baseline the job that creates nightly reports, you could use the following example, assuming that snapshots 42 and 43 mark the beginning and ending of the job:

```
BEGIN
   Exec DBMS_WORKLOAD_REPOSITORY.CREATE_BASELINE(START_SNAP_ID =>42,
     ➥END_SNAP_ID =>43,
   BASELINE_NAME => 'REPORTS');
END
```

Dropping Baselines

When a baseline is no longer needed, the DROP_BASELINE procedure can be used. This procedure removes the baseline and if specified, cascades to remove the associated snapshots.

Table 8.5 lists the parameters for the DROP_BASELINE procedure.

In this example, the baseline REPORTS will be dropped, but the associated snapshots will remain in the repository:

```
Exec DBMS_WORKLOAD_REPOSITORY.DROP_BASELINE('REPORTS',FALSE);
```

TABLE 8.5 *DROP_BASELINE* Procedure Parameters

Parameter	Description
BASELINE_NAME	Name of the baseline to be dropped
CASCADE	Boolean to determine whether the associated snapshots will be dropped (default = FALSE)
DBID	Optional database ID

Using AWR Views

AWR information can be viewed through a collection of data dictionary views provided by Oracle. These views provide a comprehensive overview of both AWR configuration settings and views of the various types of data stored inside AWR.

The following views are available:

DBA_HIST_ACTIVE_SESS_HISTORY Displays session statistics gathered from ASH.

DBA_HIST_BASELINE Displays information on baselines in the repository.

DBA_HIST_DATABASE_INSTANCE Displays database environment data.

DBA_HIST_SQL_PLAN Displays SQL execution path data.

DBA_HIST_WR_CONTROL Displays current AWR settings.

DBA_HIST_SNAPSHOT Displays information regarding snapshots stored in the AWR.

Real World Scenario

Timestamp Traps

Be cautious when using database timestamps such as those in DBA_HIST_SNAPSHOT. These times represent the wall clock time of the server, not necessarily the users, especially in a distributed environment where the users may be in a different time zone. Even if your environment is not distributed, be sure to compare the server's time to your own, as they may not be synced.

I worked in an environment where both of these situations were true. We had remote users and servers and, even on servers within the same time zone, the time of day varied by up to an hour between different servers. A situation like this could cause you to pick the wrong snapshots and end up analyzing the incorrect data. It could also cause serious issues regarding point in time recovery, as I encountered.

We had a remote developer who accidentally truncated some key production tables, and I was called upon to perform a point-in-time recovery. He said that he truncated them at "around 2:30 P.M. or so," but he wasn't really sure. Because these were the days before log miner, I figured I'd restore to about an hour before the incident, just to be safe. Just before I began, I happened to notice the time on the server. It showed the current time as about 2:45 P.M.

It then hit me that he was in a different time zone, which was two hours ahead of mine (and the server's). I also noticed that the time on the server was slightly different from the time on my PC.

Luckily, I had caught it in time, and, after making adjustments to allow for the time differences, I was able to recover to about 45 minutes before the tables were truncated.

For example, if you want to create a baseline for a given period of time, you can query the DBA_HIST_SNAPSHOT view to determine which SNAP_ID range corresponds to that period of time, as shown here:

```
SQL> select snap_id, begin_interval_time, end_interval_time
from dba_hist_snapshot
order by 1;

SNAP_ID BEGIN_INTERVAL_TIME       END_INTERVAL_TIME
------- ------------------------- ---------------------
380     14-JUN-04 11.00.37.796 AM 14-JUN-04 12.00.11.515 PM
381     14-JUN-04 12.00.11.515 PM 14-JUN-04 01.00.54.109 PM
382     14-JUN-04 01.00.54.109 PM 14-JUN-04 02.00.34.906 PM
383     14-JUN-04 02.00.34.906 PM 14-JUN-04 03.01.07.062 PM
384     14-JUN-04 03.01.07.062 PM 14-JUN-04 04.00.41.343 PM
385     14-JUN-04 04.00.41.343 PM 14-JUN-04 05.00.19.546 PM
```

```
386      14-JUN-04 05.00.19.546 PM 14-JUN-04 06.00.57.187 PM
387      14-JUN-04 06.00.57.187 PM 14-JUN-04 07.00.35.734 PM
388      14-JUN-04 07.00.35.734 PM 14-JUN-04 08.00.13.734 PM
389      14-JUN-04 08.00.13.734 PM 14-JUN-04 09.00.51.812 PM
390      14-JUN-04 09.00.51.812 PM 14-JUN-04 10.00.30.234 PM
```

Using AWR Reports

Oracle offers a standard summary report that can be run at any time against the statistics stored in the AWR. This report provides an analysis of system performance over a specified period of time.

The report is run through one of two SQL*Plus scripts:

- `awrrpt.sql`, which generates a text file report
- `awrrpti.sql`, which generates an HTML version of the report

These scripts reside in `$ORACLE_HOME/rdbms/admin` (on Unix systems) or `%ORACLE_HOME%\rdbms\admin` (on Windows systems).

The scripts will prompt for several options:

```
SQL> @$ORACLE_HOME/rdbms/admin/awrrpti.sql

Specify the Report Type
~~~~~~~~~~~~~~~~~~~~~~~

Would you like an HTML report, or a plain text report?
Enter 'html' for an HTML report, or 'text' for plain text
Defaults to 'html'
```

At this prompt, you can enter the type of report you want (either **text** for plain text or **html** for HTML output. The default is HTML. For this example, **html** is specified:

```
Enter value for report_type: html

Type Specified:  html
Instances in this Workload Repository schema
~~~~~~~~~~~~~~~~~~~~~~~~~~~~~~~~~~~~~~~~~~~~

   DB Id     Inst Num DB Name      Instance     Host
------------ -------- ------------ ------------ -----------
* 268115148         1 LNX1         lnx1         peabody

Enter value for dbid:  268115148
Using  268115148 for database Id
Enter value for inst_num: 1
Using 1 for instance number
```

```
Specify the number of days of snapshots to choose from
~~~~~~~~~~~~~~~~~~~~~~~~~~~~~~~~~~~~~~~~~~~~~~~~~~~~~~~~~~~~~~~~~~~~~~~~~~

Entering the number of days (n) will result in the most recent (n) days of
snapshots being listed. Pressing <return> without specifying a number
lists all completed snapshots.

Listing the last 3 days of Completed Snapshots
                                                                Snap
Instance     DB Name        Snap Id    Snap Started          Level
------------ ------------ --------- ------------------ ----
lnx1         LNX1               290 31 Jul 2004 00:00     1
                                291 31 Jul 2004 01:00     1
                                292 31 Jul 2004 02:00     1
                                293 31 Jul 2004 03:00     1
                                294 31 Jul 2004 04:00     1
                                295 31 Jul 2004 05:00     1

Specify the Begin and End Snapshot Ids
~~~~~~~~~~~~~~~~~~~~~~~~~~~~~~~~~~~~~~
```

The report now prompts you for a range of snapshots to include in the report. For the example, the range specified is 290 through 295:

```
Enter value for begin_snap: 290
Begin Snapshot Id specified: 290
Enter value for end_snap: 295
End   Snapshot Id specified: 295

Specify the Report Name
~~~~~~~~~~~~~~~~~~~~~~~

The default report file name is awrrpt_1_290_345.html. To use this name,
press <return> to continue, otherwise enter an alternative.
```

Lastly, you are prompted for a report name. You can accept the default shown earlier in this example or type the name you wish to call it:

```
Enter value for report_name: report.html
Using the report_name report.html
```

The AWR report provides a detailed overview of system performance. Figure 8.1 shows a section of the report in HTML format.

FIGURE 8.1 The AWR report in HTML format

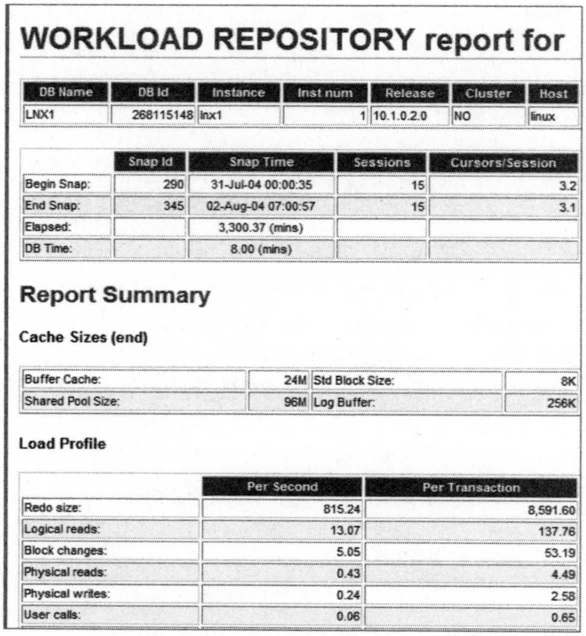

WORKLOAD REPOSITORY report for

DB Name	DB Id	Instance	Inst num	Release	Cluster	Host
LNX1	268115148	lnx1	1	10.1.0.2.0	NO	linux

	Snap Id	Snap Time	Sessions	Cursors/Session
Begin Snap:	290	31-Jul-04 00:00:35	15	3.2
End Snap:	345	02-Aug-04 07:00:57	15	3.1
Elapsed:		3,300.37 (mins)		
DB Time:		8.00 (mins)		

Report Summary

Cache Sizes (end)

Buffer Cache:	24M	Std Block Size:	8K
Shared Pool Size:	96M	Log Buffer:	256K

Load Profile

	Per Second	Per Transaction
Redo size:	815.24	8,591.60
Logical reads:	13.07	137.76
Block changes:	5.05	53.19
Physical reads:	0.43	4.49
Physical writes:	0.24	2.58
User calls:	0.06	0.65

Managing Server-Generated Alerts

Now that you've seen the role of the AWR, we can move ahead to the other elements in the CMI. The first will be server-generated alerts.

The term *server-generated alerts* refers to the database's ability to detect problematic situations and to send an alert with both notification of the problem and suggestions about how to resolve it. These alerts can be classified as either threshold or non-threshold alerts.

Threshold alerts leverage the metrics computed by the MMON process to determine potential performance problems. This is accomplished by comparing the current metrics to preset threshold levels. If the threshold is exceeded, an alarm is generated.

Non-threshold alerts are triggered by database events, as opposed to specific threshold levels. For example, when an `ORA-01555 Snapshot Too Old` error occurs, a non-threshold alert is generated.

Oracle offers a set of default alerts that are automatically generated based on predefined criteria. You can also define your own alerts, based on metric thresholds of your choice.

The following sections will discuss threshold and non-threshold alerts, as well as Oracle's default alerts. You'll also learn about the views available to access alert data. Lastly, you'll see how to manage, create, and modify your own alerts through the PL/SQL API and through EM Database Control.

Threshold and Non-Threshold Alerts

Threshold alerts are kind of like smoke detectors. Smoke detectors monitor the air in your house and generate an alert (a very loud one) if the level of smoke surpasses a certain level. A threshold alert, however, can be defined based on 161 different performance metrics and offers more civilized notification methods (such as e-mail and paging).

Let's say you are concerned with a specific performance metric such as "physical reads per second." A threshold alert can be defined to monitor this metric and raise an alert based on the current value of the metric against two threshold settings: the warning threshold and the critical threshold.

The warning threshold is the lowest level at which an alert will be generated. When physical reads are starting to creep up, for instance, a warning threshold may be exceeded. In this case, an alert is generated and notification is sent containing a predefined warning value.

When a critical threshold is exceeded, an alert is generated and notification is sent containing a predefined critical value. This may represent the level at which your instance is disk-bound and the performance impact is severe.

Threshold alerts are not limited to instance-level metrics, though. They can also be used for database-specific metrics such as tablespace usage.

Non-threshold alerts are generated based on specific database events, rather than on threshold settings. Often, these are events that are logged to the alert log such as a hung ARCH process. In fact, an alert can be generated whenever any event is logged to the alert log.

Default Alerts

Oracle comes with a set of predefined alerts, both threshold and non-threshold. These alerts represent a base set of situations that Oracle deems worthy of notification in every database. For example, any ORA-01555 (snapshot too old) situation will generate an alert. Also, if Oracle detects a certain number of blocked sessions (session waiting for resources held by another session), failed jobs, or if tablespace usage exceeds a predefined percentage, alerts will be generated. Some of these default alerts will allow user modification, though some of them are locked and cannot be altered.

An Overview of the Alert Process

The MMON process automatically computes metric values from in-memory performance statistics once every minute. If a metric has a threshold value defined (either warning, critical, or both), the MMON process compares the newly computed metric to the threshold level. If the threshold has been exceeded, an alert is generated.

Also, when a foreground process encounters certain unusual conditions, the process can invoke MMON to process the condition on its behalf.

When an alert is generated, an alert message is sent to a persistent queue called `ALERT_QUE`, which is monitored by Enterprise Manager. When the message is received, the alert is displayed on the EM Database Control console. If notification methods have been defined, the alert is also sent to the designated administrator(s) via their notification method of choice.

Depending on the alert, EM Database Control may also include corrective action suggestions in the notification.

If MMON is unable to successfully write the alert message to the queue, it will instead be written to the alert log.

Using Enterprise Manager to Configure Thresholds

Metric thresholds can be managed through the EM Database Control Manage Metrics screen. In the following sections, you will learn how to view and edit metric thresholds using EM Database Control. You will also learn to set multiple thresholds on aggregate metrics.

Viewing Metric Thresholds

From the EM Database Control console, click the Manage Metrics link, which will open the Manage Metrics screen. This screen allows you to view current metrics settings, as shown in Figure 8.2.

Notice that for each metric, a comparison operator, warning threshold, critical threshold, and response action can be assigned. For some metrics, Oracle has predefined the thresholds, as discussed earlier.

FIGURE 8.2 The Manage Metrics screen

ORACLE Enterprise Manager 10g
Database Control

Setup Preferences Help Logout

Database

Database: miisdev > Manage Metrics

Manage Metrics

Thresholds | Metric Baselines

Edit Thresholds

Pending changes: 0

Metric	Comparison Operator	Warning Threshold	Critical Threshold	Response Action
Archive Area Used (%)	>	80		
Archiver Hung Alert Log Error	Contains		ORA-	
Archiver Hung Alert Log Error Status	>	0		
Audited User	=	SYS		
Average File Read Time (centi-seconds)	>			
Average File Write Time (centi-seconds)	>			
Average Users Waiting Count				
Administrative	>	10		
Application	>	10		
Cluster	>	30		
Commit	>	30		
Concurrency	>	10		
Configuration	>	10		
Network	>	10		

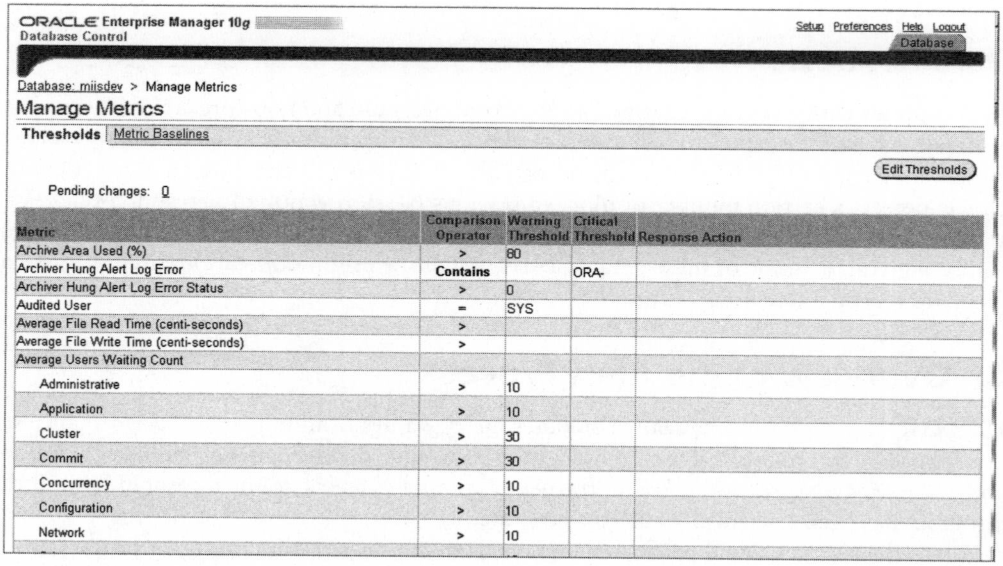

Editing Metric Thresholds

By default, many metrics do not have any thresholds defined. To set threshold levels for a metric, click the Edit Thresholds button on the Manage Metrics screen. This opens the Edit Thresholds screen (shown in Figure 8.3), which looks much like the Manage Metrics screen except that it allows edits.

FIGURE 8.3 The Edit Thresholds screen

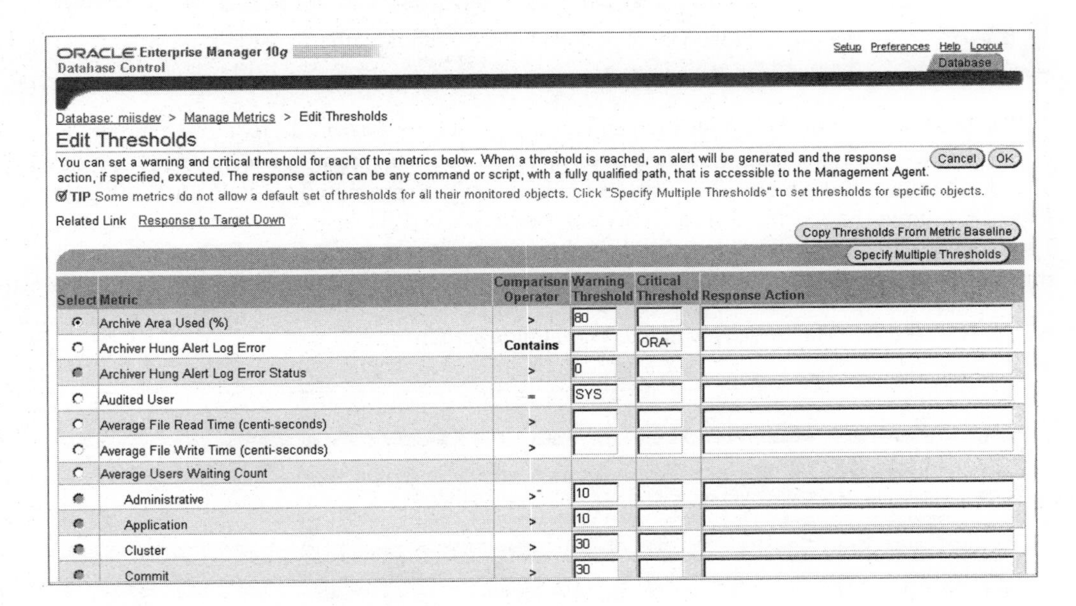

Table 8.6 lists the settings that you can edit for each metric.

To make a change, simply enter the new value(s) and click OK.

TABLE 8.6 Metric Threshold Setting Options

Setting	Description
Warning Threshold	When this threshold is exceeded, a warning alert will be generated.
Critical Threshold	When this threshold is exceeded, a critical alert will be generated.
Response Action	In response to a warning, Oracle can execute an operating system command, execute a PL/SQL procedure, or generate an SNMP trap. Response actions must be created through the Notification Methods screen prior to being assigned to a metric.

Setting Multiple Thresholds

Some metrics may contain values for multiple distinct entities. For example, `Average File Read Time` averages the metrics for all datafiles in the database. However, you may want to set thresholds for each file individually. In this case, you can select the metric and click the Specify Multiple Thresholds button, which brings up the Specify Multiple Thresholds screen. The Specify Multiple Thresholds button is located at the top right side of the metrics display area.

If a metric doesn't support multiple thresholds, the Select option will be disabled.

The Specify Multiple Thresholds screen is context-sensitive based on the selected metric. For example, if the selected metric is related to the archive, you'll be prompted for individual archive area destinations. If the metric is related to file I/O, you'll be prompted for individual filenames. Figure 8.4 shows the Specify Multiple Thresholds screen when called for the `Average File Read Time` metric. As you can see, a threshold has been set for one specific data file. You can define thresholds for each data file individually to achieve finer granularity in monitoring your data files.

FIGURE 8.4 The Specify Multiple Thresholds screen

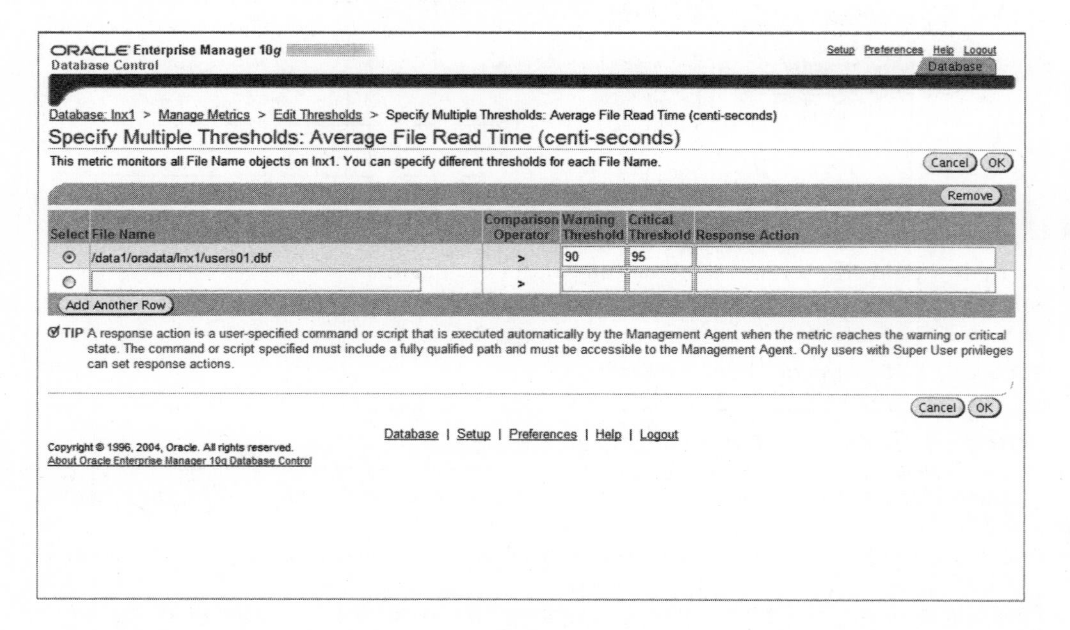

Setting Thresholds through PL/SQL

Server-generated alerts can also be set up through the DBMS_SERVER_ALERTS PL/SQL package. The package contains two procedures: SET_THRESHOLD and GET_THRESHOLD.

The SET_THRESHOLD procedure is used to define thresholds for a given metric. The GET_THRESHOLD procedure returns current threshold settings for a given metric.

As you saw previously, thresholds are set using a comparison operator. These operators determine the type of comparison to be performed between the current metrics and the threshold levels. In PL/SQL, this parameter is defined by using one of Oracle's predefined constants. Table 8.7 lists the constants and the operations that they represent.

TABLE 8.7 Comparison Operator Constants

Comparison Operator	Description
OPERATOR_CONTAINS	Metrics value is contained in the list of threshold values.
OPERATOR_DO_NOT_CHECK	Will not apply default threshold to a specified object type.
OPERATOR_EQ	Metrics value is equal to the threshold value.
OPERATOR_GE	Metrics value is greater than or equal to the threshold value.
OPERATOR_GT	Metrics value is greater than the threshold value.
OPERATOR_LE	Metrics value is less than or equal to the threshold value.
OPERATOR_LT	Metrics value is less than the threshold value.
OPERATOR_NE	Metrics value is not equal to the threshold value.

The SET_THRESHOLD procedure parameters are listed in Table 8.8.

To define multiple thresholds for an aggregate metric, the OBJECT_TYPE and OBJECT_NAME parameters are used. Otherwise, they should be left as NULL.

The following example sets the threshold for the CPU Time Per Call metric:

```
EXEC DBMS_SERVER_ALERTS.SET_THRESHOLD(
  METRICS_ID => CPU_TIME_PER_CALL,
  WARNING_OPERATOR => OPERATOR_GT,
```

```
WARNING_VALUE => '15000',
CRITICAL_OPERATOR => OPERATOR_GT,
CRITICAL_VALUE => '30000',  OBSERVATION_PERIOD => 10,
CONSECUTIVE_OCCURRENCES => 3);
```

TABLE 8.8 *SET_THRESHOLD* Procedure Parameters

Parameter	Description
METRICS_ID	The internal name of the metrics.
WARNING_OPERATOR	The operator used to compare the metrics value with the warning threshold (in other words, OPERATOR_GE).
WARNING_VALUE	The warning threshold value. Can be a list of values if the OPERATOR_CONTAINS operator is specified in the WARNING_OPERATOR parameter.
CRITICAL_OPERATOR	The operator used to compare the metrics value with the critical threshold (such as OPERATOR_GE).
CRITICAL_VALUE	The warning threshold value. Can be a list of values if the OPERATOR_CONTAINS operator is specified in the CRITICAL_OPERATOR parameter.
OBSERVATION_PERIOD	The period (in minutes) at which the metrics should be computed and verified against the threshold setting. The valid range is 1 to 60.
CONSECUTIVE_OCCURRENCES	The number of observation periods that the threshold can be violated before an alert is issued.
INSTANCE_NAME	The name of the instance for which the threshold is set. NULL for database-wide alerts.
OBJECT_TYPE	Oracle-defined constant classifying the object type. Valid values include OBJECT_TYPE_SYSTEM OBJECT_TYPE_FILE OBJECT_TYPE_SERVICE OBJECT_TYPE_TABLESPACE OBJECT_TYPE_EVENT_CLASS OBJECT_TYPE_SESSION
OBJECT_NAME	The name of the object.

This example causes a warning alert to be generated if the CPU_TIME_PER_CALL exceeds 15,000 or a critical alert to be generated if CPU_TIME_PER_CALL exceeds 30,000 for 40 minutes.

In the preceding example, CONSECUTIVE_OCCURRENCES is set to 3, allowing the threshold to be exceeded three times without an alert. Only on the fourth consecutive breach is an alert issued. Because the OBSERVATION_PERIOD is 10 minutes, it will be 40 minutes before an alert is issued.

Viewing Server Alerts

A number of dictionary views are available to access information regarding server alerts. These are listed in Table 8.9.

TABLE 8.9 Server Alert Views

View	Description
DBA_OUTSTANDING_ALERTS	Current alerts awaiting resolution
DBA_ALERT_HISTORY	Alerts that have been cleared
DBA_THRESHOLDS	Threshold settings defined for the instance
V$ALERT_TYPES	Alert type and group information
V$METRIC	System-level metric values in memory
V$METRIC_NAME	Names, identifiers, and other information about system metrics
V$METRIC_HISTORY	Historical system-level metric values in memory

Using Automatic Routine Administration Tasks

The third element in the CMI is the automatic routine administration functionality designed into Oracle 10g. Recent surveys of database administrators show that most of them spend over 50 percent of their time on routine administration functions. In response, Oracle automated many of the most time-consuming tasks, leaving you with more time to focus on other issues.

In this section, we'll discuss the automatic statistics collection feature, which automates optimizer statistics collection and maintenance. You'll also be introduced to the automatic Database Manipulation Language (DML) monitoring functionality that detects stale statistics on database objects.

Automatic Statistics Collection

Though optimizer statistics can be generated manually using the DBMS_STATS package, Oracle can do the job for you automatically through the use of its *automatic statistics collection* functionality. This is Oracle's recommended method for optimizer statistics collection.

Successful Oracle performance tuning relies heavily on the availability of accurate optimizer statistics. Optimizer statistics store detailed information about tables and indexes in your database. They provide the data that Oracle's query optimizer needs to generate efficient execution plans for SQL statements.

The different types of optimizer statistics include the following:

Dictionary statistics Dictionary statistics, new to Oracle 10*g*, are statistics that can be captured on Oracle's data dictionary objects. Because data dictionary tables are queried heavily by Oracle, having up-to-date statistics on these tables can dramatically improve overall performance.

System statistics System statistics provide the query optimizer with information on hardware characteristics such as CPU performance and disk I/O. This enables the query optimizer to estimate hardware costs more accurately when generating execution plans.

Operating system statistics Operating system statistics, new to Oracle 10*g*, offer operating system–level statistics, which were previously unavailable inside Oracle.

User-defined statistics User-defined statistics provide the optimizer with statistics on non-standard objects such as user-defined functions and packages, domain indexes, index types, datatypes, and others. User-defined statistics are used in conjunction with Oracle data cartridges and the Oracle Extensibility Services framework.

In the following sections, we'll provide an overview of the many types of optimizer statistics and their purpose. You'll look at the automatic collection process and the *automatic DML monitoring* process. To finish, we'll discuss the STATISTICS_LEVEL initialization parameter and how it affects automatic statistics collection.

Optimizer Statistics

Oracle's query optimizer is tasked with choosing the optimum execution plan for SQL statements executed against the database. To do this, it needs accurate optimizer statistics for all objects that may be used to satisfy a SQL statement. These objects include tables, columns, and indexes.

The optimizer also needs information on the system itself, such as CPU configuration and I/O speed, to apply weights to different execution methods. This information is supplied through the collection of system statistics.

Optimizer statistics differ based on the type of object on which they are collected, as shown here:

- Tables
  - Number of rows
  - Number of blocks
  - Average row length
- Columns
  - Number of distinct values in the column
  - Number of nulls in the column
  - Histograms (distribution of data)
- Indexes
  - Number of leaf blocks in the index
  - Levels
  - Clustering factor
- System
  - I/O performance/utilization
  - CPU performance/utilization

When optimizer statistics are collected on an object, Oracle will invalidate all previously parsed SQL statements that access the object. This will force the optimizer to generate a new execution plan based on the updated statistics.

The availability of accurate and up-to-date optimizer statistics significantly increases the chances that the query optimizer will generate an efficient execution plan. However, missing or stale optimizer statistics will often result in the optimizer choosing inefficient (or downright stupid) execution plans.

Let's look at a simple example of this. First, create a table called SALES and insert five rows into it:

```
SQL> create table sales
as select * from sh.sales
where rownum < 6 ;

Table created.
```

Next, use DBMS_STATS to gather statistics on the table:

```
SQL> exec dbms_stats.gather_table_stats(null, 'SALES');

PL/SQL procedure successfully completed.
```

Now, insert 40,000 rows into the table and create an index on the CUST_ID column:

```
SQL> insert into sales
select * from sh.sales
where rownum <= 40000;

40000 rows inserted.

SQL> commit;

Commit complete.

SQL> create index sales_idx on sales(cust_id)
  tablespace index;

Index created.
```

Now, suppose you want to execute the following query:

```
select *
From sample_table
Where client_id = 1234567;
```

Before executing this query, run EXPLAIN PLAN on it and view the results (note that the EXPLAIN PLAN output has been trimmed for space):

```
SQL> explain plan
  2  for
  3  select * from sales
  4  where cust_id = 123;

Explained.

SQL> @utlxpls

PLAN_TABLE_OUTPUT
-------------------------------------------------------
Plan hash value: 3099465693
```

```
---------------------------------------------------
| Id  | Operation          | Name  | Rows  | Bytes |
---------------------------------------------------
|   0 | SELECT STATEMENT   |       |     1 |    30 |
|*  1 |  TABLE ACCESS FULL| SALES |     1 |    30 |
---------------------------------------------------

Predicate Information (identified by operation id):
---------------------------------------------------

PLAN_TABLE_OUTPUT
-------------------------------------------------------
   1 - filter("CUST_ID"=123)

13 rows selected.
```

You can see that the query optimizer decided to ignore the index and to use a full table scan to fulfill this query because you didn't update the statistics after inserting the new rows. Even though you had drastically increased the number of rows, according to the statistics, the table still only has five rows in it. Therefore, it decided that a full table scan would be quicker than using the index (which would be true for a table with only five rows).

To verify this, gather the statistics and try it again:

```
SQL> exec dbms_stats.gather_table_stats(null, 'SALES');

PL/SQL procedure successfully completed.

SQL> delete from plan_table;

2 rows deleted.

SQL> commit;

Commit complete.

SQL> explain plan
  2  for
  3  select * from sales
  4  where cust_id = 123;
```

```
Explained.

SQL> @utlxpls

PLAN_TABLE_OUTPUT
-------------------------------------------------------
Plan hash value: 3208976390

-------------------------------------------------------
| Id  | Operation                    | Name       | Rows
-------------------------------------------------------
|   0 | SELECT STATEMENT             |            |
|   1 |  TABLE ACCESS BY INDEX ROWID| SALES      |
|*  2 |   INDEX RANGE SCAN           | SALES_CUST |
-------------------------------------------------------

Predicate Information (identified by operation id):

PLAN_TABLE_OUTPUT
-------------------------------------------------------
   2 - access("CUST_ID"=123)

14 rows selected.
```

This time, armed with accurate statistics, the optimizer correctly chose to make use of the index over the full table scan.

Optimizer statistics are stored in data dictionary tables and are therefore static in the sense that they will not be lost if the instance shuts down. They can be viewed using a wide variety of data dictionary views (DBA_*, ALL_*, and USER_*). The specific views are covered later in this chapter.

Dictionary Statistics

Oracle 10*g* is the first Oracle release to allow the collection of statistics on dictionary tables, both real and fixed. Because dictionary tables are heavily accessed by Oracle, the availability of these statistics can have a great impact on overall system performance. Note that because fixed tables reside only in memory, they don't have an I/O cost associated with them. Instead, the CPU cost of accessing these rows is gathered.

System Statistics

In order for the query optimizer to build optimal SQL execution plans, it needs more than just object statistics. It also needs to know something about the hardware on which it is running (in other words, CPU and I/O performance). It needs this information in order to assign weights to specific resources for comparison purposes.

This information is made available to the query optimizer through the use of system statistics. Armed with this information, Oracle can make more accurate resource estimates and, subsequently, more efficient execution plans.

As mentioned previously, system statistics are classified as optimizer statistics. Unlike other optimizer statistics, however, Oracle does not invalidate previously parsed SQL statements (in the library cache) when system statistics get updated. Only new SQL statements will be parsed using the new statistics.

System statistics can be viewed using either the V$SYSSTAT or V$SESSTAT views, as shown here:

```
SQL> select statistic#, name, value from v$sysstat
  where rownum <=20;

STATISTIC# NAME                                VALUE
---------- ------------------------------ ----------
         0 logons cumulative                    7811
         1 logons current                        964
         2 opened cursors cumulative         2115614
         3 opened cursors current                653
         4 user commits                        52290
         5 user rollbacks                       3965
         6 user calls                         801463
         7 recursive calls                  74932775
         8 recursive cpu usage               1090165
         9 session logical reads            39069641
        10 session stored procedure space          0
        11 CPU used when call started        1284787
        12 CPU used by this session          1281547
        13 DB time                          91184061
        14 cluster wait time                       0
        15 concurrency wait time                4139
        16 application wait time                3569
        17 user I/O wait time                  88034
        18 session connect time           7.1900E+12
        19 process last non-idle time     7.1900E+12

20 rows selected.
```

As you can see, the V$SYSSTAT view allows you to access system statistics values stored in dynamic performance tables.

Operating System Statistics

Oracle 10*g* has also added a new category of system statistics known as operating system statistics. Operating system statistics provide CPU, memory, and file system utilization data from the operating system. Many of these statistics were not available in previous versions of Oracle, making it difficult to investigate hardware-related issues. Instead, you had to rely on operating system–specific tools called from outside of Oracle.

Operating system statistics are described in Table 8.10 and can be seen through the V$OSSTAT view.

TABLE 8.10 *V$OSSTAT* View Operating System Statistics

Statistic Name	Description
NUM_CPUS	Number of CPUs
IDLE_TICKS	Hundredths of a second that a processor has been idle, over all processors
BUSY_TICKS	Hundredths of a second that a processor has been busy executing user or kernel code, over all processors
USER_TICKS	Hundredths of a second that a processor has been busy executing user code, over all processors
SYS_TICKS	Hundredths of a second that a processor has been busy executing kernel code, over all processors
IOWAIT_TICKS	Hundredths of a second that a processor has been waiting for I/O to complete, over all processors
NICE_TICKS	Hundredths of a second that a processor has been busy executing low-priority user code, over all processors
AVG_IDLE_TICKS	Hundredths of a second that a processor has been idle, averaged over all processors
AVG_BUSY_TICKS	Hundredths of a second that a processor has been busy executing user or kernel code, averaged over all processors
AVG_USER_TICKS	Hundredths of a second that a processor has been busy executing user code, averaged over all processors
AVG_SYS_TICKS	Hundredths of a second that a processor has been busy executing kernel code, averaged over all processors
AVG_IOWAIT_TICKS	Hundredths of a second that a processor has been waiting for I/O to complete, averaged over all processors

TABLE 8.10 *V$OSSTAT* View Operating System Statistics *(continued)*

Statistic Name	Description
AVG_NICE_TICKS	Hundredths of a second that a processor has been busy executing low-priority user code, averaged over all processors
OS_CPU_WAIT_TIME	Hundredths of a second that processes have been in a ready state (waiting to run)
RSRC_MGR_CPU_WAIT_TIME	Hundredths of a second that Oracle processes have waited for CPU allocation for their consumer group (in the currently active resource plan)
IN_BYTES	Total number of bytes that have been paged in
OUT_BYTES	Total number of bytes that have been paged out
FS_IN_BYTES	Total number of bytes that have been paged in due to the file system
FS_OUT_BYTES	Total number of bytes that have been paged out due to the file system
AVG_IN_BYTES	Number of bytes that have been paged in, averaged over all processors
AVG_OUT_BYTES	Total number of bytes that have been paged out, averaged over all processors
AVG_FS_IN_BYTES	Total number of bytes that have been paged in due to the file system, averaged over all processors
AVG_FS_OUT_BYTES	Total number of bytes that have been paged out due to the file system, averaged over all processors

The availability of all statistics except for NUM_CPUS and RSRC_MGR_CPU_WAIT_TIME is subject to the operating system platform on which Oracle Database is running.

User-Defined Statistics

Oracle 10*g* can be described as an object-relational database. This means that, in addition to the standard relational model, Oracle supports data organized under the object model. The object model allows users the flexibility to define their own objects for data storage and manipulation. It also allows them to define new datatypes to supplement the native types.

Obviously, most standard functions and index types won't know how to deal with data stored in a non-native format. Therefore, Oracle allows the creation of functions, indexes, and so on to support these new datatypes. For example, you can create your own set of aggregate functions, such as min() and max(), that will operate on custom data stored in a character large object (CLOB).

To support these user-defined objects, Oracle also allows the creation of user-defined statistics to support the optimizer in generating efficient execution plans.

Collecting Optimizer Statistics

Automated statistics collection is automatic in the truest sense of the term. No action is required on your part at all. When a database is created in Oracle 10g, Oracle creates a job called GATHER_STATS_JOB in the scheduler. This job runs whenever the Maintenance window (defined in the scheduler) is opened.

The scheduler is covered in detail in Chapter 12, "Using the Scheduler to Automate Tasks."

If the job is still running when the Maintenance window closes, it will continue to run until completion. By default, the Maintenance window is open weeknights from 10:00 P.M. until 6:00 A.M., and all day long on the weekends.

The GATHER_STATS_JOB job utilizes an internal procedure named DBMS_STATS.GATHER_DATABASE_STATS_JOB_PROC to gather the statistics. This procedure detects objects that have either no statistics or statistics that it deems stale. It then prioritizes them (so that those objects most in need will get processed first) and begins collecting statistics.

DBMS_STATS classifies statistics as "stale" when the number of rows in the object has been modified by more than 10 percent since the last statistics were gathered.

The DBMS_STATS.GATHER_DATABASE_STATS_JOB_PROC procedure is similar to the DBMS_STATS.GATHER_DATABASE_STATS procedure when called with the GATHER AUTO option. The major difference is that the latter performs no prioritization.

To verify that the job exists, query the DBA_SCHEDULER_JOBS view:

```
SELECT *
FROM DBA_SCHEDULER_JOBS
WHERE JOB_NAME = 'GATHER_STATS_JOB';
```

If you need to turn off automated statistics collection, simply disable the job by using the DBMS_SCHEDULER.DISABLE function:

```
BEGIN
  DBMS_SCHEDULER.DISABLE('GATHER_STATS_JOB');
END;
/
```

Managing Volatile Object Statistics

While automatic statistics collection works well for most tables, it falls short when dealing with volatile objects. Volatile objects are objects that can drastically change in size over the course of a day. For example, tables that are the target of a bulk-load operation (where the number of rows increases by 10 percent or more) would be considered volatile. Also, tables that are truncated or dropped, and then rebuilt, would also be considered volatile. Volatile objects run the risk of having no statistics (if they were dropped and rebuilt) or having inaccurate statistics.

Oracle 10*g* offers several options for dealing with volatile objects. The first, and most obvious, is to simply gather the statistics manually using DBMS_STATS. Beyond that however, there are two other options.

The first option is to set statistics to NULL. As part of Oracle's query optimization, any table with no statistics will have them generated dynamically via the dynamic sampling feature. This "just-in-time" statistics generation ensures that no query will be executed without statistics. The parameter OPTIMIZER_DYNAMIC_SAMPLING needs to be set to a value of 2 (the default) or higher to enable this feature.

To set statistics for a table to NULL, delete and lock the statistics as shown:

```
SQL> exec DBMS_STATS.DELETE_TABLE_STATS('BUTERTB', 'VOLATILE_TABLE');

PL/SQL procedure successfully completed

SQL> exec DBMS_STATS.LOCK_TABLE_STATS('BUTERTB', 'VOLATILE_TABLE');

PL/SQL procedure successfully completed
```

The second option is to set statistics to values that are typical for the table and lock them. To achieve this, gather statistics when the table is at a typical size. When complete, lock the table's statistics, as shown in the preceding example.

Monitoring DML Table Changes

Oracle 10*g* changes the method in which Oracle monitors tables for DML changes. Instead of using the [NO]MONITORING clause in the CREATE TABLE or ALTER TABLE statements, the STATISTICS_LEVEL initialization parameter now acts as a global switch to control monitoring for all objects. It is no longer necessary to enable/disable DML monitoring at the object level.

The following are all deprecated in Oracle 10*g*: ALTER TABLE ... MONITORING;, DBMS_STATS.ALTER_DATABASE_TAB_MONITORING();, and DBMS_STATS.ALTER_SCHEMA_TAB_MONITORING();. They can still be used, but they are considered as no operation to Oracle.

The DML monitoring feature keeps track of all DML activity (INSERT, UPDATE, DELETE) against a table since statistics were last gathered. The System Monitor (SMON) process will periodically (approximately every three hours) update the data dictionary with this information. Oracle can then use this data to identify when statistics are stale.

Monitoring data can be viewed using the DBA_TAB_MODIFICATIONS, ALL_TAB_MODIFICATIONS, or USER_TAB_MODIFICATIONS views. The ALL_TAB_MODIFICATIONS view is described in Table 8.11.

TABLE 8.11 *ALL_TAB_MODIFICATIONS* View Columns

Column	Description
TABLE_OWNER	Owner of the modified table
TABLE_NAME	Name of the modified table
PARTITION_NAME	Name of the modified partition
SUBPARTITION_NAME	Name of the modified subpartition
INSERTS	Approximate number of inserts since the last time statistics were gathered
UPDATES	Approximate number of updates since the last time statistics were gathered
DELETES	Approximate number of deletes since the last time statistics were gathered
TIMESTAMP	The last time the table was modified
DROP_SEGMENTS	Number of partition and subpartition segments dropped since the last analyze

Because of the delay in updating by the SMON process, recent DML statements may not be immediately reflected in the monitoring views.

Altering the *STATISTICS_LEVEL* Parameter

The automatic statistics collection functionality is controlled by the setting of the STATISTICS_LEVEL initialization parameter. This parameter can be set to one of three values: BASIC, TYPICAL (the default), and ALL.

BASIC This setting disables the collection of many important statistics that Oracle requires in order to provide the following functionality:

- ADDM
- Automatic optimizer statistics collection
- Automatic SGA memory management
- AWR snapshots
- Buffer cache advisory
- Database time distribution statistics
- End-to-end application tracing
- Monitoring of statistics
- MTTR advisory
- Object-level statistics
- PGA target advisory
- Segment-level statistics
- Server-generated alerts
- Service-level statistics
- Shared Pool sizing advisory
- Timed statistics

Oracle strongly advises against setting the `STATISTICS_LEVEL` parameter to `BASIC`, due to the serious loss of functionality.

TYPICAL This setting ensures collection of all major statistics that the database needs for self-management. It also provides the best performance overall. Oracle suggests that the default value of `TYPICAL` should be adequate for most environments.

ALL This setting results in the gathering of all of the `TYPICAL` statistics, as well as the operating system and plan execution statistics.

The `STATISTICS_LEVEL` setting can be dynamically altered at the system level using the `ALTER SYSTEM` statement or at the session level using the `ALTER SESSION` statement. However, the `ALTER SESSION` statement only affects the following statistics within the specified session:

- Timed statistics
- Timed operating system statistics
- Plan execution statistics

The rest of the statistics for the session are gathered as always, because they are needed by Oracle.

Viewing the Statistics Level

The V$STATISTICS_LEVEL view can be used to see which statistics are captured at each level. Table 8.12 lists the columns available in the V$STATISTICS_LEVEL view.

TABLE 8.12 *V$STATISTICS_LEVEL* View

Column Name	Description
DESCRIPTION	Description of statistics/advisory. May also list available views for the category (see STATISTICS_VIEW_NAME for details).
SESSION_STATUS	Status of the current session for the statistic/advisory (ENABLED or DISABLED).
SYSTEM_STATUS	System-wide status for the statistic/advisory (ENABLED or DISABLED).
ACTIVATION_LEVEL	STATISTICS_LEVEL setting at which the statistic/advisory is activated (BASIC, TYPICAL, or ALL).
STATISTICS_VIEW_NAME	If a single view exists for the statistic/advisory, it will be listed here. If more than one view exists, they will be listed in the DESCRIPTION column. If none exists, the column will be NULL.
SESSION_SETTABLE	Can the statistic/advisory be modified at the session level (YES or NO)?

Understanding the Advisory Framework

The final component of the CMI is the advisory framework. If you're anything like me, when you hear the term "advisor," you may be picturing an animated paper clip popping up whenever you open SQL*Plus and dispensing wisdom such as, "It looks like you're connecting to a database." But don't worry, no irritating paper clips are going to appear (or dogs or guys named Bob).

Instead, the advisors are a collection of services that aid in the optimization of different aspects of the Oracle 10*g* database. Each advisor covers a specific subsystem within the database, and can analyze, diagnose, and provide recommendations to eliminate performance issues in the database.

This section takes a quick look at some of the different advisors that are available. We'll then discuss the common interface shared by the advisors. Next, you'll learn about ADDM and see how it proactively monitors the database on your behalf. Lastly, we'll investigate the SQL Tuning Advisor and see how it automates the SQL Tuning process.

An Overview of the Advisors

The Advisory Framework offers a consistent, uniform interface across all advisors allowing them to interact with each other as needed. This framework is enhanced by the use of a common repository (the AWR).

There are a number of advisors available, some of which will be described in detail later in this chapter. The following is a brief overview of the different advisors and a description of their functionality.

Automatic Database Diagnostic Monitor (ADDM)

ADDM represents the pinnacle of automatic database performance tuning. Without any human interaction, it proactively identifies performance issues and bottlenecks within the database. In addition, ADDM works with other advisors to offer recommendations on how to resolve the problems detected.

The Segment Advisor

The Segment Advisor analyzes space fragmentation within segments and identifies the segments that are good candidates for the new online shrink operation. To put that in simpler terms, Oracle finally has online reorganization capability.

In past versions, to repair fragmentation generally meant dropping and re-creating objects or using a command such as `ALTER TABLE MOVE` (which is essentially a drop and a re-create). With the Segment Advisor, you are notified of fragmented segments and can reclaim the wasted space using the online shrink operation. There is also an option to reset the high water mark, or to leave it as before.

The Segment Advisor also reports on segment growth trends, to aid in capacity planning and resource monitoring.

The Undo Advisor

The Undo Advisor helps determine appropriate sizing for Undo tablespaces and helps determine optimal `UNDO_RETENTION` settings. This aids in the prevention of `Snapshot too old` errors. It also assists in setting the proper low threshold value of the Undo retention period for use with the flashback query feature.

The Undo Advisor assists in identifying problems relating to the Undo tablespace and offers advice to help correct those problems.

The SQL Tuning Advisor

The *SQL Tuning Advisor* is used to analyze individual SQL statements and provides recommendations to increase performance. It can be run against SQL identified as problematic by ADDM, against the most resource-intensive SQL (top SQL) from the AWR, or against any user-defined SQL.

The SQL Tuning Advisor is covered in greater detail later in this chapter.

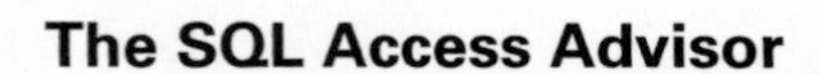

The SQL Access Advisor

The SQL Access Advisor is used to analyze a SQL workload (which can consist of one or more SQL statements) and recommend appropriate access structures to improve the performance of the workload. These access structures include, but are not limited to, materialized views and indexes.

The Memory Advisor

The Memory Advisor helps you to tune the size of the different Oracle memory structures. The Memory Advisor acts as a sort of supervising advisor with responsibility for the overall instance. Within the realm of the Memory Advisor, the following advisors are available to help optimize individual areas of memory:

- SGA Advisor
- PGA Advisor
- Buffer Cache Advisor
- Library Cache Advisor

Each of these subadvisors aids you in determining the optimum size for its associated Oracle memory structure. They also help to identify and resolve problems relating to the structure.

Note that the Memory Advisor and its associated advisors are available only if you choose not to take advantage of Automatic Shared Memory Management (ASMM). Oracle strongly encourages the use of ASMM over the use of the Memory Advisor.

In keeping with the theme of the CMI, the various advisors all expose a common, uniform interface. This shortens the learning curve and also enables seamless integration across advisors.

This uniform interface also allows the advisors to invoke each other as needed. For instance, the SQL Tuning Advisor may need to invoke the SQL Access Advisor and utilize its services directly.

In addition, the advisors all share a common repository: the AWR.

Invoking Advisors

There are several distinct contexts in which the advisors may be invoked. The first is through Oracle Enterprise Manager (EM) Database Control. EM Database Control offers graphical wizards that will guide you through all the steps required to utilize an advisor.

To access the advisors through EM Database Control, navigate to the Advisor Central home page. A link can be found on the EM Database Control home page, under Related Links, as shown in Figure 8.5.

An example of advisor usage through EM Database Control is provided later in this chapter.

FIGURE 8.5 The Advisor Central home page

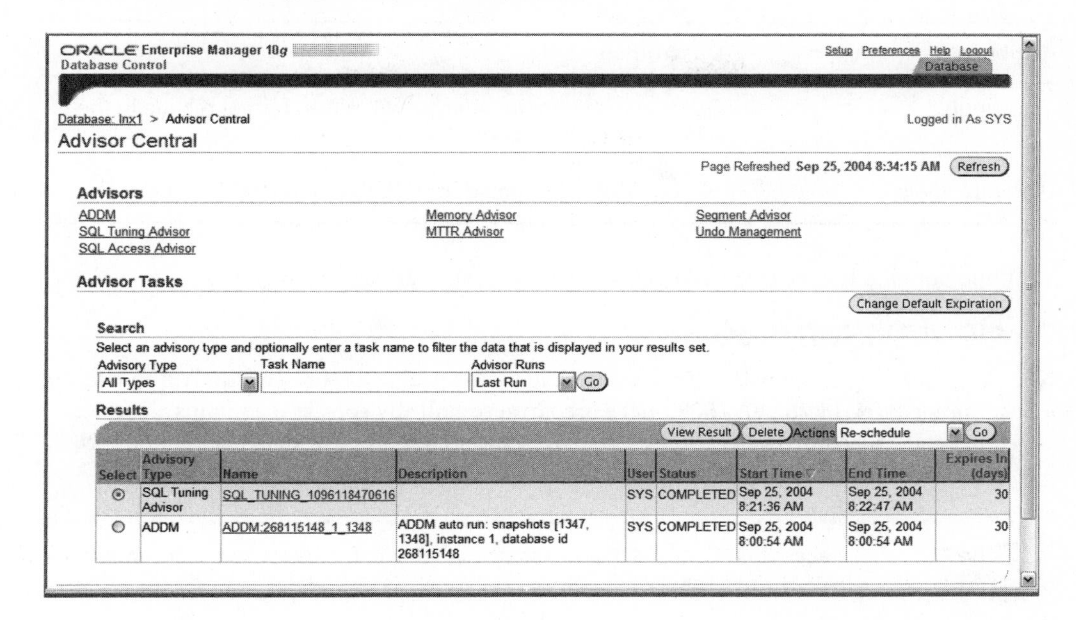

The second method advisors can be invoked is through the MMON process. As MMON monitors the system, it may trigger an advisor in response to its findings. When invoked in this manner, the advisors may execute in a limited capacity.

The third method is invocation by a Server Alert recommendation. The alert may suggest that a specific advisor be utilized in order to resolve the alert situation.

The fourth method is through the use of the DBMS_ADVISOR package.

In addition to the common invocation methods, the advisors also share common attributes, such as those listed in Table 8.13.

TABLE 8.13 Common Attributes of Advisors

Attribute	Description
Mode of operation	You can choose to run the advisor in either LIMITED or COMPREHENSIVE mode. As the names imply, LIMITED executes a fairly shallow analysis, while COMPREHENSIVE utilizes more statistics and system resources to perform a more intensive analysis.
Time limit	The maximum run time for the advisor. This attribute is useful to limit COMPREHENSIVE analysis from running for too long.

TABLE 8.13 Common Attributes of Advisors *(continued)*

Attribute	Description
Interruptible	Specifies whether an advisor will return partial results in the event of an interruption.
User directives	Specifies whether an advisor will accept user directives.

While not all advisors share all of these attributes, they are common across most of them.

DBMS_ADVISOR Package

New to Oracle 10*g* is the DBMS_ADVISOR package. This package represents an API to execute advisor procedures. DBMS_ADVISOR can be used to access all advisors, as it contains all necessary constants and procedure declarations. Table 8.14 shows the procedures available in the DBMS_ADVISOR package.

To access DBMS_ADVISOR and associated views, the user must be granted the ADVISOR privilege.

TABLE 8.14 *DBMS_ADVISOR* Procedures

Procedure	Description
CREATE_TASK	Add a new task in the repository.
DELETE_TASK	Remove a task from the repository.
EXECUTE_TASK	Execute a task.
INTERRUPT_TASK	Suspend a running task.
CREATE_TASK_REPORT	Generate a recommendations report.
RESUME_TASK	Resume execution of a suspended task.
UPDATE_TASK_ATTRIBUTES	Update the attributes of a task.
SET_TASK_PARAMETER	Set or modify parameters for a task.
MARK_RECOMMENDATION	Accept, reject, or ignore one or more recommendations.
CREATE_TASK_SCRIPT	Create a SQL script of all accepted recommendations.

To highlight the usage of the DBMS_ADVISOR package, let's look at the high-level steps that would occur during a typical tuning session:

1. CREATE_TASK: Using this procedure, a data area will be set up in the repository to store and manage your task.
2. SET_TASK_PARAMETER: Using this procedure, parameters can be defined to control the advisor's behavior. Common parameters include TIME_WINDOW, TIME_LIMIT, and TARGET_OBJECTS. For example, TIME_WINDOW tells the advisor what timeframe to use for its analysis. This determines which statistics source the advisor will utilize, repository or memory, in most cases.
3. EXECUTE_TASK: This procedure initiates synchronous execution of the task. Being synchronous, control is not returned to the user until the task has finished executing, or until it is interrupted.

Using the INTERRUPT_TASK procedure allows you to suspend a running task. You can then view the results up to that point. If you want to continue the task, just use RESUME_TASK, and the job will continue from where it left off.

4. CREATE_TASK_REPORT: This procedure creates a report of the advisor's analysis and recommendations (they can also be accessed through views) for you to view.
5. MARK_RECOMMENDATION: This procedure allows you to accept, reject, or ignore the recommendations of the advisor.
6. CREATE_TASK_SCRIPT: This procedure creates a SQL script to implement all accepted recommendations on your system.

Advisor Views

A set of advisor views is also available to view information related to the advisors. Again, the ADVISOR privilege is required to access these views. Table 8.15 lists the advisor views.

TABLE 8.15 Advisor Views

View	Description
DBA_ADVISOR_DEFINITIONS	Advisor properties
DBA_ADVISOR_TASKS	Global information about tasks
DBA_ADVISOR_LOG	Current status tasks
DBA_ADVISOR_PARAMETERS	Task parameters
DBA_ADVISOR_COMMANDS	Advisor commands and associated actions

TABLE 8.15 Advisor Views *(continued)*

View	Description
DBA_ADVISOR_OBJECTS	Objects referenced by tasks
DBA_ADVISOR_FINDINGS	Advisor findings
DBA_ADVISOR_RECOMMENDATIONS	Advisor recommendations
DBA_ADVISOR_ACTIONS	Actions associated to the recommendations
DBA_ADVISOR_RATIONALE	Reasons for the recommendations
DBA_ADVISOR_USAGE	Usage for each advisor

Though the data available through these views is accurate, Oracle still recommends the use of Enterprise Manager screens or the use of the CREATE_TASK_REPORT procedure when assessing this information.

Automatic Database Diagnostic Monitor (ADDM)

The *Automatic Database Diagnostic Monitor (ADDM)* represents another key component in Oracle's *Common Manageability Infrastructure*. ADDM provides automated proactive tuning of an Oracle 10*g* instance.

As you have already seen, Oracle 10*g* gathers an enormous amount of statistics and gathers them on a very frequent basis. Some of these statistics are self-explanatory and easy to understand. Others, however, are quite cryptic and confusing.

For anyone to understand the meaning of all those statistics is a tall order in itself. But to match ADDM, you would also have to analyze those statistics, derive the root cause of any performance problems found, produce a report encapsulating the findings, write the SQL to resolve the problem, and repeat this process every hour.

ADDM provides all of the following benefits:

- Automatic performance diagnostic report produced hourly (default setting)
- Problem diagnosis based on decades of Oracle tuning expertise
- Time-based quantification of problem impacts and recommendation benefits
- Identification of the root causes of problems, not just symptoms
- Recommendations for resolving identified problems
- Identification of non-problem areas of the system
- Minimal overhead to the system during the diagnostic process

ADDM Analysis

ADDM is automatically invoked by the MMON process after each AWR snapshot is performed. By default, this occurs every hour. Its analysis is based on the two most recent snapshots to proactively identify any performance issues.

The analysis performed by ADDM compares the most current snapshot to the one prior. It identifies system bottlenecks as well as non-problem areas of the system and identifies the root cause of problems. This is vital, as we all know the frustration in troubleshooting an issue, only to find that it was only a symptom of a totally different problem.

DB_TIME

ADDM relies heavily on Oracle's new time model statistics. Each component in Oracle has its own statistics set that capture the information relevant to that component. But, to perform analysis on the system as a whole, there is a need for a common scale of comparison that can be applied to all components. That scale is time, and the *DB_TIME* statistic is used to accomplish this.

The `DB_TIME` statistic is the most important of the time model statistics. `DB_TIME` captures total time spent in database calls for all components. `DB_TIME` represents an aggregation of CPU and non-idle wait event time. It is collected cumulatively from instance startup time.

Because `DB_TIME` is gathered for all non-idle sessions, the total time will nearly always exceed the total elapsed time since instance startup. For example, an instance that has been up for 10 hours may have had 60 sessions that were active for 30 minutes each. These would show a total time of 60 × 30 minutes, or 30 hours.

Because `DB_TIME` is common across database components, the goal of tuning can be simplified to "reducing `DB_TIME`." And because you are dealing with a common scale, the job of analysis becomes simpler and recommendations easier to quantify. The example in this section illustrates why.

In the past, aggregated statistics were used to make generalized recommendations regarding database performance improvements. Often these recommendations didn't address the real cause of the performance issue. Sometimes they were flat out wrong.

For example, a company upgrades to faster CPUs expecting to see a big increase in performance. If CPU usage wasn't the root cause of their performance issues, they may see no improvement at all.

In contrast, the time model statistics will show exactly where Oracle is spending its time. And, when taken as a percentage of the total time collected, the percentage of potential improvement can be seen immediately. Refer to the example shown in Table 8.16.

In this simplified example, let's assume that these five fictitious statistics (A, B, C, D, and E) represent a particular workload on your system. The `DB_TIME` column shows the amount of time (in seconds) that each of them used during the workload. By totaling their combined time, you can arrive at a total time of 15,000 seconds.

TABLE 8.16 Time Model Statistics Example

Statistic	*DB_TIME* (in seconds)	Total *DB_TIME*	Percentage of Total *DB_TIME*
A	10,000	15,000	66%
B	50	15,000	<1%
C	50	15,000	<1%
D	900	15,000	6%
E	4,000	15,000	26%

Then, calculate the percentage of the total time each statistic accounted for. Now you can see a clear picture of where Oracle is spending its time and where to focus your tuning efforts. For example, tuning to decrease `DB_TIME` for statistics A and E will yield the greatest results. Tuning for statistics B and C would be a waste of time. Even if `DB_TIME` for those statistics was reduced to 0, you'd see less than a 1 percent improvement. Remember that reducing `DB_TIME` means that Oracle would be able to support more user requests using the same resources (in other words, increased throughput).

Time model statistics at the session level can be viewed using the `V$SESS_TIME_MODEL` view. For time model statistics at the system level, use the `V$SYS_TIME_MODEL` view.

Wait Event Changes

ADDM also benefits greatly from the changes made in the Wait Event model in Oracle 10*g*. The first of these changes is the enhanced granularity of the statistics.

In previous versions of Oracle Database, tools such as Statspack attempted to provide diagnostic tuning services similar to those provided by ADDM. However, they fell short of their goals due to the quality of the statistics available to them. Many important statistics were either absent or were aggregated with others and therefore useless for extracting detail. This lack of granularity made it exceedingly difficult to make accurate determinations for many performance problems.

Oracle 10*g*, on the other hand, dramatically increased the granularity of the statistics collected. For example, numerous statistics related to locks and latches were aggregated into catchall statistics in Oracle 9*i*. In 10*g*, these are separated into many individual statistics. This granularity exposes a whole new level of detail never before available and makes accurate diagnosis much more likely.

The second change to the Wait Event model is the classification of wait events into high-level classes for ease of identification. Every wait event is now classified into one of the following classes:

- Application
- Administration

- Commit
- Concurrency
- Network
- User I/O
- System I/O
- Configuration

By maintaining wait event granularity but assigning wait event classes, Oracle provides the best of both worlds. Statistics can be analyzed at the class level or at the detail level, depending on the need.

ADDM Findings

When ADDM analysis is complete, ADDM will return a set of findings, recommendations, and rationales.

Findings represent the performance issues uncovered during analysis. These findings will be classified as a symptom or as a root cause, to aid in the resolution process.

Recommendations are suggestions to aid in resolving the bottleneck. These may include specifics (for example, increase the size of the Java Shared Pool) or recommendations to utilize another advisor (for example, the SQL Tuning Advisor) that can target specific types of performance issues.

Along with the recommendations, ADDM shows the benefit (performance improvement) that will result when the bottleneck is removed.

Finally, the rationale behind the recommendation is reported, to explain the reason for the recommendation.

ADDM is invoked by the MMON process each time a snapshot is taken. When invoked, ADDM will automatically begin analysis, comparing the two most recent snapshots.

Accessing ADDM through EM Database Control

Though ADDM can be accessed using the `DBMS_ADVISOR` package, Oracle recommends using EM Database Control to access ADDM. EM Database Control offers a graphical interface to ADDM (and the other advisors as well).

ADDM can be accessed from the Advisor Central page by clicking the ADDM link under the Advisors heading. This link opens the Create ADDM Task page, where new tasks can be defined.

The Advisor Central page also displays the results from recent advisor activity. If any ADDM tasks appear in this section, clicking the name of the task (or selecting the task and then clicking the View Result button) allows you to view the results of a previous ADDM task. Both options can be seen in Figure 8.6.

FIGURE 8.6 The Advisor Central screen

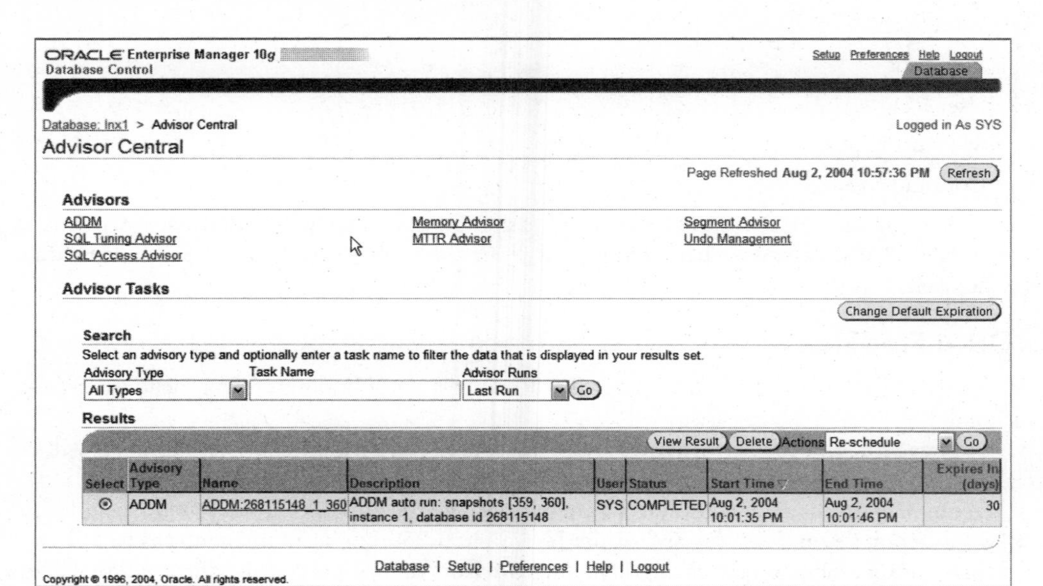

SQL Tuning Advisor

One of the greatest challenges in database administration has always been SQL statement tuning. Regardless of how well tuned your database may be, poorly written SQL can still bring it to its knees. Even properly written SQL can have a huge detrimental effect on Oracle performance if the query optimizer chooses a poor execution path. However, the introduction of *automatic SQL tuning* functionality to Oracle 10*g* promises to make SQL tuning headaches a thing of the past.

This section takes a look at the Automatic Tuning Optimizer (ATO) and the types of analysis it performs on SQL statements. Next, you'll learn how to interface with the ATO through the SQL Tuning Advisor. You'll step through the SQL Tuning Advisor using both the PL/SQL API and through EM Database Control.

Automatic Tuning Optimizer (ATO)

Automatic SQL tuning functionality has been designed into the new query optimizer that totally replaces the need for manual SQL tuning. The key to this new functionality lies in the query optimizer's choice of tuning modes.

In its normal mode, the optimizer accepts a SQL statement and generates a reasonable execution plan based on the available statistics. For the most part, it does a very good job and completes in a fraction of a second. The normal mode places a strong emphasis on returning an execution plan quickly, sometimes to the detriment of the actual execution plan itself.

When placed in tuning mode, the query optimizer is referred to as the *Automatic Tuning Optimizer (ATO)*, and its emphasis is on generating a superior execution plan. When the ATO parses a query, it performs a more thorough analysis in an attempt to improve on the execution plan.

This intensive analysis can require multiple minutes to tune a single query and is therefore recommended for complex, high-load statements that have a measurable impact on system performance.

The output from the ATO is not, however, an execution plan. Instead, it produces a group of actions, along with their expected impact, and the rationale behind each.

Automatic SQL Tuning

The Automatic SQL Tuning functionality analyzes SQL using four distinct methods:

Statistics Analysis Statistics Analysis is essential to the tuning of any SQL statement, so if essential statistics are missing or stale, the optimizer will be unable to generate an accurate execution plan. Instead, it will return a recommendation to gather the relevant statistics. It will also return additional information in the form of a SQL Profile.

SQL Profiling *SQL Profiles* contain auxiliary statistics specific to a single query that aid the optimizer in generating an optimal execution path. Through the use of sampling, partial execution, and execution history, a profile is built that will be stored in the data dictionary. When this query is executed in the future, the optimizer will include the profile in its analysis when generating an execution plan. The additional data provided by the profile helps the optimizer to generate a well-tuned plan.

Don't confuse SQL Profiles with Stored Outlines. A Stored Outline effectively freezes a particular execution plan for a query, regardless of changes made to the underlying objects. A SQL Profile can change as underlying objects change, and the data in a SQL Profile remains relevant through data distribution changes. Over a long period of time, though, a SQL Profile may indeed become outdated and require regeneration by simply running Automatic Statistics Tuning on the same SQL statement.

SQL profiles can be applied to `SELECT`, `INSERT`, `UPDATE`, `DELETE`, `CREATE TABLE AS SELECT`, and `MERGE` statements.

Access Path Analysis Access Path Analysis examines whether the addition of one or more new indexes would significantly increase performance for the query. If it identifies a promising candidate, it will return a recommendation for the creation of this new index (or indexes).

Because the addition of new indexes can also have a profound impact on other queries, the optimizer will also return a recommendation to run the SQL Access Advisor (along with a representative workload) to determine the impact of adding the new index.

SQL Structure Analysis SQL Structure Analysis looks at the syntax, semantics, and design of a query and identifies common problems associated with each. It then returns suggestions to restructure the query to achieve superior performance.

For example, consider the following query:

```
SQL> select distinct client_id from clients;
```

The inclusion of the DISTINCT clause forces Oracle to perform a sort operation to de-duplicate the result set. Through SQL Structure Analysis, the ATO can determine that CLIENT_ID is the primary key for the CLIENTS table, which ensures that no duplicate values can exist. Therefore, the query will perform exactly the same if the DISTINCT clause were removed, as shown:

```
SQL> select client_id from clients;
```

The exclusion of the DISTINCT clause allows Oracle to skip the sort operation, resulting in improved query performance.

Using the SQL Tuning Advisor

The interface to the ATO is provided by the SQL Tuning Advisor. The SQL Tuning Advisor accepts one or more SQL statements and invokes the ATO to tune them on your behalf. It then returns the advice, recommendations, rationale, and so on in the same consistent manner as the other advisors.

This section discusses the input, options, and output from the SQL Tuning Advisor.

SQL Tuning Advisor Input

Input into the SQL Tuning Advisor can come from multiple sources. First and foremost, ADDM identifies high-load SQL each time it executes. For each high-load SQL statement that it finds, it returns a recommendation to run the SQL Tuning Advisor. If you accept the recommendation, the SQL will be passed into the SQL Tuning Advisor for analysis.

High-load SQL can also be manually identified through the AWR views or through the Cursor Cache (for recent SQL not yet in the AWR). These statements can also be processed by the SQL Tuning Advisor.

A *SQL Tuning Set (STS)* allows a group of SQL statements to be passed into the SQL Tuning Advisor. SQL Tuning Sets are database objects that store information regarding a set of SQL statements (usually representing a specific workload, though not necessarily).

A SQL Tuning Set includes the following information:

- The SQL text for multiple SQL statements
- Execution context information such as schema and application information, bind variable values, and cursor compilation environment

SQL Tuning Sets are covered later in this chapter.

The SQL Tuning Advisor will not accept multiple SQL statements as input unless they are packaged in a SQL Tuning Set.

SQL Tuning Advisor Options

The scope and duration of a SQL Tuning Advisor task can be set to one of two options: limited or comprehensive.

Limited Performs statistics analysis, access path analysis, and SQL structure analysis, and returns recommendations. No SQL Profile recommendations are produced.

Comprehensive Performs all functions included in the Limited mode, but also performs full SQL Profile analysis. Also allows user-specified time limit for the tuning task, because Comprehensive analysis can be very time-consuming.

The default time limit for SQL Tuning Advisor's comprehensive SQL analysis is 30 minutes.

SQL Tuning Advisor Output

The SQL Tuning Advisor produces the following output:

- Recommendations on optimizing the execution plan
- Rationale to support the recommendations
- Estimated performance gain
- Script to implement the recommendations

The only action required on your part is to accept or reject the recommendations. If accepted, the recommendations will be implemented automatically.

DBMS_SQLTUNE Package

The DBMS_SQLTUNE package exposes the API to directly access the SQL Tuning Advisor. This package allows tuning tasks to be created and executed. It also allows for the processing of the recommendations returned from tuning tasks. This section focuses on the use of the DBMS_SQLTUNE package.

Utilizing the DBMS_SQLTUNE package requires the ADVISOR privilege.

Creating a Task

Creating a task is the first step in using the SQL Tuning Advisor. The task defines the SQL text, scope, and duration of the tuning effort, among other things. The CREATE_TUNING_TASK procedure provides the interface to define a new task. Table 8.17 describes the interface for the CREATE_TUNING_TASK procedure.

TABLE 8.17 *DBMS_SQLTUNE.CREATE_TUNING_TASK* Procedure

Argument	Type	In/Out	Default
SQL_TEXT	CLOB	In	
BIND_LIST	SQL_BINDS	In	Default
USER_NAME	VARCHAR2	In	Default
SCOPE	VARCHAR2	In	Default
TIME_LIMIT	NUMBER	In	Default
TASK_NAME	VARCHAR2	In	Default
DESCRIPTION	VARCHAR2	In	Default

Because DBMS_SQLTUNE requires the use of CLOB and SQL_BINDS datatypes, you will use a PL/SQL procedure to call the procedure, as shown here:

```
DECLARE
  task_name   varchar2(30);
sql_stmt      clob;
BEGIN
   sql_stmt := 'select /*+ full(a) use_hash(a) ' ||
' parallel(a,8) full(b) use_hash(b) parallel(b,8) ' ||
' */ a.type, sum(a.amt_paid) ' ||
' from large_table a, large_table2 b ' ||
' where a.key = b.key ' ||
' and state_id = :bnd';

task_name := DBMS_SQLTUNE.CREATE_TUNING_TASK(
  sql_text   => sql_stmt,
  bind_list   => sql_binds (anydata.ConvertNumber(32));
  user_name   => 'BUTERTB',
  scope      => 'COMPREHENSIVE',
  time_limit   => 45,
  task_name   => 'large_table_task',
  description   => 'Tune state totals query');
```

```
dbms_output.put_line('Task ' || task_name ||
' has been created.');
END;
/
```

The CREATE_TUNING_TASK procedure returns the name of the task (or a system-generated name if one is not defined) when the task is created.

Executing a Task

Once a tuning task has been created, it can be executed through the EXECUTE_TUNING_TASK procedure:

```
BEGIN
  DBMS_SQLTUNE.EXECUTE_TUNING_TASK( task_name => 'large_table_task');
END;
```

The status of the executing task can be monitored by querying the DBA_ADVISOR_LOG view or V$SESSION_LONGOPS:

```
Select status
From dba_advisor_log
Where task_name = 'large_table_task';
```

If you want to interrupt a tuning task that is currently executing, use the INTERRUPT_TUNING_TASK procedure:

```
BEGIN
  DBMS_SQLTUNE.INTERRUPT_TUNING_TASK( task_name => 'large_table_task');
END;
```

The following functions and procedures are also available to manage tuning tasks. As their names are self-explanatory, examples and descriptions are not provided.

- CANCEL_TUNING_TASK
- RESET_TUNING_TASK
- DROP_TUNING_TASK

Task Results

Results from the tuning task can be reported by using the REPORT_TUNING_TASK function. This function produces a report showing all findings and recommendations as well as the rationale, benefits, and SQL to implement the recommendations. This example shows the usage of the REPORT_TUNING_TASK function:

```
set long 1000
set longchunksize 1000
```

```
set linesize 132
select dbms_sqltune.report_tuning_task('large_table_task') from dual;
```

In the interest of space, the output from this report is not shown.

Managing SQL Profiles

If the SQL Tuning Advisor returns a recommended SQL Profile, the DBMS_SQLTUNE package can be utilized to accept it. It can also be used to alter or drop SQL Profiles.

Accepting a SQL Profile

To accept a recommended SQL Profile, use the ACCEPT_SQL_PROFILE procedure. Executing this procedure results in the creation and storage of a new SQL Profile in the database. An example is shown here:

```
DECLARE
  sqlprofile_name   varchar2(30);
BEGIN
sqlprofile_name := DBMS_SQLTUNE.ACCEPT_SQL_PROFILE(
task_name => 'large_table_task',
profile_name => 'large_table_profile');
END;
```

Altering a SQL Profile

Attributes of SQL Profiles can be altered using the ALTER_SQL_PROFILE procedure. For example, if you want to enable the STATUS attribute (to ensure that the SQL Profile will be used during SQL parsing), you could use the following code:

```
BEGIN
  DBMS_SQLTUNE.ALTER_SQL_PROFILE(
    Name => 'large_table_profile',
    Attribute_name => 'STATUS',
    Value => 'ENABLED');
END;
```

Not all attributes of a SQL Profile can be altered. Only the STATUS, NAME, DESCRIPTION, and CATEGORY attributes are eligible to be altered.

Dropping a SQL Profile

In much the same manner, a SQL Profile can be dropped using the DROP_SQL_PROFILE procedure:

```
BEGIN
  DBMS_SQLTUNE.DROP_SQL_PROFILE(
```

```
    Name => 'large_table_profile');
END;
```

Managing SQL Tuning Sets

As discussed earlier in this chapter, a SQL Tuning Set (STS) is a database object that contains a set of SQL statements along with their execution statistics and execution context information. They can optionally include a user priority ranking for each SQL statement in the set.

SQL Tuning Sets can be created on any SQL statements, but often they represent a specific workload, process, or grouping of high-load SQL. By creating sets, multiple SQL statements can be passed into the SQL Tuning Advisor at once.

SQL Tuning Sets can be managed through the use of the DBMS_SQLTUNE package.

Creating a SQL Tuning Set

The first step in the creation of an STS is to create an empty STS object in the database. This can be accomplished by using the CREATE_SQLSET procedure:

```
BEGIN
  DBMS_SQLTUNE.CREATE_SQLSET(
    Sqlset_name => 'load_proc_set',
    Description => 'SQL used in load procedure');
END;
```

Loading a SQL Tuning Set

The next step is to populate the new STS with SQL statements (and their associated execution statistics) using the LOAD_SQLSET procedure. Common sources that may be used for this step include the AWR, the Cursor Cache, or even another STS. Predefined functions are available to simplify the process of extracting and loading this information.

DBMS_SQLTUNE offers the following procedures to extract the necessary SQL information from the AWR, Cursor Cache, or from another STS:

- SELECT_WORKLOAD_REPOSITORY
- SELECT_CURSOR_CACHE
- SELECT_SQLSET

As of the time of this writing, the SELECT_CURSOR_CACHE procedure remained undocumented by Oracle, but it clearly exists in the DBMS_SQLTUNE package. As with any undocumented feature, proceed with caution.

These procedures extract all necessary SQL information from their respective containers and make the information available for loading into a new STS. To support this functionality, the LOAD_SQLSET procedure utilizes a weakly defined type known as a SQLSET_CURSOR. The

SQLSET_CURSOR type handles the results returned from queries into these non-standard repositories. The following example may clear this up a bit:

```
DECLARE

   sql_cursor   DBMS_SQLTUNE.SQLSET_CURSOR;
   begin_snap   number := 1; /* beginning snapshot id
   end_snap   number := 5; /* end snapshot id */

BEGIN

   open sql_cursor for
      select value(p)
      from table (DBMS_SQLTUNE.SELECT_WORKLOAD_REPOSITORY(
        ➥begin_snap, end_snap) p;

DBMS_SQLTUNE.LOAD_SQLSET(
      sqlset_name => 'load_proc_set',
      populate_cursor => sql_cursor);
END;
/
```

As this example shows, the SQL information is extracted for a range of snapshots stored in the AWR. The data is held in a SQLSET_CURSOR, which is then used as the source to populate the new STS.

SQL Tuning Views

Information gathered for SQL tuning tasks can be viewed through a set of SQL Tuning Information views. Some of the most common are listed here:

- SQL Tuning Information
  - DBA_SQLTUNE_STATISTICS
  - DBA_SQLTUNE_BINDS
  - DBA_SQLTUNE_PLANS
- SQL Tuning Sets
  - DBA_SQLSET
  - DBA_SQLSET_BINDS
  - DBA_SQLSET_STATEMENTS
  - DBA_SQLSET_REFERENCES
- SQL Profiles
  - DBA_SQL_PROFILES

- Advisor Information
  - DBA_ADVISOR_TASKS
  - DBA_ADVISOR_FINDINGS
  - DBA_ADVISOR_RECOMMENDATIONS
  - DBA_ADVISOR_RATIONALE
- Dynamic Views
  - V$SQL
  - V$SQLAREA
  - V$SQL_BINDS

Using SQL Tuning Advisor through EM Database Control

Oracle's recommended interface into the SQL Tuning Advisor is through EM Database Control. EM Database Control offers a graphical interface as well as context-sensitive integration with other Oracle advisors. Context-sensitive means that any EM Database Control pages displaying SQL statements, SQL Tuning Sets, or snapshots will also offer a link to the SQL Tuning Advisor. In fact, the SQL Tuning Advisor is *only* available through these screens. If you try to access it through the Advisor Central links, you'll see the screen shown in Figure 8.7, which directs you to the Top SQL, SQL Tuning Sets, Snapshots, or Preserved Snapshot Sets screens.

The process of invoking the SQL Tuning Advisor in EM Database Control is similar regardless of which screen it is called from. On any screen where you can specify one or more SQL statements (whether in a snapshot, SQL Tuning Set, AWR report, and so on), you should find a link to submit the SQL to the SQL Tuning Advisor. For this example, we'll use the AWR Snapshots screen.

The AWR Snapshots screen is designed for snapshot management. However, as shown in Figure 8.8, the Action drop-down list also includes the option of creating a SQL Tuning Set from a range of snapshots. Once an STS is created, you can then call the SQL Tuning Advisor. In this example, we select a beginning snapshot, select Create SQL Tuning Set from the Actions drop-down list, and then click Go.

FIGURE 8.7 The SQL Tuning Advisor Links screen

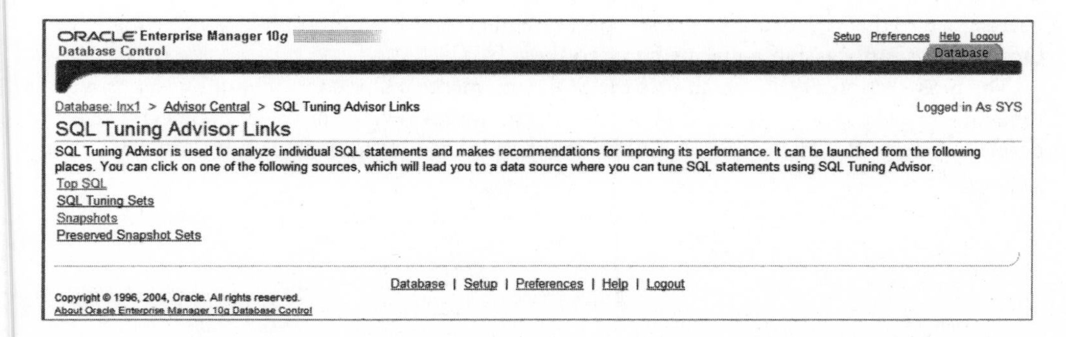

FIGURE 8.8 The AWR Snapshots screen

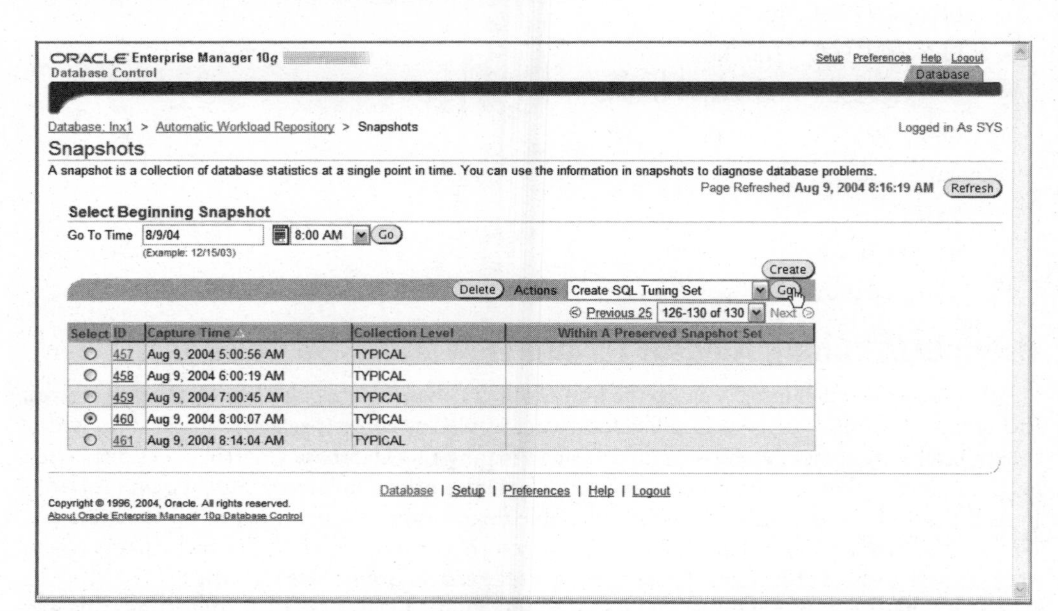

Next, you'll see the Create SQL Tuning Set screen. In this screen, you will select the ending snapshot ID and assign a name and an optional description to the STS. Technically, the name is optional as well. If it is left blank, Oracle will generate a unique name for the set. When finished, click OK to generate the STS. Figure 8.9 shows an example.

You will now be taken to the SQL Tuning Sets screen , which displays a message that the STS was successfully created. As you can see in Figure 8.10, the screen also displays a list of SQL Tuning Sets and offers a button to invoke the SQL Tuning Advisor (as well as the SQL Access Advisor). To invoke the SQL Tuning Advisor, simply select an STS from the list and then click the Run SQL Tuning Advisor button.

You should now find yourself at the Schedule Advisor screen, where you can set options for the execution of the SQL Tuning Advisor. At the top of the screen, a name and description can be assigned to the SQL Tuning Advisor job, though neither is required. If a name is not defined, Oracle will simply assign a unique name to the job.

The next section of the screen lists the SQL statements included in the tuning set as well as the name of the parsing schema. This section is strictly for review, however. You can't select or deselect statements. The entire set will be processed through the SQL Tuning Advisor.

FIGURE 8.9 The Create SQL Tuning Set screen

ORACLE Enterprise Manager 10g
Database Control
Setup Preferences Help Logout
Database
Database: lnx1 > Automatic Workload Repository > Snapshots > Create SQL Tuning Set
Logged in As SYS
Create SQL Tuning Set
Cancel OK
Beginning Snapshot ID 460
Beginning Snapshot Capture Time Aug 9, 2004 8:00:07 AM
* SQL Tuning Set Name my_sts
Description test workload
Select Ending Snapshot
Go To Time 8/9/04 8:00 AM Go
(Example: 12/15/03)

Select	ID	Capture Time	Collection Level	Within A Preserved Snapshot Set
⦿	461	Aug 9, 2004 8:14:04 AM	TYPICAL	

Cancel OK
Database | Setup | Preferences | Help | Logout
Copyright © 1996, 2004, Oracle. All rights reserved.
About Oracle Enterprise Manager 10g Database Control

FIGURE 8.10 Invoke the SQL Tuning Advisor in the SQL Tuning Sets screen.

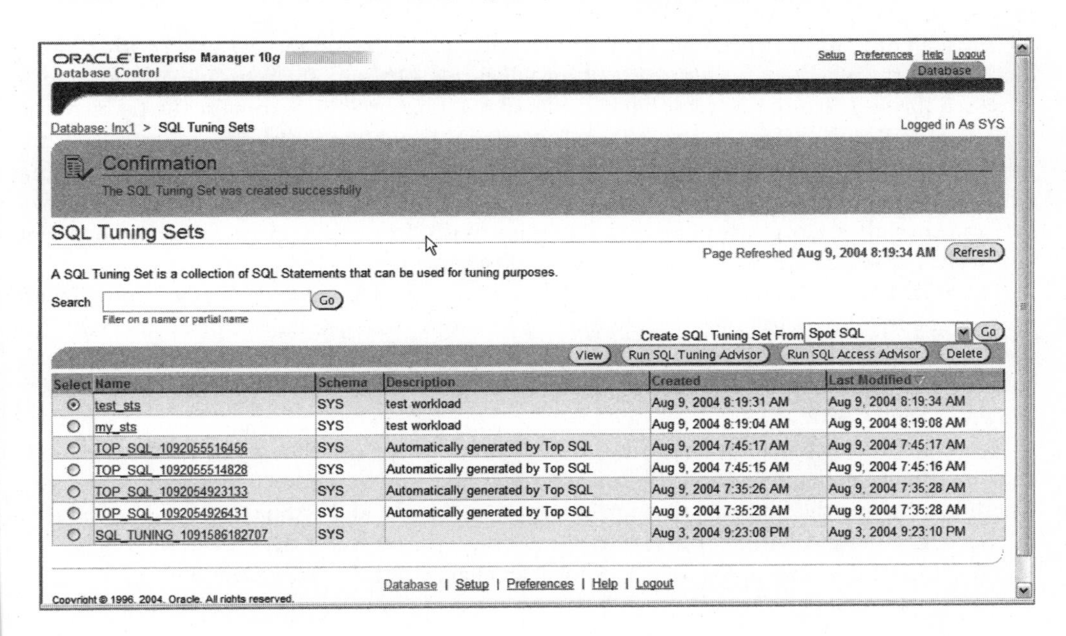

Below the SQL statements, you can define the scope for the job. As discussed earlier in this chapter, the following options are available:

Limited Perform analysis without SQL Profile recommendations. This option averages about one second per SQL statement.

Comprehensive Perform complete analysis, including SQL Profile recommendations.

Total Time Limit If the Comprehensive option is selected, the total execution time for the Schedule Advisor will not exceed the amount of time specified (in minutes). By default, this is set to 30 minutes.

Comprehensive analysis can consume a great deal of time, so Oracle strongly recommends setting the Total Time Limit to a reasonable number. Also, remember that advisor jobs can be interrupted and resumed, or cancelled altogether if necessary.

Finally, the Schedule section of the screen allows you to schedule execution time for the job. By default, the job executes immediately upon submission. More often, however, you may want the job to execute after work hours to minimize its impact on the system. The Schedule option makes this simple.

When all options have been set, clicking OK will submit the job for execution (either immediately or to the scheduler for future execution). Figure 8.11 shows the Schedule Advisor screen.

When the SQL Tuning Advisor has completed the job, you'll be automatically taken to the SQL Tuning Results screen. If the job was executed through the scheduler, you can navigate to the Advisor Central screen and use the Search option to find it. Simply select SQL Tuning Advisor from the Advisory Type drop-down list, select All from the Advisor Runs drop-down list, and then click Go. A list of all SQL Tuning Advisor jobs will appear. Select the one that you want to view and then click the View Results button.

The SQL Tuning Results screen lists all SQL statements included in the analysis, along with a series of check boxes to indicate its findings. The check boxes are labeled Statistics, SQL Profile, Index, Restructure SQL, Miscellaneous, and Error. A check mark in one or more of these columns indicates that the SQL Tuning Advisor has recommendations for the statement, as shown in Figure 8.12.

To view the recommendations, select the statement with a corresponding check mark and click the View Recommendations button. This will take you to the Recommendations screen, where you can see the findings, recommendations, rationale, and estimated benefits produced by the SQL Tuning Advisor for that statement. You can also access the execution plan for the statement from this screen. Figure 8.13 shows an example of the Recommendations screen.

FIGURE 8.11 The Schedule Advisor screen

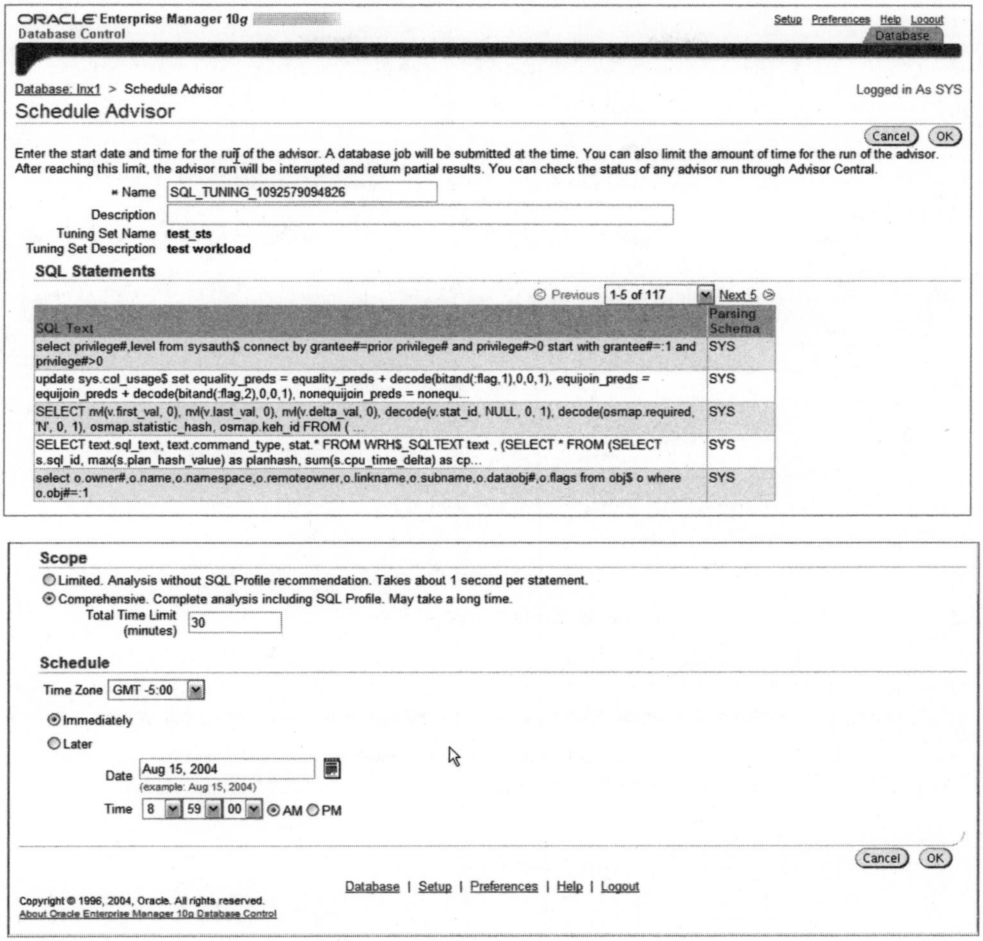

ORACLE Enterprise Manager 10g
Database Control

Setup Preferences Help Logout
Database

Database: lnx1 > Schedule Advisor

Logged in As SYS

Schedule Advisor

Cancel OK

Enter the start date and time for the run of the advisor. A database job will be submitted at the time. You can also limit the amount of time for the run of the advisor. After reaching this limit, the advisor run will be interrupted and return partial results. You can check the status of any advisor run through Advisor Central.

* Name SQL_TUNING_1092579094826

Description

Tuning Set Name **test_sts**

Tuning Set Description **test workload**

SQL Statements

Previous 1-5 of 117 Next 5

SQL Text	Parsing Schema
select privilege#,level from sysauth$ connect by grantee#=prior privilege# and privilege#>0 start with grantee#=:1 and privilege#>0	SYS
update sys.col_usage$ set equality_preds = equality_preds + decode(bitand(:flag,1),0,0,1), equijoin_preds = equijoin_preds + decode(bitand(:flag,2),0,0,1), nonequijoin_preds = nonequ...	SYS
SELECT nvl(v.first_val, 0), nvl(v.last_val, 0), nvl(v.delta_val, 0), decode(v.stat_id, NULL, 0, 1), decode(osmap.required, 'N', 0, 1), osmap.statistic_hash, osmap.keh_id FROM (...	SYS
SELECT text.sql_text, text.command_type, stat.* FROM WRH$_SQLTEXT text , (SELECT * FROM (SELECT s.sql_id, max(s.plan_hash_value) as planhash, sum(s.cpu_time_delta) as cp...	SYS
select o.owner#,o.name,o.namespace,o.remoteowner,o.linkname,o.subname,o.dataobj#,o.flags from obj$ o where o.obj#=:1	SYS

Scope

○ Limited. Analysis without SQL Profile recommendation. Takes about 1 second per statement.

⦿ Comprehensive. Complete analysis including SQL Profile. May take a long time.

Total Time Limit (minutes) 30

Schedule

Time Zone GMT -5:00

⦿ Immediately

○ Later

Date Aug 15, 2004
(example: Aug 15, 2004)

Time 8 59 00 ⦿ AM ○ PM

Cancel OK

Database | Setup | Preferences | Help | Logout

About Oracle Enterprise Manager 10g Database Control

FIGURE 8.12 The SQL Tuning Results screen

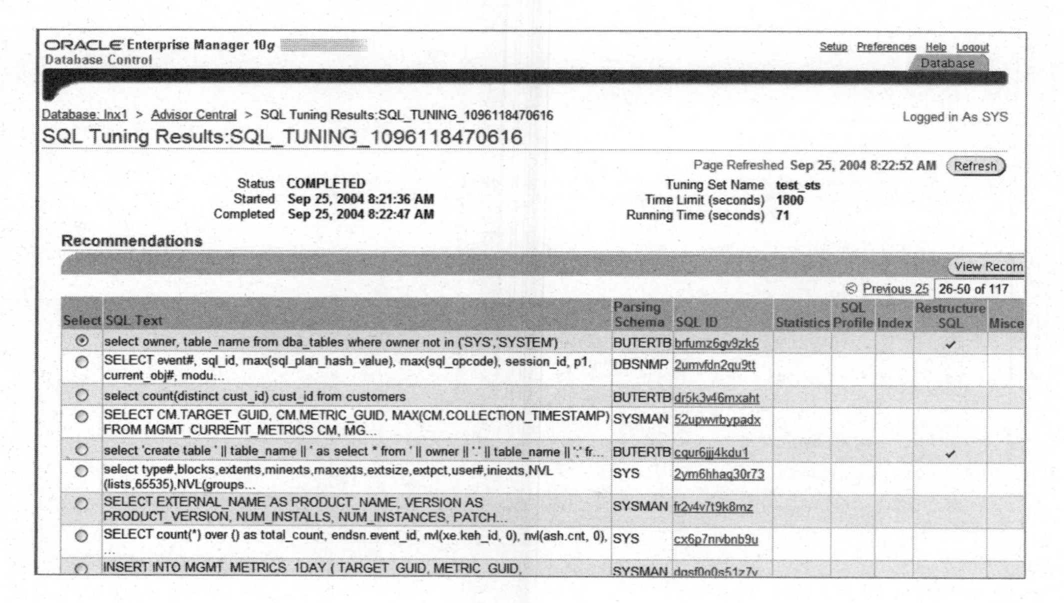

FIGURE 8.13 The Recommendations screen

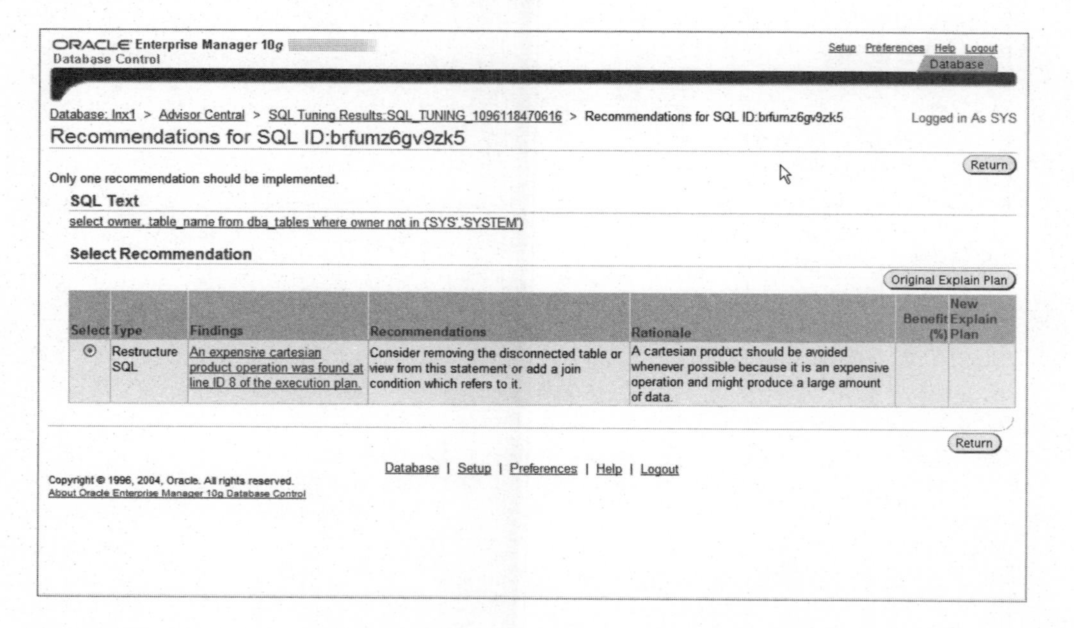

Summary

This chapter took an in-depth look at the Automatic Database Management features available in Oracle 10*g*. You saw how Oracle's Common Manageability Infrastructure (CMI) has delivered on the promise of a self-managing database. By automating many common administrative tasks and simplifying others, you saw how Oracle 10*g* has freed you to focus on the bigger issues of database management.

We covered statistics collection by first classifying the types of available statistics (optimizer statistics, performance statistics, dictionary statistics, system statistics, and user-defined statistics). You learned that without adequate, up-to-date statistics, the query optimizer often produces suboptimal execution plans.

You learned that optimizer statistics could be gathered automatically through the automatic statistics collection feature. You saw that simply setting the initialization parameter `STATISTICS_LEVEL` to `TYPICAL` (the default setting) or `ALL` enables this feature. You also learned that monitoring for stale statistics is also handled automatically, so there is no longer a need for the `MONITORING` clause to be set on tables.

Optimizer statistics can also be collected manually, when needed, through the use of the `DBMS_STATS` package. You saw how volatile tables offer special challenges to automatic statistics collection, and you learned some options for better handling them. We also discussed the changes to the `DBMS_STATS` package, including the `DEGREE` and `GRANULARITY` arguments.

This chapter also introduced you to the Automatic Workload Repository (AWR). You saw that the AWR is the primary occupant of the `SYSAUX` tablespace, and that is responsible for the collection of dynamic performance statistics. AWR also provides the repository for many performance-tuning statistics and objects. You learned that this repository offers persistence to dynamic performance statistics, allowing them to survive across instance shutdowns.

You learned about AWR snapshots and baselines and how to create, modify, and drop them. You learned how snapshots, by default, are created hourly through a job in the Oracle Scheduler and are retained for seven days. You saw how baselines could be created by identifying a range of snapshots that represent a workload. These baselines could then be used for comparisons over time. We also examined the new Memory Monitor (MMON) process and its responsibilities for snapshot retention and purging. You were exposed to many of the AWR views, and you learned to produce AWR reports in HTML and plain text.

Next, we introduced the Oracle 10*g* advisory framework and provided a brief synopsis of the various advisors. You saw how all the advisors utilized a common interface to allow consistency as well as simplified interaction between the advisors. You learned about using the `DBMS_ADVISOR` package as a common API for all the advisors. You created, adjusted, and executed advisor tasks, and learned to use the advisor views to view the results.

The Automatic Database Diagnostic Monitor (ADDM) provides proactive database performance monitoring with no human interaction required. ADDM is invoked automatically by MMON any time a snapshot is created. When invoked, ADDM identifies performance bottlenecks in the system and offers recommendations to resolve the problem.

And finally, you learned about using the SQL Tuning Advisor to tune individual SQL statements as well as SQL Tuning Sets. You learned that you could create an STS by extracting SQL text and execution statistics from the Cursor Cache, the AWR, or from another STS.

Exam Essentials

Describe the four elements that comprise the Common Manageability Infrastructure (CMI). Be able to name the individual elements of the CMI and the functionality that they offer: the AWR, server-generated alerts, automated routine maintenance tasks, and the advisory framework.

Understand the functionality provided by the advisors. Be aware of the names of the available advisors: the Segment Advisor, the Undo Advisor, the SQL Tuning Advisor, the SQL Access Advisor, and the Memory Advisor and its subadvisors. Understand the role that advisors play in the CMI. Be able to describe the functionality provided by each.

Understand the usage of the common advisor interface. Be able to create, delete, execute, interrupt and resume advisor tasks. Be able to update task parameters. Understand that advisors produce recommendations. Know how to view recommendations.

Describe the functionality of the SQL Tuning Advisor. Be able to describe the SQL Tuning Optimizer. Understand the types of analysis performed on SQL statements. Be able to describe SQL Tuning Sets.

Be aware of the advisor views. Be able to identify the advisor views. Be aware of the naming convention to which they adhere.

Be able to identify the new statistics in Oracle 10*g*. Be aware of the new time-based statistics and operating system statistics. Understand the importance of each.

Understand metrics and thresholds. Be able to describe metrics and their usage. Understand the purpose of metric thresholds and how to set them.

Review Questions

1. Which of the following is *not* a valid ADDM finding type?

   A. Error

   B. Problem

   C. Information

   D. Symptom

   E. All are valid ADDM finding types.

2. What is the default setting for the `STATISTICS_LEVEL` initialization parameter?

   A. `BASIC`

   B. `ALL`

   C. `STANDARD`

   D. `TYPICAL`

   E. None of the above

3. Which of the following would be used to set or change the value for `DBIO_EXPECTED`?

   A. The `DBIO_EXPECTED` initialization parameter

   B. The `ALTER SYSTEM` statement

   C. The `ALTER SESSION` statement

   D. All of the above will work.

   E. None of the above will work.

4. Which of the following are types of problems that the ADDM will consider? (Choose all that apply.)

   A. Database configuration issues

   B. Concurrency issues

   C. CPU bottlenecks

   D. Suboptimal use of Oracle by an application

   E. All of the above

5. The statistical data needed for ADDM to accurately diagnose problems is stored in which of the following areas?

   A. Automatic Workload Repository (AWR)

   B. Data dictionary

   C. ADDM repository

   D. PERFSTAT tables

   E. None of the above

6. Which of the following is *not* a valid DBMS_ADVISOR procedure or function?

   A. CREATE_TASK_SCRIPT

   B. RESTART_TASK

   C. INTERRUPT_TASK

   D. RESUME_TASK

   E. None of the above

7. In an RAC environment, which element(s) always uniquely identifies a snapshot?

   A. INSTANCE_ID

   B. CLUSTER_ID

   C. SNAP_ID

   D. Both A and C

   E. A, B, and C

8. If the ASH buffer is filled in less than 30 minutes, which process is responsible for flushing it?

   A. SMON

   B. MMON

   C. MMNL

   D. PMON

   E. AMON

9. Which are valid SCOPE settings for the SQL Tuning Advisor? (Choose all that apply.)

   A. Full

   B. Comprehensive

   C. Detailed

   D. Basic

   E. Limited

10. If a metrics threshold is defined with an OBSERVATION_PERIOD setting of 5 and a CONSECUTIVE_OCCURRENCES setting of 2, an alert would be generated after how many minutes of consecutive violations?

    A. 10

    B. 15

    C. 20

    D. 5

    E. None of the above

11. Which of the following statements regarding the Automatic Tuning Optimizer (ATO) is incorrect?
    - **A.** The ATO generates more efficient execution plans than the query optimizer in normal mode.
    - **B.** The ATO is nothing more than the query optimizer in tuning mode.
    - **C.** The ATO can take a long time to process a SQL statement, especially when performing a comprehensive analysis.
    - **D.** The ATO does generate a SQL Profile when performing a limited analysis.
    - **E.** All the above statements are correct.
12. The AWR resides in which tablespace?
    - **A.** `SYSTEM`
    - **B.** `TOOLS`
    - **C.** `SYSAUX`
    - **D.** `AWR`
    - **E.** None of the above
13. Which `DBMS_STATS` function is used to allow Oracle to dynamically choose an appropriate parallel degree based on the size of the object and the values of certain initialization parameters?
    - **A.** `AUTO`
    - **B.** `CHOOSE`
    - **C.** `DETECT`
    - **D.** `AUTO_DEGREE`
    - **E.** `BEST_DEGREE`
14. Which Oracle process updates the data dictionary with DML activity information gathered by the Automatic DML Monitoring feature?
    - **A.** SMON
    - **B.** PMON
    - **C.** MMNL
    - **D.** DMON
    - **E.** MMON
15. Which of the following views can be queried to display advisor findings?
    - **A.** `V$ADVISOR_FINDINGS`
    - **B.** `DBA_ADV_FINDINGS`
    - **C.** `DBA_ADV_RECOMMENDATIONS`
    - **D.** `DBA_ADVISOR_FINDINGS`
    - **E.** Findings can be viewed only through Enterprise Manager.

16. Which view shows the current AWR settings?

    A. DBA_AWR_SETTINGS

    B. DBA_AWR_CONFIG

    C. DBA_HIST_WR_CONTROL

    D. DBA_HIST_WR_SETTINGS

    E. DBA_REPOSITORY

17. On an eight-CPU system with a Shared Pool size of 1GB, what size would the ASH buffer be set to?

    A. 8MB

    B. 16MB

    C. 50MB

    D. 32MB

    E. 32KB

18. ______________ is a hash value that uniquely identifies a SQL statement in the database.

    A. SQL_HASH

    B. SQL_HASH_ID

    C. SQL_ID

    D. SID

    E. SPID

19. Which package(s) can be used to interface with the SQL Tuning Advisor? (Choose all that apply.)

    A. DBMS_ADVISOR

    B. DBMS_SQL_TUNE

    C. DBMS_SQLTUNE

    D. DBMS_SQL_ADVISOR

    E. DBMS_SQL_TUNE_ADV

20. On the Edit Thresholds screen in Oracle Enterprise Manager, what does it mean if the Select button is disabled for a specific metric?

    A. The metric is disabled on the current instance.

    B. The metric is stale.

    C. The metric does not support multiple thresholds.

    D. The threshold is locked and cannot be modified.

    E. None of the above.

Answers to Review Questions

1. A. All ADDM analysis results are categorized as Problem, Symptom, or Information findings. Problem represents the root problem identified, Symptom identifies a symptom resulting from the root problem, and Information reports on non-problem areas. ADDM does not classify its findings as Errors.

2. D. The default setting for STATISTICS_LEVEL is TYPICAL, which ensures that adequate statistics are gathered to support all of the automatic database management features.

3. E. The value for DBIO_EXPECTED is set by using the DBMS_ADVISOR.SET_DEFAULT_TASK_PARAMETER procedure. It is not an initialization parameter value, so answers A, B, and C cannot be correct, because all of them deal with initialization parameters.

4. E. ADDM considers all of these problem areas and more when performing its analysis.

5. A. ADDM, along with all the other advisors, utilize the AWR. The data dictionary stores optimizer statistics, whereas ADDM deals with performance statistics, so choice B is wrong. There is no such thing as an ADDM repository; therefore, choice C is wrong. And PERFSTAT tables are a part of Statspack, which is no longer used in Oracle 10*g*.

6. B. There is no RESTART_TASK procedure or function. Choices A, C, and D all represent valid procedures. E is obviously wrong.

7. D. Both A and C are required to uniquely identify snapshots across Real Application Clusters (RACs). In a stand-alone environment, the SNAP_ID is guaranteed to be unique. However, with RAC, a snapshot shares the same SNAP_ID across all instances, so the INSTANCE_ID is used to differentiate between them.

8. C. While MMON is normally tasked with flushing the ASH buffer every 30 minutes, the MMNL process performs the task if the buffer fills before that time. SMON and PMON don't have any interaction with the ASH flush, and AMON is not a valid Oracle process name.

9. B, E. SQL Tuning Advisor can perform either Comprehensive or Limited analysis, based on the SCOPE setting. Answers A, C, and D are all invalid settings for the SCOPE parameter.

10. B. The CONSECUTIVE_OCCURRENCES parameter defines the number of allowable violations without an alert. This number must be exceeded before an alert is generated. Because the values are checked every five minutes (as defined by the OBSERVATION_PERIOD parameter), an alert would be generated after 15 minutes.

11. A. The Automatic Tuning Optimizer (ATO) does not generate execution plans at all. Instead, it will return recommendations for optimization, along with their expected benefit and rationale.

12. C. The AWR is the primary occupant of the SYSAUX tablespace.

13. D. The AUTO_DEGREE function chooses the most appropriate degree of parallelism based on factors such as object size and init.ora settings.

14. A. The SMON process updates the data dictionary with DML activity information approximately every three hours, as well as at instance shutdown.

15. D. The `DBA_ADVISOR_FINDINGS` view shows the findings from any advisor execution. Though they can also be viewed through Enterprise Manager, answer E is incorrect.

16. C. The `DBA_HIST_WR_CONTROL` view shows information about the AWR, including the current settings.

17. B. The ASH buffer will be set to the lesser of:

    (Total number of CPUs × 2MB)

    or

    (Shared Pool size × 5%)

    8 CPUs × 2MB = 16MB

    1GB × 5% = 50MB

    Therefore, the ASH will be sized at 16MB.

18. C. `SQL_ID`, new in Oracle 10*g*, is a hash value that uniquely identifies a single SQL statement within a database.

19. A, C. `DBMS_SQLTUNE` is designed specifically as the interface to the SQL Tuning Advisor. However, the `DBMS_ADVISOR` package can be used to interface with *all* advisors, including the SQL Tuning Advisor.

20. C. Multiple thresholds can be set only on aggregated metrics with underlying granularity. For example, `Blocking Session Count` aggregates all underlying blocking sessions. Therefore, you can set thresholds for individual sessions as well as for the aggregate metric.

Chapter 9

Understanding Automatic Storage Management

ORACLE DATABASE 10*G*: ADMINISTRATION II EXAM OBJECTIVES COVERED IN THIS CHAPTER:

✓ **Automatic Storage Management**

- Set up initialization parameter files for ASM and database instances.
- Execute SQL commands with ASM filenames.
- Start up and shut down ASM instances.
- Administer ASM disk groups.
- Use RMAN to migrate your database to ASM.

Exam objectives are subject to change at any time without prior notice and at Oracle's sole discretion. Please visit Oracle's Training and Certification website (`http://www.oracle.com/education/certification/`) for the most current exam objectives listing.

One of the biggest enhancements introduced in Oracle Database 10*g* (Oracle 10*g*) is *Automatic Storage Management (ASM)*. ASM is a cluster file system that can be used either with stand-alone Oracle instances or with Oracle Real Application Clusters (RAC) to provide a vertically integrated subsystem encapsulating a file system, a volume manager, and a fault-tolerant environment specifically designed for Oracle databases. It works in concert with other Oracle features such as Oracle Managed Files (OMF) to not only make disk space management easier but also to enhance the performance of the database by automatically spreading the I/O load across all available hardware devices.

As with most features of Oracle 10*g*, Oracle Enterprise Manager (EM) Database Control provides wizards and a graphical interface for ASM, making it easy to leverage ASM features when the command-line syntax is unfamiliar or difficult to remember.

When creating a new tablespace or other database structure such as a control file or redo log file, you can specify a structure new to Oracle 10*g* called an ASM disk group as the storage area for the database structure instead of an operating system file. ASM takes the ease of use of OMF and combines it with mirroring and striping features to provide a robust file system and logical volume manager that can even support multiple nodes in an Oracle RAC. ASM eliminates the need to purchase a third-party logical volume manager. To provide further benefits beyond a typical third-party logical volume manager, ASM stripes files, not logical volumes.

In this chapter, we will delve further into the architecture of ASM. In addition, we will show you how to create a special type of Oracle instance to support ASM as well as how to start up and shut down an ASM instance. We will describe the new initialization parameters related to ASM and the existing initialization parameters that have new values to support an ASM instance. In addition, we will explain the variety of methods that you can use to refer to an ASM filename. A number of new dynamic performance views support ASM, providing different functionality depending on whether they reside in the ASM instance or in the traditional RDBMS instance. Also, we will use some raw disk devices on a development Linux server to demonstrate how disk groups are created and maintained. Finally, we will show you how to migrate your entire database to an ASM environment.

Introducing the ASM Architecture

ASM not only enhances performance by automatically spreading database objects over multiple devices, but it increases availability by allowing new disk devices to be added to the database without shutting down the database; ASM automatically rebalances the distribution of files with minimal intervention.

ASM also eases the administrative burden of managing potentially thousands of database files by creating *disk groups*, which are comprised of disk devices and the files that reside on the disk devices managed as a logical unit. ASM divides the datafiles and other database structures into extents and divides the extents among all the disks in the disk group to enhance both performance and reliability. Instead of mirroring entire disk volumes, ASM mirrors the database objects to provide the flexibility to mirror or stripe the database objects differently depending on their type. Optionally, the objects may not be striped at all if the underlying disk hardware is already RAID-enabled, for example.

Automatic rebalancing is another key feature of ASM. When you need an increase in disk space, you can add disk devices to a disk group, and ASM moves a proportional number of files from one or more existing disks to the new disks to maintain the overall I/O balance across all disks. This happens in the background while the database objects contained in the disk files are still online and available to users. If the impact to the I/O subsystem is high during a rebalance operation, the speed at which the rebalance occurs can be reduced using an initialization parameter.

As mentioned earlier in this chapter, ASM supports virtually all Oracle object types as well as RAC, eliminating the need to use any other logical volume manager or cluster file system. Figure 9.1 shows an example of a database that contains tablespaces consisting of files both from a traditional file system and from an ASM disk group, and another database that allocates all its datafiles from an ASM disk group.

Note that the example in Figure 9.1 shows that more than one database may allocate files from the same ASM disk group. An ASM file is always spread over all ASM disks in the ASM group; an ASM disk belongs to only one ASM disk group.

FIGURE 9.1 Tablespaces using ASM and traditional datafiles

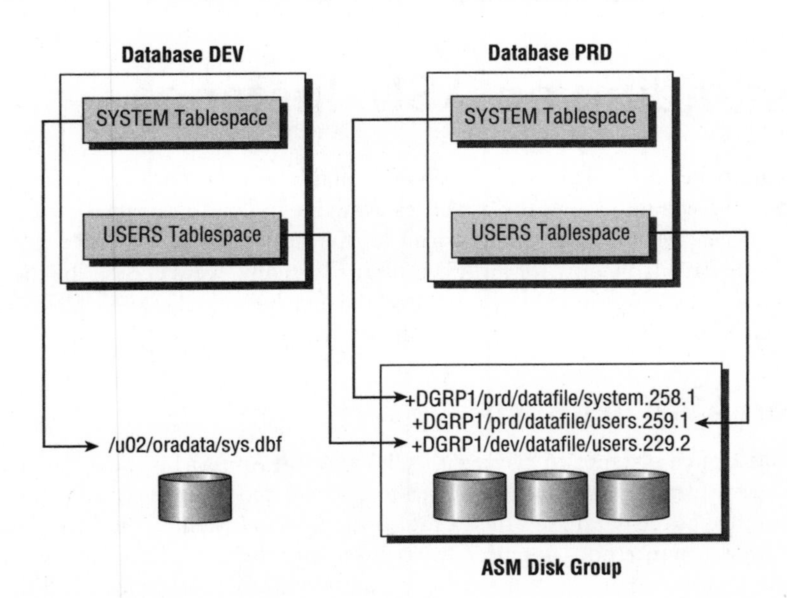

ASM disks are partitioned in units of 1MB each.

ASM requires a special type of Oracle instance to provide the interface between a traditional Oracle instance and the file system. The ASM software components are shipped with the database and are always available as a selection when choosing the storage type for the SYSTEM, SYSAUX, and other default tablespaces when the database is created.

We'll explain how an ASM instance is created in the next section.

Using ASM does not, however, preclude you from mixing ASM disk groups with manual Oracle datafile management techniques, but the ease of use and performance of ASM makes a strong case for eventually converting all your storage to ASM disk groups.

Two new background processes support ASM instances: *RBAL* and *ORBn*. RBAL coordinates the disk activity for disk groups on an ASM instance, and ORB*n*, where *n* can be from 0 to 9, performs the actual extent movement between disks in the disk groups.

For database instances that use ASM disks, two new background processes also exist: *OSMB* and RBAL. OSMB performs the communication between the database and the ASM instance, and RBAL performs the open and close of the disks in the disk group on behalf of the database instance. Note that the RBAL process exists in both ASM instances and database instances, but performs different functions on each.

Understanding an ASM Instance

ASM instances cannot be accessed using the methods available with a traditional database. In the following sections, we will talk about the privileges available to you that connect with SYSDBA and SYSOPER privileges. We will also distinguish an ASM instance by the new and expanded initialization parameters available only for an ASM instance. Finally, we will describe the procedures for starting and stopping an ASM instance and the dependencies between ASM instances and the traditional RDBMS database instances that they serve.

Creating an ASM Instance

ASM requires a dedicated instance to manage the disk groups. An ASM instance generally has a smaller memory footprint in the range of 60MB to 100MB and is automatically configured when ASM is specified as the database's file storage option when installing the Oracle software and an existing ASM instance does not already exist (see Figure 9.2).

As an example, suppose your Linux server has a number of raw disk devices with the capacities listed in Table 9.1.

FIGURE 9.2 Specifying ASM for database file storage

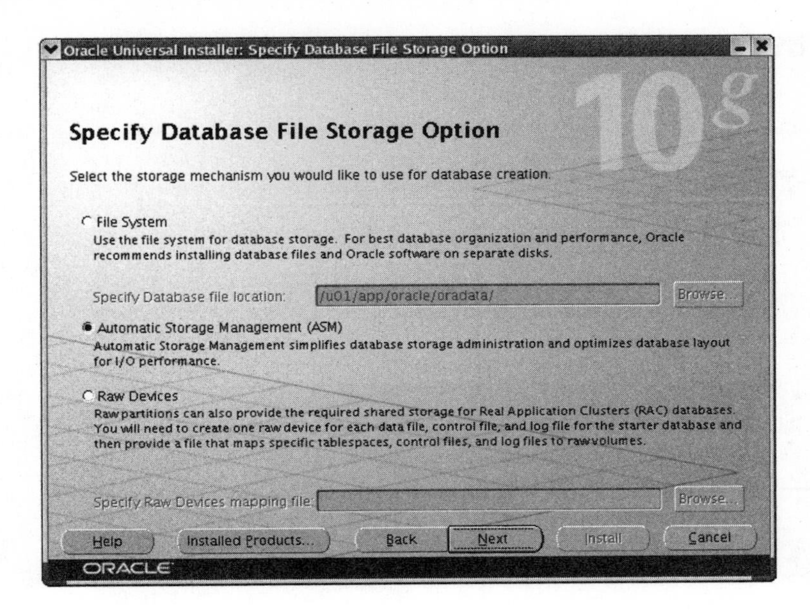

You will use these raw devices to create, alter, and delete ASM disk groups throughout the rest of this chapter.

Configure the first disk group within the Oracle Universal Installer (OUI), as shown in Figure 9.3.

TABLE 9.1 Sample Raw Devices and Capacities

Device Name	Capacity
/dev/raw/raw1	8GB
/dev/raw/raw2	8GB
/dev/raw/raw3	6GB
/dev/raw/raw4	6GB
/dev/raw/raw5	6GB
/dev/raw/raw6	6GB

FIGURE 9.3 Specifying disk group member disks

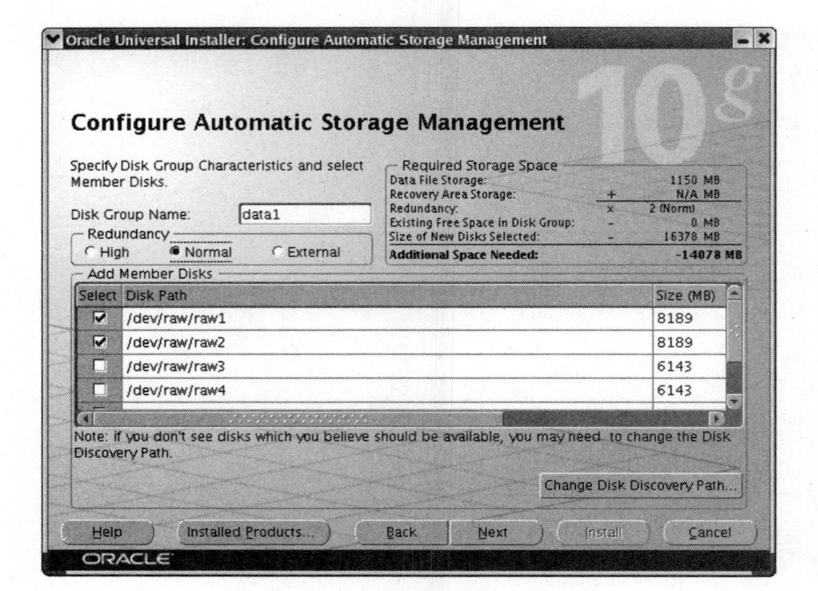

The name of the first disk group is DATA1, and you will be using /dev/raw/raw1 and /dev/raw/raw2 to create the normal redundancy disk group. After the database has been created, both the regular instance and the ASM instance are started.

An ASM instance has a few other unique characteristics. While it does have an initialization parameter file and a password file, it has no data dictionary or control file. Therefore, all connections to an ASM instance are via SYS and SYSTEM using operating system authentication only. Disk group commands such as CREATE DISKGROUP, ALTER DISKGROUP, and DROP DISKGROUP are valid only from an ASM instance. Finally, an ASM instance is in either a MOUNT state or a NOMOUNT state; it can never be in an OPEN state. The only difference between the MOUNT state and the NOMOUNT state is that the MOUNT state mounts the ASM disk groups and makes them available to other instances.

Connecting to an ASM Instance

As mentioned in the previous section, an ASM instance does not have a data dictionary, so access to the instance is restricted to users who can authenticate with the operating system—in other words, connecting as SYSDBA or SYSOPER by an operating system user that is in the dba group.

Users who connect to an ASM instance as SYSDBA can perform all ASM operations such as creating and deleting disk groups as well as adding and removing disks from disk groups.

The SYSOPER users have a much more limited set of commands available in an ASM instance. In general, the commands available to SYSOPER commands give only enough privileges to perform routine operations for an already configured and stable ASM instance. The following list contains the operations available as SYSOPER:

- Starting up and shutting down an ASM instance
- Mounting or dismounting a disk group
- Altering a disk group's disk status to ONLINE or OFFLINE
- Rebalancing a disk group
- Performing an integrity check of a disk group
- Accessing V$ASM_* dynamic performance views

Starting Up and Shutting Down an ASM Instance

An ASM instance is started much like a database instance, except that the STARTUP command defaults to STARTUP MOUNT. Because there is no control file, database, or data dictionary to mount, the ASM disk groups are mounted instead of a database. STARTUP NOMOUNT starts up the instance but does not mount any ASM disks. In addition, you can specify STARTUP RESTRICT to temporarily prevent database instances from connecting to the ASM instance to mount disk groups. If an ASM instance is already started, you can use this command in an ASM instance to prevent other database instances from connecting to the ASM instance:

```
SQL> alter system enable restricted session;
System altered.
```

Similarly, you can re-enable connections as in this example:

```
SQL> alter system disable restricted session;
System altered.
```

Performing a SHUTDOWN command on an ASM instance performs the same SHUTDOWN command on any database instances using the ASM instance; before the ASM instance finishes a shutdown, it waits for all dependent databases to shut down. The only exception to this is if you use the SHUTDOWN ABORT command on the ASM instance, the ASM instance does not pass the ABORT command to the dependent databases. However, all dependent databases immediately perform a SHUTDOWN ABORT because there is no longer an ASM instance available to manage the database's storage.

For multiple ASM instances sharing disk groups, such as in a RAC environment, the failure of an ASM instance does not cause the database instances to fail. Instead, another ASM instance performs a recovery operation for the failed instance.

Defining ASM Initialization Parameters

A number of initialization parameters either are specific to ASM instances or have new values within an ASM instance. An SPFILE is highly recommended over an initialization parameter file for an ASM instance. For example, parameters such as ASM_DISKGROUPS are automatically maintained when a disk group is added or dropped, potentially freeing you from ever having to manually change this value.

These initialization parameters include the following:

INSTANCE_TYPE For an ASM instance, the INSTANCE_TYPE parameter has a value of ASM. The default, for a traditional Oracle instance, is RDBMS.

DB_UNIQUE_NAME The default value for the DB_UNIQUE_NAME parameter is +ASM and is the unique name for a group of ASM instances within a cluster or on a single node. The default value needs to be modified only if you're trying to run multiple ASM instances on a single node.

ASM_POWER_LIMIT To ensure that rebalancing operations do not interfere with ongoing user I/O, the ASM_POWER_LIMIT parameter controls how fast rebalance operations occur. The values range from 1 to 11, with 11 being the highest possible value; the default value is 1 (low I/O overhead). Because this is a dynamic parameter, you may set this to a low value during the day and set it higher overnight whenever a disk rebalancing operation must occur.

ASM_DISKSTRING The ASM_DISKSTRING parameter specifies one or more strings, which are operating system dependent, to limit the disk devices that can be used to create disk groups. If this value is NULL, all disks visible to the ASM instance are potential candidates for creating disk groups.

Here is the value for the development server:

```
SQL> show parameter asm_diskstring

NAME                   TYPE        VALUE
---------------------- ----------- ------------------
asm_diskstring         string      /dev/raw/*
```

When creating disk groups, the only disks available on this server are raw disks.

ASM_DISKGROUPS The ASM_DISKGROUPS parameter specifies a list containing the names of the disk groups to be automatically mounted by the ASM instance at startup or by the ALTER DISKGROUP ALL MOUNT command. Even if this list is empty at instance startup, any existing disk group can be manually mounted.

LARGE_POOL_SIZE The LARGE_POOL_SIZE parameter is useful for both regular and ASM instances. However, this pool is used differently for an ASM instance. All internal ASM packages are executed from this pool, so this parameter should be set to at least 8MB.

Categorizing ASM Dynamic Performance Views

A few new dynamic performance views are associated with ASM instances. The contents of these views vary depending on whether they are displaying data for an ASM instance or a standard, non-ASM (RDBMS) instance. Table 9.2 contains the common ASM-related dynamic performance views.

We'll provide further explanation for some of these views where appropriate later in this chapter.

TABLE 9.2 ASM Dynamic Performance Views

View Name	Contents In ASM Instance	Contents In RDBMS Instance
V$ASM_DISK	One row for each disk discovered by an ASM instance, whether used by a disk group or not	One row for each disk in use by the instance
V$ASM_DISKGROUP	One row for each disk group containing general characteristics of the disk group	One row for each disk group in use, whether mounted or not
V$ASM_FILE	One row for each file in every mounted disk group	Not used
V$ASM_OPERATION	One row for each executing, long-running operation (ADD, DROP, RESIZE, or REBALANCE) in the ASM instance	Not used
V$ASM_TEMPLATE	One row for each template in each mounted disk group in the ASM instance	One row for each template for each mounted disk group
V$ASM_CLIENT	One row for each database using disk groups managed by the ASM instance	One row for the ASM instance if any ASM files are open
V$ASM_ALIAS	One row for every alias in every mounted disk group	Not used

Using ASM Filenames

All ASM files are OMF, so the details of the actual filename within the disk group are not needed for most administrative functions. When an object in an ASM disk group is dropped, the file is automatically deleted. Certain commands will expose the actual filenames, such as `ALTER DATABASE BACKUP CONTROLFILE TO TRACE`, as well as some data dictionary views. For example, the data dictionary view `V$DATAFILE` shows the actual filenames within each disk group:

```
SQL> select file#, name, blocks from v$datafile;

  FILE# NAME                                         BLOCKS
------- ---------------------------------------- ---------
      1 +DATA1/rac0/datafile/system.256.1             57600
      2 +DATA1/rac0/datafile/undotbs1.258.1            3840
      3 +DATA1/rac0/datafile/sysaux.257.1             44800
      4 +DATA1/rac0/datafile/users.259.1                640
      5 +DATA1/rac0/datafile/example.269.1            19200
      6 +DATA2/rac0/datafile/users3.256.1             12800

6 rows selected.
```

ASM filenames can be one of six different formats. In the sections that follow, we'll give an overview of the different formats and the context where they can be used:

- As a reference to an existing file
- During a single-file creation operation
- During a multiple-file creation operation

Fully Qualified Names

Fully qualified ASM filenames are used only when referencing an existing file. A fully qualified ASM filename has the format

```
+group/dbname/file type/tag.file.incarnation
```

where

- *group* is the disk group name.
- *dbname* is the database to which the file belongs.
- *file type* is the Oracle file type.
- *tag* is the type-specific information about the specific file type.
- The *file.incarnation* pair ensures uniqueness.

An example of an ASM file for the USERS3 tablespace is as follows:

```
+DATA2/rac0/datafile/users3.256.1
```

The disk group name is +DATA2, the database name is rac0, it's a datafile for the USERS3 tablespace, and the file number/incarnation pair 256.1 ensures uniqueness if you decide to create another ASM datafile for the USERS3 tablespace.

Numeric Names

Numeric names are used only when referencing an existing ASM file. It allows you to refer to an existing ASM file by only the disk group name and the file number/incarnation pair. The numeric name for the ASM file in the previous section is as follows:

```
+DATA2.256.1
```

Alias Names

You can use an alias either when referencing an existing object or when creating a single ASM file. Using the ALTER DISKGROUP ADD ALIAS command, you can create a more user-friendly name for an existing or a new ASM file; they are distinguishable from regular ASM filenames because they do not end in a dotted pair of numbers (the file number/incarnation pair). In the following example, you create a directory object to the data2 disk group, and then you use the ALTER DISKGROUP ADD ALIAS command to create a user-friendly alias in the newly created directory object to point to a fully qualified datafile name. The following example creates a directory called +data2/redempt for the ASM disk group called data2:

```
SQL> alter diskgroup data2
  2     add directory '+data2/redempt';

Diskgroup altered.
```

Using the directory created previously, this next example gives the datafile called users3.256.1 the user-friendly filename users.dbf:

```
SQL> alter diskgroup data2
  2     add alias '+data2/redempt/users.dbf'
  3     for '+data2/rac0/datafile/users3.256.1';

Diskgroup altered.
```

Alias with Template Names

You can use an alias with a template only when creating a new ASM file. Templates provide a shorthand way of specifying a file type and a tag when creating a new ASM file.

The "Understanding ASM File Types and Templates" section later in this chapter covers default ASM templates.

An example of an alias using a template for a new tablespace in the +DATA2 disk group is as follows:

```
SQL> create tablespace users4 datafile
  2      '+data2/uspare(datafile)';
Tablespace created.
```

Incomplete Names

You can use an incomplete filename format either for single-file or for multiple-file creation operations. You specify only the disk group name, and you use a default template depending on the type of file, as shown here:

```
SQL> create tablespace users5 datafile '+data1';
Tablespace created.
```

Incomplete Names with Template

As with incomplete ASM filenames, you can use an incomplete filename with a template for single-file or multiple-file creation operations. Regardless of the actual file type, the template name determines the characteristics of the file.

Even though you are creating a tablespace, the characteristics of a `tempfile` are used instead as the attributes for the datafile, as shown here:

```
SQL> create tablespace users6 datafile '+data1(tempfile)';
Tablespace created.
```

Understanding ASM File Types and Templates

ASM supports all types of files used by the database except for files such as operating system executables. Table 9.3 contains the complete list of ASM file types; *File Type* and *Tag* are those presented previously for ASM file-naming conventions.

TABLE 9.3 ASM File Types

Oracle File Type	File Type	Tag	Default Template
Control files	`controlfile`	cf (control file) or bcf (backup control file)	CONTROLFILE
Datafiles	`datafile`	*tablespace name.file#*	DATAFILE
Online logs	`online_log`	`log_`*thread#*	ONLINELOG
Archive logs	`archive_log`	Parameter	ARCHIVELOG
Temp files	`temp`	*tablespace name.file#*	TEMPFILE
RMAN datafile backup piece	`backupset`	Client-specified	BACKUPSET
RMAN incremental backup piece	`backupset`	Client-specified	BACKUPSET
RMAN archive log backup piece	`backupset`	Client-specified	BACKUPSET
RMAN datafile copy	`datafile`	*tablespace name.file#*	DATAFILE
Initialization parameters	`init`	`spfile`	PARAMETERFILE
Broker config	`drc`	`drc`	DATAGUARDCONFIG
Flashback logs	`rlog`	*thread#_log#*	FLASHBACK
Change tracking bitmap	`ctb`	`bitmap`	CHANGETRACKING
Auto backup	`autobackup`	Client-specified	AUTOBACKUP
Data Pump dumpset	`dumpset`	`dump`	DUMPSET
Cross-platform datafiles			XTRANSPORT

Table 9.4 lists the default ASM file templates referenced in the Default Template column of Table 9.3.

TABLE 9.4 ASM File Templates

System Template	External Redundancy	Normal Redundancy	High Redundancy	Striping
CONTROLFILE	Unprotected	Two-way mirroring	Three-way mirroring	Fine
DATAFILE	Unprotected	Two-way mirroring	Three-way mirroring	Coarse
ONLINELOG	Unprotected	Two-way mirroring	Three-way mirroring	Fine
ARCHIVELOG	Unprotected	Two-way mirroring	Three-way mirroring	Coarse
TEMPFILE	Unprotected	Two-way mirroring	Three-way mirroring	Coarse
BACKUPSET	Unprotected	Two-way mirroring	Three-way mirroring	Coarse
XTRANSPORT	Unprotected	Two-way mirroring	Three-way mirroring	Coarse
PARAMETERFILE	Unprotected	Two-way mirroring	Three-way mirroring	Coarse
DATAGUARDCONFIG	Unprotected	Two-way mirroring	Three-way mirroring	Coarse
FLASHBACK	Unprotected	Two-way mirroring	Three-way mirroring	Fine
CHANGETRACKING	Unprotected	Two-way mirroring	Three-way mirroring	Coarse
AUTOBACKUP	Unprotected	Two-way mirroring	Three-way mirroring	Coarse
DUMPSET	Unprotected	Two-way mirroring	Three-way mirroring	Coarse

The mirroring options in the High Redundancy column of Table 9.4 are discussed in the next section under "Understanding Disk Group Architecture."

When a new disk group is created, a set of ASM file templates copied from the default templates in Table 9.3 is saved with the disk group. As a result, individual template characteristics can be changed and apply only to the disk group where they reside. In other words, the DATAFILE system template in disk group +DATA1 may have the default coarse striping, but the DATAFILE template in disk group +DATA2 may have fine striping. You can create your own templates in each disk group as needed.

When an ASM datafile is created with the DATAFILE template, by default, the datafile is 100MB, the datafile is autoextensible, and the maximum size is unlimited.

Administering ASM Disk Groups

Using ASM disk groups benefits you in a number of ways:

- I/O performance is improved.
- Availability is increased.
- The ease with which you can add a disk to a disk group or add an entirely new disk group enables you to manage many more databases in the same amount of time.

Understanding the components of a disk group as well as correctly configuring a disk group is an important goal for a successful DBA.

In the following sections, we will delve more deeply into the details of the structure of a disk group. Also, we will review the different types of administrative tasks related to disk groups and show how disks are assigned to failure groups, how disk groups are mirrored, and how disk groups are created, dropped, and altered. We will also briefly review the Enterprise Manager (EM) Database Control interface to ASM.

Understanding Disk Group Architecture

As defined earlier in this chapter, a disk group is a collection of physical disks managed as a unit. Every ASM disk, as part of a disk group, has an ASM disk name that is either assigned by the DBA or automatically assigned when it is assigned to the disk group.

Files in a disk group are striped on the disks using either coarse striping or fine striping. *Coarse striping* spreads files in units of 1MB each across all disks. Coarse striping is appropriate for a system with a high degree of concurrent small I/O requests such as an online transaction processing (OLTP) environment. Alternatively, *fine striping* spreads files in units of 128KB and is appropriate for traditional data warehouse environments or OLTP systems with low concurrency and improves response time for individual I/O requests.

Understanding Failure Groups and Disk Group Mirroring

Before defining the type of mirroring within a disk group, you must group disks into failure groups. A *failure group* is one or more disks within a disk group that share a common resource, such as a disk controller, whose failure would cause the entire set of disks to be unavailable to the group. In most cases, an ASM instance does not know the hardware and software dependencies for a given disk. Therefore, unless you specifically assign a disk to a failure group, each disk in a disk group is assigned to its own failure group.

Once the failure groups have been defined, you can define the mirroring for the disk group; the number of failure groups available within a disk group can restrict the type of mirroring available for the disk group. The following three types of mirroring are available:

External redundancy *External redundancy* requires only one failure group and assumes that the disk is not critical to the ongoing operation of the database or that the disk is managed externally with high-availability hardware such as a RAID controller.

Normal redundancy *Normal redundancy* provides two-way mirroring and requires at least two failure groups within a disk group. The failure of one of the disks in a failure group does not cause any downtime for the disk group or any data loss other than a slight performance hit for queries against objects in the disk group.

High redundancy *High redundancy* provides three-way mirroring and requires at least three failure groups within a disk group. The failure of disks in two out of the three failure groups is for the most part transparent to the database users as in normal redundancy mirroring.

Mirroring is managed at a very low level; extents, not disks, are mirrored. In addition, each disk will have a mixture of both primary and mirrored (secondary and tertiary) extents on each disk. While there is a slight overhead incurred for managing mirroring at the extent level, it provides the advantage of spreading the load from the failed disk to all other disks instead of to a single disk.

Understanding Disk Group Dynamic Rebalancing

Whenever the configuration of a disk group changes, whether it is adding or removing a failure group or a disk within a failure group, *dynamic rebalancing* occurs automatically to proportionally reallocate data from other members of the disk group to the new member of the disk group. This rebalance occurs while the database is online and available to users; any impact to ongoing database I/O can be controlled by adjusting the value of the initialization parameter `ASM_POWER_LIMIT` to a lower value.

Not only does dynamic rebalancing free you from the tedious and often error-prone task of identifying hot spots in a disk group, it also provides an automatic way to migrate an entire database from a set of slower disks to a set of faster disks while the entire database remains online during the entire operation. The faster disks are added as two or more new failure groups in an existing disk group and the automatic rebalance occurs. The failure groups containing the slower disks are dropped, leaving a disk group with only fast disks. To make this operation even faster, both the `ADD` and `DROP` operations can be initiated within the same `ALTER DISKGROUP` command.

Creating and Deleting Disk Groups

Sometimes you may want to create a new disk group with high redundancy to hold tablespaces for an existing application. Using the view `V$ASM_DISK`, you can view all disks discovered using the initialization parameter `ASM_DISKSTRING` along with the status of the disk—in other words, whether it is assigned to an existing disk group or it is unassigned. Here is how you do that:

```
SQL> select group_number, disk_number, name,
  2      failgroup, create_date, path from v$asm_disk;
```

```
GROUP_ DISK_
NUMBER NUMBER NAME       FAILGROUP  CREATE_DA PATH

------ ------ ---------- ---------- --------- ---------
     0      0                                 /dev/raw/
                                              raw6
     0      1                                 /dev/raw/
                                              raw5
     0      2                                 /dev/raw/
                                              raw4
     0      3                                 /dev/raw/
                                              raw3
     1      1 DATA1_0001 DATA1_0001 18-APR-04 /dev/raw/
                                              raw2
     1      0 DATA1_0000 DATA1_0000 18-APR-04 /dev/raw/
                                              raw1

6 rows selected.

SQL>
```

Out of the six disks available for ASM, only two of them are assigned to a single disk group, each in their own failure group. You can obtain the disk group name from the view V$ASM_DISKGROUP, as seen here:

```
SQL> select group_number, name, type, total_mb, free_mb
  2     from v$asm_diskgroup;

GROUP_NUMBER NAME         TYPE     TOTAL_MB    FREE_MB
------------ ------------ ------ ---------- ----------
           1 DATA1        NORMAL      16378      14024

SQL>
```

Note that if you had a number of ASM disks and disk groups, you could have joined the two views on the GROUP_NUMBER column and filtered the query result by GROUP_NUMBER. Also, you see from V$ASM_DISKGROUP that the disk group DATA1 is a NORMAL REDUNDANCY group consisting of two disks.

Your first step is to create the disk group:

```
SQL> create diskgroup data2 high redundancy
  2  failgroup fg1 disk '/dev/raw/raw3' name d2a
  3  failgroup fg2 disk '/dev/raw/raw4' name d2b
  4  failgroup fg3 disk '/dev/raw/raw5' name d2c
  5  failgroup fg4 disk '/dev/raw/raw6' name d2d;

Diskgroup created.

SQL>
```

Looking at the dynamic performance views, you see the new disk group available in V$ASM_DISKGROUP and the failure groups in V$ASM_DISK:

```
SQL> select group_number, name, type, total_mb, free_mb
  2    from v$asm_diskgroup;

GROUP_NUMBER NAME         TYPE     TOTAL_MB    FREE_MB
------------ ------------ ------ ---------- ----------
           1 DATA1        NORMAL      16378      14024
           2 DATA2        HIGH        24572      24420

SQL> select group_number, disk_number, name,
  2      failgroup, create_date, path from v$asm_disk;

GROUP_ DISK_
NUMBER NUMBER NAME       FAILGROUP  CREATE_DA PATH
------ ------ ---------- ---------- --------- ---------
     2      3 D2D        FG4        11-MAY-04 /dev/raw/
                                              raw6
     2      2 D2C        FG3        11-MAY-04 /dev/raw/
                                              raw5
     2      1 D2B        FG2        11-MAY-04 /dev/raw/
                                              raw4
     2      0 D2A        FG1        11-MAY-04 /dev/raw/
                                              raw3
     1      1 DATA1_0001 DATA1_0001 18-APR-04 /dev/raw/
                                              raw2
     1      0 DATA1_0000 DATA1_0000 18-APR-04 /dev/raw/
                                              raw1

6 rows selected.
```

When you create a disk group and add a disk, you must specify FORCE if the disk has been previously used as part of a disk group. In the following example, the disk /dev/raw/raw4 was previously used as part of a disk group, so you must specify FORCE:

```
SQL> create diskgroup data2 high redundancy
  2  failgroup fg1 disk '/dev/raw/raw3' name d2a
  3  failgroup fg2 disk '/dev/raw/raw4' name d2b force
  4  failgroup fg3 disk '/dev/raw/raw5' name d2c
  5  failgroup fg4 disk '/dev/raw/raw6' name d2d;

Diskgroup created.

SQL>
```

For completeness, you can specify NOFORCE for any disk that has not been a part of a disk group in the past, but it is the default and does not need to be specified.

However, in this example, if disk space is tight, you do not need four members; for a high redundancy disk group, only three failure groups are necessary, so the disk group is dropped and recreated with only three members. Here is how you do that:

```
SQL> drop diskgroup data2;

Diskgroup dropped.

SQL> create diskgroup data2 high redundancy
  2    failgroup fg1 disk '/dev/raw/raw3' name d2a
  3    failgroup fg2 disk '/dev/raw/raw4' name d2b
  4    failgroup fg3 disk '/dev/raw/raw5' name d2c;

Diskgroup created.

SQL> select group_number, disk_number, name,
  2        failgroup, create_date, path from v$asm_disk;

GROUP_ DISK_
NUMBER NUMBER NAME       FAILGROUP  CREATE_DA PATH
------ ------ ---------- ---------- --------- ---------
     0      3                       11-MAY-04 /dev/raw/
                                              raw6
     2      2 D2C        FG3        11-MAY-04 /dev/raw/
                                              raw5
     2      1 D2B        FG2        11-MAY-04 /dev/raw/
                                              raw4
```

```
    2       0 D2A          FG1          11-MAY-04 /dev/raw/
                                                  raw3
    1       1 DATA1_0001 DATA1_0001 18-APR-04 /dev/raw/
                                                  raw2
    1       0 DATA1_0000 DATA1_0000 18-APR-04 /dev/raw/
                                                  raw1

6 rows selected.
```

If the disk group had any database objects other than disk group metadata, you would have to specify INCLUDING CONTENTS in the DROP DISKGROUP command. This is an extra safeguard to make sure that disk groups with database objects are not accidentally dropped.

Now that the configuration of the new disk group has been completed, you can create a tablespace in the new disk group from the database instance:

```
SQL> create tablespace users3 datafile '+DATA2';
Tablespace created.
```

Because ASM files are OMF, no other datafile characteristics need to be specified when creating the tablespace.

Altering Disk Groups

You can add and drop disks from a disk group. In addition, you can alter most characteristics of a disk group without recreating the disk group or impacting user transactions on objects in the disk group. In the following examples, we will show you how to perform many of the common operations that you will perform on disk groups:

- Adding a disk to a disk group
- Dropping a disk from a disk group
- Undropping a disk from a disk group
- Rebalancing an ongoing disk group operation
- Dismounting a disk group
- Checking the internal consistency of a disk group

Using *ALTER DISKGROUP … ADD DISK*

When a disk is added to a disk group, a rebalance operation is performed in the background after the new disk has been formatted for use in the disk group. As mentioned earlier in this chapter, the initialization parameter ASM_POWER_LIMIT controls the speed of the rebalance.

Continuing with one of the examples earlier in the chapter, suppose you decide to improve the I/O characteristics of the disk group DATA1 by adding the last available raw disk to the disk group, as follows:

```
SQL> alter diskgroup data1
  2     add failgroup d1fg3 disk '/dev/raw/raw6' name d1c;

Diskgroup altered.
```

The command returns immediately, and the format and rebalance continue in the background. You then check the status of the rebalance operation by checking V$ASM_OPERATION:

```
SQL> select group_number, operation, state, power, actual,
  2     sofar, est_work, est_rate, est_minutes
  3  from v$asm_operation;

GROUP_                                                EST_
NUMBER OPERA STAT POWER ACTUA SOFAR EST_WORK EST_RATE MIN
------ ----- ---- ----- ----- ----- -------- -------- ----
     1 REBAL RUN      1     1     3      964       60   16
```

This output shows that with a POWER setting of 1, the ASM operation is expected to take approximately 16 minutes more to complete. Because the estimate is a bit higher than you expected, you decide to allocate more resources to the rebalance operation and change the power limit for this particular rebalance operation:

```
SQL> alter diskgroup data1 rebalance power 8;

Diskgroup altered.
```

Checking the status of the rebalance operation confirms that the estimated time for completion in the column EST_MINUTES has been reduced to 4 minutes instead of 16:

```
SQL> select group_number, operation, state, power, actual,
  2     sofar, est_work, est_rate, est_minutes
  3  from v$asm_operation;

GROUP_                                                EST_
NUMBER OPERA STAT POWER ACTUA SOFAR EST_WORK EST_RATE MIN
------ ----- ---- ----- ----- ----- -------- -------- ----
     1 REBAL RUN      8     8    16      605      118    4
```

About four minutes later, you check the status once more:

```
SQL> /

No rows selected.
```

Finally, you can confirm the new disk configuration from the V$ASM_DISK and V$ASM_DISKGROUP views:

```
SQL> select group_number, disk_number, name,
  2   failgroup, create_date, path from v$asm_disk;

GROUP_ DISK_
NUMBER NUMBER NAME       FAILGROUP  CREATE_DA PATH
------ ------ ---------- ---------- --------- ---------
     1      2 D1C        D1FG3      11-MAY-04 /dev/raw/
                                              raw6
     2      2 D2C        FG3        11-MAY-04 /dev/raw/
                                              raw5
     2      1 D2B        FG2        11-MAY-04 /dev/raw/
                                              raw4
     2      0 D2A        FG1        11-MAY-04 /dev/raw/
                                              raw3
     1      1 DATA1_0001 DATA1_0001 18-APR-04 /dev/raw/
                                              raw2
     1      0 DATA1_0000 DATA1_0000 18-APR-04 /dev/raw/
                                              raw1

6 rows selected.

SQL> select group_number, name, type, total_mb, free_mb
  2     from v$asm_diskgroup;

GROUP_NUMBER NAME         TYPE     TOTAL_MB    FREE_MB
------------ ------------ ------ ---------- ----------
           1 DATA1        NORMAL      22521      20116
           2 DATA2        HIGH        18429      18279

SQL>
```

Note that the disk group DATA1 is still normal redundancy, even though it has three failure groups. However, the I/O performance of SELECT statements against objects in the disk group is improved because of additional copies of extents available in the disk group.

If /dev/raw/raw7 and /dev/raw/raw8 are the last remaining available disks in the command's discovery string (using the same format as the initialization parameter ASM_DISKSTRING), you can use a wildcard to add the disks:

```
SQL> alter diskgroup data1
  2      add failgroup d1fg3 disk '/dev/raw/*' name d1c;

Diskgroup altered.
```

The ALTER DISKGROUP command will ignore all disks that match the discovery string if they are already a part of this or any other disk group.

Real World Scenario

Mixing Disk Types within Disk Groups

For our shop floor scheduling and trouble ticket system, we wanted to improve the response time for technicians who checked the status of a repair job, because the application issuing the queries against the database was taking up to 10 seconds during the first shift. To help alleviate the problem, we noticed that we had two spare disk drives in the server running the Oracle 10*g* instance and put the disks to good use by using them in another failure group for the existing disk group.

After only a few minutes of testing, the performance of the queries got worse instead of better in many cases. Upon further investigation, we discovered why the extra disk drives in the server were not used for the database: They were older, slower disks, and as a rule of thumb, a disk group should not mix disk drives of different performance levels. Depending on which disk the database object's extents are mapped to, the I/O response time will vary dramatically and may actually be slower than using only the faster disks.

One situation exists where this configuration is temporarily an acceptable configuration: when converting a disk group from slower disks to faster disks. As the faster disks are added, the disk group rebalances, and once the rebalance operation is complete, the slower disks can be dropped from the disk group.

Using *ALTER DISKGROUP ... DROP DISK*

The DROP DISK clause removes a disk from a failure group within a disk group and performs an automatic rebalance. In a previous example, we dropped and re-created the entire disk group just to remove one member; it's a lot easier and less disruptive to the database to merely drop one disk from the group. Here's an example of dropping a disk from the group and monitoring the progress using the data dictionary view V$ASM_OPERATION:

```
SQL> select group_number, operation, state, power, actual,
  2      sofar, est_work, est_rate, est_minutes
```

```
  3  from v$asm_operation;

No rows selected.

SQL> alter diskgroup data2 drop disk d2d;

Diskgroup altered.

SQL> select group_number, operation, state, power, actual,
  2     sofar, est_work, est_rate, est_minutes
  3  from v$asm_operation;

GROUP_                                                EST_
NUMBER OPERA STAT POWER ACTUA SOFAR EST_WORK EST_RATE MIN
------ ----- ---- ----- ----- ----- -------- -------- ----
     2 REBAL WAIT     1     0     0        0        0    0


SQL> /

GROUP_                                                EST_
NUMBER OPERA STAT POWER ACTUA SOFAR EST_WORK EST_RATE MIN
------ ----- ---- ----- ----- ----- -------- -------- ----
     2 REBAL RUN      1     1     2      187      120    1


SQL> /

GROUP_                                                EST_
NUMBER OPERA STAT POWER ACTUA SOFAR EST_WORK EST_RATE MIN
------ ----- ---- ----- ----- ----- -------- -------- ----
     2 REBAL RUN      1     1    56      196      253    0


SQL> /

No rows selected.
SQL>
```

As you can see, the DROP DISK operation is initially in a wait state, progresses to a RUN state, and when the operation finishes, no longer appears in V$ASM_OPERATION.

Using *ALTER DISKGROUP ... UNDROP DISKS*

The UNDROP DISKS clause cancels any pending drops of a disk from a disk group. If the drop operation has completed, you must re-add the disk to the disk group manually and incur the rebalancing costs associated with adding the disk back to the disk group.

Using the example from the previous section, you will first add the disk back to the disk group, and then you will drop the disk again. Before the disk rebalance operation completes, however, you will cancel the drop with UNDROP DISKS and verify that the cancel completed successfully by joining V$ASM_DISKGROUP with V$ASM_DISK:

```
SQL> alter diskgroup data2 add failgroup fg4
  2     disk '/dev/raw/raw6' name d2d;

Diskgroup altered.

SQL> select adg.name DG_NAME,
  2      ad.name FG_NAME, path from v$asm_disk ad
  3      right outer join v$asm_diskgroup adg
  4      on ad.group_number = adg.group_number
  5  where adg.name = 'DATA2';

DG_NAME      FG_NAME      PATH
------------ ------------ --------------------
DATA2        D2A          /dev/raw/raw3
DATA2        D2B          /dev/raw/raw4
DATA2        D2C          /dev/raw/raw5
DATA2        D2D          /dev/raw/raw6

4 rows selected.

SQL> alter diskgroup data2 drop disk d2d;

Diskgroup altered.

SQL> alter diskgroup data2 undrop disks;

Diskgroup altered.
```

As you can verify with the same query you ran previously that joins V$ASM_DISKGROUP and V$ASM_DISK, the disk group still has all four disks:

```
SQL> select adg.name DG_NAME,
  2      ad.name FG_NAME, path from v$asm_disk ad
```

```
  3      right outer join v$asm_diskgroup adg
  4      on ad.group_number = adg.group_number
  5  where adg.name = 'DATA2';

DG_NAME      FG_NAME      PATH
------------ ------------ --------------------
DATA2        D2A          /dev/raw/raw3
DATA2        D2B          /dev/raw/raw4
DATA2        D2C          /dev/raw/raw5
DATA2        D2D          /dev/raw/raw6

4 rows selected.
```

If you wait too long and the DROP DISK completes, this example shows you what happens if you attempt to perform an UNDROP DISKS operation:

```
SQL> alter diskgroup data2 drop disk d2d;

Diskgroup altered.

SQL> select group_number, operation, state, power, actual,
  2     sofar, est_work, est_rate, est_minutes
  3  from v$asm_operation;

No rows selected.

SQL> select adg.name DG_NAME,
  2      ad.name FG_NAME, path from v$asm_disk ad
  3      right outer join v$asm_diskgroup adg
  4      on ad.group_number = adg.group_number
  5  where adg.name = 'DATA2';

DG_NAME      FG_NAME      PATH
------------ ------------ --------------------
DATA2        D2A          /dev/raw/raw3
DATA2        D2B          /dev/raw/raw4
DATA2        D2C          /dev/raw/raw5

3 rows selected.
```

Using *ALTER DISKGROUP ... REBALANCE POWER* n

The REBALANCE POWER *n* clause of ALTER DISKGROUP forces a rebalance operation to occur. This command is normally not necessary, because rebalance operations occur automatically when a disk is added, dropped, or modified. However, you need to use this command if you want to override the default speed of the rebalance operation as defined by the initialization parameter ASM_POWER_LIMIT. The earlier section titled "Using ALTER DISKGROUP ... ADD DISK" showed you how to perform a rebalance operation on the fly to adjust the speed of the rebalance operation.

Using *ALTER DISKGROUP ... DROP ... ADD*

The DROP and ADD combination removes a disk from a failure group and adds another disk in the same command. Instead of two rebalance operations occurring, only one occurs, saving a significant amount of CPU and I/O. In this example, you will effectively swap the disk /dev/raw/raw5 with /dev/raw/raw6:

```
SQL> select adg.name DG_NAME,
  2       ad.name FG_NAME, path from v$asm_disk ad
  3       right outer join v$asm_diskgroup adg
  4       on ad.group_number = adg.group_number
  5  where adg.name = 'DATA2';

DG_NAME      FG_NAME      PATH
------------ ------------ --------------------
DATA2        D2A          /dev/raw/raw3
DATA2        D2B          /dev/raw/raw4
DATA2        D2C          /dev/raw/raw5

3 rows selected.

SQL> alter diskgroup data2
  2     add failgroup fg4
  3        disk '/dev/raw/raw6' name d2d
  4     drop disk d2c;

Diskgroup altered.

SQL> select adg.name DG_NAME,
  2       ad.name FG_NAME, path from v$asm_disk ad
  3       right outer join v$asm_diskgroup adg
  4       on ad.group_number = adg.group_number
  5  where adg.name = 'DATA2';
```

```
DG_NAME      FG_NAME      PATH
------------ ------------ --------------------
DATA2        D2A          /dev/raw/raw3
DATA2        D2B          /dev/raw/raw4
DATA2        D2D          /dev/raw/raw6

3 rows selected.
```

As a result, only one rebalance operation is performed instead of two.

Using *ALTER DISKGROUP ... DISMOUNT*

The DISMOUNT keyword makes a disk group unavailable to all instances, as you can see in this example:

```
SQL> alter diskgroup data2 dismount;

Diskgroup altered.
```

Note that you cannot dismount a disk group unless there are no open files on the disk group and all tablespaces in the disk group are offline.

Using *ALTER DISKGROUP ... MOUNT*

The MOUNT keyword makes a disk group available to all instances. In the following example, you remount the disk group dismounted previously:

```
SQL> alter diskgroup data2 mount;

Diskgroup altered.
```

Using *ALTER DISKGROUP ... CHECK ALL*

The CHECK ALL option verifies the internal consistency of the disk group. In the following example, you will check the consistency of the DATA2 disk group:

```
SQL> alter diskgroup data2 check all;

Diskgroup altered.
```

Checking can also be specified for individual files or disks within the disk group. If any errors are found, they are automatically repaired unless you specify the NOREPAIR option. A summary message is returned from the command, and the details are reported in the alert log.

Using EM Database Control with ASM Disk Groups

You can also use EM Database Control to administer disk groups. For a database that uses ASM disk groups, the Disk Groups link in the Administration tab brings you to a login screen for the ASM instance, as shown in Figure 9.4. Remember that authentication for an ASM instance uses operating system authentication only.

After authentication with the ASM instance, you can perform the same operations that you performed earlier in this chapter at the command line: mounting and dismounting disk groups, adding disk groups, adding or deleting disk group members, and so forth. Figure 9.5 shows the ASM administration screen, and Figure 9.6 shows the statistics and options for the disk group DATA1.

Other EM Database Control ASM-related screens show information such as I/O response time for the disk group, the templates defined for the disk group, and the initialization parameters in effect for this ASM instance.

FIGURE 9.4 ASM instance authentication

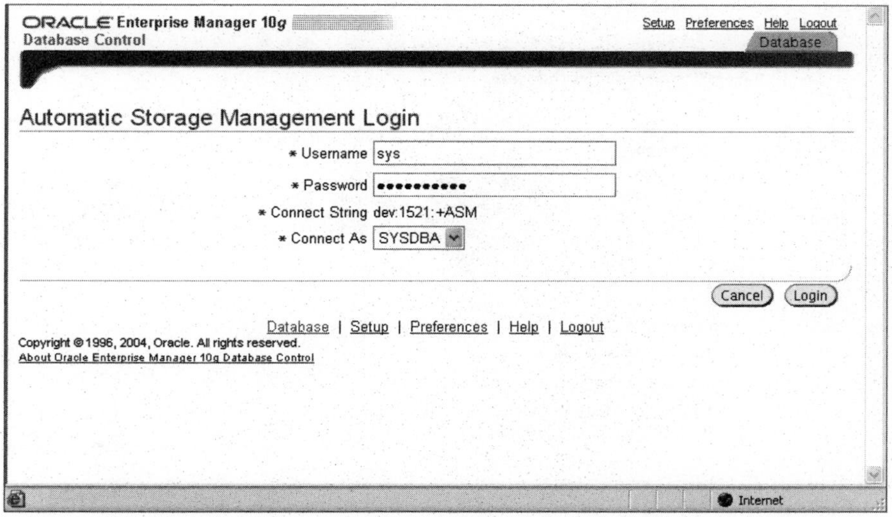

FIGURE 9.5 The ASM administration screen

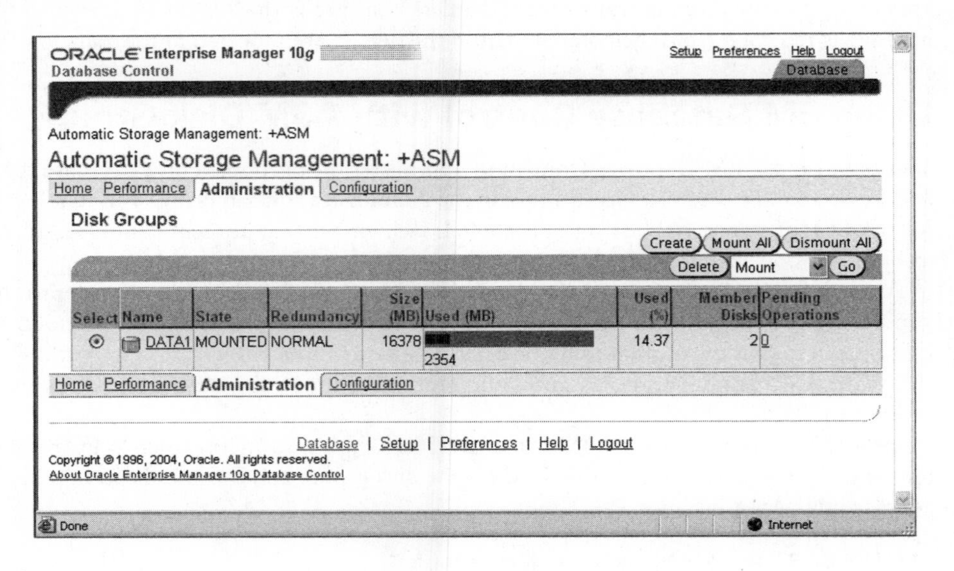

FIGURE 9.6 The disk group maintenance screen

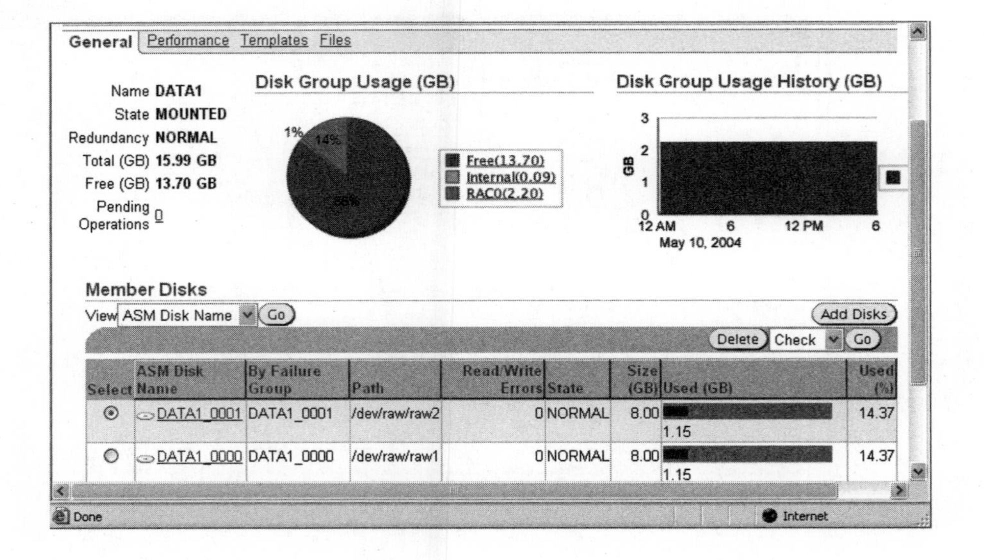

Using RMAN to Perform Database Migration to ASM

Because ASM files cannot be accessed via the operating system, you must use the Recovery Manager (RMAN) to move database objects from a non-ASM disk location to an ASM disk group. Follow these steps to move these database objects:

1. Note the filenames of the control files and the online redo log files.
2. Shut down the database using the NORMAL, IMMEDIATE, or TRANSACTIONAL keywords.
3. Back up the database.
4. Edit the SPFILE to use OMF for all file destinations.
5. Edit the SPFILE to remove the CONTROL_FILES parameter.
6. Run the following RMAN script, substituting your specific filenames as needed:

```
STARTUP NOMOUNT;
RESTORE CONTROLFILE FROM '<controlfile location>';
ALTER DATABASE MOUNT;
BACKUP AS COPY DATABASE FORMAT
   '+<disk group destination>';
SWITCH DATABASE TO COPY;
SQL "ALTER DATABASE RENAME <logfile1>
         TO '+<disk group destination>' ";
# repeat for all log file members
ALTER DATABASE OPEN RESETLOGS;
```

7. Delete or archive the old database files.

Even though all files in this example are now ASM files, you can still create a non-ASM tablespace if, for example, you want to transport a tablespace to a database that does not use ASM.

Summary

In this chapter, we showed you how Automatic Storage Management (ASM) can reduce or eliminate the headaches involved in managing the disk space for all Oracle file types, including online and archived logs, RMAN backup sets, flashback logs, and even initialization parameter files (SPFILEs).

We reviewed the concepts related to a special type of instance called an ASM instance along with the initialization parameters specific to an ASM instance. In addition, we described the dynamic performance views that allow you to view the components of an ASM disk group as well as to monitor the online rebalancing operations that occur when disks are added or removed from a disk group. Starting and stopping an ASM instance is similar to a traditional database instance, with the added dependencies of database instances that use the disk groups managed by an ASM instance and therefore will not be available to users if the ASM instance is not available to service disk group requests.

ASM filenames have a number of different formats and are used differently depending on whether existing ASM files or new ASM files are being referenced. ASM templates are used in conjunction with ASM filenames to ease the administration of ASM files.

Near the end of this chapter, we reviewed ASM disk group architecture, showing how failure groups can provide redundancy and performance benefits while at the same time eliminating the need for a third-party logical volume manager. Dynamic disk group rebalancing automatically tunes I/O performance when a disk is added or deleted from a disk group or a disk in a disk group fails. While we focused on the SQL commands necessary to manage disk groups, we also presented the EM Database Control interface for performing these same operations.

Exam Essentials

Enumerate the benefits and characteristics of Automatic Storage Management (ASM). Understand how ASM can relieve you of manually optimizing I/O across all files in the tablespace by using ASM disk groups. Show how ASM operations can be performed online with minimal impact to ongoing database transactions.

Be able to create an ASM instance and configure its initialization parameters. Understand the new initialization parameters `INSTANCE_TYPE`, `ASM_POWER_LIMIT`, `ASM_DISKSTRING`, and `ASM_DISKGROUPS`. Configure `DB_UNIQUE_NAME` and `LARGE_POOL_SIZE` for an ASM instance. Start up and shut down an ASM instance, noting the dependencies with database instances that are using the ASM instance's disk groups.

Understand the architecture of an ASM instance. Enumerate the different states for an ASM instance. Describe what happens when an ASM instance is shut down normally or is aborted. List the differences between an RDBMS instance and an ASM instance.

Understand how ASM filenames are constructed and used when creating Oracle objects. Differentiate how different ASM filename formats are used and files are created depending on whether the file is an existing ASM file, whether a new ASM file is being created, or whether multiple ASM files are being created. Understand the different system templates for creating ASM files with the associated filename and how the characteristics are applied to the ASM files. Show how ASM files are used in SQL commands.

Be able to create, drop, and alter ASM disk groups. Define multiple failure groups for new disk groups and make sure you understand how the number of failure groups is different for two-way and three-way mirroring. Show how disk rebalancing can be controlled or rolled back.

Identify the steps involved in converting non-ASM files to ASM files using RMAN. Migrate a database to ASM disk groups by shutting down the database, editing the SPFILE, running an RMAN script for each file to be converted, and opening the database with `RESETLOGS`.

Review Questions

1. Extents in an ASM file are allocated in units of which size?

   A. 100KB

   B. 10MB

   C. 1MB

   D. 64KB

2. To prevent connections to an ASM instance, you can use which of the following commands? (Choose the best answer.)

   A. ALTER SYSTEM ENABLE RESTRICTED SESSION

   B. SHUTDOWN IMMEDIATE

   C. ALTER SYSTEM DISABLE CONNECTIONS

   D. ALTER DATABASE ENABLE RESTRICTED SESSION

3. Which initialization parameter in an ASM instance specifies the disk groups to be automatically mounted at instance startup?

   A. ASM_DISKMOUNT

   B. ASM_DISKGROUP

   C. ASM_DISKSTRING

   D. ASM_MOUNTGROUP

4. Which of the following command options is not valid for an ASM instance?

   A. STARTUP OPEN

   B. STARTUP NOMOUNT

   C. STARTUP MOUNT

   D. STARTUP OPEN RESTRICT

   E. SHUTDOWN ABORT

5. When an ASM instance receives a SHUTDOWN NORMAL command, what command does it pass on to all database instances that rely on the ASM instance's disk groups?

   A. TRANSACTIONAL

   B. IMMEDIATE

   C. ABORT

   D. NORMAL

   E. None of the above

6. When creating a disk group, what keyword must be specified if you need to reuse a disk that has previously been used as part of another disk group?

   A. NOFORCE

   B. REUSE

   C. USE

   D. FORCE

   E. INCLUDING CONTENTS

7. Which of the following ASM file templates is not striped as fine?

   A. FLASHBACK

   B. ARCHIVELOG

   C. CONTROLFILE

   D. ONLINELOG

8. You want to migrate your database to ASM, so you've done a clean shutdown, made a closed backup of the entire database, noted the location of your control files and online redo log files, and changed your SPFILE to use OMF. The last step is running an RMAN script to do the conversion. Using the following steps, what is the correct order in which the following RMAN commands should be executed?

   1. STARTUP NOMOUNT

   2. ALTER DATABASE OPEN RESETLOGS

   3. SQL "ALTER DATABASE RENAME 'logfile1 path' TO '+dgrp4 '"   # plus all other log files

   4. SWITCH DATABASE TO COPY

   5. BACKUP AS COPY DATABASE FORMAT '+dgrp4'

   6. ALTER DATABASE MOUNT

   7. RESTORE CONTROLFILE FROM 'controlfile_location'

   A. 2, 5, 3, 1, 7, 6, 4

   B. 1, 7, 6, 5, 4, 3, 2

   C. 5, 1, 2, 7, 4, 6, 3

   D. 7, 3, 1, 5, 6, 2, 4

9. How can you reverse the effects of an ALTER DISKGROUP ... DROP DISK command if it has not yet completed?

   A. Issue the ALTER DISKGROUP ... ADD DISK command.

   B. Issue the ALTER DISKGROUP ... UNDROP DISKS command.

   C. Issue the ALTER DISKGROUP ... DROP DISK CANCEL command.

   D. Retrieve the disk from the recycle bin after the operation completes.

10. To reference existing ASM files, you need to use a fully qualified ASM filename. Your development database has a disk group named DG2A, the database name is DEV19, and the ASM file that you want to reference is a datafile for the USERS02 tablespace. Which of the following is a valid ASM filename for this ASM file?

    A. dev19/+DG2A/datafile/users02.701.2

    B. +DG2A/dev19/datafile/users02.701.2

    C. +DG2A/dev19/users02/datafile.701.2

    D. +DG2A.701.2

    E. +DG2A/datafile/dev19.users.02.701.2

11. Which background process coordinates the rebalance activity for disk groups?

    A. ORB*n*

    B. OSMB

    C. RBAL

    D. ASM*n*

12. On the development database rac0 there are six raw devices: /dev/raw/raw1 through /dev/raw/raw6. /dev/raw/raw1 and /dev/raw/raw2 are 8GB each, and the rest are 6GB each. An existing disk group +DATA1, of NORMAL REDUNDANCY, uses /dev/raw/raw1 and /dev/raw/raw2. Which series of the following commands will drop one of the failure groups for +DATA1, create a new disk group +DATA2 using two of the remaining four raw devices, and then cancel the drop operation from +DATA1?

    A.
    ```
    ALTER DISKGROUP DATA1 DROP DISK DATA1_0001;
    CREATE DISKGROUP DATA2 NORMAL REDUNDANCY
      FAILGROUP DATA1A DISK '/dev/raw/raw3'
      FAILGROUP DATA1B DISK '/dev/raw/raw4';
    ALTER DISKGROUP DATA1 UNDROP DISKS;
    ```

    B.
    ```
    ALTER DISKGROUP DATA1 DROP DISK DATA1_0001;
    CREATE DISKGROUP DATA2 HIGH REDUNDANCY
      FAILGROUP DATA1A DISK '/dev/raw/raw3'
      FAILGROUP DATA1B DISK '/dev/raw/raw4'
    ALTER DISKGROUP DATA1 UNDROP DISKS;
    ```

    C.
    ```
    ALTER DISKGROUP DATA1 DROP DISK DATA1_0001;
    CREATE DISKGROUP DATA2 NORMAL REDUNDANCY
      FAILGROUP DATA1A DISK '/dev/raw/raw3'
      FAILGROUP DATA1B DISK '/dev/raw/raw4';
    ALTER DISKGROUP DATA1 UNDROP DATA1_0001;
    ```

    D.
    ```
    ALTER DISKGROUP DATA1 DROP DISK DATA1_0001
      ADD DISKGROUP DATA2 NORMAL REDUNDANCY
      FAILGROUP DATA1A DISK '/dev/raw/raw3'
      FAILGROUP DATA1B DISK '/dev/raw/raw4';
    ALTER DISKGROUP DATA1 UNDROP DISKS;
    ```

13. Which type of database file is spread across all disks in a disk group?

    A. All types of files are spread across all disks in the disk group.

    B. Datafiles

    C. Redo log files

    D. Archived redo log files

    E. Control files

14. How can you reverse the effects of an ALTER DISKGROUP ... DROP DISK command if it has already completed?

    A. Issue the ALTER DISKGROUP ... ADD DISK command.

    B. Issue the ALTER DISKGROUP ... UNDROP DISKS command.

    C. Issue the ALTER DISKGROUP ... DROP DISK CANCEL command.

    D. Retrieve the disk from the recycle bin after the operation completes.

15. Which of the following ALTER DISKGROUP commands does *not* use V$ASM_OPERATION to record the status of the operation?

    A. ADD DIRECTORY

    B. DROP DISK

    C. RESIZE DISK

    D. REBALANCE

    E. ADD FAILGROUP

16. If you use ALTER DISKGROUP ... ADD DISK and specify a wildcard for the discovery string, what happens to disks that are already a part of the same or another disk group?

    A. The command fails unless you specify the FORCE option.

    B. The command fails unless you specify the REUSE option.

    C. The command must be reissued with a more specific discovery string.

    D. The other disks already part of the disk group are ignored.

17. Choose the set of the following initialization parameters that is valid and recommended for an ASM instance.

    A.
    ```
    INSTANCE_TYPE=RDBMS
    ASM_POWER_LIMIT=2
    LARGE_POOL_SIZE=8MB
    DB_UNIQUE_NAME=+ASM
    ASM_DISKGROUPS=DATA1,DATA2
    ```

    B.
    ```
    INSTANCE_TYPE=ASM
    ASM_POWER_LIMIT=2
    LARGE_POOL_SIZE=8MB
    DB_UNIQUE_NAME=+ASM
    ASM_DISKGROUPS=DATA1,DATA2
    ```

C. INSTANCE_TYPE=ASM
ASM_POWER_LIMIT=15
LARGE_POOL_SIZE=8MB
DB_UNIQUE_NAME=+ASM
ASM_DISKGROUPS=DATA1,DATA2

D. INSTANCE_TYPE=ASM
ASM_POWER_LIMIT=2
LARGE_POOL_SIZE=4MB
DB_UNIQUE_NAME=+ASM
ASM_DISKGROUPS=DATA1,DATA2

18. Which of the following scenarios concerning ASM instance shutdown is correct?

A. When an ASM instance is shut down with NORMAL, IMMEDIATE, or TRANSACTIONAL, the same shutdown command is passed to the dependent instances and the ASM instance waits for all dependent instances to shut down before it shuts down.

B. When an ASM instance shuts down with NORMAL, an alert is sent to all dependent instances, notifying the DBA to shut down the dependent instances manually before the ASM instance shuts down.

C. When an ASM instance shuts down with the TRANSACTIONAL option, all dependent instances shut down with NORMAL, IMMEDIATE, or TRANSACTIONAL, depending on the dependent database's default.

D. When an ASM instance is shut down with NORMAL, IMMEDIATE, or TRANSACTIONAL, the same shutdown command is passed to the dependent instances and the ASM instance does not wait for all dependent instances to shut down before it shuts down.

E. When an ASM instance shuts down with the IMMEDIATE option, the ASM instance shuts down immediately and all dependent instances shut down with ABORT.

19. A database can create datafiles in how many different disk groups? (Choose the best answer.)

A. Each datafile in the database can reside in a different disk group.

B. One

C. Disk groups manage tablespaces, not datafiles.

D. A maximum of two, one for SYSTEM and SYSAUX and the other tablespaces in another disk group.

20. ASM supports all of the following file types except for which of the following? (Choose all that apply.)

A. Database files

B. SPFILEs

C. Redo log files

D. Archived log files

E. RMAN backup sets

F. Password files

G. init.ora files

Answers to Review Questions

1. C. ASM disks are partitioned in allocation units of one megabyte each.

2. A. Similar to an RDBMS instance, you can use ALTER SYSTEM ENABLE RESTRICTED SESSION to prevent connections to the instance. While SHUTDOWN IMMEDIATE will prevent connections to the ASM instance, this is most likely overkill if all you want to do is temporarily prevent connections. Choices C and D are not valid commands and will generate an error message.

3. B. The initialization parameter ASM_DISKGROUP, valid only in an ASM instance, specifies the disk groups to be automatically mounted when the ASM instance starts. ASM_DISKSTRING is operating system dependent and restricts the file system devices that can be used to create disk groups. ASM_DISKMOUNT and ASM_MOUNTGROUP are not valid initialization parameters.

4. A. An ASM instance can be started up and shut down in the same way that an RDBMS database can, except that an ASM instance cannot be in the OPEN state because it does not have a data dictionary or a control file.

5. D. When an ASM instance receives a SHUTDOWN command, it passes the same option (NORMAL, IMMEDIATE or TRANSACTIONAL) to all database instances that rely on the ASM instance for disk group services.

6. D. You must use FORCE if the disk has previously been used as part of a disk group. If the disk has never been used as part of a disk group, using the FORCE keyword returns an error.

7. B. Files such as ARCHIVELOG files use coarse-grained striping. Fine striping stripes the files every 128KB while coarse striping stripes the files every 1MB. All file types with the exception of FLASHBACK, CONTROLFILE, and ONLINELOG are striped coarse.

8. B. After the RMAN script is run and the database is up and running successfully, you may delete the old database files.

9. B. If the DROP DISK operation has not yet completed, you can cancel and roll back the entire DROP DISK operation by using ALTER DISKGROUP ... UNDROP DISKS, with the disk group still being continuously available to all users.

10. B. A fully qualified existing ASM filename has the format *+group/dbname/filetype/tag.file.incarnation*. In this case, *filetype* is datafile, and *tag* is the tablespace name to which it belongs, or users02.

11. C. RBAL coordinates rebalance activity for a disk group in an ASM instance, ORB*n* actually performs the extent movement in an ASM instance, and OSMB acts as a bridge between the ASM instance and the RDBMS instance. There is no such process name ASM*n*.

12. A. Note that the UNDROP operation will cancel a drop operation in progress but cannot reverse a drop operation that has already completed. For HIGH REDUNDANCY, at least three failure groups must be specified. While you can combine a drop and add operation into one command, the command can reference only one disk group.

13. A. All types of database files are spread across all disks in the disk group to ensure redundancy unless the redundancy is set to EXTERNAL.

14. A. If the DROP DISK operation has already completed, you must use ALTER DISKGROUP … ADD DISK to add the disk back to the disk group. In any case, the disk group is continuously available to all users.

15. A. The ADD DIRECTORY command does not use V$ASM_OPERATION to track its progress, because this operation adds only a small amount of metadata—a directory object—to the disk group and takes a minimal amount of time to complete.

16. D. The ALTER DISKGROUP … ADD DISK command adds all disks that match the discovery string but are not already part of the same or another disk group.

17. B. The INSTANCE_TYPE for an ASM instance is ASM; otherwise, it is RDBMS, whether it uses ASM or not. The ASM_POWER_LIMIT command controls the speed of a disk group rebalance, but its maximum value is 11. For an ASM instance, the minimum recommended value for LARGE_POOL_SIZE is 8MB.

18. A. When an ASM instance shuts down with NORMAL, IMMEDIATE, or TRANSACTIONAL, the same shutdown option is passed to all dependent instances and the ASM instance waits for the dependent instances to shut down before shutting itself down. If an ASM instance shuts down with ABORT, it immediately shuts down, the dependent instances lose their connection to the ASM instance, and as a result, they shut down with ABORT either before or after the ASM instance shuts down completely.

19. A. Each database datafile can reside in a different disk group; each disk group can also contain datafiles from other databases.

20. F, G. ASM supports datafiles, log files, control files, archive logs, RMAN backup sets, SPFILEs, and other Oracle database file types, but not password files or init.ora files.

Understanding Globalization Support

ORACLE DATABASE 10*G*: ADMINISTRATION II EXAM OBJECTIVES COVERED IN THIS CHAPTER:

✓ **Using Globalization Support**

- Customize language-dependent behavior for the database and individual sessions.
- Specify different linguistic sorts for queries.
- Use datetime datatypes.
- Query data using case-insensitive and accent-insensitive searches.
- Obtain Globalization support configuration information.

Exam objectives are subject to change at any time without prior notice and at Oracle's sole discretion. Please visit Oracle's Training and Certification website (`http://www.oracle.com/education/certification/`) for the most current exam objectives listing.

Doing business on a global scale presents a new set of challenges to any company, especially to the DBA. Beyond the obvious issues of language lie a host of less obvious but equally important issues that must be addressed—time zone differences, mixed currency types, and differing calendars, just to name a few. But Oracle's globalization support features provide the tools needed to meet these challenges.

Globalization support enables you to manage data in multiple languages. It provides the functionality to ensure that native language and locale conventions are followed when dealing with date, time, currency, numeric, and calendar data.

Globalization support also offers new *datetime datatype* options for handling transactions crossing time zones. It also provides a rich set of options for *linguistic sorts* and searching.

In this chapter, you will see how, with the release of Oracle Database 10*g* (Oracle 10*g*), Oracle has positioned itself as the database of choice for companies doing business internationally. You'll learn what globalization support entails and how it all fits together. You'll see how *National Language Support (NLS)* parameter settings can change the functionality of many of Oracle's operations. You will learn about datetime datatypes and how they can be used to synchronize data around the globe. You'll also learn about new linguistic sorting and searching options that allow multilingual data to be searched, sorted, and managed simply and efficiently.

An Overview of Globalization Support

Oracle's globalization support is a collection of features that allow you to manage data in multiple native languages within the same database instance. It also greatly simplifies application development by offering a rich set of globalization functionality to the developer.

Globalization support provides the character sets and datatypes needed to store multilingual data. It ensures that date, time, monetary, numeric, and calendar data will follow any supported *locale* conventions and display properly. It provides utilities and error messages translated to many different languages. It also provides the internal functionality to sort and to query multilingual data using proper linguistic rules.

In the following sections, you will learn about Oracle's globalization support features. You will get an overview of each feature and the functionality that it provides.

You will learn about the underlying architecture upon which globalization support is built. You'll be introduced to the *National Language Support Runtime Library (NLSRTL)* and see how its modular design provides flexibility and saves resources.

You will also learn how applications interact with Oracle from a globalization perspective.

And finally, you will be introduced to *Unicode* and the advantages that it offers in a multilingual environment.

Globalization Support Features

Globalization support provides a rich set of functionality to the Oracle database. But it is important to make two distinctions perfectly clear regarding what globalization support does not do:

- Globalization support does not translate text into different languages.
- Globalization does not control how multilingual text is displayed on client machines.

Globalization support simply provides the infrastructure to allow text to be stored, manipulated, sorted, and searched in many languages using linguistically significant means. It also allows the data to be displayed using the standard conventions for a specific region.

Globalization support includes these features:

Language support Globalization support allows data to be stored, processed, and retrieved in virtually any scripted language. For many of these languages, Oracle also provides additional support such as text-sorting conventions, date-formatting conventions (including translated month names), and even error message and utility interface translation.

Territory support Cultural conventions often differ between geographical locations. For example, local time format, date format, and numeric and monetary conventions can differ significantly between regions, even though they may share a common language. To allow for these differences, the `NLS_TERRITORY` parameter can be used to define which conventions to follow.

However, these default settings can still be overridden through the use of NLS parameter settings. Overriding the default settings allows finer granularity in defining and customizing display formats to account for special circumstances. For example, it is possible to set the primary currency to the Japanese yen and the secondary currency to the dollar even with the territory defined as India.

Linguistic sorting and searching Globalization support offers culturally accurate case conversion, sorting, and searching for all supported languages. It offers the ability to search and sort based on the rules of language rather than simply on the order in which the characters are encoded in the character set. It also offers *case-insensitive sorts* and searches as well as *accent-insensitive sorts* and searches.

Linguistic sorts are defined separately from the language itself, allowing the ability to share sort definitions between languages. Linguistic sort defaults can also be overridden through the use of NLS parameter settings. This allows you the flexibility to customize your environment as needed.

Character sets and semantics Oracle supports a vast number of character sets based on national and international standards, including Unicode. Being offered a wide variety of *character sets*, users can often find one that supports all of the languages needed in a single set.

Unicode is a universal character set that supports all known written languages. Oracle offers full support of the Unicode 3.2 standard and offers several Unicode encoding options.

Unicode can be defined as the database character set, making it the default datatype for all character columns. If Unicode is not defined as the database character set, it can still be used by defining specific columns as *Unicode datatypes* (in other words, NCHAR, NVARCHAR2, NCLOB).

Many multi-byte character sets use variable widths when storing data. This means that, depending on the character being stored, Oracle may use anywhere from one to four bytes to store it. Therefore, defining column widths in terms of the number of characters, rather than the number of bytes, becomes crucial. *Character semantics* allow character data to be specified in terms of the number of characters, regardless of the number of bytes actually required. *Byte semantics*, the default, assume a single byte character set, where one character always requires one byte of storage.

While Unicode may seem like the logical choice for any database, the decision to use it needs to be weighed carefully. There are performance and space usage penalties associated with using Unicode. If a smaller code set is available that encompasses all of the languages you are likely to ever need, then the overhead of Unicode makes it an illogical choice.

Calendars Different geographic areas often utilize different calendar systems, which can make international transactions hard to synchronize. Oracle supports seven distinct calendar systems: Gregorian, Japanese Imperial, ROC (Republic of China) Official, Thai Buddha, Persian, English Hijrah, and Arabic Hijrah. Globalization support offers functionality to resolve calendar system differences.

Locale and calendar customization Oracle's Locale Builder utility allows customization of globalization definitions, including language, character set, territory, and linguistic sorting. Calendars can also be customized using the NLS Calendar utility. Coverage of Locale Builder and the NLS Calendar utilities fall outside the scope of this book.

Globalization Support Architecture

Globalization support in Oracle 10*g* is implemented through the Oracle National Language Support Runtime Library (NLSRTL). The NLSRTL offers a set of language-independent text and character-processing functions, as well as functions for language convention manipulation. The behavior of these algorithms is determined at runtime (database startup), as the name suggests.

At database startup time, NLSRTL looks for a file named *lx1boot.nlb*. This file defines the set of locale definitions available to the database. To determine where to look for this file, NLSRTL will first check the environment for the existence of an ORA_NLS10 variable.

If ORA_NLS10 is defined, it will contain the path to where the lx1boot.nlb file resides. If the variable is not set, the default location of $ORACLE_HOME/nls/data will be used instead.

By default, ORA_NLS10 is not set. It should be set only in a multi-homed environment where the locale-specific files are shared.

The `lx1boot.nlb` file identifies the set of locales available to the NLSRTL. These locales are defined in a collection of *locale definition files* that reside in the same directory as the `lx1boot.nlb` file.

There are four types of locale definition files:

- Language
- Territory
- Character set
- Linguistic sort

Each file contains data relating to only one particular locale type. For each locale type, there can be many different definition files.

For example, one language file will exist for French, one for Italian, and so on. In fact, there are approximately 66 different language files, 120 different territory files, 86 different character sets, and 8 different linguistic sorts.

This modular design of the locale definition files offers several distinct benefits, including the following:

- By using only the set of locales that you need, memory won't be wasted on unnecessary locales.
- Locale definitions can be mixed and matched.
- Locale files can be modified without affecting any other files.
- New locale files can be created without affecting existing files.

All the locale definition files follow the common naming convention:

Code	Position	Meaning
`lx`	1–2	The standard prefix for all locale definition files
t	3	Represents the locale type: 0 = language 1 = territory 2 = character set 3 = linguistic sort
nnnn	4–7	The object ID (in Hex)
`.nlb`	8–11	The standard extension for all locale definition files

For example, the file `lx1001b.nlb` would represent a territory with a territory ID of 0x001B (decimal 27), as shown in Figure 10.1. This happens to be the territory of Algeria.

The complete set of locale definition files represents the globalization options available inside the database. Locale definitions can also be added or modified to support new functionality.

FIGURE 10.1 Locale definition file lx001b.nlb

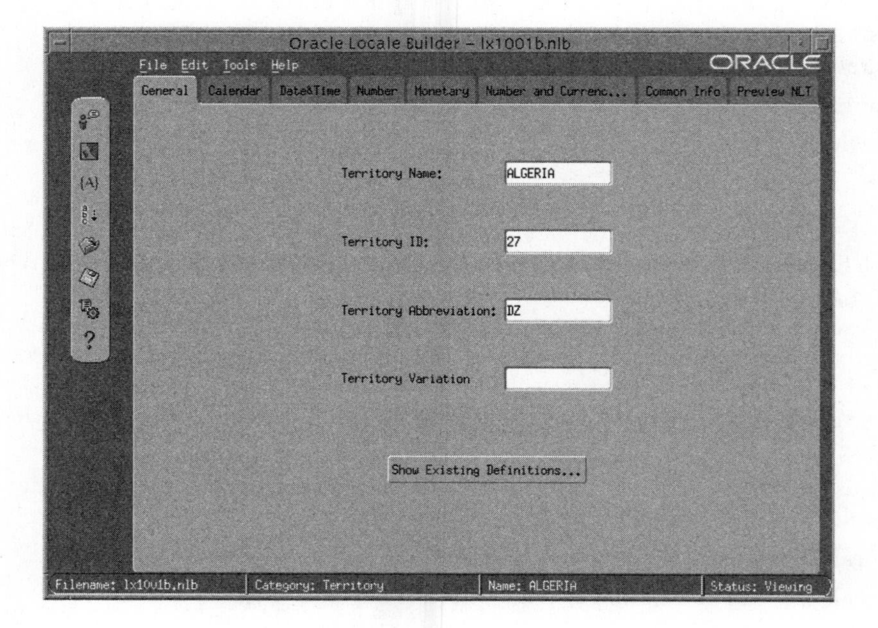

Supporting Multilingual Applications

Globalization allows the database to support multi-tier and client/server applications in any language for which it is configured. Locale-dependent operations are governed by NLS parameters and NLS environment variables set on both the client and server sides.

In this section, you will learn how client applications interact with the server from a globalization viewpoint. You will learn the purpose of the character sets defined at database creation time. You'll learn how data conversion issues can affect session performance. And finally, you'll learn how clients resolve globalization environment differences when they connect to a server.

Database Character Sets

When a database is created, two session-independent NLS parameters are specified: the *database character set* and the *national character set*.

The database character set defines the character set that will govern default text storage in the database. This includes all CHAR, VARCHAR2, LONG, and fixed-width CLOB data as well as all SQL and PL/SQL text.

The national character set is an alternate Unicode character set that governs NCHAR, NVARCHAR2, and NCLOB data.

Together, these two settings define the available character sets for the database.

Automatic Data Conversion

When a client makes a connection to a database server, the character sets used on both the client and server are compared. If they do not match, Oracle will need to perform automatic data conversion to resolve the difference. There is overhead involved in this conversion process as well as a risk of data loss. Performance will be affected relative to the level of conversion required.

The exception to this rule is when the database character set is a strict *superset* of the client character set. Two things must be true in order to classify a character set as a strict superset of another:

- The superset must contain all of the characters defined in the subset.
- The encoded values of all characters defined in the subset must match their encoded values in the superset.

If Oracle determines that both of these requirements are met, it will not perform automatic data conversion, because it is not necessary.

Resolving Client/Server Settings

Any application that connects to the server is considered to be a client, in terms of globalization. Even if the application lives on the same physical machine as the server, it will still be classified as a client. This includes middle-tier application servers. Therefore, from a globalization perspective, all applications are governed by client-side NLS parameters.

When a client application is run, the client NLS environment is initialized from the environment variable settings. All local NLS operations are executed using these settings. *Local NLS operations* are client operations performed independently of any Oracle server session (for example, display formatting in Oracle Developer applications).

When the application completes a connection to the database server, the resulting session is initialized with the NLS environment settings of the server.

However, immediately after the session is established, the client implicitly issues an ALTER SESSION statement to synchronize the session NLS environment to match the client's NLS environment. In fact, the session environment can be modified at any time by using the ALTER SESSION statement, as shown here:

```
SQL*Plus: Release 10.1.0.2.0 - Production on Sat Aug 28 14:02:56 2004

Copyright (c) 1982, 2004, Oracle.  All rights reserved.
```

```
Connected to:
Oracle Database 10g Enterprise Edition Release 10.1.0.2.0 - Production
With the Partitioning, OLAP and Data Mining options

SQL> select sysdate from dual;

SYSDATE
---------
28-AUG-04

SQL> alter session set NLS_LANGUAGE=French;

Session altered.

SQL> select sysdate from dual;

SYSDATE
-----------
28-AOÛT -04

SQL> alter session set NLS_LANGUAGE=Italian;

Session altered.

SQL> select sysdate from dual;

SYSDATE
---------
28-AGO-04
```

Remember, however, that using `ALTER SESSION` changes only the session NLS environment. It does not change the client NLS environment.

Using Unicode in a Multilingual Database

Unicode is a universal character set that encompasses all known written languages in the world. Historically, dealing with multiple languages in a database or an application has been a difficult proposition. Existing character sets have always been too limited. Many don't even offer all the characters required for a single language, much less for all languages!

To support a wide variety of languages, it often meant that applications, databases, and programs using different character sets would have to be able to interact and exchange data, all with proper data conversion taking place every step of the way.

To address this problem, Unicode was created with this simple motto:

> Unicode provides a unique number for every character,
> no matter what the platform,
> no matter what the program,
> no matter what the language.
>
> Source: `http://www.unicode.org/standard/WhatIsUnicode.html`

Unicode assigns a guaranteed unique value (known as a *code point*) to every character to assure that no conflicts exist. Oracle supports version 3.2 of Unicode and offers the encoding methods listed in Table 10.1.

Unicode can be used in Oracle in several ways:

- It can be defined as the database character set, thereby becoming the default for all SQL `CHAR` datatypes (`CHAR`, `VARCHAR2`, `CLOB`, and `LONG`). In this setup, the UTF-8 encoding method will be used.
- It can be used as needed by creating columns using the `NCHAR` datatypes, also known as Unicode datatypes (`NCHAR`, `NVARCHAR2`, and `NCLOB`). Unicode data can be encoded as either UTF-8 or UTF-16 when used in this scenario.

TABLE 10.1 Oracle-Supported Unicode Encoding Methods

Encoding Method	Description
UTF-8	An eight-bit encoding method that uses one to four bytes to store characters, as needed. UTF-8 is a strict superset of ASCII, meaning that every character in the ASCII character set is not only represented in the UTF-8 character set, but that they have the same code point value in both character sets. UTF-8 is supported on Unix platforms, HTML, and most Internet browsers.
UCS-2	A fixed-width, 16-bit encoding method, meaning that each character is stored in two bytes. Both Microsoft Windows NT and Java support UCS-2 encoding. UCS-2 supports the older Unicode 3 standard; therefore it does not support supplementary characters.
UTF-16	A strict superset of UCS-2 and offers support of supplementary characters by using two UCS-2 code points for each supplementary character. Newer versions of Windows (2000, XP) are based on this encoding method.

Using NLS Parameters

Ultimately, Oracle globalization support options are defined by NLS parameter settings. By assigning values to specific NLS parameters, you can control when, where, and how Oracle will utilize globalization support functionality. These settings can be specified in a variety of ways, and their effects may vary accordingly.

On the server side, NLS parameters are read from initialization parameter settings at instance startup time. The values are stored in the data dictionary, as are the database and national character set settings.

On the client side, NLS parameters can be defined as environment variables (such as `NLS_LANG`), or they can be set at the session level by using the `ALTER SESSION` statement. NLS parameters can also be defined inside SQL function calls with a scope limited to only the current function. Therefore, it is vital to understand the order of precedence that Oracle follows concerning NLS parameter settings.

In the following sections, you'll learn about many of the different NLS parameters, how to set them, and what effect they will have on the system. You'll also learn how Oracle prioritizes NLS parameter settings. Lastly, you will learn how to use NLS data dictionary and dynamic performance views to access NLS information from the database.

Setting NLS Parameters

Oracle's globalization support is designed to be very simple to use. In many environments, globalization needs can be met by setting a single client side parameter (`NLS_LANG`). This is because Oracle automatically derives lower-level specifics from the high-level settings. For instance, if the `NLS_TERRITORY` parameter is set to `AMERICA`, Oracle assumes that currency should be displayed as dollars, commas should be used to separate thousands of dollars, and so on.

However, the granularity provided by Oracle's globalization support allows almost unlimited variations for users with even the most demanding globalization needs.

NLS parameters can be classified into the following categories:

- Language and territory parameters
- Date and time parameters
- Calendar parameters
- Numeric, list, and monetary parameters
- Length semantics

Each category offers one or more individual parameters that can be set to meet your exact globalization needs.

In the following sections, you will learn how to set the `NLS_LANG` client-side environment variable to specify the NLS environment for your session. You'll also learn about each of the different categories of NLS parameter settings, and the different options they offer.

Using the *NLS_LANG* Parameter

NLS_LANG is a client-side environment variable that defines the language, territory, and character set for the client. It is functionally equivalent to setting the NLS_LANGUAGE, NLS_TERRITORY, and NLS_CHARACTERSET parameters individually.

For most clients, the NLS_LANG parameter is all that needs to be set to define the entire globalization environment. This is true because the NLS_LANGUAGE and NLS_TERRITORY settings define the default settings for nearly all other NLS parameters.

The NLS_LANGUAGE parameter, for instance, specifies the default conventions to be used for all of the following globalization elements:

- Language for server messages
- Day and month names and abbreviations
- Symbols to represent AM, PM, AD, and BC
- Sorting sequence for character data
- Affirmative and negative response strings (YES, NO)

The NLS_TERRITORY parameter specifies the default conventions used for these globalization elements:

- Date format
- Decimal character
- Group separator
- Local currency symbol
- ISO currency symbol
- Dual currency symbol
- First day of the week
- Credit/debit symbols
- ISO week flag
- List separator

Therefore, no other NLS parameters need to be set unless the default settings don't meet your needs.

The format for setting the NLS_LANG parameter is as follows:

```
NLS_LANG = language_territory.characterset
```

For example, the following are all valid:

```
NLS_LANG=AMERICAN_AMERICA.US7ASCII
NLS_LANG=JAPANESE_JAPAN.JA16EUC
NLS_LANG=FRENCH_CANADA.WE8ISO8859P1
```

The language element controls the conventions used for Oracle messages, sorting, day, and month names. If language is not set, Oracle will default to AMERICAN. Each language is identified by a unique name such as FRENCH or GERMAN. Languages also impose a default territory and character set that will be used unless overridden.

The territory element determines the default date, monetary format, and numeric format conventions. If the territory is not defined, the default territory value from the language setting will be used. Territories carry distinct names such as AMERICA, CANADA, or GERMANY.

The character set element determines the client character set. Normally this would be the Oracle character set that matches the character set of the operating system or terminal. Character sets have unique identifiers such as WE8ISO8859P1, US7ASCII, or JA16EUC.

All NLS_LANG definition components are optional. For example, the following is valid to set the language component independently of the other components:

```
NLS_LANG=FRENCH
```

It is also possible to set the territory and character set components independently, but the following conventions must be followed:

- Territory must be preceded by an underscore character (_).
- Character set must be preceded by a period (.).

For example, to set the territory to AMERICA, you could use this syntax:

```
NLS_LANG=_AMERICA
```

Oracle Character Set Naming Convention

The naming convention for Oracle character sets is as follows:

```
region number_of_bits standard_character_set_name [S][C]
```

where

- *region* is generally a two-character abbreviation (US, WE, JA).
- *number_of_bits* represents the number of bits used to store one character.
- *standard_character_set_name* represents the common name for the character set. This name can vary in length (ASCII, ISO8859P1, SJIS).
- The optional S and C are used to specify character sets that are exclusive to the server (S) or the client (C) side.

For example, US7ASCII is a seven-bit United States code commonly referred to as ASCII (American Standard Code for Information Interchange).

The Unicode character sets UTF-8 and UTF-E defy Oracle's standard character set naming convention.

To set the client character set to UTF-8, you could use this syntax:

```
NLS_LANG=.UTF8
```

Use caution when setting NLS_LANG. It is possible to make combinations that will not function correctly, such as specifying a character set that does not support the specified language.

In the following example, you'll set the NLS_LANG parameter to FRENCH_FRANCE.WEISO8859P1 and see how this affects your session. Remember that NLS_LANG is an environment variable setting, so it must be set in the operating system before connecting to Oracle:

```
$ export NLS_LANG=French_France.WE8ISO8859P1
$ sqlplus "/ as sysdba"

SQL*Plus: Release 10.1.0.2.0 - Production on Dim. Août 29 23:11:07 2004

Copyright (c) 1982, 2004, Oracle.  All rights reserved.


Connected to:
Oracle Database 10g Enterprise Edition Release 10.1.0.2.0 - Production
With the Partitioning, OLAP and Data Mining options

SQL> select prod_id, time_id,
round(sum(amount_sold),2) amount
from sh.sales
group by prod_id, time_id;

   PROD_ID TIME_ID  AMOUNT
---------- -------- -------------------------
       140 23/02/98                    831,08
       140 02/03/98                   1427,66
       140 08/03/98                   1432,76
       140 18/03/98                    1916,1
       140 23/03/98                    894,18
       140 27/03/98                   1234,82
       146 02/01/98                    587,39
       146 18/01/98                     606,6
       146 23/01/98                    419,75
       146 27/01/98                    436,54
```

```
146 02/02/98                    402,96
140 02/02/98                   1091,74
140 03/02/98                     247,5
140 14/02/98                   1447,72
140 16/02/98                     41,09
```

As you can see in this example, the date and number formats follow the conventions established in the NLS_LANG settings.

Using Language and Territory Parameters

NLS language and territory functionality can also be defined individually using the NLS_LANGUAGE and NLS_TERRITORY parameters.

On the server side, these parameters can be set as initialization parameters. They will then become the default settings for the Oracle instance. For example, the following lines could be inserted into the INIT.ORA file:

```
NLS_LANGUAGE=French
NLS_TERRITORY=France
```

When the database instance is next started, these settings will become the default settings for the instance.

On the client side, these parameters can be set within a session by using the ALTER SESSION statement, as shown here:

```
SQL> alter session set NLS_LANGUAGE=French;

Session altered.

SQL> alter session set NLS_TERRITORY=France;

Session altered.
```

NLS parameters modified using ALTER SESSION have a higher precedence than those set through environment variables such as NLS_LANG. Therefore, they will override the previously set parameter values. This topic will be covered later in this chapter.

Using Date and Time Parameters

NLS date and time functionality can also be defined individually using the following NLS parameters:

- NLS_DATE_FORMAT
- NLS_DATE_LANGUAGE

- NLS_TIMESTAMP_FORMAT
- NLS_TIMESTAMP_TZ_FORMAT

All of these parameters can be set within a session by using the ALTER SESSION statement. They can also be defined as initialization parameters and will then become default settings for the entire instance.

NLS_DATE_FORMAT

The NLS_DATE_FORMAT parameter specifies the default format for dates in the current session. It can be defined as any valid date format mask such as:

```
SQL> ALTER SESSION SET NLS_DATE_FORMAT = MM/DD/YY;

Session altered.
```

You can even append text literals into the date format, if you wish, by enclosing the literal in double quotes. You must also enclose the entire format string in apostrophes (single quotes), as shown here:

```
SQL> alter session set NLS_DATE_FORMAT ='"Today''s date is "MM/DD/YYYY';

Session altered.

SQL> select sysdate from dual;

SYSDATE
--------------------------
Today's date is 08/30/2004
```

Note that normal quoting rules apply inside the text literal. Therefore, two apostrophes were required to create the string "Today's".

NLS_DATE_LANGUAGE

The NLS_DATE_LANGUAGE parameter governs the language used in the following situations:

- Day and month names and abbreviations displayed by the functions TO_CHAR and TO_DATE
- Day and month names returned by the default date format (NLS_DATE_FORMAT)
- Abbreviations for AM, PM, AD, and BC

NLS_DATE_LANGUAGE accepts any valid language as a value and can be set as shown here:

```
SQL> alter session set nls_date_language=Italian;

Session altered.
```

```
SQL> select to_char(sysdate,'Day:Dd Month YYYY') from dual;

TO_CHAR(SYSDATE,'DAY:DDMONT
---------------------------
Lunedì    :30 Agosto    2004
```

NLS_TIMESTAMP_FORMAT

The NLS_TIMESTAMP_FORMAT parameter is used to set the default date format for both TIMESTAMP and TIMESTAMP WITH TIME ZONE datatypes. An example is shown here:

```
SQL> alter session set nls_timestamp_format='MM/DD/YYYY HH24:MI:SS.FF';

Session altered.

SQL> select startup_time
  2  from sys.dba_hist_snapshot
  3  where rownum < 3;

STARTUP_TIME
---------------------------------------------------------------------------
10/22/2004 08:06:09:000
10/22/2004 08:06:09:000


SQL> select next_run_date
  2  from sys.dba_scheduler_jobs;

NEXT_RUN_DATE
---------------------------------------------------------------------------
2004/11/12 03:00 -05:00
```

The TIMESTAMP and TIMESTAMP WITH TIME ZONE datatypes will be covered later in this chapter.

NLS_TIMESTAMP_TZ_FORMAT

Like the NLS_TIMESTAMP_FORMAT parameter, the NLS_TIMESTAMP_TZ_FORMAT parameter is used to set the default date format for TIMESTAMP and TIMESTAMP WITH TIME ZONE datatypes. However, as the name suggests, it adds the option of time zone formatting, as shown here:

```
SQL> alter session set nls_timestamp_tz_format = 'YYYY/MM/DD HH:MI TZH:TZM';

Session altered.
```

```
SQL> select startup_time
  2  from sys.dba_hist_snapshot
  3  where rownum < 3;

STARTUP_TIME
---------------------------------------------------------------------------
10/22/2004 08:06:09:000
10/22/2004 08:06:09:000


SQL> select next_run_date
  2  from sys.dba_scheduler_jobs;

NEXT_RUN_DATE
---------------------------------------------------------------------------
2004/11/12 03:00 -05:00
```

As you can see in the example, the `TZH:TZM` element shows the time zone offset in hours and minutes.

Using Calendar Parameters

Different geographical areas can use different calendaring systems. Oracle 10*g*'s globalization support defines seven distinct calendars, all of which are fully supported:

- Gregorian
- Japanese Imperial
- ROC Official
- Persian
- Thai Buddha
- Arabic Hijrah
- English Hijrah

For each of these calendars, the following information is maintained:

First day of the week While the United States and many other countries consider Sunday to represent the first day of the week, other countries, such as Germany, consider Monday to be the first day of the week.

First calendar week of the year Many countries use the week number for things like bookkeeping and scheduling. However, an International Standards Organization (ISO) week can differ from the calendar week number. (ISO weeks run from Monday through Sunday.) Oracle supports both conventions.

Number of days/months in a year The number of days and months in a year can differ between calendars, as shown in Table 10.2.

First year of the era Different regions may also choose a notable year in which to start, much like the Gregorian calendar starts with Anno Domini (Latin for "the year of the Lord"), also known as the Common Era. The Islamic calendar, for example, starts with the year of the Hegria (622 AD, when the prophet Mohammed and his followers migrated from Mecca to Medina).

The NLS_CALENDAR parameter is used to specify which calendar Oracle should use, as shown here:

```
SQL> alter session set NLS_CALENDAR = 'Persian';

Session altered.

SQL> select sysdate from dual;

SYSDATE
------------------
10 Shahruoar  1383
```

TABLE 10.2 International Calendar Days/Months in a Year

Calendar	Description
Gregorian	The standard calendar used by most of the world. The Gregorian calendar has 365 days in each year, with 366 days on leap years. The number of days in a month varies. Years are counted from the beginning of the common era or Anno Domini.
Japanese Imperial	Same as Gregorian, but the year starts with the beginning of each Imperial era.
ROC Official	Same as Gregorian, but the year starts with the founding of the Republic of China.
Persian	The first six months have 31 days each. The next five have 30 days each. The last month has 29 days (30 in a leap year).
Thai Buddha	Same as Gregorian, but the year begins with B.E. (Buddhist Era), which starts with the death of Gautama Buddha.
Arabic Hijrah	Has 12 months with 354 or 355 days.
English Hijrah	Has 12 months with 354 or 355 days.

Using Numeric, List, and Monetary Parameters

Number-formatting conventions define how Oracle should display large numbers and numeric lists.

In the United States, for example, the following convention is followed:

1,234,567.89

Germany, on the other hand, uses a convention that is diametrically opposite:

1.234.567,89

In this section, you'll learn to use the various numeric, list, and monetary NLS parameters.

NLS_NUMERIC_CHARACTERS

The NLS_NUMERIC_CHARACTERS parameter defines the characters that represent the decimal and group separator (for example, thousands, millions, and so on) elements in the number format mask. These elements are represented by the letters *D* and *G* respectively in the number format mask. Any single-byte character can be assigned, with the following exceptions:

- The decimal character and the group separator cannot be the same character.
- They cannot be numeric.
- They cannot have mathematical significance (+, –, <, >).

When setting this parameter, the decimal character comes before the group separator, as shown here:

```
SQL> alter session set NLS_NUMERIC_CHARACTERS=",.";

Session altered.

SQL> select cust_id, to_char(sum(amount_sold), '9G999G999D99') big_sales
from sales
group by cust_id
having sum(amount_sold) > 30000;

CUST_ID    BIG_SALES
---------- -------------
      2994     30.200,18
      3618     30.312,59
      9038     45.075,65
     12783     33.611,56
```

As you can see, the decimal character is now represented by a comma. The group separator, on the other hand, is now represented by a period.

NLS_LIST_SEPARATOR

The NLS_LIST_SEPARATOR parameter specifies the character used to separate values in a list of values. The following restrictions apply to the NLS_LIST_SEPARATOR parameter:

- It cannot be numeric.
- It cannot be the same character as the numeric or monetary decimal character.
- It cannot have mathematical significance (+, –, <, >).

The NLS_LIST_SEPARATOR parameter is strictly a client-side setting. It has no meaning on the server. Therefore, it is set through a client-side environment variable but does not execute an implicit ALTER SESSION when a server connection is established.

NLS_CURRENCY

The NLS_CURRENCY parameter defines the currency symbol that will be displayed by the element *L* in the number format mask, as shown here:

```
SQL> alter session set NLS_CURRENCY = "£";

Session altered.

SQL> select to_char(123.45,'L9G999G999D99') amount
from dual;

AMOUNT
-----------------------
                £123.45
```

The NLS_CURRENCY parameter is not limited to a single character. It can be set to a string as well:

```
SQL> alter session set NLS_CURRENCY = " USD";

Session altered.

SQL>  select to_char(123.45,'9G999G999D99L') amount
  2   from dual;

AMOUNT
-----------------------
             123.45 USD
```

Notice in the example that a space is embedded at the beginning of the string. Without the space, the output would appear as shown here:

```
AMOUNT
-----------------------
             123.45USD
```

NLS_ISO_CURRENCY

The NLS_ISO_CURRENCY parameter is used to prevent ambiguity in the currency symbol. For example, the dollar sign ($) can be used for both Australian and American dollars. NLS_ISO_CURRENCY uses a unique text string in place of the currency sign. Several common examples are shown here:

USD: United States

AUD: Australia

EEK: Estonia

EUR: Germany

GBP: United Kingdom

The NLS_ISO_CURRENCY parameter defines the currency symbol that will be displayed by the *C* element of the number format mask. It can be modified using the ALTER SESSION statement, but instead of a text string, it requires a valid territory name, as follows:

```
SQL>  alter session set NLS_ISO_CURRENCY=France;

Session altered.

SQL> select to_char(123.45,'9G999G999D99C') amount
  2  from dual;

AMOUNT
--------------------
           123.45EUR
```

Using the *NLS_LENGTH_SEMANTICS* Parameter

Single-byte character sets always use one byte to store one character. This makes storage calculation a breeze. But when using a multi-byte character set, such as Unicode, a single character may use several bytes of storage. Column sizing becomes much more difficult in this situation.

Length semantics, originally introduced in Oracle 9*i*, make it possible to size columns using either bytes or characters. The method of calculating the length of character strings in bytes is known as byte semantics. Calculating the length in characters is referred to as character semantics.

The NLS_LENGTH_SEMANTICS parameter defines the default method of length semantics to either BYTE (the default) or CHAR. An example is shown here:

```
SQL> alter system set NLS_LENGTH_SEMANTICS = CHAR;

System altered.
```

Consider the following example:

```
SQL> create table test_table (
Last_name VARCHAR2(25));

Table created.
```

When length semantics are set to CHAR, the LAST_NAME column in this table will hold 25 characters, no matter how many actual bytes of storage are required.

When length semantics are set to BYTE, the LAST_NAME column will allocate 25 bytes of storage. If the character set requires 3 bytes to store a single character (or symbol), only eight characters can be stored.

The default setting can be overridden by declaring the length semantics directly in the CREATE TABLE statement. For example, when defining a character column, character semantics can be forced using the following syntax:

```
SQL> create table test_table (
Last_name VARCHAR2(25 CHAR));

Table created.
```

This example forces the use of character semantics, regardless of the setting of the NLS_LENGTH_SEMANTICS parameter.

There are a few exceptions to consider when dealing with length semantics:

- NCHAR, NVARCHAR, CLOB, and NCLOB datatypes are not affected by the NLS_LENGTH_SEMANTICS parameter value. These are datatypes designed specifically for multi-byte character data; therefore they will always use character semantics.
- Tables in the SYS and SYSTEM tablespaces are not governed by the NLS_LENGTH_SEMANTICS parameter. All Data dictionary tables always use byte semantics.

Prioritizing NLS Parameters

Oracle databases often represent only one tier in a multi-tier environment. For instance, let's assume that Arren is a user in France. He uses a custom, client-side application that connects to an application server in Italy. The application server connects to a transaction-processing gateway in Sweden. The transaction-processing gateway connects to the Oracle database in the United States.

Each of these machines may have NLS settings appropriate for their respective locale, none of which match the settings of the database server. How does the database server determine the NLS settings to honor?

There are several different ways in which NLS parameters can be specified. Therefore, when conflicting settings are issued, Oracle needs to have a method of prioritizing to determine which setting will ultimately be used.

NLS parameters can be defined using any of the following methods:

- Server initialization parameters
- Client environment variables
- Using the ALTER SESSION statement
- In SQL functions
- Default values

In the following sections, you will learn about each of the methods of setting NLS parameter values, as well as how Oracle chooses to prioritize them.

Setting Server Initialization Parameters

NLS settings can be defined as initialization parameters on the server. Initialization parameters are loaded at instance startup time, as in this example:

```
NLS_LANGUAGE=FRENCH
```

The effect of initialization parameter settings will be seen only on the server. They have no effect on the client side. They will, however, govern sessions created by the client to the server, unless the client NLS environment overrides them.

Setting Client Environment Variables

Environment variables on the client side will govern local client-side NLS operations (operations that don't involve the database). They will also override server-side NLS settings for sessions created from the client.

In the following example, the environment variable NLS_LANGUAGE is set to French before opening a session. Note that in a Windows environment, the environment variable could be set either using the set command or in the Environment tab in the System Properties window.

```
$ export NLS_LANGUAGE=French

$ sqlplus "/ as sysdba"

SQL*Plus: Release 10.1.0.2.0 - Production on Dim. Août 29 09:26:48 2004

Copyright (c) 1982, 2004, Oracle.  All rights reserved.
```

```
Connected to:
Oracle Database 10g Enterprise Edition Release 10.1.0.2.0 - Production
With the Partitioning, OLAP and Data Mining options

SQL> select to_char(sysdate, 'Mon') from dual;

TO_CH
-----
Août
```

By setting the client-side environment variable NLS_LANG, the server's NLS settings were overridden for the session. The client program accomplishes this by issuing an implicit ALTER SESSION statement when a new session is opened.

Using the *ALTER SESSION* Statement

Setting NLS parameters using the ALTER SESSION statement also overrides the server-side NLS settings for the current session, as in this example:

```
SQL> ALTER SESSION set NLS_SORT = FRENCH;

Session altered.
```

Using ALTER SESSION also overrides any previous ALTER SESSION settings. Therefore, an explicit ALTER SESSION statement overrides settings from the client environment variables (which perform an implicit ALTER SESSION call).

Setting NLS Parameters in SQL Functions

NLS parameters can also be set inside certain SQL functions. Inline NLS parameter settings have the highest priority and will override any other NLS settings. However, their scope is limited to the immediate SQL function, as shown here:

```
SQL> select to_char(sysdate, 'DD/MON/YYYY','nls_date_language=Italian')
  ➥from dual;

TO_CHAR(SYS
-----------
29/AGO/2004

SQL> select to_char(sysdate, 'DD/MON/YYYY') from dual;

TO_CHAR(SYS
-----------
29/AUG/2004
```

As you can see in this example, the inline NLS parameter setting affected only the function in which it was called. It had no effect on the subsequent statement.

Only specific SQL functions will accept inline NLS parameter settings.

Prioritization Summary

As you learned in the preceding sections, there are five distinct methods in which NLS parameters can be specified. Oracle prioritizes these methods to ensure that conflicting settings can be resolved. Table 10.3 encapsulates these methods for NLS parameter prioritization, as well as the scope for each method.

TABLE 10.3 NLS Parameter Setting Precedence

Method	Priority	Scope
Set in SQL functions	1	Current SQL function
Explicit `ALTER SESSION` statement	2	Current session
Client environment variable (implicit `ALTER SESSION` statement)	3	Current session
Set by server initialization parameter	4	Instance
Default	5	Instance

Using NLS Views

Information relating to Oracle NLS settings is stored in the data dictionary and inside fixed tables in memory. This information consists of NLS settings for the session, instance, and database. You can also view a list of the valid values that may be specified when setting NLS parameters.

The following views can be queried to find NLS information from the data dictionary and from dynamic performance tables:

- `NLS_SESSION_PARAMETERS`
- `NLS_INSTANCE_PARAMETERS`
- `NLS_DATABASE_PARAMETERS`
- `V$NLS_VALID_VALUES`

We will look at each of these views in the following sections.

NLS_SESSION_PARAMETERS

The NLS_SESSION_PARAMETERS view offers an insight into the current NLS settings for your session. Here is an example:

```
SQL> select * from nls_session_parameters;

PARAMETER                      VALUE
------------------------------ ---------------------------
NLS_LANGUAGE                   AMERICAN
NLS_TERRITORY                  AMERICA
NLS_CURRENCY                   $
NLS_ISO_CURRENCY               AMERICA
NLS_NUMERIC_CHARACTERS         .,
NLS_CALENDAR                   GREGORIAN
NLS_DATE_FORMAT                DD-MON-RR
NLS_DATE_LANGUAGE              AMERICAN
NLS_SORT                       BINARY
NLS_TIME_FORMAT                HH.MI.SSXFF AM
NLS_TIMESTAMP_FORMAT           DD-MON-RR HH.MI.SSXFF AM
NLS_TIME_TZ_FORMAT             HH.MI.SSXFF AM TZR
NLS_TIMESTAMP_TZ_FORMAT        DD-MON-RR HH.MI.SSXFF AM TZR
NLS_DUAL_CURRENCY              $
NLS_COMP                       BINARY
NLS_LENGTH_SEMANTICS           BYTE
NLS_NCHAR_CONV_EXCP            FALSE

17 rows selected.
```

You will notice that the NLS_SESSION_PARAMETERS view is restricted to show only the current session and nothing more. You may also see settings here that you don't remember specifying. If so, the values represent either the default setting or the value derived from a higher level NLS parameter. For example, if NLS_TERRITORY is set to AMERICA, the NLS_CURRENCY parameter will automatically be set to use dollars.

NLS_INSTANCE_PARAMETERS

The NLS_INSTANCE_PARAMETERS view returns NLS settings for the entire instance, rather than for a single session. These are settings that have been set explicitly through initialization parameters or ALTER SYSTEM statements. Here is an example:

```
SQL> select * from nls_instance_parameters;
```

```
PARAMETER                      VALUE
------------------------------ --------------
NLS_LANGUAGE                   AMERICAN
NLS_TERRITORY                  AMERICA
NLS_SORT
NLS_DATE_LANGUAGE
NLS_DATE_FORMAT
NLS_CURRENCY
NLS_NUMERIC_CHARACTERS
NLS_ISO_CURRENCY
NLS_CALENDAR
NLS_TIME_FORMAT
NLS_TIMESTAMP_FORMAT
NLS_TIME_TZ_FORMAT
NLS_TIMESTAMP_TZ_FORMAT
NLS_DUAL_CURRENCY
NLS_COMP
NLS_LENGTH_SEMANTICS           BYTE
NLS_NCHAR_CONV_EXCP            FALSE

17 rows selected.
```

The results from the NLS_INSTANCE_PARAMETERS view show that many parameters have not been explicitly set. Instead, they derive their value from higher-level parameters. For example, NLS_SORT derives its value from NLS_LANGUAGE, while the currency-, date-, and time-related parameters are derived from NLS_TERRITORY.

NLS_DATABASE_PARAMETERS

The NLS_DATABASE_PARAMETERS view shows NLS settings for the database itself. These represent the default values that will govern the instance, unless they are overridden by initialization parameter settings.

An example is shown here:

```
SQL> select * from nls_database_parameters;

PARAMETER                      VALUE
------------------------------ ----------------------------
NLS_LANGUAGE                   AMERICAN
NLS_TERRITORY                  AMERICA
NLS_CURRENCY                   $
NLS_ISO_CURRENCY               AMERICA
```

```
NLS_NUMERIC_CHARACTERS          .,
NLS_CHARACTERSET                WE8ISO8859P1
NLS_CALENDAR                    GREGORIAN
NLS_DATE_FORMAT                 DD-MON-RR
NLS_DATE_LANGUAGE               AMERICAN
NLS_SORT                        BINARY
NLS_TIME_FORMAT                 HH.MI.SSXFF AM
NLS_TIMESTAMP_FORMAT            DD-MON-RR HH.MI.SSXFF AM
NLS_TIME_TZ_FORMAT              HH.MI.SSXFF AM TZR
NLS_TIMESTAMP_TZ_FORMAT         DD-MON-RR HH.MI.SSXFF AM TZR
NLS_DUAL_CURRENCY               $
NLS_COMP                        BINARY
NLS_LENGTH_SEMANTICS            BYTE
NLS_NCHAR_CONV_EXCP             FALSE
NLS_NCHAR_CHARACTERSET          AL16UTF16
NLS_RDBMS_VERSION               10.1.0.2.0

20 rows selected.
```

The values shown in the NLS_DATABASE_PARMETERS view are set at database creation time, based on the parameters used in the CREATE DATABASE statement.

V$NLS_VALID_VALUES

The V$NLS_VALID_VALUES dynamic performance view lists all valid values for each of the following NLS parameters: NLS_LANGUAGE, NLS_SORT, NLS_TERRITORY, and NLS_CHARACTERSET.

The following example shows a truncated listing:

```
SQL> select *
  from v$nls_valid_values
  where value like '%GER%';

PARAMETER                       VALUE
------------------------------ ------------------
LANGUAGE                        GERMAN
LANGUAGE                        GERMAN_DIN
TERRITORY                       GERMANY
TERRITORY                       ALGERIA
SORT                            GERMAN
SORT                            XGERMAN
SORT                            GERMAN_DIN
SORT                            XGERMAN_DIN
```

Using Datetime Datatypes

A challenge in managing data in a global environment is synchronizing transactions that occur across time zones. Oracle's globalization support offers special datatypes and functionality to manage dates and times across differing time zones.

In the following sections, you'll learn about the Oracle datatypes that store date and time information. The data stored using these datatypes are often called datetimes, and you'll learn about the following:

- DATE
- TIMESTAMP
- TIMESTAMP WITH TIME ZONE
- TIMESTAMP WITH LOCAL TIME ZONE

You'll also be introduced to several datetime SQL functions. Lastly, time zone parameters and files will be covered.

DATE Datatype

The DATE datatype is used to store date information as well as time information in the database. In fact, every date stored as a DATE datatype will have an accompanying time, even if no time was specified when the date was stored. See the following sidebar "Time Elements in DATE Datatypes" for further information on time elements.

To define a column using the DATE datatype, use the DATE keyword as shown here:

```
SQL> create table birthdates (
  client_id NUMBER,
  birthdate DATE);

Table created.
```

Oracle dates consist of seven parts: century, year, month, day, hours, minutes, and seconds (elapsed since midnight). In fact, they are stored internally in the database as seven separate elements.

To demonstrate, insert a row into the BIRTHDATES table that was created earlier:

```
SQL> insert into birthdates
  2  values(1, sysdate);

1 row created.

SQL> commit;

Commit complete.
```

Next, select the date from the table using the following TO_CHAR formatting option:

```
SQL> select to_char(birthdate,'YYYY-MM-DD:HH24:MI:SS')
  2  from birthdates;

TO_CHAR(BIRTHDATE,'
-------------------
2004-10-22:11:29:44
```

You can see the elements displayed clearly when using this formatting option. However, that doesn't tell you anything about how the data is stored internally. To see that, use the DUMP function, as shown here:

```
SQL> select dump(birthdate)
  2  from birthdates;

DUMP(BIRTHDATE)
---------------------------------------------------
Typ=12 Len=7: 120,104,10,22,12,30,45
```

The DUMP function shows the datatype, length (number of bytes), and the actual byte values for a particular element. So, the example shows that the BIRTHDATE element is stored internally as a DATE datatype (typ=12). It occupies seven bytes (Len=7) of storage, and the values stored in those bytes are: 120, 104, 10, 22, 12, 30, and 45.

Oracle stores the century and the year elements using excess 100 notation, which means that it adds 100 to the number before storing it. Also, the hours, minutes, and seconds elements are stored using excess 1 notation. As you probably guessed, that means that it adds one to each number before storing it. Therefore, if the stored values were converted to standard decimal notation, this is what we would see:

```
DUMP(BIRTHDATE)
---------------------------------------------------
Typ=12 Len=7: 20,04,10,22,11,29,44
```

Now, you can see that the stored values do indeed match the original date, as shown here:

```
SQL> select to_char(birthdate,'YYYY-MM-DD:HH24:MI:SS')
  2  from birthdates;

TO_CHAR(BIRTHDATE,'
-------------------
2004-10-22:11:29:44
```

By better understanding how the data is stored internally, you can think of dates as collections of individual elements that can be accessed together or individually.

Time Elements in *DATE* Datatypes

DATE datatypes always store both a date and a time. If no time is specified when storing a date, Oracle will use a default time of midnight. This can be problematic if you're not careful, as the next example will demonstrate.

First, confirm the date by selecting SYSDATE from dual:

```
SQL> select sysdate from dual;

SYSDATE
----------
09-02-2004
```

Next, insert the current date into a table column defined as a datatype of DATE:

```
SQL> insert into conv_dates
  values ('09-02-2004', to_date('09-02-2004','MM-DD-YYYY'));

1 row created.

SQL> commit;

Commit complete.
```

Now, execute the following SQL:

```
SQL> select * from conv_dates where converted_date = sysdate;

no rows selected
```

Even though the two dates appear identical, the query fails to return any matching rows. The following queries will show you the reason:

```
SQL> select
  to_char(converted_date, 'MM-DD-YYYY HH24:MI')
  from conv_dates;

TO_CHAR(CONVERTE
----------------
12-07-1941 00:00
06-06-1944 00:00
09-02-2004 00:00
```

```
SQL> select
  to_char(sysdate,'MM-DD-YYYY HH24:MI')
  from dual;

TO_CHAR(SYSDATE,
----------------
09-02-2004 16:47
```

Because no time element was defined when you inserted the rows into the CONV_DATES table, Oracle defaulted the time to midnight. SYSDATE, on the other hand, returns the current date and the current time. Therefore, unless you happen to run the query at exactly midnight, the query returns no rows.

To resolve this problem, you can use the TRUNC function, as shown here:

```
SQL> select * from conv_dates
  where trunc(converted_date) = trunc(sysdate);

DATESTRING      CONVERTED_
--------------- ----------
09-02-2004      09-02-2004
```

The TRUNC function removes the time element from the date element in a DATE value. With the time element gone, the query returns one row, as expected.

When entering date information into a DATE datatype, you can specify it in several ways:

Literal The date can be entered as a literal, which matches the NLS_DATE_FORMAT. For example, if NLS_DATE_FORMAT is defined as 'MM-DD-YYYY', then a literal of '12-30-1972' would be acceptable. For example:

```
SQL> alter session set NLS_DATE_FORMAT = "MM-DD-YYYY";

Session altered.

SQL> insert into birthdates
values(2, '12-30-1972');

1 row created.
```

Note that in this example, because no time portion was specified, Oracle will set the time elements to represent midnight.

ANSI date literal An ANSI (American National Standards Institute) date literal contains no time element. It must be formatted exactly as shown here:

```
DATE 'YYYY-MM-DD'
```

Dates can be entered using the ANSI date literal format at any time, regardless of the NLS_DATE_FORMAT setting. For example:

```
SQL> insert into birthdates
  2  values(3, DATE '1966-08-25');

1 row created.
```

***TO_DATE* function** Dates can also be entered by using the TO_DATE function. This function converts text strings to DATE types based on the format specified. An example is shown here:

```
SQL> insert into birthdates
  values(4,
  to_date('09-29-1993 13:45', 'MM-DD-YYYY HH24:MI');
```

This example specifies not only the date, but also the hours and minutes elements of the time.

The TO_DATE function can also be handy for converting dates that have been stored as character types. Consider the following examples:

```
SQL> create table conv_dates (
  datestring varchar2(15),
  converted_date date);

Table created.
```

This table will hold a string of 15 characters, and a date. Now, a string representation of two dates will be inserted in the table. Note that they are being stored as VARCHAR2 character data, not as dates.

```
SQL> insert into conv_dates (datestring)
  values ('08-25-2000');

1 row created.

SQL> insert into conv_dates (datestring)
  values ('07-25-2001');

1 row created.
```

```
SQL> commit;

Commit complete.
```

Next, the strings will be converted and stored as dates by using the TO_DATE function:

```
SQL> update conv_dates
  set converted_date =
  to_date(datestring,'MM-DD-YYYY');

2 rows updated.

SQL> commit;

Commit complete.
```

Now, both will be selected, as shown here:

```
SQL> select * from conv_dates;

DATESTRING      CONVERTED_D
--------------- -----------
08-25-2000      25-AUG-2000
07-25-2001      25-JUL-2001
```

As you can see in this example, the TO_DATE function converted the dates stored as VARCHAR2 data in the DATESTRING column into the DATE datatype format, which was subsequently stored in the CONVERTED_DATE column.

TIMESTAMP Datatype

The TIMESTAMP datatype offers all the date and time elements found in the DATE datatype, but offers the extended functionality of storing fractional seconds.

By default, the TIMESTAMP datatype stores fractional seconds to six digits of precision. This can be changed, however, by specifying a number between 0 and 9 in parentheses after the TIMESTAMP keyword. This number determines the digits of precision for the fractional seconds, as shown here:

```
SQL> create table test_stamp (stamp timestamp(2));

Table created.
```

```
SQL> insert into test_stamp
select to_timestamp('09-SEP-2004 17:54.38.92',
'DD-MON-YYYY HH24:MI:SS:FF')
from dual;

1 row created.

SQL> commit;

Commit complete.

SQL> select * from test_stamp;

STAMP
-----------------------------------
09-SEP-04 05.54.38.92 PM
```

As you can see, the timestamp was entered using the TO_TIMESTAMP function (which is similar to the TO_DATE function). Notice that fractional seconds can be specified by using the FF element in the date mask.

The TIMESTAMP datatype should be used when locale information (time zone) is not required, but fractional second granularity is. For example, application event logging is a common use of the TIMESTAMP datatype.

TIMESTAMP WITH TIME ZONE Datatype

The TIMESTAMP WITH TIME ZONE datatype extends the functionality of the TIMESTAMP datatype by including time zone information. The time zone data is stored as an offset (hours and minutes) between the local time and the UTC (Coordinated Universal Time, formerly known as Greenwich Mean Time). It can be displayed either in this form or in the form of a region name.

Like the TIMESTAMP datatype, the TIMESTAMP WITH TIME ZONE datatype stores fractional seconds to six digits of precision. This can be changed by specifying a number between 0 and 9 in parentheses between the TIMESTAMP keyword and the WITH TIME ZONE keywords. This number determines the digits of precision for the fractional seconds. For example:

```
SQL> create table stamp_tz (stamp_tz TIMESTAMP(4) WITH TIME ZONE);
Table created.
```

The TIMESTAMP WITH TIME ZONE is recommended when local information and precise time transactions across time zones need to be synchronized. For example, a bank with branches in different time zones needs to post transactions in real time, regardless of location.

TIMESTAMP WITH LOCAL TIME ZONE Datatype

The `TIMESTAMP WITH TIME ZONE` doesn't actually store time zone information at all. Instead, when a record is inserted into a column defined with a datatype of `TIMESTAMP WITH LOCAL TIME ZONE`, the following happens:

- If the incoming data has no time zone element, it is assumed to be local time and is stored as is.
- If the incoming data has a time zone element but the time zone matches the local time zone, the time zone element is dropped and the data is stored.
- If the incoming data has a time zone element and the time zone does not match the local time zone, the timestamp is adjusted to local time. The data is then stored without a time zone element.

Using this method synchronizes all time elements to the local time, allowing a company that spans multiple time zones to see data in real time relative to the local time zone.

For example, suppose your company is headquartered in London and you have a branch office in New York. Transactions from the branch office need to be stored in your London database and synchronized to London time.

The time zone information for London is as follows:

Element	Value
Standard time zone	No UTC offset
Daylight Savings Time	+1 hour
Current time zone offset	UTC +1 hour
Time zone abbreviation	BST (British Summer Time)
Current time	Friday, September 3, 2004, at 1:15:14 pm BST

The time zone information for New York is as follows:

Element	Value
Standard time zone	UTC –5 hours
Daylight Savings Time	+1 hour
Current time zone offset	UTC –4 hours
Time zone abbreviation	EDT (Eastern Daylight Time)
Current time	Friday, September 3, 2004, at 8:15:14 am EDT

As you can see, London is currently one hour ahead of UTC, whereas New York is four hours behind. Therefore, London's time is five hours ahead of New York's.

Now, suppose a transaction comes in from your New York branch to your London office. The timestamp data will be stored in a column `defined with the TIMESTAMP WITH LOCAL TIME ZONE` datatype. Before storing the data, Oracle synchronizes the time by adding five hours to the timestamp value and drops the time zone element.

Using Linguistic Sorts and Searches

Different languages follow different rules when it comes to sorting text. Unfortunately, that means that there is no "one-size-fits-all" algorithm that can be used. Instead, Oracle's global support functionality allows not only binary sorting methods, but also linguistic sorting and searching methodologies to provide the flexibility to support the needs of many languages.

In the following sections, you will learn the methods that Oracle uses when it performs text-sorting operations. You will also learn about the different NLS parameters that impact linguistic sorting and searching. Next, you will learn about the different types of linguistic sorts supported by Oracle. Lastly, you will learn about linguistic text searches.

An Overview of Text Sorting

There are many ways in which text sorting can be accomplished. Sort order can be case-sensitive or case can be ignored. *Diacritics* (accent marks) can be considered or ignored. Sorting can be done phonetically or based on the appearance of the character.

Some languages even consider groupings of characters to have a specific sort order. For example, traditional Spanish treats *ch* as a character that sorts after the letter C. Therefore, when sorting the words *cat*, *dog*, *cow*, and *chinchilla*, the correct sort sequence would be *cat*, *cow*, *chinchilla*, and *dog*.

To support these different sorting methods, Oracle offers two basic categories of sorting: binary and linguistic.

Binary Sorts

Binary sorts are the fastest and most efficient sorting method offered by Oracle. However, they are also the most limited. Binary sorts perform a numeric sort based on the encoded value (in the character set) for each character. As long as the character set encodes all of the characters in the proper sort order, this method works very well. The performance is also exceptional.

For example, in the US7ASCII character set, alphabetical characters are encoded as shown in Table 10.4. Note that this is just a subset of the character set.

Because the encoded values ascend in correlation with the characters, a binary sort will always perform a proper alphabetical sort. In addition, uppercase characters will always sort higher than lowercase characters.

However, different languages may share the same alphabet (and therefore, the same character set), yet utilize a sort order that deviates from the encoding order of the character set. In this situation, binary sorting will fail to produce an acceptable result.

Binary sorting is Oracle's default sorting method.

TABLE 10.4 US7ASCII Alphabetical Characters

Char	Value	Char	Value	Char	Value	Char	Value
A	65	N	78	a	97	n	110
B	66	O	79	b	98	o	111
C	67	P	80	c	99	p	112
D	68	Q	81	d	100	q	113
E	69	R	82	e	101	r	114
F	70	S	83	f	102	s	115
G	71	T	84	g	103	t	116
H	72	U	85	h	104	u	117
I	73	V	86	j	105	v	118
J	74	W	87	j	106	w	119
K	75	X	88	k	107	x	120
L	76	Y	89	l	108	y	121
M	77	Z	90	m	109	z	122

Linguistic Sorts

Linguistic sorts, unlike binary sorts, operate independently of the underlying encoded values. Instead, they allow character data to be sorted based on the rules of specific languages. Linguistic sorts offer the flexibility to deal with the caveats imposed by different languages.

Oracle provides a rich set of linguistic sort definitions that cover most of the languages of the world. However, it also provides the ability to define new definitions or to modify existing definitions. The Oracle Locale Builder, a graphical tool that ships with Oracle 10g, can be used to view, create, and modify sort definitions and other locale definitions. However, as mentioned earlier, Locale Builder is not covered in this book.

Linguistic sorts are defined using a variety of rules that govern the sorting process. The following elements are available and can be used to create a comprehensive linguistic sort:

Base letters Base letters are the individual letters upon which other characters are based. The derived characters would map back to the base letter to determine the sorting value. For example, the character *A* is a base letter, while *À Á Ã Ä a à á ä* would all map to *A* as a base letter.

Ignorable characters Ignorable characters, just as the name implies, can be defined as having no effect on sort order. Diacritics, such as the umlaut, can be classified as ignorable, as can certain punctuation characters such as the hyphen. Therefore, a word such as *e-mail* would be sorted the same as *email*.

Contracting characters Contracting characters represent two or more characters that are treated linguistically as a single character. An example—the traditional Spanish *ch* string—was explained earlier in this section. Contracting characters require flexibility in the sorting algorithm to read ahead to the next character to determine if a contracting character has been found.

Expanding characters Some locales choose to compress repeating or commonly occurring strings of characters into a single character for brevity's sake. When sorting, however, the character needs to sort as if all characters are present. These are referred to as expanding characters.

For example, the *ö* character should be treated as the string *oe* for sorting purposes.

Context-sensitive characters Certain languages sort characters differently based upon their relationship to other characters. These are generally characters that modify the preceding character. For example, a Japanese length mark is sorted according to the vowel that precedes it.

Canonical equivalence When using a Unicode character set, the character *ö* and the string *o¨* can be considered equal from a sorting perspective. This is because the code points of the two-character string match the code point of the individual character. The two are said to have canonical equivalence.

In situations of canonical equivalence, the value of the `CANONICAL_EQUIVALENCE` linguistic flag (with a value of `TRUE` or `FALSE`) determines whether the rules of canonical equivalence should be followed.

Reverse secondary sorting In some languages, strings containing diacritics will be sorted from left to right on the base characters, and then from right to left on the diacritics. This is referred to as reverse secondary sorting. For example, resumé would sort before résume because of the position of the diacritic from left to right.

The `REVERSE_SECONDARY=TRUE` linguistic flag enables this functionality.

Character rearrangement In certain languages (notably Thai and Laotian dialects), sorting rules declare that certain characters should switch places with the following character before sorting. This generally happens when a consonant is preceded by a vowel sound. In this case, the consonant is given priority, forcing the characters to be switched before the sort begins. The SWAP_WITH_NEXT linguistic flag can determine whether character rearrangement will occur within a sort definition.

Don't confuse linguistic flags with Oracle parameter settings. Linguistic flags are defined for specific sort order definitions when they are created.

These different sorting methods represent the toolset available to sort and search text. Different languages may use one or more of the linguistic methods listed here. But as long as the rules of a language can be described using these methods, Oracle is able to perform linguistic sorts, either through an existing sort definition or through a custom sort definition.

Using Linguistic Sort Parameters

Linguistic sorts are generally applicable to a specific language or to a specific character set. And, as mentioned previously, there are many pre-defined linguistic sort definitions that may be utilized. Therefore, it is unlikely that you would ever need to define your own.

You can instruct Oracle to utilize specific linguistic sorts by setting the appropriate NLS sort parameters. In this section, you will learn about the NLS_SORT and NLS_COMP parameters, and how they affect linguistic sorting operations.

NLS_SORT

The NLS_SORT parameter defines which type of sorting—binary or linguistic—should be performed for SQL sort operations. By default, the value for NLS_SORT is the default sort method defined for the language identified in the NLS_LANGUAGE parameter. For example, if the NLS_LANGUAGE parameter is set to AMERICAN, the default value for the NLS_SORT parameter will be BINARY.

To instruct Oracle to use linguistic sorting, this parameter can be set to the name of any valid linguistic sort definition, as shown here:

```
SQL> alter session set NLS_SORT = German;
Session altered.
```

A list of valid sort definition names is shown here. You could also query the V$NLS_VALID_VALUES views (as shown earlier in this chapter).

```
ARABIC              GERMAN       SWISS
ARABIC_ABJ_MATCH    GERMAN_DIN   TCHINESE_RADICAL_M
```

ARABIC_ABJ_SORT
ARABIC_MATCH
ASCII7
AZERBAIJANI
BENGALI
BIG5
BINARY
BULGARIAN
CANADIAN FRENCH
CANADIAN_M
CATALAN
CROATIAN
CZECH
CZECH_PUNCTUATION
DANISH
DANISH_M
DUTCH
EBCDIC
EEC_EURO
EEC_EUROPA3
ESTONIAN
FINNISH
FRENCH
FRENCH_M
GBK
GENERIC_BASELETTER
GENERIC_M
GREEK
HEBREW
HKSCS
HUNGARIAN
ICELANDIC
INDONESIAN
ITALIAN
JAPANESE
JAPANESE_M
KOREAN_M
LATIN
LATVIAN
LITHUANIAN
MALAY
NORWEGIAN
POLISH
PUNCTUATION
ROMANIAN
RUSSIAN
SCHINESE_PINYIN_M
SCHINESE_RADICAL_M
SCHINESE_STROKE_M
SLOVAK
SLOVENIAN
SPANISH
SPANISH_M
SWEDISH
TCHINESE_STROKE_M
THAI_DICTIONARY
THAI_M
THAI_TELEPHONE
TURKISH
UKRAINIAN
UNICODE_BINARY
VIETNAMESE
WEST_EUROPEAN
XAZERBAIJANI
XCATALAN
XCROATIAN
XCZECH
XCZECH_PUNCTUATION
XDANISH
XDUTCH
XFRENCH
XGERMAN
XGERMAN_DIN
XHUNGARIAN
XPUNCTUATION
XSLOVAK
XSLOVENIAN
XSPANISH
XSWISS
XTURKISH
XWEST_EUROPEAN

By using the NLS_SORT parameter, you can make the following changes to Oracle's default functionality:

- Set the default sort method for all ORDER BY operations.
- Set the default sort value for the NLSSORT function.

It is important to note that not all SQL functionality supports linguistic sorting. Certain functions support only binary sorts. However, most of the commonly used methods are supported. Also, all NLS-specific SQL functions (for example, NLSSORT) will support linguistic sorts.

The methods listed here support linguistic sorting:

- ORDER BY
- BETWEEN
- CASE WHEN
- HAVING
- IN/OUT
- START WITH
- WHERE

By default, all of these operations will perform binary sorts. By setting the NLS_SORT parameter, SQL statements using the WHERE operation will perform linguistic sorts by default.

The following example demonstrates the use of the NLS_SORT parameter. Initially, you can see that your session has no value set for NLS_SORT. Therefore, it will inherit the default setting from the NLS_LANGUAGE parameter (BINARY).

```
SQL> show parameters NLS_LANGUAGE

NAME                                 TYPE        VALUE
------------------------------------ ----------- ----------
nls_language                         string      AMERICAN

SQL> show parameters NLS_SORT

NAME                                 TYPE        VALUE
------------------------------------ ----------- ----------
nls_sort                             string
```

As you learned earlier, the default sort for the language AMERICAN is BINARY. The default setting for NLS_COMP is BINARY as well. Therefore, you can expect that, by default, Oracle will perform a binary sort unless otherwise specified, as shown here:

```
SQL> select * from sort_test
  order by name;
```

```
NAME
--------------------------------
Finsteraarhornhutte
Grünhornlücke
einschließlich
finsteraarhornhütte
grünhornlücke

5 rows selected.
```

As expected, Oracle sorted the rows based on the encoded value of the characters in the US7ASCII character set. Therefore, all uppercase characters sort before lowercase characters.

Because the words in this table are of German origin, it is logical that you might want to sort them using a German sorting method. To change the sorting method for a GROUP BY clause, the NLS_SORT parameter can be set as shown here:

```
SQL> alter session set NLS_SORT=German_din;

Session altered.

SQL> select * from sort_test
  order by name;

NAME
--------------------------------------------
einschließlich
Finsteraarhornhutte
finsteraarhornhütte
Grünhornlücke
grünhornlücke

5 rows selected.
```

As you can see, setting the NLS_SORT parameter changed the default sorting method to a linguistic sort instead of a binary sort.

In the next step, another query is executed, this time using a WHERE condition rather than an ORDER BY clause:

```
SQL> select * from sort_test
  2  where name > 'einschließlich';
```

```
NAME
----------------------------------------
finsteraarhornhütte
grünhornlücke

2 rows selected.
```

The result of this query might not be what you expect. Instead of the expected four rows (which a linguistic sort would have returned), only two rows are returned, indicating that a binary sort took place instead.

Remember, the NLS_SORT parameter overrides the default sorting method for ORDER BY operations and for the NLSSORT function, but has no effect on other sort operations, such as WHERE conditions. Therefore, this query ignored the parameter entirely.

To perform a linguistic sort, you call the NLSSORT function. Normally, the function would be called like this:

```
SQL> select * from sort_test
  where nlssort(name, 'NLS_SORT=German_din') >
  nlssort('einschließlich','NLS_SORT=German_din');

NAME
----------------------------------------------------
Finsteraarhornhutte
finsteraarhornhütte
Grünhornlücke
grünhornlücke

4 rows selected.
```

However, because the NLS_SORT parameter defines the default sort for the NLSSORT function, specifying the sort inside the function is unnecessary. The following method works as well:

```
SQL> select * from sort_test
  where nlssort(name) > nlssort('einschließlich');

NAME
----------------------------------------------------
Finsteraarhornhutte
finsteraarhornhütte
Grünhornlücke
grünhornlücke

4 rows selected.
```

As you can see, in both queries, the sort was performed linguistically and returned the expected rows.

The NLS_SORT parameter is very limited in relation to linguistic sorting. The NLS_COMP parameter, on the other hand, makes linguistic sorting much easier.

NLS_COMP

The NLS_COMP parameter works in conjunction with the NLS_SORT parameter to make linguistic sorts easier to use. When the NLS_COMP parameter is set to a value of ANSI, all of the following SQL operations will default to linguistic sorting (using the language specified in NLS_SORT parameter):

- ORDER BY
- BETWEEN
- CASE WHEN
- HAVING
- IN/OUT
- START WITH
- WHERE

Setting the NLS_COMP parameter makes it unnecessary to call the NLSSORT function when using these sort operations. As you can guess, this makes linguistic sorting much easier to perform.

The NLS_COMP parameter can be set to either BINARY (the default) or ANSI.

The following example shows the usage of the NLS_COMP parameter:

```
SQL> alter session set NLS_SORT=German_din;

Session altered.

SQL> alter session set NLS_COMP=ANSI;

Session altered.

SQL> select * from sort_test
  2  where name > 'einschließlich';

NAME
----------------------------------------
Finsteraarhornhutte
finsteraarhornhütte
Grünhornlücke
grünhornlücke

4 rows selected.
```

As you can see, the query performed the linguistic sort and returned the expected results, even without using the NLSSORT function.

If the NLS_COMP parameter is set back to BINARY, binary sorting occurs once again:

```
SQL> alter session set NLS_COMP=BINARY;

Session altered.

SQL> select * from sort_test
  2  where name > 'einschließlich';

NAME
------------------------------------------------
finsteraarhornhütte
grünhornlücke

2 rows selected.
```

Linguistic Sort Types

When performing linguistic sorts, Oracle uses different methodologies, depending upon the number of languages involved in the sort. If character data in only one language is being sorted, this is classified as a monolingual linguistic sort. If more than one language is involved in the sort, it is classified as a multilingual linguistic sort.

In the following sections, you will learn the methodology that Oracle implements in performing both monolingual and multilingual linguistic sorts. You will also learn about accent-insensitive and case-insensitive linguistic sorts.

Monolingual Linguistic Sorts

When dealing with only a single language inside a sort, Oracle performs a two-step process to compare character strings. First, the major value of the strings is compared. Next, if necessary, the minor value of the strings is compared.

Major and minor values are sort values assigned to letters in the character set. A base letter and those derived from it will generally share a common major value, but they will have different minor values based on the desired sort order.

Here's an example:

Letter	Major Value	Minor Value
a	30	10
A	30	20

ä	30	30
Ä	30	40
b	40	10

The example shows that all four variations of the letter *A* have identical major values, but differing minor values. When two letters share a major value, the minor value will determine the sort order.

The major value numbers are assigned to a *Unicode code point* (a 16-bit binary value that defines a character in a Unicode character set).

Multilingual Linguistic Sorts

Multilingual sorts offer the ability to sort mixed languages within the same sort. For example, if you have a table that stores names in both English and Spanish, a multilingual sort should be used.

Multilingual sorts perform three levels of evaluation: primary, secondary, and tertiary.

Primary sorts assign a primary sort value based on the base letter of each character (diacritics and case are ignored). If a character is defined as ignorable, it is assigned a primary value of zero.

Secondary level sorts consider diacritics to differentiate accented letters from base letters in assigning a secondary sort level. For example, *A* and *ä* share the same base letter, so they have the same primary sort level, but they will have different secondary levels.

Tertiary level sorts consider character case to differentiate uppercase and lowercase letters. Tertiary sorts also handle special characters such as *, +, and -.

Consider the following words:

Fahrvergnügen

Fahrvergnugen

farhrvergnugen

fahrvergnügen

Because all of these words share the same base letters in the same order, all of them would be considered equivalent at the primary sort level. After a secondary level sort, they would be ordered similarly to the following list:

Fahrvergnugen

farhrvergnugen

Fahrvergnügen

fahrvergnügen

The secondary level sort is concerned only with diacritics, so it will sort characters without diacritics above those with diacritics. After that, the words are displayed in their primary sort order. Because the words in this example have identical primary sort orders, there is no guarantee which word will appear before the other. The only guarantee is that those with diacritics will sort after those without.

After the tertiary level sort is performed, the list should look exactly like this:

farhrvergnugen

Fahrvergnugen

fahrvergnügen

Fahrvergnügen

The tertiary level sort applies the case rule to the data, forcing lowercase letters to sort before uppercase letters. This is the final result of the sort after applying all three multilingual sorting levels.

In keeping with the ISO 14651 standard for multilingual sorting, Oracle appends an _M to the sort name to identify it as multilingual. For example, FRENCH_M identifies a French multilingual sort, whereas FRENCH identifies a French monolingual sort. Table 10.5 shows the multilingual sorts predefined in Oracle 10*g*.

TABLE 10.5 Multilingual Sorts Available in Oracle 10*g*

Multilingual Sort Name	Description
CANADIAN_M	Canadian French
DANISH_M	Danish
FRENCH_M	French
GENERIC_M	Generic based on ISO14651
JAPANESE_M	Japanese
KOREAN_M	Korean
SPANISH_M	Traditional Spanish
THAI_M	Thai
SCHINESE_RADICAL_M	Simplified Chinese
SCHINESE_STROKE_M	Simplified Chinese
SCHINESE_PINYIN_M	Simplified Chinese
TCHINESE_RADICAL_M	Traditional Chinese
TCHINESE_STROKE_M	Traditional Chinese

Case-Insensitive and Accent-Insensitive Linguistic Sorts

Oracle, by default, will always consider both the case of the characters and any diacritics when performing sort operations. As you've seen in previous examples, linguistic sorts have rules to govern precedence between uppercase and lowercase words, as well as those words containing diacritics.

However, you may wish to override this functionality from time to time and choose to ignore case and/or diacritics. Oracle 10*g* offers case-insensitive and accent-insensitive sorting options to allow for these cases.

To specify case-insensitive or accent-insensitive sorts, the `NLS_SORT` parameter is used, but with the following changes:

- For a case-insensitive linguistic sort, append the string `_CI` to the sort name.
- For an accent-insensitive linguistic sort, append the string `_AI` to the sort name.

Accent-insensitive sorts are also case-insensitive by default.

For example, to specify a French, multilingual, accent-insensitive sort, use the following:

```
NLS_SORT = French_M_AI
```

Here is how to specify a German, monolingual, case-insensitive sort:

```
NLS_SORT = German_CI
```

Case-Insensitive and Accent-Insensitive Binary Sorts

Binary sorts can also be designated as case-insensitive or accent-insensitive. The `NLS_SORT` parameter can be set to `BINARY_CI` or `BINARY_AI`. Table 10.6 shows how the sort will be affected by these settings.

TABLE 10.6 Binary Case and Accent-insensitive Sort Options

Sort Name	Sort type	Case-insensitive?	Accent-Insensitive?
BINARY_CI	Binary	Yes	No
BINARY_AI	Binary	Yes	Yes

As you can see, using the `BINARY_AI` sort will result in both an accent-insensitive and case-insensitive sort.

Searching Linguistic Strings

Linguistic searches are closely related to linguistic sorts and are directly affected by the NLS_SORT setting. To accomplish linguistically meaningful searches, Oracle must apply the same rules it applies for linguistic sorts.

Earlier in this section, you saw several examples of linguistic string searching, including the following:

```
SQL> select * from sort_test
  2  where name > 'einschließlich';

NAME
------------------------------------------
Finsteraarhornhutte
finsteraarhornhütte
Grünhornlücke
grünhornlücke

4 rows selected.
```

By setting the NLS_COMP parameter to ANSI and the NLS_SORT parameter to the desired sort language, the WHERE operator (as well as several others) will perform linguistic searching by default.

And, just as you did with sorts, if the NLS_SORT is set to ignore case or accents, linguistic searches will follow suit, as in this example:

```
SQL> alter session set NLS_COMP=ANSI;

Session altered.
SQL> alter session set NLS_SORT=German_din_ci;

Session altered.

SQL> select * from sort_test
  2  where name = 'Grünhornlücke';

NAME
-----------------------------------------
Grünhornlücke
grünhornlücke
```

As you can see, the search ignored the case and returned both rows that matched. This is the expected functionality of the case-insensitive search.

In the next example, the NLS_SORT parameter will be set to define an accent-insensitive search:

```
SQL> alter session set NLS_SORT=German_din_ai;

Session altered.

SQL> select * from sort_test
  where name = 'Finsteraarhornhutte';

NAME
-----------------------------------------------
Finsteraarhornhutte
finsteraarhornhütte
```

When the NLS_SORT parameter defined an accent-insensitive search, both accents and case were ignored. This is the expected functionality for accent-insensitive searches.

Summary

In this chapter, you learned about Oracle's global support functionality and how it simplifies the issues related to multilingual databases. You learned about the internal architecture that makes globalization support possible. You saw how the NLS Runtime Library (NLSRTL) integrates with the Oracle locale definition files to provide functionality. You also learned that the modular nature of the locale definition files provides great flexibility while reducing memory usage.

You learned about the main components of globalization support: language, territory, character set, and linguistic sorts. You saw how these four components provide default settings for all the other NLS options. You then learned that those default settings can be overridden in a variety of methods.

We introduced you to the many character sets that Oracle supports, including the important Unicode character set. You saw how the Unicode character set can support all known written languages in the world.

You also learned about using NLS parameters to modify your globalization environment as needed. You learned about the different categories of NLS parameters, including language and territory parameters, date and time parameters, linguistic sort parameters, calendar parameters, and more.

This chapter introduced you to the datetime datatypes and explained how the TIMESTAMP WITH TIME ZONE and TIMESTAMP WITH LOCAL TIME ZONE datatypes can be used to synchronize transactions occurring across time zones.

Lastly, you learned about linguistic sorting and searching and how globalization support allows culturally appropriate sorting and searching. You also learned about monolingual and multilingual sorts and how each evaluates text strings when performing a sort operation. You learned that multilingual sorts can be identified by the _M appended to the sort definition name.

You learned how, in conjunction with linguistic sorting and searching, you can perform case-insensitive and accent-insensitive operations by appending an _CI or _AI to the end of the NLS_SORT parameter value.

Exam Essentials

Be able to customize language-dependent behavior for the database and individual sessions. Be aware of the different NLS parameters and the different ways that they can be set (initialization parameters, environment variables, the ALTER SESSION statement). Know the order of precedence for NLS parameter settings. Know which parameters apply only to the client or the server.

Know how to specify different linguistic sorts for queries. Understand the mechanisms for producing linguistic sorts versus binary sorts. Know how to specify both case-insensitive and accent-insensitive linguistic sorts. Know how to differentiate between multilingual and monolingual sort definitions.

Understand how to use datetime datatypes. Understand the purpose of datetime datatypes. Know the different datetimes covered in this chapter: DATE, TIMESTAMP, TIMESTAMP WITH TIME ZONE, and TIMESTAMP WITH LOCAL TIME ZONE. Understand the differences between the various datetime datatypes and how they relate to globalization.

Know how to query data using case-insensitive and accent-insensitive searches. Know the syntax for specifying case-insensitive and accent-insensitive operations. Understand which SQL operations support linguistic operations. Know which NLS parameters control case-insensitive and accent-insensitive searching.

Understand how to obtain globalization support configuration information. Know the views available to see globalization information: NLS_SESSION_PARAMETERS, NLS_INSTANCE_PARAMETERS, NLS_DATABASE_PARAMETERS, and V$NLS_VALID_VALUES. Understand the information returned by each of these views.

Understand globalization support architecture. Know the purpose of the NLSRTL. Understand the location, purpose, and file-naming conventions of locale definition files. Know the four types of locale definition files.

Review Questions

1. Globalization support is implemented through the text- and character-processing functions provided by which Oracle feature?

   A. RSTLNE

   B. NLSRTL

   C. LISTENER

   D. NLSSORT

   E. Linguistic sorts

2. What three elements of globalization can be explicitly defined using the NLS_LANG environment variable?

   A. NLS_LANGUAGE

   B. NLS_SORT

   C. NLS_CALENDAR

   D. NLS_CHARACTERSET

   E. NLS_TERRITORY

3. Given two different character sets (*A* and *B*), which of the following must be true for *A* to be considered a strict superset of *B*? (Choose all that apply.)

   A. *A* must contain all of the characters defined in *B*.

   B. *A* must be Unicode.

   C. The encoded values in *A* must match the encoded values in *B* for all characters defined in *B*.

   D. *A* must be a multi-byte character set.

   E. The encoded values in *A* must match the encoded values in *B* for all numeric and alphabetic characters in *B*.

4. The NLS_SORT parameter sets the default sort method for which of the following operations? (Choose all that apply.)

   A. WHERE clause

   B. ORDER BY clause

   C. BETWEEN clause

   D. NLSSORT function

   E. NLS_SORT function

5. Which view shows all valid values for the NLS_LANGUAGE, NLS_SORT, NLS_TERRITORY, and NLS_CHARACTERSET parameters?

   A. V$VALID_NLS_VALUES

   B. NLS_VALID_VALUES

   C. NLS_VALUE_OPTIONS

   D. V$NLS_VALUE_OPTIONS

   E. V$NLS_VALID_VALUES

6. Which of the following datatypes store time zone information in the database?

   A. TIMESTAMP

   B. DATE

   C. TIMESTAMP WITH TIME ZONE

   D. TIMESTAMP WITH LOCAL TIME ZONE

   E. DATETIME

7. Which of the following are valid settings for the NLS_COMP parameter? (Choose all that apply.)

   A. ASCII

   B. ANSI

   C. BINARY

   D. MONOLINGUAL

   E. MULTILINGUAL

8. NLS parameters can be set using the five methods listed below. Put the methods in order from highest to lowest according to Oracle's order of precedence:

   1. Default setting
   2. Client environment variable
   3. Explicit ALTER SESSION statement
   4. Inside SQL function
   5. Server initialization parameter

   A. 2, 4, 5, 1, 3

   B. 5, 1, 2, 3, 4

   C. 4, 3, 2, 5, 1

   D. 1, 2, 4, 3, 5

   E. 4, 3, 2, 1, 5

9. What can you determine about the following linguistic sorts based only on their names?

   1. GERMAN
   2. FRENCH_M

   Select all the true statements:

   A. 1 is a monolingual sort.

   B. 2 is a monolingual sort.

   C. 1 is case-insensitive.

   D. Both 1 and 2 are case-insensitive.

   E. Case-sensitivity is unknown.

10. In a database with the database character set of US7ASCII and a national character set of UTF-8, which datatypes would be capable of storing Unicode data by default?

    A. VARCHAR2

    B. CHAR

    C. NVARCHAR2

    D. CLOB

    E. LONG

11. Automatic data conversion will occur if

    A. The client and server have different NLS_LANGUAGE settings.

    B. The client and server character sets are not the same, and the database character set is not a strict superset of the client character set.

    C. The client and server are in different time zones.

    D. The client requests automatic data conversion.

    E. The AUTO_CONVERT initialization parameter is set to TRUE.

12. Which of the following NLS_SORT parameter values would result in case-insensitive and accent-insensitive binary sorts?

    A. NLS_SORT = BINARY

    B. NLS_SORT = BINARY_AI

    C. NLS_SORT = BINARY_CI

    D. NLS_SORT = BINARY_AI_CI

    E. Binary sorts are case and accent-insensitive by default.

13. Which NLS parameter can be used to change the default Oracle sort method from binary to linguistic for the SQL SELECT statement?

    A. NLS_LANG

    B. NLS_SORT

    C. NLS_COMP

    D. NLS_SORT

    E. None of the above

14. Which of the following would be affected by setting NLS_LENGTH_SEMANTICS=CHAR?

    A. All objects in the database

    B. Tables owned by SYS and SYSTEM

    C. Data dictionary tables

    D. NCHAR columns

    E. CHAR columns

15. Which is not a valid locale definition file type?

    A. Language

    B. Linguistic sort

    C. Calendar

    D. Territory

    E. Character set

16. How many different calendars does Oracle 10*g* support?

    A. 22

    B. 7

    C. 6

    D. 15

    E. 2

17. Which NLS parameter directly governs linguistic searches?

    A. NLS_SEARCH_L

    B. NLS_SORT

    C. NLS_SEARCH

    D. NLS_SORT_L

    E. None of the above

18. Case-insensitive sorts are always accent-insensitive by default.

    A. True

    B. False

19. What is the name of the file that identifies the set of available locale definitions?

    A. `locale.def`

    B. `lxdef.ora`

    C. `lx1boot.nlb`

    D. `lx1boot.ora`

    E. `lang.def`

20. Which of the following is not a valid linguistic sort element?

    A. Accent expansion

    B. Canonical equivalence

    C. Reverse secondary sorting

    D. Ignorable characters

    E. Character rearrangement

Answers to Review Questions

1. B. The NLS Runtime Library (NLSRTL) provides the language-independent text and character-processing functionality for Oracle.

2. A, D, E. The client-side NLS_LANG parameter can define language, territory, and character set all at once. Though the value for NLS_SORT is derived from the NLS_LANGUAGE parameter setting, it is not *explicitly* set by NLS_LANG. NLS_CALENDAR is not affected by the setting of NLS_LANG.

3. A, C. A strict superset must contain all characters found in the other character set *and* have matching encoded values for those characters.

4. A, D. The NLS_SORT parameter defines the default sort method (binary or linguistic) for both SQL WHERE clause operations and NLSSORT function operations. The default sort method for ORDER_BY and BETWEEN (and all other SQL operations that support linguistic sorts) is defined by the NLS_COMP parameter. NLS_SORT is an invalid function name.

5. E. The V$NLS_VALID_VALUES view shows the names of all language, territory, sort, and character set definitions that are available in the database.

6. C. Only TIMESTAMP WITH TIME ZONE datatype actually stores time zone information in the database. The TIMESTAMP WITH LOCAL TIME ZONE datatype converts the timestamp to local time and drops the time zone information before storing it in the database. DATE and TIMESTAMP datatypes do not deal with time zone information at all. DATETIME is not a valid datatype.

7. B, C. The NLS_COMP parameter can be set to BINARY or ANSI. This parameter determines the default sort type for certain SQL functions. (A setting of ANSI specifies that linguistic sorts should be used.)

8. C. NLS settings embedded in a SQL function have the highest precedence, followed by explicit ALTER SESSION statements, client environment variables (which execute an implicit ALTER SESSION statement), server initialization parameters, and finally default settings.

9. A. A is the only true statement. The _M appended to the end of a sort name denotes a multilingual sort. Its absence denotes a monolingual sort. Case-sensitive and accent-insensitive sorts have _CI or _AI appended to the name. Its absence denotes case- and accent-sensitivity.

10. C. NLS datatypes (NCHAR, NVARCHAR, and NCLOB) store data using the character set defined as the national character set by default. Because the national character set is UTF-8 (a Unicode character set), data stored in these datatypes will be Unicode data by default. All other datatypes use the character set defined as the database character set. Because US7ASCII is not a Unicode character set, it does not store Unicode data by default.

11. B. Automatic data conversion occurs when data is moved between character sets. However, if the server character set is a strict superset of the client character set, no conversion is necessary.

12. B. The _AI suffix implies that an accent-insensitive sort will be performed. Accent-insensitive sorts are also case-insensitive by default. The _CI suffix implies that a case-insensitive sort will be performed, but it will not be accent-insensitive. Specifying both suffixes (_AI_CI) is illegal.

13. E. The SQL SELECT statement does not invoke a sort.

14. E. Only option E is correct. Tables owned by the SYS and SYSTEM users are not affected by default-length semantics. Data dictionary tables always use byte semantics, and NCHAR columns always use character semantics. Therefore, neither is affected by the setting of the NLS_LENGTH_SEMANTICS parameter.

15. C. Calendar definitions are not stored as locale definition files. Only languages, linguistic sorts, territories, and character set definitions are stored as locale definition files.

16. B. Oracle supports 7 distinct calendars: Gregorian, Japanese Imperial, ROC Official, Persian, Thai Buddha, Arabic Hijrah, and English Hijrah.

17. B. Linguistic searches are closely related to linguistic sorts and are governed by the NLS_SORT parameter.

18. B. Accent-insensitive sorts are always case-insensitive, not the other way around.

19. C. The `lx1boot.nlb` file identifies the available locale definitions to the NLSRTL.

20. A. Linguistic sort elements define the rules for linguistic sorting. There is no linguistic sort element named "accent expansion." The other choices are all valid rules.

Managing Resources

ORACLE DATABASE 10G: ADMINISTRATION II EXAM OBJECTIVES COVERED IN THIS CHAPTER:

✓ **Managing Resources**

- Configure the Resource Manager.
- Assign users to Resource Manager groups.
- Create resource plans within groups.
- Specify directives for allocating resources to consumer groups.

Exam objectives are subject to change at any time without prior notice and at Oracle's sole discretion. Please visit Oracle's Training and Certification website (`http://www.oracle.com/education/certification/`) for the most current exam objectives listing.

As a database administrator, it is your job to maintain a given level of performance from the database. To successfully accomplish this mission requires close management of scarce hardware resources.

In the past, management of Oracle resources fell upon the operating system. The operating system not only had to juggle resources between the different Oracle processes, but also between Oracle and all other processes running on the system. As if that weren't enough, it also had no way of differentiating one Oracle process from another. Therefore, allocating resources between user groups or applications was impossible.

In addition, resource management performed by the operating system has a tendency to cause certain performance problems. Excessive context switching can occur when the number of server processes is high. Server processes holding latches can be de-scheduled, resulting in further inefficiency. And inappropriate resource allocation is common, due to the inability to prioritize Oracle tasks.

Oracle's Database Resource Manager (DRM) circumvents the inefficient operating system management process by giving the Oracle database server more control over resource management decisions. It also allows you to distribute available system resources among your users and applications based on business needs (or whatever criteria you wish to base it on).

This chapter describes the different elements of DRM and how to use them. In the overview section, you'll learn about the elements that comprise the DRM and see, at a high level, how they interact. You will be introduced to the pending area, a work area that must be established prior to the creation or modification of DRM objects.

Next, you will learn about resource consumer groups, which allow you to classify users based on their resource requirements. You'll learn how to set up resource plans that direct the allocation of resources among the resource consumer groups. You'll learn about resource allocation options offered by the database and the methods you can define to apply them.

You will also learn about resource plan directives that associate resource consumer groups, resource plans, and resource allocation methods. Finally, you'll learn the PL/SQL interface to manage DRM, as well as the views available to query DRM information.

Keep in mind when reading this chapter that the elements of DRM constitute a "chicken or the egg" situation in terms of the ordering of the topics. For instance, the pending area must be established before anything else is done. However, discussion of the pending area assumes knowledge of the objects defined later in the chapter. In the interest of organization and ease of use, each topic will be covered separately in its own section. Then, a final section will show how the elements integrate.

An Overview of the Database Resource Manager

The *Database Resource Manager (DRM)* offers a component-based approach to resource allocation management. By defining distinct, independent components representing the DRM elements, the result is an extremely flexible and easy-to-use system.

There are three main elements that comprise the DRM:

- Resource consumer groups
- Resource plans
- Resource plan directives

DRM allocates resources among resource consumer groups based on a resource plan. A resource plan consists of resource plan directives that specify how resources should be distributed among the groups. Resource consumer groups are categories to which user sessions can be assigned. These groups can then be allocated resources through plan directives.

Plan directives define resource allocation rules by assigning resource allocation methods to specific resource consumer groups. They connect resource plans to consumer groups and define the resource allocation method to be used.

Resource allocation methods are methods that can be used to allocate resources such as CPU usage, number of sessions, idle time, operation execution time, etc. Resource allocation methods are predefined by Oracle, but plan directives determine which ones to apply and the allocation amounts. For example, a plan named NIGHT_PLAN may contain a directive allocating a percentage of CPU to a consumer group named MANAGERS.

Working with the Pending Area

Before defining or updating any DRM objects, you must first establish a *pending area*. A pending area is a staging area where resource management objects can be defined and validated before they are activated. If you forget to create the pending area, you will receive the following error message if you try to create or update a DRM object:

```
ERROR at line 1:
ORA-29371: pending area is not active
ORA-06512: at "SYS.DBMS_RMIN", line 115
ORA-06512: at "SYS.DBMS_RESOURCE_MANAGER", line 108
ORA-06512: at line 1
```

The next sections explain how to manage pending areas. You will learn to create, validate, submit, and clear them.

Creating a Pending Area

To create a pending area, simply execute the DBMS_RESOURCE_MANAGER.CREATE_PENDING_AREA procedure. This procedure accepts no parameters, so it can be called as follows:

```
SQL> exec dbms_resource_manager.create_pending_area();

PL/SQL procedure successfully completed.
```

Once a pending area has been created, all changes will automatically be stored there until they are validated and submitted.

Validating Changes

After changes have been made in the pending area, they need to be checked for validity before being activated. This can be accomplished through the DBMS_RESOURCE_GROUP.VALIDATE_PENDING_AREA procedure.

The validation process verifies that any changes in the pending area will not result in a violation of any of the following rules:

- No plan schema can contain a loop.
- All DRM objects identified in a plan directive must exist.
- All plan directives refer to either plans or resource groups.
- Allocation percentages for a given level cannot exceed 100.
- Deletes are not allowed for top plans being used by an active instance.
- Only plan directives that refer to consumer resource groups are allowed to set the following parameters:
  - ACTIVE_SESS_POOL_P1
  - MAX_EST_EXEC_TIME
  - MAX_IDLE_BLOCKER_TIME
  - MAX_IDLE_TIME
  - PARALLEL_DEGREE_LIMIT_P1
  - QUEUEING_P1
  - SWITCH_ESTIMATE
  - SWITCH_GROUP
  - SWITCH_TIME
  - SWITCH_TIME_IN_CALL
  - UNDO_POOL
- An active plan schema can contain no more than 32 resource consumer groups.

- Plan names cannot conflict with resource consumer group names.
- There must be a plan directive for the OTHER_GROUPS group to allocate resources for sessions not identified in the active plan.

If any of the preceding rules are violated, the VALIDATE_PENDING_AREA procedure will return errors for each violation. Here's an example:

```
SQL> exec dbms_resource_manager.validate_pending_area;
BEGIN dbms_resource_manager.validate_pending_area; END;

*
ERROR at line 1:
ORA-29382: validation of pending area failed
ORA-29377: consumer group OTHER_GROUPS is not part of top-plan OLTP_PLAN
ORA-29383: all leaves of top-plan OLTP_PLAN must be consumer groups
ORA-29374: resource plan OLTP_PLAN in top-plan OLTP_PLAN has no plan directives
ORA-29377: consumer group OTHER_GROUPS is not part of top-plan OFF_HOURS_PLAN
ORA-29383: all leaves of top-plan OFF_HOURS_PLAN must be consumer groups
ORA-29374: resource plan OFF_HOURS_PLAN in top-plan OFF_HOURS_PLAN has no plan
  directives

ORA-29377: consumer group OTHER_GROUPS is not part of top-plan DAY_PLAN
ORA-29383: all leaves of top-plan DAY_PLAN must be consumer groups
ORA-29374: resource plan DAY_PLAN in top-plan DAY_PLAN has no plan directives
ORA-06512: at "SYS.DBMS_RMIN", line 402
ORA-06512: at "SYS.DBMS_RESOURCE_MANAGER", line 437
ORA-06512: at line 1
```

If validation is successful, no error messages will be returned.

Submitting the Pending Area

When you are ready to make your changes active, you can use the DBMS_RESOURCE_MANAGER.SUBMIT_PENDING_AREA procedure, as shown here:

```
SQL> exec dbms_resource_manager.submit_pending_area;

PL/SQL procedure successfully completed.
```

As you can see, no parameters are required when submitting the pending area.

Submitting the contents of the pending area will activate those objects (move them to the data dictionary). Active objects are stored in the data dictionary and can be enabled by DRM.

Just because a DRM object is active does not mean it is enabled. It simply means it can be enabled or be included in an enabled plan.

Submitting the pending area actually performs three distinct actions: It validates, submits, and clears the pending area. Therefore, it is not required to perform a separate validation before submitting. However, from a debugging standpoint, it is beneficial to validate changes on an incremental basis rather than waiting until submit time.

Clearing the Pending Area

To clear the pending area without submitting your changes, you can use the DBMS_RESOURCE_MANAGER.CLEAR_PENDING_AREA procedure, as shown here:

```
SQL> exec dbms_resource_manager.clear_pending_area;

PL/SQL procedure successfully completed.
```

Clearing the pending area drops everything in the pending area irretrievably, so use this procedure with caution. As mentioned earlier, submitting the pending area also clears the pending area, so it is not necessary to use this procedure after a successful submit is performed.

The name of this procedure is somewhat misleading. It seems to imply that the objects in the pending area will be cleared, but that the pending area will remain intact. This is not true. Once the pending area is cleared, a new pending area must be created before making any new changes.

Resource Consumer Groups

Resource consumer groups represent the next step in defining a DRM strategy. They allow you to classify users into logical groupings based on resource consumption requirements or business needs.

There are two ways to define *resource consumer groups*:

- A resource consumer group is a method of classifying users based on their resource consumption tendencies or requirements.
- A resource consumer group is a method of prioritizing database resource usage by classifying users based on business needs.

For instance, in most companies, payroll users tend to have high priority, because no one wants their paychecks to be late. Therefore, a resource consumer group named PAYROLL can be created and all payroll users assigned to it.

This does not imply anything about the resource consumption tendencies or the requirements of payroll users. Instead, it identifies them based on a business need.

On the other hand, a group of inexperienced users may have a habit of executing queries without first checking join conditions. Their resultant Cartesian products tend to run for hours, wasting system resources. For these users, a group named NOVICE could be created. This group could then have resource limitations placed upon it.

In this situation, group classification is directly related to the consumption tendencies of the users.

In either situation, users can be assigned to one or more resource consumer groups, although each active session can be assigned to only one resource consumer group at a time. A user may, for example, use the system in an online transaction processing (OLTP) capacity for part of the day, perhaps entering orders or doing account maintenance. The rest of the day, the same user may switch to an online analytical processing (OLAP) capacity, running reports and statistical queries. This user could be a member of both the OLTP and OLAP resource consumer groups, but could be assigned to only one for any session.

The following sections explain how to manage resource consumer groups using PL/SQL packages.

Managing Resource Consumer Groups

Resource consumer groups can be managed by using the *DBMS_RESOURCE_MANAGER* PL/SQL package. This package offers procedures that allow the creation, deletion, and modification of resource consumer groups. It also provides functionality for assigning users to groups and switching the group for user sessions.

In the next few sections, you'll learn how to add, modify, and delete resource consumer groups using the DBMS_RESOURCE_MANAGER package. You will also learn to assign users to groups as well as how to switch user sessions between groups.

You must have the ADMINISTER_RESOURCE_MANAGER system privilege to administer Database Resource Manager. This privilege is granted by default to the DBA role.

Creating Resource Consumer Groups

To create a new resource consumer group, use the DBMS_RESOURCE_MANAGER.CREATE_CONSUMER_GROUP procedure. All that is required when defining a new group is a unique name and a description. It is not necessary (nor possible) to define how this group will be used at this point.

There are three parameters that you can specify when creating a resource consumer group. Table 11.1 describes these parameters.

The *CPU_MTH* parameter defines the resource scheduling method used between sessions within a resource group. This method governs only CPU resources between group members.

TABLE 11.1 *CREATE_CONSUMER_GROUP* Parameters

Parameter	Description
CONSUMER_GROUP	Consumer group name.
COMMENT	Any comment (usually a description of the group).
CPU_MTH	Method used to schedule CPU resources between sessions in the group. Valid values are: ROUND_ROBIN (the default) ensures fair distribution by using a round-robin schedule. RUN_TO_COMPLETION schedules the most active sessions ahead of other sessions.

Be aware that a CPU allocation method can also be defined at the plan level. Therefore, the total CPU available to the resource group may already have been limited by the active resource plan.

To create a new resource consumer group named DEVELOPERS that uses a round-robin CPU methodology, see the following example:

```
SQL> begin
  dbms_resource_manager.create_consumer_group('developers',
    'application developers');
 end;
SQL>/

PL/SQL procedure successfully completed.
```

To verify that the command succeeded, you can use the DBA_RSRC_CONSUMER_GROUPS view:

```
SQL>  select consumer_group, cpu_method, comments from dba_rsrc_consumer_groups
  where consumer_group = 'DEVELOPERS';

CONSUMER_GROUP  CPU_METHOD      COMMENTS
--------------- --------------- ------------------------
DEVELOPERS      ROUND-ROBIN     application developers
```

By default, there are four resource consumer groups predefined in the database. They are defined in Table 11.2.

As you can see in the description, all users who are not assigned to a group will become part of the *DEFAULT_CONSUMER_GROUP* group. And users who are not assigned to a group in the currently active plan will be assigned to the *OTHER_GROUPS* group.

The remaining two groups, SYS_GROUP and LOW_GROUP, were defined to support a predefined resource plan provided by Oracle.

TABLE 11.2 Predefined Resource Consumer Groups

Group Name	Description
DEFAULT_CONSUMER_GROUP	Default group for all users/sessions not assigned to an initial consumer group.
OTHER_GROUPS	Catch-all group for users assigned to groups that are not part of the currently active plan. This group cannot be explicitly assigned to users.
SYS_GROUP	Used by the Oracle-provided SYSTEM_PLAN plan.
LOW_GROUP	Used by the Oracle-provided SYSTEM_PLAN plan.

Updating Resource Consumer Groups

Consumer resource groups can be updated using the DBMS_RESOURCE_MANAGER.UPDATE_CONSUMER_GROUP procedure. This procedure allows you to change the comment and/or the CPU allocation method for a particular group. Table 11.3 describes the parameters for the DBMS_RESOURCE_MANAGER.UPDATE_CONSUMER_GROUP procedure.

For instance, to change the CPU allocation method for the DEVELOPERS group, the following SQL could be used:

```
SQL> begin
  dbms_resource_manager.update_consumer_group(
  CONSUMER_GROUP => 'DEVELOPERS',
  NEW_CPU_MTH => 'RUN-TO-COMPLETION');
 end;
SQL> /

PL/SQL procedure successfully completed.
```

TABLE 11.3 *UPDATE_CONSUMER_GROUP* Procedure Parameters

Parameter	Description
CONSUMER_GROUP	The name of consumer group
NEW_COMMENT	Updated comment
NEW_CPU_MTH	Updated method for CPU resource allocation

As you can see in this example, the NEW_COMMENT parameter was omitted because no change was being made to it. By the same token, the NEW_CPU_MTH parameter could be omitted if only the comment was being updated.

Deleting a Resource Consumer Group

Consumer resource groups can be deleted using the DBMS_RESOURCE_MANAGER.DELETE_CONSUMER_GROUP procedure. Deleting a resource group has a couple of implications that are important to understand:

- Users assigned to the deleted group as their initial consumer resource group will be assigned to the DEFAULT_CONSUMER_GROUP group.
- Current sessions assigned to the deleted group will be switched to the DEFAULT_CONSUMER_GROUP group.

Don't worry if you don't understand the implications of these changes right now. They will be made clear as this chapter progresses.

Table 11.4 shows the single parameter required by the DBMS_RESOURCE_MANAGER.DELETE_CONSUMER_GROUP procedure.

TABLE 11.4 *DELETE_CONSUMER_GROUP* Procedure Parameter

Parameter	Description
CONSUMER_GROUP	The name of the consumer group to be deleted

Only the name of the group to be deleted needs to be passed to the procedure, as you can see in this example:

```
SQL> begin
  dbms_resource_manager.delete_consumer_group('DEVELOPERS');
 end;
SQL>/

PL/SQL procedure successfully completed.
```

The DEVELOPERS group should now be deleted from the system.

Assigning User Sessions to Consumer Groups

Creating resource consumer groups is only half the battle. You still need a method of assigning consumer groups to user sessions. DRM can be configured to automatically assign consumer groups to sessions based on specific session attributes. This process is called *consumer group mapping*. In the following sections, you will learn how to create consumer group mappings. You will also learn how to set priorities so DRM knows which mapping has precedence in case of conflicts.

Creating Consumer Group Mappings

Consumer group mappings can be created by using the DBMS_RESOURCE_MANAGER.SET_CONSUMER_GROUP_MAPPING procedure. This procedure allows you to map sessions to consumer groups based on login or runtime *session attributes*. Table 11.5 shows the available attributes that can be mapped.

TABLE 11.5 *SET_CONSUMER_GROUP_MAPPING* Session Attributes

Attribute	Type	Description
CLIENT_OS_USER	Login	Operating system username.
CLIENT_PROGRAM	Login	Name of the client program.
CLIENT_MACHINE	Login	Name of machine from which the client is logging in.
MODULE_NAME	Runtime	Module name that is currently executing, as defined by the DBMS_APPLICATION_INFO.SET_MODULE_NAME procedure.
MODULE_NAME_ACTION	Runtime	Module name and module action that are currently executing, as defined by the DBMS_APPLICATION_INFO.SET_MODULE_NAME/SET_ACTION procedures. Attribute is specified in the format *SERVICE_NAME.ACTION*.
ORACLE_USER	Login	Oracle username.
SERVICE_NAME	Login	Client service name used to establish a login.
SERVICE_MODULE	Runtime	Service name and module name in the format SERVICE_NAME.MODULE_NAME.
SERVICE_MODULE_ACTION	Runtime	Service name, module name, and action name in the format SERVICE_NAME.MODULE_NAME.ACTION_NAME.

Mappings simply define a session attribute, a value for the attribute, and a consumer group. For example, if the session attribute CLIENT_OS_USER has a value of graciej, then assign the OLAP_GROUP to the session. The following code would create this mapping:

```
SQL> begin
  dbms_resource_manager.set_consumer_group_mapping(ATTRIBUTE => CLIENT_OS_USER,
    VALUE => 'graciej', CONSUMER_GROUP => 'OLAP_GROUP');
 end;
SQL>/

PL/SQL procedure successfully completed.
```

Note that session attributes are defined as Oracle constants and are therefore specified without surrounding single quotes.

Establishing Mapping Priorities

It is possible that a session may map to more than one consumer group based on mapping rules. Therefore, Oracle allows the creation of *mapping priorities* through the use of the DBMS_ RESOURCE_MANAGER.SET_MAPPING_PRIORITY procedure, as follows:

```
SQL> begin
  dbms_resource_manager.set_mapping_priority(
    EXPLICIT => 1,
    CLIENT_OS_USER => 2,
    CLIENT_MACHINE => 3,
    CLIENT_PROGRAM => 4,
    ORACLE_USER => 5,
    MODULE_NAME => 6,
    MODULE_NAME_ACTION => 7,
    SERVICE_NAME => 8,
    SERVICE_MODULE => 9,
    SERVICE_MODULE_ACTION => 10);
 end;
SQL>/

PL/SQL procedure successfully completed.
```

The priorities defined in the SET_MAPPING_PRIORITY procedure are used to resolve any conflicting mapping rules. The EXPLICIT attribute refers to an explicit consumer group switch (using one of the switching methods described in the next section).

Changing Resource Consumer Groups

Two procedures are provided in the DBMS_RESOURCE_MANAGER package to allow you to explicitly change consumer groups for currently active user sessions: the SWITCH_CONSUMER_GROUP_FOR_SESS and SWITCH_CONSUMER_GROUP_FOR_USER procedures.

In addition, users can be granted the privilege to change their own consumer group. When a user is granted the *switch privilege*, they can use the DBMS_SESSION.SWITCH_CURRENT_CONSUMER_GROUP procedure to change the consumer group for their current session.

In the following sections, you will learn how to use each of these methods to explicitly change consumer groups. You will also learn how to grant and revoke the switch privilege.

Switching Groups using *DBMS_RESOURCE_MANAGER* Procedures

The first procedure, SWITCH_CONSUMER_GROUP_FOR_SESS, explicitly assigns an active session to a new consumer group. The session is identified by the session identifier (SID) and serial number (SERIAL#), both of which can be derived from the V$SESSION table. This procedure is described in Table 11.6.

For example, the following SQL switches a session to the LOW_GROUP group:

```
SQL> begin
  dbms_resource_manager.switch_consumer_group_for_sess (
     SESSION_ID => '56',
     SESSION_SERIAL=> '106',
     CONSUMER_GROUP => 'LOW_GROUP');
 end;
SQL>/

PL/SQL procedure successfully completed.
```

TABLE 11.6 *SWITCH_CONSUMER_GROUP_FOR_SESS* Procedure Parameters

Parameter	Description
SESSION_ID	Session identifier (SID column from the view V$SESSION)
SESSION_SERIAL	Serial number of the session (SERIAL# column from view V$SESSION)
CONSUMER_GROUP	The name of the target consumer group

The second method of changing the consumer group for an active session is the SWITCH_CONSUMER_GROUP_FOR_USER procedure. This procedure changes all active sessions for a given Oracle username. Here's an example:

```
SQL> begin
  dbms_resource_manager.switch_consumer_group_for_user (
     USER => 'BRANDON',
     CONSUMER_GROUP => 'LOW_GROUP');
 end;
SQL>/

PL/SQL procedure successfully completed.
```

This procedure identifies all sessions running under the username of BRANDON and switches them to the LOW_GROUP.

Both of these procedures also switch all parallel sessions that may have been spawned by the session or user.

Explicit consumer group changes are not persistent. They affect only current sessions.

Switching Groups Using *DBMS_SESSION*

If a user has been granted the switch privilege, they can use the DBMS_SESSION.SWITCH_CURRENT_CONSUMER_GROUP procedure to explicitly change the group for their current session. Table 11.7 describes the parameters for this procedure.

TABLE 11.7 *SWITCH_CURRENT_CONSUMER_GROUP* Procedure Parameters

Parameter	Description
NEW_CONSUMER_GROUP	The name of the consumer group to which the session is switching.
OLD_CONSUMER_GROUP	An output parameter that returns the name of the original consumer group (before the switch).
INITIAL_GROUP_ON_ERROR	If the switch fails, this parameter controls the outcome. If TRUE, the session reverts to its original group. If FALSE, an error is raised.

When this procedure completes, it returns the name of the original consumer group back to the calling program. This is presumably so the program can retain the original group and use it to revert back later in the program, if so desired. The following example shows how to call this procedure from a PL/SQL block:

```
DECLARE
   original_group varchar2(30);
   junk           varchar2(30);
BEGIN
  DBMS_SESSION.SWITCH_CURRENT_CONSUMER_GROUP(
  'MARKETING', original_group, FALSE);

< execute some SQL>

  DBMS_SESSION.SWITCH_CURRENT_CONSUMER_GROUP(
  original_group, junk, FALSE);

END;
```

This PL/SQL block switches from the current consumer group to the MARKETING group and saves the original group name in a variable named ORIGINAL_GROUP. After executing some SQL, it uses the ORIGINAL_GROUP variable to switch back to the original group.

Managing the Switch Privilege

Before a user can switch their own consumer group, they must have been granted the switch privilege directly, or be granted a role that has been granted the switch privilege. The switch privilege is granted to users and/or to roles through the DBMS_RESOURCE_MANAGER_PRIVS.GRANT_SWITCH_CONSUMER_GROUP procedure. The parameters for this procedure are described in Table 11.8.

TABLE 11.8 *GRANT_SWITCH_CONSUMER_GROUP* Procedure Parameters

Parameter	Description
GRANTEE_NAME	Username or role name receiving the grant.
CONSUMER_GROUP	Name of the consumer group to which the grantee will be allowed to switch.
GRANT_OPTION	Determines whether the grantee can, in turn, grant the switch privilege to another user. If TRUE, the grantee can grant the switch privilege to another user. If FALSE, the grantee cannot grant the switch privilege to another user.

By granting the switch privilege to roles, it is much easier to grant the privilege to entire groups of users, as shown here:

```
SQL> begin
  dbms_resource_manager_privs.grant_switch_consumer_group(
    'PROG_ROLE', 'DEVELOPERS', FALSE);
 end;
SQL>/

PL/SQL procedure successfully completed.
```

In this example, the switch privilege is granted to the PROG_ROLE role. Any user granted that role will be able to switch to the DEVELOPERS group, but they cannot grant the privilege to any other users. If the *GRANT_OPTION* parameter was set to TRUE, the user could, in turn, grant the same privilege to another user.

If the switch privilege is granted to PUBLIC for any consumer group, any user will be able to switch to the specified consumer group.

The switch privilege can also be revoked by using the DBMS_RESOURCE_MANAGER_PRIVS .REVOKE_SWITCH_CONSUMER_GROUP procedure. The parameters for this procedure are described in Table 11.9.

This procedure revokes a user or role's privilege to switch to the specified consumer group. Here's an example:

```
SQL> begin
  dbms_resource_manager_privs.revoke_switch_consumer_group(
    'PROG_ROLE', 'DEVELOPERS');
 end;
SQL>/

PL/SQL procedure successfully completed.
```

This example revokes the privileges granted in the preceding example.

TABLE 11.9 *REVOKE_SWITCH_CONSUMER_GROUP* Procedure Parameters

Parameter	Description
REVOKEE_NAME	Name of user or role with privileges being revoked
CONSUMER_GROUP	Name of consumer group being revoked

Resource Plans

DRM allocates resources among resource consumer groups based on a resource plan. A *resource plan* consists of directives specifying how resources should be distributed among resource consumer groups or other resource plans.

Resource plans prioritize resource allocation through the use of levels, with level 1 being the highest priority and level 8 being the lowest.

Simple resource plans are limited to allocating only CPU resources to a small number of consumer groups. However, they are very simple to set up and represent a good starting place if you're new to DRM. Simple resource plans define the resource plan, resource plan directives, and resource consumer groups all with one procedure, whereas complex plans define each separately. Simple resource plans are also classified as *single-level resource plans* because there are no sub-plans involved.

Complex resource plans can use any of Oracle's predefined resource allocation methods and can include up to 32 consumer groups. Complex resource plans can also contain *sub-plans*. If sub-plans are defined, the plan would be classified as a multi-level resource plan.

There is no difference between a plan and a sub-plan. They are defined in exactly the same manner. A sub-plan is simply a plan that is nested within the scope of a top-level plan, so it is allocated resources from the top-level plan.

Resource plans have two options regarding the CPU allocation method—EMPHASIS and RATIO—as described in Table 11.10.

The EMPHASIS method is used most often and can be used for either single- or multi-level plans. Under the EMPHASIS method, CPU resource allocations are expressed as percentages in the plan directives.

The RATIO method can be used only on single-level plans (plans that contain directives that allocate CPU resources at level 1 only). Under the RATIO method, the CPU resource allocations are expressed as a weight in the plan directives.

TABLE 11.10 Resource Plan CPU Allocation Methods

CPU Allocation Method	Description
EMPHASIS	The allocated amount is treated as a percentage (in other words, 80 = 80 percent) of available CPU. EMPHASIS is valid for both single and multi-level plans, and is the only option for simple resource plans (the default).
RATIO	The allocated amount is treated as a ratio of the total CPU resources. The RATIO method can be defined only on single-level plans.

For example, assume a plan containing plan directives for the PAYROLL, MARKETING, and OTHER_GROUPS consumer groups. The plan is defined to use the RATIO method for CPU allocation. Assume that the directives contain the allocations listed in Table 11.11.

The result of these directives will allocate CPU resources using a 10:2:1 ratio. The MARKETING group will get only two CPU cycles for every 10 that the PAYROLL group receives. The OTHER_GROUPS group will get one cycle for every for every two that the MARKETING group receives.

Examples of resource directives using both the EMPHASIS and RATIO methods are provided in the "Resource Plan Directives" section later in this chapter.

In the following sections, you will learn how to create both simple and complex resource plans. You'll also learn how to update and delete resource plans.

TABLE 11.11 Plan Directives Using the *RATIO* Method

Consumer Group	*CPU_P1* Parameter Setting
PAYROLL	10
MARKETING	2
OTHER_GROUPS	1

Creating Simple Resource Plans

Simple resource plans, though limited in their abilities and scope, offer an adequate solution for environments with only basic resource management needs. They are distinct from complex plans in that they create a resource plan, resource plan directives, and resource consumer groups in one simple procedure.

Simple resource plans are limited to using only the CPU resource plan directive. This means that the only resource that can be allocated is the CPU. Simple plans also limit the total number of resource groups to eight.

To create a simple resource plan, Oracle provides the DBMS_RESOURCE_MANAGER.CREATE_SIMPLE_PLAN procedure, whose parameters are described in Table 11.12.

This procedure allows for the creation of up to eight consumer groups, along with their CPU allocations.

Simple resource plans always use the EMPHASIS CPU resource allocation policy. This means that the value entered for the CPU allocations will be interpreted as a percentage of total CPU. For example, if you want to implement the specifications shown in Table 11.13, a simple resource plan can be created in the example that follows.

```
SQL> begin
DBMS_RESOURCE_MANAGER.CREATE_SIMPLE_PLAN(
```

```
  SIMPLE_PLAN => 'DEPARTMENTS',
  CONSUMER_GROUP1 => 'PAYROLL',
  GROUP1_CPU => 50,
  CONSUMER_GROUP2 => 'SALES',
  GROUP2_CPU => 25,
  CONSUMER_GROUP3 => 'MARKETING',
  GROUP3_CPU => 25);
end;
SQL> /

PL/SQL procedure successfully completed.
```

TABLE 11.12 *CREATE_SIMPLE_PLAN* Procedure Parameters

Parameter	Description
SIMPLE_PLAN	The name assigned to the plan
CONSUMER_GROUP1	The name of the first consumer group
GROUP1_CPU	CPU allocation for the first consumer group
CONSUMER_GROUP2	The name of the second consumer group
GROUP2_CPU	CPU allocation for the second consumer group
CONSUMER_GROUP3	The name of the third consumer group
GROUP3_CPU	CPU allocation for the third consumer group
CONSUMER_GROUP4	The name of the fourth consumer group
GROUP4_CPU	CPU allocation for the fourth consumer group
CONSUMER_GROUP5	The name of the fifth consumer group
GROUP5_CPU	CPU allocation for the fifth consumer group
CONSUMER_GROUP6	The name of the sixth consumer group
GROUP6_CPU	CPU allocation for the sixth consumer group
CONSUMER_GROUP7	The name of the seventh consumer group

TABLE 11.12 *CREATE_SIMPLE_PLAN* Procedure Parameters *(continued)*

Parameter	Description
GROUP7_CPU	CPU allocation for the seventh consumer group
CONSUMER_GROUP8	The name of the eighth consumer group
GROUP8_CPU	CPU allocation for the eighth consumer group

TABLE 11.13 *DEPARTMENTS* Plan Specification

Group	CPU Allocation
PAYROLL	50%
SALES	25%
MARKETING	25%

When a simple plan is created, the results might be somewhat surprising. Table 11.14 shows the finished plan, and you can see that Oracle has added two additional consumer groups to it: SYS_GROUP and OTHER_GROUPS.

SYS_GROUP represents the users SYS and SYSTEM.

OTHER_GROUPS is a required group that must be included in any resource plan. It ensures that users who are not assigned to any group in the active resource plan will still have resources allocated.

Notice also that the final plan is a multi-level plan and the elements that you defined are assigned to the second level. This ensures that members of the SYS_GROUP (at level 1) will have no CPU restrictions. Groups at level 2 will share CPU resources not used by level 1 groups. Likewise, users not assigned to any group in the plan (at level 3) will receive CPU time only after levels 1 and 2 have satisfied their requirements.

TABLE 11.14 Final *DEPARTMENTS* Plan

Level	*Sys_Group*	*Payroll*	*Sales*	*Marketing*	*Other_Groups*
1	100%				
2		50%	25%	25%	
3					100%

Creating Complex Resource Plans

Complex resource plans differ from simple resource plans in how they are defined. Simple plans can create the plan, resource groups, and plan directives in one operation. For complex plans, each of these elements is defined and stored separately. This method offers more flexibility when building resource plans.

This method also allows for the nesting of plans, so one plan can act as a sub-plan of another. When plans are nested in this manner, it is referred to as a multi-level plan.

Creating a plan involves defining the name of the plan, a comment or description regarding the plan, and the methods that the plan will follow when allocating specific resources. Notice that the plan does not determine which resources it will manage. Those are predefined by Oracle. A plan defines only the method it will apply when allocating those resources.

To create a new plan, use the DBMS_RESOURCE_MANAGER.CREATE_PLAN procedure, whose parameters are described in Table 11.15.

TABLE 11.15 *CREATE_PLAN* Procedure Parameters

Parameter	Description
PLAN	The name of the resource plan.
COMMENT	Comment or description of plan.
CPU_MTH	The method of allocating CPU resources. EMPHASIS (default): CPU will be distributed on a percentage basis. RATIO: CPU will be distributed on a ratio basis.
ACTIVE_SESS_POOL_MTH	The method of allocating session pool resources (limiting the number of active sessions). ACTIVE_SESS_POOL_ABSOLUTE: The only method available. Treats the number specified in a plan directive as the maximum number of active sessions allowed.
PARALLEL_DEGREE_LIMIT_MTH	The method of specifying degree of parallelism for any operation. PARALLEL_DEGREE_LIMIT_ABSOLUTE: The only method available. Treats the number specified in plan directives as the maximum degree of parallelism that will be allowed.
QUEUEING_MTH	Method of allocating execution of queued sessions. FIFO_TIMEOUT: The only method available. Uses a first-in/first-out method for prioritizing sessions waiting in queue due to resource limitations.

As you can see, only the first three parameters (PLAN, COMMENT, and CPU_MTH) actually have any effect on the plan. The others (ACTIVE_SESS_POOL_MTH, PARALLEL_DEGREE_LIMIT_MTH, and QUEUEING_MTH) offer only one option, which is also the default. It is expected that future releases will expand the choices for these parameters.

Therefore, a plan can be created as follows:

```
SQL> begin
  dbms_resource_manager.create_plan(
    PLAN => 'DAY',
    COMMENT => 'CREATED BY TBB');
  end;
SQL>/

PL/SQL procedure successfully completed.
```

To verify that the resource plan was actually created, you can use the DBA_RSRC_PLANS view:

```
SQL> select plan, num_plan_directives, cpu_method
  2  from dba_rsrc_plans;

PLAN                     NUM_PLAN_DIRECTIVES CPU_METHOD
-------------------- ------------------- ----------
SYSTEM_PLAN                            3 EMPHASIS
INTERNAL_QUIESCE                       2 EMPHASIS
INTERNAL_PLAN                          1 EMPHASIS
DAY                                    1 EMPHASIS
```

As you can see, the plan was indeed created, and in fact it already has one plan directive assigned to it. Remember that Oracle requires all plans to have a directive for the OTHER_GROUPS resource group. Therefore, Oracle automatically creates this directive for you.

Creating Resource Sub-Plans

A resource sub-plan is created in exactly the same manner as a resource plan. That's because there is no difference between them. A sub-plan is a plan. It only becomes a sub-plan if a higher level plan allocates resources to it (through a resource plan directive).

For example, plan A can allocate resources to consumer groups A and B, and to plan B. Plan B is now classified as a sub-plan. The difference is that a top-level plan always has 100 percent of the resources available to allocate, whereas a sub-plan can allocate only the resources that have been allocated to it by the top-level plan.

Modifying Resource Plans

Resource plans can be modified by using the DBMS_RESOURCE_MANAGER.UPDATE_PLAN procedure. The parameters for this procedure are described in Table 11.16.

Again, keep in mind that only the first three parameters will have any effect on resource plans because there are no other valid options for the others. To verify this, you can use any of the following views:

- V$ACTIVE_SESS_POOL_MTH
- V$PARALLEL_DEGREE_LIMIT_MTH
- V$QUEUEING_MTH
- V$RSRC_PLAN_CPU_MTH

These views display the valid values for each of the resource plan allocation methods.

To change the comment on the DAY plan, see the following example:

```
SQL> exec dbms_resource_manager.update_plan(
  PLAN => 'DAY',
  NEW_COMMENT => 'Plan for scheduled work hours');

PL/SQL procedure successfully completed.
```

TABLE 11.16 *UPDATE_PLAN* Procedure Parameters

Parameter	Description
PLAN	Name of the resource plan
NEW_COMMENT	New comment
NEW_CPU_MTH	New method of allocating CPU resources
NEW_ACTIVE_SESS_POOL_MTH	New method of allocating session pool resources
NEW_PARALLEL_DEGREE_LIMIT_MTH	New method of specifying the degree of parallelism for any operation
NEW_QUEUEING_MTH	New method of allocating the execution of queued sessions

Deleting Resource Plans

Resource plans can be deleted by using either the DBMS_RESOURCE_MANAGER.DELETE_PLAN procedure or the DBMS_RESOURCE_MANAGER.DELETE_PLAN_CASCADE procedure. The former removes the resource plan but leaves all subordinate objects (consumer groups, plan directives, and sub-plans) intact. The latter removes the resource plan, along with all subordinate objects.

If the DELETE_PLAN_CASCADE procedure attempts to delete a subordinate object that happens to also be part of the currently active plan, the delete will fail and the entire plan will be restored.

The only parameter accepted by these procedures is a valid resource plan name, as shown in this example:

```
SQL>  exec dbms_resource_manager.delete_plan('DAY');

PL/SQL procedure successfully completed.
```

Resource Plan Directives

Resource plan directives are the key element in creating complex resource plans. As you saw earlier in this chapter, a resource plan by itself does very little, until it has resource plan directives assigned to it. Resource plan directives assign consumer groups to resource plans and define the resource allocations for each. In addition to consumer groups, plan directives can allocate resources to sub-plans.

Resource plan directives work by specifying the owning resource plan, the target consumer group or sub-plan, and the resource allocations assigned to the target. Resources are allocated to the target by setting parameters for the various resource allocation methods.

Resource allocation methods are predefined by Oracle and, as such, are not modifiable. These represent the various methods available to DRM to allocate resources. The following methods are available:

CPU The CPU method specifies how CPU resources are to be allocated among consumer groups or sub-plans. Up to eight levels can be defined, allowing for the prioritization of CPU resources. For example, level 2 gets CPU only if level 1 is unable to utilize all of its allocated CPU. Therefore, level 1 has the highest priority, while level 8 has the lowest priority.

Active session pool with queuing The active session pool with queuing method limits the number of concurrent active sessions available to a consumer group. If the allocated number of sessions is reached, new session requests will be placed in a queue until an active session completes.

Degree of parallelism limit The degree of parallelism limit method specifies the maximum parallel degree for any operation within a consumer group. If a higher degree is specified, it will automatically be altered down to the value specified for this parameter.

Automatic consumer group switching The automatic consumer group switching method allows sessions exceeding certain execution time criteria to be dynamically switched to a different group. For example, if a session exceeds the defined execution time threshold, it can be automatically switched to a lower priority group. This method can also be used to automatically cancel the operation or even kill the offending session.

Canceling SQL and terminating sessions This method specifies that long-running queries or long-running sessions will be automatically terminated if the execution time threshold is exceeded.

Execution time limit The execution time limit method specifies the maximum estimated execution time allowed for any operation. If Oracle estimates that an operation will exceed the specified execution time, it will terminate the operation and return an error. It does this before actual execution begins.

Undo pool The undo pool method specifies the amount of undo that can be generated by a consumer group. If the group exceeds the allocated amount, the current DML statement is terminated and no other group members may perform data manipulation until undo space is freed.

Idle time limit The idle time limit method specifies the maximum amount of time that a session can remain idle. If this limit is exceeded, the session will automatically be terminated. This method can also be limited to terminating only idle sessions that are blocking other sessions.

Resource plan directives can set levels for one or more of these methods for each consumer group or sub-plan. However, only CPU methods may be defined for sub-plans. The other methods are invalid for assigning resources to sub-plans.

In the following sections, you will learn how to create the various types of resource plan directives. You'll also learn how plan directives can be used to monitor and manage long-running operations. Finally, you'll learn to update and delete plan directives.

Creating Resource Plan Directives

To create a resource plan directive, the DBMS_RESOURCE_MANAGER.CREATE_PLAN_DIRECTIVE procedure is used. Table 11.17 describes the interface for this procedure.

TABLE 11.17 *CREATE_PLAN_DIRECTIVE* Procedure Parameters

Parameter	Description
PLAN	The name of the resource plan to which this directive belongs.
GROUP_OR_SUBPLAN	The name of the consumer group or sub-plan being allocated resources by this directive.
COMMENT	Comment or description of plan directive.

TABLE 11.17 *CREATE_PLAN_DIRECTIVE* Procedure Parameters *(continued)*

Parameter	Description
CPU_P1	This parameter represents either the CPU allocated at level 1 or the ratio weight for CPU resources, depending on the allocation method defined for the resource plan. If the resource plan uses the EMPHASIS allocation method for CPU resources, this parameter defines the percentage of CPU allocated at level 1 for the group/sub-plan. If the plan uses the RATIO allocation method for CPU resources, this parameter defines the weight of CPU usage for the group/sub-plan. The default is NULL, which provides no allocation of CPU resources.
CPU_P2	The percentage of CPU allocated at level 2 for the group/sub-plan (if the plan uses the EMPHASIS method). Not applicable for the RATIO method. The default is NULL.
CPU_P3	The percentage of CPU allocated at level 3 for the group/sub-plan (if the plan uses the EMPHASIS method). Not applicable for the RATIO method. The default is NULL.
CPU_P4	The percentage of CPU allocated at level 4 for the group/sub-plan (if the plan uses the EMPHASIS method). Not applicable for the RATIO method. The default is NULL.
CPU_P5	The percentage of CPU allocated at level 5 for the group/sub-plan (if the plan uses the EMPHASIS method). Not applicable for the RATIO method. The default is NULL.
CPU_P6	The percentage of CPU allocated at level 6 for the group/sub-plan (if the plan uses the EMPHASIS method). Not applicable for the RATIO method. The default is NULL.
CPU_P7	The percentage of CPU allocated at level 7 for the group/sub-plan (if the plan uses the EMPHASIS method). Not applicable for the RATIO method. The default is NULL.
CPU_P8	The percentage of CPU allocated at level 8 for the group/sub-plan (if the plan uses the EMPHASIS method). Not applicable for the RATIO method. The default is NULL.
ACTIVE_SESS_POOL_P1	Specifies the maximum number of concurrently active sessions for a consumer group or sub-plan. The default is NULL, which means unlimited.
QUEUEING_P1	The number of seconds before a job in the inactive session queue times out. The default is NULL, meaning that queued jobs will never time out.

TABLE 11.17 *CREATE_PLAN_DIRECTIVE* Procedure Parameters *(continued)*

Parameter	Description
PARALLEL_DEGREE_LIMIT_P1	The maximum degree of parallelism that can be defined for any operation. The default is NULL, meaning that no limit is imposed.
SWITCH_GROUP	The consumer group to which this session will be switched if the switch criteria is met. The default is NULL. Other options are CANCEL_SQL, which will kill the query when switch criteria is met, and KILL_SESSION, which will kill the session when the switch criteria is met.
SWITCH_TIME	The number of seconds that a session can execute an operation before a group switch will occur. The default is NULL, meaning that there is no limit on execution time. After the operation is complete, the session remains in the new consumer group, rather than reverting to its original consumer group.
SWITCH_ESTIMATE	Directs Oracle to estimate the execution time for an operation before execution begins. If the estimated time exceeds the value set for SWITCH_TIME, Oracle will perform the switch before execution of the query begins. Valid settings are TRUE or FALSE. The default is FALSE.
MAX_EST_EXEC_TIME	Directs Oracle to estimate the execution time for an operation before execution begins. If the estimated time exceeds the number of seconds defined in this parameter, the operation is not started and an ORA-07455 error is issued. The default is NULL, meaning that no estimate limit is imposed.
UNDO_POOL	Maximum kilobytes (KB) of undo that can be generated by the consumer group/sub-plan. The default is NULL, meaning that no limit is imposed.
MAX_IDLE_TIME	The number of seconds that a session can remain idle before the session is killed. The default is NULL, meaning that no idle time limit is imposed.
MAX_IDLE_BLOCKER_TIME	The number of seconds that a blocking session can remain idle before the session is killed. (A blocking session is a session that is locking a resource that is needed by another session.) The default is NULL, meaning that no idle time limit is imposed.
SWITCH_TIME_IN_CALL	The number of seconds that a session can execute before a group switch will occur. When the top call has completed, the session will revert to its original consumer group. The default is NULL, meaning that no limit is imposed.

Both SWITCH_TIME_IN_CALL and SWITCH_TIME cannot be specified in the same resource directive, because they represent conflicting actions.

The following example creates a resource plan directive for the DAY plan, which limits the parallel degree settings for the DEVELOPERS group:

```
SQL> begin
  dbms_resource_manager.create_plan_directive(
    PLAN => 'DAY',
    COMMENT => 'DEVELOPERS DAY PLAN',
    GROUP_OR_SUBPLAN => 'DEVELOPERS',
    PARALLEL_DEGREE_LIMIT_P1 => '4');
  end;
SQL> /

PL/SQL procedure successfully completed.
```

In the following sections, you will learn to create directives, which define sub-plans. You'll also learn to create directives that create multi-level plans. Finally, you'll learn to create plans that use the consumer group switching method to manage long-running operations.

Creating Sub-Plan Directives

To create a sub-plan directive, a plan directive is created, which allocates CPU resources to another plan (which is then referred to as a sub-plan). The sub-plan still retains all of its original functionality. However, the total CPU resources it can allocate are limited to those it receives from the top-level plan.

For example, to define a sub-plan under the DAY plan, you would set the GROUP_OR_SUBPLAN parameter to the name of the target plan, as follows:

```
SQL> begin
  dbms_resource_manager.create_plan_directive(
    PLAN => 'DAY',
    COMMENT => 'DEPARTMENTS SUB-PLAN',
    GROUP_OR_SUBPLAN => 'DEPARTMENTS',
    CPU_P2=> 50);
  end;
SQL> /

PL/SQL procedure successfully completed.
```

In this example, the plan DEPARTMENTS was defined as a sub-plan of the DAY plan and limited to 50 percent of the level 2 CPU resources.

Sub-plan directives can allocate only CPU resources to a sub-plan.

Creating Multi-Level Plan Directives

Multi-level plan directives are used to prioritize CPU allocation for consumer groups and sub-plans. When a plan directive is created, the parameters CPU_P1 through CPU_P8 determine the level at which the CPU resources will be allocated to the specified group or sub-plan. The total of resources allocated at any one level cannot exceed 100 percent.

Up to eight levels can be specified, with level 1 being the highest priority and level 8 being the lowest. Level 1 recipients share the total available CPU based on their respective CPU_P1 parameter value. Level 2 recipients share only the CPU resources that are not consumed at level 1, and so on.

Consider this example:

```
SQL> begin
  dbms_resource_manager.create_plan_directive(
    PLAN => 'DAY',
    COMMENT => 'SYSTEM USERS',
    GROUP_OR_SUBPLAN => 'SYS_GROUP',
    CPU_P1=> 100);
  end;
SQL> /

PL/SQL procedure successfully completed.

SQL> begin
  dbms_resource_manager.create_plan_directive(
    PLAN => 'DAY',
    COMMENT => 'DEPARTMENTS SUB-PLAN',
    GROUP_OR_SUBPLAN => 'DEPARTMENTS',
    CPU_P2=> 50);
  end;
SQL> /

PL/SQL procedure successfully completed.

SQL> begin
  dbms_resource_manager.create_plan_directive(
    PLAN => 'DAY',
```

```
    COMMENT => 'DEVELOPERS GROUP CPU ALLOCATION',
    GROUP_OR_SUBPLAN => 'DEVELOPERS',
    CPU_P2=> 50);
  end;
SQL> /

PL/SQL procedure successfully completed.

SQL> begin
  dbms_resource_manager.create_plan_directive(
    PLAN => 'DAY',
    COMMENT => 'OTHER_GROUPS CPU ALLOCATION',
    GROUP_OR_SUBPLAN => 'OTHER_GROUPS',
    CPU_P3=> 100);
  end;
SQL> /

PL/SQL procedure successfully completed.
```

In this example, four directives are created for the DAY plan. The first directive allocates 100 percent of level 1 CPU resources to the SYS_GROUP group. The second directive allocates 50 percent of level 2 CPU resources to the DEPARTMENTS sub-plan. The third directive allocates the other 50 percent of level 2 CPU resources to the DEVELOPERS consumer group. Finally, the fourth directive allocates 100 percent of level 3 CPU resources to the OTHER_GROUPS group. Figure 11.1 shows a representation of the multi-level DAY plan.

Creating Automatic Consumer Group Switching Directives

Plan directives can include options for automatically switching consumer resource groups for sessions that exceed defined thresholds. For example, a directive can dictate that any session that has an operation executing for more than 10 minutes should automatically be switched into a lower priority group. They can also dictate that Oracle will automatically kill the query or even the session when switching thresholds are exceeded.

The key parameters in defining automatic consumer group switching are as follows:

SWITCH_TIME The SWITCH_TIME parameter sets the maximum execution time (in seconds) allowed for any operation. A session violating this threshold is automatically switched to the group defined by the SWITCH_GROUP parameter.

The switch group is generally a group with lower priority so that the long-running operation will be allocated fewer resources. However, the switch group can also be set to the Oracle constants KILL_SESSION or CANCEL_SQL, which would result in the offending session being killed or the offending SQL operation being cancelled.

Once a session has been switched to another group using this method, it will not switch back to its original consumer group, even after the offending operation has completed.

FIGURE 11.1 Multi-level resource plan

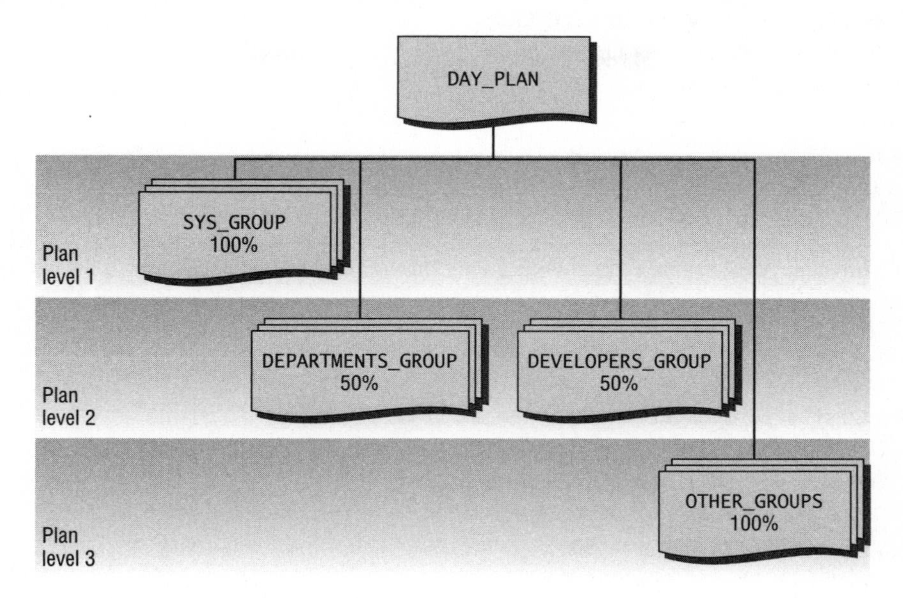

SWITCH_TIME_IN_CALL The SWITCH_TIME_IN_CALL parameter works similarly to the SWITCH_TIME parameter, except that the offending session remains in the switch group only until the operation has completed. After the operation completes, the session reverts to its original consumer group.

The SWITCH_TIME and SWITCH_TIME_IN_CALL methods are mutually exclusive. Only one method may be defined in a plan directive.

SWITCH_ESTIMATE The SWITCH_ESTIMATE parameter specifies that the Oracle optimizer should estimate the execution time of an operation before actually executing it. If the estimated time exceeds the value set in the SWITCH_TIME or SWITCH_TIME_IN_CALL parameter, then the consumer group switch will occur prior to execution of the operation.

When a session is switched using this method, it will not revert to its original consumer group if the SWITCH_TIME parameter is set. It will revert to its original consumer group if the SWITCH_TIME_IN_CALL parameter is set.

To create a plan directive that automatically cancels operations that execute for more than one hour, see the following example:

```
SQL> begin
  dbms_resource_manager.create_plan_directive(
    PLAN => 'DAY',
```

```
    COMMENT => 'LIMIT DEVELOPERS EXECUTION TIME',
    GROUP_OR_SUBPLAN => 'DEVELOPERS',
    SWITCH_GROUP => 'CANCEL_SQL',
    SWITCH_TIME => 3600);
  end;
SQL> /

PL/SQL procedure successfully completed.
```

To create a plan directive that temporarily moves DEVELOPERS sessions to a lower priority group whenever Oracle estimates that an operation will execute for more than 15 minutes, see this example:

```
SQL> begin
  dbms_resource_manager.create_plan_directive(
    PLAN => 'DAY',
    COMMENT => 'SWITCH DEVELOPERS TEMPORARILY',
    GROUP_OR_SUBPLAN => 'DEVELOPERS',
    SWITCH_TIME_IN_CALL => 900,
    SWITCH_GROUP => 'LOW_GROUP',
    SWITCH_ESTIMATE => TRUE);
  end;
SQL> /

PL/SQL procedure successfully completed.
```

This example switches the session to the LOW_GROUP consumer group prior to execution of any operation that Oracle estimates will exceed 15 minutes (900 seconds). When the operation has completed, the session will revert to the DEVELOPERS group.

Updating Resource Plan Directives

Resource plan directives can be updated using the DBMS_RESOURCE_MANAGER.UPDATE_PLAN_DIRECTIVE procedure. The parameters for this procedure are identical to the parameters for the CREATE_PLAN_DIRECTIVE procedure, except that the prefix NEW_ has been added to all of the modifiable parameters (for example, NEW_COMMENT, NEW_CPU_P1, and so on).

The only parameters that cannot be modified are the PLAN and GROUP_OR_SUBPLAN parameters. All of the others can be updated.

Consider the following example:

```
SQL> begin
  dbms_resource_manager.update_plan_directive(
    PLAN => 'DAY',
    GROUP_OR_SUBPLAN => 'DEVELOPERS',
```

```
    NEW_SWITCH_ESTIMATE => FALSE);
 end;
SQL>/

PL/SQL procedure successfully completed.
```

In this example, the SWITCH_ESTIMATE setting is updated to a value of FALSE. Notice that the parameter used is NEW_SWITCH_ESTIMATE rather than SWITCH_ESTIMATE.

Real World Scenario

Runaway Processes

In my current job, my team administers (among other things) a data warehouse totaling approximately five billion rows. Due to the size of many of the tables, parallel queries drastically reduce runtime for most queries. However, we seem to encounter our share of Oracle bugs, resulting in runaway parallel processes.

For example, a query will spawn eight parallel processes and proceed normally until very near the end of the processing. Then, one process will slowly start spinning CPU cycles. If not caught early, it will eventually consume all CPU and bring the system grinding to a halt.

We've applied several patches that seem to fix the problem, but in reality we just encounter the bug (or a different one with similar effects) less often.

By using Database Resource Monitor, we were able to devise a relatively simple plan that killed sessions if they reached a very high CPU percentage threshold. Now the runaway processes are automatically killed, and the beauty of it is that no DBA involvement is required.

Deleting Resource Plan Directives

Resource plan directives can be deleted using the DBMS_RESOURCE_MANAGER.DELETE_PLAN_DIRECTIVE procedure. The only parameters required are the PLAN and GROUP_OR_SUBPLAN parameters, as shown here:

```
SQL> begin
  dbms_resource_manager.delete_plan_directive(
    PLAN => 'DAY',
    GROUP_OR_SUBPLAN => 'DEVELOPERS');
 end;
SQL>/

PL/SQL procedure successfully completed.
```

Putting the Pieces Together

Now that you've learned about all of the various elements of DRM individually, it's time to put them all together.

For most companies, database requirements differ depending on the time of day. For example, during normal daytime business hours, online transaction processing (OLTP) may be mission-critical, along with a small amount of report processing. After hours, however, bulk data loads and online analytical processing (OLAP) reports may take priority.

In this section, you'll learn how to develop complex multi-level resource plans to accommodate these types of business requirements. You'll see how all of the elements are created and associated to the plan. You'll also learn how to enable the finalized plan.

Creating the Elements

In this section, you will be provided step-by-step instructions for the creation of the plans shown in Figures 11.2 and 11.3. First, the pending area will be created. Next, the consumer resource groups will be created. After that, the resource plans will be created. And, finally, the resource plan directives will be created to tie them all together.

Once all of the elements are in place, they will be validated and activated. Finally, you'll learn to enable the resource plans, as well as how to switch the enabled resource plan.

FIGURE 11.2 *OFF_HOURS_PLAN* high-level design

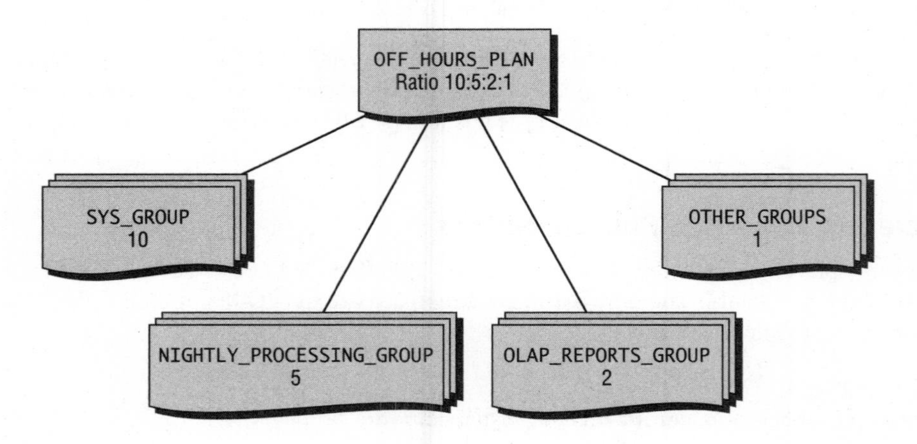

FIGURE 11.3 *DAY_PLAN* high-level design

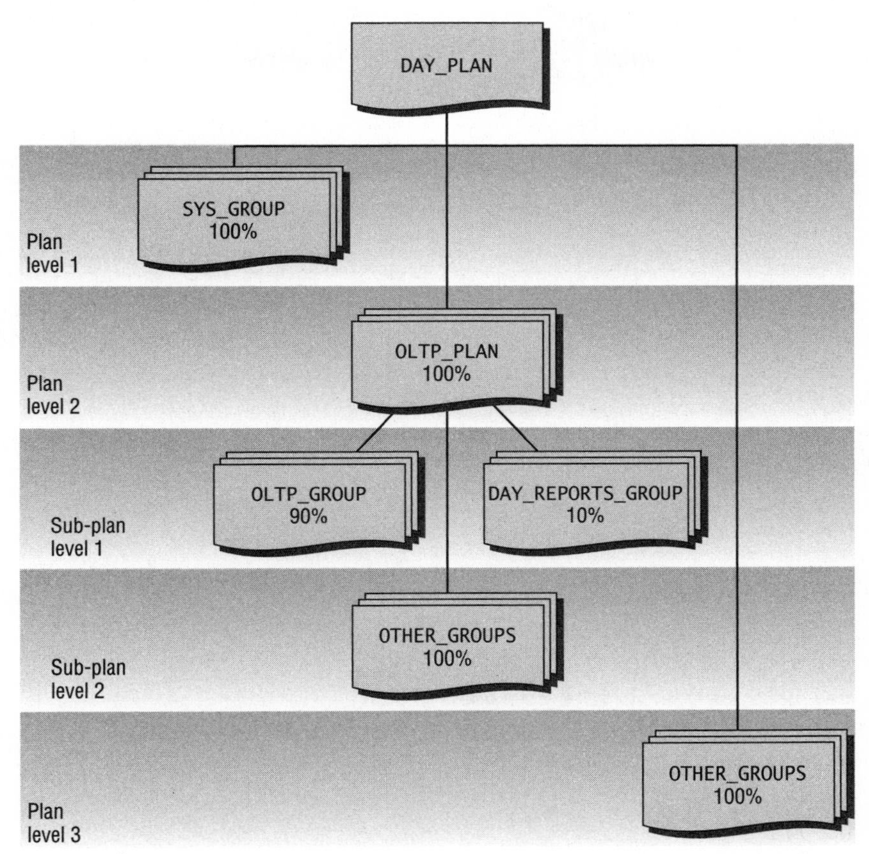

Creating the Pending Area

Before creating any new DRM elements, a pending area must be established to hold your new plans. The pending area is a development area where you can work on DRM elements without affecting the active DRM plan. It can be created as shown here:

```
SQL> exec dbms_resource_manager.create_pending_area();

PL/SQL procedure successfully completed.
```

Once the pending area is in place, new elements will reside there until the plan is enabled.

Creating the Consumer Resource Groups

Next, the consumer resource groups can be created. In this step, all consumer resource groups required by both resource plans will be created.

These groups can be created as follows:

```
SQL> begin
  dbms_resource_manager.create_consumer_group(
  'OLTP_GROUP','Incoming orders');
 end;
SQL>/

PL/SQL procedure successfully completed.

SQL> begin
  dbms_resource_manager.create_consumer_group(
  'DAY_REPORTS_GROUP','DAYTIME REPORTS');
 end;
SQL>/

PL/SQL procedure successfully completed.

SQL> begin
  dbms_resource_manager.create_consumer_group(
  'NIGHTLY_PROCESSING_GROUP','BULK LOADS, ETL, ETC.');
 end;
SQL>/

PL/SQL procedure successfully completed.

SQL> begin
  dbms_resource_manager.create_consumer_group(
  'OLAP_REPORTS_GROUP','OFF HOURS REPORTS');
 end;
SQL>/

PL/SQL procedure successfully completed.
```

Because the SYS_GROUP and the OTHER_GROUPS consumer groups are created automatically at Oracle installation time, there is no need to create them.

Creating the Resource Plans

Now that all the necessary consumer groups are in place, the next step is to create the resource plans. Three distinct plans are required. Both the DAY_PLAN and OLTP_PLAN plans use the default EMPHASIS CPU allocation method, whereas the OFF_HOURS_PLAN plan utilizes the RATIO method. Remember that the CPU resource allocation method (CPU_MTH) sets the type of allocation used only if there is a resource plan directive which specifies CPU allocation.

These plans can be created as shown here:

```
SQL> begin
  dbms_resource_manager.create_plan(
    PLAN => 'DAY_PLAN',
    COMMENT => 'GOVERNS NORMAL WORKING HOURS ');
  end;
SQL> /

PL/SQL procedure successfully completed.

SQL> begin
  dbms_resource_manager.create_plan(
    PLAN => 'OLTP_PLAN',
    COMMENT => 'ORDER ENTRY SUB-PLAN');
  end;
SQL> /

PL/SQL procedure successfully completed.

SQL> begin
  dbms_resource_manager.create_plan(
    PLAN => 'OFF_HOURS_PLAN',
    COMMENT => 'GOVERNS NON-WORKING HOURS',
    CPU_MTH => 'RATIO');
  end;
SQL> /

PL/SQL procedure successfully completed.
```

Because the default CPU allocation method is EMPHASIS, the CPU_MTH parameter was left out when creating the first two plans. For the OFF_HOURS_PLAN plan, the CPU_MTH parameter was explicitly set.

Creating the Resource Plan Directives

Next, the resource plan directives need to be created. This will be done in three steps. First, the directives for the OFF_HOURS_PLAN plan will be created. Next, the directives for the OLTP_PLAN plan will be created. Finally, the directives for the DAY_PLAN plan will be created.

Creating the *OFF_HOURS_PLAN* Plan Directives

The OFF_HOURS_PLAN plan is a single-level plan using the RATIO method for CPU allocation. The plan directives can be created as follows:

```
SQL> begin
  dbms_resource_manager.create_plan_directive(
    PLAN => 'OFF_HOURS_PLAN',
    GROUP_OR_SUBPLAN => 'SYS_GROUP',
    COMMENT => 'CPU ALLOCATION FOR SYS_GROUP',
    CPU_P1 => 10);
 end;
SQL>/

PL/SQL procedure successfully completed.

SQL> begin
   dbms_resource_manager.create_plan_directive(
     PLAN => 'OFF_HOURS_PLAN',
     GROUP_OR_SUBPLAN => 'NIGHTLY_PROCESSING_GROUP',
     COMMENT => 'CPU ALLOCATION FOR NIGHTLY JOBS',
     CPU_P1 => 5);
  end;
SQL>/

PL/SQL procedure successfully completed.

SQL> begin
   dbms_resource_manager.create_plan_directive(
     PLAN => 'OFF_HOURS_PLAN',
     GROUP_OR_SUBPLAN => 'OLAP_REPORTS_GROUP',
     COMMENT => 'CPU ALLOCATION FOR NIGHTLY REPORTS',
     CPU_P1 => 2);
  end;
SQL>/

PL/SQL procedure successfully completed.
```

```
SQL> begin
   dbms_resource_manager.create_plan_directive(
     PLAN => 'OFF_HOURS_PLAN',
     GROUP_OR_SUBPLAN => 'OTHER_GROUPS',
     COMMENT => 'CPU ALLOCATION FOR OTHER_GROUPS',
     CPU_P1 => 1);
  end;
SQL>/

PL/SQL procedure successfully completed.
```

The CPU allocation ratio for the OFF_HOURS_PLAN plan will be 10:5:2:1.

Creating the *OLTP_PLAN* Plan Directives

Next, the plan directives for the OLTP_PLAN plan can be created:

```
SQL> begin
   dbms_resource_manager.create_plan_directive(
     PLAN => 'OLTP_PLAN',
     GROUP_OR_SUBPLAN => 'OLTP_GROUP',
     COMMENT => 'CPU ALLOCATION FOR OLTP USERS',
     CPU_P1 => 90);
  end;
SQL>/

PL/SQL procedure successfully completed.

SQL> begin
   dbms_resource_manager.create_plan_directive(
     PLAN => 'OLTP_PLAN',
     GROUP_OR_SUBPLAN => 'DAY_REPORTS_GROUP',
     COMMENT => 'CPU ALLOCATION FOR DAYTIME REPORTING',
     CPU_P1 => 10);
  end;
SQL>/

PL/SQL procedure successfully completed.

SQL> begin
   dbms_resource_manager.create_plan_directive(
     PLAN => 'OLTP_PLAN',
     GROUP_OR_SUBPLAN => 'OTHER_GROUPS',
```

```
    COMMENT => 'CPU ALLOCATION FOR OTHER_GROUPS',
    CPU_P2 => 100);
 end;
SQL>/

PL/SQL procedure successfully completed.
```

As you can see, the directives for the OLTP_PLAN plan allocate 90 percent of level 1 CPU resources to the OLTP_GROUP group, and the other 10 percent to the DAY_REPORTS_GROUP group. 100 percent of level 2 CPU resources are allocated to the OTHER_GROUPS group.

Creating the *DAY_PLAN* Plan Directives

Now, the directives for the DAY_PLAN plan can be created:

```
SQL> begin
  dbms_resource_manager.create_plan_directive(
    PLAN => 'DAY_PLAN',
    GROUP_OR_SUBPLAN => 'SYS_GROUP',
    COMMENT => 'CPU ALLOCATION FOR SYS_GROUP',
    CPU_P1 => 100);
 end;
SQL>/

PL/SQL procedure successfully completed.

SQL> begin
  dbms_resource_manager.create_plan_directive(
    PLAN => 'DAY_PLAN',
    GROUP_OR_SUBPLAN => 'OLTP_PLAN',
    COMMENT => 'CPU ALLOCATION FOR OLTP_PLAN SUB-PLAN',
    CPU_P2 => 100);
 end;
SQL>/

PL/SQL procedure successfully completed.

SQL> begin
  dbms_resource_manager.create_plan_directive(
    PLAN => 'DAY_PLAN',
    GROUP_OR_SUBPLAN => 'OTHER_GROUPS',
    COMMENT => 'CPU ALLOCATION FOR OTHER_GROUPS',
    CPU_P3 => 100);
```

```
 end;
SQL>/

PL/SQL procedure successfully completed.
```

You may have noticed that both the DAY_PLAN and OLTP_PLAN plans allocate resources to the OTHER_GROUPS group. Remember that *every* resource plan must have an allocation to the OTHER_GROUPS group. In fact, any consumer group can be assigned to more than one plan, as long as no loops are created as a result.

Validating the Pending Area

Now that all of the necessary elements have been created and defined, the contents of the pending area must be validated. Validation checks for any rule violations that may exist when the elements are grouped under their respective plans.

Validation will be done for all elements in the pending area, as shown here:

```
SQL> exec dbms_resource_manager.validate_pending_area;

PL/SQL procedure successfully completed.
```

When validating the pending area, no news is good news. As long as the procedure completes and no error messages are returned, the pending area has passed inspection.

If you are using SQL*Plus, make sure that the SERVEROUTPUT option is on before validating. Otherwise, any error messages will not be displayed on-screen. Use the SET SERVEROUTPUT ON statement to turn it on.

Submitting the Pending Area

The final step is to activate the plans by submitting the pending area. This step moves the DRM elements to the data dictionary. Once the elements are in the data dictionary, they are considered active and eligible to be enabled (resource plans) or referenced by enabled plans (resource consumer groups and resource plan directives). Remember that this step does not actually enable a plan, it only makes it eligible to be enabled.

Also, when submitting a pending area, Oracle automatically performs the same validation that was done in the previous step. Therefore, the validation step above is technically unnecessary. However, it is still a good idea from a debugging standpoint, especially when designing very complex plans.

The pending area can be submitted as shown:

```
SQL> exec dbms_resource_manager.submit_pending_area;

PL/SQL procedure successfully completed.
```

Again, the absence of error messages signifies successful submission of the pending area to the data dictionary. The plans are now active (in other words, residing in the data dictionary) and can be enabled at any time.

Enabling the Resource Plans

When a resource plan is enabled, it governs all resource allocation for the Oracle instance. Only one resource plan may be enabled at any given time, and the enabled plan can be switched at any time.

There are two methods in which resource plans can be enabled:

- Initialization parameter (at instance startup time)
- ALTER SYSTEM statement

Initialization Parameter Method

In the init.ora file, the RESOURCE_MANAGER_PLAN initialization variable can be set to the name of any active plan. For example, the following code can be added to the init.ora file:

```
RESOURCE_MANAGER_PLAN = DAY_PLAN;
```

When the instance is restarted, DAY_PLAN will be the enabled plan for the instance.

ALTER SYSTEM Statement Method

Resource plans can also be enabled dynamically by using the ALTER SYSTEM statement, as shown here:

```
ALTER SYSTEM SET RESOURCE_MANAGER_PLAN = 'DAY_PLAN' [SCOPE = BOTH];
```

This dynamically enables the DAY_PLAN plan for the instance. There is no need to shut down the instance in this case. The optional SCOPE clause can be used in an SPFILE environment to change the setting both in memory and in the SPFILE (to make the change persist through a shutdown).

Switching the Enabled Resource Plan

The top-level plans that were created in this section are designed to govern specific times of the day. The DAY_PLAN plan is to be used during normal business hours, while the OFF_HOURS plan is to be used on nights and weekends.

The enabled plan can be changed at any time by using the ALTER SYSTEM command, as you saw earlier, but it would be very inconvenient to have to always make this change manually. Instead, Oracle's scheduler can be used to schedule the switch so that it is executed automatically based on a specific schedule.

One caveat of scheduling resource plan switches, however, is that you may encounter a situation where you don't want the plans to change.

For instance, if your nightly data loads are larger than normal and might exceed the cutoff time, you may want to delay the switch until the loads have finished. This will ensure that the loads have all the resources necessary to complete.

Rather than having to alter the job in the scheduler, you can simply execute the following statement:

```
SQL> ALTER SYSTEM
  SET RESOURCE_MANAGER_PLAN = 'FORCE:OFF_HOURS_PLAN';

System altered.
```

By adding the prefix FORCE: to the name of the plan, Oracle will restrict the active plan from being changed by the scheduler. The scheduler will still attempt to make the change, but it will fail.

When the nightly loads are finished, the restriction can be lifted by reissuing the identical ALTER SYSTEM statement without the FORCE: prefix, as shown here:

```
SQL> ALTER SYSTEM
  SET RESOURCE_MANAGER_PLAN = 'OFF_HOURS_PLAN';

System altered.
```

With the restriction lifted, the resource plan can now be changed manually (or by the scheduler).

Summary

In this chapter, you learned about the Oracle Database Resource Manager (DRM) and how to configure it to manage resources on your Oracle database. You learned about setting up a pending area to hold all of the DRM objects as they are created or modified. You learned that objects in the pending area need to be validated before moving them into the data dictionary. You also learned the requirements that each object must pass before being declared valid by DRM. You learned that submitting the pending area activates all the objects therein and moves them into the data dictionary.

We taught you how to create and manage consumer resource groups and how these groups are used by DRM. You saw that consumer resource groups can be assigned to sessions based on a variety of session attributes. You learned that applications as well as users can be defined through these attributes. You also learned the different methods that can be used to switch the consumer group for a session. You learned to grant switch privileges to users and roles so that users can switch to specific groups themselves.

Next, we showed you how to create and manage resource plans. You learned about simple plans, which allow up to eight levels of CPU resources to be allocated to consumer groups. You also learned that simple plans can also create consumer groups and resource plan directives all in one procedure. You learned that complex resource plan definitions only define the CPU allocation resource method (either RATIO or EMPHASIS), and the real power lies in the resource plan directives.

You learned about resource plan directives and how they connect consumer groups to resource plans as well as define the resource allocation for the consumer group. We showed you that plan directives can allocate resources at up to eight levels and can allocate resources to sub-plans as well as to consumer groups. You learned the various resource allocation methods available, including CPU methods, active session pool with queuing, degree of parallelism limit, automatic consumer group switching, canceling SQL and terminating sessions, execution time limit, undo pool, and idle time limit (blocking and non-blocking).

Lastly, you learned to put all of the elements together to build a complex resource plan schema using PL/SQL packages. Then you learned to enable the plan on the database.

Exam Essentials

Know how to configure the Database Resource Manager. Be able to create, update, and delete DRM objects. Be aware of the pending area and the need to validate and submit objects to the data dictionary to make them active. Know that submitting the pending area enforces validation, so it isn't strictly necessary to validate as a separate step. Know the various methods of enabling DRM (through `ALTER SYSTEM` and through initialization parameters). Understand the various allocation methods.

Be able to assign users to Database Resource Manager groups. Know all the methods of assigning user sessions to DRM groups. Know the names of the `DBMS_RESOURCE_MANAGER` procedures for assigning groups. Be aware of the switch privilege and how it is granted. Be aware of the `DBMS_SESSION` procedure that users can use to change their own group.

Know how to create resource plans within groups. Understand all the steps involved in creating resource plans, both simple and complex. Know the difference between single- and multi-level resource plans. Understand the allocation methods used. Know what constitutes a top-level plan and a sub-plan.

Be able to specify directives for allocating resources to consumer groups. Know how to create and manage plan directives to allocate resources to consumer groups and sub-plans. Understand which allocation methods are available for directives to groups as opposed to directives to sub-plans.

Review Questions

1. Which system privileges allow you to administer the Database Resource Manager?

   A. DBA

   B. ADMINISTER_ANY_RESOURCE

   C. ADMINISTER_RESOURCE_MANAGER

   D. RESOURCE_MANAGER_ADMIN

   E. All of the above

2. When creating a plan directive, which of the following resource allocation methods are valid when the target of the directive is a sub-plan?

   A. Execution time limit

   B. Undo pool

   C. Automatic consumer group switching

   D. Canceling SQL and terminating sessions

   E. CPU method

3. Which of the following is *not* a valid consumer group mapping attribute?

   A. CLIENT_OS_USER

   B. MODULE_NAME

   C. CLIENT_PROGRAM

   D. MODULE_ACTION

   E. SERVICE_MODULE_ACTION

4. Which of the following methods of CPU allocation can be defined for a single-level resource plan?

   A. RATIO

   B. EMPHASIS

   C. BASIC

   D. A, B, and C

   E. Both A and B

5. What is the effect of the following statement?

```
ALTER SYSTEM SET RESOURCE_MANAGER_PLAN = 'FORCE:NIGHT_PLAN';
```

   A. DRM will be enabled with NIGHT_PLAN as the top-level plan. Changes to the top-level plan will be restricted.

   B. NIGHT_PLAN will be moved into the data dictionary, and DRM will be enabled with NIGHT_PLAN as the top-level plan. Changes to the top-level plan will be restricted.

C. The current DRM top-level plan will be changed to NIGHT_PLAN, in spite of restrictions.

D. NIGHT_PLAN will be moved into the data dictionary, and the current DRM top-level plan will be changed to NIGHT_PLAN, in spite of restrictions.

E. NIGHT_PLAN will be made active.

6. A simple resource plan can define how many CPU allocation levels?

A. 1

B. 2

C. 4

D. 8

E. 16

7. A session assigned to the MARKETING group is switched to the LOW_GROUP because it exceeded the execution time set in the SWITCH_TIME_IN_CALL parameter of the plan directive. When the long-running operation completes, which group will the session be assigned to?

A. MARKETING

B. LOW_GROUP

C. DEFAULT_GROUP

D. None, the session would have been killed.

8. Where are active DRM objects are located?

A. V$ tables

B. Pending area

C. Data dictionary

D. DRM_OBJECTS table

E. None of the above

9. Consumer groups can be automatically assigned to sessions based on the mappings created through which DBMS_RESOURCE_MANAGER procedure?

A. CREATE_CONSUMER_GROUP_MAPPING

B. CREATE_GROUP_MAPPING

C. SET_CONSUMER_GROUP_MAPPING

D. MAP_CONSUMER_GROUPS

E. CREATE_CONSUMER_RSRC_GROUP_MAPPING

10. Every resource plan must contain an allocation to which consumer group?

A. LOW_GROUP

B. SYS_GROUP

C. DEFAULT_GROUP

D. BASE_GROUP

E. OTHER_GROUPS

11. Which DBMS_RESOURCE_MANAGER procedure prioritizes consumer group mappings?
    A. CREATE_MAPPING_PRIORITY
    B. SET_MAPPING_PRIORITY
    C. SET_MAPPING_ORDER
    D. PRIORITIZE_MAPPING_ORDER
    E. This functionality is not available through the DBMS_RESOURCE_MANAGER package.
12. Which of the following are valid methods of switching consumer groups for one or more sessions? (Choose all that apply.)
    A. SWITCH_CONSUMER_GROUP_FOR_SESS procedure of DBMS_RESOURCE_MANAGER
    B. SWITCH_CONSUMER_GROUPS procedure of DBMS_RESOURCE_MANAGER
    C. SWITCH_CONSUMER_GROUP_FOR_USER procedure of DBMS_RESOURCE_MANAGER
    D. ALTER SESSION SWITCH CONSUMER GROUP command
    E. All of the above
13. If a session is assigned to a consumer group that is not included in the enabled plan, which group will it be considered part of?
    A. None
    B. BASE_GROUP
    C. DEFAULT_GROUP
    D. OTHER_GROUPS
    E. SWITCH_GROUP
14. Within a resource plan definition, what differentiates a top-level plan from a sub-plan?
    A. A sub-plan has the PLAN_SUB parameter value set to SUB.
    B. A top-level plan has the GROUP_OR_PLAN parameter set to the name of the sub-plan in the resource plan definition.
    C. There is no difference in the resource plan definition.
    D. A sub-plan always has the CPU_MTH parameter value set to RATIO.
    E. The string TOP_LEVEL is appended to the name of top-level resource plans.
15. Which DBMS_RESOURCE_MANAGER procedure deletes a plan along with all of its subordinate objects?
    A. DELETE_PLAN_CASCADE
    B. DELETE_RESOURCE_PLAN_CASCADE
    C. DROP_PLAN
    D. DROP_PLAN_CASCADE
    E. Subordinate objects must be deleted separately.

16. Which DRM object ties a plan to a resource group and also defines the allocation method to be utilized?

A. Resource plan

B. Resource plan directive

C. Resource plan rule

D. Consumer group directive

E. None of the above

17. Which view displays the resource consumer groups currently assigned to sessions?

A. `V$SESS_GROUP`

B. `DBA_RSRC_GROUP`

C. `DBA_RSRC_PLANS`

D. `V$RSRC_CONSUMER_GROUPS`

E. `V$SESSION`

18. The switch privilege can be granted to a user or role by using which method(s)? (Choose all that apply.)

A. `GRANT` statement

B. `DBMS_RESOURCE_MANAGER` procedure

C. `DBMS_RESOURCE_MANAGER_PRIVS` procedure

D. `DBMS_SESSION` procedure

E. All of the above

19. Which of the following statements are true regarding users who have been granted the switch privilege? (Choose all that apply.)

A. They can switch only to a consumer group with equal or lower priority.

B. They can switch the group for any session as long as they have been granted the privilege `ADMIN` option.

C. They can switch to any consumer group for which they have been granted the switch privilege.

D. They can grant the switch privilege to another user if they have been granted the privilege with the `ADMIN` option.

E. All of the above are true.

20. If the switch privilege has been granted to `PUBLIC` for a specific consumer group, which of the following statements is true?

A. Any user assigned to that group can switch to another group.

B. Any user can switch to the specified group.

C. Any user with a `SWITCH_PUBLIC` grant can switch to the specified group.

D. Both A and B are true.

E. A, B, and C are true.

Answers to Review Questions

1. C. While the DBA role will grant the ADMINISTER_RESOURCE_MANAGER privilege, DBA is not a valid system privilege name.

2. E. A plan directive can only allocate CPU resources to a sub-plan. A, B, C, and D are all valid allocation methods, but they can only be defined for a resource consumer group, not for a sub-plan.

3. D. MODULE_ACTION is not a valid attribute by itself. The DBMS_APPLICATION_INFO package allows applications to define an application name and, secondarily, the action that they are currently performing. In general, the action without a corresponding name isn't useful. Therefore, MODULE_NAME and MODULE_NAME_ACTION are both useful and valid mapping attributes, but not MODULE_ACTION.

4. E. A single-level resource plan can allocate CPU resources to consumer groups using either the RATIO or the EMPHASIS (percentage) method. A multi-level resource plan is limited to using the EMPHASIS method exclusively. BASIC is not a valid CPU allocation method.

5. A. The ALTER SYSTEM statement sets NIGHT_PLAN as the enabled plan. The FORCE: prefix restricts the setting from being changed.

6. D. Simple resource plans can define up to eight levels of CPU allocation.

7. A. The SWITCH_TIME_IN_CALL parameter will cause the offending session to be switched for the duration of the current operation. It will then revert to its original group.

8. C. When objects in the pending area are submitted, they become active and are stored in the data dictionary.

9. C. The SET_CONSUMER_GROUP_MAPPING procedure is used to map session attributes to consumer groups.

10. E. The OTHER_GROUPS consumer group is assigned to sessions whose assigned group is not contained in the enabled plan. Therefore, Oracle requires that an allocation be made so that no sessions will be completely deprived of resources.

11. B. The SET_MAPPING_PRIORITY procedure allows for prioritization based on the session attribute type.

12. A, C. The SWITCH_CONSUMER_GROUP_FOR_SESS procedure will switch a single session. The procedure SWITCH_CONSUMER_GROUP_FOR_USER will switch all sessions owned by a user.

13. D. If a session belongs to a consumer resource group that receives no allocation of resources from the enabled plan, their session could not function. Therefore, Oracle switches them to the OTHER_GROUPS group. Because all resource plans are required to allocate resources to the OTHER_GROUPS group, the session will receive at least some level of resources.

14. C. There is no concept of sub-plan in the resource plan definition. Only in a resource plan directive can a sub-plan be identified.

15. A. The DELETE_PLAN_CASCADE procedure removes a plan along with any subordinate objects that it may reference. Using the DELETE_PLAN procedure, on the other hand, removes the plan but leaves the subordinate objects in place.

16. B. A resource plan directive identifies a plan, a consumer group (or sub-plan), and defines the allocation method for a resource.

17. E. The V$SESSION view contains a CONSUMER_GROUP column that displays the value of the consumer group currently assigned to the session.

18. C. The GRANT_SWITCH_CONSUMER_GROUP procedure in the DBMS_RESOURCE_MANAGER_PRIVS package is the only way to grant the switch privilege to users or roles.

19. C, D. The switch privilege allows the user to switch their own session to the specified consumer group. They can grant this privilege to another user if they have ADMIN rights. They cannot, however, switch consumer groups for sessions other than their own. Also, they are not limited to switching only to a lower priority group.

20. B. Only option B is true. The switch privilege granted to PUBLIC allows any user the privilege of switching to the group.

Using the Scheduler to Automate Tasks

ORACLE DATABASE 10*G*: ADMINISTRATION II EXAM OBJECTIVES COVERED IN THIS CHAPTER:

✓ **Automating Tasks with the Scheduler**

- Simplify management tasks by using the Scheduler.
- Create a job, program, schedule, and window.
- Reuse Scheduler components for similar tasks.
- View information about job executions and job instances.

Exam objectives are subject to change at any time without prior notice and at Oracle's sole discretion. Please visit Oracle's Training and Certification website (`http://www.oracle.com/education/certification/`) for the most current exam objectives listing.

As an Oracle database administrator, you might find that an inordinate amount of your time is spent performing routine tasks. Unfortunately, routine tasks come with the territory, and that is unlikely to change in the foreseeable future. Handling these routine tasks manually is an invitation for problems. Mistakes can be made, or even worse, the tasks will be forgotten and not run at all.

To resolve this dilemma, Oracle Database 10*g* (Oracle 10*g*) introduced the Oracle Scheduler, a new feature that makes the scheduling of routine tasks a simple matter. The Oracle Scheduler is a major advancement over the old `DBMS_JOB` scheduling system found in previous Oracle versions. It corrects many of the nagging idiosyncrasies while adding powerful new features such as the calendaring syntax, a flexible method of defining repeat intervals for Scheduler jobs.

In this chapter, you will learn how the Scheduler works and how to create and manage Scheduler elements. First, you will get an overview of the terminology and components that make up the Scheduler. You will learn the underlying architecture of the Scheduler and how all the pieces fit together.

Next, you will learn about Scheduler jobs and how to create and manage them. You will also learn about job groups and how they can be used to simplify the management of jobs, as well as to prioritize job execution.

You will also learn about Scheduler programs, which define the work that will be performed. You'll learn to create and manage schedules, which define when jobs will be run and how often they will be repeated. You'll learn how to define complex repeat intervals using Oracle's new calendaring syntax.

Next, you will learn about windows and window groups, which allow you to switch resource plans based on a schedule. And, lastly, you will learn about the Scheduler views that are available to you.

Scheduler Overview

The main functionality of any enterprise scheduling system is the ability to schedule tasks to execute at a specific date and time. These can be recurring tasks that run at preset intervals or one-time tasks set to execute immediately or at some point in the future.

To achieve this functionality, the Scheduler uses several distinct components to specify scheduled tasks:

Jobs A *job* instructs the Scheduler to run a specific program at a specific time on a specific date.

Programs A *program* contains the code (or a reference to the code) that needs to be run to accomplish a task. It can also contain parameters that should be passed to the program at runtime. A program can be stored as an independent object that can be referenced by many jobs.

Schedules A *schedule* contains a start date, an optional end date, and a repeat interval. With these elements, an execution schedule can be calculated. A schedule can be stored as an independent object that can be referenced by many jobs.

Windows A window identifies a recurring block of time during which a specific resource plan should be enabled to govern resource allocation for the database. For instance, the weekend may be classified as a maintenance window, and you can enable a resource plan that allocates the bulk of the system resources to administrative users.

Job groups A *job group* is a logical method of classifying jobs with similar characteristics. Job groups define specific characteristics that will be inherited by all jobs assigned to the group. They also simplify management by allowing collections of jobs to be manipulated as one object.

Window groups A *window group* is a logical method of grouping windows. They simplify the management of windows by allowing the members of the group to be manipulated as one object. Unlike job groups, window groups don't set default characteristics for windows that belong to the group.

These basic components comprise the bulk of Oracle's Scheduler facility. Their design encourages building flexible, reusable components shared by many scheduled jobs.

The Scheduler also offers a powerful and flexible *calendaring syntax* that is used to specify recurring task executions. This new syntax allows for the specification of complex date and time requirements. It also eliminates many of the shortcomings of `DBMS_JOB` such as schedule creep (where the start time of a task was directly affected by the start time of the previous execution of that task).

Lastly, the Scheduler allows the execution of non-Oracle-related programs and scripts. This means that the Scheduler can be used not only to execute SQL and PL/SQL, but also operating system executable programs. Therefore, most all of your tasks can be scheduled in a common place.

Scheduler Architecture

Understanding how to use the Scheduler begins with understanding the underlying architecture upon which the Scheduler functionality is built. This is not to say that you have to be able to name every locking mechanism and memory structure used in the Scheduler, any more than a person needs to know the ignition sequence of their car in order to drive it. Rather, it implies that a high-level knowledge of the underlying Scheduler processes will help you create more logical Scheduler objects and enable you to troubleshoot problems associated with the Scheduler.

In these sections, you will learn about

- The job table, which houses all the active jobs within the database
- The job coordinator, a key Oracle process that ensures that jobs are being run on schedule
- Job slaves, processes that carry out the execution of jobs under the guidance of the job coordinator
- The architecture in Real Application Cluster (RAC) environments and how it differs only slightly from a stand-alone database environment

The Job Table

The Scheduler *job table* is the master container for all enabled jobs in the database. This table stores information about all jobs, including the objects referenced by the job, the owner of the job, and the next run date. It also stores statistical information about jobs such as the number of times the job has run and the number of times the job has failed. It also contains the STATE column that contains the current state of the job (for example, RUNNING, SCHEDULED, BROKEN).

The information stored in the job table can be viewed through the *_SCHEDULER_JOBS view. For example, the following query will show the state of all jobs in the table, as well as their next run date:

```
SQL> select owner, job_name, state
  2  from dba_scheduler_jobs;

OWNER      JOB_NAME             STATE
---------- -------------------- ------------
SYS        PURGE_LOG            SCHEDULED
SYS        GATHER_STATS_JOB     RUNNING
```

As you can see in this example, the GATHER_STATS_JOB is currently running, while the PURGE_LOG job is scheduled to run at some point in the future. If you really want to know when the PURGE_LOG job will run, you could include the NEXT_RUN_DATE column in your query and see exactly when it will run next.

The Job Coordinator

The *job coordinator* is an Oracle background process with the responsibility of ensuring that jobs are run on schedule. The job coordinator regularly queries the job table and copies job information to a memory cache for improved performance when the job is executed.

The Oracle database itself monitors job schedules and starts the job coordinator process (if it is not already started) when a job needs to be executed. The job coordinator pulls the job information from the memory cache and passes it to a job slave (described in the next section) process for execution.

The job coordinator controls all aspects of the job slave pool of processes, so it can remove dormant slave processes and spawn new processes as needed to meet the needs of the Scheduler.

The Job Slave Processes

Job slave processes are tasked with carrying out the execution of job programs assigned to them by the job Scheduler. When a job slave receives the job information from the coordinator, it sets to work collecting all the metadata that it needs to carry out the request. This metadata includes things such as the program arguments and privilege information.

When it is ready to execute the program, the job slave creates a new session as the owner of the job, starts a transaction within the session, and then executes the job. When the job is complete, the transaction is committed and the session is closed by the job slave. Next, the slave performs the following actions:

- Update the STATUS column to a value of COMPLETED in the job table for the current job.
- Update the RUN_COUNT column to increment the current value by 1 in the job table for the current job.
- Insert an entry into the job log table.
- Look for any new work that needs to be done.

If no new work is found, the job slave process will sleep until it is called again by the coordinator or until it is removed from the system by the job coordinator.

RAC Considerations

The Scheduler architecture in an Oracle Real Application Cluster (RAC) environment is the same as in a stand-alone instance, with the following exceptions:

- Each instance in the cluster will have its own job coordinator.
- The job coordinators can communicate with one another to share information.
- Jobs can be defined with a service affinity (they should run on a specific service) as opposed to an instance affinity (they should run on a specific instance). If a job is assigned to a service consisting of two instances, even if one instance is down, the other can execute the job normally.

Aside from these exceptions, the Scheduler architecture in a RAC environment is the same as described previously.

Common Administration Tools

The Oracle Scheduler is implemented through a PL/SQL package named DBMS_SCHEDULER. This package offers a collection of procedures that are used to create and manage Scheduler objects (jobs, programs, schedules, windows, job groups, and window groups). Each of these object types will be covered thoroughly in this chapter.

Most of the procedures in the DBMS_SCHEDULER package are specific to a certain object type. The object type can be derived from the name of the procedure. For example, the CREATE_PROGRAM procedure is obviously specific to program objects.

However, because all Scheduler objects share some common attributes, there are also procedures that work with any Scheduler object type. Because these procedures play an important role in the management of Scheduler objects, they warrant thorough coverage. However, due to their "global" nature, they will be covered in this section, separate from any specific object type.

In the following sections, you will learn about the following DBMS_SCHEDULER procedures:

- ENABLE
- DISABLE
- SET_ATTRIBUTE
- SET_ATTRIBUTE_NULL

You will also learn about any special cases that may exist within the different Scheduler object types.

Using the *ENABLE* Procedure

With the exception of schedules, all Scheduler objects have a common attribute named ENABLED. The attribute is a Boolean (TRUE or FALSE) value that identifies whether the object is eligible for use by the Scheduler.

Because schedule objects do not have an ENABLED attribute, they cannot be enabled or disabled. They are always enabled by default.

Therefore, to be eligible for use in the Scheduler, the ENABLED attribute must be set to TRUE. By default, only schedule objects are enabled at creation time, because they cannot be disabled. All other objects will be disabled by default when they are created.

To enable an object, the DBMS_SCHEDULER.ENABLE procedure is used. The procedure accepts only one argument, NAME, which designates one of the following:

- The name of one specific object
- A comma-separated list of objects

For example, here's how to enable one specific object:

```
SQL> begin
  2  dbms_scheduler.enable('BACKUP_JOB');
  3  end;
  4  /

PL/SQL procedure successfully completed.
```

To enable multiple objects, a comma-separated list can be passed in. Note that the entire list is enclosed in single quotes. Therefore, the list is submitted as a single parameter, as shown here:

```
SQL> begin
  2  dbms_scheduler.enable(
  3   'BACKUP_PROGRAM, BACKUP_JOB, STATS_JOB');
```

```
  4  end;
  5  /

PL/SQL procedure successfully completed.
```

The list of objects can also contain both groups and individual objects:

```
SQL> begin
  2  dbms_scheduler.enable(
  3   'BACKUP_JOB_GROUP, STATS_JOB, SYS.WINDOW_GROUP_1');
  4  end;
  5  /

PL/SQL procedure successfully completed.
```

There are a couple of special cases that should be noted about enabling group objects:

- When a job group is enabled, all members of that job group will be enabled.
- When a window group is enabled, only the window group object is enabled. Windows that are members of the group are not enabled.
- When a window or window group is referenced in the ENABLE procedure, it must always be prefixed with the SYS schema name as shown in the preceding example (SYS.WINDOW_GROUP_1).

Using the *DISABLE* Procedure

When a Scheduler object is disabled, it is ineligible for use by the Scheduler. Disabling a Scheduler object is accomplished by setting the object's ENABLED attribute to FALSE.

To disable an object, the DBMS_SCHEDULER.DISABLE procedure is used. This procedure accepts two parameters: NAME and FORCE. The NAME parameter designates one of the following:

- The name of one specific object
- A comma-separated list of objects

The FORCE parameter is a Boolean (TRUE or FALSE) value that tells the procedure how to handle the request if dependencies exist. The default value is FALSE.

There are two situations that could be classified as dependencies:

- A job object that references a program object is considered to be dependent on that object.
- If an instance of an object is currently running (for example, a window is open or a job is running), there may be a dependency issue.

If any dependencies are found, the value of the FORCE parameter will determine the ultimate outcome of the DISABLE procedure.

The purpose of the FORCE parameter is not to cascade the changes to dependent objects. The purpose is to make you aware of dependencies. No changes will be made to dependent objects.

The effect of the FORCE option varies between object types. The differences are listed in Table 12.1.

If an object has no dependencies, using the DISABLE procedure will disable any valid Scheduler object, regardless of the value of the FORCE parameter.

For example, use the following command to disable one specific object:

```
SQL> begin
  2  dbms_scheduler.disable('BACKUP_JOB');
  3  end;
  4  /

PL/SQL procedure successfully completed.
```

To disable multiple objects, a comma-separated list can be passed in. Note that the entire list is enclosed in single quotes. Therefore, the list is submitted as a single parameter. In this example, the FORCE option is also set to TRUE:

```
SQL> begin
  2  dbms_scheduler.disable(
  3   'BACKUP_PROGRAM, BACKUP_JOB, STATS_JOB',TRUE);
  4  end;
  5  /

PL/SQL procedure successfully completed.
```

The list of objects can also contain both groups and individual objects:

```
SQL> begin
  2  dbms_scheduler.disable(
  3   'BACKUP_JOB_GROUP, STATS_JOB, SYS.WINDOW_GROUP_1');
  4  end;
  5  /

PL/SQL procedure successfully completed.
```

TABLE 12.1 Effects of *DISABLE* with the *FORCE* Option

Object Type	Effect
Job	If the FORCE attribute is FALSE: If an instance of the job is currently running, the procedure will fail. TRUE: The job is disabled, but the currently running instance is allowed to finish.
Schedule	N/A
Program	If the FORCE attribute is FALSE: If the program is referenced by any job, the procedure will fail. TRUE: The program will be disabled. Jobs that reference the program will not be disabled, but will fail at runtime if the program is still disabled.
Window	If the FORCE attribute is FALSE: If the window is open or referenced by any job, the procedure will fail. TRUE: The procedure will succeed in disabling the window. If that window is open at the time the DISABLE procedure is called, it will not be affected. Jobs that reference the window will not be disabled.
Window Group	If the FORCE attribute is: FALSE: If any member windows are open or if any member windows are referenced by a job object, the DISABLE procedure will fail. TRUE: The window group will be disabled. Any open window that is a member of the group will continue to its end. Jobs that reference the window group as their schedule will not be disabled.

There are a couple of special cases that should be noted about disabling group objects:

- Disabling a window group does not disable jobs that reference the group. However, those jobs will fail when they try to execute.
- Disabling a window group does not affect members of the group. They will continue to function normally.

Setting Attributes

You might be surprised to find that the DBMS_SCHEDULER package does not have an ALTER procedure of any kind. This is because Scheduler objects are collections of attributes. To make a change to an object requires setting its *attributes*. Therefore, to alter a Scheduler object, the DBMS_SCHEDULER.SET_ATTRIBUTE and DBMS_SCHEDULER.SET_ATTRIBUTE_NULL procedures are used.

In the following sections, you will learn to use these procedures with all types of Scheduler objects.

The SET_ATTRIBUTE procedure sets an attribute for any type of Scheduler object. The SET_ATTRIBUTE_NULL procedure, on the other hand, sets any attribute to NULL for any type of Scheduler object. This is useful for "unsetting" an attribute.

The only attribute that cannot be altered (for any type of Scheduler object) is the name of the object.

When the attributes on an object are changed, Oracle will attempt to disable the object before making the changes. When the attribute has been successfully altered, Oracle will re-enable the object automatically. If the SET_ATTRIBUTE procedure fails, the object will remain disabled (and an error message is returned).

Using the SET_ATTRIBUTE procedure does not affect instances of the object that are currently executing. Changes made will only affect future instantiations of the object.

The SET_ATTRIBUTE procedure accepts three parameters:

NAME The name of the Scheduler object.

ATTRIBUTE The name of the attribute to be changed.

VALUE The new value for the attribute. The procedure is overloaded to accept a value of any applicable datatype, so no conversion is necessary when setting values for different datatypes.

The SET_ATTRIBUTE_NULL procedure accepts only two parameters:

NAME The name of the Scheduler object.

ATTRIBUTE The name of the attribute, which should be set to NULL.

In the last section, you learned that an object was considered enabled when the ENABLED attribute was set to a value of TRUE. Therefore, you can enable or disable an object by using the SET_ATTRIBUTE procedure, as shown here:

```
SQL> begin
  2  dbms_scheduler.set_attribute (
  3  name => 'TEST_JOB',
  4  attribute => 'ENABLED',
  5  value => TRUE);
  6 end;
  7 /

PL/SQL procedure successfully completed.
```

To remove the end date from a schedule, the SET_ATTRIBUTE_NULL procedure can be used to set the attribute to NULL, as shown here:

```
SQL> begin
  2  dbms_scheduler.set_attribute_null (
  3  name => 'TEST_SCHEDULE',
```

```
  4  attribute => 'END_DATE');
  5  end;
  6  /

PL/SQL procedure successfully completed.
```

Using Scheduler Jobs

A Scheduler job defines a specific program to be executed, the arguments (or parameters) to be passed to the program, and the schedule defining when the program should be executed. It also specifies other characteristics such as logging options, job priority, and so on.

Many of these characteristics are explicitly set at job creation time through the CREATE_JOB procedure. However, others are inherited from the job class to which the job is assigned. If a job is not explicitly assigned to a job class, these characteristics will be inherited from a job class named DEFAULT_JOB_CLASS.

In the following sections, you will learn how to administer the various aspects of Scheduler jobs. You will learn to create, copy, and alter jobs to achieve your scheduling needs. You will learn how to run jobs and how to stop jobs that are running. You will learn how to enable and disable jobs, and finally, how to drop jobs that are no longer needed.

Creating Jobs

Scheduler jobs can be created by using the DBMS_SCHEDULER.CREATE_JOB procedure. As you will recall, a job combines a program and a schedule for execution of that program. Therefore, these are the elements that you must define when creating a new job.

Depending on the program that the job uses, you may also need to set job arguments. These are parameters that will be passed to the program at execution time. Job arguments can be set by using the SET_JOB_ARGUMENT and/or SET_JOB_ANYDATA_VALUE procedures in the DBMS_SCHEDULER package.

Jobs also have *job attributes* that control certain behaviors of the job. Many of these can be set through the CREATE_JOB procedure, while others are inherited from the job class to which the job is assigned (or from the DEFAULT_JOB_CLASS class, as mentioned previously).

For example, job attributes such as the JOB_TYPE, JOB_ACTION, and REPEAT_INTERVAL can all be defined at job creation time. Other attributes such as MAX_FAILURES, LOGGING_LEVEL, and JOB_PRIORITY are inherited from the job class.

A job is stored like any other database object, so it is vital that a valid object name is used when creating jobs. The job name must also be unique within the schema in which it is created. Like other database objects, jobs can be created in a different schema by prefixing the job name with a schema name. For example, specifying a job name of BUTERTB.STATS_JOB would cause the job to be created in the BUTERTB schema.

In the following sections, you will learn which attributes define a Scheduler job. You will also learn how to administer all aspects of Scheduler job objects.

Job Attributes

Scheduler jobs have a specific set of attributes that you can set to define the characteristics of the job. These attributes can be set at job creation time through the following CREATE_JOB procedure parameters:

JOB_NAME The JOB_NAME parameter specifies the name assigned to the new job. Because jobs are stored like any other database object, standard Oracle naming requirements are enforced for jobs. This means that the job name must not only be a valid Oracle object name, it must also be unique within the schema.

JOB_TYPE The JOB_TYPE parameter specifies the type of job that will be created. This is a required parameter and cannot be excluded. It can be any one of the following:

PLSQL_BLOCK The job will execute an anonymous PL/SQL block. Anonymous PL/SQL block jobs do not accept job or program arguments, so the number of arguments attribute must be set to 0.

STORED_PROCEDURE The job will execute a PL/SQL stored procedure. By using PL/SQL's External Procedure feature, the PL/SQL procedure could be a wrapper to call a Java stored procedure or an external C routine.

EXECUTABLE The job will execute a program that is external to the database. An external job is any program that can be executed from the operating system's command line. ANYDATA arguments are not supported with a job or program type of executable.

JOB_ACTION The JOB_ACTION attribute specifies the code to be executed for this job.

For a PL/SQL block, the Scheduler will automatically wrap the JOB_ACTION code in its own PL/SQL block prior to execution. Therefore, JOB_ACTION can be a complete PL/SQL block, or one or more lines of valid PL/SQL code. Therefore, both of the following examples are valid:

```
'BEGIN update employee set salary = salary*2 where employee_name like
'BUTERBAUGH'; commit; END;'

'update employee set salary = salary*2 where employee_name like 'BUTERBAUGH';
commit;'
```

For a stored procedure, the value should be the name of the stored procedure, as in this example:

```
'DBMS_SESSION.SET_ROLE(''PAYROLL_USER'');'
```

For an executable, the value is the name of the executable, including the full path name and applicable command-line arguments. If environment variables are required, we suggest that the executable be wrapped in a shell script that defines the environment before executing the program.

For example, specifying '/prod/bin/big_load.sh full' would execute the big_load.sh script and pass in one argument with the value of full.

NUMBER_OF_ARGUMENTS The NUMBER_OF_ARGUMENTS parameter specifies the number of arguments that the job accepts. The range is 0 (default) to 255.

PROGRAM_NAME The PROGRAM_NAME parameter specifies the name of the program associated with this job. The program name must be the name of an existing program object.

START_DATE The START_DATE parameter specifies the first date that the job should be run. If both the START_DATE and REPEAT_INTERVAL parameters are NULL, the job will be run as soon as it is enabled.

The START_DATE parameter is used as a reference date when the REPEAT_INTERVAL parameter uses a calendaring expression. In this situation, the job will run on the first date that matches the calendaring expression *and* is on or after the date specified in the START_DATE parameter.

The Scheduler cannot guarantee that a job will execute at an exact time, because the system may be overloaded and thus resources may be unavailable.

REPEAT_INTERVAL The REPEAT_INTERVAL parameter specifies how often the job should be repeated. This parameter can be specified using either a calendaring or a PL/SQL expression. If this parameter is NULL, the job will run only once (at the scheduled start time).

SCHEDULE_NAME The SCHEDULE_NAME parameter specifies the name of the schedule associated with this job. It can optionally specify a *window* or window group associated with the job.

END_DATE The END_DATE parameter specifies the date when the job will expire. After the date specified, the job will no longer be executed; the STATE of the job will be set to COMPLETED, and the ENABLED flag will be set to FALSE.

If this parameter is set to NULL, the job will repeat forever. However, if the MAX_RUNS or MAX_FAILURES parameters are set, the job will stop if either of these thresholds is met.

JOB_CLASS The JOB_CLASS parameter specifies the class to which the job is assigned. If this parameter is NULL, the job is assigned to the default class.

COMMENTS The COMMENTS parameter allows the entry of a comment to document the job.

ENABLED The ENABLED parameter specifies whether the job is created in an enabled state. A value of TRUE means the job will be enabled. By default, all jobs are created disabled, so the default value for this parameter is FALSE. A disabled job will exist as an object in the database, but it will never be processed by the job coordinator.

AUTO_DROP The AUTO_DROP parameter specifies whether the job will be automatically dropped once it has been executed (for non-repeating jobs) or when its status is changed to COMPLETED (for repeating jobs).

The default value for this parameter is TRUE, meaning the job will be dropped from the database. If it is set to FALSE, the jobs are not dropped and their metadata is retained in the database until it is explicitly dropped using the DBMS_SCHEDULER.DROP_JOB procedure.

Identifying the *CREATE_JOB* Procedure Options

Jobs are created by using the DBMS_SCHEDULER.CREATE_JOB procedure. The CREATE_JOB procedure is an *overloaded procedure*. If you are not familiar with procedure overloading, it simply means that the procedure can accept a variety of different parameter combinations. Oracle will execute the version of the procedure that matches the parameter list that is passed in. For a more thorough explanation, see the following sidebar titled "Overloading Procedures and Functions."

Real World Scenario

Overloading Procedures and Functions

Overloading allows you to create multiple versions of a procedure or function. Each version has the same name but a different parameter list. When an overloaded procedure or function is called, Oracle will execute the version with the parameter list matching the parameters that have been passed in.

The power of overloading lies in the ability to make a single function or procedure that will work with differing datatypes or data elements. For example, if you want to create a function that returns a date in *DD-MM-YYYY* format, you could overload the function to accept date, string, or numeric datatypes. For example, the function could be defined as shown here:

```
FUNCTION conv_date (dt IN DATE)
   <CODE GOES HERE>
   RETURN VARCHAR2;

FUNCTION conv_date (dt IN VARCHAR2)
   <CODE GOES HERE>
   RETURN VARCHAR2;

FUNCTION conv_date (
   mon IN NUMBER,
   day IN NUMBER,
   year IN NUMBER
   )
   <CODE GOES HERE>
   RETURN VARCHAR2;
```

By overloading the function, the same function name can be used, regardless of how the date is passed in.

By overloading the CREATE_JOB procedure, the Scheduler allows four distinct methods in which jobs can be created:

- Method 1 allows the use of *inline program* and *inline schedule* definitions. This means that the program and schedule for the job are defined strictly within the confines of the CREATE_JOB procedure. They do not exist as independent Scheduler program or schedule objects.
- Method 2 allows the creation of jobs using an existing program object and schedule object. This method shows how the component nature of the Scheduler can be leveraged through object reuse. Rather than recreate an identical schedule or program, an existing one can be utilized instead.
- Method 3 combines an existing program with an inline schedule definition.
- Method 4 combines an inline program definition with an existing schedule.

Table 12.2 shows the available parameters for each variation of the procedure.

TABLE 12.2 *CREATE_JOB* Procedure Parameter Options

Parameter	Method 1	Method 2	Method 3	Method 4
JOB_NAME	✔	✔	✔	✔
JOB_TYPE	✔		✔	✔
JOB_ACTION	✔			✔
NUMBER_OF_ARGUMENTS	✔			✔
PROGRAM_NAME		✔	✔	
START_DATE	✔		✔	
REPEAT_INTERVAL	✔		✔	
SCHEDULE_NAME		✔		✔
END_DATE	✔		✔	
JOB_CLASS	✔	✔	✔	✔
ENABLED	✔	✔	✔	✔
AUTO_DROP	✔	✔	✔	✔
COMMENTS	✔	✔	✔	✔

Using the *CREATE_JOB* Procedure

Now that you have been introduced to the options available with the CREATE_JOB procedure, you should have a feel for how Scheduler jobs are created. The following example creates a job that will run once every year to enact cost of living adjustments for all employees:

```
SQL> begin
  2  dbms_scheduler.create_job (
  3  job_name => 'cola_job',
  4  job_type => 'PLSQL_BLOCK',
  5  job_action => 'update employee set salary = salary*1.05;',
  6  start_date => '10-OCT-2004 06:00:00 AM',
  7  repeat_interval => 'FREQ=YEARLY',
  8  comments => 'Cost of living adjustment');
  9  end;
 10  /

PL/SQL procedure successfully completed.
```

To verify that the job was created, the DBA|ALL|USER_SCHEDULER_JOBS view can be queried, as shown here:

```
SQL> select job_name, enabled, run_count
  from user_scheduler_jobs;

JOB_NAME                  ENABLED  RUN_COUNT
------------------------- ----------
COLA_JOB                  FALSE            0
```

As you can see from the results, the job was indeed created, but is not enabled because the ENABLE attribute was not explicitly set in the CREATE_JOB procedure.

Copying Jobs

Jobs can be copied by using the DBMS_SCHEDULER.COPY_JOB procedure. This procedure accepts only two parameters: OLD_JOB and NEW_JOB. These parameters represent the name of the source and destination job names, respectively.

A copied job will be identical to the original job, with the following exceptions:

- The new job will have a different name.
- The new job will be created in a disabled state.

The COPY_JOB procedure can be used as shown in the following example:

```
SQL> begin
  2  dbms_scheduler.copy_job('COLA_JOB','RAISE_JOB');
  3  end;
  4  /

PL/SQL procedure successfully completed.
```

In the example, a new job named RAISE_JOB was created as a copy of the COLA_JOB job. To verify, the USER_SCHEDULER_JOBS view can be queried, as shown here:

```
SQL> select job_name, enabled
  2  from user_scheduler_jobs;

JOB_NAME                       ENABL
------------------------------ -----
COLA_JOB                       TRUE
RAISE_JOB                      FALSE
```

As you can see, the job was indeed created, and even though the COLA_JOB job is enabled, the RAISE_JOB job is disabled.

Running Jobs

The Scheduler allows scheduled jobs to be run outside of their normal schedule through the DBMS_SCHEDULER.RUN_JOB procedure. This procedure is useful for testing a newly created job or for re-executing a job that failed previously. It doesn't affect the existing schedule of the job, nor does it require the creation of a separate, one-time-only job.

The RUN_JOB procedure accepts the JOB_NAME and USE_CURRENT_SESSION parameters. While JOB_NAME is self-explanatory, the USE_CURRENT_SESSION parameter is new to Oracle 10*g*.

The USE_CURRENT_SESSION parameter is a Boolean (TRUE or FALSE) value that determines the method in which the job will be run. If this parameter is set to FALSE (the default value), the job will be submitted to the job Scheduler for normal asynchronous execution.

If the parameter is set to TRUE, the job will be executed in a synchronous fashion using the current user session. This means that as soon as the procedure is executed, the job will run. Therefore, control will not be returned to your user session until the job execution is complete, as you can see here:

```
SQL> begin
  2  dbms_scheduler.run_job('COLA_JOB',TRUE);
  3  end;
  4  /
```

```
<JOB RUNS HERE>

PL/SQL procedure successfully completed.
SQL>
```

Keep in mind that only an enabled job may be run using the RUN_JOB procedure.

Stopping Jobs

A running job can be stopped by using the DBMS_SCHEDULER.STOP_JOB procedure. When a job is stopped in this manner, the Scheduler attempts to stop the job in a graceful manner by means of an interrupt mechanism. When successful, control is returned to the slave process running the job, which will set the status of the job to STOPPED.

Optionally, a user with the MANAGE_SCHEDULER privilege can set the FORCE parameter to TRUE. This causes Oracle to terminate the process running the job and stops the job much faster, in most cases.

The STOP_JOB procedure can be called as follows:

```
SQL> begin
  2  dbms_scheduler.stop_job(job_name => 'COLA_JOB',
  3  force => TRUE);
  4  end;
  5  /

PL/SQL procedure successfully completed.
```

When a job is stopped using the STOP_JOB procedure, only the most recent transaction is rolled back. If the job has performed any commits prior to the time when it is stopped, data inconsistency may result.

Dropping Jobs

Jobs can be dropped by using the DBMS_SCHEDULER.DROP_JOB procedure. This procedure removes the job object completely from the database. If an instance of the job is running when you issue the DROP_JOB procedure, an error will result. If you set the FORCE option to TRUE, Oracle will issue an implicit STOP_JOB procedure to kill the current instance and then drop the job.

The DROP_JOB procedure can be called as follows:

```
SQL> begin
  2  dbms_scheduler.drop_job(job_name => 'COLA_JOB',
  3  force => TRUE);
```

```
  4  end;
  5  /

PL/SQL procedure successfully completed.
```

Using Job Classes

A job class is a container object for the logical grouping of jobs into a larger unit. Classifying jobs in this manner offers several advantages:

- From an administrative perspective, it is easier to manage a small number of job groups than a large number of individual jobs. Certain job characteristics can be assigned at the group level and will be inherited by all jobs within the group. Certain administrative procedures will also operate at the group level, making administrative functions easier.
- Job classes can be assigned to a resource consumer group. This allows you to control resource allocation for all jobs within the group.
- Jobs can be prioritized within the job class. This gives you more control over which jobs should take precedence in case of a conflict. For example, if a conflict occurs, the `JOB_PRIORITY` attribute of each job will be evaluated. A job with a value of `HIGH` takes priority over a job with a value of `LOW`.

All jobs must belong to exactly one job class. Any job not explicitly assigned to a job class will belong to the `DEFAULT_JOB_CLASS` class, and they will inherit the characteristics of that job class. In the following sections, you will learn to create and administer job classes.

Job Class Parameters

Job classes have a specific set of attributes that you can set to define the characteristics of the class. These attributes will be inherited by all jobs assigned to the job class, thereby saving you the work of setting them individually on each job. The available attribute parameters are described here:

JOB_CLASS_NAME The `JOB_CLASS_NAME` parameter uniquely identifies the job class in the SYS schema. The name has to be unique in the SYS schema.

RESOURCE_CONSUMER_GROUP The `RESOURCE_CONSUMER_GROUP` parameter associates the job group with a specific consumer group. All jobs assigned to the job group will automatically be governed by this consumer group.

SERVICE The `SERVICE` parameter specifies the service to which the job class belongs. This means that, in a RAC environment, the jobs in this class will have affinity to the particular service specified. Therefore, they will run only on those database instances that are assigned to the specific service. If this attribute is not set, the default service will be used, meaning that the jobs have no service affinity and can be run by any instance within the cluster. If the SERVICE parameter is specified, the RESOURCE_CONSUMER_GROUP attribute cannot be set. They are mutually exclusive.

LOGGING_LEVEL The Oracle Scheduler can optionally maintain *job logs* of all job activities. Job logging is determined by the setting of the LOGGING_LEVEL attribute of the job class. The LOGGING_LEVEL parameter specifies how much job information is logged. There are three valid settings for this attribute:

DBMS_SCHEDULER.LOGGING_OFF No logging will be performed for any jobs in this class.

DBMS_SCHEDULER.LOGGING_RUNS Detailed information will be written for all runs of each job in the class.

DBMS_SCHEDULER.LOGGING_FULL Detailed information will be written for all runs of each job in the class, and every operation performed on any job in the class (create, enable, drop, and so on) will be logged.

Note that the valid values for this parameter are all constants defined within the DBMS_SCHEDULER package. Therefore, they must be referenced exactly as shown, with no quotes around them.

LOG_HISTORY The LOG_HISTORY parameter determines the number of days logged information should be retained. The default value is 30 days. Valid values are 1 to 999. When records have exceeded this age, the Scheduler will automatically purge them.

COMMENTS The COMMENTS parameter specifies an optional comment about the job class.

Creating Job Classes

Job classes can be created through the DBMS_SCHEDULER.CREATE_JOB_CLASS procedure, as shown in the following example:

```
SQL> begin
  2    dbms_scheduler.create_job_class(
  3  job_class_name => 'LOW_PRIORITY_CLASS',
  4  resource_consumer_group => 'LOW_GROUP',
  5  logging_level => DBMS_SCHEDULER.LOGGING_FULL,
  6  log_history => 60,
  7  comments => 'LOW PRIORITY JOB CLASS');
  8 end;
SQL> /

PL/SQL procedure successfully completed.
```

In this example, a job class named LOW_PRIORITY_CLASS was created that will assign all jobs in the group to the LOW_GROUP consumer group.

Dropping Job Classes

Job classes can be dropped by using the DBMS_SCHEDULER.DROP_JOB_CLASS procedure. Dropping a job class that has jobs assigned to it will result in an error. However, it is allowed if the FORCE parameter is set to TRUE. In this case, the job class will be dropped and the jobs assigned to the class will be disabled. Dropping the class has no effect on any currently running instances of member jobs.

Several job classes can also be dropped at the same time by separating the names of the job classes by a comma, as shown in the following example:

```
SQL> begin
  2  dbms_scheduler.drop_job_class(
  3    'LOW_PRIORITY_CLASS, HIGH_PRIORITY_CLASS');
  4  end;
SQL> /

PL/SQL procedure successfully completed.
```

Note that if a list of job classes is used, as in this example, there is no rollback available. For instance, if the first job class dropped but the second job class failed to drop, the procedure will return an error, but the first job class will not be restored.

Using Scheduler Programs

A program defines the action that will occur when a job runs. It can be a PL/SQL block, a stored procedure, or an operating system executable. In the previous section, you learned to define a program within the confines of the CREATE_JOB procedure. However, programs can also be created as independent objects that can be reused by many different jobs. And because programs can also accept arguments, they offer flexibility and encourage reuse.

In the following sections, you will learn the different attributes that define a Scheduler program object. You will learn how to create new programs and how to drop them. Finally, you will also learn to define arguments for programs.

Program Attributes

Scheduler programs have a specific set of attributes that you can set to define the characteristics of the program. These attributes can be set at creation time through the following CREATE_PROGRAM procedure parameters:

PROGRAM_NAME The PROGRAM_NAME parameter specifies the name assigned to the new program. Because programs are stored like any other database object, standard Oracle object naming requirements are enforced for programs. This means that the program name must not only be a valid Oracle object name, it must also be unique within the schema.

PROGRAM_TYPE The PROGRAM_TYPE parameter specifies the type of program that will be created. This is a required parameter and cannot be excluded. It can be any one of the following:

PLSQL_BLOCK The program is an anonymous PL/SQL block. Anonymous PL/SQL block jobs do not accept job or program arguments, so the NUMBER_OF_ARGUMENTS attribute must be set to 0.

STORED_PROCEDURE The program is a PL/SQL stored procedure. By using PL/SQL's External Procedure feature, the PL/SQL procedure could be a wrapper to call a Java stored procedure or an external C routine.

EXECUTABLE The program is external to the database. An external program is any program that can be executed from the operating system's command line.

PROGRAM_ACTION The PROGRAM_ACTION attribute specifies the code to be executed. For a PL/SQL block, the Scheduler automatically wraps the PROGRAM_ACTION code in its own PL/SQL block prior to execution. Therefore, this attribute can be a complete PL/SQL block or one or more lines of valid PL/SQL code.

NUMBER_OF_ARGUMENTS The NUMBER_OF_ARGUMENTS parameter specifies the number of arguments that the job accepts. The range is 0 (the default) to 255.

ENABLED The ENABLED parameter specifies whether the job is created in an enabled state. A value of TRUE means the program will be enabled. By default, all programs are created disabled, so the default value for this parameter is FALSE.

COMMENTS The COMMENTS parameter allows the entry of a comment to document the program.

Creating Programs

New programs can be created by using the DBMS_SCHEDULER.CREATE_PROGRAM procedure. This procedure creates a new program object that can in turn be called by job objects. The procedure's parameters match the list of attributes described in the previous section.

Programs, like jobs, are stored as independent schema objects. Therefore, they must have unique names within the schema, and they must conform to Oracle's standards for valid object naming.

To create a program that executes a stored procedure, see the following example:

```
SQL> begin
  2  dbms_scheduler.create_program(
  3  program_name => 'STATS_PROGRAM',
  4  program_type => 'STORED_PROCEDURE',
  5  program_action => 'DBMS_STATS.GATHER_SCHEMA_STATS',
  6  number_of_arguments => 1,
  7  comments => 'Gather stats for a schema');
```

```
  8  end;
  9  /

PL/SQL procedure successfully completed.
```

This example creates a reusable program that will gather statistics for a schema. As you can see, the program requires one argument, which is the name of the schema. The argument can be defined by using the DEFINE_PROGRAM_ARGUMENT procedure, as shown here:

```
SQL> begin
  2  dbms_scheduler.define_program_argument(
  3  program_name => 'STATS_PROGRAM',
  4  argument_position => 1,
  5  argument_type => 'VARCHAR2');
  6  end;
SQL> /

PL/SQL procedure successfully completed.
```

You may have noticed that the preceding example doesn't specify a name for the argument. The ARGUMENT_NAME parameter is available, but is completely optional.

This program can now be used by a job object, and the schema name can be passed in as an argument. Therefore, the same program can be used by many jobs, each gathering statistics for a different schema.

Arguments can be dropped from programs as well. The DBMS_SCHEDULER.DROP_PROGRAM_ARGUMENT procedure allows arguments to be dropped by either name or by the position of the argument. The following examples show how an argument may be dropped by specifying either its position:

```
SQL> begin
  2  dbms_scheduler.drop_program_argument(
  3  program_name => 'STATS_PROGRAM',
  4  argument_position => 1,
  5  end;
SQL> /

PL/SQL procedure successfully completed.
```

or its name:

```
SQL> begin
  2  dbms_scheduler.drop_program_argument(
  3  program_name => 'STATS_PROGRAM',
  4  argument_name => 'SCHEMA_NAME',
  5  end;
SQL> /

PL/SQL procedure successfully completed.
```

Dropping Programs

Program objects can be dropped through the use of the DBMS_SCHEDULER.DROP_PROGRAM procedure. This procedure removes the procedure entirely from the database. If existing job definitions include the program that you are attempting to drop, the drop will fail. However, if you set the FORCE parameter to TRUE, the program will be dropped and the referencing jobs will become disabled.

The following example drops the STATS_PROGRAM program and disables any referencing jobs:

```
SQL> begin
  2  dbms_scheduler.drop_program (
  3  program_name => 'STATS_PROGRAM',
  4  force => TRUE
  5  end;
SQL> /

PL/SQL procedure successfully completed.
```

Using Schedules

Schedules define when jobs run as well as when windows are opened. (Windows will be covered later in this chapter.) Like jobs and programs, schedules are stored objects and follow all the same naming requirements. By saving schedules as independent objects, they can be used by multiple jobs.

Schedules define not only when a job will start, but also how often the job will be repeated. This is known as the repeat interval. Oracle's Scheduler offers two ways to define the interval: using PL/SQL expressions or using the powerful new calendaring syntax introduced in Oracle 10*g*.

In the following sections, you will learn which attributes define a schedule object. You will learn how to create and drop schedules. You will also learn how to define repeat intervals using the calendaring syntax.

Schedule Attributes

Schedule objects have a specific set of attributes that you can set to define the characteristics of the schedule. These attributes can be set at creation time through the following CREATE_SCHEDULE procedure parameters:

SCHEDULE_NAME The SCHEDULE_NAME parameter specifies the name of the schedule. Because schedules are stored like any other database object, standard Oracle object naming requirements are enforced for schedules. This means that the program name must not only be a valid Oracle object name, it must also be unique within the schema.

START_DATE The START_DATE parameter specifies the first date that the schedule is valid. The START_DATE parameter is used as a reference date when the REPEAT_INTERVAL parameter uses a calendaring expression. In this situation, the job runs on the first date that matches the calendaring expression and is on or after the date specified in the START_DATE parameter.

END_DATE The END_DATE parameter specifies the date when the schedule will expire. After the date specified, the job will no longer be executed; the STATE of the job will be set to COMPLETED, and the ENABLED flag will be set to FALSE.

If this parameter is set to NULL, the job will repeat forever. However, if the MAX_RUNS or MAX_FAILURES parameter is set, the job will stop if either of these thresholds is met.

REPEAT_INTERVAL The REPEAT_INTERVAL parameter specifies how often the schedule should be repeated. This parameter can be specified using either a calendaring or a PL/SQL expression. If this parameter is NULL, the job will run only once (at the scheduled start time).

COMMENTS The COMMENTS parameter allows the entry of a comment to document the schedule.

Creating Schedules

Schedules are created using the DBMS_SCHEDULER.CREATE_SCHEDULE procedure. By default, schedules are created with access to the PUBLIC role. Therefore, no privileges need to be granted to allow other users to use the schedule.

To create a schedule that repeats every night at 8:00 P.M., use the following example:

```
SQL> begin
  2  dbms_scheduler.create_schedule(
  3  schedule_name => 'NIGHTLY_8_SCHEDULE',
  4  start_date => SYSTIMESTAMP,
```

```
  5  repeat_interval => 'FREQ=DAILY; BYHOUR=20',
  6  comments => 'Runs nightly at 8:00 PM');
  7  end;
SQL> /

PL/SQL procedure successfully completed.
```

Setting Repeat Intervals

Oracle's new calendaring syntax offers tremendous flexibility when it comes to defining repeat intervals. However, the syntax does require a certain amount of getting used to. The syntax offers a set of elements that offer different methods of specifying repeating dates. By mixing and matching these elements, you can generate fairly complex repeat intervals. Table 12.3 describes the clauses and describes their usage.

TABLE 12.3 Calendaring Syntax Element Descriptions

Name	Description
FREQ	The FREQ parameter defines the frequency type. This parameter is required. The following values are valid: YEARLY, MONTHLY, WEEKLY, DAILY, HOURLY, MINUTELY, and SECONDLY.
INTERVAL	The INTERVAL element specifies how often the recurrence repeats. For example, if the FREQ is set to DAILY, then an INTERVAL of 1 (the default value) means that the job will execute every day. A value of 2 means that the job would execute every other day, and so on. The maximum value is 999.
BYMONTH	The BYMONTH element specifies the month or months in which you want the job to execute. The months can be represented numerically (1–12) or using three-letter abbreviations (JAN–DEC). Multiple months should be separated by commas.
BYWEEKNO	The BYWEEKNO element specifies the week of the year as a number. It follows the ISO-8601 standard, which defines the week as starting with Monday and ending with Sunday. It also defines the first week of a year as the first week in which the majority of days fall within the Gregorian year.
BYYEARDAY	The BYYEARDAY element specifies the day of the year as a number. Positive numbers that are greater than 59 will be affected by leap day. For example, 60 would evaluate to March 1 on non-leap years, but would evaluate to February 29 on leap years. Instead, negative numbers can be used. For example, –7 will always evaluate to December 25.

TABLE 12.3 Calendaring Syntax Element Descriptions *(continued)*

Name	Description
BYMONTHDAY	The BYMONTHDAY element specifies the day of the month as a number. Negative numbers can be used to count backward. For example, -1 will always evaluate to the last day of the month.
BYDAY	The BYDAY element specifies the day of the week using a three-letter abbreviation (MON, TUE, and so on). Monday is always the first day of the week. You can also prepend the BYDAY element with a number representing the occurrence of the specified day. For example, if FREQ is set to MONTHLY, you can specify the last Friday of the month by using -1FRI.
BYHOUR	The BYHOUR element specifies the hour on which the job is to run. Valid values are 0–23.
BYMINUTE	The BYMINUTE element specifies the minute on which the job is to run. Valid values are 0–59.
BYSECOND	The BYSECOND element specifies the second on which the job is to run. Valid values are 0–59.

Keep in mind that certain rules apply when using the calendaring syntax. These rules will aid you in creating accurate schedules:

- The first element defined must always be the frequency. All other elements are optional and can appear in any order.
- Elements should be separated by a semi-colon, and each element can be represented no more than once.
- Lists of values within an element should be separated by commas. They do not need to be ordered.
- Calendaring statements are case-insensitive, and white space is allowed between elements.
- The BYWEEKNO element can be used only when the FREQ element is set to YEARLY. By default, it returns all days in the week, so a BYDAY setting would be required to limit the days.
- Negative numbers are allowed with certain BY elements. For example, months have different numbers of days, so defining the last day of every month is not possible by using a single, positive number. Instead, you can specify BYMONTHDAY=-1, which will always return the last day of the month. Fixed-size elements such as BYMONTH, BYHOUR, and so on, do not support negative numbers.
- The BYDAY element generally specifies the day of the week. However, when used in conjunction with a frequency of YEARLY or MONTHLY, you can add a positive or negative number in front of the day to achieve greater specificity. For example, a FREQ value set to MONTHLY and a BYDAY value set to -1SAT would specify the last Saturday of every month.

- The calendaring syntax always considers Monday the first day of the week.
- The calendaring syntax does not allow you to specify time zones or Daylight Savings Time adjustments. Instead, the region defined in the schedule's START_DATE attribute is used to determine the time zone/Daylight Savings Time adjustments.

To help you get more familiar with the calendaring syntax, examples will be provided that demonstrate different repeat intervals and the syntax used to achieve it. Table 12.4 offers a variety of examples.

TABLE 12.4 Calendaring Syntax Examples

Goal	Expression
Every Monday	FREQ=WEEKLY; BYDAY=MON;
Every other Monday	FREQ=WEEKLY; BYDAY=MON; INTERVAL=2;
Last day of each month	FREQ=MONTHLY; BYMONTHDAY=-1;
Every January 7	FREQ=YEARLY; BYMONTH=JAN; BYMONTHDAY=7;
Second Wednesday of each month	FREQ=MONTHLY; BYDAY=2WED;
Every hour	FREQ=HOURLY;
Every 4 hours	FREQ=HOURLY; INTERVAL=4;
Hourly on the first day of each month	FREQ=HOURLY; BYMONTHDAY=1;
15th day of every other month	FREQ=MONTHLY; BYMONTHDAY=15; INTERVAL=2

Testing Repeat Intervals

One issue inherent in defining schedule repeat intervals is testing. How do you make sure you didn't make a mistake in your logic? To address that issue, Oracle offers the DBMS_SCHEDULER.EVALUATE_CALENDAR_STRING procedure. This procedure allows you to pass in a calendaring syntax expression and a start date, and it will return the time and date that the job will execute next. Optionally, you can also instruct the procedure to show the next execution time after a certain date, thereby allowing you to see execution dates in the future. Table 12.5 lists the parameters for the EVALUATE_CALENDAR_STRING procedure and describes their usage.

TABLE 12.5 *EVALUATE_CALENDAR_STRING* Procedure Parameters

Parameter	Description
CALENDAR_STRING	The calendar expression to be evaluated.
START_DATE	The date after which the repeat interval becomes valid.
RETURN_DATE_AFTER	Instructs the procedure to return only execution dates that will occur after the date specified in this parameter. This allows you to see dates and times far out into the future. By default, Oracle uses the current SYSTIMESTAMP.
NEXT_RUN_DATE	This is an out parameter (the procedure will return this value to the calling program) of type TIMESTAMP that shows the date and time of the next execution.

To use the EVALUATE_CALENDAR_STRING procedure, you will need to use PL/SQL that accepts a return value of type TIMESTAMP, as shown here:

```
SQL> DECLARE
  2   start_date TIMESTAMP;
  3   return_date_after TIMESTAMP;
  4   next_run_date TIMESTAMP;
  5  BEGIN
  6   start_date := to_timestamp_tz(
  7  '10-OCT-2004 10:00:00','DD-MON-YYYY HH24:MI:SS');
  8   DBMS_SCHEDULER.EVALUATE_CALENDAR_STRING(
  9   'FREQ=MONTHLY; INTERVAL=2; BYMONTHDAY=15',
 10   start_date, null, next_run_date);
 11   DBMS_OUTPUT.PUT_LINE('next_run_date: ' ||
 12   next_run_date);
 13   END;
SQL> /
next_run_date: 15-OCT-04 10.00.00.000000 AM

PL/SQL procedure successfully completed.
```

As you can see, line 9 contains the actual calendar expression that is being evaluated. Also, because a value of NULL was submitted for the RETURN_DATE_AFTER parameter, Oracle uses the current date and time as the default.

The procedure returns only a single value for NEXT_RUN_DATE, but you may want to see more than one. If so, you can use the SQL shown here:

```
SQL> DECLARE
  2   start_date TIMESTAMP;
  3   return_date_after TIMESTAMP;
  4   next_run_date TIMESTAMP;
  5  BEGIN
  6   start_date := to_timestamp_tz(
  7   '10-OCT-2004 10:00:00','DD-MON-YYYY HH24:MI:SS')
  8   return_date_after := start_date;
  9   FOR i IN 1..10 LOOP
 10   DBMS_SCHEDULER.EVALUATE_CALENDAR_STRING(
 11   'FREQ=MONTHLY; INTERVAL=2; BYMONTHDAY=15',
 12   start_date, return_date_after, next_run_date);
 13   DBMS_OUTPUT.PUT_LINE(
 14    'next_run_date: ' || next_run_date);
 15   return_date_after := next_run_date;
 16   END LOOP;
 17  END;
SQL> /
next_run_date: 15-OCT-04 10.00.00.000000 AM
next_run_date: 15-DEC-04 10.00.00.000000 AM
next_run_date: 15-FEB-05 10.00.00.000000 AM
next_run_date: 15-APR-05 10.00.00.000000 AM
next_run_date: 15-JUN-05 10.00.00.000000 AM
next_run_date: 15-AUG-05 10.00.00.000000 AM
next_run_date: 15-OCT-05 10.00.00.000000 AM
next_run_date: 15-DEC-05 10.00.00.000000 AM
next_run_date: 15-FEB-06 10.00.00.000000 AM
next_run_date: 15-APR-06 10.00.00.000000 AM

PL/SQL procedure successfully completed.
```

This example calls the procedure inside of a loop, and each time through, it uses the NEXT_RUN_DATE returned from the prior call as the value for the RETURN_DATE_AFTER parameter. This tells Oracle to only return a date that is farther in the future than the date specified. Therefore, you will get each successive execution date.

Using Scheduler Windows

In Chapter 11, "Managing Resources," you learned to create and manage resource plans to allocate system resources. Scheduler windows allow you to change the active resource plan based on defined schedules. In general, resource plans tend to be created with specific time windows in mind. For instance, assume that your system performs heavy transaction processing between the hours of 8:00 A.M. and 5:00 P.M. but runs mostly batch processing and reports after hours. It would make sense to create a separate resource plan to govern resource allocation for each time period. Scheduler windows can then be used to switch automatically between the two.

Unlike most of the other Scheduler objects that you've seen so far, windows are created in the SYS schema. They are stored as database objects and therefore must have a valid name that is unique within the SYS schema.

In the following sections, you will learn to create, open, and close scheduler windows. You'll also learn about scheduler window logging and how to manage window logs. Lastly, you'll learn about purging scheduler logs.

Creating Windows

Windows can be created by using the `DBMS_SCHEDULER.CREATE_WINDOW` procedure. When creating a window, you have the choice of either using an existing schedule or defining an inline schedule. However, an existing schedule may not be used if the schedule has a repeat interval based on a PL/SQL expression.

The parameters for the `CREATE_WINDOW` procedure are described here:

WINDOW_NAME The `WINDOW_NAME` parameter uniquely identifies the window in the SYS schema. The name has to be unique in the SYS schema.

RESOURCE_PLAN The `RESOURCE_PLAN` parameter specifies the name of the resource plan that will govern the timeframe of the window. When the window opens, the system switches to the specified resource plan. When the window closes, the system either switches back to the prior resource plan or, if another window is opening, to the resource plan of the new window. If the current resource plan has been set through the use of the `ALTER SYSTEM SET RESOURCE_MANAGER_PLAN FORCE` statement, the Scheduler will not be allowed to change the resource plan. If no resource plan is defined for the window, the current resource plan will remain in effect when the window opens and will stay in effect for the duration of the window.

START_DATE The `START_DATE` parameter specifies the first date that the window is scheduled to open. If `START_DATE` is `NULL` or references a date in the past, the window will open as soon as it is created. The `START_DATE` parameter is used as a reference date when the `REPEAT_INTERVAL` parameter uses a calendaring expression. In this situation, the window will open on the first date that matches the calendaring expression *and* is on or after the date specified in the `START_DATE` parameter.

DURATION The DURATION attribute specifies how long the window will remain open. There is no default value, so a value must be provided. The value should be specified as an INTERVAL DAY TO SECOND datatype (for example, interval '10' hour or interval '20' minute).

SCHEDULE_NAME The SCHEDULE_NAME parameter specifies the name of the schedule associated with the window.

REPEAT_INTERVAL The REPEAT_INTERVAL parameter specifies how often the window should repeat. It is defined using the calendaring syntax only; PL/SQL expressions cannot be used in conjunction with a window. If the REPEAT_INTERVAL parameter is NULL, the window will open only once at the specified start date.

END_DATE The END_DATE parameter specifies the date when the window will be disabled. If the END_DATE parameter is NULL, a repeating window will repeat forever.

WINDOW_PRIORITY The WINDOW_PRIORITY parameter is relevant only when two windows overlap each other. Because only one window can be in effect at a time, the window priority determines which window will be opened. The valid values are LOW (the default) and HIGH. A high priority window has precedence.

COMMENTS The COMMENTS parameter specifies an optional comment about the window.

To create a window that activates the DAY_PLAN resource plan and uses a schedule named WORK_HOURS_SCHEDULE, see the following example:

```
SQL> begin
  2  dbms_scheduler.create_window (
  3  window_name => 'WORK_HOURS_WINDOW',
  4  resource_plan => 'DAY_PLAN',
  5  schedule_name => 'WORK_HOURS_SCHEDULE',
  6  duration => INTERVAL '10' HOUR,
  7  window_priority => 'HIGH');
  8  end;
  SQL> /

PL/SQL procedure successfully completed.
```

This newly created window will be started based on a schedule named WORK_HOURS_SCHEDULE and will remain in effect for 10 hours. During those 10 hours, the DAY_PLAN resource plan will be in effect. Also, because the priority for this window is set to HIGH, it will take precedence over any overlapping window that has a priority setting of LOW.

Opening and Closing Windows

There are two distinct ways that a window can be opened. The first is based on the window's schedule. The second is they can be opened manually by using the DBMS_SCHEDULER.OPEN_WINDOW procedure.

The OPEN_WINDOW procedure opens a window independent of its schedule. The associated resource plan is enabled immediately, and currently executing jobs are subjected to the change in resource plan, just as if the window had opened based on its schedule.

When opening a window manually, you can specify a new duration for the window to remain open; otherwise it will remain open for the duration defined when the window was created.

If the FORCE parameter is set to TRUE in the OPEN_WINDOW procedure, the Scheduler will automatically close any currently open window, even if it has a higher priority. Also, it will not allow any other windows to be opened for the duration of the manually opened window.

The OPEN_WINDOW procedure accepts only three parameters: WINDOW_NAME, DURATION, and FORCE. An example of its usage is as follows:

```
SQL>  begin
  2  dbms_scheduler.open_window (
  3  window_name => 'WORK_HOURS_WINDOW',
  4  duration => INTERVAL '20' MINUTE,
  5  force => TRUE);
  6  end;
  SQL> /

PL/SQL procedure successfully completed.
```

This example forces the WORK_HOURS_WINDOW to be opened and any current window to close. The new window will remain open for a duration of 20 minutes.

In a similar manner, windows can be manually closed by using the DBMS_SCHEDULER.CLOSE_WINDOW procedure. This procedure accepts the window name as a parameter, as shown here:

```
SQL>  begin
  2  dbms_scheduler.close_window (
  3  window_name => 'WORK_HOURS_WINDOW');
  4  end;
  SQL> /

PL/SQL procedure successfully completed.
```

Window Logging

The Oracle Scheduler maintains *window logs* of all window activities. The DBA_SCHEDULER_WINDOW_LOG view can be used to view log entries for all of the following window activities:

- Creating a new window
- Dropping a window
- Opening a window
- Closing a window

- Overlapping windows
- Disabling a window
- Enabling a window

For example, use the following query to view window log entries:

```
SQL> select log_id, trunc(log_date) log_date,
  window_name, operation
  from dba_scheduler_window_log;

  LOG_ID LOG_DATE  WINDOW_NAME          OPERATION
  ------ --------- -------------------- ---------
     527 25-SEP-04 WEEKEND_WINDOW       OPEN
     544 28-SEP-04 WEEKNIGHT_WINDOW     OPEN
     547 28-SEP-04 WEEKNIGHT_WINDOW     CLOSE
     548 29-SEP-04 WEEKNIGHT_WINDOW     OPEN
     551 29-SEP-04 WEEKNIGHT_WINDOW     CLOSE
     552 30-SEP-04 WEEKNIGHT_WINDOW     OPEN
     559 01-OCT-04 WEEKNIGHT_WINDOW     CLOSE
     560 02-OCT-04 WEEKNIGHT_WINDOW     OPEN
     563 02-OCT-04 WEEKNIGHT_WINDOW     CLOSE
     555 30-SEP-04 WEEKNIGHT_WINDOW     CLOSE
     564 02-OCT-04 WEEKEND_WINDOW       OPEN
```

For each CLOSE operation logged in the DBA_SCHEDULER_WINDOW_LOG view, there will be an associated record in the DBA_SCHEDULER_WINDOW_DETAILS view, as shown here:

```
SQL> select log_id, trunc(log_date) log_date,
  window_name, actual_duration
  from dba_scheduler_window_details;

 LOG_ID LOG_DATE  WINDOW_NAME          ACTUAL_DURATION
------- --------- -------------------- ---------------
    547 28-SEP-04 WEEKNIGHT_WINDOW     +000 08:00:00
    551 29-SEP-04 WEEKNIGHT_WINDOW     +000 08:00:00
    559 01-OCT-04 WEEKNIGHT_WINDOW     +000 08:00:00
    563 02-OCT-04 WEEKNIGHT_WINDOW     +000 08:00:00
    555 30-SEP-04 WEEKNIGHT_WINDOW     +000 07:59:58
```

Purging Logs

As with any automatic logging system, window logs must be purged on a regular basis to prevent excessive table growth. Oracle provides an automatic method to purge the log files after a specified number of days.

Scheduler job and window logs will be automatically purged based on the setting of the LOG_HISTORY attribute of the Scheduler itself. The value of this parameter determines the number of days that log data should be retained, after which it will be purged. To set this value, use the SET_SCHEDULER_ATTRIBUTE procedure, as in the following example:

```
SQL> begin
  2   DBMS_SCHEDULER.SET_SCHEDULER_ATTRIBUTE(
  3   'LOG_HISTORY','60');
  4  end;
SQL> /

PL/SQL procedure successfully completed.
```

This example instructs Oracle to automatically purge all records that are over 60 days old.

By default, this procedure sets the history retention period for both Scheduler window logs and Scheduler job logs. To set only one, the WHICH_LOG parameter may be included to specify either WINDOW_LOG or JOB_LOG.

Using Scheduler Views

Oracle offers a wide variety of views to access information regarding the Scheduler and its associated objects. These views allow you to see information about currently running jobs and past runs of jobs. Table 12.6 describes the available Scheduler views.

To see information on completed instances of a job, use the example shown here:

```
SQL> select job_name, status, error#
  2  from dba_scheduler_job_run_details
  3   where job_name = 'FAIL_JOB';

JOB_NAME      STATUS              ERROR#
--------      --------------      ------
FAIL_JOB      FAILURE              20000
```

To see the current state of all jobs, use the following example:

```
SQL> select job_name, state
  2  from dba_scheduler_jobs;

JOB_NAME          STATE
----------------- ---------------
PURGE_LOG         SCHEDULED
GATHER_STATS_JOB  SCHEDULED
COLA_JOB          SCHEDULED
RAISE_JOB         DISABLED
```

TABLE 12.6 Scheduler Views Available

View	Description
*_SCHEDULER_SCHEDULES	Shows information on all defined schedules.
*_SCHEDULER_PROGRAMS	Shows information on all defined programs.
*_SCHEDULER_PROGRAM_ARGUMENTS	Shows all registered program arguments, and the default values if they exist.
*_SCHEDULER_JOBS	Shows all defined jobs, both enabled and disabled.
*_SCHEDULER_GLOBAL_ATTRIBUTE	Shows the current values of all Scheduler attributes.
*_SCHEDULER_JOB_ARGUMENTS	Shows the arguments for all defined jobs.
*_SCHEDULER_JOB_CLASSES	Shows information on all defined job classes.
*_SCHEDULER_WINDOWS	Shows information about all defined windows.
*_SCHEDULER_JOB_RUN_DETAILS	Shows information about all completed (failed or successful) job runs.
*_SCHEDULER_WINDOW_GROUPS	Shows information about all window groups.
*_SCHEDULER_WINGROUP_MEMBERS	Shows the members of all window groups.
*_SCHEDULER_RUNNING_JOBS	Shows the state information on all jobs that are currently being run.

To view windows and their next start dates, the following SQL can be used:

```
SQL> select window_name, next_start_date
  2  from dba_scheduler_windows;

WINDOW_NAME          NEXT_START_DATE
-------------------- ------------------------------------
WEEKNIGHT_WINDOW     12-OCT-04 10.00.00.300000 PM -08:00
WEEKEND_WINDOW       16-OCT-04 12.00.00.500000 AM -08:00
```

The DBA_SCHEDULER_JOB_LOG view can be used to view log entries for previously executed jobs, as shown here:

```
SQL> select log_id, trunc(log_date) log_date, owner, job_name, operation
  ➥from dba_scheduler_job_log;

LOG_ID LOG_DATE   OWNER JOB_NAME            OPERATION
------- ---------- ----- -----------------   ---------
    522 25-SEP-04  SYS     PURGE_LOG         RUN
    524 25-SEP-04  SYS     ADV_SQL_TUNING    SUCCEEDED
    525 25-SEP-04  SYS     ADV_SQL_TUNING    DROP
    528 25-SEP-04  SYS     GATHER_STATS_JOB  RUN
    484 18-SEP-04  SYS     GATHER_STATS_JOB  RUN
    541 26-SEP-04  SYS     PURGE_LOG         RUN
    543 27-SEP-04  SYS     PURGE_LOG         RUN
    545 28-SEP-04  SYS     GATHER_STATS_JOB  RUN
    546 28-SEP-04  SYS     PURGE_LOG         RUN
    553 30-SEP-04  SYS     GATHER_STATS_JOB  RUN
    622 10-OCT-04  BUTERTB COLA_JOB          RUN
    549 29-SEP-04  SYS     GATHER_STATS_JOB  RUN
```

Summary

In this chapter, you learned about the new Oracle 10*g* Scheduler. You learned how it resolves issues such as schedule creep that existed in its predecessor, the DBMS_JOB package.

This chapter also explained the new architecture that underlies the Scheduler. You learned how the job table stores all enabled jobs within the database, and you learned how the job coordinator process queries the job table on a regular basis and stores the job information in a memory cache for faster access. When a job is scheduled to run, the job coordinator process is automatically started (if it is not already active). It will pass the job information to a job slave process for execution.

You learned that the job slave process will gather all the metadata for the job, start a session as the owner of the job, begin a transaction within the session, and then execute the job. When the job completes, the slave commits the transaction and closes the session. The slave then updates the job entry in the job table to show a COMPLETE status. It inserts a new entry into the job log, updates the run count for the job, and then looks for any new work that needs to be done. If none is found, the job slave process returns to a sleep state.

You also learned that, in a RAC environment, each instance has its own job coordinator, and the job coordinators have the ability to communicate with each other to keep information current. You learned that a RAC environment will still have only one job table that is shared by all the instances. You also learned that jobs can be assigned to a service, as opposed to an instance, ensuring that the job can be run by a different node if an instance is down.

Next, you learned about job objects and how they are created and administered. You learned that the CREATE_JOB procedure is overloaded and allows jobs to be created in four different ways:

- Specifying an inline program and an inline schedule
- Specifying an inline program and a stored schedule
- Specifying a stored program and an inline schedule
- Specifying a stored program and a stored schedule

You also learned to set job arguments using the SET_JOB_ARGUMENT_VALUE and the SET_JOB_ANYDATA_VALUE procedures, as well as how to copy, run, disable, enable, and drop jobs.

You learned about program objects and how they define PL/SQL blocks, stored procedures, or external operating system executables, as well as their arguments and other metadata. You also learned to administer all aspects of program objects.

You also learned about schedule objects and how they are created. You learned that schedules specify a start date, an optional end date, and a repeat interval. Together, these elements are used to calculate run dates. You learned to use the new calendaring syntax to define repeat intervals within the schedules.

Finally, you learned about windows and how they can be used to switch resource plans at scheduled intervals to control resource allocation for the system. You learned that only one window can be open at any given time and that, when overlapping windows exist, a window with a priority of HIGH will take precedence over a window with a priority of LOW.

Exam Essentials

Know how to simplify management tasks by using the Scheduler. Understand how the Scheduler can be used to automate routine management tasks to run on a repeating basis. Know the types of programs that can be run through the Scheduler (PL/SQL blocks, stored procedures, and external operating system executables).

Be able to create a job, program, schedule, and window. Know the various CREATE procedures in the DBMS_SCHEDULER package (CREATE_JOB, CREATE_PROGRAM, CREATE_SCHEDULE, and CREATE_WINDOW). Understand the different options that can be used when creating a job (inline definitions versus stored objects). Understand that only a subset of attributes can be defined at creation time. The other attributes can be set by altering the object through the SET_ATTRIBUTE and SET_ATTRIBUTE_NULL procedures.

Know how to reuse Scheduler components for similar tasks. Understand the difference between inline schedule and program definitions and stored Scheduler object components. Know that a job can reference stored schedule and program objects. Know that a window can reference a stored schedule object. Understand that a job can be reused with different parameters.

Understand how to view information about job executions and job instances. Be aware of the different views available to view Scheduler information. Know that the views use the naming convention of DBA|ALL|USER_SCHEDULER_ as a prefix for all views (for example, DBA_SCHEDULER_JOBS, DBA_SCHEDULER_PROGRAMS, and so on). Know that the DBA_SCHEDULER_JOB_RUN_DETAILS view shows information about job executions and that the DBA_SCHEDULER_RUNNING_JOBS view shows information on jobs that are currently running.

Review Questions

1. When setting arguments for a job, which procedure do you use for types that cannot be implicitly converted to and from a VARCHAR2 datatype?

   A. SET_JOB_ARGUMENT_VALUE

   B. SET_JOB_VALUE_ANYDATA

   C. SET_JOB_ANYDATA_VALUE

   D. SET_SPECIAL_JOB_VALUE

   E. SET_JOB_ANYTYPE_VALUE

2. Which DBMS_SCHEDULER procedures can be used to enable a program? (Choose all that apply.)

   A. ENABLE

   B. ENABLE_PROGRAM

   C. VALIDATE_PROGRAM

   D. SET_ATTRIBUTE

   E. SET_ENABLED

3. Which of the following is not a valid calendaring syntax element?

   A. FREQ

   B. BYHOUR

   C. RUNDATE

   D. INTERVAL

   E. BYMINUTE

4. Which Scheduler view(s) can be queried to see which jobs are currently executing? (Choose all that apply.)

   A. DBA_SCHEDULER_JOB_RUN_DETAILS

   B. DBA_SCHEDULER_RUNNING_JOBS

   C. DBA_SCHEDULER_CURRENT_JOBS

   D. DBA_SCHEDULER_JOBS

   E. DBA_SCHEDULER_EXECUTING_JOBS

5. A schedule defined entirely within the confines of a Scheduler job object is known as a(n) ____ ________________.

   A. Fixed schedule

   B. Inline schedule

   C. Stored schedule

   D. Hard-coded schedule

   E. None of the above

6. Which DBMS_SCHEDULER procedure(s) can be used to alter an existing job? (Choose all that apply.)

   A. SET_ATTRIBUTE_NULL

   B. ALTER_JOB

   C. ALTER_JOB_PARAMETERS

   D. ALTER

   E. SET_ATTRIBUTE

7. What is the default value for the ENABLED attribute of a job or program when it is created?

   A. TRUE

   B. FALSE

   C. There is no default. It must be defined at creation time.

   D. PENDING

   E. NULL

8. To set the history retention period for either window logging or job logging individually, which two parameters of the SET_SCHEDULER_ATTRIBUTE procedure need to be used?

   A. LOG_HISTORY

   B. JOB_LOG_RETENTION

   C. WINDOW_LOG_RETENTION

   D. WHICH_LOG

   E. LOG_NAME

9. Consider the following code snippet:

```
begin
dbms_scheduler.run_job('COLA_JOB',TRUE);
end;
```

   If this code were executed, which of the following statements would be true? (Choose all that apply.)

   A. The COLA_JOB job would be executed asynchronously.

   B. The COLA_JOB job would be executed synchronously.

   C. The COLA_JOB job would run in the user's current session.

   D. The COLA_JOB job would run with the FORCE option.

   E. The user could continue to issue SQL statements in the session while the COLA_JOB job was executing.

10. Which of the following calendaring syntax expressions would evaluate to the last day of every month?

    A. `FREQ = MONTHLY; BYMONTHDAY = 31`
    B. `FREQ = MONTHLY; BYMONTHDAY = -1`
    C. `FREQ = DAILY; BYDAY = -1`
    D. `FREQ = MONTHLY; BYDAY = 31`
    E. `FREQ = DAILY; BYMONTHDAY = LAST_DAY`

11. Which of the following tasks is *not* performed by the job coordinator?

    A. Update job log when a job completes
    B. Spawn and remove job slaves
    C. Write/read job info to/from memory cache
    D. Query job table
    E. Pass job information to job slaves

12. Which of the following objects can be directly referenced by a window object? (Choose all that apply.)

    A. Schedule object
    B. Program object
    C. Job object
    D. Resource plan
    E. Resource Consumer Group

13. Which `DBMS_SCHEDULER` procedure is available for testing repeat intervals produced by calendaring syntax expressions?

    A. `EVALUATE_REPEAT_INTERVAL`
    B. `VALIDATE_CALENDAR_EXPRESSION`
    C. `EVALUATE_CALENDAR_STRING`
    D. `VALIDATE_CALENDAR_STRING`
    E. `EVALUATE_INTERVAL_EXPRESSION`

14. Which of the following is not a valid setting for the `PROGRAM_TYPE` parameter in a program object or the `JOB_TYPE` parameter in a job object?

    A. `PLSQL_BLOCK`
    B. `JAVA_STORED_PROCEDURE`
    C. `STORED_PROCEDURE`
    D. `EXECUTABLE`
    E. None of the above are invalid settings.

15. Which of the following Scheduler elements encourage object reuse? (Choose all that apply.)

A. Schedule objects

B. Program arguments

C. Job classes

D. Job arguments

E. All of the above

16. What is the danger associated with stopping a running job by using the STOP_JOB procedure?

A. The job will need to be re-enabled before it will execute again.

B. The job may hold locks on objects referenced within the job.

C. All jobs within the job group will also be stopped.

D. The job may leave data in an inconsistent state.

E. There is no danger in using the STOP_JOB procedure.

17. If a job references a schedule that has been disabled, what will be the result?

A. The job will be automatically disabled.

B. The job will never execute.

C. The job will attempt to execute, but will fail.

D. The job will inherit the DEFAULT_SCHEDULE schedule.

E. A schedule object cannot be disabled.

18. When a job exceeds the date specified in its END_DATE attribute, which of the following will happen? (Choose all that apply.)

A. The job will be dropped automatically if the value of the AUTO_DROP attribute is TRUE.

B. The job will be disabled if the value of the AUTO_DROP attribute is FALSE.

C. The STATE attribute of the job will be set to COMPLETED if the value of the AUTO_DROP attribute is FALSE.

D. All objects referenced by the job will be dropped if the value of the AUTO_DROP attribute is TRUE and the value of the CASCADE attribute is TRUE.

E. The STATE column of the job table will be set to COMPLETED for the job.

19. Which view can you query to see information on Scheduler windows?

A. DBA_WINDOWS

B. DBA_SCHEDULER_WINDOWS

C. DBA_WINDOW_OBJECTS

D. DBA_SCHEDULER_WINDOW_OBJECTS

E. DBA_ALL_SCHEDULER_WINDOWS

20. If two windows overlap, which window attribute will determine if one should be chosen over the other?

A. WINDOW_PRIORITY

B. PRIORITY

C. PRIORITY_LEVEL

D. WINDOW_PRIORITY_LEVEL

E. OVERLAP_RULE

Answers to Review Questions

1. C. The SET_JOB_ANYDATA_VALUE procedure allows you to set job arguments that don't easily convert to and from a string (VARCHAR2) datatype.

2. A, D. Programs (as well as jobs) can be enabled in two ways: by using the ENABLE procedure or by using the SET_ATTRIBUTE procedure to set the ENABLED attribute to TRUE.

3. C. The calendaring syntax does not support an element named RUNDATE. It does not support the concept of specifying a single run date at all. The purpose of the calendaring syntax is to define repeat intervals that will be used to calculate run dates.

4. B, D. The DBA_SCHEDULER_RUNNING_JOBS view shows detailed information about all jobs currently executing. The DBA_SCHEDULER_JOBS view contains the STATE column, which shows a value of RUNNING for an executing job.

5. B. A schedule defined within a job object is known as an inline schedule, whereas an independent schedule object is referred to as a stored schedule. Inline schedules cannot be referenced by other objects.

6. A, E. A job can be altered only by changing the value of one or more of its attributes. This is accomplished by using the SET_ATTRIBUTE and SET_ATTRIBUTE_NULL procedures.

7. B. Jobs and programs are created in a disabled state by default. They must be enabled by setting the ENABLE parameter to TRUE in their respective CREATE statements, or by altering the object after creation.

8. A, D. The LOG_HISTORY parameter defines the retention period for both job logging and window logging by default. However, the WHICH_LOG parameter can be used to specify either JOB_LOG or WINDOW_LOG.

9. B, C. The RUN_JOB procedure accepts two parameters: JOB_NAME and USE_CURRENT_SESSION. In this example, the USE_CURRENT_SESSION parameter is set to a value of TRUE. This causes the job to be executed synchronously in the user's current session. Because the job runs synchronously, control would not return to the user until the job was completed. Therefore, the user could not continue to execute SQL statements while the job was running.

10. B. The BYMONTHDAY element accepts negative values that represent a specific count of days from the end of the month. Also, the FREQ parameter must be set to MONTHLY, because it will execute every month.

11. A. The job coordinator does not update the job log when a job completes. That function is performed by the job slave that has been assigned to the job.

12. A, D. A window does not execute programs or jobs. It specifies a resource plan that will be enabled based on a schedule. Therefore, it can reference both a schedule object and a resource plan object. And while the resource plan may reference one or more resource consumer groups, the window object does not directly reference them.

13. C. The EVALUATE_CALENDAR_STRING procedure will generate execution dates from a calendaring syntax expression.

14. B. Java stored procedures cannot be executed by the job Scheduler unless they are called from within a PL/SQL procedure wrapper. This can be done in a stored procedure using PL/SQL's external procedure feature. Therefore, the job or program type setting would be STORED_PROCEDURE.

15. A, B, D. Schedule objects do not specify any action to be performed; they simply generate execution dates that any job can use. Program and job arguments allow the jobs and programs to be reused by simply changing the arguments that are passed in. Job classes simplify the management of jobs, but they do not specifically encourage job reuse.

16. D. The Scheduler will attempt to wrap the job within a transaction and will execute a rollback if a job is stopped. However, if the job has performed commits, the rollback will only roll back any uncommitted changes. This could result in inconsistent data.

17. E. A schedule object does not possess the ENABLED attribute. It is therefore enabled upon creation and can never be disabled.

18. A, B, E. When a job exceeds its end date, it will be dropped only if the AUTO_DROP attribute is set to TRUE. Otherwise, it will be disabled. In either case, the STATE column will be set to COMPLETED in the job table. A job object does not possess a CASCADE attribute or a STATE attribute.

19. B. The DBA_SCHEDULER_WINDOWS view shows information on window objects defined in the Scheduler.

20. A. The WINDOW_PRIORITY attribute can be set to either HIGH or LOW for a window. If two windows overlap and only one of the windows has a priority of HIGH, it will be chosen.

Chapter 13

Monitoring and Managing Storage

ORACLE DATABASE 10G: ADMINISTRATION II EXAM OBJECTIVES COVERED IN THIS CHAPTER:

✓ **Monitoring and Managing Storage**

- Tune redo writing and archiving operations.
- Issue statements that can be suspended upon encountering space condition errors.
- Reduce space-related error conditions by proactively managing tablespace usage.
- Reclaim wasted space from tables and indexes using the segment shrink functionality.
- Estimate the size of new tables and indexes.
- Use different storage options to improve the performance of queries.
- Rebuild indexes online.

Exam objectives are subject to change at any time without prior notice and at Oracle's sole discretion. Please visit Oracle's Training and Certification website (`http://www.oracle.com/education/certification/`) for the most current exam objectives listing.

Oracle Database 10*g* (Oracle 10*g*) provides a number of automated enhancements to help you manage the disk space in the database, both at the tablespace level and at the segment level.

Proactive tablespace monitoring uses the `DBMS_SERVER_ALERT PL/SQL` package to set up thresholds at which you are notified of a potential space issue; ideally, this happens long before a user calls you because they cannot create a table because of lack of space in a tablespace.

To make table access more space efficient and reduce the amount of I/O needed to access a table, Oracle provides segment shrink functionality to compress a table whose data blocks are sparsely populated. The Segment Advisor notifies you of segments—either table or index segments—that would benefit from a shrink operation.

Other automated advisors introduced in Oracle 10*g* include the Redo Logfile Size Advisor. The Redo Logfile Size Advisor helps you optimize the size of your redo log files so they are not too big or too small; redo log files that are too small can have an impact on system performance.

As of Oracle 9*i*, you can prevent the failure of long-running operations that run out of disk space by leveraging Resumable Space Allocation. Instead of rolling back the entire long-running operation, the operation is paused until the DBA can allocate another disk volume or increase a user's quota. Once the disk space is available, the long-running operation resumes where it left off.

In all of these cases, the Oracle Enterprise Manager (EM) Database Control provides wizards and a graphical interface for these enhancements, making it easy to leverage these enhancements when the command-line syntax is unfamiliar or difficult to remember.

In this chapter, we will review how to set up server alerts, both with the PL/SQL interface and with EM Database Control. We will also explain how to identify segments that can benefit from space reclamation using the Segment Advisor and how to shrink these segments with segment shrink operations. We will present a few other table types that can optimize space usage, performance, or both; these table types include index-organized tables and clustered tables, including hash clusters and sorted hash clusters. Finally, we will provide an in-depth look at Resumable Space Allocation and how it can save both time and wasted effort when a long-running operation runs out of disk space.

Monitoring Tablespace Storage

Oracle 10*g* manages the disk space in two ways: reactively and proactively. Through database alerts, you are notified of tablespace disk space usage at two different levels: warning level and critical level. By default, the warning level is 85 percent, and the critical level is 97 percent. While these levels are by definition reactive, they can arguably be considered proactive in that you will have an opportunity to increase the amount of space in the tablespace before it runs out of space.

In a truly proactive manner, Oracle 10*g* collects statistics on space usage in the *Automatic Workload Repository (AWR)* at 30-minute intervals to assist you with tablespace and segment growth trend analysis and capacity planning. The AWR collects vital statistics and workload information, including CPU usage, user sessions, I/O usage, and many other metrics at 30-minute intervals and stores them in the SYSAUX tablespace for later analysis.

In the following sections, we will go into some of the details of how Oracle monitors tablespace usage. In addition, we will show you how you can view and modify the alert thresholds—both for an individual tablespace and for the database default—via the EM Database Control interface as well as via the PL/SQL package DBMS_SERVER_ALERT.

Space Usage Monitoring

If a tablespace does not have specific percentage thresholds defined, the database defaults of 85 percent for the warning level and 97 percent for the critical level apply. You can also change these default thresholds, as you will see in the next couple of sections.

The background process *MMON* checks for tablespace space problems every 10 minutes; alerts are triggered both when a threshold is exceeded and once again when the space usage for a tablespace falls back below the threshold. For example, assume that the default thresholds of 85 percent and 97 percent are in effect. Within a five-minute period, the USERS tablespace reaches 86 percent full, and MMON generates an alert. Fifteen minutes later, the USERS tablespace reaches 99 percent full, and MMON signals a second alert, this time a critical alert. You allocate a new datafile to the USERS tablespace to bring the overall space usage to 92 percent. The next time MMON checks for space problems in the USERS tablespace, the space usage has fallen back below the 97 percent threshold, and a third alert is sent to denote that the critical alert has been cleared. Note that the threshold is dynamically recalculated when storage is added to a tablespace that is under space pressure.

For Oracle databases that have been upgraded from a previous version to Oracle 10*g*, all tablespace alerts are off by default.

Alerts are not necessary under a few conditions. For example, tablespaces that are read-only or are offline do not need thresholds defined, because their contents will not increase or decrease while they are read-only or offline.

Some tablespaces are defined as autoextensible. This presents a challenge to tablespace threshold monitoring, because even though the space usage of the datafile at a particular point in time may be at a warning or critical level, the datafile will automatically autoextend when it runs out of space. To avoid generating false alerts, thresholds on these tablespaces are computed in one of two ways: based on the maximum size specified when the tablespace was created or based on the maximum operating system file size, whichever is smaller.

Dictionary-managed tablespaces do not support server-generated alerts, which is yet another good reason to convert tablespaces from a previous version of Oracle to locally managed and to create all new tablespaces as locally managed.

Editing Thresholds with Enterprise Manager Database Control

You can edit space usage thresholds for tablespaces in one of two ways via EM Database Control: one from an overall threshold perspective and the other from an individual tablespace perspective.

To access the thresholds from a database-wide point of view, click the Manage Metrics link at the bottom of the EM Database Control database Home tab, and you'll see all possible database alerts listed as shown in Figure 13.1.

Clicking the Edit Thresholds button brings up the Edit Thresholds screen, where you can change one or more of these thresholds, as you can see in Figure 13.2.

FIGURE 13.1 All database thresholds

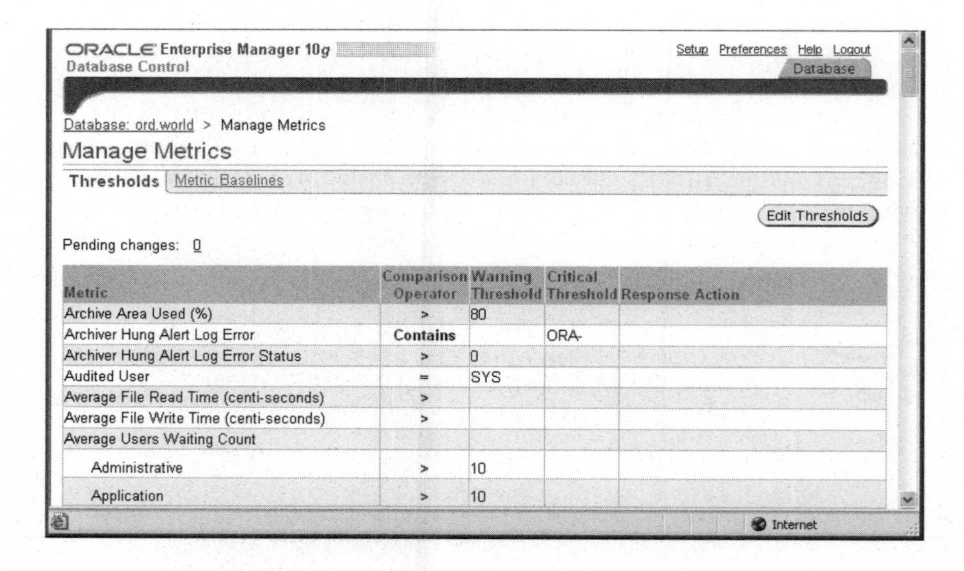

FIGURE 13.2 Editing thresholds

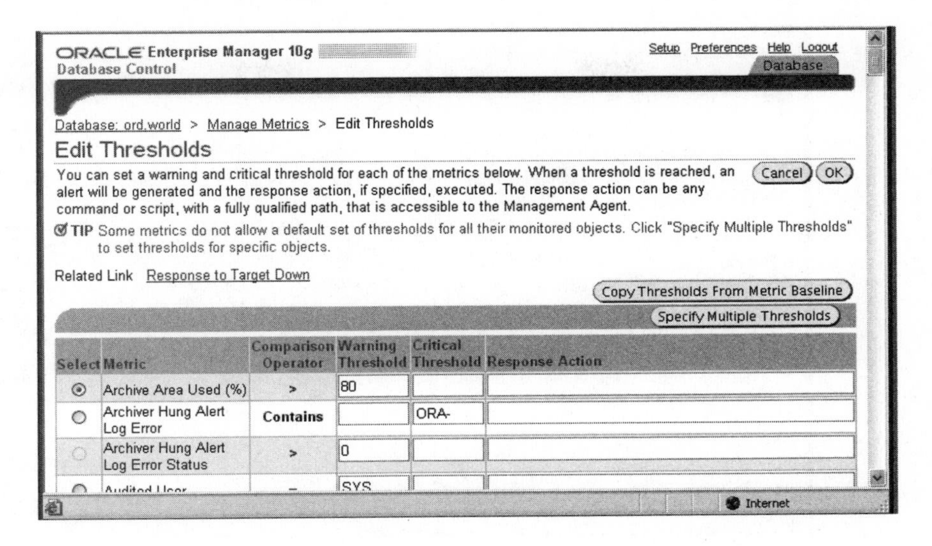

As the tip on this screen indicates, some metrics allow different thresholds for different objects of the same type such as tablespaces. For instance, if you select the Tablespace Space Used (%) metric (see Figure 13.3) and then click the Specify Multiple Thresholds button on the Edit Thresholds screen, you arrive at the Specify Multiple Thresholds: Tablespace Space Used (%) screen, shown in Figure 13.4.

FIGURE 13.3 Selecting the Tablespace Space Used (%) metric

○	Soft Parse (%)	<			
○	Sorts in Memory (%)	<			
○	Sorts to Disk (per second)	>			
○	Sorts to Disk (per transaction)	>			
○	State	Contains	MOUNTEI		
○	System Response Time (centi-seconds)	>			
◉	Tablespace Space Used (%)	>	85	97	
○	Tablespace Space Used (%) (dictionary managed)	>	85	97	
○	Total Index Scans (per second)	>			
○	Total Index Scans (per transaction)	>			
○	Total Invalid Object Count	>			
○	Total Parses (per second)	>			
○	Total Parses (per	>			

Internet

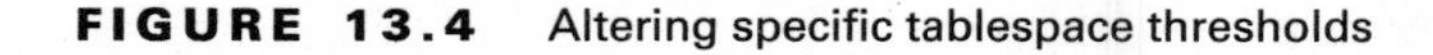

FIGURE 13.4 Altering specific tablespace thresholds

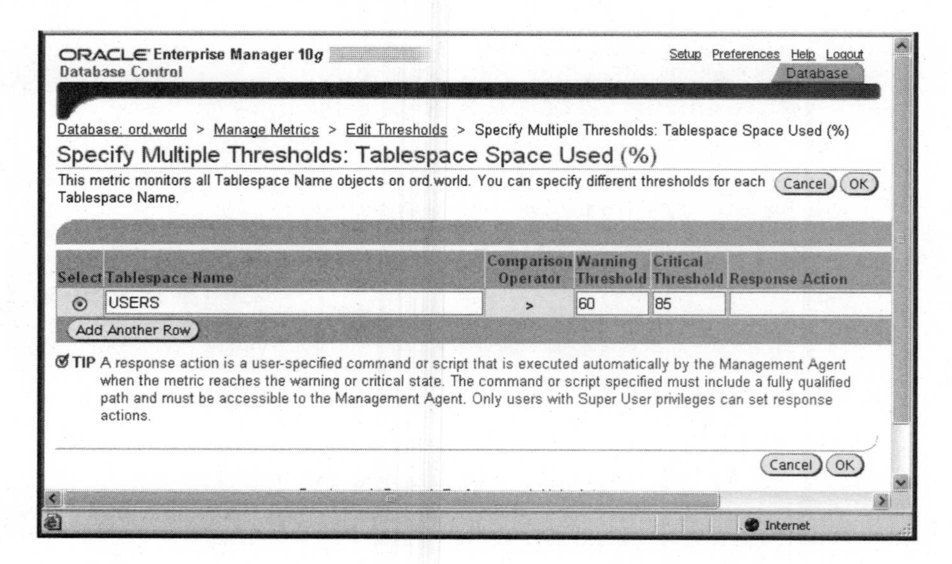

Because the USERS tablespace tends to grow quickly, notice in Figure 13.4 that you set the thresholds for the tablespace at 60 percent and 85 percent, a bit lower than the defaults, so that you will have more time to allocate the space for the USERS tablespace when the alert is generated. Also, note that this screen has a place for a response action: It can range from a script containing a SQL command to automatically freeing up the space in the tablespace or adding a new datafile to the tablespace.

You can also edit the thresholds for a tablespace by clicking the Tablespaces link on the Administration tab of the EM Database Control Database Administration page. Clicking the link for the USERS tablespace, you see the general characteristics of the tablespace as shown in Figure 13.5.

Clicking the Thresholds link brings you to the Edit Tablespace: USERS screen (see Figure 13.6). Here, you can see the current space usage for the USERS tablespace and change the thresholds for the warning and critical levels. As with the previous example, the thresholds for the USERS tablespace were changed to 60 percent and 85 percent.

On this same screen, you have the option to change the database-wide defaults by clicking the Modify Database Defaults button, which opens the Modify Database Defaults screen (see Figure 13.7). Using this screen, you can edit the database's default thresholds or disable them completely.

FIGURE 13.5 Tablespace general characteristics

ORACLE Enterprise Manager 10*g*
Database Control
Setup Preferences Help Logout
Database
Database: ord.world > Tablespaces > Edit Tablespace: USERS
Logged in As SYSTEM
Edit Tablespace: USERS
Show SQL Revert Apply
General Storage Thresholds
Name USERS
Bigfile tablespace **No**
Extent Management
Locally Managed
Dictionary Managed
Type
Permanent
Set as default permanent tablespace
Temporary
Set as default temporary tablespace
Status
Read Write
Read Only
Offline
Offline Mode Normal
Internet

FIGURE 13.6 Editing tablespace thresholds

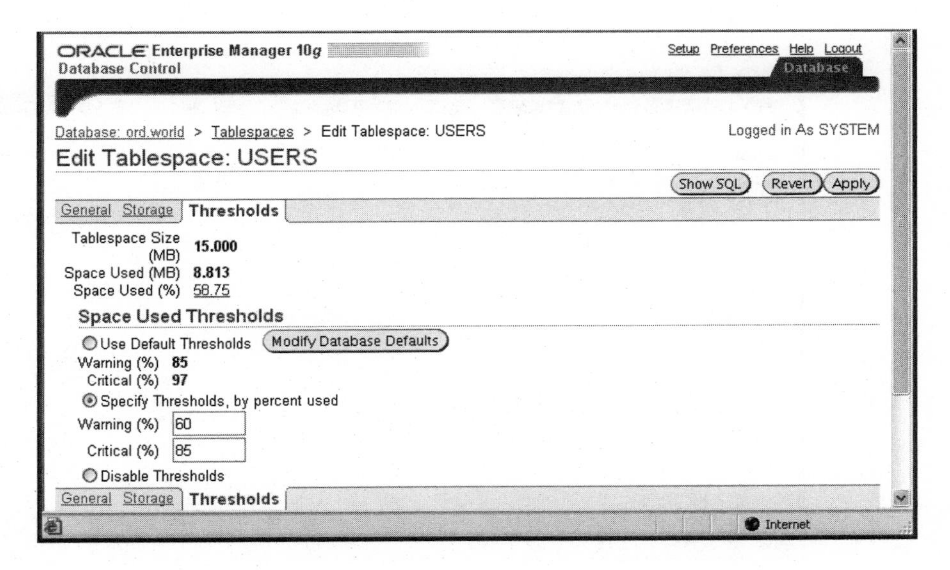

Referring to the Edit Tablespace: USERS screen (shown earlier in Figure 13.6), you want to apply your changes for the USERS tablespace thresholds. But before you do, you want to look at the SQL commands that will be executed by clicking the Show SQL button. As with most EM Database Control screens, you can brush up on the command-line syntax while enjoying the ease of use of a graphical user interface (GUI). Figure 13.8 shows the command that will be run when you click the Apply button.

Referring back to Figure 13.6, note that the USERS tablespace is already at 58.75 percent full. Let's see what happens when you add a few more segments to the USERS tablespace:

```
SQL> create table oe.customers_archive
  2       tablespace users
  3       as select * from oe.customers;
Table created.
```

The thresholds screen for the USERS tablespace in Figure 13.9 shows that you have not only exceeded the warning level but also the critical level.

Within 10 minutes, the MMON process will notify you of the critical tablespace problem in one of three ways: via the EM Database Control Home tab, via an e-mail message sent to the e-mail address configured when the database was created, or using the script in the Response Action column, if one was specified, shown in Figure 13.4 when the tablespace thresholds were modified.

FIGURE 13.7 Editing database default thresholds

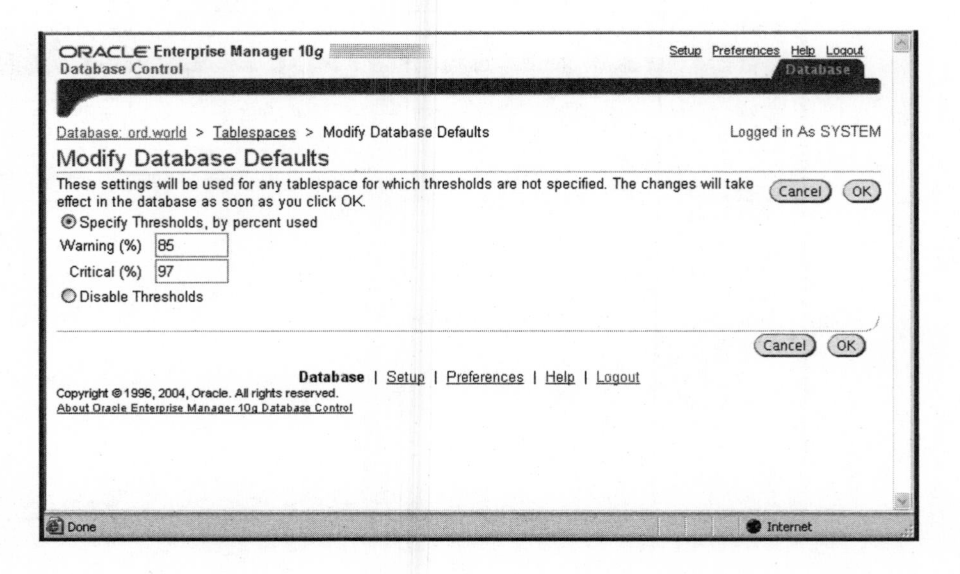

FIGURE 13.8 Showing SQL for tablespace thresholds

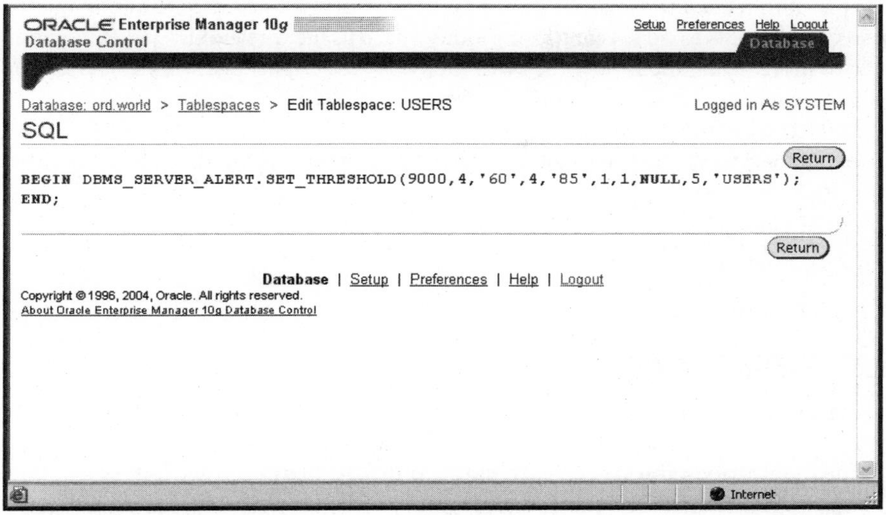

ORACLE Enterprise Manager 10g
Database Control
Setup Preferences Help Logout
Database

Database: ord.world > Tablespaces > Edit Tablespace: USERS
Logged in As SYSTEM

SQL

Return

```
BEGIN DBMS_SERVER_ALERT.SET_THRESHOLD(9000,4,'60',4,'85',1,1,NULL,5,'USERS');
END;
```

Return

Database | Setup | Preferences | Help | Logout
Copyright © 1996, 2004, Oracle. All rights reserved.
About Oracle Enterprise Manager 10g Database Control

Internet

FIGURE 13.9 Viewing current tablespace usage

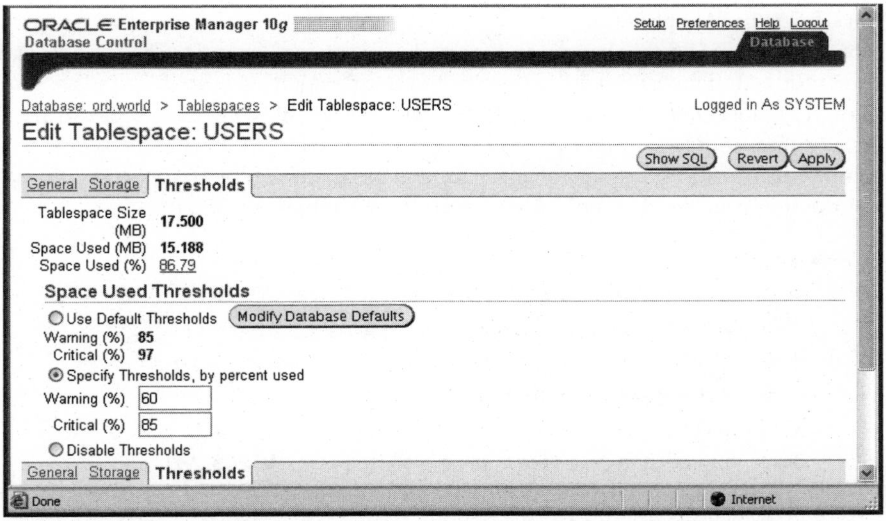

ORACLE Enterprise Manager 10g
Database Control
Setup Preferences Help Logout
Database

Database: ord.world > Tablespaces > Edit Tablespace: USERS
Logged in As SYSTEM

Edit Tablespace: USERS

Show SQL Revert Apply

General Storage **Thresholds**

Tablespace Size (MB) **17.500**
Space Used (MB) **15.188**
Space Used (%) 86.79

Space Used Thresholds

Use Default Thresholds Modify Database Defaults
Warning (%) **85**
Critical (%) **97**
Specify Thresholds, by percent used
Warning (%) 60
Critical (%) 85
Disable Thresholds

General Storage **Thresholds**

Done Internet

Using *DBMS_SERVER_ALERT*

The previous section demonstrated how you could view the actual SQL commands that EM Database Control uses to add, change, or modify space usage thresholds. The following sections will go into more detail about how the DBMS_SERVER_ALERT package works. The *DBMS_SERVER_ALERT* package contains a number of procedures that allow you to set, view, and modify a variety of alert conditions.

For managing space usage alerts, as with every other type of alert, the three procedures available are as follows:

- SET_THRESHOLD
- GET_THRESHOLD
- EXPAND_MESSAGE

SET_THRESHOLD

As the name implies, the *SET_THRESHOLD* procedure sets the threshold for a particular alert type. Table 13.1 describes the parameters for SET_THRESHOLD.

For monitoring tablespace space usage, only one metric object type is available: the TABLESPACE_PCT_FULL metric. The operators for exceeding a threshold are either OPERATOR_GE or OPERATOR_GT. OPERATOR_GE indicates that the current value of the metric is compared to the WARNING_VALUE or CRITICAL_VALUE using the greater than or equal to operator (>=); similarly, OPERATOR_GT indicates that the current value of the metric is compared to WARNING_VALUE or CRITICAL_VALUE using the greater than operator (>). The object type is always OBJECT_TYPE_TABLESPACE.

Because the USERS2 tablespace in the database is an infrequently used tablespace and not part of the production environment, you want to raise the alert thresholds for space usage to reduce the total number of alerts you receive every day. In the following example, you are changing the warning threshold to 90 percent and the critical threshold to 99 percent. These thresholds will be compared to the percentage of space used in the USERS2 tablespace every minute, causing an alert the first time the threshold is exceeded for the tablespace USERS2:

```
SQL> execute
  2     dbms_server_alert.set_threshold(
  3     dbms_server_alert.tablespace_pct_full,
  4     dbms_server_alert.operator_ge, 90,
  5     dbms_server_alert.operator_ge, 99,
  6     1, 1, null,
  7     dbms_server_alert.object_type_tablespace,'USERS2');
PL/SQL procedure successfully completed.
```

The new threshold goes into effect immediately. The next time MMON runs, an alert will be generated if the space usage on the USERS2 tablespace is at 90 percent or higher.

TABLE 13.1 *SET_THRESHOLD* Parameters

Parameter Name	Description
METRICS_ID	The name of the metric, using an internally defined constant.
WARNING_OPERATOR	The comparison operator for comparing the current value to the warning threshold value.
WARNING_VALUE	The warning threshold, or NULL if no warning threshold exists.
CRITICAL_OPERATOR	The comparison operator for comparing the current value to the warning threshold value.
CRITICAL_VALUE	The critical threshold, or NULL if no critical threshold exists.
OBSERVATION_PERIOD	The timer period at which the metrics are computed against the threshold; the valid range is 1 to 60 minutes.
CONSECUTIVE_OCCURRENCES	How many times the threshold needs to be exceeded before the alert is issued.
INSTANCE_NAME	The name of the instance for which the threshold applies; this value is NULL for all instances in a RAC database and is NULL for database-wide alerts.
OBJECT_TYPE	The type of object—for example, a tablespace, session, or service—using a set of internally defined constants.
OBJECT_NAME	The name of the object, such as the tablespace name.

GET_THRESHOLD

Similar to SET_THRESHOLD, the *GET_THRESHOLD* procedure retrieves the values of a defined alert. Table 13.2 describes the parameters for GET_THRESHOLD.

Not surprisingly, the parameters for GET_THRESHOLD are identical to SET_THRESHOLD, except that the values of WARNING_OPERATOR through CONSECUTIVE_OCCURRENCES are OUT parameters instead of IN. In the following example, you will retrieve the threshold values you set for the USERS tablespace earlier in this chapter:

```
SQL> begin
  2     dbms_server_alert.get_threshold(
  3      dbms_server_alert.tablespace_pct_full,
  4      :warn_oper, :warn_value, :crit_oper, :crit_value,
```

```
  5      :obs_per, :cons_oc, null,
  6      dbms_server_alert.object_type_tablespace,'USERS');
  7   end;
  8   /

PL/SQL procedure successfully completed.

SQL> print warn_value

WARN_VALUE
--------------------------------
60

SQL> print crit_value

CRIT_VALUE
--------------------------------
85
```

Setting the last parameter to NULL instead of to the tablespace name will retrieve the database-wide default values instead of the values for a particular tablespace.

TABLE 13.2 *GET_THRESHOLD* Parameters

Parameter Name	Description
METRICS_ID	The name of the metric, using an internally defined constant.
WARNING_OPERATOR	The comparison operator for comparing the current value to the warning threshold value.
WARNING_VALUE	The warning threshold, or NULL if no warning threshold exists.
CRITICAL_OPERATOR	The comparison operator for comparing the current value to the warning threshold value.
CRITICAL_VALUE	The critical threshold, or NULL if no critical threshold exists.
OBSERVATION_PERIOD	The timer period at which the metrics are computed against the threshold; the valid range is 1 to 60 minutes.

TABLE 13.2 *GET_THRESHOLD* Parameters *(continued)*

Parameter Name	Description
CONSECUTIVE_OCCURRENCES	How many times the threshold needs to be exceeded before the alert is issued.
INSTANCE_NAME	The name of the instance for which the threshold applies; this value is NULL for all instances in a RAC database.
OBJECT_TYPE	The type of object—for example, a tablespace, session, or service—using a set of internally defined constants.
OBJECT_NAME	The name of the object, such as the tablespace name.

EXPAND_MESSAGE

The EXPAND_MESSAGE procedure is very straightforward, translating a numeric message number to a text format. Table 13.3 describes the parameters for EXPAND_MESSAGE.

If additional values are returned along with the alert code number, they are specified using ARGUMENT_1 through ARGUMENT_5 and are substituted into the alert message as needed. For server alert message number 6, you can retrieve the text of the message as follows:

```
SQL> select dbms_server_alert.expand_message
  2       (null,6,null,null,null,null,null) alert_msg
  3  from dual;

ALERT_MSG
-----------------------------------
Read and write contention on database
blocks was consuming significant
database time. However, no single
object was the predominant cause for
this contention.
```

Rarely will you have to call EXPAND_MESSAGE; it is primarily used for third-party applications that read alert messages from the alert queue. The EM Database Control automatically retrieves the text of all alert messages.

TABLE 13.3 *EXPAND_MESSAGE* Parameters

Parameter Name	Description
USER_LANGUAGE	The current session's language
MESSAGE_ID	The alert message ID number
ARGUMENT_1	The first argument returned in the alert message
ARGUMENT_2	The second argument returned in the alert message
ARGUMENT_3	The third argument returned in the alert message
ARGUMENT_4	The fourth argument returned in the alert message
ARGUMENT_5	The fifth argument returned in the alert message

Using Segment Management Tools

Oracle 10*g* provides a number of new ways to manage segments in the database. To use disk space more efficiently and to reduce the I/O required to access a segment, segment shrink functionality compacts the space within a segment and optionally moves the high watermark (HWM), freeing up space for other segments.

The Segment Advisor, one of many advisors in Oracle 10*g*, can analyze one segment or all the segments within a tablespace and determine if a segment is a good candidate for a segment shrink operation. In addition, the Segment Advisor can help you estimate the initial size of a table, as well as predicting growth patterns given your estimates for table inserts, updates, and deletes over time.

Finally, Oracle 10*g* provides a way to both monitor index space usage as well as to help you identify whether an index is used at all. We will also present the pros and cons of rebuilding the index versus coalescing the index.

Segment Shrink

If rows were added only to tables, then segment shrink would not be needed. However, deletes and updates to a table—and ultimately the index—leave many blocks with fewer or no rows. While this space can be used by future inserts or updates, you have no guarantee that the space will be reused, if ever. In addition, because the HWM only stays the same or gets larger, full table scans must read every block, whether or not it is empty.

The following sections discuss the benefits of segment shrink and cover a few of the restrictions regarding the types of segments you can shrink and where the segments must reside. Finally, you will see some practical examples of how segment shrink works, both using the command line and EM Database Control.

An Overview of Segment Shrink

Segment shrink compresses the data blocks in a table or index and optionally moves the HWM down, making the unused space available for other segments in the tablespace. In addition to making full table scans more efficient, a shrunken segment makes even single I/Os for individual data blocks more efficient, because more rows are retrieved for each I/O. Indexes that are shrunk are also more efficient for the same reason: During an index range scan operation, more index entries are read for each I/O, reducing overall I/O for the query.

There are other benefits to segment shrink. Some or all chained rows in a table may be eliminated by performing a segment shrink operation, however, it is not guaranteed that all chained rows will be repaired because not all blocks may be accessed in a segment shrink operation.

Figure 13.10 shows a sparsely populated table segment before and after a shrink operation.

Before Oracle 10*g*, the HWM could be moved down only if the segment was moved or truncated. While online table redefinition or Create Table As Select (CTAS) operations can provide similar results to segment shrink, those methods must temporarily provide double the amount of space occupied by the table. Segment shrink is online and in place, requiring a negligible amount of extra space and remaining available during the entire operation, except for a brief period when the HWM is moved.

FIGURE 13.10 Segment before and after shrink

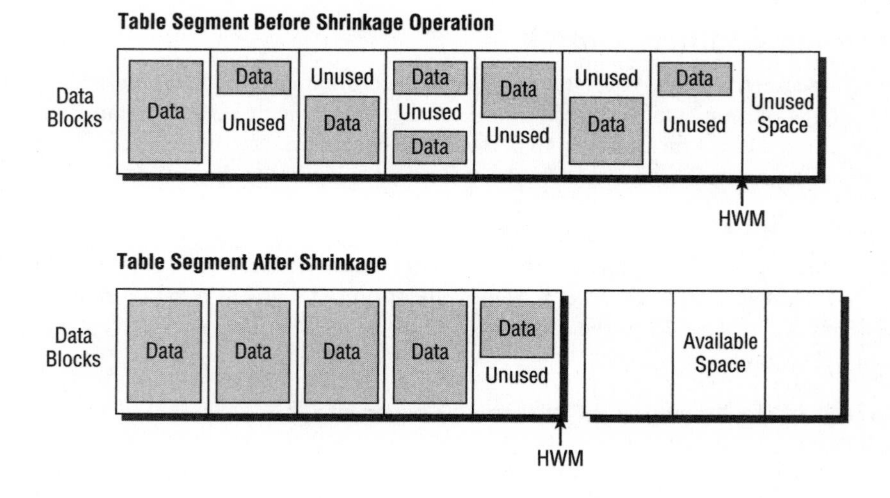

Segment Shrink Restrictions and Considerations

Segment shrink operations have one major restriction: Segments managed with freelists cannot be shrunk; in other words, the tablespace containing the segment must be defined with automatic segment space management.

The most common types of segments can be shrunk, such as

- Heap-organized and index-organized tables
- Indexes
- Partitions and subpartitions
- Materialized views and materialized view logs

Other segment types or segment with specific characteristics cannot be shrunk, such as

- Clustered tables
- Tables with LONG columns
- Tables with on-commit or ROWID-based materialized views
- LOB segments
- IOT mapping tables or overflow segments
- Tables with function-based indexes

During a segment shrink operation, the ROWID may change for a row when it moves between blocks. Therefore, segments that rely on ROWIDs being constant, such as an application that maintains ROWIDs as pointers in another table, cannot be shrunk. In any case, ROW MOVEMENT must be enabled for table segments that are candidates for shrink operations.

All indexes are maintained and useable both during and after the shrink operation.

Performing Segment Shrink

To perform segment shrink, you can use either SQL commands or EM Database Control. If you have hundreds of segments to shrink, a series of batch jobs with SQL commands submitted overnight is most likely the best way to perform the operation. For only one or two shrink operations on an occasional basis, EM Database Control is probably the fastest and easiest to use.

SQL Commands and Segment Shrink

As mentioned previously, segment shrink operations may change the ROWID of one or more rows of a table segment. Therefore, row movement on the segment must be enabled before the segment can be shrunk. In the following example, you'll enable row movement for the HR.EMPLOYEES table:

```
SQL> alter table hr.employees enable row movement;
Table altered.
```

The ROW MOVEMENT capability appeared in Oracle 8*i* to allow rows to move between partitions of a partitioned table.

Shrinking the space in a segment is performed as an extension to the ALTER TABLE or ALTER INDEX command, with the SHRINK SPACE clause, as shown here:

```
SQL> alter table hr.employees shrink space;
Table altered.
```

In this example, the table HR.EMPLOYEES is shrunk, and the HWM is moved in the same operation.

Although the table is available for use by all users while the shrink operation is in progress, the I/O throughput may be decreased. Therefore, it may be advantageous to split the operation into two commands using the COMPACT clause to compress the rows without moving the HWM, as shown here:

```
SQL> alter table hr.employees shrink space compact;
Table altered.
```

At a later time, when the database is not as busy, you can complete the rest of the operation by omitting the COMPACT clause.

```
SQL> alter table hr.employees shrink space;
Table altered.
```

Any fragmentation that has occurred in the mean time is addressed, and the HWM is moved. Whether the operation is performed all at once or in two steps, only a small number of rows are locked at any given time. Conversely, a user DML command may lock one or more rows and temporarily prevent segment shrink from completing compaction of the rows. When the HWM is moved, the entire table is locked for a brief amount of time.

Another potential benefit of splitting the operation into two parts is based on PL/SQL code that may have cursors open while the segment is being accessed. With the COMPACT option, all cursors defined on the segment remain valid; without the COMPACT option, all cursors on the segment are invalidated.

Another option available with the ALTER TABLE … SHRINK SPACE command is the CASCADE keyword. When CASCADE is specified, all dependent objects, such as indexes, are also shrunk. In the following example, you'll use the CASCADE example to shrink all the indexes defined on the HR.EMPLOYEES table:

```
SQL> alter table hr.employees shrink space cascade;
Table altered.
```

Without the CASCADE keyword, you would have to identify all the indexes defined on the table and execute a series of commands instead of just one command.

```
SQL> select index_name from dba_indexes where
  2       table_name = 'EMPLOYEES' and owner = 'HR';

INDEX_NAME
------------------------------
EMP_EMAIL_UK
EMP_EMP_ID_PK
EMP_DEPARTMENT_IX
EMP_JOB_IX
EMP_MANAGER_IX
EMP_NAME_IX

6 rows selected.

SQL> alter index hr.emp_email_uk shrink space;
Index altered.

SQL> alter index hr.emp_emp_id_pk shrink space;
Index altered.

SQL> alter index hr.emp_department_ix shrink space;
Index altered.

SQL> alter index hr.emp_job_ix shrink space;
Index altered.

SQL> alter index hr.emp_manager_ix shrink space;
Index altered.

SQL> alter index hr.emp_name_ix shrink space;
Index altered.
```

EM Database Control and Segment Shrink

Performing segment shrink with EM Database Control is even easier. From the Administration tab on the EM Database Control database Home tab, click the Tables link under the Schema heading. Search for the tables you want to shrink and select the Shrink Segment action, as shown in Figure 13.11.

The EM Database Control screen gives you all the options that are available on the command line, including the COMPACT and the CASCADE options (see Figure 13.12).

FIGURE 13.11 Selecting tables for segment shrink

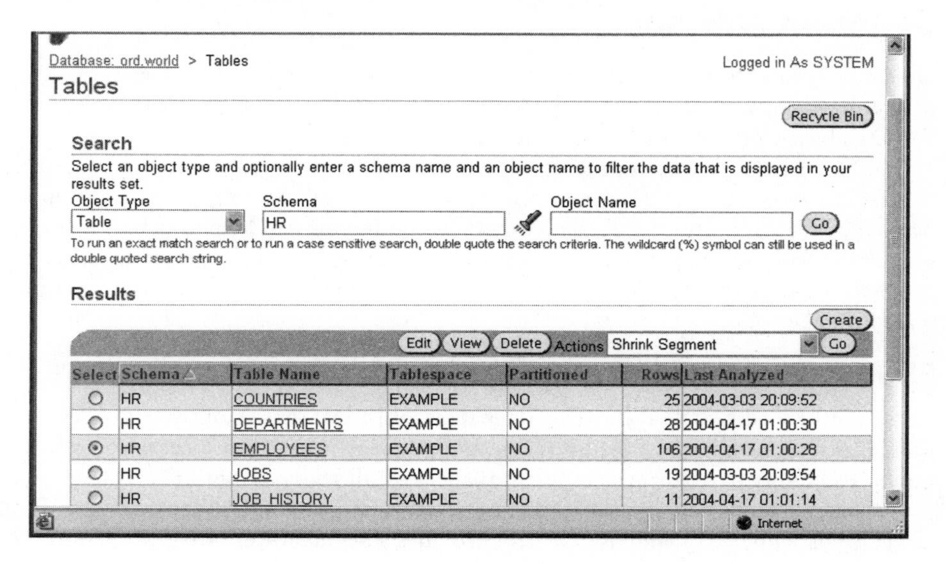

FIGURE 13.12 The EM Database Control segment shrink options

Another benefit to using EM Database Control is that the segment shrink operation will be submitted as a job and run in the background, allowing you to immediately perform other tasks with EM Database Control.

Segment Advisor

Oracle's *Segment Advisor* provides several types of functionality to manage the space occupied by database segments such as tables and indexes. This functionality is available through both EM Database Control and PL/SQL procedures.

The Segment Advisor can provide advice regarding a particular table, schema, or tablespace that contains segments that are good candidates for shrink operations. In addition, using the data collected within the AWR, the Growth Trend Report can help predict how much space a segment will occupy based on previous growth patterns. Finally, Segment Resource Estimation can help make preliminary sizing estimates for a table given the column datatypes and the estimated number of rows in the table.

EM Database Control and Segment Advisor

As with nearly all Oracle Database 10*g* features, EM Database Control provides an intuitive graphical interface to make the most common segment analysis tasks easy to perform. In addition to the ability to perform a complete analysis on all segments within a tablespace, EM Database Control can use data in the AWR to use segment growth patterns to predict future space usage needs. Plus, EM Database Control provides a Segment Resource Estimation tool to help size a table's space usage needs even before it is created.

Segment Advisor

To use the Segment Advisor, select the Advisor Central link under any tab. Click Segment Advisor, which brings you to the Segment Advisor screen (see Figure 13.13).

Click Continue, which brings you to the Segment Advisor: Tablespaces screen, where you select the tablespaces to be analyzed (see Figure 13.14). In this example, the USERS tablespace is added to the list.

After clicking Next, you can specify how long to run the analysis on the Segment Advisor: Options screen (see Figure 13.15). Because the USERS tablespace is relatively small, you will not specify a time limit. But for much larger tablespaces, you may want to prevent I/O contention—even during a non-peak time interval—and settle for a limited analysis. In Figure 13.15, the results of the analysis are to be retained for 30 days.

Clicking Next opens the Segment Advisor: Schedule screen (see Figure 13.16). Here, you can set up the task name and the scheduling options; in this example, the job will run immediately.

FIGURE 13.13 Segment Advisor

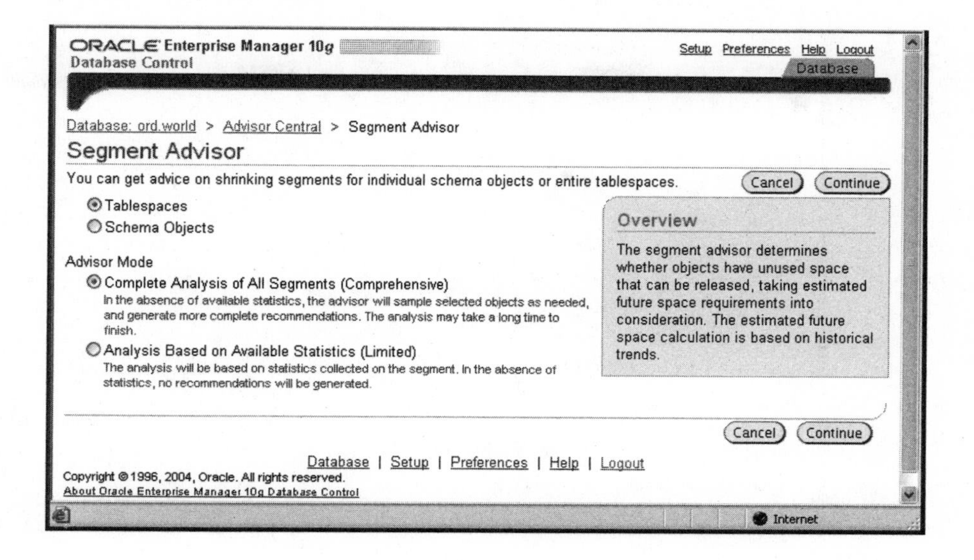

FIGURE 13.14 Selecting tablespaces for the Segment Advisor

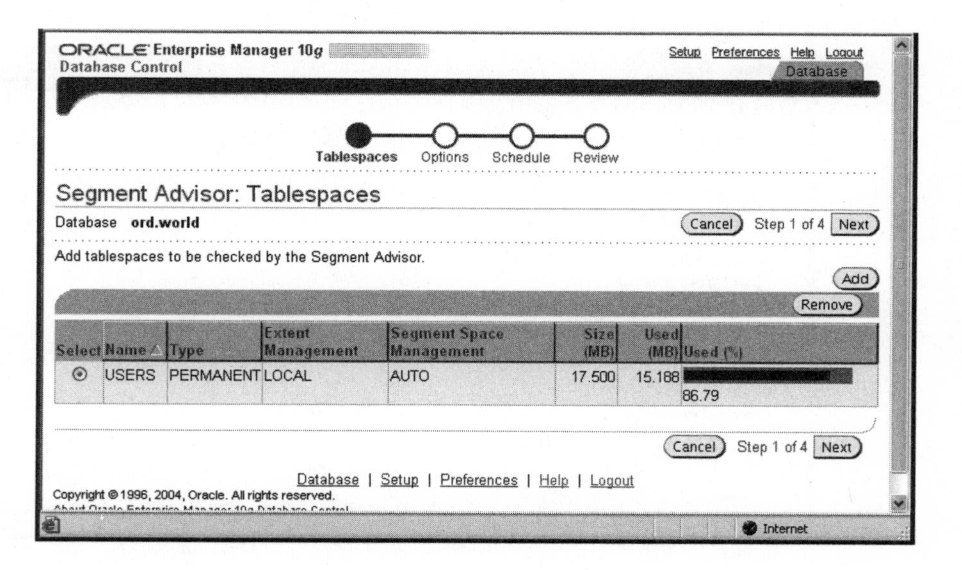

FIGURE 13.15 Segment Advisor options

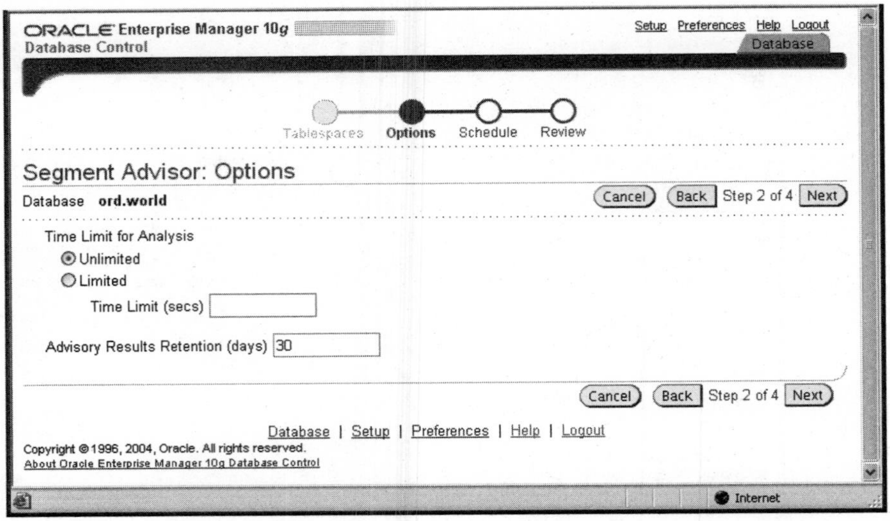

FIGURE 13.16 Task scheduling options

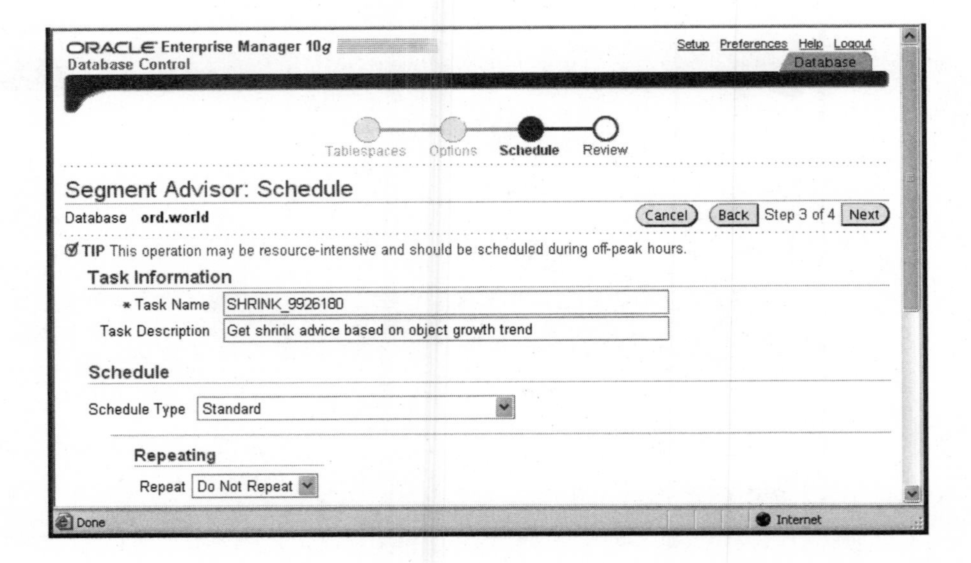

In the last screen of the Segment Advisor—Segment Advisor: Review—you have one more chance to review the analysis options and to review the SQL commands that will be submitted to perform the analysis. Figure 13.17 shows the summary.

FIGURE 13.17 Segment Advisor task summary

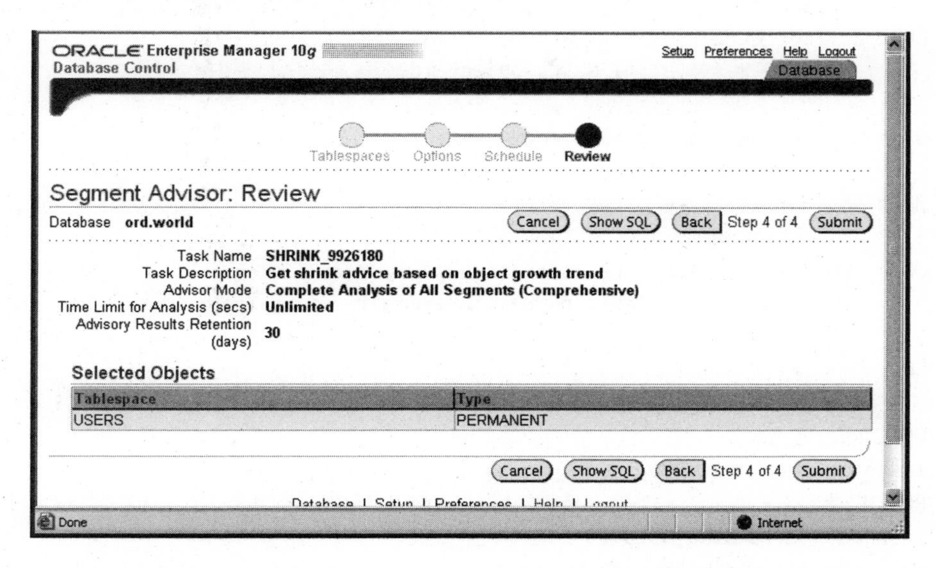

Clicking the Show SQL button, you can review the anonymous PL/SQL procedures that will perform the tasks just configured:

```
DECLARE
taskname varchar2(100);
taskdesc varchar2(128);
task_id number;
object_id number;
advMode varchar2(25);
timeLimit varchar2(25);
numDaysToRetain varchar2(25);
objectName varchar2(100);
objectType varchar2(100);
BEGIN
taskname := 'SHRINK_9926180';
```

```
taskdesc := 'Get shrink advice based on object growth trend';
advMode :='COMPREHENSIVE';
numDaysToRetain :='30';
dbms_advisor.create_task('Segment Advisor',?,
       taskname,taskdesc,NULL);
dbms_advisor.create_object(taskname, 'TABLESPACE',
       'USERS', ' ', ' ', NULL, object_id);

dbms_advisor.set_task_parameter(taskname,
          'MODE', advMode);
dbms_advisor.set_task_parameter(taskname,
          'RECOMMEND_ALL', 'TRUE');
dbms_advisor.set_task_parameter(taskname,
          'DAYS_TO_EXPIRE', numDaysToRetain);

END;

DECLARE
taskname varchar2(100);
BEGIN
taskname := 'SHRINK_9926180';
dbms_advisor.reset_task(taskname);
dbms_advisor.execute_task(taskname);
END;
```

Clicking Submit submits the SQL commands to be run. A few moments later, click the Refresh button on the Advisor Central screen. In Figure 13.18, notice that the Segment Advisor task has completed.

Click the link containing the job name of the task you just ran—in this case, SHRINK_9926180—to see that there are no segments in the USERS tablespace that can benefit from a shrink operation early in the evening (see Figure 13.19).

Emphasizing the dynamic nature of space management in any database, you may run the analysis again and find that there is now a table that can benefit from a shrink operation: the HR.EMPLOYEES_HIST table. You can shrink the HR.EMPLOYEES_HIST table by selecting one of the recommendations at the bottom of the results screen for task name SHRINK_6871100 in Figure 13.20. These options are identical to those used in Figures 13.11 and 13.12, except that you can perform a shrink operation on more than one table at a time.

FIGURE 13.18 Advisor Central task completion

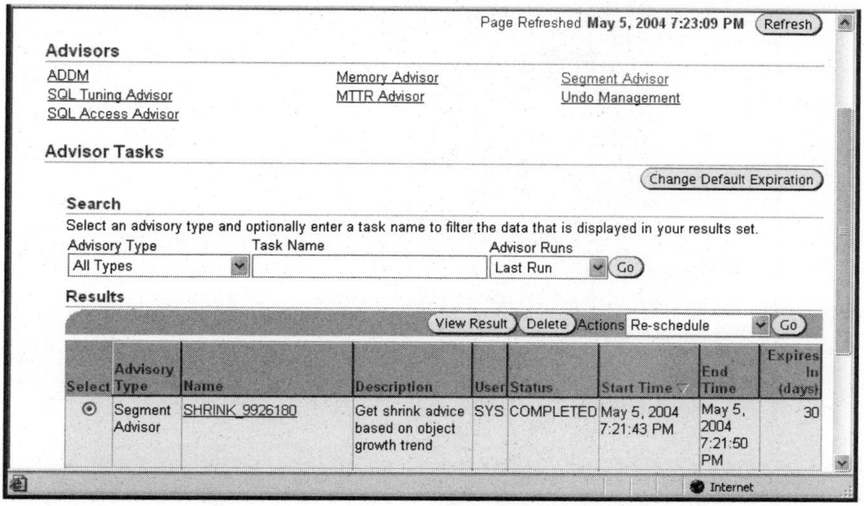

Page Refreshed **May 5, 2004 7:23:09 PM** Refresh

Advisors

ADDM
SQL Tuning Advisor
SQL Access Advisor
Memory Advisor
MTTR Advisor
Segment Advisor
Undo Management

Advisor Tasks

Change Default Expiration

Search

Select an advisory type and optionally enter a task name to filter the data that is displayed in your results set.

Advisory Type: All Types | Task Name | Advisor Runs: Last Run | Go

Results

View Result | Delete | Actions Re-schedule | Go

Select	Advisory Type	Name	Description	User	Status	Start Time	End Time	Expires In (days)
⦿	Segment Advisor	SHRINK_9926180	Get shrink advice based on object growth trend	SYS	COMPLETED	May 5, 2004 7:21:43 PM	May 5, 2004 7:21:50 PM	30

Internet

FIGURE 13.19 Segment Advisor recommendations at 7:21 P.M.

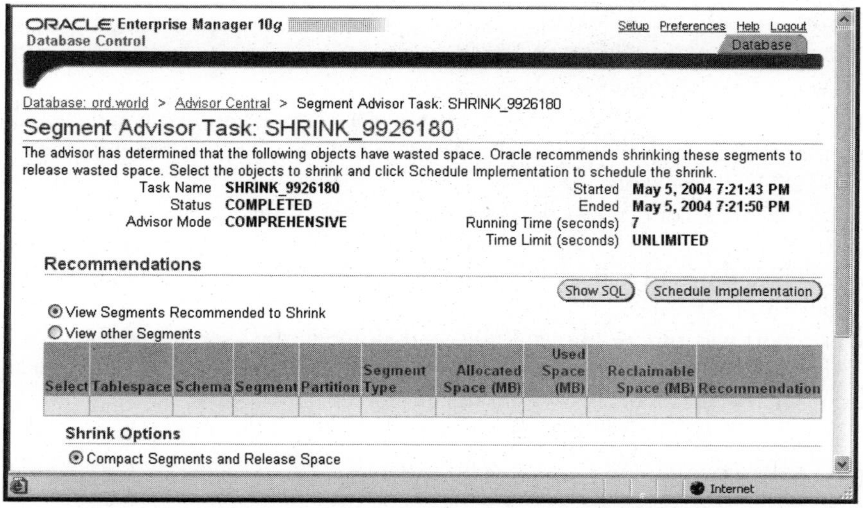

ORACLE Enterprise Manager 10*g*
Database Control

Setup Preferences Help Logout
Database

Database: ord.world > Advisor Central > Segment Advisor Task: SHRINK_9926180

Segment Advisor Task: SHRINK_9926180

The advisor has determined that the following objects have wasted space. Oracle recommends shrinking these segments to release wasted space. Select the objects to shrink and click Schedule Implementation to schedule the shrink.

Task Name **SHRINK_9926180**
Status **COMPLETED**
Advisor Mode **COMPREHENSIVE**
Started **May 5, 2004 7:21:43 PM**
Ended **May 5, 2004 7:21:50 PM**
Running Time (seconds) **7**
Time Limit (seconds) **UNLIMITED**

Recommendations

Show SQL | Schedule Implementation

⦿ View Segments Recommended to Shrink
○ View other Segments

Select	Tablespace	Schema	Segment	Partition	Segment Type	Allocated Space (MB)	Used Space (MB)	Reclaimable Space (MB)	Recommendation

Shrink Options

⦿ Compact Segments and Release Space

Internet

FIGURE 13.20 Segment Advisor recommendations at 11:12 P.M.

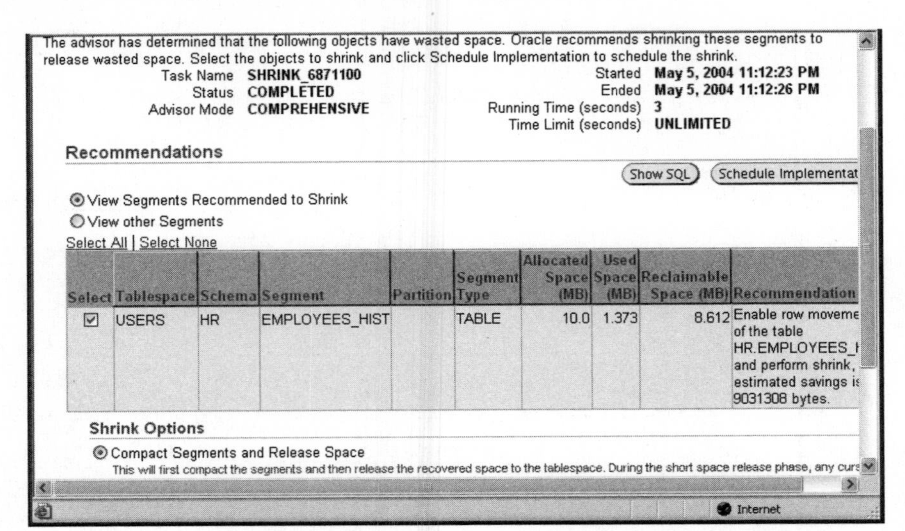

Growth Trend Report

The *Growth Trend Report*, based on the AWR data collected at 30-minute intervals or when space-related server-generated alerts are triggered, helps to predict future growth trends for selected segments. Given the predicted growth pattern, you know when space will need to be added to support segment growth.

To access the Growth Trend Report, start at the Administration tab and click the Tables link under the Schema heading. In Figure 13.21, you want to predict the growth of the `HR.EMPLOYEES_HIST` table.

Click the table name, select the Segments tab, and enter a future date to see when more space should be allocated to the segment. In this example, the user entered **5/16/04**. Once you've clicked the Refresh button, the results of the analysis appear, as shown in the example in Figure 13.22.

This report was run on May 8, 2004, and although the overall usage is predicted to be relatively flat, the Segment Advisor has predicted that the amount of space allocated for the segment will rise dramatically within the next week.

As with the Segment Advisor, the Growth Trend Report is supported only for locally managed tablespaces.

FIGURE 13.21 Growth Trend Report segment selection

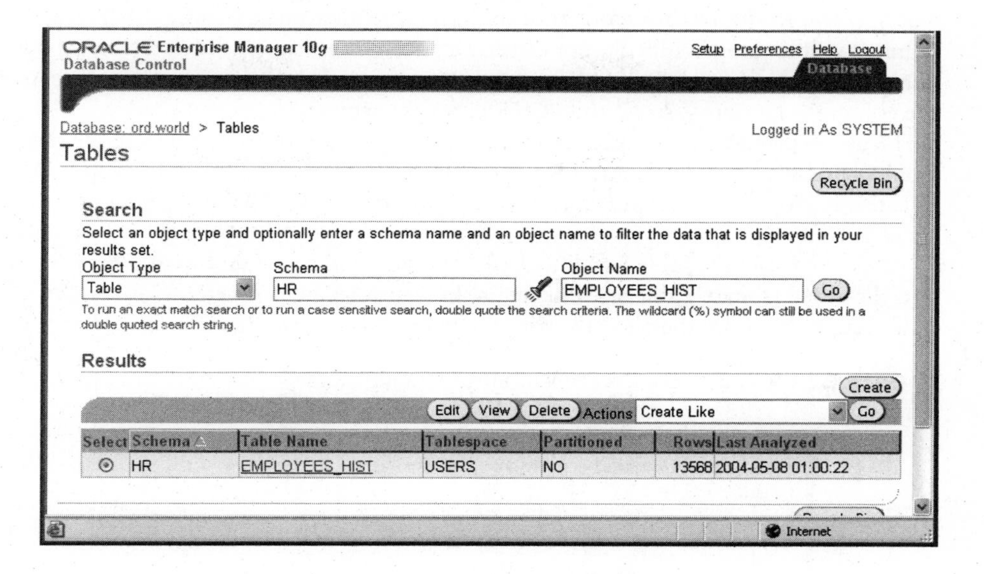

FIGURE 13.22 Growth Trend Report segment analysis

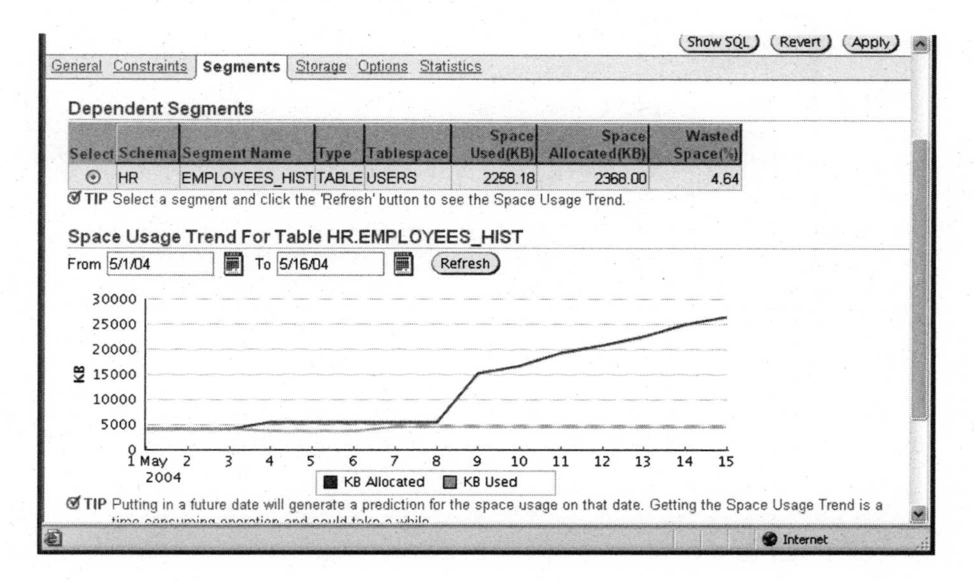

Segment Resource Estimation

The *Segment Resource Estimation* tool gives you a good estimate of how much disk space a new segment will require. While it is not directly a part of the Segment Advisor, it is a point-in-time analysis tool to give you sizing advice so you can estimate space usage for a new segment given the columns, datatypes, sizes, and PCTFREE for the segment.

To use Segment Resource Estimation, start at the Administration tab from the EM Database Control home page and click the Tables link. Instead of searching for an existing table, click the Create link. As you can see in Figure 13.23, a table called HR.EMPLOYEE_REVIEW with three columns is created.

Click the Estimate Table Size link, enter an estimated row count of 5000 for the first year, and click the Estimate Table Size link again. In Figure 13.24, notice that 5,000 rows of the table will occupy just more than 13MB, with the allocated space at 14MB.

FIGURE 13.23 EM Database Control: Create Table

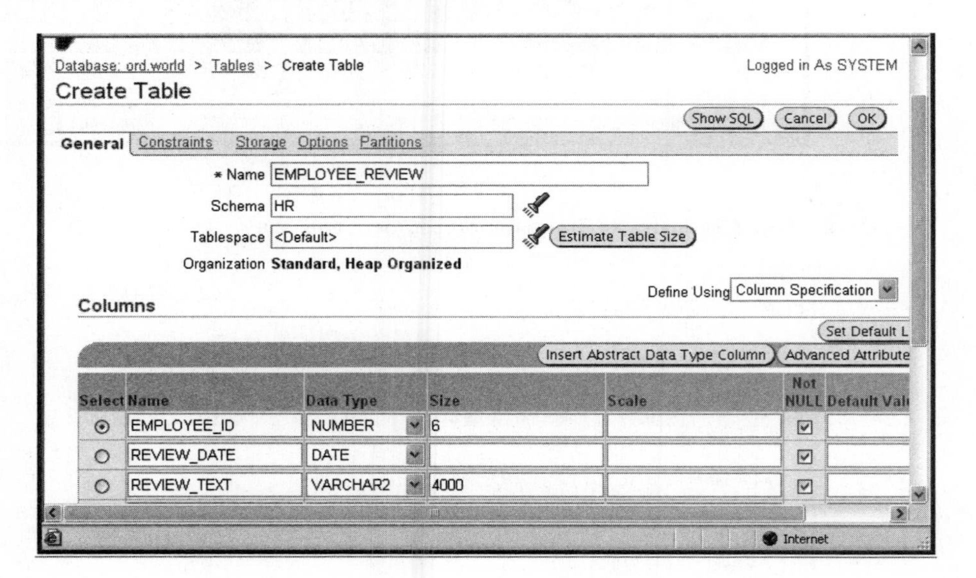

FIGURE 13.24 Estimating table size

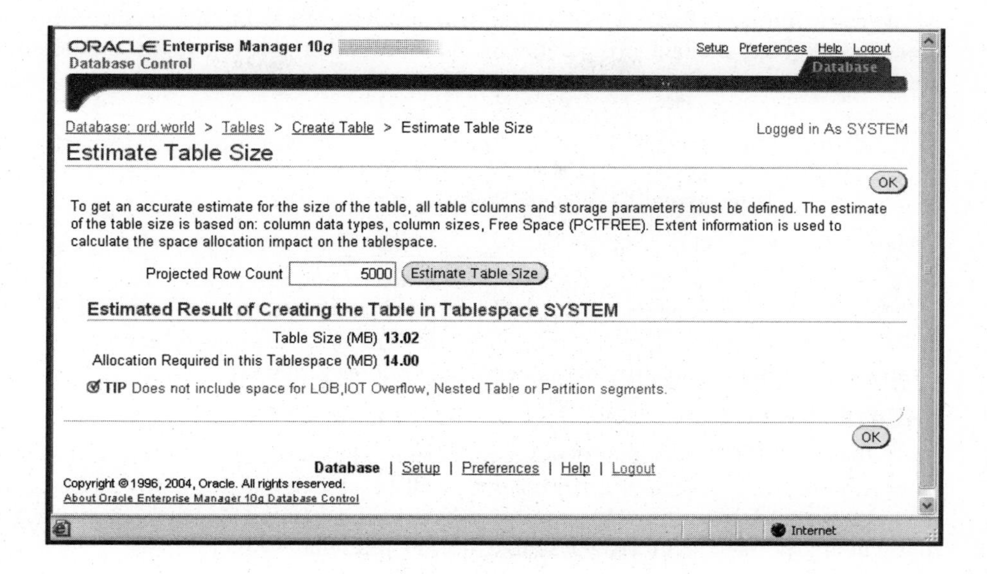

Segment Advisor within PL/SQL

Although the Segment Advisor is easy to use from EM Database Control, sometimes you may want to perform some of these operations from within a PL/SQL procedure. For example, you may want to automate the advisors in a nightly batch job.

To access the Segment Advisor functionality within PL/SQL, use the package DBMS_ADVISOR. Because DBMS_ADVISOR is used with the AWR for all advisors within the Oracle 10*g* advisory framework, not all procedures within DBMS_ADVISOR are applicable to all advisors, and the parameters for a particular procedure will also vary depending on the advisor. For the Segment Advisor, you typically use the following procedures:

- CREATE_TASK
- CREATE_OBJECT
- SET_TASK_PARAMETER
- EXECUTE_TASK
- DELETE_TASK
- CANCEL_TASK

We will explain each of these procedures in the following sections and provide two examples of analyzing a table using the Segment Advisor and implementing Segment Advisor recommendations.

CREATE_TASK

As the name implies, CREATE_TASK creates a new advisor task. For the Segment Advisor, the procedure requires the text string Segment Advisor, a variable to contain the assigned task number, a task name, and a description. Here is an example:

```
dbms_advisor.create_task
        ('Segment Advisor', :task_id, task_name,
            'Free space in OE.CUSTOMERS', NULL);
```

After the task is created, the assigned task number is stored in the SQL*Plus variable task_id. The unique task name is automatically generated if you leave task_name null; otherwise, Oracle will use the task name specified. In both cases, the task name must be unique among all tasks created by a particular user. Assigning a task name or description can help identify the results when querying the advisor-related data dictionary views.

CREATE_OBJECT

The CREATE_OBJECT procedure specifies an object to be analyzed within the task. For the Segment Advisor, the object to be analyzed is typically a table or index; for other advisors, such as the SQL Access Advisor, the object to be analyzed is a SQL statement. To create a task object that will analyze the OE.CUSTOMERS table, use the following syntax:

```
dbms_advisor.create_object
        (task_name, 'TABLE', 'OE', 'CUSTOMERS',
           NULL, NULL, object_id);
```

The PL/SQL variable object_id is assigned a unique identifier for this object. The NULL parameters are not needed for advisor objects within the Segment Advisor.

SET_TASK_PARAMETER

The SET_TASK_PARAMETER procedure allows you to specify any additional parameters needed to run the analysis for the database objects specified with CREATE_OBJECT. In the case of the Segment Advisor, you have a Boolean parameter called RECOMMEND_ALL that you set to TRUE for the analysis on the table. Here is an example:

```
dbms_advisor.set_task_parameter
     (task_name, 'RECOMMEND_ALL', 'TRUE');
```

When set to TRUE, the parameter RECOMMEND_ALL provides recommendations for all objects specified by the user, not just the objects eligible for segment shrink. Objects not eligible for segment shrink include objects such as tables that don't have ROW MOVEMENT enabled or tables that reside in tablespaces that do not have automatic segment space management enabled.

EXECUTE_TASK

Once all the tasks are created and their parameters specified, EXECUTE_TASK performs the analysis. The only parameter specified is the task name generated in a previous step in your code by the CREATE_TASK procedure. Here is an example:

```
dbms_advisor.execute_task(task_name);
```

To view the status of the executing task, especially for a long-running task such as a full tablespace analysis, the data dictionary view DBA_ADVISOR_LOG contains the task name, the start and stop time, the current status, and estimated percentage complete for the task.

DELETE_TASK

The DELETE_TASK procedure removes a single advisor task from the AWR, even if the task has not been executed yet. Here is an example:

```
dbms_advisor.delete_task(task_name);
```

CANCEL_TASK

The CANCEL_TASK procedure terminates a currently executing task. Because all advisor procedures are synchronous, the CANCEL_TASK procedure must be called from a different session for the same user account. Here is an example:

```
dbms_advisor.cancel_task(task_name);
```

Analyzing a Table Using Segment Advisor

The code examples that follow call these procedures to determine if the table OE.CUSTOMERS needs to be shrunk.

The last change to the table OE.CUSTOMERS added a field called CUST_COMMENTS to contain any suggestions, complaints, or information about the customer:

```
SQL> alter table oe.customers
          add (cust_comments varchar2(2000));
Table altered.
```

After a number of months using this new field, you realize that the comments should be broken out by date and decide to create a new table to hold a timestamp and a comment for that particular date and time. After the new table is implemented and the comments moved to the new table, drop the column from the OE.CUSTOMERS table:

```
SQL> alter table oe.customers drop (cust_comments);
Table altered.
```

You realize that this table may be a good candidate for segment shrink and decide to use a PL/SQL procedure to analyze the table:

```
-- SQL*Plus variable to contain the task ID
variable task_id number

-- PL/SQL block follows
declare
    task_name  varchar2(100);
    task_descr varchar2(100);
    object_id  number;
begin
    task_name := ''; -- unique name generated
                     -- by create_task
    task_descr := 'Free space in OE.CUSTOMERS';
    dbms_advisor.create_task
        ('Segment Advisor', :task_id, task_name,
           task_descr, NULL);
    dbms_advisor.create_object
        (task_name, 'TABLE', 'OE', 'CUSTOMERS',
             NULL, NULL, object_id);
    dbms_advisor.set_task_parameter
         (task_name, 'RECOMMEND_ALL', 'TRUE');
    dbms_advisor.execute_task(task_name);
end;

PL/SQL procedure successfully completed.
```

Using the SQL*Plus `PRINT` command, identify the task ID number to use in your data dictionary queries:

```
SQL> print task_id

   TASK_ID
----------
       680
```

Using this task number, you can query the data dictionary view `DBA_ADVISOR_FINDINGS` to see the recommendations:

```
SQL> select owner, task_id, task_name, type,
  2         message, more_info from dba_advisor_findings
  3         where task_id = 680;
```

```
OWNER        TASK_ID TASK_NAME    TYPE
---------- ---------- ------------ -----------
SYS              680 TASK_680     INFORMATION

MESSAGE
----------------------------------------------------------
Enable row movement of the table OE.CUSTOMERS and perform
shrink, estimated savings is 775878 bytes.

MORE_INFO
----------------------------------------------------------
Allocated Space:983040: Used Space:205110:
Reclaimable Space :775878:


1 row selected.
```

Note that the Segment Advisor reminds you to enable row movement for the table; this is a required prerequisite before a shrink can be performed. The space in each block occupied by the CUST_COMMENTS column is unused, and by compacting this table, you can reclaim almost 80 percent of the allocated space.

Implementing Segment Advisor Recommendations

To shrink the table OE.CUSTOMERS, you need to enable row movement:

```
SQL> alter table oe.customers enable row movement;
Table altered.
```

Because you have no applications or triggers that depend on the ROWIDs of this table, leave row movement enabled.

Next, perform the shrink operation; the data dictionary view DBA_ADVISOR_ACTIONS provides the SQL for the shrink operation:

```
SQL> select task_id, task_name, command, attr1 from
  2       dba_advisor_actions where task_id = 680;

   TASK_ID TASK_NAME    COMMAND
---------- ------------ ---------------
       680 TASK_680     SHRINK SPACE

ATTR1
----------------------------------------------------------
alter table "OE"."CUSTOMERS" shrink space
```

```
1 row selected.

SQL> alter table "OE"."CUSTOMERS" shrink space;
Table altered.
```

The shrink operation requires a negligible amount of disk space, and the table is available to other users during the shrink operation, except for a short period of time at the end of the shrink operation to move the HWM. Because this table is relatively large, you may consider performing this operation in two steps, the first time with the COMPACT option to free the space and the second time without the COMPACT option to move the HWM.

Finally, remove this task from the AWR, because you have no need to retain this information once the segment has been shrunk:

```
SQL> execute dbms_advisor.delete_task('TASK_680');

PL/SQL procedure successfully completed.
```

Index Space Monitoring

While you may use Segment Advisor to analyze a table and its associated indexes, you can perform this analysis manually for an individual index of interest by using data dictionary views and some specific SQL commands, as we will demonstrate in this section. We will also show you how to rebuild and coalesce an index and show you the SQL commands that you can use to determine if an index has been used or not.

Monitoring Index Space Usage

If index entries are inserted, updated, and deleted frequently, an index may lose its space efficiency over time; Oracle b-tree indexes, however, will always stay balanced. For a given index, you can determine if an index needs to be rebuilt by validating the structure of the index and checking the value of PCT_USED in the data dictionary view INDEX_STATS, as in this example:

```
SQL> analyze index emp_name_ix validate structure;

Index analyzed.

SQL> select pct_used from index_stats where name = 'EMP_NAME_IX';

  PCT_USED
----------
        33
```

Over time, if the PCT_USED value starts to decline, you can either rebuild the index, or drop and re-create the index.

Rebuilding versus Coalescing Indexes

Both rebuilding an index or coalescing the index have their pros and cons. Table 13.4 compares the two methods.

If you decide to coalesce the index, you can do it using an ALTER INDEX command, as in this example:

```
SQL> alter index emp_name_ix coalesce;

Index altered.
```

TABLE 13.4 Rebuilding versus Coalescing an Index

Rebuilding an Index	Coalescing an Index
Can move index to another tablespace	Cannot move index to another tablespace
Requires double the amount of disk space if performed online	Does not require additional disk space
Creates a new tree and adjusts tree height if necessary	Coalesces index leaf blocks within each branch

If you decide to rebuild the index, you can do it online, as in this example:

```
SQL> alter index emp_name_ix rebuild online;

Index altered.
```

Because you are using the ONLINE keyword, the current index is left intact while a new copy of the index is built, allowing users to access the old index with SELECT statements or other DML statements. Any changes to the old index are saved in a special table known as a *journal table*. Once the index rebuild is complete, the changes recorded in the journal table are merged into the new index. Once the merge operation is complete, the data dictionary is updated and the old index is dropped. The index is available nearly 100 percent of the time that the rebuild operation is in progress, other than a very short amount of time at the end of the rebuild when the old index is swapped with the new copy of the index. One of the downsides, however, of rebuilding an index online is that you temporarily need enough disk space to store another copy of the index while the rebuild occurs.

Identifying Unused Indexes

Starting with Oracle 9*i*, Oracle has a feature that can monitor an index and set a flag in the dynamic performance view V$OBJECT_USAGE. To turn on the monitoring process, you use the MONITORING USAGE clause of the ALTER INDEX statement.

To see if the EMP_NAME_IX index is going to be used during the day, turn on the monitoring process with this statement:

```
SQL> alter index hr.emp_name_ix monitoring usage;

Index altered.
```

Next, check V$OBJECT_USAGE to make sure the index is being monitored:

```
SQL> select index_name, table_name, monitoring,
  2          used, start_monitoring
  3  from v$object_usage where index_name = 'EMP_NAME_IX';

INDEX_NAME    TABLE_NAME       MON USE START_MONITORING
------------- ---------------- --- --- -------------------
EMP_NAME_IX   EMPLOYEES        YES NO  06/02/2004 08:57:44

1 row selected.
```

During the day, one of the HR employees runs this query:

```
SQL> select employee_id from employees
  2  where last_name = 'King';

EMPLOYEE_ID
-----------
        100
        156

2 rows selected.
```

At around 5 P.M., check V$OBJECT_USAGE again to see if the index was used:

```
SQL> select index_name, table_name, monitoring,
  2        used, start_monitoring
  3  from v$object_usage where index_name = 'EMP_NAME_IX';

INDEX_NAME    TABLE_NAME       MON USE START_MONITORING
------------- ---------------- --- --- -------------------
EMP_NAME_IX   EMPLOYEES        YES YES 06/02/2004 08:57:44

1 row selected.
```

Because V$OBJECT_USAGE is a dynamic performance view, the contents will not be retained in the view once the database is shut down and restarted.

Because the index is being used at least once during the day, you probably want to keep the index pending further analysis. Your last step is to turn off monitoring with the NOMONITORING USAGE clause and check the V$OBJECT_USAGE view one more time to verify this:

```
SQL> alter index hr.emp_name_ix nomonitoring usage;

Index altered.

SQL> select index_name, table_name, monitoring,
  2       used, end_monitoring
  3  from v$object_usage where index_name = 'EMP_NAME_IX';

INDEX_NAME   TABLE_NAME        MON USE END_MONITORING
------------ ----------------- --- --- -------------------
EMP_NAME_IX  EMPLOYEES         NO  YES 06/02/2004 17:00:40

1 row selected.
```

The SQL Access Advisor, new to Oracle 10*g*, can help to identify indexes that should be created and indexes that are not needed.

Understanding Special Table Types

Two special table types—index-organized tables and clustered tables—provide a number of performance-related and space-related benefits compared to the traditional heap-based tables. In the sections that follow, we will show you how to create, maintain, and use both of these table types in your database to maximize your disk space usage.

Index-Organized Tables

An *index-organized table (IOT)* is one special type of table that is most effective when the access of the table is primarily by the primary key and the primary key columns constitute a large part of the table's columns. In the following sections, we will present an overview of IOTs, show you how to create an IOT, manage the non-primary key columns of an IOT by using an overflow area, and show you how to retrieve the metadata about IOTs from the data dictionary.

An Overview of Index-Organized Tables

You can store index and table data together in an IOT. IOTs are suitable for tables in which the data access is mostly through its primary key, such as lookup tables. An IOT is a b-tree index, much like a traditional stand-alone index. However, instead of storing the ROWID of the table where the row belongs, the entire row is stored as part of the index. In addition, you can also build additional indexes on the columns of an IOT. Accessing an IOT is identical to accessing a heap-based table, and no special syntax is required in your SQL statements.

Because the row is stored along with the b-tree index, there is no physical ROWID for each row. The primary key identifies the rows in an IOT. Oracle "guesses" the location of the row and assigns a *logical ROWID* for each row, which permits the creation of secondary indexes. As with heap-based tables, you can partition an IOT, but the partition columns must be the same as or a subset of the primary key columns.

Creating Index-Organized Tables

To create an IOT, you use the `CREATE TABLE` command, adding the `ORGANIZATION INDEX` keyword as part of the command. A primary key must be specified as part of the table definition. In this example, you create an index-organized table that stores sales summaries by division for a given sales date; the primary key is a composite primary key. Here is an example:

```
create table sales_summary_by_date_division
    (sales_date        date,
     division_id       number,
     total_sales       number(20,2),
     constraint ssum_dt_div_pk primary key
         (sales_date, division_id))
organization index
tablespace users;
```

Each entry in the IOT contains a date, a division number, and a total sales amount for the day. All three of these column values are stored in each IOT row, but the IOT is built based on only the date and division number. Only one segment is used to store an IOT; if you build a secondary index on this IOT, then a new segment is created.

IOT Row Overflow

To further improve the performance benefits provided by an IOT, you can create an *IOT overflow area.* If an IOT row's data exceeds the threshold of available space in a block, the row's data will be dynamically and automatically moved to the overflow area. When you create an

IOT, you specify a tablespace to hold the IOT overflow segment. Expanding on the previous example, you will re-create the IOT and specify an overflow area in this example:

```
create table sales_summary_by_date_division
    (sales_date       date,
     division_id      number,
     total_sales      number(20,2),
     constraint ssum_dt_div_pk primary key
         (sales_date, division_id))
organization index
tablespace users
pctthreshold 25
overflow tablespace users2;
```

The default value for PCTTHRESHOLD is 50.

Notice that you are also including the PCTTHRESHOLD clause. This is the percentage of space reserved in the index block of an IOT; this value must be high enough to at least store the primary key. Any columns that cause this threshold to be exceeded are stored in the overflow area. In this example, 25 percent of each block is reserved to hold the key and the row data for the row.

IOT Mapping Tables

To create bitmap indexes on an IOT, you must use an *IOT mapping table*. In a heap-based table, the index stores the bitmaps with the physical ROWID. Because an IOT does not have physical ROWIDs, you must create a mapping table. The mapping table maps the IOT's physical ROWIDs to the corresponding logical ROWIDs used by the IOT. IOTs use logical ROWIDs to manage index access to their rows because the physical ROWIDs can change as data is added to, or removed from, the IOT.

Only one mapping table is required per IOT, regardless of the number of bitmap indexes defined on the IOT.

In this example, you will further refine the IOT that you created previously by adding a mapping table:

```
create table sales_summary_by_date_division
    (sales_date       date,
     division_id      number,
```

```
     total_sales       number(20,2),
     constraint ssum_dt_div_pk primary key
         (sales_date, division_id))
organization index
tablespace users
pctthreshold 25
overflow tablespace users2
mapping table;
```

Oracle creates the mapping table in the same tablespace as its parent IOT. You cannot query, perform DML operations on, or modify the storage characteristics of the mapping table—it is created and maintained automatically and is dropped automatically when the IOT is dropped.

Data Dictionary Views for IOTs

A number of data dictionary views contain metadata concerning an IOT, its overflow segment, and its mapping table. Each of these views—DBA_INDEXES, DBA_SEGMENTS, and DBA_TABLES—reveal different parts of the structure of an IOT, as you will see in the following examples.

DBA_INDEXES

The view DBA_INDEXES contains most of the information you need about IOTs. Note that because an IOT is an index and a table at the same time, you will see an entry in DBA_INDEXES and in DBA_TABLES for an IOT. Here is a query where you can retrieve information about the table named SALES_SUMMARY_BY_DATE_DIVISION that you created earlier:

```
SQL> select index_name, index_type, tablespace_name
  2  from dba_indexes
  3  where table_name = 'SALES_SUMMARY_BY_DATE_DIVISION';

INDEX_NAME             INDEX_TYPE       TABLESPACE_NAME
---------------------- ---------------- ------------------
SSUM_DT_DIV_PK         IOT - TOP        USERS

1 row selected.
```

DBA_SEGMENTS

The view DBA_SEGMENTS helps you identify an IOT's related segments: the IOT itself and the overflow segment. You can see both of these segments in the following query against DBA_SEGMENTS:

```
SQL> select segment_name, segment_type, tablespace_name
  2  from dba_segments
  3  where segment_name LIKE '%_IOT_%' or
  4        segment_name = 'SSUM_DT_DIV_PK';
```

```
SEGMENT_NAME         SEGMENT_TYPE      TABLESPACE_NAME
-------------------- ----------------- ---------------------
SYS_IOT_MAP_59990    TABLE             USERS
SYS_IOT_OVER_59990   TABLE             USERS2
SSUM_DT_DIV_PK       INDEX             USERS

3 rows selected.
```

Notice that the mapping table resides in the same tablespace as the IOT itself and that the overflow segment resides in a different tablespace, as you specified when you created the IOT.

DBA_TABLES

The DBA_TABLES view, similar to the DBA_SEGMENTS view, provides you with the information about the IOT itself, the mapping table, and the associated overflow segment, as in this example:

```
SQL> select table_name, iot_name, iot_type, tablespace_name
  2  from dba_tables
  3  where table_name = 'SALES_SUMMARY_BY_DATE_DIVISION'
  4     or iot_name = 'SALES_SUMMARY_BY_DATE_DIVISION';

TABLE_NAME     IOT_NAME       IOT_TYPE     TABLESPACE_NAME
-------------- -------------- ------------ ---------------
SALES_SUMMARY_                IOT
BY_DATE_DIVISI
ON

SYS_IOT_MAP_59 SALES_SUMMARY_ IOT_MAPPING  USERS
990            BY_DATE_DIVISI
               ON

SYS_IOT_OVER_5 SALES_SUMMARY_ IOT_OVERFLOW USERS2
9990           BY_DATE_DIVISI
               ON

3 rows selected.
```

Clustered Tables

Clustered tables provide another alternative to the traditional heap-based table to provide performance benefits as well as optimizing the usage of your disk space. In this section, we will provide an architectural overview of clusters and describe the different types of clusters and in which situations each is appropriate.

Clusters Overview

A cluster consists of a group of two or more tables that share the same data blocks. If you are using hash clusters, as you will see later in this section, you can have only one table in the cluster. In other words, rows from two different tables in the cluster may reside in the same block on disk. The tables are logically grouped together because they share one or more common columns and are often used together in a join, such as an ORDER table and an ORDER_ITEM table. In most cases, the retrieval of a customer's order will include rows from both tables when they are joined on the ORDER_NUMBER column.

An alternative to creating a cluster for tables that are frequently or always queried together is to create a single table.

Before you add tables to a cluster, you specify a *cluster key* containing the common columns for all tables that will reside in the cluster. When you add a table to a cluster, you specify the column in the table that corresponds to the cluster key.

A cluster provides two primary benefits:

- Because rows from both tables on the join column are stored in the same block, disk I/O is dramatically reduced since a given query may need to read only a single block instead of at least two blocks for a join using traditional heap-based tables.
- The disk space required to store the cluster is significantly reduced because each cluster key value is stored only once each in the cluster and in the cluster index, no matter how many rows of each table in the cluster contain the value.

Creating a clustered table requires three steps:

1. Create the cluster definition.
2. Create the index on the cluster. (This step is skipped for hash clusters.)
3. Create tables within the cluster.

Once the cluster is created, you may add and remove indexes on tables in the cluster as with any heap-based table.

Cluster Types

Clusters can be divided into two broad categories: index clusters and hash clusters. Index clusters use a traditional b-tree index to find rows in the cluster, and hash clusters use a hashing function to determine the physical location where a given row is stored. Each has their own benefits depending on the type of data stored in the cluster; we will show you how each of these clusters is created and show you a special type of hash cluster called a sorted hash cluster.

Index Clusters

An *index cluster* performs much like a b-tree index to ensure quick access to the rows in each cluster table. Consider an index cluster in these situations:

- The tables in the cluster are always queried together and only infrequently on their own.
- The tables have little or no insert, update, or delete activity performed on them after the initial load of the cluster.
- The child tables have roughly equal numbers of rows for each parent key in the parent table.

The following example shows the SQL commands necessary to create a cluster called ORD_ITEM, an index on the cluster called ORD_ITEM_IDX, and tables ORD and ITEM in the cluster:

```
SQL> create cluster ord_item
  2  (ord_number number) size 500
  3  tablespace app_data;

Cluster created.
```

The preceding command creates a cluster called ORD_ITEM and specifies that the column ORD_NUMBER is the cluster key or column around which the two tables' data will be clustered; in this case, the ORD_NUMBER column is the common column for all tables that will be stored in this cluster. The parameter SIZE specifies how many cluster keys you expect to have per Oracle block. In this example, you create the index for all tables in the cluster:

```
SQL> create index ord_item_idx
  2     on cluster ord_item
  3     tablespace app_idx;

Index created.
```

Notice that the indexed column is not specified when creating an index on a cluster segment. The index is automatically created on the cluster key column, ORD_NUMBER.

Now that the cluster structure exists, you can create the ORD and ITEM tables in the cluster:

```
SQL> create table ord
  2  (ord_number       number,
  3   cust_last_name   varchar2(40),
  4   cust_first_name  varchar2(30),
  5   ord_date         date,
  6   ord_total        number(15,2))
  7  cluster ord_item (ord_number);
```

```
Table created.

SQL> create table item
  2  (item_id          number,
  3   ord_number       number,
  4   catalog_number   number,
  5   item_price       number(7,2))
  6  cluster ord_item (ord_number);

Table created.
```

Note that no tablespace specification is allowed when creating the tables in the cluster: The cluster table is stored in the tablespace specified in the cluster definition. Storing each table in a different tablespace is logically incorrect; it also does not make sense, because that would defeat the purpose of storing each table's row in the same data block to improve I/O performance.

Hash Clusters

A *hash cluster* is similar to an index cluster, except that a hash cluster uses a hashing algorithm on the row's cluster key to find the physical location of the row in the table. Hash clusters work best for queries with equivalence operators, as in this example:

```
select cust_last_name from ord
      where ord_number = 681107;
```

Here are the attributes of a table that make it suitable for use in a hash cluster:

- The tables in the cluster have a relatively uniform distribution of values in the indexed column.
- The tables have little or no insert, update, or delete activity performed on them after the initial load of the cluster.
- The tables in the cluster have a predictable number of values in the indexed column.
- The queries against the clustered table almost exclusively use an equality operator to retrieve the desired row.

Using a hash cluster, the desired row can usually be found with one I/O read, in contrast to a traditional indexed heap-based table, which may require several I/O operations on the index itself and another I/O on the table to retrieve the desired row.

Because you are using a hashing function to find rows in a cluster's table, you cannot create a cluster index on a hash cluster. To create a hash cluster, you add the `HASH IS` clause when creating the cluster. To create an `ORD_ITEM2` table using hashing, you can use a `CREATE CLUSTER` command similar to the following:

```
create cluster ord_item2
   (ord_number number(6,0)) size 500
   hash is ord_number hashkeys 100000
   tablespace users;
```

The HASHKEYS keyword specifies the number of unique hash values that can be generated by the cluster's hash function, in this case, 100,000. Note that if a cluster's table has more rows than the maximum number of hash keys, performance may begin to suffer because more than one row may map to the same location, potentially increasing the number of I/O reads necessary to retrieve the desired row.

Sorted Hash Clusters

Sorted hash clusters, introduced in Oracle 10*g*, extend the functionality of hash clusters that have been available since Oracle 8*i* by maintaining a sort order for rows that are retrieved by the same cluster key. In heap-organized tables and traditional hash clusters, the order in which rows are returned is not under user control and depends on internal algorithms and the relative physical location of data blocks on disk. For each hash cluster key, Oracle maintains a list of rows sorted by one or more sort columns.

Maintaining the sort order of rows upon insert incurs minimal overhead but provides a tangible benefit when the data is updated or queried: CPU time and private memory requirements are reduced because no additional sorts are required, as long as the ORDER BY clause references the sort key columns or the sort key columns prefix. In fact, the ORDER BY clause is not required if you are retrieving rows only for a single hash cluster key and want to order the rows by the sort key columns. This processing implies another valuable benefit of sorted hash clusters in that it supports FIFO processing: The sort order within each cluster key guarantees that rows are returned in the same order in which they were inserted.

For queries with an ORDER BY clause using non-prefixed sort key columns, you can use a traditional index to maintain the performance of queries on the table in the cluster.

A couple of examples will help demonstrate the value of sorted hash clusters. In the sample order entry system, you want to make sure to process the customer orders for a given customer in the order in which the orders were received without the extra overhead of sorting on the timestamp of the order.

The first step is to create a single table sorted hash cluster, as follows:

```
create cluster order_cluster
   (customer_number       number,
    order_timestamp       timestamp sort)
hashkeys 10000000
single table hash is customer_number
size 500;
```

You expect at most 10 million unique customer numbers, and the average size of the row in your cluster will be 500 bytes. The next step is to create the order table itself:

```
create table orders
   (cust_number      number,
```

```
    order_date        timestamp,
    order_number      number,
    spec_instr        varchar2(1000))
cluster order_cluster(cust_number, order_date);
```

Note that the names of the cluster keys do not have to match as long as the relative positions match and the datatypes are compatible.

Next, add a few orders with the following INSERT statements. Depending on when the orders were submitted and the locations where the orders are placed, the orders may not necessarily be inserted in chronological order:

```
insert into orders values(3045,
     timestamp'2004-05-05 15:04:14',
     405584,'Reorder from last month');
insert into orders values(1958,
     timestamp'2004-05-05 15:05:01',
     348857,'New customer');
insert into orders values(3045,
     timestamp'2004-05-04  9:26:59',
     938477,'GGT Promotion');
insert into orders values(3045,
     timestamp'2004-05-07 12:33:23',
     703749,'');
insert into orders values(3045,
     timestamp'2004-05-02 19:47:09',
     389233,'Needs order in time for Mothers Day');
```

However, because you are storing the orders in a sorted hash cluster, they are automatically maintained in the order of the sort key columns for each customer without specifying an ORDER BY clause:

```
SQL> select cust_number,
  2       to_char(order_date,'yyyy-mm-dd hh:mi pm')
  3                   order_date,
  4       order_number, spec_instr
  5  from orders where cust_number = 3045;

CUST_NUMBER ORDER_DATE          ORDER_NUMBER SPEC_INSTR
----------- ------------------- ------------ -------------
       3045 2004-05-02 07:47 pm       389233 Needs order i
                                             n time for Mo
                                             thers Day
```

```
      3045 2004-05-04 09:26 am       938477 GGT Promotion
      3045 2004-05-05 03:04 pm       405584 Reorder from
                                            last month
      3045 2004-05-07 12:33 pm       703749

4 rows selected.

Execution Plan
----------------------------------------------------------
   0      SELECT STATEMENT Optimizer=ALL_ROWS
             (Cost=0 Card=4 Bytes=2164)
   1    0   TABLE ACCESS (HASH) OF 'ORDERS'
                     (CLUSTER (HASH))
```

Even though you had no ORDER BY clause, all rows selected using a specific customer number (in this case, customer number 3045) will automatically return the rows ordered by the sort keys, because the sorted hash cluster maintains the order within the customer number cluster key.

To make sure the new access path is used, you must ensure that the cost-based optimizer is enabled and statistics are gathered for the table. An EXPLAIN PLAN of any query on a sorted hash cluster will show an access method of TABLE ACCESS HASH without a sort operation. Also, any queries must use an equality predicate; if the previous query was instead written as follows, then an ORDER BY clause would be necessary to keep the rows in the desired sequence:

```
SQL> select cust_number,
  2     to_char(order_date,'yyyy-mm-dd hh:mi pm')
  3            order_date,
  4     order_number, spec_instr
  5  from orders where cust_number >= 3045;

CUST_NUMBER ORDER_DATE          ORDER_NUMBER SPEC_INSTR
----------- ------------------- ------------ -------------
       3045 2004-05-05 03:04 pm       405584 Reorder from
                                             last month
       3045 2004-05-04 09:26 am       938477 GGT Promotion
       3045 2004-05-07 12:33 pm       703749
       3045 2004-05-02 07:47 pm       389233 Needs order i
                                             n time for Mo
                                             thers Day

4 rows selected.
```

Similarly, if you accessed the table using a reference to only the SPEC_INSTR column in the WHERE clause, a sort would be necessary to return the rows in the desired order.

To make further improvements in performance, you may consider creating a multi-table hash cluster to hold both the orders and the order items, but for now the improvements in processing orders alone will help you avoid new hardware acquisitions for a few months.

Using Miscellaneous Space Management Tools

Two other automated space management features fall into the advisor category: the Undo Advisor and the Redo Logfile Size Advisor. In both cases, Oracle collects statistics on a continuous basis to help you size the undo tablespace and the online redo logs to enhance both performance and availability.

In the following sections, we'll show you how to manage the size of your undo tablespace using the Undo Advisor. After we present an overview of how online redo log files are configured and managed, we'll explain how the Redo Logfile Size Advisor can help you tune the configuration of your online redo log files.

Controlling Undo Space

Undo tablespaces are monitored just like any other tablespace: If a specific set of space thresholds is not defined, the database default values are used; otherwise, a specific set of thresholds can be assigned.

Running out of space in an undo tablespace, however, may also trigger an ORA-01555 Snapshot too old error. Long-running queries that need a read-consistent view of one or more tables can be at odds with ongoing transactions that need undo space. Unless the undo tablespace is defined with the RETENTION GUARANTEE parameter, ongoing DML can use undo space that may be needed for long-running queries. As a result, a Snapshot too old error is returned to the user executing the query, and an alert is generated. This alert is also known as a *long query warning alert*.

This alert may be triggered independently of the space available in the undo tablespace if the UNDO_RETENTION initialization parameter is set too low.

Regardless of how often the Snapshot too old error occurs, the alert is generated at most once per 24-hour period. Increasing the size of the undo tablespace or changing the value of UNDO_RETENTION does not reset the 24-hour timer. For example, an alert is generated at 10 A.M. and you add undo space at 11 A.M. The undo tablespace is still too small, and users are still receiving Snapshot too old errors at 2 P.M. You will not receive a long query warning alert until 10 A.M. the next day, but chances are you will get a phone call before then!

To help you maintain the best balance between disk space in the undo tablespace and user query performance, EM Database Control *Undo Advisor* helps you determine how large of an undo tablespace is necessary given adjustments to the undo retention setting.

In Figure 13.25, the Undo Advisor screen shows the autotuned undo retention of 753 minutes and an undo tablespace size of 94MB. If you don't expect your undo usage to increase or you don't expect to need to retain undo information longer than 753 minutes, you can drop the size of the undo tablespace if it is significantly more than 94MB.

On the other hand, if you expect to need undo information for longer than 753 minutes, you can see the impact of this increase by either entering a new value for undo retention and refreshing the page or by clicking a point on the graph corresponding to the estimated undo retention. Figure 13.26 shows the results of increasing the undo retention to 103,204 minutes.

To support an undo retention setting of 103,204 minutes given the current undo usage, the undo tablespace will have to be increased in size to 8,625MB, or 8.625GB.

FIGURE 13.25 Autotuned undo retention settings

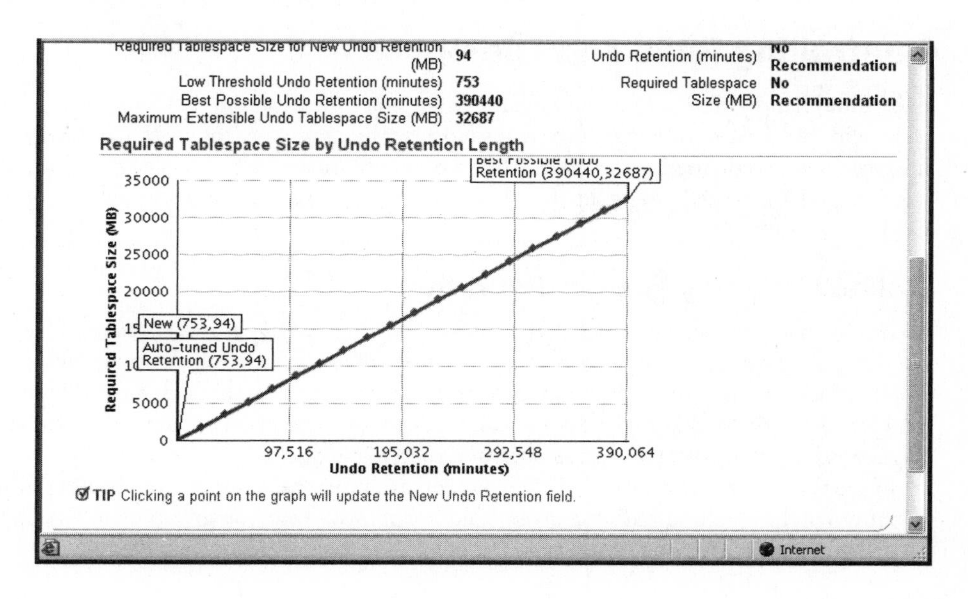

FIGURE 13.26 Specifying new undo retention settings

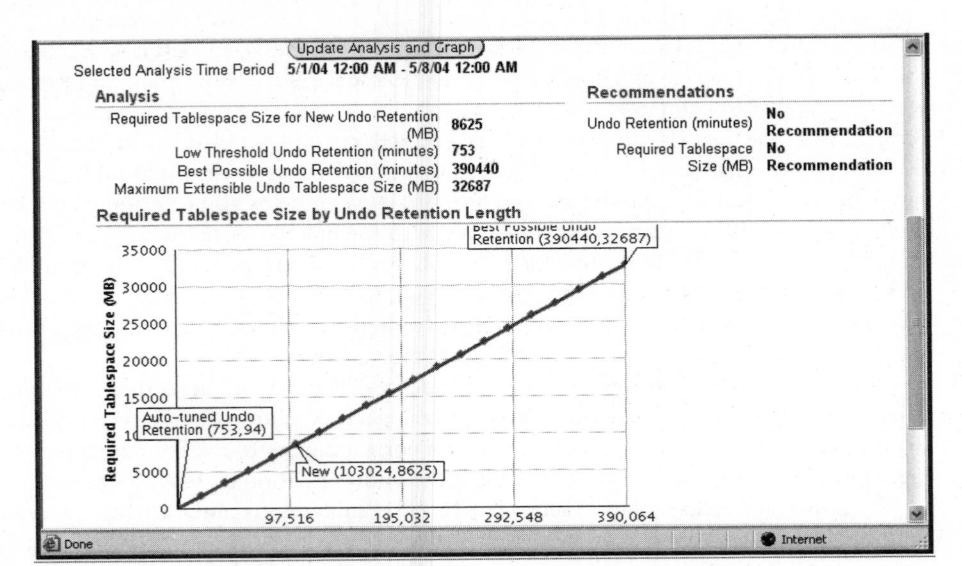

Controlling Redo Log File Space

Even though individual online redo log files do not use much space, they must still be optimized to provide the best performance for transactions while ensuring the instance recovery capabilities that online redo log files provide. After we provide an in-depth overview of how online redo log files are configured, we will show you how to optimize their performance using the Redo Logfile Size Advisor.

Online Redo Log File Configuration

A *redo log file* records all changes to the database, in most cases before the changes are written to the datafiles. To recover from an instance or a media failure, redo log information is required to roll datafiles forward to the last committed transaction. Ensuring that you have at least two members for each redo log file group dramatically reduces the likelihood of data loss, because the database continues to operate if one member of a redo log file is lost.

In the following sections, we will give you an architectural overview of redo log files, as well as show you how to add redo log groups, add or remove redo log group members, and clear a redo log group in case one of the redo log group's members becomes corrupted.

Redo Log File Architecture

Online redo log files are filled with redo records. A *redo record*, also called a *redo entry*, is made up of a group of *change vectors*, each of which describes a change made to a single block in the database. Redo entries record data that you can use to reconstruct all changes made to the database, including the undo segments. When you recover the database by using redo log files, Oracle reads the change vectors in the redo records and applies the changes to the relevant blocks.

The LGWR process writes redo information from the redo log buffer to the online redo log files under a variety of circumstances:

- When a user commits a transaction, even if this is the only transaction in the log buffer.
- When the redo log buffer becomes one-third full.
- When the buffer contains approximately 1MB of *changed* records. This total does not include deleted or inserted records.

LGWR always writes its records to the online redo log file *before* DBW*n* writes new or modified database buffer cache records to the datafiles.

Each database has its own online *redo log groups*. A redo log group can have one or more *redo log members* (each member is a single operating system file). If you have a RAC configuration, in which multiple instances are mounted to one database, each instance has one online redo thread. That is, the LGWR process of each instance writes to the same online redo log files, and hence Oracle has to keep track of the instance from where the database changes are coming. Single instance configurations will have only one thread, and that thread number is 1. The redo log file contains both committed and uncommitted transactions. Whenever a transaction is committed, a system change number is assigned to the redo records to identify the committed transaction.

The redo log group is referenced by an integer; you can specify the group number when you create the redo log files, either when you create the database or when you create a redo log group after you create the database. You can also change the redo log configuration (add, drop, or rename files) by using database commands. The following example shows a CREATE DATABASE command:

```
CREATE DATABASE "MYDB01"
. . .
LOGFILE '/ora02/oradata/MYDB01/redo01.log' SIZE 10M,
        '/ora03/oradata/MYDB01/redo02.log' SIZE 10M;
```

Two *log file groups* are created here; the first file is assigned to group 1, and the second file is assigned to group 2. You can have more files in each group; this practice is known as the multiplexing of redo log files, which we'll discuss later in this chapter in the section "Multiplexing Redo

Log Files." You can specify any group number—the range will be between 1 and the initialization parameter MAXLOGFILES. Oracle recommends that all redo log groups be the same size. The following is an example of creating the log files by specifying the group number:

```
CREATE DATABASE "MYDB01"
. . .
LOGFILE GROUP 1 '/ora02/oradata/MYDB01/redo01.log' SIZE 10M,
        GROUP 2 '/ora03/oradata/MYDB01/redo02.log' SIZE 10M;
```

Log Switch Operations

The LGWR process writes to only one redo log file group at any time. The file that is actively being written to is known as the *current* log file. The log files that are required for instance recovery are known as the *active* log files. The other log files are known as *inactive*. Oracle automatically recovers an instance when starting up the instance by using the online redo log files. Instance recovery can be needed if you do not shut down the database cleanly or if your database server crashes.

The log files are written in a circular fashion. A log switch occurs when Oracle finishes writing to one log group and starts writing to the next log group. A log switch always occurs when the current redo log group is completely full and log writing must continue. You can force a log switch by using the ALTER SYSTEM command. A manual log switch can be necessary when performing maintenance on the redo log files by using the ALTER SYSTEM SWITCH LOGFILE command. Figure 13.27 shows how LGWR writes to the redo log groups in a circular fashion.

Whenever a log switch occurs, Oracle allocates a sequence number to the new redo log group before writing to it. As stated earlier, this number is known as the log sequence number. If there are lots of transactions or changes to the database, the log switches can occur too frequently. Make sure to size the redo log files appropriately to avoid frequent log switches. Oracle writes to the alert log file whenever a log switch occurs.

Redo log files are written sequentially on the disk, so the I/O will be fast if there is no other activity on the disk. (The disk head is always properly positioned.) Keep the redo log files on a separate disk for better performance. If you have to store a datafile on the same disk as the redo log file, do not put the SYSTEM, UNDOTBS, SYSAUX, or any very active data or index tablespace file on this disk. A commit cannot complete until a transaction's information has been written to the redo logs, so maximizing the throughput of the redo log files is a top priority.

Database checkpoints are closely tied to redo log file switches. A checkpoint is an event that flushes the modified data from the buffer cache to the disk and updates the control file and datafiles. The CKPT process updates the headers of datafiles and control files; the actual blocks are written to the file by the DBW*n* process. A checkpoint is initiated

- When the redo log file is filled and a log switch occurs.
- When the instance is shut down with NORMAL, TRANSACTIONAL, or IMMEDIATE.

- When a tablespace status is changed to read-only or put into BACKUP mode.
- When other values specified by certain parameters (discussed later in this section) are reached.

You can force a checkpoint if needed, as shown here:

```
ALTER SYSTEM CHECKPOINT;
```

Forcing a checkpoint ensures that all changes to the database buffers are written to the datafiles on disk.

Another way to force a checkpoint is by forcing a log file switch:

```
ALTER SYSTEM SWITCH LOGFILE;
```

The size of the redo log affects the checkpoint performance. If the size of the redo log is smaller compared to the number of transactions, a log switch occurs often, and so does the checkpoint. The DBW*n* process writes the dirty buffer blocks whenever a checkpoint occurs. This situation might reduce the time required for instance recovery, but it might also affect the runtime performance. You can adjust checkpoints primarily by using the initialization parameter FAST_START_MTTR_TARGET. This parameter replaces the deprecated parameters FAST_START_IO_TARGET and LOG_CHECKPOINT_TIMEOUT in previous versions of the Oracle database. It is used to ensure that recovery time at instance startup (if required) will not exceed a certain number of seconds.

FIGURE 13.27 Redo log file usage

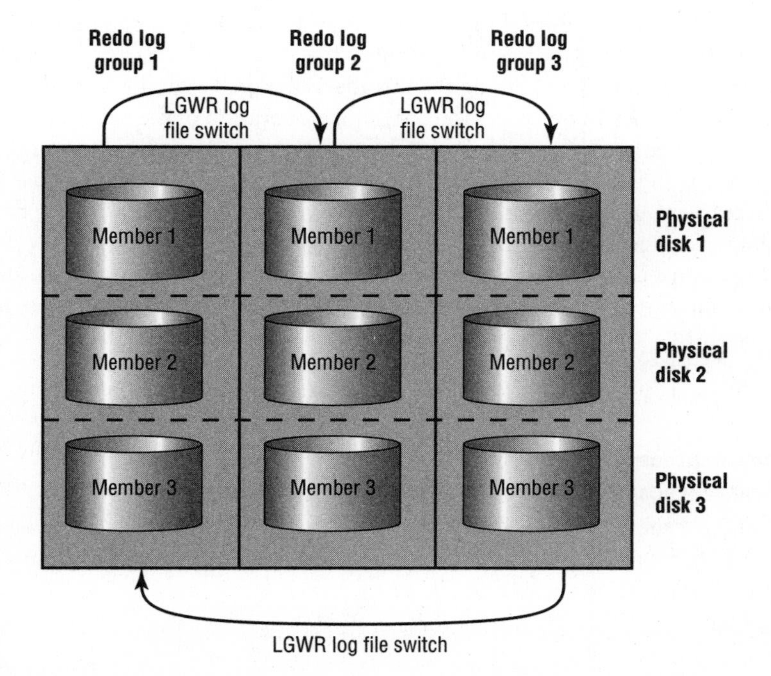

Real World Scenario

Redo Log Troubleshooting

In the case of redo log groups, it's best to be generous with the number of groups and the number of members for each group. After estimating the number of groups that would be appropriate for your installation, add one more. I can remember many database installations in which I was trying to be overly cautious about disk space usage, not putting things into perspective and realizing that the slight additional work involved in maintaining either additional or larger redo logs is small in relation to the time needed to fix a problem when the number of users and concurrent active transactions increase.

The space needed for additional log file groups is minimal and is well worth the effort up front to avoid the undesirable situation in which writes to the redo log file are waiting on the completion of writes to the database files or to the archived log file destination.

Multiplexing Redo Log Files

You can keep multiple copies of the online redo log file to safeguard against damage to these files. When multiplexing online redo log files, LGWR concurrently writes the same redo log information to multiple identical online redo log files, thereby eliminating a single point of redo log failure. All copies of the redo file are the same size and are known as a *group*, which is identified by an integer. Each redo log file in the group is known as a *member*. You must have at least two redo log groups for normal database operation.

When multiplexing redo log files, keeping the members of a group on different disks is preferable so that one disk failure will not affect the continuing operation of the database. If LGWR can write to at least one member of the group, database operation proceeds as normal; an entry is written to the alert log file. If all members of the redo log file group are not available for writing, Oracle hangs, crashes, or shuts down. An instance recovery or media recovery can be needed to bring up the database, and you can lose committed transactions.

You can create multiple copies of the online redo log files when you create the database. For example, the following statement creates two redo log file groups with two members in each:

```
CREATE DATABASE "MYDB01"
...
LOGFILE
  GROUP 1 ('/ora02/oradata/MYDB01/redo0101.log',
           '/ora03/oradata/MYDB01/redo0102.log') SIZE 10M,
  GROUP 2 ('/ora02/oradata/MYDB01/redo0201.log',
           '/ora03/oradata/MYDB01/redo0202.log') SIZE 10M;
```

The maximum number of log file groups is specified in the clause MAXLOGFILES, and the maximum number of members is specified in the clause MAXLOGMEMBERS. You can separate the filenames (members) by using a space or a comma.

In the following sections, we will show you how to create a new redo log group, add a new member to an existing group, rename a member, and drop a member from an existing group. In addition, we'll show you how to drop a group and clear all members of a group in certain circumstances.

Creating New Groups

You can create and add more redo log groups to the database by using the ALTER DATABASE command. The following statement creates a new log file group with two members:

```
ALTER DATABASE ADD LOGFILE
  GROUP 3 ('/ora02/oradata/MYDB01/redo0301.log',
           '/ora03/oradata/MYDB01/redo0302.log') SIZE 10M;
```

If you omit the GROUP clause, Oracle assigns the next available number. For example, the following statement also creates a multiplexed group:

```
ALTER DATABASE ADD LOGFILE
     ('/ora02/oradata/MYDB01/redo0301.log',
      '/ora03/oradata/MYDB01/redo0302.log') SIZE 10M;
```

To create a new group without multiplexing, use the following statement:

```
ALTER DATABASE ADD LOGFILE
     '/ora02/oradata/MYDB01/redo0301.log' REUSE;
```

You can add more than one redo log group by using the ALTER DATABASE command—just use a comma to separate the groups.

If the redo log files you create already exist, use the REUSE option and don't specify the size. The new redo log size will be the same as that of the existing file.

Adding a new redo log group is straightforward using the EM Database Control interface. To do so, click the Administration tab on the database home page, and then click the Redo Log Groups link. You can view and add another redo log group, as you can see in Figure 13.28 on the Redo Log Groups screen.

FIGURE 13.28 The Redo Log Groups maintenance screen

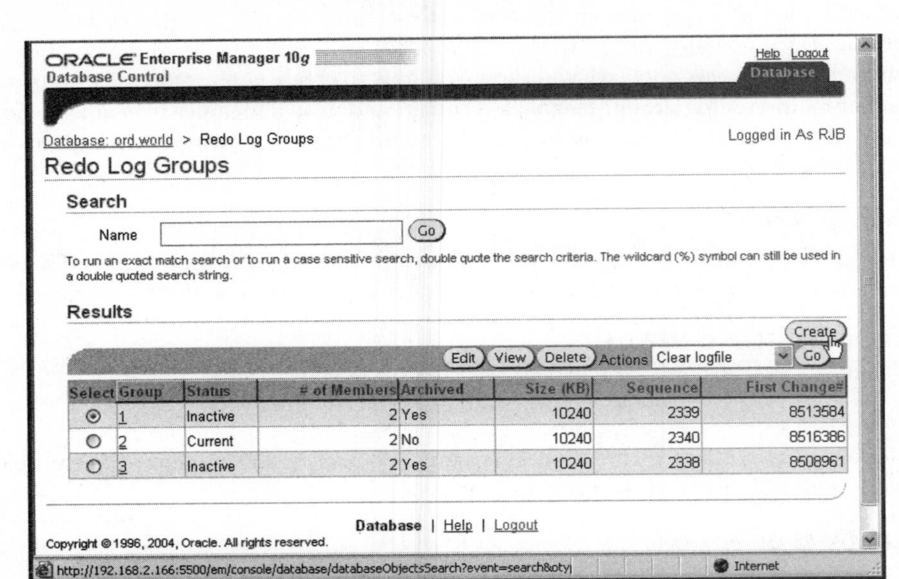

Adding New Members

If you forgot to multiplex the redo log files when creating the database (multiplexing redo log files is the default when you use DBCA) or if you need to add more redo log members, you can do so by using the ALTER DATABASE command. When adding new members, you do not specify the file size, because all group members will have the same size.

If you know the group number, use the following statement to add a member to group 2:

```
ALTER DATABASE ADD LOGFILE MEMBER
'/ora04/oradata/MYDB01/redo0203.log' TO GROUP 2;
```

You can also add group members by specifying the names of other members in the group instead of specifying the group number. Specify all the existing group members with this syntax:

```
ALTER DATABASE ADD LOGFILE MEMBER
 '/ora04/oradata/MYDB01/redo0203.log' TO
('/ora02/oradata/MYDB01/redo0201.log',
 '/ora03/oradata/MYDB01/redo0202.log');
```

You can add a new member to a group in EM Database Control by clicking the Edit button in Figure13.28 and then clicking Add.

Renaming Log Members

If you want to move the log file member from one disk to another or you just want a more meaningful name, you can rename a redo log member. Before renaming the online redo log members, the new (target) online redo files should exist. The SQL commands in Oracle change only the internal pointer in the control file to a new log file; they do not change or rename the operating system file. You must use an operating system command to rename or move the file.

Follow these steps to rename a log member:

1. Shut down the database.
2. Copy/rename the redo log file member to the new location by using an operating system command.
3. Start up the instance and mount the database (`STARTUP MOUNT`).
4. Rename the log file member in the control file. Use the `ALTER DATABASE RENAME FILE 'old_redo_file_name' TO 'new_redo_file_name';` command.
5. Open the database (`ALTER DATABASE OPEN`).
6. Back up the control file.

Another way to achieve the same result is to add a new member to the group and then drop the old member from the group, as discussed in the "Adding New Members" section earlier in this chapter and the "Dropping Redo Log Members" section, which you'll read shortly.

You can rename a log group member in EM Database Control by clicking the Edit button in Figure 13.28, then clicking Edit again, and then changing the filename in the File Name box.

Dropping Redo Log Groups

You can drop a redo log group and its members by using the `ALTER DATABASE` command. Remember that you should have at least two redo log groups for the database to function normally. The group that is to be dropped should not be the active group or the current group—that is, you can drop only an inactive log file group. If the log file to be dropped is not inactive, use the `ALTER SYSTEM SWITCH LOGFILE` command.

To drop the log file group 3, use the following SQL statement:

```
ALTER DATABASE DROP LOGFILE GROUP 3;
```

When an online redo log group is dropped from the database, the operating system files are not deleted from disk. The control files of the associated database are updated to drop the members of the group from the database structure. After dropping an online redo log group, make sure that the drop is completed successfully and then use the appropriate operating system command to delete the dropped online redo log files.

You can delete an entire redo log group in EM Database Control by clicking the Edit button in Figure 13.28 and then clicking the Delete button.

Dropping Redo Log Members

In much the same way that you drop a redo log group, you can drop only the members of an inactive redo log group. Also, if there are only two groups, the log member to be dropped should not be the last member of a group. Each redo log group can have a different number of members, though this is not advised. For example, say you have three log groups, each with two members. If you drop a log member from group 2 and a failure occurs to the sole member of group 2, the instance will hang, crash, and potentially cause loss of committed transactions when attempts are made to write to the missing redo log group, as discussed earlier in this chapter. Even if you drop a member for maintenance reasons, ensure that all redo log groups have the same number of members.

To drop a redo log member, use the `DROP LOGFILE MEMBER` clause of the `ALTER DATABASE` command:

```
ALTER DATABASE DROP LOGFILE MEMBER
'/ora04/oradata/MYDB01/redo0203.log';
```

The operating system file is not removed from the disk; only the control file is updated. Use an operating system command to delete the redo log file member from disk.

If a database is running in `ARCHIVELOG` mode, redo log members cannot be deleted unless the redo log group has been archived.

You can drop a member of a redo log group in EM Database Control by clicking the Edit button in Figure 13.28, selecting the member to be dropped, and then clicking the Remove button.

Clearing Online Redo Log Files

Under certain circumstances, a redo log group member (or all members of a log group) can become corrupted. To solve this problem, you can drop and re-add the log file group or group member. It is much easier, however, to use the `ALTER DATABASE CLEAR LOGFILE` command. The following example clears the contents of redo log group 3 in the database:

```
ALTER DATABASE CLEAR LOGFILE GROUP 3;
```

Another distinct advantage of this command is that you can clear a log group even if the database has only two log groups and only one member in each group. You can also clear a log group member even if it has not been archived by using the `UNARCHIVED` keyword. In this case, it is advisable to do a full database backup at the earliest convenience, because the unarchived redo log file is no longer usable for database recovery.

Redo Logfile Size Advisor

The *Redo Logfile Size Advisor* provides an automatic method for sizing redo log files. In general, redo logs should be sized large enough so that checkpoints do not occur too frequently; if the logs switch more often than every 20 minutes, performance of the database may be affected.

On the other hand, redo logs that are too big may impact disk space usage without a measurable benefit.

In addition to the amount of redo generated, the other factor that directly affects the proper sizing of the redo logs is the initialization parameter FAST_START_MTTR_TARGET. A parameter available since Oracle *9i*, FAST_START_MTTR_TARGET indicates the time, in seconds, that instance recovery should take after a crash or instance failure. For the Redo Logfile Size Advisor to provide a value for the optimal log file size, this parameter must be non-zero. As one of Oracle's automated advisors, statistics for optimizing the redo log file size are collected automatically and continually.

The initialization parameters FAST_START_IO_TARGET and LOG_CHECKPOINT_INTERVAL can still be specified to control instance recovery, but setting either of these parameters disables FAST_START_MTTR_TARGET.

In the sample order database, the redo log files are sized as follows:

```
SQL> select member from v$logfile;

MEMBER
----------------------------------------
/u07/oradata/ord/redo03.log
/u07/oradata/ord/redo02.log
/u07/oradata/ord/redo01.log
/u08/oradata/ord/redo01.log
/u08/oradata/ord/redo02.log
/u08/oradata/ord/redo03.log

6 rows selected.

SQL> !ls -l /u07/oradata/ord/redo03.log
-rw-r-----    1 oracle   oinstall 10486272 Apr 20 14:01
                                   /u07/oradata/ord/redo03.log
```

The redo log files are sized at 10MB each, the default size for redo log files when the database was created. The parameter FAST_START_MTTR_TARGET is set for 30 seconds; in other words, you don't want instance recovery to take more than 30 seconds after a crash or instance failure:

```
SQL> show parameter fast_start_mttr_target

NAME                         TYPE        VALUE
---------------------------- ----------- ---------------
fast_start_mttr_target       integer     30
SQL>
```

You have two ways to retrieve the optimal log file size calculated by the Redo Logfile Size Advisor: using a new column in the view V$INSTANCE_RECOVERY or using EM Database Control. The view V$INSTANCE_RECOVERY contains a new column, OPTIMAL_LOGFILE_SIZE, which recommends a minimum size for the redo log files:

```
SQL> select optimal_logfile_size from v$instance_recovery;
OPTIMAL_LOGFILE_SIZE
--------------------
                  49

1 row selected.
```

Given the current log file size of 10MB, you should probably increase the log file size to at least 49MB to reduce the number of log file switches.

Using EM Database Control, you can retrieve the same information via a graphical interface. In Figure 13.29, review the Redo Log Groups screen containing the number and size of each redo log file.

In the Actions drop-down list on the right, select Sizing Advice and click Go. Figure 13.30 shows the recommendation for the redo log file size, which coincidentally corresponds with the information obtained from the view V$INSTANCE_RECOVERY.

FIGURE 13.29 Redo Log Groups screen

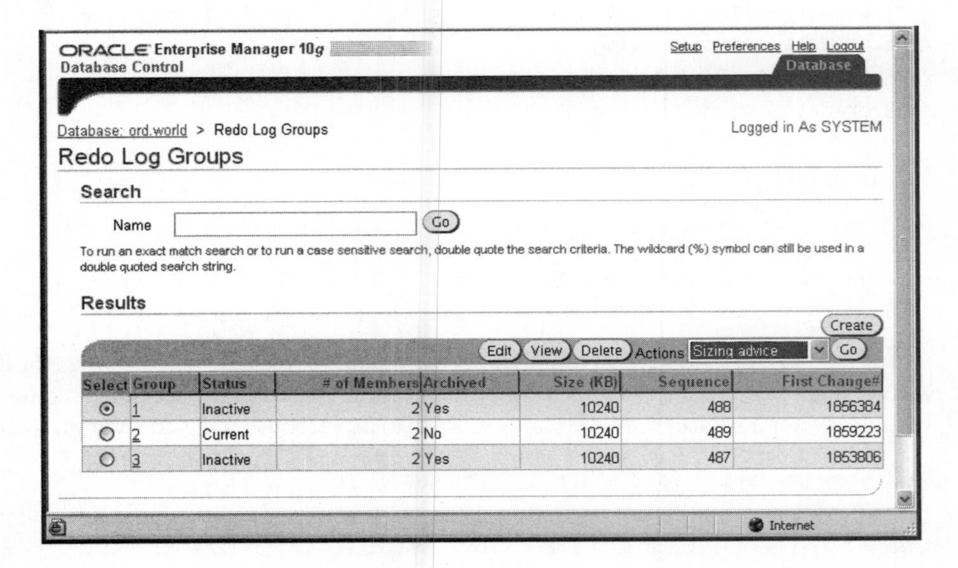

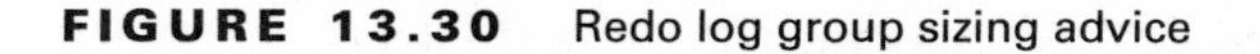

FIGURE 13.30 Redo log group sizing advice

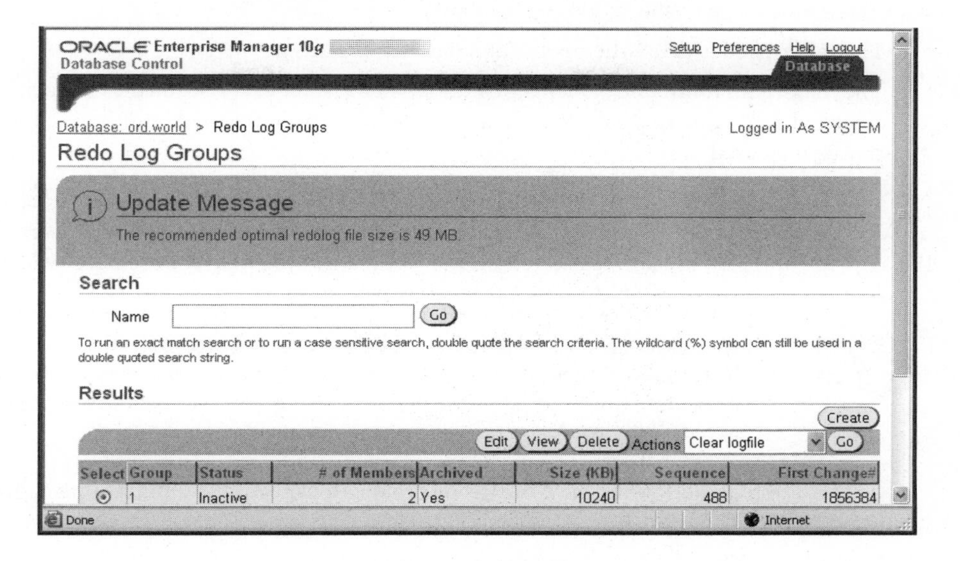

Leveraging Resumable Space Allocation

Until Resumable Space Allocation was introduced in Oracle 9*i*, you had to implement workarounds to prevent a long-running operation from failing from a space-related error condition, for example, artificially splitting up a job into smaller pieces so that a failure of one piece of the job would not require you to rerun the earlier parts of the job. Using Resumable Space Allocation, your developers can design their applications from a logical transaction point of view and give you an opportunity to fix the out-of-space condition while the application's long-running operation is temporarily suspended.

In the following sections, we will give you an overview of the Resumable Space Allocation architecture, show you how to use Resumable Space Allocation, and show you both the SQL and PL/SQL interfaces for Resumable Space Allocation. Finally, we will review the data dictionary views related to Resumable Space Allocation.

An Overview of Resumable Space Allocation

Resumable Space Allocation allows you to suspend and resume execution of large database operations that fail due to errors related to space limits and out-of-space conditions. Once you repair the condition by either adjusting quotas, or adding disk space to a tablespace, or both, the suspended operation automatically resumes where it left off.

When a session is enabled for Resumable Space Allocation, the long-running operation is suspended when one of the following occurs:

- The tablespace used by the operation runs out of space.
- The maximum number of extents in a table, index, temporary segment, rollback segment, cluster, LOB, table partition, or index partition has been reached, and no further extents can be allocated.
- The quota for the user executing the long-running operation has been reached.

When a statement is suspended under Resumable Space Allocation, the error is reported in the alert log and any triggers registered on the resumable system event are executed.

An operation on a remote database executed by a local session running in Resumable Space Allocation mode does not itself run in Resumable Space Allocation mode; in other words, Resumable Space Allocation is not supported across databases.

The types of SQL statements and operations that can trigger a Resumable Space Allocation condition include the following:

- SQL queries that run out of temporary space, such as for sorting
- DML commands such as INSERT, UPDATE, and DELETE
- Import/export operations, when Resumable Space Allocation is specified
- SQL*Loader jobs, when Resumable Space Allocation is specified
- DDL operations such as CREATE TABLE, CREATE INDEX, ALTER TABLE, ALTER INDEX, and CREATE MATERIALIZED VIEW

Also, a timeout parameter is associated with each Resumable Space Allocation suspension. If the space condition is not corrected within the timeout period, the transaction in progress is cancelled and rolled back as if Resumable Space Allocation was not enabled.

Using Resumable Space Allocation

Resumable Space Allocation is enabled via a new option of the ALTER SESSION command:

```
ALTER SESSION ENABLE RESUMABLE
    [TIMEOUT timeout] [NAME name];
```

The value for timeout is specified in seconds; if it is not specified, it defaults to the value stored in the initialization parameter RESUMABLE_TIMEOUT. You can specify a name for the resumable session; if it is not specified, a system-assigned name is used. In the following example, you enable Resumable Space Allocation in your session and set the timeout to 10 minutes (600 seconds):

```
SQL> alter session enable resumable timeout 600 name 'Short Timeout';
Session altered.
```

If any space-related condition occurs in this session that is not resolved within 10 minutes, the transaction is cancelled and rolled back. The value for NAME is stored in the data dictionary views USER_RESUMABLE and DBA_RESUMABLE.

Disabling Resumable Space Allocation in a session uses a different option of the ALTER SESSION command:

```
SQL> alter session disable resumable;
Session altered.
```

For a user to use Resumable Space Allocation, the user must be granted the RESUMABLE system privilege, as in this example:

```
SQL> grant resumable to scott;
Grant succeeded.
```

DBMS_RESUMABLE Package

The PL/SQL package DBMS_RESUMABLE gives you more control over sessions running in Resumable Space Allocation mode. The procedures within DBMS_RESUMABLE are as follows:

ABORT Cancels a suspended Resumable Space Allocation transaction.

GET_SESSION_TIMEOUT Returns the timeout value for a given session.

GET_TIMEOUT Returns the timeout value for the current session.

SET_SESSION_TIMEOUT Sets the timeout value for a given session.

SET_TIMEOUT Sets the timeout value for the current session.

SPACE_ERROR_INFO Returns an error code for a particular object if it is currently triggering Resumable Space Allocation.

In the following example, you retrieve the timeout value for your session and double it:

```
SQL> select dbms_resumable.get_timeout() from dual;

DBMS_RESUMABLE.GET_TIMEOUT()
----------------------------
                         600
1 row selected.

SQL> exec dbms_resumable.set_timeout(1200);
PL/SQL procedure successfully completed.

SQL> select dbms_resumable.get_timeout() from dual;
```

```
DBMS_RESUMABLE.GET_TIMEOUT()
----------------------------
                        1200
1 row selected.
```

Using the *AFTER SUSPEND* System Event

A system event called AFTER SUSPEND, first introduced in Oracle 9*i*, is triggered at the database or schema level when a correctable Resumable Space Allocation error occurs. The trigger defined on this system event can take a number of corrective actions such as adjusting the timeout value and sending an e-mail to the DBA requesting assistance while the session is suspended. In the following example, you create a trigger to set the timeout to eight hours and send an e-mail to the DBA:

```
CREATE OR REPLACE TRIGGER resumable_default_timeout
   AFTER SUSPEND ON DATABASE
BEGIN
   /* set timeout to 8 hours */
   DBMS_RESUMABLE.SET_TIMEOUT(28800);
   /* prepare e-mail to DBA on call */
   . . .
   UTL_MAIL.SEND (. . .);
END;
```

Resumable Space Allocation Data Dictionary Views

The data dictionary views DBA_RESUMABLE and USER_RESUMABLE display the set of Resumable Space Allocation statements in the system. The view contains all currently executing or suspended statements that are running in Resumable Space Allocation mode. In the following query against DBA_RESUMABLE, you can review the user number, session number, name, status, timeout value, and the current SQL statement for all sessions that have enabled Resumable Space Allocation:

```
SQL> select user_id, session_id, name, status,
  2      timeout, sql_text
  3  from dba_resumable;

 USER_ID  SESSION_ID NAME     STATUS TIMEOUT SQL_TEXT
-------- ----------- -------- ------ ------- ------------
      58         258 Short Ti NORMAL     600 select dbms_
                     meout                   resumable.ge
                                             t_timeout()
                                             from dual
```

```
      64          239 Short Ti NORMAL    1200 select user_
                      meout                     id, session_
                                                id, name, st
                                                atus, timeou
                                                t, sql_text
                                                from dba_res
                                                umable

2 rows selected.
```

Summary

This chapter presented an in-depth tour of the automatic features that can help you manage tablespaces and the segments in the tablespaces in a proactive, instead of a reactive, manner.

Tablespaces can be monitored proactively when they reach one of two thresholds, and an alert can be generated to notify you that a tablespace has crossed the warning or critical threshold level. We showed how the PL/SQL package DBMS_SERVER_ALERT gives you a way to programmatically change these thresholds.

The Segment Advisor and segment shrink work together to not only find segments that have unused space but also to compact the space in a segment and free up the space for other database objects. We also showed you how other advisors such as the Undo Advisor and the Redo Logfile Size Advisor can help you manage and optimize disk space and performance for the undo tablespace and the redo log files, respectively.

We described a number of alternatives to the standard heap-based tables: index-organized tables and clustered tables. Index-organized tables provide a distinct performance and space usage benefit for those tables frequently accessed by the primary key because the row data is stored within the index itself. Clustered tables provide a distinct benefit for tables that are frequently queried together by storing those tables within the same segment. A variation on clustered tables—sorted hash clusters—provides you not only with another way to use disk space efficiently but also to optimize the performance of applications that use data in a first-in, first-out (FIFO) fashion.

Finally, we explained an Oracle feature that prevents rework when out-of-space conditions occur: Resumable Space Allocation. For those sessions with Resumable Space Allocation enabled, the long-running operation that runs out of disk space is temporarily suspended until the DBA provides additional disk space, allowing the long-running operation to complete successfully.

Exam Essentials

Be able to monitor space usage in a tablespace. Respond to space warning and critical alerts by adding disk space or removing objects. Adjust the space thresholds using either DBMS_SERVER_ALERT or the EM Database Control interface.

Describe two types of segments that can provide benefits beyond the traditional heap-based table segments. Use index-organized tables to maximize performance and space usage for tables exclusively accessed by the primary key. Leverage clustered tables to maximize performance for tables that are frequently joined in a query.

List the tools and methods available to monitor and maintain indexes. Be able to list the pros and cons of rebuilding an index versus coalescing an index. Identify the dynamic performance view used to determine if an index is accessed. Write a SQL query to determine the percentage of space used in each index block.

Understand how the Segment Advisor and segment shrink work together to optimize space usage and performance. Use the Segment Advisor to analyze one segment or an entire tablespace, and then use segment shrink functionality to compress one or more segments and optionally move the HWM.

Describe how sorted hash clusters—a special type of clustered table—are created and used. Identify the types of applications that can benefit from hash clusters whose elements are maintained in a sorted list for each value of the cluster key.

Identify the purpose of the redo log files. Describe the redo log file architecture. Provide details about how to create new redo log file groups and add new members to redo log file groups. Be able to drop redo log group members. Know how to clear online redo log file groups when a log file member becomes corrupted.

Identify the purpose of the Undo Advisor and Redo Logfile Size Advisor within the Oracle advisory framework. Be able to optimize the UNDO_RETENTION parameter as well as the size of the undo tablespace by using the Undo Advisor. Use the Redo Logfile Size Advisor to maximize performance by optimizing the time between log file switches.

Be able to leverage Resumable Space Allocation to correct repairable space-related errors while the statement that triggered the error is suspended. List the key columns of the data dictionary view containing information about Resumable Space Allocation sessions. Enable and disable Resumable Space Allocation for a session. Set up a system-level trigger to trap Resumable Space Allocation errors and take corrective action.

Review Questions

1. Which data dictionary view provides the recommended action, as a SQL statement, from the Segment Advisor?
   - **A.** `DBA_ADVISOR_FINDINGS`
   - **B.** `DBA_ADVISOR_RECOMMENDATIONS`
   - **C.** `DBA_ADVISOR_ACTIONS`
   - **D.** `DBA_ADVISOR_RATIONALE`

2. Which of the following statements is *not* true about sorted hash clusters?
   - **A.** The new access path is used regardless of the type of predicate in the `WHERE` clause.
   - **B.** You are allowed to create indexes on sorted hash clusters.
   - **C.** The cost-based optimizer must be used to take advantage of the new access path.
   - **D.** Additional sorts are not necessary if you access the cluster by one of the lists of hash key columns.
   - **E.** More than one table can be stored in a sorted hash cluster.

3. Consider the following scenario. The user `SCOTT` runs a query at 8:25 A.M. that receives an `ORA-01555: Snapshot too old` error after running for 15 minutes. An alert is sent to the DBA that the undo tablespace is incorrectly sized. At 10:15 A.M., the DBA checks the initialization parameter `UNDO_RETENTION`, and its value is 3600; the parameter is sized correctly. The DBA doubles the size of the undo tablespace by adding a second datafile. At 1:15 P.M., the user `SCOTT` runs the same query and once again receives an `ORA-01555: Snapshot too old` error. What happens next? (Choose the best answer.)
   - **A.** The DBA receives another alert indicating that the undo tablespace is still undersized.
   - **B.** The user `SCOTT` calls the DBA to report that the query is still failing.
   - **C.** The second datafile autoextends so that future queries will have enough undo space to complete when there is concurrent DML activity.
   - **D.** Resumable Space Allocation suspends the query until the DBA adds another datafile to the undo tablespace, and then the query runs to completion.

4. The background process __________ checks for tablespace threshold violation or clearance every __________ minutes.
   - **A.** MMON, 10
   - **B.** SMON, 10
   - **C.** TMON, 30
   - **D.** PMON, 15
   - **E.** MMON, 30

5. Which of the following initialization parameters influences the recommended redo log file size provided by the Redo Logfile Size Advisor?

   A. LOG_CHECKPOINT_INTERVAL

   B. OPTIMAL_LOGFILE_SIZE

   C. FAST_START_IO_TARGET

   D. FAST_START_MTTR_TARGET

   E. None of the above

6. Which of the following is *not* a benefit of segment shrink?

   A. Full table scans will take less time.

   B. Better index access takes place because of a smaller b-tree.

   C. Space is freed up for other database objects.

   D. All chained rows are fixed.

   E. Space below the HWM is released, and the HWM is moved down.

7. The EM Database Control Segment Resource Estimation feature uses all the following characteristics of the proposed table except for which one?

   A. Column datatypes

   B. PCTUSED

   C. PCTFREE

   D. Column sizes

   E. Estimated number of rows

8. Which of the following is not a benefit of sorted hash clusters? (Choose the best answer.)

   A. Rows within a given cluster key value are sorted by the sort key(s).

   B. The ORDER BY clause is not required to retrieve rows in ascending or descending order of the sort key(s).

   C. Cluster key values are hashed.

   D. Rows selected by a cluster key value using an equality operator are returned in ascending or descending order.

9. In the following scenario, the DBA wants to reclaim a lot of wasted space in the HR.EMPLOYEES table by using the segment shrink functionality. Which of the following is the correct order of the steps?

   1. ALTER TABLE HR.EMPLOYEES SHRINK SPACE;

   2. ALTER TABLE HR.EMPLOYEES DISABLE ROW MOVEMENT;

   3. ALTER TABLE HR.EMPLOYEES ENABLE ROW MOVEMENT;

4. `ALTER TABLE HR.EMPLOYEES SHRINK SPACE COMPACT;`
5. `ALTER TABLE HR.EMPLOYEES SHRINK SPACE CASCADE;`

A. 3, 4, 1, 5, 2

B. 4, 1, 3, 2, 5

C. 5, 2, 1, 3, 4

D. 4, 1, 2, 3, 5

10. Which of the following calls to `DBMS_SERVER_ALERT.SET_THRESHOLD` will set the thresholds for the `UNDOTBS1` tablespace to 60 percent and 90 percent? (Choose the best answer.)

A.
```
dbms_server_alert.set_threshold(
   dbms_server_alert.tablespace_pct_full,
   dbms_server_alert.operator_ge, 60,
   dbms_server_alert.operator_ge, 90,
   1, 1, null,
   dbms_server_alert.object_type_tablespace,
   null);
```

B.
```
dbms_server_alert.set_threshold(
   dbms_server_alert.tablespace_pct_full,
   dbms_server_alert.operator_le, 60,
   dbms_server_alert.operator_le, 90,
   1, 1, null,
   dbms_server_alert.object_type_datafile,
   'UNDOTBS1');
```

C.
```
dbms_server_alert.set_threshold(
   dbms_server_alert.tablespace_full,
   dbms_server_alert.operator_ge, 60,
   dbms_server_alert.operator_ge, 90,
   1, 1, null,
   dbms_server_alert.object_type_tablespace,
   'UNDOTBS1');
```

D.
```
dbms_server_alert.set_threshold(
   dbms_server_alert.tablespace_pct_full,
   dbms_server_alert.operator_ge, 60,
   dbms_server_alert.operator_ge, 90,
   1, 1, null,
   dbms_server_alert.object_type_tablespace,
   'UNDOTBS1');
```

11. Which of the following statements is *not* true about segment shrink operations? (Choose the best answer.)
    A. Tables with ROWID-based materialized views are maintained.
    B. Segment shrink is allowed only on segments whose space is automatically managed.
    C. Heap-organized and index-organized tables can be shrunk.
    D. `ROW MOVEMENT` must be enabled for heap-organized segments.
    E. Chained rows may be repaired during a segment shrink operation.
    F. Triggers are not fired during a segment shrink operation.

12. Which of the following is *not* a feature of the Segment Advisor within EM Database Control?
    A. Growth trend analysis
    B. Segment Resource Estimation
    C. Finding candidates for segment shrink
    D. Finding table segments with chained rows

13. Which of the following conditions will trigger an additional sort on a sorted hash cluster? (Choose two.)
    A. The `ORDER BY` clause specifies non-sort columns that are not indexed.
    B. An `ORDER BY` clause is used in the query, although the sort may still fit in memory.
    C. The cost-based optimizer is in effect.
    D. The `ORDER BY` clause is omitted, and the `WHERE` clause does not reference the cluster key.
    E. The `ORDER BY` clause specifies trailing sort columns.

14. Which of the following statements is *not* true about segment shrink operations in tablespaces with automatic segment space management?
    A. Clustered tables cannot be shrunk.
    B. LOB segments can be shrunk.
    C. IOT mapping tables and overflow segments cannot be shrunk.
    D. Tables with function-based indexes cannot be shrunk.
    E. `ROW MOVEMENT` must be enabled for heap-based segments.

15. Which of the following is a disadvantage of rebuilding an index instead of coalescing an index?
    A. You temporarily need twice as much disk space to rebuild the index.
    B. You cannot move the index to another tablespace.
    C. The storage characteristics of the index cannot be changed.
    D. The rebuild operation only coalesces index leaf blocks within each branch instead of re-creating the entire tree.

16. Which of the following commands adds a member /logs/redo22.log to redo log file group 2?

    A. ALTER DATABASE ADD LOGFILE '/logs/redo22.log' TO GROUP 2;

    B. ALTER DATABASE ADD LOGFILE MEMBER '/logs/redo22.log' TO GROUP 2;

    C. ALTER DATABASE ADD MEMBER '/logs/redo22.log' TO GROUP 2;

    D. ALTER DATABASE ADD LOGFILE '/logs/redo22.log';

17. Which of the following is *not* a benefit of index clusters?

    A. The tables in the cluster are always queried together.

    B. Queries with an equivalence operator will perform better.

    C. The tables in the cluster have little or no DML activity.

    D. The child tables have roughly the same number of rows for each parent key in the parent table.

18. Which of the following scenarios will never trigger Resumable Space Allocation? (Choose all that apply.)

    A. SELECT * FROM HR.EMPLOYEES;

    B. DELETE FROM HR.EMPLOYEES;

    C. DROP TABLE HR.EMPLOYEES;

    D. SELECT * FROM HR.DEPARTMENTS ORDER BY DEPARTMENT_NUMBER;

    E. ALTER INDEX HR.EMP_NAME_IX REBUILD ONLINE;

    F. ALTER INDEX HR.EMP_NAME_IX REBUILD;

19. An AFTER SUSPEND trigger can be defined at what level? (Choose all that apply.)

    A. Instance

    B. Schema

    C. Table

    D. Session

    E. Database

20. Which of the following statements is *not* true about index-organized tables?

    A. An index-organized table can have additional indexes defined on other columns in the table.

    B. An index-organized table has both physical and logical ROWIDs.

    C. An index-organized table without secondary indexes is stored in a single segment.

    D. The space requirements for an index-organized table are reduced in part because the data is stored in the same segment as the index, and therefore no physical ROWID is required.

Answers to Review Questions

1. C. The data dictionary view DBA_ADVISOR_ACTIONS contains the SQL statement(s) that the Segment Advisor supplies to implement its recommendation for segment maintenance. DBA_ADVISOR_FINDINGS contains the results of the analysis, but no SQL. DBA_ADVISOR_RECOMMENDATIONS presents one or more findings and the benefits for performing the recommendation. DBA_ADVISOR_RATIONALE provides a more detailed set of reasons why the recommendation should be implemented, along with the impact of not performing the recommendation.

2. A. The new access path in a sorted hash cluster is used only if an equality predicate is used.

3. B. Even if the size of the undo tablespace is adjusted after an undo space problem, only one alert is sent for each 24-hour period. Therefore, the only way that the problem will be resolved promptly is for SCOTT to call the DBA, because the DBA will not receive another alert until the next day when another query fails.

4. A. The new background process MMON checks for threshold violations every 10 minutes. An alert is triggered when the threshold is reached or is cleared.

5. D. FAST_START_MTTR_TARGET specifies the desired time, in seconds, for instance recovery after a crash or an instance failure. Therefore, the Redo Logfile Size Advisor uses this value to determine the optimal log file size. OPTIMAL_LOGFILE_SIZE is not an initialization parameter but a column in the view V$INSTANCE_RECOVERY. The initialization parameter FAST_START_IO_TARGET specifies recovery at the I/O level, and LOG_CHECKPOINT_INTERVAL specifies the frequency of checkpoints in terms of redo log file blocks used.

6. D. While some chained rows may be fixed with segment shrink functionality, it is not guaranteed that all chained rows will be fixed, because not all blocks may be read in a segment shrink operation.

7. B. Only PCTFREE is used in the calculation, because it is the amount of space to leave free in the block for updates to existing rows. PCTUSED is not needed unless the segment space management is not AUTO. In addition, extent sizes calculated by this feature help assess the impact on the tablespace where this segment will be stored.

8. C. While cluster key values in a sorted hash cluster are hashed, this is also true of regular hash clusters, and therefore is not a benefit unique to sorted hash clusters.

9. A. While the segment shrink operation could combine steps 1 and 4, the impact to the users will most likely be lessened by performing two smaller operations instead of one by specifying SHRINK SPACE COMPACT before specifying SHRINK SPACE in a subsequent operation.

10. D. The call to DBMS_SERVER_ALERT.SET_THRESHOLD must specify the metric TABLESPACE_PCT_FULL, the two thresholds, an object type of tablespace, and the tablespace name itself. Specifying NULL for the tablespace name will set the threshold for all tablespaces, not just the UNDOTBS1 tablespace.

11. A. Because the ROWIDs are changed with a segment shrink operation, tables with ROWID-based materialized views cannot be shrunk unless the materialized views are dropped and re-created after the segment shrink operation.

12. D. The Segment Advisor is not used to find tables with chained rows, but instead is used for finding segments that are good candidates for segment shrink or may be growing too fast.

13. A, E. If a query on a sorted hash cluster retrieves rows and an `ORDER BY` clause specifies either non-sort columns or a suffix of the sort columns, additional sorting is required, assuming that indexes are not defined on the columns in the `ORDER BY` clause.

14. B. For segments in tablespaces with automatic segment space management, LOB segments cannot be shrunk. In addition, tables with LONG columns, on-commit materialized views, and ROWID-based materialized view cannot be shrunk. In all cases, shrink operations cannot be performed on segments managed by freelists.

15. A. Whether you rebuild the index offline or online, you temporarily need twice as much disk space. If you rebuild the index online, you also need disk space to support a journal table to hold the intermediate changes to the index while the index is being rebuilt.

16. B. When adding log file members, specify the group number or specify all the existing group members.

17. B. Hash clusters, not index clusters, use a hashing function to find a row in a cluster and perform best for equivalence queries.

18. A, C. Unless an `ORDER BY` clause forces a sort operation and uses up temporary space, a `SELECT` command will not otherwise trigger Resumable Space Allocation. Dropping a table does not use any additional disk space in a tablespace; it frees up disk space. Therefore, it will not trigger Resumable Space Allocation.

19. B, E. The `AFTER SUSPEND` system-level trigger can be defined only at the database level or at the schema level.

20. B. An index-organized table (IOT) does not have a physical ROWID; instead, a logical ROWID is constructed based on the value of the primary key.

Securing the Oracle Listener, Diagnostic Sources, and Memory

ORACLE DATABASE 10*G*: ADMINISTRATION II EXAM OBJECTIVES COVERED IN THIS CHAPTER:

✓ **Securing the Oracle Listener**
- Secure the listener.
- Remove default EXTPROC entry and add a separate listener to handle external procedure calls.

✓ **Diagnostic Sources**
- Use the alert log and database trace files for diagnostic purposes.
- View alerts using Enterprise Manager.
- Control the size and location of trace files.

✓ **Monitoring and Managing Memory**
- Implement Automatic Shared Memory Management.
- Manually configure SGA parameters for various memory components in the SGA.
- Use Automatic PGA Memory Management.

Exam objectives are subject to change at any time without prior notice and at Oracle's sole discretion. Please visit Oracle's Training and Certification website (`http://www.oracle.com/education/certification/`) for the most current exam objectives listing.

In this chapter, three distinct topics will be addressed: listener security, diagnostic sources, and automatic memory management.

Security is a topic that seems to be on everyone's mind lately, and with good reason. Many network elements once thought to be secure are being proved otherwise at an alarming rate. Oracle's TNS (Transparent Network Substrate) listener is no exception.

Historically, the listener has received little attention or fanfare. However, with the advent of the Internet, security holes have been discovered that could be putting your database at risk. In this section, you will learn the security issues surrounding the listener, as well as how to address them to make your database more secure.

Also in this chapter, you will learn about Oracle's diagnostic sources. When problems in the database come up, it is important to know what sources of information are available to aid in the troubleshooting process. Oracle provides a wealth of data in the form of logs and trace files that you can use to resolve database issues, or you can go to Oracle technical support. In this section, you will learn the types of diagnostic data that Oracle provides. You'll also learn how to locate and view the information.

Lastly, you will learn about the automatic memory management options provided in Oracle 10g. As you are probably well aware, the sizing and management of SGA and PGA memory has historically been one of the most time-consuming elements in the life of a DBA. Oracle's new automatic memory management options relieve you of this task, and will do a better job. In this section, you will learn about the Automatic Shared Memory Management (ASMM) feature, which simplifies memory management for the SGA. You'll also learn about the Automatic PGA Memory Management (APMM) feature, which simplifies and optimizes PGA memory allocation.

Securing the Oracle Listener

The role of the *TNS listener* in an Oracle environment cannot be overstated. In fact, it is arguably one of the most critical elements in any Oracle environment. From a security standpoint, it is easily the most important. Yet, in spite of all this, it remains one of the least understood.

For many, listener configuration consists of little more than clicking a few selections in the `netca` utility. Afterward, testing usually consists of connecting from a remote workstation. Beyond that, little thought is given to the listener.

What they don't realize is that, in its default configuration, the Oracle listener presents an enormous security risk. The listener can be compromised in a number of ways, allowing attackers unauthorized access to your server.

In the following sections, you will learn the recommended methods of securing the listener. First, you'll get an overview of the functionality that the listener provides. You'll also learn how simple it is to manage an unprotected listener remotely. Next, you'll learn the steps to securing the listener, including listener passwords, logging, external procedure restrictions, and a few others.

This chapter is not intended to provide thorough coverage of TNS listener setup, configuration, and usage. It assumes that you already have a familiarity with Oracle Net Services and the listener. It also assumes that you are familiar with basic TCP/IP networking concepts.

An Overview of the TNS Listener

The Oracle TNS listener is a server process that provides network connectivity to the Oracle database. The listener is configured to listen for connection requests on a specified port on the database server. When an incoming connection request is received on the port, the listener will attempt to resolve the request and forward the connection information to the appropriate database instance.

A connection request will provide a username, a password, and an Oracle SID or service name. If the listener has been configured to listen for that particular SID or service name, it will forward the login information to that instance. If not, it will return an error message to the requester.

Once the database authenticates the login information, the listener will negotiate with the client to redirect their communications to another port, thus freeing up port 1521. Once the listener and the client agree on a new port, a session will be created between the client and the server on the new port.

By default, the listener will use port 1521 to listen for incoming connection requests. As you should be aware, the listener can easily be configured to use other ports instead. For this chapter, all examples assume that port 1521 is being used, unless otherwise specified.

The listener is not limited to database connections, however. It can also be used to access executable programs on the database server. This functionality, known as *external procedures*, was originally introduced to support Oracle Applications, which needed to call binary executables from within PL/SQL packages.

The Oracle listener is invoked through the *lsnrctl* program. The `lsnrctl` program resides in the `$ORACLE_HOME/bin` directory on Unix systems, and in the `%ORACLE_HOME%\bin` directory on Windows systems. This program is used to stop and start the listener. It can also be used to configure and manage the listener.

When the listener is started, it reads the contents of the `listener.ora` file, which is located in the `$ORACLE_HOME/network/admin` directory in Unix, or the `%ORACLE_HOME%\network\admin` directory in Windows, by default. The `listener.ora` file, in general, will instruct the listener as to the services for which it needs to listen. However, this is not always the case. If no `listener.ora` file is found, or if the file is empty, Oracle will use its default settings. These defaults will instruct the listener to use the TCP/IP protocol and listen on port 1521. In this configuration, the listener will not support any services at startup time. However, database instances can register themselves with the listener, if appropriately configured.

From a security standpoint, it is important to note that the listener process runs under the user ID of the owner of the `lsnrctl` executable. This is usually the `oracle` account on Unix or the `administrator` account in Windows. Therefore, if the listener is exploited by a buffer overflow or similar attack, the hacker would gain the privileges of these accounts.

But this is not the only security risk. If an intruder can simply gain access to the listener using simple management tools, any of the following could be accomplished:

- Stopping the listener
- Locking out legitimate administrators by setting a password
- Writing to any disk location available to the process owner (usually the `oracle` or `administrator` user)
- Obtaining detailed information on database and application setup
- Setting up external process definitions that allow execution of binary executables on the server

As you will see in the next section, this access is surprisingly easy to obtain if proper security measures are not in place.

Managing the Listener Remotely

The listener plays a key role in allowing external access to the Oracle database and to the database server itself. Therefore, restricting access to the listener configuration tools (for example, `lsnrctl`) seems like a logical step in securing the database server.

What many people are unaware of, however, is that the listener can be managed remotely through port 1521. The `lsnrctl` program, or a program that provides similar functionality, can be used from a remote site to manage a listener. This means that an intruder would not need to gain access to your server in order to modify your listener.

Remote management can be accomplished by simply following these steps:

1. Install Oracle software (either client or server) on a remote machine. The machine needs to have Oracle Net Services connectivity, as well as the `lsnrctl` executable.
2. On the remote machine, configure the `listener.ora` file so that it can resolve to the address of the database server. For this example, assume that the IP address of the database server is 192.168.1.200.

The following lines can be added to the `listener.ora` file to accomplish this step:

```
REMOTE_LISTENER =
  ADDRESS_LIST =
    (ADDRESS =
      (PROTOCOL = TCP)
      (HOST =192.168.1.200)
      (PORT = 1521)
    )
  )
```

You may have noticed that the syntax is identical to the syntax used in the TNSNAMES.ORA file when creating TNS aliases. In fact, that is exactly what is being done. The only difference is that no SID or service name is specified. In the preceding example, the alias name is REMOTE_LISTENER.

3. Start the `lsnrctl` program and specify the alias defined in step 2, as shown here:

```
lsnrctl remote_listener
```

The `lsnrctl` program will now be accessing the listener on the database server. It can process all commands, with the exception of the `start` command.

While remote management is a very convenient feature for managing remote servers, it also makes the server highly susceptible to outside attacks unless properly secured.

Setting the Listener Password

The most important step in securing the Oracle listener is to set a password for the listener. This step patches the biggest security hole relating to the listener—the fact that no password is required.

Setting the password for the listener can be accomplished using several different methods. The first method is to manually edit the `listener.ora` file and add the following line:

```
PASSWORDS_LISTENER = shazam
```

Obviously, you can set the password to anything you like, and Oracle recommends following standard password security conventions. Once the file has been saved, restart the listener as follows:

```
lsnrctl> reload
Connecting to (DESCRIPTION=(ADDRESS=(PROTOCOL=IPC)(KEY=EXTPROC)))
The command completed successfully
```

This process will successfully set the password, but there is one drawback that you may have already noticed: The password is stored in plaintext inside the file, another security faux pas. The second method of setting the listener password is to use the CHANGE_PASSWORD command from the lsnrctl prompt:

```
LSNRCTL> change_password
Old password:
New password:
Reenter new password:
 Connecting to (DESCRIPTION=(ADDRESS=(PROTOCOL=IPC)(KEY=EXTPROC)))
Password changed for LISTENER
The command completed successfully
```

As you can see in this example, the command prompts for the old password, if one was previously set. If not, you can just press the Enter key. You will be prompted to enter the new password and then to confirm it by entering it a second time. The command does not echo the characters back to the screen, so enter them carefully.Once the password has been set, the change must be saved, otherwise it will exist only for the duration of the current listener session. In order to save the change, you must first use the SET PASSWORD command. Because the listener is now governed by a password, certain administrative commands require that the password be set (entered) before executing. The SET PASSWORD command allows you to enter the password; then you can use the SAVE_CONFIG command to save the change to the listener.ora file, as follows:

```
LSNRCTL> set password
Password:
The command completed successfully
LSNRCTL> save_config
Connecting to (DESCRIPTION=(ADDRESS=(PROTOCOL=IPC)(KEY=EXTPROC)))
Saved LISTENER configuration parameters.
Listener Parameter File   /apps/oracle/product/10g/network/admin/listener.ora
Old Parameter File   /apps/oracle/product/10g/network/admin/listener.bak
The command completed successfully
```

Once these steps have been completed, you will notice a new section has been added to your listener.ora file. An example is shown here:

```
#----ADDED BY TNSLSNR 24-OCT-2004 10:23:01---
PASSWORDS_LISTENER = 64F4692D9E64433F
LOGGING_LISTENER = ON
#--------------------------------------------
```

As you can see, with this method, the password is stored in an encrypted format in the file.

The third method of setting the listener password is to use one of Oracle's graphical tools such as Net Manager (netmgr), Network Creation Assistant (netca), or the Oracle Enterprise Manager (EM) Database Control application.

In this chapter, all graphical examples will use the Oracle EM Database Control application.

To set the listener password using EM Database Control, follow these steps:

1. Navigate to the Database Home screen.
2. In the General section of the screen, click the listener name displayed next to the label Listener. The Listener screen (shown in Figure 14.1) appears.
3. In the General section of the screen, click the Edit button. The Edit Listener: LISTENER screen appears.
4. Click the Authentication tab (shown in Figure 14.2).
5. Enter the old password (or leave it null if there was no previous password), enter the new password, and confirm the new password where indicated.
6. Click the OK button. The Edit Confirmation: LISTENER screen appears (shown in Figure 14.3).
7. Click the OK button to restart the listener with the changes in place.

FIGURE 14.1 Oracle EM Database Control Listener screen

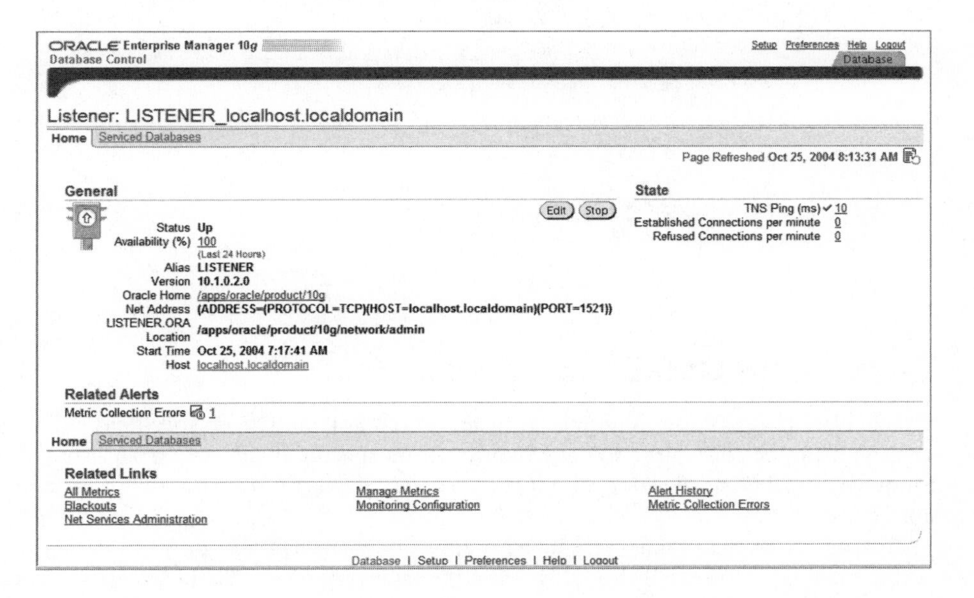

FIGURE 14.2 Oracle EM Database Control Edit Listener: LISTENER screen

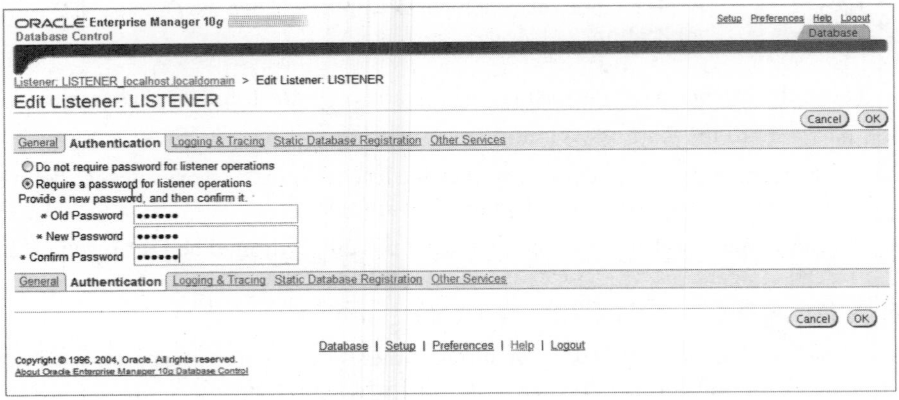

FIGURE 14.3 Oracle EM Database Control Edit Confirmation: LISTENER screen

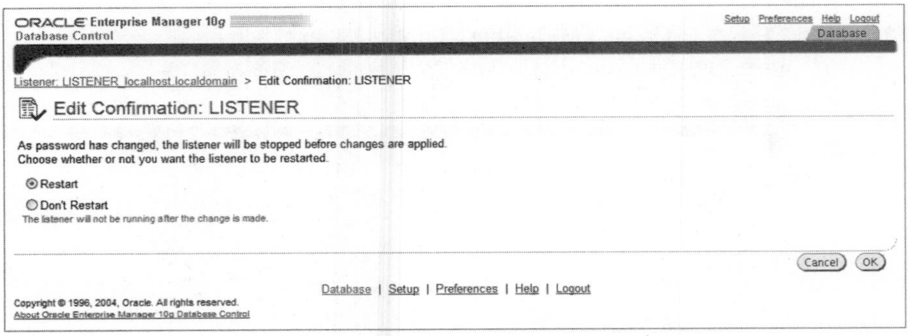

Controlling Database Access

Oracle Net Services can be configured to accept requests only from specific IP addresses. Conversely, it can be configured to deny requests from specific IP addresses. This functionality is known as *valid node checking*, and it can be a very powerful security tool in specific network configurations.

In general, databases that serve Internet applications lie behind a firewall. By design, the only access through the firewall should be from the application servers that reside in the demilitarized zone (DMZ). Figure 14.4 shows an example of this configuration.

FIGURE 14.4 Common Internet application setup

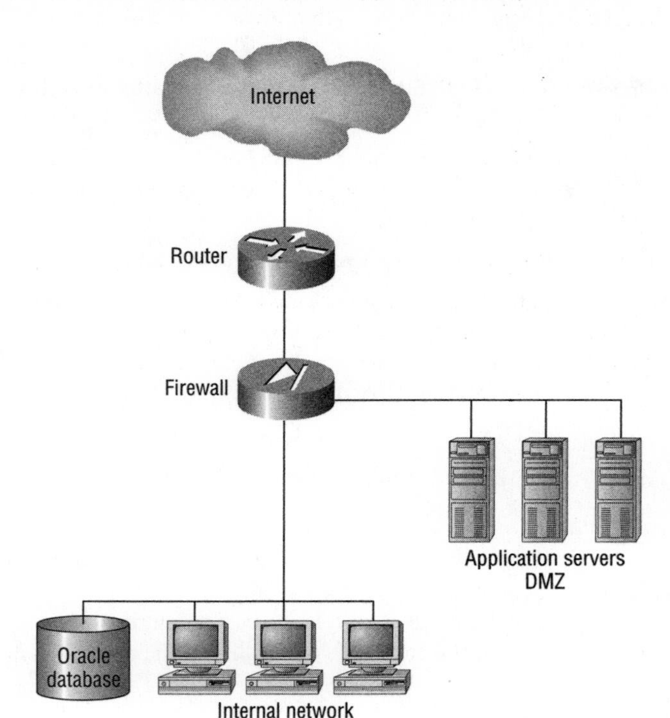

By implementing valid node checking, only requests coming from the application servers would be accepted, and all others would be denied. This measure will prevent unauthorized access from the Internet.

Valid node checking is implemented by manually modifying the `$ORACLE_HOME/network/admin/sqlnet.ora` file to add the following settings:

TCP.VALIDNODE_CHECKING This option should be set to a value of YES to enable valid node checking.

TCP.INVITED_NODES This option specifies the addresses from which requests should be accepted. These can be explicit IP addresses or host names. If host names are used, SQL*NET must have a method of resolving them (DNS, hosts file, and so on). Wildcard settings are not supported.

TCP.EXCLUDED_NODES This option specifies the addresses from which requests should not be accepted. These can be explicit IP addresses or node names. If names are used, they must be resolvable by the Oracle environment (using DNS, hosts file, and so on). Wildcard settings are not supported.

By defining the values for these options, you can control which machines have access to the database. There are, however, several important caveats that must be addressed regarding valid node checking:

- The `TCP.INVITED_NODES` and `TCP.EXCLUDED_NODES` options are mutually exclusive. Only one may be defined. Do not use both.
- Wildcard values cannot be used. Each individual host name or IP address needs to be specified. Therefore, valid node checking is not a good choice for databases being accessed by a large number of hosts (or by unknown hosts).
- If more sophisticated address verification is required, use Oracle Connection Manager.

If you can deal with these limitations, valid node checking may be a good option.

For example, to instruct the listener to accept requests only from an application server (159.158.212.1) and from the administrative team (Jeaneanne, Nicholas, Gillian, and Murphy), the following lines could be added to the `sqlnet.ora` file:

```
tcp.validnode_checking = yes
tcp.invited_nodes = (159.158.216.12, jeaneanne, nicholas,
  gillian, murphy)
```

This example assumes that each of the administrative team members have host-name aliases that match their names. IP addresses could also have been used.

To enact these changes, the listener must be restarted. Upon restarting, the listener will compare the IP address of incoming requests to the `INVITED_NODES` list. If the address is not found in the list, the request will be denied.

Using Listener Logging

The listener logging feature creates and maintains a log file showing all listener activity, including incoming requests and administrative commands. Enabling this feature is highly recommended. However, it is also imperative that you monitor the log file on a regular basis for suspicious activity.

For example, any failed password attempt on the listener will produce a TNS-01169 error message in the log file. If a brute force password attack is being used against your listener, the log file will show a high number of TNS-01169 errors. A simple shell script could be used to periodically scan the log file and count these errors. If the count exceeds a certain threshold, the script could shut down the listener and raise an alert.

The log file also shows administrative commands that have been executed on the listener (both authorized and unauthorized). Therefore, you can monitor the log file for unauthorized modifications made to the listener (such as new external process definitions to execute malicious code).

In the following sections, you will learn to enable listener logging using both the `lsnrctl` program and the EM Database Console application.

Enabling Logging Using the *lsnrctl* Program

Logging can be turned on through the `lsnrctl` program, or through any of the graphical tools mentioned earlier in the chapter. To turn on logging through `lsnrctl`, the following parameters can be used:

LOG_DIRECTORY The `LOG_DIRECTORY` parameter allows you to specify the location where the log file should be created. If this parameter is not set, Oracle will use the default location of `$ORACLE_HOME/network/log` (on Unix systems) or `%ORACLE_HOME%\network\log` (on Windows systems).

When using this parameter, make sure that the Oracle process owner has privileges to write files in this location.

LOG_FILE The `LOG_FILE` parameter allows you to specify the name of the log file. If this parameter is not specified, the name of the listener will be used, with the filename extension `.log` appended to the end. For example, if your listener uses the default name of listener, the log file name will default to `listener.log`.

LOG_STATUS The `LOG_STATUS` parameter controls whether logging is turned on or off. The parameter can be set to the values `ON` or `OFF`. When this parameter is set to a value of `ON`, logging will be enabled.

Changes made to any of these parameters take effect immediately. The listener does not need to be restarted. The following example shows how the parameters can be set:

```
LSNRCTL> set log_directory /oralogs
Connecting to (DESCRIPTION=(ADDRESS=(PROTOCOL=TCP)(HOST=linux)
   (PORT=1521)))
LISTENER parameter "log_directory" set to /oralogs
The command completed successfully
LSNRCTL> set log_file listener_lnx1.log
Connecting to (DESCRIPTION=(ADDRESS=(PROTOCOL=TCP)(HOST=linux)
   (PORT=1521)))
LISTENER parameter "log_file" set to listener_lnx1.log
The command completed successfully
LSNRCTL> set log_status on
Connecting to (DESCRIPTION=(ADDRESS=(PROTOCOL=TCP)(HOST=linux)
   (PORT=1521)))
LISTENER parameter "log_status" set to ON
The command completed successfully
```

The steps in this example would enable listener logging to a log file named `listener_lnx1.log` in the `/oralogs` directory. Remember that you also need to save the configuration to make the changes persistent.

Enabling Listener Logging Using EM Database Control

Listener logging can also be enabled through the EM Database Control application by following these steps:

1. Navigate to the Database Home screen.
2. In the General section of the screen, click the listener name displayed next to the label Listener. The Listener screen appears.
3. In the General section of the screen, click the Edit button. The Edit Listener: LISTENER screen appears.
4. Click the Logging & Tracing tab.
5. Under the Logging section, click the Logging Enabled radio button.
6. If you want to change the location or name of the log file, enter the new path and log file filename in the Log File text box. Figure 14.5 shows an example.
7. When all changes have been made, click the OK button. You will be prompted to restart the listener for the changes to take effect. Click the OK button to proceed.

FIGURE 14.5 EM Database Control Logging & Tracing screen

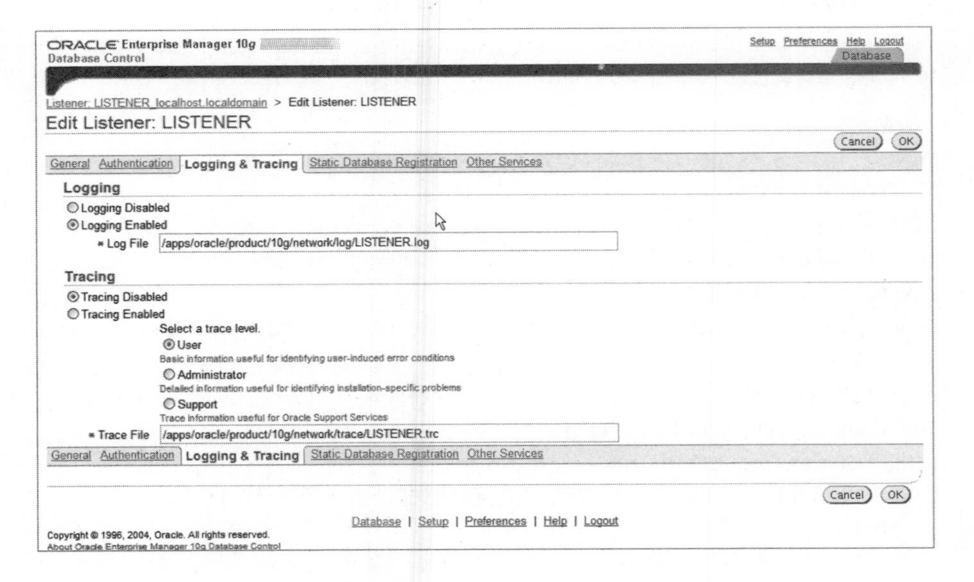

Removing Unneeded External Procedure Services

The listener can do more than just listen for database requests. It can also be used to run binary executable programs on the database server and to return the output back to the caller. This functionality is referred to as external procedure support.

By definition, an external procedure is a program called by a program that is written in a different language. For example, if a PL/SQL procedure calls a C function stored in a *shared library*, the C function would be considered an external procedure. Oracle supports external procedures that are written in C and stored in shared library objects or .DLL files.

This functionality was designed to allow command-line executables to be run from within a PL/SQL procedure. In Oracle Applications environments, this technique is commonly used. It is also used in Windows environments to implement Component Object Model (COM) functionality within Oracle.

As you can well guess, external procedure functionality poses a great security risk. Because the external procedures run with the rights of the oracle process owner, the level of damage that an unauthorized user can cause is extremely high.

An intruder may also attempt to modify the listener to define new external procedure services that could be used to execute malicious code.

By default, Oracle creates a service for external procedures in the listener. For the majority of users, this service is never used. Therefore, the service should be removed from the listener.

If your environment requires the use of external procedures, then removing the service entirely is not an option. However, there are other steps that can be taken to decrease your risk. The service can be configured under a separate listener and can be run by a less-powerful operating system account.

In the next sections, you will learn how to remove external procedure services from the listener manually and through the EM Database Control application. You will also learn how to configure external procedure services on a separate listener with greater security measures in place.

Manually Removing External Procedure Services

External procedure service definitions can be found in the listener.ora configuration file. The entry name generally will be set to PLSExtProc and the program name will be extproc.

For example, a sample listener.ora file is shown here with the external process definitions underlined:

```
# listener.ora Network Configuration File:
  /apps/oracle/oracle10gR1/network/admin/listener.ora
# Generated by Oracle configuration tools.

SID_LIST_LISTENER =
  (SID_LIST =
    (SID_DESC =
      (SID_NAME = PLSExtProc)
      (ORACLE_HOME = /apps/oracle/oracle10gR1)
      (PROGRAM = extproc)
    )
    (SID_DESC =
      (GLOBAL_DBNAME = lnx1)
```

```
      (ORACLE_HOME = /apps/oracle/oracle10g)
      (SID_NAME = lnx1)
    )
  )

LISTENER =
  (DESCRIPTION_LIST =
    (DESCRIPTION =
      (ADDRESS_LIST =
        (ADDRESS = (PROTOCOL = ICP)(KEY = EXTPROC))
      )
      (ADDRESS_LIST =
        (ADDRESS = (PROTOCOL = TCP)(HOST =lnx1)
        (PORT = 1521))
      )
    )
  )
```

As you can see, there is an entry in both sections of the file. The highlighted areas need to be removed from the file using a text editor. Make sure you delete the enclosing parentheses as well.

Whenever you are manually editing the `listener.ora` file, be very careful that the appropriate parentheses are maintained. Mismatched parentheses can cause unexpected results.

After making the changes, the file contents should look like the following example:

```
# listener.ora Network Configuration File:
  /apps/oracle/oracle10gR1/network/admin/listener.ora
# Generated by Oracle configuration tools.

SID_LIST_LISTENER =
  (SID_LIST =
    (SID_DESC =
      (GLOBAL_DBNAME = lnx1)
      (ORACLE_HOME = /apps/oracle/oracle10g)
      (SID_NAME = lnx1)
    )
  )

LISTENER =
  (DESCRIPTION_LIST =
```

```
    (DESCRIPTION =
      (ADDRESS_LIST =
        (ADDRESS = (PROTOCOL = TCP)(HOST =lnx1)
        (PORT = 1521))
      )
    )
  )
```

Removing External Procedure Services Using EM Database Control

External procedure services can also be removed through the Oracle EM Database Control application by following these steps:

1. Navigate to the Database Home screen.
2. In the General section of the screen, click the listener name displayed next to the label Listener. The Listener screen appears.
3. In the General section of the screen, click the Edit button. The Edit Listener: LISTENER screen appears.
4. Click the Other Services tab.
5. Select the row with a program name of `extproc`.
6. Click the Remove button.

The external process service should now have been removed from the listener.

Creating a Separate Listener for External Procedures

To provide higher security for external procedures, a separate listener can be configured that handles strictly external procedure requests. By separating external procedures from the standard listener functionality, you have more options in terms of securing the listener. One option is to have the new listener executed by a user with very limited operating system privileges. Another is to limit the libraries from which procedures can be executed.

In the following sections, you will learn how these options can be used to secure your environment. You will then learn how to create a new listener incorporating these methods.

Executing the Listener with a Restricted Account

The first option is to execute the new listener using an account with restricted operating system privileges. When an external process is called, the listener spawns an `extproc` agent process to execute the procedure. This process inherits the operating system privileges of the listener process owner. Therefore, by executing this listener under an account with minimal operating system privileges, the potential damage caused by an intruder is drastically reduced.

The user who executes the listener process should not have general access to files owned by the `oracle` user account. It should not have permission to read or write to database files, nor to the Oracle server address space. It needs to have read access to the `listener.ora` file and should not have write access to it. This will prevent configuration changes via the SET command in `lsnrctl` for this listener.

Limiting the Available Libraries

Another option is to explicitly define which procedure libraries can be accessed through the listener. By default, the `extproc` agent can execute procedures from any DLL or shared object library stored in the following locations:

- `$ORACLE_HOME/lib` directory in Unix
- `%ORACLE_HOME%\bin` directory in Windows

However, you can limit the listener to accessing only the libraries explicitly specified in the `listener.ora` file. This can be done by editing the file manually, or through the EM Database Control application.

Whichever method that is used, the following `listener.ora` file settings will need to be defined:

PROGRAM The PROGRAM setting specifies the name of the external procedure agent. The external procedure agent is an executable program that will call the external procedure on behalf of the listener. When finished, the agent returns the output from the procedure back to the caller.

Oracle supplies an external procedure agent named `extproc`, which is used almost exclusively. However, other agent programs can be used as well. The `extproc` agent program resides in the `%ORACLE_HOME%\bin` directory in Windows and in the `$ORACLE_HOME/lib` directory in Unix.

In Windows environments, it is a requirement that the external procedure agent must reside in the `%ORACLE_HOME%\bin` directory. Unix environments do not share this restriction.

ENVS The ENVS setting is used to define any environment variables required by the agent. These variables will be set prior to execution of the agent.

One particular environment variable that can be defined is the *EXTPROC_DLLS* variable. This environment variable is used to restrict access to DLL and shared library files for the external procedure agent.

If the ENVS setting is not defined, the agent will be able to access any DLL or shared library file in the `$ORACLE_HOME/lib` directory in Unix or the `%ORACLE_HOME%\bin` directory in Windows.

If the ENVS setting is defined, the agent's access will be governed by the rules defined in it. There are several options available for this setting:

Colon-separated list This option allows you to specify specific library files that can be accessed by the agent, in addition to those found in `$ORACLE_HOME/lib` or `%ORACLE_HOME%/bin` directories. You must specify the complete path, as well as the library name.

The libraries can be specified as a list, with a colon separating the entries, as in the following example:

```
/usr/lib/libjava.so:/apps/ora/libsql.so
```

ONLY **directive** The ONLY directive allows the agent to access only the specific libraries listed. This means that the agent is denied the default access to the libraries in the $ORACLE_HOME/lib (Unix) and %ORACLE_HOME%\bin (Windows) directories (except ones that are explicitly specified in this setting).

The ONLY directive offers the highest level of security, as it is the most restrictive.

This setting requires the ONLY directive to precede a colon-separated list of library files. You must also specify the complete path, as well as the library name, as in the following example:

```
ONLY:/usr/libjava.so:/apps/ora/libsql.so
```

ANY **directive** The ANY directive is the least restrictive of the settings. It allows access to any library file.

If you attempt to set the ENVS parameter by manually editing the listener.ora file, it is crucial that the formatting in the file is correct. Remember that the name of the environment variable must be provided, as well as the value. Also, multiple variables can be set, as long as they are separated by a comma. The entire value should be enclosed in double quotes, as in the following example:

```
(ENVS="EXTPROC_DLLS=ONLY:/usr/libjava.so:/usr/lib/libz.so,
ORACLE_SID=lnx1,PATH=$PATH:/usr/bin:/usr/sql")
```

In this example, the environment variables EXTPROC_DLLS, ORACLE_SID, and PATH are all defined.

ORACLE_HOME The ORACLE_HOME setting specifies the Oracle home location for the agent program.

SID_NAME The SID_NAME setting specifies a unique system identifier name for the external procedure agent.

Creating the Listener Using EM Database Control

The new listener can be created through the EM Database Control application by following these steps:

1. Navigate to the Database Home screen.
2. In the General section of the screen, click the host name displayed next to the label Host. The Host screen appears.
3. In the Related Links section near the bottom of the screen, click the Net Services Administration link. The Net Services Administration screen appears (shown in Figure 14.6).
4. Verify that the value Listeners appears in the Administer drop-down box and click the Go button. The Listeners screen now appears.
5. Click the Create button. The Create Listener screen appears.

FIGURE 14.6 EM Database Control Net Services Administration screen

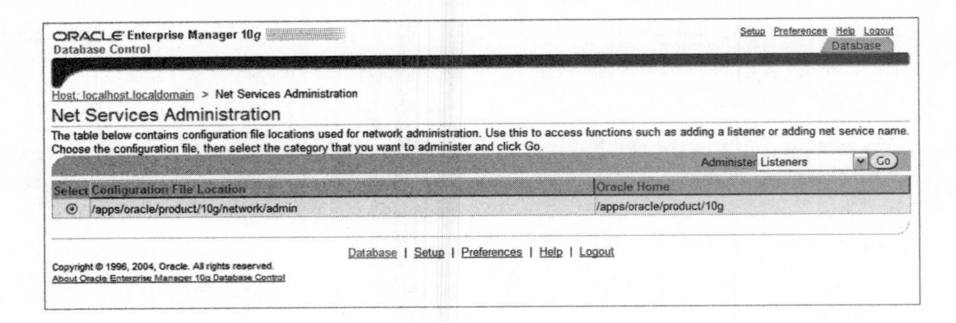

6. Enter a unique listener name in the Listener Name field.
7. In the Addresses section, click the Add button. The Add Addresses screen appears.
8. Select IPC from the Protocol drop-down list.
9. In the Key field, enter a unique key value. Oracle suggests using `extproc1` for the first listener, `extproc2` for the second listener, and so on. Click the OK button when you are done. The Create Listener screen will appear again.
10. Click the Other Services tab and then click the Add button. The Create Other Service screen appears.
11. Provide values for the Program Name, Oracle Home Directory, and Oracle System Identifier (SID) fields, as shown in Figure 14.7.

FIGURE 14.7 EM Database Control Create Other Service screen

ORACLE Enterprise Manager 10g
Database Control
Setup Preferences Help Logout
Database
Host: ir2-dbx > Net Services Administration > Listeners: /apps/oracle/oracle10gR1/network/admin > Create Listener > Create Other Service
Create Other Service
Cancel OK

Field	Value
* Program Name	extproc
Service Name	
Oracle Home Directory	/apps/oracle/oracle10g/bin
Oracle System Identifier (SID)	ext_proc
Program Argument Zero	
Program Arguments	

Environment Variables
Enter any environment variables that should be set prior to starting the service.

Name	Value	Delete

Add Another Row
Cancel OK
Database | Setup | Preferences | Help | Logout

About Oracle Enterprise Manager 10g Database Control

12. In the Environment Variables section, click the Add Another Row button.
13. Enter the value **EXTPROC_DLLS** in the Name field.
14. Enter your desired library list values in the Value field.
15. When finished adding environment variables, click the OK button. The Listeners screen should once again appear, with a message notifying you that your listener was successfully created.

Using the *ADMIN_RESTRICTIONS* Parameter

The `ADMIN_RESTRICTIONS` parameter can be set to a value of `ON` in the `listener.ora` file. This parameter disallows all SET commands executed through the `lsnrctl` program or through Oracle's graphical utilities. Therefore, when `ADMIN_RESTRICTIONS` is enabled, changes to the listener configuration can only be made by manually editing the `listener.ora` file.

Securing the Listener Directory

The directory containing the `listener.ora` and `sqlnet.ora` files should be protected so that no user (other than the Oracle administrative account) can read or write files in the directory. This is generally the `$ORACLE_HOME/network/admin` (Unix) or the `%ORACLE_HOME%\network\admin` directory (Windows).

Applying Oracle Listener Patches

Always be vigilant about applying security patches as they are released by Oracle. If the listener is susceptible to buffer overflow exploits (or similar attacks that attempt to cause the program itself to fail), the only solution may be a patched version of the program.

Blocking SQL*NET Traffic on Firewalls

Internet firewalls should be configured so that they do not allow SQL*NET traffic to pass through, except from known application servers. If the database isn't accessed by an application server, disable all SQL*NET traffic through the router. This ensures that only users on the local network will be able to access the database.

Diagnostic Sources

Database problems are unavoidable. No matter how well your system may be configured and managed, problems will still occur. As an Oracle DBA, it is your responsibility to resolve database issues in a timely manner to ensure maximum database uptime. To do this, you need to be aware of the diagnostic data that Oracle provides to aid in the troubleshooting process.

The alert log provides a high-level record of the significant events that occur in a database instance. It is not relegated to strictly logging errors. The alert log is an excellent source of diagnostic data and is generally considered the first place to check when an error occurs.

When more detailed diagnostic data is required, Oracle's tracing functionality provides an in-depth view into the internal workings of the database. *Trace files* are automatically produced when background processes encounter problem situations. Trace files can also be produced to analyze SQL execution for performance purposes. The data in these trace files can provide an overwhelming amount of diagnostic data.

In the following sections, you will learn to work with the alert log and with Oracle trace files. You'll learn what types of diagnostic data they provide, how to control their size and location, and how they can be used to troubleshoot database problems.

Using the Oracle Alert Log

A primary source of database diagnostic information is the *alert log*. The alert log is a log file created and maintained by Oracle that logs and timestamps significant events that occur in the database. These significant events include all of the following (and more):

- Administrative create, alter, and drop events
- Redo log switches
- Checkpoints (optional)
- Recovery operations
- Database startup and shutdown
- `ALTER SYSTEM` operations
- Database errors
- `DBMS_JOB` and `DBMS_SCHEDULER` job errors

Therefore, the alert log represents a valuable record of database events that can be utilized for diagnostic purposes.

In the following sections, you will learn how the alert log is used by Oracle. You will also learn how you can use the alert log for diagnostic purposes. You will see different ways of viewing alert log data, and you will learn how to search for specific entries. Lastly, you'll learn a few alert log maintenance techniques.

An Overview of the Alert Log

The alert log file is automatically created by Oracle. By default, the file will be named `alert_SID.log`, where *SID* is the Oracle system identifier. The file is created using the path identified in the `BACKGROUND_DUMP_DEST` initialization parameter. For example, assume that the following entries exist in your `init.ora` or SPFILE file:

```
DB_NAME=lnx1
BACKGROUND_DUMP_DEST=/data1/admin/lnx1/bdump
```

From this information, you can determine that the full path to your alert log would be

```
/data1/admin/lnx1/bdump/alert_lnx1.log
```

When Oracle needs to write an alert log entry, it will attempt to open this file in APPEND mode. If it isn't found, it will create a new file using the naming method described at the beginning of this section. It will then write the entry and close the file.

Alert Log Usage

The alert log can provide a wealth of information regarding your database instance. Because it stores a timestamped record of all the significant events in the database, it is invaluable as a diagnostic aid.

For example, suppose you arrive at work one morning and are immediately greeted by the boss, wondering why his nightly sales report wasn't in his e-mail inbox this morning. You check the alert log and find the following (the underlined entries will be discussed following the code):

```
Wed Oct  6 01:37:04 2004
Shutting down instance: further logons disabled
Wed Oct  6 01:37:06 2004
Stopping background process QMNC
Wed Oct  6 01:37:06 2004
Stopping background process CJQ0
Wed Oct  6 01:37:08 2004
Stopping background process MMNL
Wed Oct  6 01:37:09 2004
Stopping background process MMON
Wed Oct  6 01:37:10 2004
Shutting down instance (immediate)
License high water mark = 93
Wed Oct  6 01:37:10 2004
Stopping Job queue slave processes
Wed Oct  6 01:37:10 2004
Job queue slave processes stopped
Wed Oct  6 01:42:43 2004
Shutting down instance (abort)
License high water mark = 93
Instance terminated by USER, pid = 6132
Wed Oct  6 06:17:47 2004
Starting ORACLE instance (normal)
LICENSE_MAX_SESSION = 0
LICENSE_SESSIONS_WARNING = 0
Picked latch-free SCN scheme 3
KCCDEBUG_LEVEL = 0
Using LOG_ARCHIVE_DEST_1 parameter default value as
  /apps/oracle/oracle10gR1/dbs/arch
```

```
Autotune of undo retention is turned on.
Dynamic strands is set to TRUE
Running with 2 shared and 42 private strand(s). Zero-copy
  redo is FALSE
IMODE=BR
ILAT =42
LICENSE_MAX_USERS = 0
SYS auditing is disabled
Starting up ORACLE RDBMS Version: 10.1.0.2.0.
System parameters with non-default values:
  processes                = 350
  __shared_pool_size       = 150994944
  __large_pool_size        = 4194304
  __java_pool_size         = 8388608
  filesystemio_options     = setall
  dbwr_io_slaves           = 2
  sga_target               = 524288000
  control_files
  /data1/oradata/incdev/control01.ctl,
  /data1/oradata/incdev/control02.ctl,
  / apps/oracle/oradata/incdev/control01.ctl,
  /apps/oracle/oradata/incdev/control02.ctl
  db_block_size            = 8192
  __db_cache_size          = 356515840
  compatible               = 10.1.0.2.0
  log_buffer               = 2097152
  db_file_multiblock_read_count= 16
  undo_management          = AUTO
  undo_tablespace          = UNDOTBS1
  remote_login_passwordfile= EXCLUSIVE
  db_domain                =
  dispatchers              = (PROTOCOL=TCP)
   (SERVICE=irdbXDB)
  job_queue_processes      = 3
  background_dump_dest     = /data1/admin/incdev/bdump
  user_dump_dest           = /data1/admin/incdev/udump
  max_dump_file_size       = 250M
  core_dump_dest           = /data1/admin/incdev/cdump
  sort_area_size           = 65536
  db_name                  = incdev
```

```
  open_cursors             = 1500
  optimizer_mode           = CHOOSE
  parallel_automatic_tuning= TRUE
  pga_aggregate_target     = 262144000
Deprecated system parameters with specified values:
  parallel_automatic_tuning
End of deprecated system parameter listing
PMON started with pid=2, OS id=6136
MMAN started with pid=3, OS id=6138
DBW0 started with pid=4, OS id=6140
LGWR started with pid=5, OS id=6142
CKPT started with pid=6, OS id=6144
SMON started with pid=7, OS id=6146
RECO started with pid=8, OS id=6148
Wed Oct  6 06:17:50 2004
starting up 1 dispatcher(s) for network address
  '(ADDRESS=(PARTIAL=YES)(PROTOCOL=TCP))'...
CJQ0 started with pid=9, OS id=6150
Wed Oct  6 06:17:51 2004
starting up 1 shared server(s) ...
Wed Oct  6 06:17:51 2004
ALTER DATABASE   MOUNT
Wed Oct  6 06:17:51 2004
Controlfile identified with block size 16384
Wed Oct  6 06:17:55 2004
Setting recovery target incarnation to 1
Wed Oct  6 06:17:55 2004
Successful mount of redo thread 1, with mount id 2177287387
Wed Oct  6 06:17:55 2004
Database mounted in Exclusive Mode.
Completed: ALTER DATABASE   MOUNT
Wed Oct  6 06:17:56 2004
ALTER DATABASE OPEN
Wed Oct  6 06:17:56 2004
Beginning crash recovery of 1 threads
 attempting to start a parallel recovery with 3 processes
 parallel recovery started with 3 processes
Wed Oct  6 06:17:57 2004
Started first pass scan
Wed Oct  6 06:17:57 2004
```

```
Completed first pass scan
 4 redo blocks read, 3 data blocks need recovery
Wed Oct  6 06:17:57 2004
Started redo application at
 Thread 1: logseq 88, block 64844, scn 0.0
Recovery of Online Redo Log: Thread 1 Group 1 Seq 88 Reading mem 0
  Mem# 0 errs 0: /data1/oradata/incdev/redo01.log
  Mem# 1 errs 0: /apps/oracle/oradata/incdev/redo01.log
Wed Oct  6 06:17:57 2004
Completed redo application
Wed Oct  6 06:17:58 2004
Completed crash recovery at
 Thread 1: logseq 88, block 64848, scn 0.1205991
 3 data blocks read, 3 data blocks written, 4 redo blocks read
Wed Oct  6 06:17:59 2004
Thread 1 advanced to log sequence 89
Maximum redo generation record size = 132096 bytes
Maximum redo generation change vector size = 116476 bytes
Private_strands 19 at log switch
Thread 1 opened at log sequence 89
  Current log# 2 seq# 89 mem# 0: /data1/oradata/incdev/redo02.log
  Current log# 2 seq# 89 mem# 1: /apps/oracle/oradata/incdev/redo02.log
Successful open of redo thread 1
Wed Oct  6 06:17:59 2004
MTTR advisory is disabled because FAST_START_MTTR_TARGET is not set
Wed Oct  6 06:17:59 2004
SMON: enabling cache recovery
Wed Oct  6 06:18:00 2004
Successfully onlined Undo Tablespace 1.
Wed Oct  6 06:18:00 2004
SMON: enabling tx recovery
Wed Oct  6 06:18:00 2004
Database Characterset is WE8ISO8859P1
Wed Oct  6 06:18:00 2004
Published database character set on system events channel
Wed Oct  6 06:18:00 2004
All processes have switched to database character set
Wed Oct  6 06:18:04 2004
Starting background process QMNC
QMNC started with pid=19, OS id=6170
```

```
Wed Oct  6 06:18:05 2004
replication_dependency_tracking turned off (no async
  ➥multimaster replication found)
Wed Oct  6 06:18:06 2004
Starting background process MMON
Starting background process MMNL
MMON started with pid=20, OS id=6172
MMNL started with pid=21, OS id=6174
Wed Oct  6 06:18:07 2004
Completed: ALTER DATABASE OPEN
```

From the information in this alert log, you can determine a great deal of detailed information regarding the events of the previous night (note that each number in the following list represents a highlighted section in the preceding alert log snippet):

1. At 1:37:04 A.M., the database was issued a `shutdown` command (most likely using the `immediate` clause, because it mentions that further logons are disabled).
2. Six seconds later (at 1:37:10 A.M.), you can confirm that it was indeed a `shutdown immediate` request. You can also see that the licensing high water mark reached 93 for the duration of the instance.
3. About five minutes later, at 1:42:43 A.M., you can see that the `shutdown immediate` request was replaced with a `shutdown abort` request. Apparently, whoever was shutting down the instance got tired of waiting for things to shut down gracefully.

   Just below that, you'll find the entry:

   ```
   instance terminated by USER, pid = 6132
   ```

   While this entry doesn't necessarily identify which user was responsible, it does confirm that it was indeed a user process that issued the `shutdown` command. If this line had identified a background process name such as PMON or SMON, we could surmise that the background process had an error that forced the instance to be shut down. You could then look to the appropriate process trace file for details.
4. At 6:17:47 A.M., the database was restarted. You can see the startup process as it occurs. You can also see the initialization parameters used at startup time.
5. You can see that the instance has a deprecated initialization parameter (`parallel_automatic_tuning`) defined. This parameter should be removed from your `init.ora` file.
6. At 6:17:56 A.M., Oracle started crash recovery on the instance. This is standard whenever an instance is brought down with the abort option.
7. At 6:17:58 A.M., Oracle completed the crash recovery and continued with the instance startup procedures.
8. At 6:18:07 A.M., the database was opened successfully.

As you can see, the alert log provides you with a wealth of information about your database, much of which is not available by any other means.

Checking the Alert Log Using EM Database Control

The alert log should be checked on a daily basis for errors or other events that may have occurred without your knowledge. To view the alert log, you can open the file directly through the operating system using any text editor or viewer. To view the alert log through the EM Database Control application, do the following:

1. Navigate to the Database Home screen.
2. Under Related Links at the bottom of the screen, select Alert Log Content. The contents of the alert log will be displayed on the screen, as shown in Figure 14.8.

Be aware that when viewing the alert log content through EM Database Control, only 100K of data will be displayed. Therefore, the entire contents of the file may not be viewable.

Viewing Alert Log Entries in the Database

If you prefer to view alert log data through the database itself, you can take advantage of Oracle's external tables feature. This technique creates a table named ALERT_LOG that will access the alert log file stored externally to the database. Keep in mind that this is just one of the many ways in which this can be accomplished.

FIGURE 14.8 EM Database Control Most Recent Alert Log Entries screen

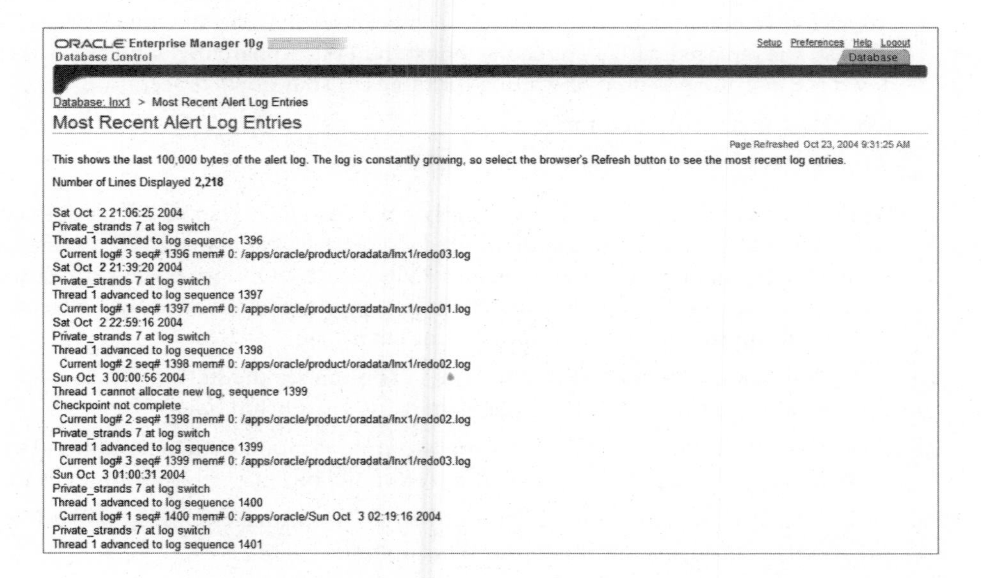

To create the table, you must first create a directory object that references the location of the alert log file. Remember that this will be the location defined in the BACKGROUND_DUMP_DEST initialization parameter. Here's an example:

```
SQL> create directory BDUMP as '/data1/admin/lnx1/bdump';

Directory created.
```

Next, you can create the table, referencing the directory object that you just created. The table will have a single column named log_line that holds one line of the alert log, as shown here:

```
SQL> create table alert_log ( log_line varchar2(80) )
   organization external (
   type oracle_loader
   default directory BDUMP
   access parameters (records delimited by newline)
   location('alert_lnx1.log')
   )
   reject limit 1000;

Table created.
```

The table can now be queried, as follows:

```
SQL> select * from alert_log
     where log_line like '%ORA-%';

LOG_LINE
-----------------------------------------------------------
ORA-12012: error on auto execute of job 756
ORA-04068: existing state of packages has been discarded
ORA-04063: package body "JNEXUS.PKG_AC_DIFF" has errors
ORA-06508: PL/SQL: could not find program unit being called
ORA-06512: at line 1

5 rows selected.
```

In this example, you can see that five lines contained ORA errors.

Keep in mind that the preceding example does not represent a thorough search of the alert log. The file may contain warnings, actions, or errors that do not contain the string ORA- in the text.

Maintaining Historical Alert Log Data

Early in my DBA career, I created a simple web-based tool to allow me to perform certain administrative functions from a browser (this was back before Enterprise Manager was available through a browser). One of the functions I wanted to be able to perform was to browse the alert log and search for ORA errors. To accomplish this, the alert log data was loaded into a database table on a nightly basis.

This functionality worked well, and I was happy with the results. However, I never got around to coding any maintenance routines to purge the old data, so my historical data grew quite large. This wasn't a requirement, just the product of my laziness.

As fate would have it, my boss came to me with a strange request. Apparently, our applications group was having ongoing issues with a third-party application that had been installed about six months earlier. The vendor was trying to convince my boss that the problems were due to a certain Oracle error that could occur when their application was installed. In other words, he was saying that it wasn't their problem; it was our problem.

"If you can track down your old alert logs," he said, "you'll see that I'm right. There will be an ORA error." Our suspicion was that he was trying to buy time, assuming that we'd have to restore backup tapes and pore through files for some time.

I knew that my application had been collecting the alert log data for some time, but I wasn't sure how far back it went. I asked for the date, keyed it into my application, and Shazam! There it was. We searched through the log file and located a `CREATE TABLESPACE` command which we recognized as part of the vendor's installation procedure. However, there was no sign of the alleged Oracle error to be found. We were vindicated.

Alert Log Maintenance

As new events are recorded in the alert log, they are appended to the end of the existing alert log file. Over time, this file can grow to a significant size and therefore requires periodic maintenance to prevent this from occurring.

Alert log maintenance is relatively simple, but it requires some knowledge of the underlying mechanism used by Oracle to write to the file. When Oracle logs an event to the alert log, it performs the following operations on the file:

- Open the alert log file using `APPEND` mode. If the file exists, move the file pointer to the end of the file. If the file doesn't exist, create it.
- Write the alert data to the file.
- Close the file.

Now, compare Oracle's method with the following method:

- Mount the database.
- Open the alert log file using APPEND mode. If the file exists, move the file pointer to the end of the file. If the file doesn't exist, create it.
- Open the database.
- Write the alert data to the file as events occur.
- Close the file when database shutdown occurs.

In the first method, Oracle has almost no relationship with the alert log file. Oracle doesn't care if it even exists. It will just create a new one. The only relationship to the file is for the few microseconds that the log entry is being written.

In the second method, Oracle has a strong relationship with the file and requires that the file exist for the duration of the instance (much like a database datafile). This method would likely require file maintenance to be performed when the database is down.

Because Oracle uses the first method, maintenance is much simpler. The only real question is how long to keep the alert log data.

A historical alert log file is of dubious value, and how long alert log data should be maintained is more a question of company policy than anything else. However, as the preceding Real World Scenario testified, you never know when having historical alert log data may be useful.

As an example, let's assume that you are required to keep the last 30 days' worth of log information. Let's also assume that you want each file to represent one day of database usage. The following pseudocode could be used to build a rudimentary maintenance script:

```
1. Every night at midnight, rename the current alert log file to alert_
log.YYYYMMDD (where YYYYMMDD represents the current date).
2. Check to see if any existing logs are older than 30 days.
3. If found, delete the old logs.
4. End.
```

As you can see, the alert log file can simply be renamed (or deleted) without incident. When Oracle needs to write a new alert log entry, it will create a new one.

If searching historical alert log entries is important, you could also store alert log entries into a database table (or external table, as shown earlier in this chapter). This will allow you to use standard SQL to query the alert log history.

Using Server-Generated Alerts

A server-generated alert is a notification from Oracle that indicates a potential problem in the database. These alerts generally indicate that the threshold level for a monitored metric has been exceeded.

Server-generated alerts were covered in detail in Chapter 8, "Understanding Automatic Database Management."

By default, Oracle computes seven distinct metrics based on the contents of the alert log. Where indicated, these metrics have thresholds defined to automatically generate alerts in certain conditions. In short, this means that Oracle automatically monitors the alert log file for you and notifies you if it finds troublesome messages.

These alert log metrics include the following:

Alert log error trace file Oracle detects any references to system-generated trace files. These are generally trace files produced by a background process that encounters an error situation.

Alert log name Oracle checks the name and location of the alert log file.

Archiver hung alert log error Oracle detects any ORA-00257 messages (indicating that an ARCH archiver process is hung) in the alert log. Because a hung archiver process will suspend the database, this metric has a critical threshold set. Any appearance of an ORA-00257 message will generate a critical alert.

Data block corruption alert log error Oracle detects error messages relating to database block corruption in the alert log. This metric has a critical threshold set and will generate a critical alert when any block corruption messages appear.

Generic alert log error Oracle detects the presence of any ORA errors in the alert log. This metric has a warning threshold set and will generate a warning alert if the error is an ORA-00600.

Session-terminated alert log error Oracle detects any ORA-00603 session unexpectedly terminated messages in the alert log. This metric has a warning threshold set and will generate a warning alert if any ORA-00603 messages appear.

You can also add your own threshold settings to these metrics to instruct Oracle to monitor for other types of messages.

Server-generated alerts can be viewed through EM Database Control by following these steps:

1. Navigate to the Database Home screen.
2. In the Alerts section of the screen, you can see the most recent server-generated alert notifications, as shown in Figure 14.9.
3. If any alert log messages are found in this section, you can click the message to see further details. If not, click the Alert History link at the bottom of the screen to display the Alert History screen.
4. Under the Metric column, look for an entry labeled Generic Alert Log Error Status. If one is found, click it. The Generic Alert Log Error Status screen is displayed, as shown in Figure 14.10. This screen shows you the appearances of ORA messages in the alert log.

FIGURE 14.9 EM Database Control Alerts screen

Alerts

Severity	Category	Name	Message	Alert Triggered	Last Value	Time
⚠	Waits by Wait Class	Database Time Spent Waiting (%)	Metrics "Database Time Spent Waiting (%)" is at 100 for event class "Other"	Oct 29, 2004 12:43:07 PM	97	Nov 3, 2004 9:53:28 AM
⚠	User Audit	Audited User	User SYS logged on from ir2-dbx.	Nov 3, 2004 10:00:40 AM	0	Nov 3, 2004 10:00:40 AM
⚠	Invalid Objects by Schema	Owner's Invalid Object Count	19 object(s) are invalid in the PUBLIC schema.	Oct 29, 2004 12:51:47 PM	19	Oct 29, 2004 12:51:47 PM
⚠	Invalid Objects by Schema	Owner's Invalid Object Count	92 object(s) are invalid in the SE_IROWNER schema.	Oct 29, 2004 12:51:47 PM	92	Oct 29, 2004 12:51:47 PM
⚠	Invalid Objects by Schema	Owner's Invalid Object Count	84 object(s) are invalid in the STAGING_IROWNER schema.	Oct 29, 2004 12:51:47 PM	84	Oct 29, 2004 12:51:47 PM
⚠	Invalid Objects by Schema	Owner's Invalid Object Count	21 object(s) are invalid in the SYS schema.	Oct 29, 2004 12:51:47 PM	21	Oct 29, 2004 12:51:47 PM

Related Alerts

Severity	Target Name	Target Type	Category	Name	Message	Alert Triggered	Last Value	Time
(No alerts)								

Performance Analysis

Period Start Time **Nov 3, 2004 9:00:54 AM** Period Duration (minutes) **59.6**

Impact (%)	Finding	Recommendations
99.9	Wait class "Other" was consuming significant database time.	
98.89	Wait event "i/o slave wait" in wait class "Other" was consuming significant database time.	2 Application Analysis

FIGURE 14.10 EM Database Control Generic Alert Log Error Status screen

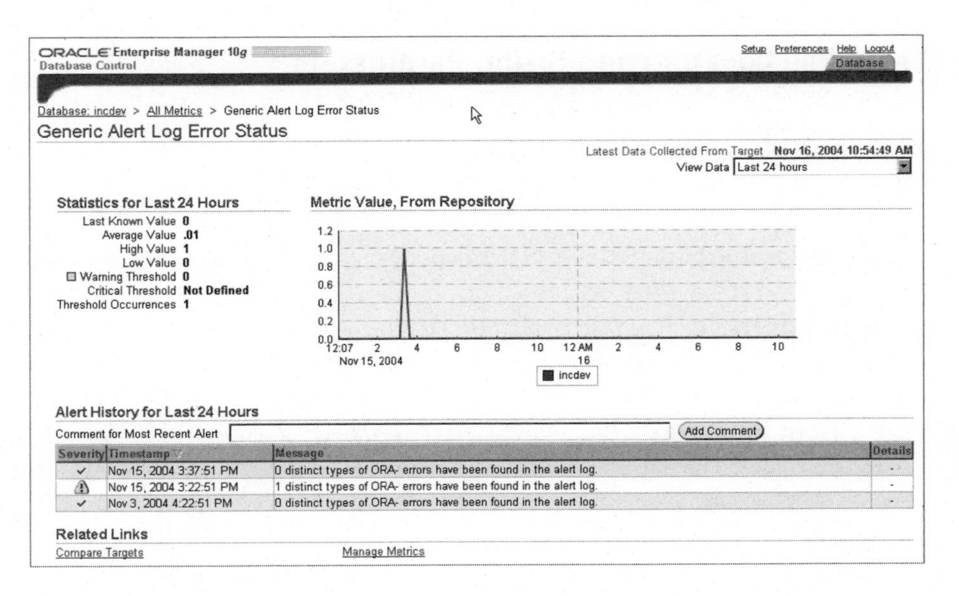

Using Oracle Trace Files

When an Oracle *background process* encounters an error situation, it will generate a trace file. The trace file contains in-depth details about the error and the state of the process at the time of the error. These trace files are intended to help you and/or Oracle Support to diagnose the cause of the error.

However, tracing is not delegated strictly to error diagnosis, as you are probably well aware. Oracle's *SQL trace* functionality allows you to trace user processes (sessions) as well. SQL trace produces incredibly detailed output of all SQL executed by a session (or for all sessions, if enabled). These trace files can be used to diagnose poorly performing SQL statements. They can also help you locate inefficient code in applications such as excessive parsing, unnecessary database calls, and so on.

In the following sections, you will learn how to control the location and sizing of trace files. You'll also learn the naming conventions Oracle follows when creating trace files. Next, you'll learn how to add an identifier to user session trace files to make them easier to identify.

Please note that the purpose of this section is not to analyze the contents of trace files. That is beyond the scope of this book.

Trace File Location and Sizing Parameters

The location and sizing of trace files is controlled by the following initialization parameters:

BACKGROUND_DUMP_DEST The *BACKGROUND_DUMP_DEST* parameter defines the operating system path where background process trace files will be created. Trace files associated with parallel query slave processes and job queue processes are also created in this location.

This also happens to be the location of the alert log file. This is because Oracle classifies the alert log as a special type of trace file.

USER_DUMP_DEST The *USER_DUMP_DEST* parameter defines the operating system path where user session trace files will be created. User session trace files are created automatically when the SQL trace feature is enabled for a session (or for the instance).

MAX_DUMP_FILE_SIZE The *MAX_DUMP_FILE_SIZE* parameter specifies the maximum size for trace files. The default value for this parameter is `UNLIMITED`, which places no restriction on trace file size.

This parameter applies to all types of trace files.

If a value is specified for this parameter, it must be a numeric value, optionally suffixed with the letter `K` (specifying kilobytes) or the letter `M` (specifying megabytes). If no suffix is provided, the value will be interpreted as number of blocks.

When a session trace file reaches the maximum size, tracing will cease. The resultant trace file is truncated at the point when it reached maximum size. This can result in important tracing data being lost.

Trace File Naming

Oracle trace files receive system-generated filenames. These names follow one of two formatting conventions, depending on the type of process being traced. Background processes use this format:

sid_process_name_process_id.trc

User processes use this format:

*sid*_ora_*process_id*.trc

Table 14.1 shows some examples.

TABLE 14.1 Trace File Naming Examples

SID	Session Type	PID	Trace File Name	Trace File Location
lnx1	User	12995	lnx1_ora_12995.trc	USER_DUMP_DEST
lnx1	PMON	1766	lnx1_pmon_1766.trc	BACKGROUND_DUMP_DEST
lnx1	User	4867	lnx1_ora_4867.trc	USER_DUMP_DEST
lnx1	LGWR	2247	lnx1_lgwr_2247.trc	BACKGROUND_DUMP_DEST

Given Oracle's somewhat cryptic file-naming conventions, it can be difficult to locate a specific trace file, unless you happen to know the process ID for the session. To alleviate this problem, the *TRACEFILE_IDENTIFIER* parameter can be used.

The TRACEFILE_IDENTIFIER parameter allows you specify a text string that will be appended to the names of user session trace files. This identifier makes it easier to locate specific trace files, especially on busy systems.

For example, suppose you have a script that runs each night at midnight. It usually runs in about five minutes, but lately it has been taking considerably longer to finish. You decide to use SQL tracing to diagnose the problem. At the beginning of your SQL script, add the following lines:

```
ALTER SESSION SET SQLTRACE = TRUE
ALTER SESSION SET TIMED_STATISTICS = TRUE
ALTER SESSION SET TRACEFILE_IDENTIFIER = 'TIM'
```

Assuming that the process ID for your job was 10322, you should find a file named lnx1_ora-10322_TIM.trc in the USER_DUMP_DEST directory.

The TRACEFILE_IDENTIFIER parameter applies only to user session trace files. It has no effect on background process trace files.

Automatic Memory Management

Oracle performance (and, for that matter, computer performance in general) can be summed up in two basic tenets:

- Memory is fast.
- Disk is slow.

In fact, accessing data from memory tends to be approximately 10,000 times faster than accessing data from disk. So why is disk usage so prevalent if it is so slow? This is because of a couple of other basic tenets:

- Memory is expensive.
- Disk is cheap.

The terms "expensive" and "cheap" carry a deeper connotation than simply the purchase price. They also refer to the availability of the item. In fact, it might be more accurate to say that memory is scarce, while disk is plentiful.

For example, consider Oscar, the avid fisherman. He lives an hour away from the nearest lake, and he is growing tired of the long drive. Oscar decides to buy a house on the lakefront, thereby making access to the lake nearly instantaneous. When he contacts his realtor, however, he is shocked to discover that only one small property is for sale, and the price is astronomical.

Lakefront property is limited and, therefore very expensive. In the same way, servers are limited in the amount of memory that they can physically accommodate. Likewise, CPUs are limited in the amount of memory that they can address. Once these limits are reached on a server, the price of memory is a moot point. No more can be added, just as no new property can be added to the lakefront.

Memory management, therefore, is a critical element in any Oracle environment. If the database has insufficient memory to meet its needs, performance will suffer. Conversely, if too much memory is allocated to a little-used memory structure, valuable resources are wasted.

To make matters worse, Oracle uses a myriad of memory pools, each specific to a particular class of memory allocation requests. For example, the Java pool handles Java-related requests, while the library cache (part of the shared pool) stores SQL statements and PL/SQL procedures and packages. And because memory needs fluctuate constantly as workloads change, monitoring memory allocation and usage could easily become a full-time job.

To meet these challenges, Oracle 10*g* introduced *Automatic Shared Memory Management (ASMM)* and *Automatic PGA Memory Management (APMM)*. Instead of allocating memory to a myriad of diverse memory structures, and constantly monitoring those components for changes in demand, Oracle's automatic memory management features greatly simplify the process of memory management.

In the following sections, you will learn how to configure Oracle's ASMM functionality to provide dynamic SGA memory allocation and management for the database. You'll also learn to configure APMM to provide dynamic PGA memory allocation and management.

Oracle Memory Usage

Oracle classifies available memory into one of two memory structures: the *System Global Area (SGA)* or the *Program Global Area (PGA)*. Within each of these structures, Oracle divides available memory into smaller structures known as pools, each designated to satisfy a particular class of memory allocation request.

In the following sections, you will be given an overview of the SGA and the PGA. You will also learn how Oracle simplifies the management of these memory structures through ASMM and APMM.

An Overview of the SGA

The System Global Area (SGA) is the largest single memory structure in an Oracle database instance. It handles the majority of Oracle's memory needs. Internally, the SGA is divided into a series of smaller memory pools such as the database buffer cache, shared pool, large pool, Java pool, streams pool, and the redo log buffer. Each of these pools handles specific types of memory requests, as discussed next.

Database Buffer Cache

The database buffer cache is a shared memory component that stores data blocks retrieved from datafiles. When an Oracle operation requires a data block from a datafile, it will first check to see if a copy of the block is currently residing in the database buffer cache. If the block is found, the operation does not need to perform a disk read operation to retrieve the block. This situation is referred to as a cache hit, and the I/O operation is classified as a logical I/O (LIO).

If the block is not found in the buffer cache, it is referred to as a cache miss and results in a physical I/O (PIO) operation (a disk read) being performed. As you should well know, LIOs are much faster than PIOs. However, keep in mind that blocks retrieved through LIOs had to have been retrieved by a PIO at some time in the past.

Memory in the database buffer cache is tracked by two internal lists: the write list and the least recently used (LRU) list.

The write list tracks dirty blocks. These are blocks whose data has been modified. When a DML statement is executed, the blocks are modified in the buffer cache, not in the datafile itself. They must be written back to the datafile at some point. The write list keeps track of these blocks until a database writer (DBW0) process can write them back to the datafile.

The LRU list is a FIFO (first in, first out) list used to age out the least recently used blocks from the buffer cache. The LRU list also tracks unused memory buffers in the database buffer cache.

When a block needs to be read into the buffer cache, Oracle must first find a free buffer in which to store the block. The process searches the LRU list, beginning at the least recently used end. It will search until it finds a free buffer. If it cannot find any, it will signal the DBW0 process to flush any dirty blocks back to disk in order to make room. If no dirty blocks exist, the least recently used block will be aged out to make room. The block will then be written to the buffer, and the buffer moves to the most recently used end of the LRU list.

The exception to this rule is when a full table scan operation is performed. Blocks retrieved from a full table scan are added to the least recently used end of the LRU list, so they will be aged out quickly. This is because full table scan blocks are generally scanned quickly and are no longer needed. This functionality can cause problems for small tables that are accessed frequently, such as lookup tables. Small tables are meant to be accessed via full table scans. This is because a full table scan will outperform an index lookup on a very small table.

Because Oracle 10*g* will put these blocks at the least recently used end of the LRU list, they will age out quickly. As a result, the next time that the table is accessed, Oracle 10*g* may likely have to perform PIO to retrieve the blocks again. In this situation, you can add the `CACHE` clause to the table (either via `ALTER TABLE` or in the `CREATE TABLE` statements) to circumvent this behavior. You can also choose to pin the table in memory.

Shared Pool

The shared pool contains the library cache and the data dictionary cache, as well as buffers for parallel execution messages and other control structures.

Library Cache

The library cache holds shared SQL areas, PL/SQL procedures and packages, and associated control structures such as library cache handles and locks. In a shared server environment, the library cache also holds private SQL areas.

When a SQL statement is parsed, the resultant parse tree and execution plan are stored (along with the statement itself) in a shared SQL area. Therefore, future executions of the statement need not be parsed, but can be executed immediately. The library cache uses a special LRU algorithm to age out shared SQL areas to make room for new entries.

PL/SQL program units are treated similarly to SQL statements within Oracle. A shared area is used to store the compiled and parsed code, while a private area is used to hold session-specific values such as program arguments and variables. SQL statements executed within a PL/SQL program unit will utilize shared SQL areas, just like individual SQL statements.

Data Dictionary Cache

The data dictionary cache stores rows from data dictionary tables and views. Because it stores rows, rather than blocks, it is also referred to as the row cache.

Because data dictionary objects are queried very frequently, caching data dictionary rows is crucial to performance. Therefore, it was allotted its own cache dedicated solely to data dictionary data.

Redo Log Buffer

The redo log buffer holds information about all changes made to the database via `INSERT`, `UPDATE`, `DELETE`, `CREATE`, `ALTER`, or `DROP` operations. The information is stored as a series of timestamped records called redo entries. These redo entries are what make point-in-time recovery operations possible.

The redo log buffer holds these changes until the log writer (LGWR) process can write the redo entries to redo log files.

Java Pool

The Java pool provides memory for all session-specific Java code and data within the Java Virtual Machine (JVM). An internal advisor known as the Java Pool Advisor maintains statistics on Java memory usage, which can be used to manage and tune the Java pool.

Large Pool

The large pool is an optional memory area that can be allocated to increase performance for the following:

- Shared server environments
- Oracle XA Distributed Transaction Processing
- Oracle backup and restore operations

Memory requests in these situations tend to be larger (several hundred kilobytes, on average). Rather than forcing the shared pool to deal with these requests, the large pool can handle them, and do so more efficiently.

Streams Pool

The streams pool is an optional pool dedicated to handling memory requests for Oracle streams. Like the large pool, the streams pool can relieve the shared pool of the added overhead of dealing with streams memory requests. However, in environments where Oracle streams functionality is not utilized, the pool is unnecessary.

Fixed SGA

The fixed SGA area stores information relating to the state of the database instance and is primarily accessed by Oracle's background processes. Dynamic performance data is stored in fixed tables (V$ tables) in this area.

With all of these diverse structures requiring memory allocation and with the constant fluctuations in workload requirements, manual memory management of the SGA is a difficult and time-consuming task. ASMM simplifies these tasks by dynamically sizing SGA elements to ensure that each has the resources needed to meet demand.

An Overview of the PGA

A Program Global Area (PGA) stores data and control information for a single server process. Therefore, every session and background process has an associated PGA.

Because PGA memory is specific to a single process, it is not shared with any other process. Internally, each PGA houses two smaller memory structures: the private SQL area and the SQL work area.

Private SQL area The private SQL area is used to hold runtime memory structures and bind variables for SQL and PL/SQL executed by the process.

SQL work area The SQL work area provides memory in which SQL operations can be performed. Complex queries often perform memory-intensive operations such as sort operations, hash-joins, bitmap merges, bitmap creates, and bulk load operations. If insufficient memory is available to these operations, they will have to utilize disk for temporary segment storage to complete the operation. There is a huge performance penalty when this situation occurs.

Appropriate sizing of the SQL work area has historically been problematic due to the fact that every process would receive an identical allocation. For example, let's say that your current SORT_AREA_SIZE initialization parameter is set to 64K. You notice that large sort operations seem to take excessive time and suspect (correctly so) that disk sorts are occurring. To remedy the situation, you boost the SORT_AREA_SIZE setting to 4MB. With the new setting, the sorts can be performed in memory and run much faster.

So what's the problem? The problem lies in the fact that this increase in sort space is allocated to every server process, not just to the handful of users who run large sorts. On a relatively busy system, it is not uncommon to have over 500 server processes running. This being the case, 2GB (500 × 4MB) of memory is consumed.

To alleviate PGA memory management issues, Oracle's APMM functionality can be implemented to allow Oracle to automatically manage PGA memory allocation.

An Overview of Automatic Memory Management

To alleviate memory sizing issues, Oracle 10*g* provides two automatic memory management features:

- Automatic Shared Memory Management (ASMM) simplifies configuration of the SGA by allowing you to specify the total size of the SGA without worrying about the underlying memory structures. ASMM handles all the details of monitoring memory usage by the internal structures and allocating memory to each in order to meet demands.
- Automatic PGA Memory Management (APMM) eliminates the problems of PGA sizing by allowing you to specify a single memory allocation for the entire database instance. APMM allocates memory to sessions on an as-needed basis to meet their SQL work area needs.

Using ASMM

To take advantage of Oracle's ASMM functionality requires the setting of only a single initialization parameter: *SGA_TARGET*. The SGA_TARGET parameter specifies the total memory size for the SGA. The memory allocated through this setting is managed by Oracle to meet the needs of all the underlying memory structures.

By default, the SGA_TARGET parameter is set to a value of zero. A setting of zero indicates that ASMM is not enabled for the instance. In this case, Oracle looks to the values set in traditional initialization parameters such as SHARED_POOL_SIZE, JAVA_POOL_SIZE, and so on.

A non-zero value in the SGA_TARGET parameter indicates that ASMM is enabled. It is also imperative that the STATISTICS_LEVEL parameter is set to a value of either TYPICAL (the default value) or ALL. If the STATISTICS_LEVEL parameter is set to value of BASIC, ASMM will not be enabled.

ASMM divides the SGA memory pools into two groups: *automatically sized components* and *manually sized components*.

Automatically sized components are SGA memory pools for which ASMM will provide automatic sizing functionality. These are considered by Oracle to be the SGA components that have the most impact on database performance.

The automatically sized components are

- Database buffer cache
- Shared pool
- Large pool
- Java pool

Keep in mind that some of these higher level components also contain subcomponents that are also automatically sized. For example, both the library cache and data dictionary cache are contained in the shared pool; therefore, they are also automatically sized by ASMM.

In previous versions of Oracle, the initialization parameters DB_CACHE_SIZE, SHARED_POOL_SIZE, LARGE_POOL_SIZE, and JAVA_POOL_SIZE were used to size these SGA components. These parameters are, in fact, still valid initialization file parameters in Oracle 10*g*. However, the purpose that they serve depends on whether ASMM is enabled or not.

If ASMM is not enabled, these parameters will behave as they did in previous versions of Oracle. This means that the values set for these parameters will define the amount of memory allocated to each component.

However, when ASMM is enabled, a non-zero value in any of these parameters is interpreted as a minimum memory allocation for the component. For example, if the value for the SGA_TARGET parameter is 12G, and the value for the DB_CACHE_SIZE parameter is 4G, ASMM will never shrink the database buffer cache to a size smaller than 4GB, even if the memory would be better utilized elsewhere.

Manually sized components are SGA components that are not automatically sized by ASMM. These components continue to be sized using the traditional initialization parameter settings.

These components are

- Streams pool
- Keep buffer cache
- Recycle buffer cache
- Other caches

Unlike the automatically sized components, these components are sized based strictly on the setting of their associated initialization file parameters. These parameters include

- DB_KEEP_CACHE_SIZE
- DB_RECYCLE_CACHE_SIZE
- DB_*n*K_CACHE_SIZE (where *n* = 2, 4, 8, 16, or 32)
- STREAMS_POOL_SIZE

Any memory allocations made to these components are taken from the total memory allocated in the SGA_TARGET parameter. For example, suppose your initialization file contained the following directives:

```
SGA_TARGET=10G
DB_RECYCLE_CACHE_SIZE=1G
```

The recycle cache would be statically sized at 1GB. That amount is deducted from the total SGA_TARGET amount, leaving 9GB to be allocated to the automatically sized components.

As you have already seen, ASMM can be implemented by simply setting the initialization parameter SGA_TARGET to a non-zero value. This can be done in the `init.ora` file, or by using the `ALTER SYSTEM` statement.

ASMM can also be configured through the EM Database Control application by following these steps:

1. Navigate to the Database Home screen.
2. Click the Administration tab. The Administration screen now appears.
3. Under the Instance heading, select Memory Parameters. The Memory Parameters screen appears.
4. Click the SGA tab.
5. Click the Enable button to enable ASMM. The Enable Automatic Shared Memory Management screen (see Figure 14.11) appears.
6. A new value can be entered for the SGA size can be entered, if desired. It can also be left at the same amount.
7. Click the OK button to activate the change.

FIGURE 14.11 EM Database Control Enable Automatic Shared Memory Management screen

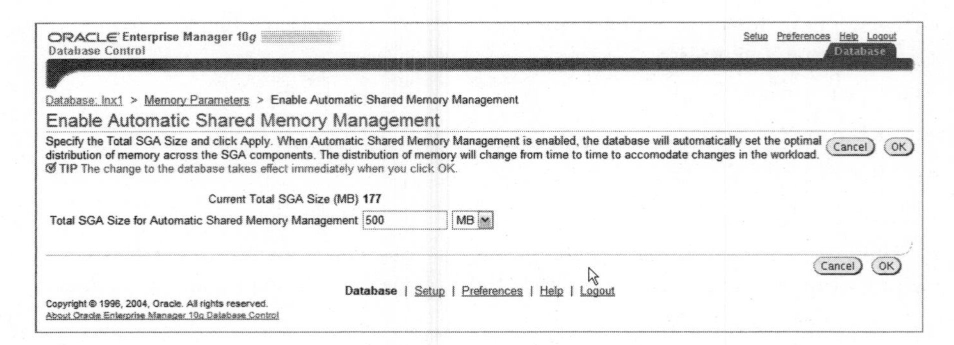

Using APMM

APMM functionality is implemented through the use of the *PGA_AGGREGATE_TARGET* initialization parameter. The memory allocated to APMM through this parameter is dynamically managed by Oracle and allocated to meet the SQL work area requirements of all Oracle sessions.

APMM is always enabled (although the functionality can be overridden). If the PGA_AGGREGATE_TARGET parameter is not explicitly set, it will default to either 10MB or 20 percent of the SGA size, whichever is larger.

Historically, PGA memory allocation has been done through the use of the following initialization parameters:

- SORT_AREA_SIZE
- HASH_AREA_SIZE
- BITMAP_MERGE_AREA_SIZE
- CREATE_BITMAP_AREA_SIZE

In Oracle 10*g*, these parameters are still valid, although their use is not encouraged. These parameters can be used in conjunction with the WORKAREA_SIZE_POLICY parameter to override the functionality of APMM.

When a query is executed within a session, APMM needs to allocate a SQL work area for the session. Before doing so, it will reference the WORKAREA_SIZE_POLICY initialization parameter to determine how to handle the request. The WORKAREA_SIZE_POLICY parameter can be set to either AUTO or MANUAL. The values of this parameter have the following effect:

AUTO If the WORKAREA_SIZE_POLICY initialization parameter is set to AUTO, APMM will dynamically allocate memory as needed to fulfill the request. This is the default setting and is highly recommended.

In this situation, the historical PGA memory parameters are ignored completely. They have no meaning.

MANUAL If the WORKAREA_SIZE_POLICY initialization parameter is set to MANUAL, APMM will allocate memory for the operation based on the value of the corresponding historical PGA memory parameter. For instance, if a hash-join operation is required, the HASH_AREA_SIZE parameter setting will determine the amount of memory allocated.

This setting effectively overrides the APMM functionality. Its use is strongly discouraged by Oracle.

While Oracle discourages overriding APMM functionality, it is worth mentioning that the WORKAREA_SIZE_POLICY parameter can be set at the session level as well as at the instance level. Therefore, it is possible to override APMM for only a single session. This may be useful for specific tasks.

Implementing APMM

To implement APMM, simply set the total memory allocation for APMM in the initialization file, as in this example:

```
PGA_AGGREGATE_TARGET=2G
```

The value of PGA_AGGREGATE_TARGET can also be modified dynamically by using the ALTER SYSTEM statement:

```
SQL> alter system set PGA_AGGREGATE_TARGET = 2G;

System altered.
```

Either method allocates 2GB of memory to APMM to be shared by all sessions in the instance. For an online transaction processing (OLTP) system, this may be too large of a value. However, for a decision support system (DSS), the SQL work area needs tend to be much greater.

Implementing APMM Through EM Database Control

APMM can also be implemented through the EM Database Control application by following these steps:

1. In the Database Home screen, click the Administration tab. The Administration screen appears.
2. Under the Instance heading, click Memory Parameters. The Memory Parameters screen appears.
3. In the Memory Parameters screen, click the PGA tab (shown in Figure 14.12).
4. Enter the desired size in the Aggregate PGA Target box.

   This screen also offers an Advice button and a PGA Memory Usage Details button. These can be useful aids in deciding how to size your PGA.
5. Click the Apply button when finished.

FIGURE 14.12 EM Database Control Memory Parameters screen

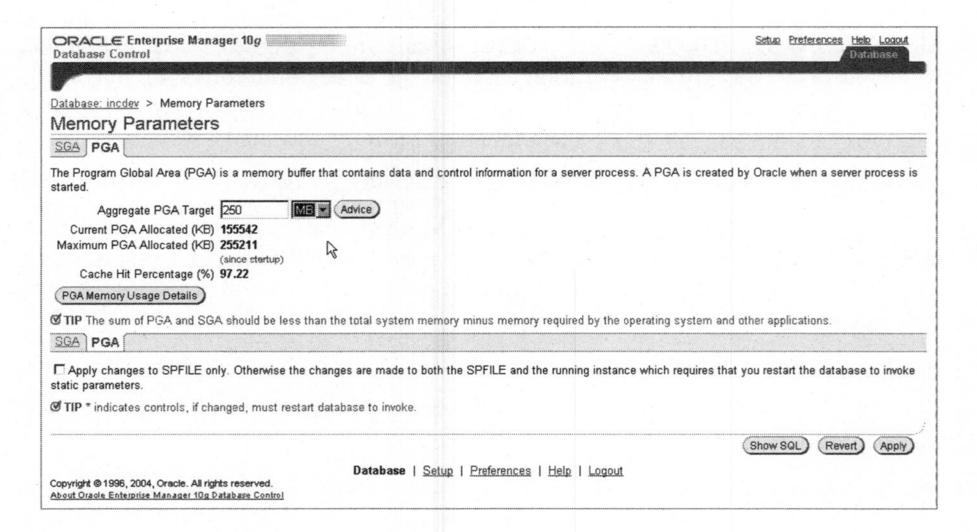

Summary

In this chapter, you learned about many of the vulnerabilities of the Oracle 10*g* listener and the steps that you can take to secure the listener. You learned about the role that the listener plays in the database, and that it can do more than simply handle database session requests. You learned that the listener can be controlled remotely and about the risks inherent in that capability.

You learned the importance of setting a password for the listener to prevent unauthorized usage. You saw that you can control database access by using the `TCP.VALIDNODE_CHECKING`, `TCP.INVITED_NODES`, and `TCP.EXCLUDED_NODES` options in your `sqlnet.ora` file. You saw that these options allow you to specify which hosts the listener would accept or which hosts the listener would deny by listing them in the appropriate section.

You learned to enable listener logging to ensure that a log file would be produced of all listener activity. You learned simple methods to monitor the log file for anomalies. You saw that failed password attempts produce a TNS-01169 error in the log file. Therefore, brute force password attacks could be identified by a large number of TNS-01169 messages in the log file.

Next, you learned that, by default, the listener is configured to accept external procedure requests. You saw that these external procedure requests can call C procedures from shared library and DLL files. Because many Oracle environments have no need for external procedures, you learned how to remove external procedure services from the listener.

For environments where external procedures are required, you learned that you could create a separate listener to handle only external procedure requests. You saw that this listener could be secured by executing it from an operating system account with only minimal privileges. You also discovered that you could limit the libraries accessible through external procedure requests through the `EXTPROC_DLLS` environment variable.

We wrapped up our look at listener security by discussing a few other standard security measures. These measures included using the `ADMIN_RESTRICTIONS` parameter to disable listener configuration changes through the `lsnrctl` program. Other measures include removing write privileges from the `$ORACLE_HOME/network/admin` directory, keeping up-to-date on listener-related security patches, and blocking SQL*NET traffic through your firewalls.

Next, we moved on to Oracle diagnostic sources. You learned about the alert log and how it logs significant events in the database. You learned the importance of checking the alert log on a regular basis. We discussed the options available for viewing the contents of the alert log. You also saw methods in which the alert log content could be loaded as an external table and viewed using standard SQL statements.

We also discussed alert log monitoring options through the EM Database Control application. You learned about predefined alert log metrics that are computed automatically. You also discovered that threshold settings on alert log metrics could be used to generate alerts when specific values are found.

Next, you took a quick look at Oracle trace files. We discussed the differences between background session trace files and user session trace files. You learned that background sessions will dump a trace file when an error is encountered. These trace files can be used to diagnose system problems.

You learned that user session trace files are created when the SQL_TRACE parameter is set to TRUE. These trace files can be used to view in-depth execution information for the session. SQL tracing can be enabled for the entire instance or for specific user sessions.

You learned about the parameters that control the sizing and location of trace files. You saw that the TRACEFILE_IDENTIFIER parameter could be used to append a character string to the name of user session trace files to make them easier to identify. However, the TRACEFILE_IDENTIFIER setting has no effect on background session trace files.

Then we discussed memory management in Oracle 10*g*. You learned about all of the major memory structures in both the SGA and PGA. You saw how manually managing memory is problematic due to the granularity of memory pools and the constant fluctuations in workload requirements.

You learned that ASMM can be used to dynamically size the major SGA memory structures as workload requirements change. You saw that ASMM identifies memory structures as automatically sized components and manually sized components. Manually sized components continue to be set using traditional Oracle memory-sizing methods. You learned that ASMM will be enabled if the initialization parameter SGA_TARGET is set to a non-zero value. You also learned that statistics collection functionality must be set to TYPICAL or ALL in order for ASMM to function.

Lastly, you learned about the PGA and how APMM is Oracle's default method of managing SQL work area sizing. You saw how APMM dynamically allocates PGA memory to meet workload demands. APMM sizing is based on the value set for the SGA_TARGET initialization parameter. If the parameter is not set, it defaults to the greater of 10MB or 20 percent of the SGA size. You also learned that APMM can be overridden through the use of the WORKAREA_SIZE_POLICY parameter, though this practice is strongly discouraged by Oracle.

Exam Essentials

Understand how to secure the listener. Be aware of the security issues that affect the listener and how to address them. Understand the methods that can be used to set a password on the listener. Be aware of valid node checking and how it is used. Know the methods for securing the new listener by limiting the libraries that it can access and by executing the process from an account with minimal operating system privileges. Know the other methods for securing the listener such as applying patches, blocking SQL*NET traffic, and so on.

Be able to remove a default *EXTPROC* entry and add a separate listener to handle external procedure calls. Understand the purpose of external process services. Know how to remove the default external process services from the listener. Be able to add a separate listener to handle external process requests.

Know how to use the alert log and database trace files for diagnostic purposes. Understand the use of the alert log and the types of information that it contains. Know that startup and shutdown operations are logged in detail to the alert log. Know how to view the alert log through multiple methods, including EM Database Control.

Be able to view alerts using Enterprise Manager. Be aware of the metrics and thresholds established for the alert log. Know how to view server-generated alerts in EM Database Control.

Describe how to control the size and location of trace files. Know the difference between background session trace files and user session trace files. Understand both the BACKGROUND_DUMP_DEST and USER_DUMP_DEST parameters used to control the location of trace files. Be aware of the MAX_DUMP_FILE_SIZE parameter to control sizing of trace files. Know how to append identifying text to trace file names for user session trace files.

Be able to implement Automatic Shared Memory Management. Understand how Oracle uses memory. Know the structures in the SGA. Understand which SGA components are automatically sized by ASMM and which remain manually sized. Know how initialization parameters are interpreted in conjunction with ASMM, both for manually sized components and automatically sized components. Know how to enable ASMM.

Know how to manually configure SGA parameters for various memory components in the SGA. Understand which SGA structures are manually sized. Be aware of how to size them using initialization parameters. Know how the use of initialization parameters may affect automatically sized components.

Describe how to use Automatic PGA Memory Management. Be aware of PGA memory structures and their purpose. Understand APMM and how it is configured. Be aware of the initialization parameters that affect PGA memory. Know how APMM can be overridden.

Review Questions

1. Your database instance has the following initialization parameter set:

```
MAX_DUMP_FILE_SIZE = 1000
```

What effect will this setting have on user session trace files?

A. No effect. MAX_DUMP_FILE_SIZE affects only background process trace files.

B. Trace files will be limited to 1000 bytes.

C. Trace files will be limited to 1000 kilobytes.

D. Trace files will be limited to 1000 megabytes.

E. Trace files will be limited to 1000 blocks.

2. The following initialization parameters reside in your initialization file:

```
SGA_TARGET=8G
STREAMS_POOL_SIZE=500M
JAVA_POOL_SIZE=1G
SHARED_POOL_SIZE=3G
```

Which of the following statements will be true when your instance is started? (Choose all that apply.)

A. The automatically sized components will have 6.5GB allocated among them.

B. The total SGA size will be 9GB.

C. The total SGA size will be 8GB.

D. The JAVA_POOL_SIZE will never shrink below 1GB.

E. The STREAMS_POOL_SIZE will always stay at 500MB.

3. ASMM cannot be started on your instance. What might be the reason?

A. The shared pool is sized larger than the database buffer cache size.

B. The DB_KEEP_CACHE_SIZE parameter is not expressed as a power of 2.

C. The STATISTICS_LEVEL parameter is set to BASIC.

D. An invalid sizing parameter is specified.

E. The ASMM option is not installed.

4. You wish to limit database access to a select group of hosts. The following lines have been added to your sqlnet.ora file:

```
tcp.validnode_checking = yes
tcp.invited_nodes = (peabody, 159.162.210.24,
  ➥159.162.211.*, 159.163.*.*)
```

From which of the following hosts will database requests be allowed?

A. peabody

B. 159.162.210.22

C. 159.162.211.44

D. 159.163.212.6

E. None. Valid node checking is defined in the `tnsnames.ora` file.

5. Your external procedure agent is governed by the following listener setting:

```
ENVS="EXTPROC_DLLS=/lib/javalib.so:/lib/tlib.so"
```

Which of the following statements is true regarding external procedure requests handled by this listener?

A. They can access procedures only in the `/lib/javalib.so` and `/lib/tlib.so` shared library files.

B. They can access procedures in the `/lib/javalib.so` and `/lib/tlib.so` shared libraries, as well as in any external libraries referenced by these procedures.

C. They can access procedures in the `/lib/javalib.so` or `/lib/tlib.so` shared libraries, as well as in any libraries in the `$ORACLE_HOME/lib` directory.

D. They can access procedures in the `/lib/javalib.so` or `/lib/tlib.so` shared libraries, as well as in any libraries in the `$ORACLE_HOME/lib` directory. They can also access any external libraries referenced by these procedures.

6. You are working with Oracle Support to resolve a database issue. The support technician asks you to forward any diagnostic files that might help them resolve the issue. Which two of the following choices represent the best files to send?

A. Alert log

B. Trace files from the `USER_DUMP_DEST` directory

C. Trace files from the `BACKGROUND_DUMP_DEST` directory

D. Files from both the `USER_DUMP_DEST` directory and the `BACKGROUND_DUMP_DEST` directory

E. External procedure files

7. You notice that a lot of disk space is being used up on one of your mount points. Upon investigating, you find that SQL tracing is turned on for the instance. You issue an `ALTER SYSTEM` statement to turn it off. In an SPFILE environment, how can you determine if it was turned on at startup or if it was turned on using an `ALTER SYSTEM` statement? Select the best answer.

A. User process trace file

B. Alert log

C. System log

D. Background process trace file

E. `init.ora` file

8. Your instance does not have a value set for the PGA_AGGREGATE_TARGET initialization parameter. The server has 8GB of memory and the SGA is using 4GB. Which of the following statements is true regarding APMM for this instance?

A. It will not be enabled.

B. It will use the default size of 10MB.

C. It will always use the *_AREA_SIZE parameters.

D. It will use the default size of 800MB.

E. It will dynamically allocate unused SGA memory.

9. Your junior DBA accidentally deleted the alert log file. How do you ensure that Oracle will continue to function? Choose the best answer.

A. Restore the most recent backup.

B. Shut down the instance. A new file will be created on startup.

C. Create a new alert log file using EM Database Control.

D. Create a new alert log file using the ALTER SYSTEM statement.

E. Do nothing.

10. You execute a Java stored procedure consisting of a single SQL statement using a large hash-join operation and a large sort operation. Which memory structure will have the most impact on your performance?

A. Shared pool

B. Java pool

C. SQL work area

D. Private SQL area

E. Shared SQL area

11. The following initialization parameters are set on your database instance:

```
DB_NAME=LNX1
SQL_TRACE=FALSE
BACKGROUND_DUMP_DEST=/data1/admin/lnx1/bdump
USER_DUMP_DEST=/data1/admin/lnx1/udump
TRACEFILE_IDENTIFIER='prod'
```

An archiver (ARCH) process encounters an error situation. Its process ID is 32123. Which of the following is true?

A. The trace file /data1/admin/lnx1/bdump/lnx1_arch_32123.trc will be created.

B. The trace file /data1/admin/lnx1/bdump/arch_lnx1_32123_prod.trc will be created.

C. The trace file /data1/admin/lnx1/udump/arch_lnx1_32123.trc will be created.

D. The trace file /data1/admin/lnx1/bdump/lnx1_arch_32123_prod.trc will be created.

E. No trace file will be created.

12. Which of the following could be found in the alert log? (Choose all that apply.)

A. Evidence of a brute force attack against the listener

B. External procedure executions

C. Tablespace creation events

D. Evidence of recovery operations

E. Initialization parameter values

13. You need to secure your listener. Which of the following is *not* a recommended security measure? (Choose the best answer.)

A. Enable Listener logging.

B. Remove unnecessary external procedure services.

C. Configure listener on a non-standard port.

D. Apply patches.

E. Block SQL*NET traffic on firewalls.

14. You want to set a password on the listener. Why might you want to use `lsnrctl` rather than manually editing the `listener.ora` file? (Select the best two answers.)

A. It is easier.

B. It will encrypt the password in the `listener.ora` file.

C. You don't have access to the operating system.

D. `lsnrctl` will log the event to the alert log.

E. The `listener.ora` file is stored in binary format.

15. Which of the following are *not* automatically sized components of ASMM?

A. Streams pool

B. Keep buffer cache

C. SQL work area

D. Recycle buffer cache

E. All of the above

16. Which of the following operations is *not* impacted by the size of the SQL work area? (Select the best answer.)

A. Index lookups

B. Sort operations

C. Bitmap merges

D. Bitmap creation

E. Bulk load operations

17. You want to change the password for your listener. The `listener.ora` file contains the following entries:

```
PASSWORDS_LISTENER=64F4692D9E6443F
LOGGING_LISTENER=ON
ADMIN_RESTRICTIONS=ON
```

Which of the following methods can you use to change the password?

A. `lsnrctl`

B. EM Database Control

C. Manually editing the `listener.ora` file

D. `netmgr`

E. `netca`

18. Dirty blocks in the database buffer cache are tracked by which component?

A. Dirty block list

B. Block list

C. LRU list

D. Write list

E. Dirty list

19. While performing routine management tasks on your database, you discover a high concentration of ORA-01169 messages in the listener log. What might be the cause?

A. Invalid setting in the `sqlnet.ora` file.

B. Mismatched parentheses in the `listener.ora` file.

C. Valid node checking has denied connection requests based on their host addresses.

D. A brute force password attack has been attempted.

E. The database is down.

20. The following parameters are set in your instance:

```
SGA_TARGET=3G
HASH_AREA_SIZE=100M
SORT_AREA_SIZE=100M
WORKAREA_SIZE_POLICY=AUTO
PGA_AGGREGATE_TARGET=600M
```

A user session executes a SQL statement that performs a large sort operation. What can be determined from these settings? (Select the best two answers.)

A. The operation will be allocated 100MB.

B. The operation will be allocated a minimum of 100MB.

C. The *_AREA_SIZE parameters will be ignored.

D. The *_AREA_SIZE parameters will not be ignored.

E. The amount of memory allocated is not known.

Answers to Review Questions

1. E. The default unit type for the MAX_DUMP_FILE_SIZE parameter is blocks.

2. C, D, E. The SGA_TARGET parameter specifies total memory available for sizing the SGA. This includes both automatically sized and manually sized components. The Java pool is an automatically sized component, so its size is unknown, but it will never shrink below the size specified in the JAVA_POOL_SIZE parameter. The streams pool is a manually sized component, so it receives a static allocation of 500MB.

3. C. ASMM is dependent on Oracle statistics and requires a STATISTICS_LEVEL of either TYPICAL or ALL. If the STATISTICS_LEVEL parameter is set to BASIC, ASMM will not function.

4. A. Only option A is correct. Wildcards are not allowed in the tcp.invited_nodes parameter, so only exact matches will be allowed.

5. C. The EXTPROC_DLLS environment variable limits the available shared libraries that the agent can access. Since the ONLY option is not included in the example, the specified libraries are available in addition to the default libraries (those in the $ORACLE_HOME/lib directory).

6. A, C. The alert log can be used to find error messages and other significant events, along with a timestamp. Trace files from background sessions may also be helpful to determine the cause of the problem. User trace files can be helpful to resolve errant SQL statements, but those are not classified as database problems. External procedure files do not exist.

7. B. The alert log details all startup events, including listing all of the non-default initialization parameters that were set.

8. D. If the PGA_AGGREGATE_TARGET parameter is not explicitly set, it will default to the greater of 10MB or 20 percent of the SGA size (800MB). Therefore, it will default to 800MB.

9. E. A new alert log will be created automatically the next time Oracle needs to write an alert log entry, so no action is required. You may indeed wish to restore the last backup of the alert log if you want it for historical purposes, but that has no effect on the Oracle instance itself.

10. C. Though Java stored procedures utilize Java pool memory, the usage is minimal. A large sort operation, on the other hand, is greatly impacted by the size of the SQL work area available to it.

11. B. Because the archiver is a background process, it will follow the naming conventions and storage locations used by all background processes. The TRACEFILE_IDENTIFIER parameter has no effect on background processes, so it is ignored.

12. C, D, E. All of the information specified in C, D, and E is logged to the alert log. Listener attacks would be logged in the listener log, not the alert log. External procedure executions are not logged.

13. C. Configuring the listener on a non-standard port may offer a slight security increase, but port-scanning programs could still easily locate the listener. Therefore, it is not a recommended security measure.

14. B, C. Manually editing the listener.ora file will result in a password that is stored in plaintext, whereas lsnrctl will store the password in an encrypted format. Also, you cannot manually edit the listener.ora file if you don't have access to the operating system (for example, if you need to perform the change remotely, but don't have an operating system account). In this situation, lsnrctl could be used from a remote location.

15. E. None of these components are automatically sized by ASMM. They are all manually sized SGA components, except for the SQL work area. The SQL work area isn't a part of the SGA at all. It is managed by APMM.

16. A. Index lookups are not memory intensive, whereas sort operations, bitmap merges, bitmap creation, and bulk load operations tend to be very memory intensive. Therefore, the SQL work area size has a major impact on their performance.

17. C. When the ADMIN_RESTRICTIONS option is enabled, all changes to the listener are disabled, except through manually editing the listener.ora file. This protects from changes being made remotely by unauthorized individuals.

18. D. Dirty blocks in the database buffer are tracked in the write list. The write list is accessed by the DBWR process to write dirty blocks back to disk.

19. D. The ORA-01169 message indicates a failed password attempt. Repeated occurrences of the message likely indicate that someone is trying to hack the password through a brute force attack.

20. C, E. When the WORKAREA_SIZE_POLICY parameter is set to AUTO (the default setting), APMM will dynamically size the SQL work area. Therefore, the amount of memory actually allocated is unknown. The *_AREA_SIZE parameters have no meaning unless the WORKAREA_SIZE_POLICY is set to MANUAL.

Glossary

1x1boot.nlb A binary file that identifies the available locale definition files for NLSRTL.

A

accent-insensitive sort A sort operation that uses information only about base letters, not diacritics or case.

Active Session History (ASH) A rolling buffer in memory that captures session statistics for all active sessions. ASH gathers the statistics from fixed tables once every second. See also *Manageability Monitor process*; *Manageability Monitor Light process.*

ADDM See *Automatic Database Diagnostic Monitor.*

advisors A collection of services that aid in the optimization of different aspects of the database. Each advisor covers a specific subsystem within the database and can analyze, diagnose, and provide recommendations to eliminate performance issues in the database.

alert log A special type of Oracle trace file that logs significant database events.

ALTER DATABASE BACKUP CONTROL FILE TO TRACE See *ASCII backup control file.*

ANALYZE A command that analyzes the integrity of a database object.

APMM See *Automatic PGA Memory Management.*

ASCII backup control file A readable character representation of the binary control file. This file is created by the command `ALTER DATABASE BACKUP CONTROL FILE TO TRACE`.

ASH See *Active Session History.*

ASM See *Automatic Storage Management.*

ASMM See *Automatic Shared Memory Management.*

asynchronous Asynchronous execution means that a process proceeds independently from another process. For example, a job submitted to the scheduler executes independently from the process that submitted the job.

ATL See *automated tape library.*

ATO See *Automatic Tuning Optimizer.*

attributes The characteristics of any scheduler object. These characteristics are defined through procedure parameters when creating the object or through the `SET_ATTRIBUTE` and `SET_ATTRIBUTE_NULL` procedures once the object has been created. For example, an object's name, repeat interval, and start date would be some of the object's attributes.

automated channel fail over An RMAN feature that allows a backup job to complete successfully on one of the remaining allocated channels if one of the allocated channels fails.

automated tape library (ATL) Third-party tape hardware that automates the backup and recovery to tape process.

automatic channel allocation Performed by setting the Recovery Manager (RMAN) configuration at the RMAN command prompt. This is done by using the `CONFIGURE DEFAULT DEVICE` or `CONFIGURE DEVICE` commands. Automatic channel allocation is automatically used when executing the `BACKUP`, `RESTORE`, or `DELETE` commands.

Automatic Database Diagnostic Monitor (ADDM) Performs proactive database diagnosis to identify performance issues and bottlenecks within the database. In addition, ADDM will work with other advisors to offer recommendations on how to resolve the problems detected.

Automatic DML Monitoring One of the Common Manageability Infrastructure's Automated Maintenance Tasks, it will detect stale and/or missing statistics on database objects.

Automatic PGA Memory Management (APMM) Oracle functionality that simplifies PGA memory management by dynamically allocating SQL work area memory to user sessions. See also *PGA_AGGREGATE_TARGET*.

Automatic Shared Memory Management (ASMM) Oracle functionality that simplifies SGA memory management by dynamically sizing SGA memory components for optimum performance.

Automatic SQL Tuning SQL tuning functionality designed into the query optimizer. By switching the query optimizer into tuning mode, the query optimizer becomes the Automatic Tuning Optimizer (ATO). The ATO performs analysis on SQL statements and produces recommendations to improve performance. See also *Automatic Tuning Optimizer*.

automatic statistics collection One of the Common Manageability Infrastructure's Automated Maintenance Tasks, it is responsible for gathering optimizer statistics for objects in the database and storing them in the data dictionary.

Automatic Storage Management (ASM) A cluster file system that can be used with either stand-alone Oracle instances or with Oracle RAC to provide a vertically integrated subsystem encapsulating a file system, a volume manager, and a fault-tolerant environment specifically designed for Oracle databases.

Automatic Tuning Optimizer (ATO) The name for the Oracle query optimizer when it is in tuning mode. In this mode, the optimizer analyzes SQL statements for ways to improve performance. Rather than an execution plan, however, the ATO returns recommendations to implement SQL changes. See also *Automatic SQL Tuning*; *SQL Tuning Advisor*.

Automatic Workload Repository (AWR) The central element of Oracle Database 10*g*'s Common Manageability Infrastructure. AWR provides services to collect, process, maintain, and access performance statistics for the database. These statistics can be used to detect performance problems and for self-tuning purposes. AWR is made up of two distinct parts: the statistics collection facility and the workload repository. AWR collects statistics every 30 minutes.

automatically sized components SGA memory components that are dynamically sized by ASMM. These include the database buffer cache, the shared pool, the Java pool, and the large pool.

AWR See *Automatic Workload Repository*.

B

BACKGROUND_DUMP_DEST An initialization parameter that specifies the location of both the alert log and all background process trace files.

background process Any Oracle process spawned by the database server other than user session processes. These include parallel query slave processes and job slave processes, as well as the standard background processes (PMON, SMON, DBWR, and so on).

backup piece A physical file stored in a Recovery Manager (RMAN) format that belongs to a backup set. Usually there is only one backup piece per backup set unless the MAXPIECESIZE option is utilized.

backup sets A Recovery Manager (RMAN) backup of datafiles, control files, and/or archive logs that are produced by the RMAN BACKUP command.

baseline A range of snapshots preserved for future comparison. A baseline generally represents a specific workload and is defined during a normal execution of that workload. Later, it can be used for comparison if the workload encounters performance issues.

block change tracking The process of recording blocks that have been modified since the last backup and storing them in a block change tracking file. See also *block change tracking file*.

block change tracking file The file that records the changes that occur to blocks in the Oracle database when block change tracking is enabled. See also *block change tracking*.

block corruption When a block on a physical disk becomes unreadable (physically corrupted) or inconsistent (logically corrupted) so that the data is unusable.

Block Media Recovery (BMR) Used to recover an individual or a group of corrupt blocks in a datafile.

BMR See *Block Media Recovery*.

byte semantics The treatment of character strings as a sequence of bytes.

C

calendaring syntax A powerful, flexible mini-language used to define repeat intervals for Oracle schedules. Repeat intervals can also be defined using PL/SQL expressions.

case-insensitive sort A sort operation that uses information about base letters and diacritics (accents) but not case.

change vectors A description of a change made to a single block in the database.

channel allocation A method of connecting Recovery Manager (RMAN) and the target database while also determining the type of I/O device that the server process will use to perform the backup or restore operation.

channel control options or commands These options or commands are used to control operating system resources that Recovery Manager (RMAN) uses when performing RMAN operations.

channel fail over The automated process that Recovery Manager (RMAN) uses to identify another channel and continue with the restore or backup operation instead of failing.

character semantics The treatment of strings as a sequence of characters, regardless of byte size.

character set A collection of characters that represent textual information for one or more specific languages. Each character is encoded with a distinct character code.

circular reuse records Information used by Recovery Manager (RMAN) in the target database's control file that is not critical for RMAN to function and can be overwritten.

CLI See *command-line interface.*

cluster key A unique key defined for a cluster that contains the common columns for all tables that will reside in the cluster.

CMI See *Common Manageability Infrastructure.*

coarse striping An ASM striping method for higher latency objects that uses a stripe size of 1MB.

code point The unique value assigned to each element in Unicode code sets. The code point value is used to determine the sorting order for the element within the code set.

command-line interface (CLI) The command-line interface to Recovery Manager that includes the `BACKUP`, `RECOVER`, and `RESTORE` commands.

Common Manageability Infrastructure (CMI) A sophisticated self-management infrastructure allowing the database to automatically resolve performance issues and to dynamically adjust to workload changes to ensure peak performance. The CMI is composed of the AWR, the advisory framework, Automated Maintenance Tasks, and server-generated alerts.

complex resource plan Any resource plan that is referenced by independent resource plan directives is classified as a complex resource plan. It is the opposite of a simple resource plan, in which the plan directives are self-contained. See also *simple resource plan.*

compressed backup A new Oracle Database10*g* feature that actually compresses the backup to a smaller size. This feature is used with the `BACKUP AS COMPRESSED BACKUPSET` command.

consumer group mapping A method of automatically assigning consumer groups to user sessions based on session attributes.

control file autobackup The process that automatically makes a backup of the control file along with a backup of other database objects.

CPU_MTH The parameter used to define the resource scheduling method used within a resource group. This method governs only CPU resources.

cumulative incremental backup A type of incremental backup that backs up all blocks changed since the last level 1 incremental backup.

D

database character set The encoded character set that is used to store text in the database. This includes CHAR, VARCHAR2, LONG, and fixed-width CLOB column values and all SQL and PL/SQL text.

database incarnation A separate version of a physical database that is created every time the database is opened with the RESETLOGS option. New with Oracle Database10*g*, you can recover backups from prior incarnations if the redo log information is available.

database point-in-time recovery (DBPITR) See *incomplete recovery*.

Database Resource Manager (DRM) An Oracle service that allows the management and prioritization of resources to be controlled by Oracle as opposed to being controlled by the operating system.

datetime datatype Standard Oracle datatypes used to store date- and time-related data. Datetime datatypes include DATE, TIMESTAMP, TIMESTAMP WITH TIME ZONE, and TIMESTAMP WITH LOCAL TIME ZONE.

DB_BLOCK_CHECKING A database parameter that sets block checking at the database level. This causes Oracle to checksum a block every time it is modified.

DB_FLASHBACK_RETENTION_TARGET A parameter value that determines how far back in time you can recover the flashback database.

DB_TIME The most important of all the time model statistics, DB_TIME tracks the total time spent in database calls for all statistics categories. This allows system analysis based on time metrics and enables Oracle to accurately calculate time-savings benefits through optimization recommendations.

***DBMS_REPAIR* package** A PL/SQL package that is made up of a set of procedures to detect and fix corrupt blocks.

***DBMS_RESOURCE_MANAGER* package** An Oracle PL/SQL package that constitutes the application programming interface (API) to the Database Resource Manager. This package contains procedures used to manage most of the functionality in DRM.

***DBMS_RESOURCE_MANAGER_PRIVS* package** An Oracle PL/SQL package used to manage Database Resource Manager privileges.

***DBMS_SERVER_ALERT* package** A PL/SQL package to configure and retrieve warning and critical threshold levels for tablespace space usage and other database resources.

DBPITR See *incomplete recovery*.

DBVERIFY utility An Oracle utility that is used to see whether corruption exists in a particular datafile.

DEFAULT_CONSUMER_GROUP The resource consumer group assigned automatically to any session not assigned to a resource consumer group.

diacritic A mark near or through a character or combination of characters that alters the sound of the character. Also called an accent.

differential incremental backup A type of incremental backup that backs up all blocks changed since the last level 0 or level 1 incremental backup. See also *incremental backup*.

disk group A group of disks treated as a unit in an ASM instance for both redundancy and performance.

DRM See *Database Resource Manager*.

dynamic rebalancing An ASM feature that automatically reallocates extents within an ASM file when a disk in an ASM disk group is added, deleted, or fails.

E

EM See *Enterprise Manager*.

Enterprise Manager (EM) A GUI-based DBA tool that performs backups, exports/imports, data loads, performance monitoring/tuning, job and event scheduling, and most other routine DBA management tasks.

EXPORT utility A backup utility that backs up only logical components of the database, such as tables, indexes, and privileges.

external procedures Shared library procedures called from an executable program written in a different language.

external redundancy For an ASM disk group with only one failure group, relying on the external disk hardware subsystem to provide mirroring.

EXTPROC_DLLS An environment variable that can be defined to limit access to shared library objects for external procedures.

F

failure group Disks as part of an ASM disk group that share a common resource whose failure causes the entire set of disks to be unavailable to the disk group.

fine striping An ASM striping method for low-latency objects that uses a stripe size of 128KB.

fixed tables Memory structures that emulate tables in that they can be queried and can be the object of views. Oracle uses fixed tables to store dynamic performance statistics.

flash recovery area The centralized storage area for Oracle Database 10*g* backups where recovery-related files can be managed. This is also the area where flashback database logs are written to.

flashback database A new Oracle Database 10*g* recovery mechanism that allows you to recover to a point-in-time by using "before" block images.

flashback database logs Logs that contain the "before" block images required to recover with the flashback database.

Flashback Drop The process of saving a copy of the dropped database object and dependent objects in the Recycle Bin so that the object can be recovered. Oracle overwrites these objects to ensure that there is enough free space for existing objects in the tablespace. See also *Recycle Bin*.

Flashback Table A flashback technology that allows you to recover a table or set tables to a specific point-in-time without performing an incomplete recovery.

Flashback Transaction Query A query designed to be a diagnostic tool to help identify changes made to the database at the transaction level.

***FLASHBACK_TRANSACTION_QUERY* view** A view that can be queried to perform diagnostics and analysis on a version of data in a particular table.

Flashback Versions Query A query that allows you to retrieve all of the versions of the rows that exist or existed between the times the query was executed to a determined point-in-time in the past.

***format* option** An option that allows for making backup sets, copies, and pieces unique with options that format the filenames according to specified naming options.

full backup A non-incremental Recovery Manager (RMAN) backup. This can be for a whole database or for individual database files or components.

G

GET_THRESHOLD A procedure within the DBMS_SERVER_ALERT package to retrieve the threshold levels for a tablespace or other database resource.

GRANT_OPTION An optional privilege that authorizes the grantee (recipient of a privilege) to grant the same privilege to other users.

Growth Trend Report A report available within EM Database Control that uses AWR data to show segment growth in the past and predict segment growth in the future. See also *Automatic Workload Repository*.

H

hash cluster A cluster that uses a hashing algorithm on the row's cluster key to find the physical location of the row in the table.

high redundancy For an ASM disk group, a level of redundancy that requires at least three failure groups in the disk group.

I

image copy A bit-for-bit copy that is similar to an operating system file copy of a database file like a datafile, archived redo log, or control file. This is generated by the `BACKUP AS COPY` command. This type of backup is quicker for recovery purposes because it is not stored in a Recovery Manager (RMAN) proprietary format.

incarnation See *database incarnation*.

incomplete recovery A recovery that stops before the point of failure that forced recovery or a recovery that does not have available all committed transactions performed before the failure occurred. Incomplete recovery is sometimes called *database point-in-time recovery (DBPITR)* because this is recovery to a specific point-in-time.

incremental backup A Recovery Manager (RMAN) backup that only backs up modified blocks. Incremental backups are performed by levels. A level 0 backup backs up all blocks much like a full backup. Level 1 backups back up only the blocks that have changed since the last incremental backup. See also *differential incremental backup*.

index cluster A cluster type that performs much like a b-tree index to ensure quick access to the rows in each cluster table. An index cluster is beneficial if the tables in the cluster are always queried together.

index-organized table (IOT) A type of table that is most effective when the access of the table is primarily by the primary key and the primary key columns constitute a large part of the table's columns. An IOT uses a single segment to store the data and the index information.

index tablespace A tablespace that should only contain indexes to improve performance.

indexes Database objects that provide referential integrity and performance benefits to tables. These non-critical database objects can be rebuilt based on the table's existence.

inline program A program defined within the confines of a scheduler job object. An inline program is not stored as an independent program object and therefore cannot be referenced by any other jobs.

inline schedule A schedule defined within the confines of a job object. An inline schedule is not stored as an independent program object and therefore cannot be referenced by any other jobs.

Inter Process Control (IPC) A local connection type that connects directly to the database not using networking connectivity.

IOT See *index-organized table.*

IOT mapping table A special type of table required when you create bitmap indexes on an IOT.

IOT overflow area A segment used when the IOT's row data exceeds the threshold of available space in a block; the row's data is dynamically and automatically moved to the overflow area. When you create an IOT, you specify a tablespace to hold the IOT overflow segment.

IPC See *Inter Process Control.*

J

job An Oracle scheduler object that specifies a program to be run, and a schedule to determine when the program should be run and how often it should be repeated.

job attributes A group of modifiable job characteristics that define the job's behavior.

job coordinator A background process (with the format `cjq`*nnn*) that is automatically started when jobs must be run, or job windows must be opened. It is automatically suspended after the scheduler is inactive for a period of time. It controls and starts the job slaves and queries the job table for new jobs.

job group A logical grouping of individual job objects used to simplify management and prioritize execution of the objects.

job instance A single execution of a program by a job.

job logs Tables populated by the scheduler that maintain information about job executions.

job slave process A process that executes the submitted jobs and updates the job table when the submitted job completes.

job table A table that contains one entry for a job definition, regardless of how many times a job runs. The job log contains an entry each time the job runs.

journal table A table used during an online index rebuild to capture changes to the index that occur while the rebuild operation is in progress.

L

linguistic sort The ordering of character strings based on locale requirements instead of the binary representation of the strings.

***list* command** A Recovery Manager (RMAN) command that allows the query of the RMAN repository to get the data regarding the BACKUP command and database incarnations.

listener.ora The default name of Oracle's TNS listener configuration file. See also *TNS listener*.

locale A collection of information about the linguistic and cultural preferences from a particular region.

locale definition files Binary files that define NLS locale specifics relating to language, territory, character set, or linguistic sort. These files are used by the NLSRTL to implement globalization support. See also *National Language Support Runtime Library*.

local NLS operations Client-side NLS operations that occur outside of a session to an Oracle server.

log file groups Two or more log files, usually stored on different physical disks, that are written in parallel and are considered multiplexed for the purposes of database recovery Also known as *redo log file groups*.

logical corruption See *block corruption*.

logical ROWID A "guess" of the location of the row in an IOT, since there is no physical ROWID; the primary key identifies the rows in an IOT. A logical ROWID permits the creation of secondary indexes on the IOT.

long query warning alert An alert generated when a user receives a `Snapshot too old` error. This alert is generated at most once per 24-hour period.

lsnrctl An executable program used to manage listener functionality.

M

Manageability Monitor (MMON) process The process responsible for a host of tasks, including invoking ADDM after each snapshot collection, snapshot retention and purging, and ASH purging (under normal circumstances). When purging ASH, MMON also filters the data and stores a portion of it in the AWR. See also *Active Session History*; *Automatic Database Diagnostic Monitor*.

Manageability Monitor Light (MMNL) process The process responsible for purging the ASH when it fills before the scheduled MMON purge takes place. Like the MMON process, MMNL filters the data in the ASH before purging and stores a portion of it in the AWR. See also *Active Session History*; *Automatic Workload Repository*.

manual channel allocation A type of channel allocation that is performed any time you issue the command `ALLOCATE CHANNEL`. The manual command for allocating a channel is `ALLOCATE CHANNEL` *`channel_name`* `TYPE DISK`.

manually sized components SGA memory components that are not dynamically sized by ASMM. Instead, they are sized according to their associated initialization parameter settings. These include the streams pool, the keep and recycle caches, and a few other miscellaneous components.

mapping priorities A method used to resolve mapping rule conflicts. When a user session maps to more than one resource consumer group, mapping priorities are used to make the final determination.

MAX_DUMP_FILE_SIZE An initialization parameter used to define the maximum size that a trace file can reach.

media management layer (MML) An API that interfaces Recovery Manager (RMAN) with different hardware vendors' tape devices.

mirrored redo logs At least one additional log member per log group. Also referred to as *multiplexed redo logs*.

MML See *media management layer*.

MMNL See *Manageability Monitor Light process*.

MMON See *Manageability Monitor process*.

multiplexed redo logs See *mirrored redo logs*.

multiplexing A process by which multiple database files are read simultaneously and all of the blocks are written to the same RMAN backup set.

N

national character set An alternate character set from the database character set that can be specified for the `NCHAR`, `NVARCHAR2`, and `NCLOB` columns. National character sets are always Unicode.

National Language Support (NLS) NLS allows users to interact with the database in their native languages and cultural conventions.

National Language Support Runtime Library (NLSRTL) A library that provides locale-independent algorithms for global support functionality.

NLS See *National Language Support*.

NLSRTL See *National Language Support Runtime Library*.

non-circular reuse records Information used by Recovery Manager (RMAN) in the target database's control file that is not written over because these records are critical to RMAN's ability to back up and recover a database.

non-current redo log file members Redo log file group members that are not currently being used by the log writer process for ongoing transactions are considered non-current redo log file members.

normal redundancy For an ASM disk group, a level of redundancy that requires at least two failure groups in the disk group.

O

Oracle Managed Files (OMF) Eliminates the need to specify file locations and names for database objects. Initialization parameters specify the default file system directories for each type of database file.

ORB*n* In an ASM instance, this performs the actual extent movement between disks in the disk groups managed by the ASM instance. *n* can be from 0 to 9.

OSMB The background process on a database instance that performs the communication between the database instance and the ASM instance.

OTHER_GROUPS The consumer group assigned to sessions that are not assigned to any consumer group included in the enabled resource plan.

overloaded procedure A procedure that accepts different parameter lists as arguments. Oracle matches the parameter list submitted with the defined parameter lists and chooses the correct version of the procedure to execute.

overloading A programming method that entails the creation of objects, procedures, etc. that can accept diverse sets of arguments and/or datatypes. For example, a function that accepts character, numeric, or date data for a particular argument is overloading.

P

password file A text-based operating system file that contains passwords for administrative accounts that need SYSDBA privileges, especially for database shutdown and startup and other maintenance operations that must be performed when the data dictionary is not available.

pending area A staging area where Database Resource Manager objects can be created, modified, deleted, and validated before being activated and moved into the data dictionary. See also *Database Resource Manager*.

permanent Oracle files in the Flash Recovery Area that cannot be deleted without causing the instance to fail, such as multiplexed copies of control files and the online redo log files. All other files in the Flash Recovery Area will eventually be deleted when they become obsolete due to the retention policy or when they are moved to tape.

persistent settings or parameters Configuration settings for each database that are maintained after Recovery Manager (RMAN) stops and restarts.

PGA See *Program Global Area.*

PGA_AGGREGATE_TARGET An initialization parameter used to define the total amount of memory available to APMM. See also *Automatic PGA Memory Management.*

physical corruption See *block corruption.*

PL/SQL expression A snippet of PL/SQL code that evaluates to a desired datatype value. For example, repeat intervals can be defined by PL/SQL expressions that evaluate to a valid date.

program An Oracle scheduler object that specifies a PL/SQL block, stored procedure, or external operating system executable, and its associated arguments and metadata.

Program Global Area (PGA) A private memory area allocated to each process. The PGA contains a private SQL area (for bind variables and so on) and a SQL work area (for intensive SQL operations).

R

***rate* option** An option designed to limit Recovery Manager (RMAN) from using excessive system resources during backup and restore operations.

RBAL In an ASM instance, this background process coordinates the disk activity for disk groups.

read-only tablespace A tablespace that contains static information and is not updated.

recovery catalog Recovery information that is stored inside an Oracle database that is different from the database being backed up. This is similar to the RMAN repository residing in the target database's control file, but the metadata about backups and restores of one or many target databases is stored in an Oracle database.

RECOVER DATABASE A user-managed and Recovery Manager (RMAN) command that initiates the recovery process by applying archived redo logs to the appropriate database files in the recovery process.

Recovery Manager (RMAN) The recommended backup and recovery tool provided with the Oracle Database Server software.

Recycle Bin A logical storage container for all dropped tables and their dependent objects. See also *Flashback Drop*; *SHOW RECYCLEBIN*; *space pressure*.

redo entry A group of *change vectors*. Redo entries record data that you can use to reconstruct all changes made to the database, including the undo segments. Also known as a *redo record*.

redo log file One of the files that comprises a redo log group. A database needs at least two redo log groups. Also known as a *redo log member*.

redo log file groups See *log file groups*.

redo log members See *redo log file*.

Redo Logfile Size Advisor An advisor within the Oracle advisory framework that analyzes redo log file usage and recommends an optimal redo log file size to minimize I/O and log file switches.

redo record See *redo entry*.

***report* command** A Recovery Manager (RMAN) command used to query the RMAN repository and get the data regarding which files need a backup, unneeded backups, database physical schema, and whether or not unrecoverable operations were performed on files.

RESETLOGS A method of opening the database after incomplete recovery that resets the redo log sequence. This has been modified in Oracle Database 10*g* to allow recovery from a prior backup through the incomplete recovery opening the database with `RESETLOGS`.

resource allocation methods A group of Oracle-defined methods of resource allocation that can be utilized in plan directives.

resource consumer groups A method of grouping user sessions, usually based on their resource consumption needs.

resource plan A DRM object that contains directives to allocate resources to consumer groups and sub-plans.

resource plan directive A rule for the allocation of resources to a consumer group or to a sub-plan from a resource plan.

retention period The amount of time that database performance snapshots will be retained in the AWR. By default, the retention period is set to 10,080 minutes (7 days). See also *Automatic Workload Repository*.

retention policy The determined length of time that a database file backup is retained for use in a potential restore operation.

RMAN See *Recovery Manager*.

RMAN backup A physical backup method using the Recovery Manager (RMAN) utility to perform the backup to tape or disk.

RMAN repository The information that Recovery Manager (RMAN) needs to function to perform backup and recovery operations. This information is stored in the database's control file or in the optional recovery catalog.

RVWR The database background process that writes to the flashback database logs and performs the flashback database recovery.

S

schedule An Oracle scheduler object that specifies a start date, optional end date, and repeat interval that can be used to generate dates and times for job execution.

Segment Advisor A tool available either via a PL/SQL package or within EM Database Control that analyzes a segment or all segments within a tablespace and recommends remedial action to optimize the space within the segments.

Segment Resource Estimation A tool available only within EM Database Control that can estimate space usage for a new table segment given the column datatypes, sizes, and the estimated row count.

segment shrink The functionality using either `ALTER TABLE` or the EM Database Control interface to reclaim wasted space within a segment and optionally move the high watermark (HWM) down.

server-generated alerts Oracle functionality that allows the database to detect problematic situations and issue alerts accordingly. Server-generated alerts are created by establishing threshold settings on specific metrics.

server-managed recovery Recovery Manager (RMAN) recovery that is initiated by a server process that interacts with the target database, the repository, and the media manager.

session attributes A group of session characteristics that can be used to identify types of sessions for the purpose of assigning consumer resource groups.

SET_THRESHOLD A procedure within the `DBMS_SERVER_ALERT` package to set the threshold levels for a tablespace or other database resource.

SGA See *System Global Area*.

SGA_TARGET An initialization parameter used to define the total amount of memory available to ASMM. See also *Automatic Shared Memory Management*.

shared library A collection of precompiled procedures and functions stored in a single file. Shared library routines can be called externally from other programs.

SHOW RECYCLEBIN A special command that displays the contents of the Recycle Bin. See also *Recycle Bin.*

simple resource plan A resource plan in which all the plan directives are self-contained. In other words, the plan has no externally stored resource plan directives. Simple resource plans are created by using the DBMS_RESOURCE_MANAGER.CREATE_SIMPLE_PLAN procedure. See also *complex resource plan.*

single-level resource plan Any resource plan that does not allocate resources to a sub-plan.

snapshot Interval The frequency with which the AWR produces snapshots for proactive monitoring. By default, the snapshot interval is set to 60 minutes. See also *Automatic Workload Repository.*

sorted hash clusters A hash cluster—either single-table or multiple-table—that maintains rows ordered by one or more sort keys for each value of the cluster key to minimize memory usage and sort operations when the rows are retrieved from the cluster. Sorted hash clusters support applications that process data in a first in, first out (FIFO) manner.

space pressure A low disk space condition in a tablespace that may cause objects in the Recycle Bin to be removed before additional space is allocated to the tablespace if AUTOALLOCATE is in effect. Oracle removes these objects if necessary on a first in, first out (FIFO) basis to maintain enough space for existing objects in the tablespace. See also *Recycle Bin.*

SQL Profile Data dictionary objects that store auxiliary statistics relating to a specific query that is utilized by the query optimizer when generating an execution plan. Unlike a Stored Outline, which instructs the optimizer to always use a specific execution plan, a SQL Profile is treated as a source of statistics that will be considered by the optimizer when generating an execution plan.

SQL trace Oracle functionality that produces verbose trace files detailing SQL execution. SQL trace files can be used to diagnose poorly running SQL statements.

SQL Tuning Advisor The interface to the Automatic Tuning Optimizer (ATO), the SQL Tuning Advisor offers functionality to submit SQL statements to the ATO and to display and process results. See also *Automatic Tuning Optimizer*; *SQL Tuning Set.*

SQL Tuning Set (STS) A collection of SQL statements, along with their associated execution statistics and execution context. SQL Tuning Sets can be used to pass a group of SQL statements into the SQL Tuning Advisor, rather than submitting them individually. See also *SQL Tuning Advisor.*

STS See *SQL Tuning Set.*

sub-plan A resource plan that is allocated resources from a top-level plan.

superset A grouping of elements that contains all of the elements contained in another group (the subset). A character set that contains all characters defined in another character set and assigns identical encoded values to those characters is considered a superset of the other character set.

switch privilege The privilege granted to a user or role enabling them to switch their consumer group.

synchronous Synchronous execution means that a process is dependent on another process and the two must remain in sync. For example, when executing a query from SQL*Plus, the query runs synchronously with the SQL*Plus program. Therefore, control does not return to SQL*Plus until the query has completed.

SYSDBA A connection privilege that has full database administration privileges.

SYSOPER A connection privilege that has partial database administration privileges. This account is good for operators who need to support a database application.

System Global Area (SGA) A shared memory area used by Oracle for the majority of its memory needs. The SGA contains a number of memory subcomponents, including the database buffer cache, the shared pool, the large pool, the Java pool, and several other memory caches.

T

***tag* option** A command option that allows for making backups unique with a user-defined character string.

target database The database that is identified or targeted by Recovery Manager (RMAN) to perform backup and recovery operations.

tempfile A type of tablespace where management occurs locally or in the tablespace, as opposed to in the data dictionary like a permanent tablespace.

temporary tablespace The tablespace that is responsible for sorting operations.

TNS listener An Oracle process that listens for requests from Oracle clients and forwards them to their appropriate destination.

trace file A detailed file containing diagnostic information relating to an Oracle process.

TRACEFILE_IDENTIFIER An initialization parameter used to append an identifying text string to the name of the user process trace files.

transient Oracle files in the Flash Recovery Area that will eventually be deleted when they become obsolete or are moved to tape. Transient files include all files stored in the Flash Recovery Area except for multiplexed copies of control files and the copies of the online redo log files stored in the Flash Recovery Area. Data files, flashback logs, and RMAN backups are considered transient files.

U

Undo Advisor A tool within the Oracle advisory framework that uses past undo usage to recommend settings for the UNDO_RETENTION parameter as well as an optimal size for the undo tablespace.

undo data The record of changes to database blocks recorded in the undo tablespace to facilitate reverting the effect of an insert, update, or delete operation on the block.

Unicode A universal encoded character set that allows you to store information from any known written language. Unicode provides a unique code value for every character, regardless of the platform, program, or language.

Unicode code point A unique value assigned to every character in a Unicode character set.

Unicode datatype Oracle datatypes used to store Unicode data when the database uses a non-Unicode character set by default. These datatypes include NCHAR, NVARCHAR, and NCLOB.

UNTIL CANCEL A user-managed incomplete recovery command that uses a random point determined by the administrator to designate the stopping point in the incomplete recovery process.

UNTIL CHANGE A user-managed incomplete recovery using the ALTER DATABASE command that uses the SCN to designate the stopping point in the incomplete recovery process.

UNTIL SCN A Recovery Manager (RMAN)-based incomplete recovery command that uses an SCN to designate the stopping point in the incomplete recovery process.

UNTIL SEQUENCE A Recovery Manager (RMAN)-based incomplete recovery command that uses a redo log sequence to designate the stopping point in the incomplete recovery process.

UNTIL TIME A user-managed and Recovery Manager (RMAN)-based incomplete recovery command that uses time to designate the stopping point in the incomplete recovery process.

USER_DUMP_DEST An initialization parameter used to specify the location of the user process trace files.

user error An error introduced to the database by the user. This error often must be resolved with unique techniques such as incomplete recovery, the Log Miner utility, or database exports. The flashback database is well suited for recovering from user errors.

user-managed backups Customized scripts that interact with the operating system's capabilities to copy and save files for later access.

user-managed recovery The traditional non-Recovery Manager (RMAN) recovery where the DBA directly manages the database files required to recover the database.

V

Valid Node Checking Optional SQL*NET functionality used to filter listener requests based on the host IP address.

VERSIONS BETWEEN A clause that is used for the Flashback Versions Query to determine the timeframe between version data in a table.

W

window An Oracle scheduler object stored in the SYS schema that defines a schedule, a time duration, and a resource plan. When a window is opened, it switches the resource plan for the duration of the window.

window group A logical grouping of individual scheduler window objects used to simplify the management of the objects.

window logs Tables populated by the scheduler that maintain information about window actions.

Index

Note to Reader: **Bolded** page references indicate definitions and main discussions of a topic. *Italicized* page references indicate tables and illustrations.

Numbers

A

B

C

D

E

G

M

N

O

P

R

T

U

V

W